ELUSIVE HUNTERS

In memory of Johannes Nicolaisen
- a fine anthropologist and companion

IDA NICOLAISEN

ELUSIVE HUNTERS

The Haddad of Kanem and The Bahr el Ghazal

THE CARLSBERG FOUNDATION'S
NOMAD RESEARCH PROJECT

AARHUS UNIVERSITY PRESS

ELUSIVE HUNTERS

Layout and cover design by Hanne Kolding

Photos: Janne Klerk (JK); Krarup Mogensen (KM); Lennart Larsen (LL);

Johannes Nicolaisen (JN) and, where no credits, the photos are taken by the author.

Type face: Minion Pro

Paper: BVS Matt from Scheufelen

Printed in Denmark by Narayana Press, Gylling

ISBN 978 87 7934 394 8

AARHUS UNIVERSITY PRESS

Langelandsgade 177

DK-8200 Aarhus N

White Cross Mills

Lancaster LA1 4XS

England

Box 511

Oakville, CT 06779

USA

www.unipress.dk

THE CARLSBERG FOUNDATION'S NOMAD RESEARCH PROJECT

Editor-in-chief: Ida Nicolaisen

The publication of this volume has been made possible by a generous grant from

The Carlsberg Foundation

CONTENTS

EDITOR'S PREFACE

DANISH NOMAD RESEARCH - AN OVERVIEW

Pastoral nomads have always fascinated the more earthbound peoples among whom they live. Forever on the move with tents and belongings, and with their flocks of goats, sheep, cattle, yaks, camels, horses or reindeer, these elusive people have captured our imagination. They call into question the very way of life that we peasant or urban people live and defy our ideas of stable and secure homesteads. They stir our emotions by questioning values that we take for granted, and by offering a vision of an alternative and, as we tend to believe, carefree existence.

Awe and respect for the Scythians, Huns, Old-Turks, Mongols, and the Arab Bedouins, who all carved out a prominent place in the history of the Old World, lie deep in the Western mind. Images of Tibetan nomads and their yaks surviving at altitudes where agriculture is impossible, of veiled Tuareg men mounted on the camels with which they held sway over the Sahara desert for centuries controlling caravans and trade between the Atlas Mountains and the West African states, or of Masai families wandering with their cattle through the tall grasses of the East African savannah are part of our perception of the world. Some of these images are out of date but persist because these are people who arouse our curiosity. Although far away in space and time they enrich our lives.

Pastoral nomadism is a way of life confined to the Old World. Until the first decades of the 20th century, pastoral nomads pursued their way of life throughout the arid and semi-arid zone which stretches from North Africa through the Middle East and the heart of Central Asia. Other pastoralists wandered with their cattle on the East African plains and in South Africa, while a range of nomadic groups whose lives were based on reindeer herding lived in Northern Scandinavia and across the taiga and forests of Russia and Siberia. The living conditions have changed for all these peoples, but some still keep livestock and continue a migratory or semi-migratory way of life.

Each of these pastoral societies represents or represented a unique adaptation to the environment, understood in the widest sense of the word, i.e. as the natural, social, and cultural surroundings which have an impact on their way of life. Pastoral nomadism and the societies and cultures of pastoral peoples are fascinating fields of research. Scholars have long been intrigued by the social organization, values, beliefs and knowledge systems of pastoralists, of their environmental know-how and sophisticated veterinary skills in handling domesticated animals, as well as of the strategies which they deploy to survive under conditions which are unforeseeable and often very harsh. Pastoral nomadism is a highly specialized occupation yet one which nevertheless relies heavily on exchanges with agricultural and urban communities. Pastoral nomads do not live apart from the wider world but are important players in the political, social and economic life of surrounding communities and the states of which they are now part.

In Denmark serious scholarly interest in the cultures and societies of pastoral nomads, including the nature, history, and transformation of nomadism, dates back almost a century. During this period explorers, photographers, and scientists - geographers, archaeologists, linguists, botanists, zoologists, and not least anthropologists - have made a substantial contribution to the documentation and understanding of a range of pastoral societies and of pastoral nomadism as such.

Geographically, Danish research efforts have centred on three areas: Central Asia, South West Asia, and North Africa. Some scholars conducted lengthy in-depth studies of the ecology, culture, and social organization of pastoral groups. A good number brought back rich collections of artefacts to Danish museums which, together with field notes, photographs, films, and recordings document the ingenious technical, esthetical, and symbolic expressions of a range of nomadic societies.

A substantial part of these studies and unique collections remained unpublished, however. To remedy this, the Carlsberg Foundation supported a major research project to mine and publish a considerable part of these rich data bases. The current volume is the 14th in the series of publications which so far has been the outcome of the research initiative. The project deals with the cultures of pastoralists as different as the Mongols, Tibetans, Kirghiz and Turkmen of Central Asia, the Pashtun of Afghanistan, the Lurs of Iran, the Bedouin of Qatar, the Tuareg of the Sahara, and the Kreda and nomadic Haddad of Chad.

Just as the lives of nomadic peoples have changed over time, so have the theoretical interests of the Danish scholars and explorers who endeavoured to record, understand and describe these societies. The issues which captured their imagination and the questions they asked were long influenced by culture-historical ethnology, a school of thought which dominated Danish anthropology until the early 1950s with an emphasis on subsistence systems and material culture studies.

Anthropology was established as a discipline at the University of Copenhagen as late as in 1945. Prior to that time it was pursued by scholars who had been trained as geographers. These were either employed or associated with the Institute of Geography or curators at the Department of Ethnography at the National Museum of Denmark. Among the former were Professor H. P. Steensby (1875-1920) and Professor Gudmund Hatt (1884-1960) who both had a keen interest in arctic societies. Most notably among the latter were Dr Carl Gunnar Feilberg (1894-1972), who became Professor of Human Geography, and Dr Kaj Birket-Smith (1893-1977) also an Inuit specialist, who became the first Lecturer in Ethnography.

The institutional roots of Danish anthropology had a marked influence on the theoretical perspectives which scholars brought to the study of pastoral societies. It characterized their concept of nomadism, defined the scientific problems which occupied them and made them focus initially on the material culture, origin, and historical transformation of pastoralism. On the basis of data gathered on an expedition to North Africa in 1908, H. P. Steensby argued, as had the French scholars A. Bernard and N. Lacroix that the various forms of pastoral nomadism found in that region had developed from subsistence systems based on both agriculture and animal husbandry in adaptation to increasingly scarce resources. Gudmund Hatt concluded from his studies of reindeer nomadism that this had its root in a hunting culture in which tame reindeer were used as decoys. Although he discussed the origin of nomadism in more general terms in later publications, Hatt ultimately linked this to aspects of hunting cultures. Feilberg, who carried out fieldwork among Lur pastoralists in Persia in 1935, dealt with the history of nomadism through an intricate analysis of the structure and distribution of the black tent.

Parallel with this theoretical interest in pastoral nomadism in the early part of the 20th century, impressive collections of ethnographic specimens from a wide range of pastoral peoples found their way into the National Museum of Denmark. The most important of these were collected by Ole Olufsen (1865-1929) in the Pamirs, West Turkestan, and North Africa, by Henning Haslund-Christensen (1896-1948) in Mongolia, and by C. G. Feilberg (1894-1972) among the Lur. After the Second World War, the National Museum and the Prehistoric Museum, Moesgaard in Jutland received new collections. A Tibetan treasure of specimen was donated by His Royal Highness Prince Peter of Greece and to Denmark (1908-1980). The collections were further enriched by the botanist Lennart Edelberg (1915-1981) and by Klaus Ferdinand (1926-2005) who began their work among Afghan nomads in the late 1940s and early 1950s respectively. Subsequently Edelberg collected specimen among the Lur and Ferdinand among the Bedouin of Qatar. Finally, Johannes Nicolaisen (1921-1980) and Ida Nicolaisen (b.1940) brought back collections from the Tuareg of the Sahara and the Sahel as well as from the Kreda and Haddad of Chad.

The earliest of the major Danish collections of nomad artefacts are those from Ole Olufsen's expeditions to the Pamirs and West Turkestan in the late 1890s if we forego the collections from the Same of northern Norway from the 17th century. Olufsen was a military man with a keen interest in geography and the exploration of little known regions of the earth. He was appointed honorary professor of geography at Copenhagen University. In 1896-97 and 1898-99 he organised and led two expeditions to the Pamirs and West Turkestan. In the course of these he gathered topographical, meteorological, hydrographical, zoological, botanical and ethnographical data. Olufsen travelled widely within the Emirate of Bokhara and Russian Turkestan. He was interested in the cultures of the various ethnic groups and collected some 700 artefacts among the pastoral Kyrgyz and Turkmen, the Uzbeks, and various urban ethnic groups. Later expeditions in 1908 and 1922-23 took Olufsen to North Africa where he also made collections of botanical, mineralogical, and ethnographic specimens including a tent from among the Tuareg. Although Olufsen published accounts of his travels, his most enduring contributions lie in the opening up of new research areas for others and in the ethnographic collections which he brought back. Olufsen's expeditions to the Pamirs and West Turkestan and the magnificent collections he brought back from here are described by Esther Fihl in *Exploring Central Asia* I-II, published in this series in 2002.

A unique Mongol collection of some 3,000 artefacts was put together by the Danish explorer and ethnographer Henning Haslund-Christensen with the help of Georg Söderbom, his Swedish colleague on the Sven Hedin expeditions. Unlike most other collectors of museum specimens of the time, Haslund-Christensen understood the necessity of providing detailed information on the use, the place of origin, and the circumstances under which the artefacts were obtained. The collection includes objects of everyday life such as tools, costumes, jewelry, and household utensils from most of the twenty or so Mongol groups, but largely from the Chahar Mongols. The exquisite garments of this fine collection, a total of more than 400 items, are analysed and presented by Henny Harald Hansen (1900-1993) in *Mongol Costumes,* published in 1993. The refined jewellry is treated by Martha Boyer (1911-1995) in *Mongol Jewelry,* which came out in 1995.

Haslund, as he was called among colleagues, had come to Mongolia in 1923 with five other adventurous young Danes on the initiative of the physician Carl I. Krebs (1889-1971) to establish a farm South-West of Lake Baikal in Uriankhai. During the three years he spent there, Haslund came to know and admire the Mongols. He learned the language and a good deal about the culture. In 1926 he left the farm, went to Ulan Bator and later to Peking, where he was engaged by the Swedish geographer and explorer Sven Hedin as a caravaneer for the Sino-Swedish Expedition. In the years 1927-1935 this expedition went from Kalgan through the Gobi Desert to Xinjiang and to the Torgut Mongols in the Tien Shan Mountains. Sven Hedin was mainly occupied with exploration and mapping the areas the expedition covered, while Haslund-Christensen cultivated his interest in the cultural life of the peoples they met on their way, realizing the significance of gathering ethnographic data in the field. He made recordings of sixty folk songs on wax cylinders and collected ethnographic specimen for the Riksmuseet in Stockholm along the way.

In 1936-37 Haslund-Christensen was back in Mongolia, this time on his own, to collect artefacts for the new National Museum in Copenhagen, which was to open in 1938 with a great expansion of its exhibition space. Despite difficulties caused by the Japanese occupation of Manchuria and Inner Mongolia, he was able to spend several months with the Eastern Mongols. In 1938-39 he launched a second expedition to Central Asia, this time under the auspices of the Royal Danish Geographical Society, together with the linguist Kaare Grønbech (1901-1957) and the archaeologist Werner Jacobsen (1914-1979). During this expedition the southern part of Inner Mongolia was surveyed and additional ethnographic collections secured for the National Museum. Thanks to Georg Söderbom, still another considerable collection of artefacts was obtained, representing the daily life of the nomads.

In the years 1947-56 a major Danish research programme was carried out in Central Asia. This, the Third Danish Expedition to Central Asia was organized and led by Haslund-Christensen. The research covered fields as diverse as ethnographical, botanical, zoological, geographical, physical-anthropological, and linguistic studies in Afghanistan, Chitral, Kashmir, Ladakh, Sikkim, and Assam. Sadly enough, Haslund-Christensen was not to see the results of his efforts as he passed away in

Kabul already in 1948. About dozen scholars participated in the expedition and two of them developed an interest in nomadism and the culture of nomadic peoples. One was H.R.H. Prince Peter (1908-1980), the only trained anthropologist on the team, the other my father's brother, the botanist Lennart Edelberg. Prince Peter was familiar with the work of Freud and Jung through his mother, Princess Marie Bonaparte but chose the study of social anthropology with Bronislaw Malinowski in London. He developed a research interest in polyandry which he pursued among the Toda in southern India and among Tibetans in and passing through Kalimpong where he was settled in 1949-1951, (see *A Study of Polyandry,* The Hague 1963). During his stay here, Prince Peter was able to purchase an exquisite collection of Tibetan clothing, tools, implements, and household belongings which has been analysed and published in this series by the former director of the Pitt Rivers Museum in Oxford, Shuyler Jones in a volume entitled *Tibetan Nomads* (1996). Upon Haslund-Christensen's untimely death, Prince Peter was appointed leader of the expedition and he devoted some time to documentaries in the northern parts of the country. Lennart Edelberg had joined the expedition in 1947 as a botanist, but his interests switched to the material culture of transhumant Nuristan and Afghan nomads and he began shipping collections back to Denmark. Upon his return to Denmark in 1949, Edelberg advocated for further, in-depth studies of these peoples and his visions informed the programme of still another Danish expedition to Afghanistan, the Haslund-Christensen Memorial Expedition 1953-55. In 1964, Edelberg joined a Danish Archaeological Expedition to Luristan for a brief study of the Lur among whom Feilberg had worked thirty years earlier, and adding to the collections already in the possession of the National Museum. The two studies and the collections from the Lur inform Inge Demant Mortensen's book in this series, *Nomads of Luristan,* published in 1993.

In the 1950's Danish research among pastoral peoples began to change its theoretical and methodological scope. The first generation of academically trained anthropologists emerged, spearheaded by Johannes Nicolaisen who was to become the first professor of anthropology at Copenhagen University. It was to include Klaus Ferdinand who established the discipline at Aarhus University and directed the Ethnographic Department at the Prehistoric Museum at Moesgaard. With them began the kind of prolonged field research and empirical in-depth studies of pastoral peoples considered indispensable today if an understanding of another culture is to be achieved. Although both Nicolaisen and Ferdinand maintained an interest in historical analysis and the study of material culture, their emphasis was different. Nicolaisen, in particular, devoted himself to problems of social organization and cultural perceptions, while both of them were interested in the ongoing changes that nomadic societies were undergoing.

Johannes Nicolaisen began his studies of North African nomads in 1947 with fieldwork among Berber and Arabic speaking pastoral groups in and just South of the Atlas Mountains in Algeria, an area he revisited in 1950. It was the Tuareg, however, who captured his fascination and heart and whose society and culture became the main subject of his research after he had earned his degree as the first academically trained anthropologist in Denmark. Nicolaisen spent more than three years among these people between 1951 and 1964, living and travelling with them on camelback. All in all he visited the Tuareg nine times, studying their society and the changes which in particular the Ahaggar and Ayr groups were experiencing.

Johannes Nicolaisen had familiarized himself with British social anthropology at University College, London where he studied for a good two years from 1952 to 1954, and the theoretical and methodological discussion there had a profound impact on his theoretical development and future analysis of Tuareg society. In his own words, he had to start all over again academically in England that is how differently anthropology was pursued in the culture-historically oriented Danish environment and the structural-functional schools dominating British anthropology at the time. Although maintaining an interest in historical anthropology and ecology, it was the organization of society and Tuareg behaviour which became the focus of his data collecting. His works examine in detail the intricate kinship systems and kinship behaviour, socio-political organization, slavery, and the beliefs of these nomads, as well as the ecological adaptations and socio-economic transformations of various Tuareg groups. Despite a substantial contribution to nomad studies, Nicolaisen left a considerable part of his data unpublished. Part of his field notes and unpublished materials were analysed and published by the editor of this series as the ninth and tenth volumes of the series entitled Johannes Nicolaisen & Ida Nicolaisen: *The Pastoral Tuareg, I-II,* (1997). This is a considerably enlarged edition of Nicolaisen's book: *The Pastoral Tuareg. Ecology, Culture and Society* (Copenhagen 1963). As soon as this work was completed, Nicolaisen set out to carry out fieldwork among the hunting and gathering Haddad of Kanem, Chad of whom very little was known at the time. He had a long-standing interest in hunting-gathering societes and in the summer of 1963 he and Ida Nicolaisen, his wife and a fellow anthropologist, took up a study among the Haddad, who lived in part among the pastoral Kreda on terms similar to slavery. The results of this joined effort are finally presented in this volume.

For Klaus Ferdinand Afghan nomadism, in particular the form practised by Pashtun and Aimaq groups, became the main focus of his research interests for years to come. He began fieldwork in Afghanistan in 1953-55 as member of the Henning Haslund-Christensen Memorial Expedition under the leadership of H.R.H. Prince Peter. The other members were Lennart Edelberg and the photographer Peter Rasmussen (1918-1992). He focused on culture-historical studies of various forms of pastoral nomadism: semi-nomadism, trading nomadism, and 'true' pastoral nomadism. Inspired by Feilberg's work on the black tent, he devoted time to the study the tent types among the various groups. Prince Peter and Ferdinand were the first to document the existence of special summer trading bazaars set up and managed by the nomads in Central Afghanistan.

Klaus Ferdinand continued his ethnographic studies and museum collecting activities in 1960, 1965-66, and 1974, partly together with his wife Marianne, among nomads in East and Central Afghanistan. Little was known at that time of the social and economic life or the culture of these people despite the fact that pastoral nomads had played an integrative economic role in the history of modern Afghanistan. Over time his studies turned increasingly to the trade and trading systems of the nomads and the socio-political conditions which shape these. In 1975 Ferdinand returned to Afghanistan to pursue the study of nomadic traders and the now rapidly changing economies the nomads. This time he was accompanied by three of his students: Birthe Frederiksen (b.1949), Asta Olesen (b.1952), and Gorm Pedersen (b.1949), who took up studies among different pastoral peoples, itinerant groups

and migrating artisans. Birthe Frederiksen carried out her work among the Hazarbuz of the Mohmand tribe, Gorm Pedersen among the Zala Khan Khel of the Ahmadzai tribe, both groups which relied on or had been heavily involved in trading in the past. Asta Olesen took up the study of non-pastoral nomads, the highly specialized itinerant craftsmen and peddlers who practice so-called peripatetic nomadism. Ferdinand devoted his own time to the collecting of information on the history of nomad bazaars and traditional caravan activities and trade routes. All of these studies will be published in this series.

In 1959 Ferdinand took part in a Danish Archaeological Expedition to Qatar, which was part of a programme of extensive archaeological investigations in the Gulf States, initiated by Professor P. V. Glob. Together with the photographer Jette Bang (1914-1964) he studied both Northern and Southern groups of Bedouin and collected ethnographic specimens. His study of these little known and nowadays sedentarized nomads, *Bedouins of Qatar* appeared as the first volume of the series in 1993.

Taken as a whole, these early Danish studies of nomadic societies and cultures are widely different in scope, as we have seen, reflecting the educational background, interests, and theoretical orientation of the explorers or scholars, the length of time they spent in the field, and the historical period in which they carried out their work. As ethnographic statements, the studies must be appreciated and analysed against this background. This goes for the museum collections as well. These cannot be fully evaluated by viewing them uncritically as objective representations of the cultures which produced them. Invariably, each collection is a result of selection by the fieldworker, who has made choices on the basis of implicit or explicit criteria of representation. As such each collection to some degree reflects Western cultural principles, scientific ideas, and aesthetic values over time. Removed from their original context, moreover, the objects are rearranged in exhibitions where they purport to faithfully replicate such abstract entities as, for example, Mongol culture. The interpretations and evaluations of the ethnographic collections and other ethnographic data which are to be presented in this series of publications take such issues into consideration.

In the early 1980s it became apparent that Danish research among pastoral peoples had reached a new phase.

Afghanistan, a country where no less than eight Danish anthropologists had been working during the 1970s, became sealed off to researchers after the communist takeover in 1979, and is likely to be so for the foreseeable future. Afghan refugees, including pastoral nomads, poured by the millions into neighbouring Pakistan and Iran upon the Soviet invasion and the ensuing war. Luristan, another core area of Danish research interest, was likewise barred to foreign researchers due to the political changes which followed the coming to power of Ayatollah Khomeni and his government. At the same time, the situation of pastoral nomads all over the world was undergoing rapid transformation in the wake of changing ecological, demographic, economic, social, and not least political conditions. In the Sahel region severe droughts brought starvation to man and beast both in the 1970s and the 1980s and several pastoral groups were at the brink of extinction. Demographic pressure and the ensuing competition over land and pastures between nomads and peasants put severe strain on many a pastoral economy. Trade and transport, a significant economic activity for pastoralists in many regions, had run into difficulties. Camels and horses lost out in competition with trucks, trade routes were closed by political decree, and traditional items of local manufacture and trade were replaced by new, industrially produced goods. In the Gulf region, the oil adventure put an end to the traditional way of life of the Bedouins. The Bedouin of Qatar, among whom Klaus Ferdinand had carried out research in 1959, gave up migration in the 1960s as the men obtained employment at the refineries and in other petroleum related fields. A main obstacle to the continuous existence of a pastoral way of life was and is nevertheless the development of modern bureaucratic administrations in areas where pastoral nomads have had virtual autonomy, and the interests of governments in getting the nomads settled and under control.

In view of these challenges, anthropological research must reinvent itself. New problems of inquiry and analysis force themselves upon the scholar, not only in the wake of insights already gained and current theoretical agendas, but first and foremost because of the socio-economic changes and political obstacles that pastoral nomads are facing all over the world, and the radical transformations that their cultures have undergone within living memory. It is evident at the same time, that ethnographic collections

and unpublished data on the lives, values and knowledge of pastoral peoples, which in some cases are already of the past, attain new significance. Each of these books and museum collections embody a singular social and cultural experiment in the history of mankind. As such each one of them will hopefully be of value to ongoing scientific endeavours to explore and explain the cultural and social variability of human society, and the factors which curb the latter, which is the ultimate goal of anthropological research. Hopefully, the greatest significance of the Danish contributions will be the use that the pastoral groups themselves make of the books and collections as documentation of their unique social and cultural achievements and their contributions to the history of mankind.

In 1986 the Carlsberg Foundation decided to support a research initiative to publish a substantial part of the results from the above mentioned Danish expeditions to Central and South-West Asia, Iran, Qatar, and North Africa, many of which had been funded by the Foundation in the past. A substantial grant was given for a five year period and later extended for another five years. The CARLSBERG FOUNDATION NOMAD RESEARCH PROJECT was born.

Initially, the work was supervised by a committee chaired first by Professor Henrik Glahn, and later by Professor Poul Christian Matthiessen, both members of the board of the Carlsberg Foundation. Over the ten year period other members have been the late Professor Tove Birkelund, Associate Professor Klaus Ferdinand, Curator of the Ethnographic Department of the Prehistoric Museum, Moesgaard, who initially took the initiative to the project, Curator Rolf Gilberg of the Danish National Museum, and Asssociate Professor Ida Nicolaisen of Copenhagen University. Niels Petri and later Gunver Kyhn carried the secretarial burden, assisted initially by Sven Dindler. In 1990 an editorial committee was formed with Poul Christian Matthiessen and Ida Nicolaisen as members. In 1993, Professor Per Øhrgaard took over from Matthiessen and Ida Nicolaisen was appointed Editor-in-Chief of the publications.

It may come as no surprise to anyone who has undertaken a major research project, that unforeseen problems do turn up and that it may end up taking much more time than originally planned for. Unfortunately, this has been the case with The Carlsberg Foundation Nomad Research Project. Over the years some researchers had to leave the project, and although others came onboard the speed of the publication process did suffer from this change of guards. Most sadly, some colleagues passed away before their work was completed and this too has caused serious delays. Not only did we loose fine colleagues, the very completion of their work became a challenge. Although the funding for the research programme as such came to an end after ten years, the remaining work has gone on with the generous support to the remaining publications by Carlsberg Foundation. This has also been the case with the present volume, which took me longer to complete than anticipated. Changes have also occurred in respect to publishing. The first ten volumes were published jointly by Rhodos International Science and Art Publishers A/S and Hudson & Tames London and New York, the next three volumes by Rhodos International Science and Art Publishers alone, while the current volume is published by Aarhus University Press.

A research project of this kind and magnitude relies on the collaboration not only of the participating scholars but also on extensive support by many institutions. I take this opportunity to thank the key players: the National Museum of Denmark, the Prehistoric Museum at Moesgaard, the Institute of Asian Studies and the Institute of Anthropology both at Copenhagen University, the Institute of Social Anthropology, University of Aarhus, as well as Danish and foreign colleagues for help and interest in the work presented here. I wish moreover to express my sincere gratitude to the Carlsberg Foundation for the generous support it has offered to the Danish Nomad Research Project throughout the years, both in terms of human investment by the board and secretariat and in terms of funding for the research and publication of the work. Throughout the past years, I and my colleagues have strived to live up to the vision and achieve the goals initially set for the project. Over the past century, the Carlsberg Foundation has enabled the National Museum of Denmark and the Prehistoric Museum, Moesgaard to acquire collections which are now jewels in their ethnographic crowns. It has offered Danish scientists unique opportunities to record the way of life of a range of pastoral peoples in the Pamirs, in Mongolia, Afghanistan, Iran, Qatar, and North Africa. Last but not least, it has provided scholars with the opportunity to subsequently analyse these field data and/or the museum collections for publication in this series. It has been deeply gratifying to be part of this major effort.

Ida Nicolaisen
Editor-in-Chief

Copenhagen, February 2010

Equality breeds no war
Solon (Plutarch, *Lives*: Solon. Sec. 14)

History is a cyclic poem written by Time upon the memories of man
Shelley (*Orbiter Dicta*: Ser. II, 203, 2005)

ACKNOWLEDGEMENTS

This book is about the Haddad of Kanem and the Bahr el Ghazal, an indigenous people whose entire way of life, social position within the society at large and view of themselves and the world is or has been associated with hunting. It is based on ethnographic fieldwork conducted in Chad in the summer and early autumn of 1963 with my late husband and fellow anthropologist, Johannes Nicolaisen (1921-1980).

Our study was carried out under the kind auspices of the Institut National Tchadien des Sciences Humaines, N'Djamena (then Fort-Lamy). Both the director of the institute at the time, Professor, Dr Jean-Paul Lebeuf and Colonel Jean Chapelle, who during Jean-Paul Lebeuf's absence acted on his behalf, were supportive of our work. Many Africans and Europeans showed us hospitality and cared for us during our visit: Mr Tarensaud, on whose ship our luggage was brought to Bol, Mr Derier who kindly put us up in this tiny town when we got stranded for a few days, and Mr Van Aubel, who gave us a lift to Mao, where we began our explorations. In Mao we found our first travel companions: Ali, always cheerful and easy going, who accompanied us on the first part of our journey as interpreter and cook, and Ganai, a charming and screwed old Tubu from the Tibesti mountains, who was to guide us to Haddad camps and take care of the camels during the second part of our travel – and about whom I could write a novel. With Ganai there was never a dull moment, although he caused us problems once in a while, in particular at the outset, when he led us astray to further his private business of blackmailing Kreda pastoralists. It was when Bogar Béchir joined us, however, that our research truly picked up. He

had worked among the Tubu with Colonel Chapelle and was familiar with the role and work of an interpreter. Apart from spoken and written French, he mastered Kreda and Kanembu, the latter being his mother tongue. It was due to his fine personality and expertise that we were able to forge closer ties with the Haddad and learn as much as we did about these people. Without his assistance our notes would have been scantier and less reliable. Working with an interpreter never yields the same faceted and subtle insights as when the anthropologist masters the local medium and is able to listen in on discussions between man and wife, parents and children, chiefs and subjects etc. without a go-between. Johannes had worked previously on his own for years among the Tuareg, and I was to do so several years later as an adopted member of an extended Punan Bah family in a longhouse in Central Borneo. During our stay in Chad, however, we were not able to work without an interpreter. Sources on Kanemese linguistic structures and vocabularies were scanty and our proficiency in Kreda or Kanembu remained insufficient. We were most fortunate therefore to have Bogar Bechir at our side.

A number of institutions, colleagues and friends have supported our initial work and/or assisted me later. Initially, our good friend, the late P.V. Glob, showed interest in acquiring ethnographic specimens from Chad, in line with his support of Johannes' previous work among the Tuareg. Incidentally, the specimens that he brought back from these great pastoralists were to form the very first ethnographic collection of the Moesgaard Museum. Upon our return our specimen from Chad were divided between the Moesgaard Museum and the National Museum of

Denmark, the former receiving most of the objects from the Haddad, the latter our collection from Kreda pastoralists. I take this opportunity to thank the various directors of these institutions with whom I have collaborated over the years. At the National Museum Olaf Olsen, Steen Hvass and Carsten U. Larsen have all been extremely supportive of my work as editor-in-chief of the Carlsberg Foundation's Nomad Research Project, which has ensured that not only this work but a considerable part of Moesgaard's and the National Museum's ethnographic collections have been analyzed and published. I am beholden to the former chief curator of the foreign department of the National Museum, Torben Lundbæk, the former chief curator of the ethnographic department, Espen Wæhle, former curators of the African and Asian sections, Poul Mørk and Rolf Gilberg, and the head of the museum's storage facilities, Ingegerd Marxen. I have been received similarly well by the staff of the Moesgaard Museum, Aarhus. Most of our specimens from the Haddad were collected for this institution, as just intimated. The late curator of the ethnographic department, Klaus Ferdinand, an old friend and colleague was able to support the purchase financially, something which we truly appreciated, as we had very little money at our disposal. My warm thanks extend to the present director of the Moesgaard Museum, Jan Skamby Madsen for taking an interest in my work. I want to thank another friend at this institution, the former curator of the conservation department, Jesper Trier for his practical assistance and unfailing interest in the project. I am indebted moreover to Rockefeller University, in particular to Dr Nicola Khuri and Dr Mitchell Feigenbaum, both professors at this great institution, for kindly providing me with office space and facilities in New York. Last but not least, I am most grateful for the never-failing assistance I receive at the Nordic Institute of Asian Studies, Copenhagen University, where I have had my academic home since 1997. Its successive directors have offered me optimal working conditions, most lately Jørgen Delholm and Geir Helgesen. I am particularly grateful for their unfailing support of the Carlsberg Foundation's Nomad Research Project. My gratitude extends to all the researchers at NIAS and to the excellent staff of the library, in particular Per Hansen, who has spared no effort to locate obscure sources for me.

I am also beholden to his Royal Highness, Crown Prince Frederik for lecturing me on bow hunting, a field in which I have no experience. Professor Ib Friis, Copenhagen University kindly identified some magical plants for me and my old friend Jesper Düring-Jørgensen and Torsten Schlichtkrull at the Royal Library located old illustrations of birds and animals for me. I am thankful, moreover, for useful comments offered by Christel Braae, who kindly read the first draft of the manuscript. It has been a delight to work with Janne Klerk, who breathed life into Haddad culture with her sensitive photographs of their material objects, as has Thomas Otte Stensager with his drawings. I am also indebted to Jens Kirkeby for drawing diagrams and maps, to John Irons and Gerald Jackson for their tweaking of the English language, to Martine Petrod for translating the resumé into French, to Niels Peder Jørgensen for copy-editing the manuscript and to Irene Ring for helping me out with the indexes. Finally, I want to thank Aarhus Universitetsforlag, its director Claes Hvidbak and its marketing director and editor Sanne Lind Hansen for professional assistance in producing this book and to Hanne Kolding for her fine graphic design.

The initial fieldwork was made possible by a grant from the Rask-Ørsted Foundation. The financial support covered Johannes' airfare plus some of our modest expenses in Ch'ad, while I earned my way to Chad (airfares to the former French West Africa were highly expensive in those days) by taking various jobs as a student. The French Air Force gave us a lift from Fort-Lamy to Bol and the Danish-French Shipping Co. transported our ethnographic specimens free of charge from Douala in Cameroun to Copenhagen.

In the year 2000, I was granted a two-month stay at the Aage V. Jensen Foundation in Imperia, which provided optimal working conditions both for me and incidentally also for my second husband, Abraham Pais, for which I am most grateful. The present publication had not seen the light of the day, however, had it not been for a grant from the Carlsberg Foundation, which enabled me to write up the material and also supported the printing of the book.

1:

1: STUDYING THE HADDAD

FIELDWORK AND ITS RAMIFICATIONS

It was my first visit to Chad – to Africa for that matter. I still recall a feeling of awe as I set foot on the continent and tried to take in the dusty, greyish-green savanna in the early morning light: the peculiar smells, the immobility of the standing and squatting men along the runway – all in blue, brown or white caftans except for the few officials at the tiny airport, who were in uniform – French style, of course, shorts and képi. Most vivid, actually, is the memory of the heat which slammed me in the face like a door the very moment I stepped out of the cool plane. I had a sense of transfer to an age-old world, worn to the bone by time, yet it was to prove intensely alive and seductive, as soon as we came into contact with the wonderful people living here.

I learned to appreciate and would later, at times, long intensely for the Sahelian plains, the delicate shades of colours of the landscape, and, not least, the company of the Haddad, their savoir vivre, generosity and sense of humour. They received us hesitantly but cordially and taught us gradually about their way of life. Despite the physical hardships which we endured, I found myself in a blissful mental state: unhampered, spiritually set free – a feeling promoted, I believe, by days on end on camel back, dreamless nights under a starry sky, by the cheerful company of our hosts, and, not least, by the incredibly fascinating challenge of trying to make sense of an entirely different way of life, that of the Haddad. The experience of traversing the docile Kanemese plains and dum palm groves, of living with Haddad families in their beehive huts or sharing the teeming life of the joint camps of foragers and pastoral-

ists, of hunting for gazelle with Haddad families and trying to make scholarly sense of all that we saw and heard had probably a slightly different feel to it for Johannes. I know that he utterly enjoyed himself still to him our travel was blessed by a sense of intimacy, of belonging, derived from many years of work among the Tuareg in neighbouring Niger and southern Algeria. To me it was all new and overwhelming.

We had come to Chad to undertake a preliminary study of the foraging Haddad about who very little was known then as now. Anthropological sources have claimed, in fact, that no foraging communities exist in West Africa. Peter Robertshaw states, for instance in the *Cambridge Encyclopedia of Hunters and Gatherers* that: "In North and West Africa, hunters and gatherers adopted pastoralism or agriculture or were submerged within farming societies in prehistory such that there were no autonomous hunting and gathering groups by the time of European contact." (Robertshaw 1999: 187) This view can be disputed, as our work demonstrates, but written sources on foragers in this part of the world are limited. Little was known of Haddad culture, social life, subsistence pattern, values and beliefs and of their whereabouts. Just to locate these people, in particular those who were nomadic, was to prove difficult and time-consuming. It was very difficult to obtain reliable information on the Haddad even locally and administrative and transport difficulties caused us further complications. We had read of the Haddad in a few administrative accounts, however, and knew that we had to look for them in Kanem and the Bahr el Ghazal. Full of enthusiasm we set out to do so.

1,1. Making camp in the late afternoon.

Kanem proper[1] is a loosely defined area stretching from the north-eastern shores of Lake Chad slightly up towards the Sahara desert and west somewhat beyond the southern parts of the Bahr el Ghazal, literally 'the river of the gazelle', a broad valley that marks the transition from a more lush savanna to the sparse vegetation of the Sahel. The Bahr el Ghazal stretches some 500 kilometres from the eastern part of Lake Chad towards the north-east, where it opens into two inundations known as Eguei and Bodele. Fresh-water deposits show that these were previously flooded by water that came through the Bahr el Ghazal. In the present administrative set-up, Kanem proper covers but a southerly part of a larger prefecture of the same name.

Historically, Kanem and the Bahr el Ghazal have formed a hub of migration and trade routes and the core of the ancient Kanem-Bornu Empire, known to us as far back in time as AD 872 through Arab writers. It has offered livelihood to a multitude of fascinating ethnic groups, witnessed the comings and

joy of independence in 1960, only soon after to be trapped by insurgency, a devastating civil war, severe droughts and a lack of interest on the part of the outside world.

The gently rolling yet diversified landscape has offered an ample source of subsistence that has been exploited with ingenuity by pastoralists, agriculturalist and foraging groups and by fishing communities near and on islands in Lake Chad. Kanem and Bahr el Ghazal are essentially divided along the 14 20 N. Parallel into a northern, largely pastoral zone and, to the south of this, a predominantly agricultural zone. To the far north along the fringes of the Sahara roam camel-herding Arabs such as the Awlad Sliman and Hassauna (Choas). Further south one finds numerous migrating cattle-owning Tubu groups. These belong mostly to the Daza category, as do the Kreda, with some of whom the Haddad camp. The Kreda graze their livestock, horses, donkeys, and camels throughout the southern parts of the Bahr el Ghazal. They are culturally related to the camel-breeding Teda living to the north in Tibesti, Kufra, Djado, Kawar, Borku, Erdi Ma, Murdi and Basso Erdébé, to the Daza exploiting the Sahel both to the east in Niger where the Tumnelia, Cherda, Wandalla and Dietko clans herd their cattle, and in Kanem itself, where we find the Tubu of Chitati, the Djagada and a number of Kecherda clans. The Kreda are also culturally related to groups living further to the east such as e.g. the Noarma and the Beri (Zaghawa and Bideyat) who live in Wadai. Southwest of the Bahr el Ghazal and the territory of the Kreda, one finds the largest of the ethnic groups in Kanem, the agro-pastoral Kanembu who grow millet on the sandy grass-land and let cattle graze in the vicinity of their villages. A similar subsistence strategy is employed by the Tundjur, an Arab population which came from Wadai in the 17th century.

In the vast archipelago in the lake itself lie the hamlets of the Yedina (popularly known as the Buduma - lit. the grass people), who make a living by fishing, agriculture and breeding cattle. They migrate with papyrus boats or swim holding on to bundles of papyrus from one uninhabited island to the other with their herds on the lookout for good pastures (Chapelle 1957: 154; Conte 1991: 228). Along the southern shores of Lake Chad live sedentary agro-pastoral Shuwa Arabs and riverine Kuri, who are culturally and linguistically close to the Kanembu. Although these possess substantial herds, they place as much or more emphasis on the intensive cultivation of the rich, periodically dried-up

goings of political dynasties, profited from and endured the miseries of the slave trade - northwards along ancient caravan trails which since the time of the Romans until well into the 19th century have linked Kanem with Tripoli via Tibesti, and eastwards through Dafur to Khartoum. For more than a thousand years, the eastbound trails were used by thousands of faithful pilgrims on foot, horse- or camelback on their way to and from Mecca. Kanem and Bahr el Ghazal were subject to the colonial rule of the French from 1902 and witnessed the or dammed-off channels and inlets of their marshy archipelago (cf. Conte 1991: 228).

Dispersed among these many ethnic groups one finds the Haddad. The sources available to us in 1963 divided these into three categories, a classification which turned out to coincide with Haddad perceptions as being of 'three stocks'. One group, the Haddad Kreda camp with Kreda and Kecherda pastoralists for most of the year and sustain themselves largely by foraging. They hunt collectively with nets for gazelle, antelope and other animals. According to their oral traditions, they came to the Bahr el Ghazal with the Kreda. At the turn of the 19th century, they lived in fairly large camps near Mussoro for security reasons, but later, during French colonial rule, they were able to range more freely and went up north for seasonal hunts for antelope. The other 'stock', the ones known as Haddad Kanembu, sustain themselves in an entirely different way. Game is pursued in ways similar to those so well known from prehistoric rock engravings from the Sahara. Disguised in sheep-skins and masks, the hunters sneak up upon the animals and kill them with bow and poisoned arrows. At the time of our study game had become so scarce, however, that the Haddad Kanembu subsisted largely by agriculture and lived a settled life, much like that of the agro-pastoral Kanembu. Both Haddad groups had forged asymmetrical relationships with the Kreda and Kanembu respectively. A third 'stock' of Haddad is comprised of smiths, artisans and craftsmen living in villages and towns and a few who earn a living as travelling troubadours. The latter visit the isolated camps of pastoralists and scattered beehive huts of settled agriculturalists bringing news, festivity and poetry into peoples' lives. They play music and sing poems that recapitulate historical events, venerated traditions, cherished love stories or are discourses on current political events. The relationship between the three 'stocks' of Haddad is rather obscure. The Haddad Kreda and Haddad Kanembu regularly dispute a common origin and discuss whether they are affiliated to the local smiths. Their worldviews, perceptions of themselves and artistic modes of expression are still intimately connected with the surrounding nature and the animal world that they exploit or have exploited for a living, however. They also share a caste-like status within the wider society. They have all embraced Islam although some did so only at the beginning of the 20th century.

There were only a dozen passengers that got off the Air France plane together with us that day, July 8th, 1963, and not many more were crowding on the runway to fly back to Paris. The airport consisted of a single airstrip, a hangar, and just as modest an arrival and departure building. A rattling scrapheap of a Peugeot 404 took us the few miles to town, past huts and flat-roofed mud houses, women carrying water, men squatting in tiny groups next to fires or herding sheep and goats by the roadside, if not on their way with livestock, camels and donkeys loaded with firewood, freshly cut fodder, bricks and other merchandise to the huge market place, which we later located on the outskirts of the town.

The capital, Fort-Lamy, now N'Djamena, was a city of some 60,000 souls back then.[2] It spread out along green banks at the confluence of the Logone and Shari rivers, a good one hundred kilometres below the point where they flow into Lake Chad. Small vessels navigate these waters, but they are mainly left to Kotoko fishermen, who try their luck from dug-out canoes in competition with flocks of pelicans and, previously, a fair number of crocodiles. The town itself turned out to be a loose conglomerate of spread-out government buildings along sandy roads that we hurried along to gain government approval of our research plans. It had tiny shops run by Arab and Libyan merchants, sprawling residential areas with rectangular adobe houses with bright green and blue window frames all shielded from the outside by straw or brick walls. The market was huge and buzzing with life, stocked with livestock and poultry, rice, millet, vegetables, spices, baskets, and household utensils. Here we met Haddad smiths for the first time, squatting around the anvils where they made hoes, knives and other iron tools. An open-air cinema showed Egyptian tear-jerkers and an occasional French gangster movie with Eddie Constantine. A few stores catered for Europeans, almost all of them French, some still employed by the Government, others in private business, running import-export and transport companies. The selection of merchandise was modest both in kind and number, but we supplemented our camp equipment of two blankets (which we mainly used as saddle covers), a primus, mosquito-nets, one large and two small canteens for water, a filter, torches and, of course, some packs of gauloise to keep Johannes going. There was one modern high-rise of a hotel with a great view over the Chari river, and an old, modest, but cosy one with bungalows and a French patron, where we stayed. Here you could get an omelette, a tough steak or chicken and the indispensable baguette, cheese and a bottle of wine, which the waiter marked and kept for the next meal, had you not consumed it all.

Then as now, Chad was one of the poorest countries in the world with a population of a mere 2,675,000 million (1961 census). Scattered over the sizeable territory of 1,284,000 sq. km it was not only one of Africa's largest but also one of its least populated states.[3] Historically, an intersection of equatorial and Saharan trade routes, which supported flourishing city states in its northern regions and adjacent parts of Central Sudan from the Middle Ages into the 20th century, it was also the arena of constant violence and war, spurred on by slave-raiding and religious proselytizing - the two often going hand in hand - and the comings and goings of regional potentates. From the late 19th century, it became a victim of disengaged and damaging French mal-administration that neglected education, socio-economic development and the democratization of its society. The country's land-locked location and great distance from the coast posed problems in itself for modern economic development. Chad was – and is – largely an agricultural society. The main export commodities were cotton grown in the South and cattle bred in the North. These were worth US$ 11.5 million and US$ 14.5 million respectively, and amounted to 69 % and 9 % of total exports. The industrial labour-force numbered only about 4,500 individuals (1962 census, cf. Fuchs 1966: 83, 87-8). Today, after more than forty years of political instability, civil war and the human and economic disasters following in the wake of the droughts which hit the Sahel region between 1969 and 1973 and again in the early 1980s, the basic economic structure and performance has changed precious little in the northern parts of the country. An estimated 200,000 and 400,000 of the Chadian people perished during this period, and it is only with the relative stability brought to the country since 1990 by the government of Idriss Deby that economic development is slowly picking up. Still, Chad ranks among the least developed of the Sahelien states. Life expectancy is a mere 47 years, infant mortality 122 per 1000 live births, and 70 % of the adult population is illiterate (Leisinger and Schmitt 1995). Rural poverty and high population growth rates (2.4 1980-92) have led to rapid urbanization since the

1,2. Bogar Bechir, our invaluable interpreter during the second half of our travel.

1960s, the urban population comprising about 33.8% in 1992. Migration to the urban centres and, for that matter to coastal countries, by younger men has increased women's work loads and responsibilities. Given their poor nourishment, hard labour, frequent childbirths and the poor medical care they are offered, it is no wonder that Sahelien women are often in alarmingly poor health. The maternal mortality rate, for example, is 800 per 100,000 live births, exceeding that of women in Switzerland 100 to 200 fold (UNDP, *Human Development Report 1994*, Table 11).

Moreover, Chad is far from being a tranquil place, and genuine reconciliation between the North and the South has not taken place. In 1993, democratic reforms were introduced, but the GDP per head remained low. In 1995 it was a mere US$ 165 and hence among the lowest in the world. Cotton contributes some 43 %, meat and live animals 13% of the total export earnings (Hodgkinson 1997: 303).[4] Great hopes are being pinned on oil production (ibid. 304). In June 2000, the World Bank gave its backing to a 3.7 billion US$ project at the Doba oil-field in southern Chad plus a 1,080 km pipeline to transport the oil from Doba through the rainforest of Cameroun to an offshore storage and export facility on the Atlantic coast. The support was given on the condition that 70 % of the revenue would be spent on health, education, agriculture and infrastructure. The production is estimated at 225,000 barrels a day and potential earnings for Chad of around two billion during a 25-year production period. A year later, a 600 million US$ deal was made to initiate work on the controversial oil pipeline (*Financial Times, June 21st, 2001*). But the prospects for making good use of this major source of income for the Chadian state and applying it to further economic development may not be all in the clear due to the political situation. The Movement for Democracy and Justice in Chad still maintains bases in the mountainous desert of the North, from where they launch attacks on government troops under the leadership of Youssouf Togoimi, a former defence minister. To curb these, the Chadian government stepped up its campaign against the rebels in the closing months of 2000, using new weapons paid for out of the 25 million US$ advance it had received on oil royalties. This brought criticism raining down on Mr. Deby from all sides (*The Economist, January 6th-12th 2001: 32-3*). Rebel attacks from Sudan and the ongoing fighting in Chad in 2008 has not made the prospect of development any brighter.

Chad quit its past as part of French Equatorial Africa to become an independent state on August 11, 1960, i.e. only three years prior to our arrival. However, the Saharan territory of the North, the Borku-Ennedi-Tibesti prefecture, comprising about half the country, remained under French military administration until 1964. The French kept garrisons in the area, including one in Mao manned by the French Foreign Legion. The precarious political situation of the new nation was noticeable. A few years later, it was to erupt into a full-fledged rebellion in the North, where the Front de libération nationale du Tchad (FROLINAT) had its stronghold, backed by Colonel Ghadafi of Libya.

We noticed the tense atmosphere upon our arrival in 1963. President Tombalbaye had arrested three cabinet ministers and the Speaker of the National Assembly, Mahamat Abdelkerim, and many other Christian and Muslim leaders on March 23rd that year. Three days later, he dissolved the National Assembly to hold an election to give him extended powers. The visibility of the police was striking. We learned of police intimidation, the rounding up of arms, even spears and throwing knives including part of the collections we had made for the museums in N'Djamena and Denmark. When we returned to Fort-Lamy in September a nightly curfew had been imposed and the atmosphere was unpleasant. Tombalbaye had just arrested Djebrine Ali Kerallah, a minister of the North, and Jean Baptiste, the major of Fort-Lamy who was widely respected, moves which spread dissatisfaction and rioting in the capital, resulting in the deaths of an estimated 100 to 500 people (cf. Azevedo 1998: 91). In practical terms, the lurking instability and administrative inexperience and uncertainty as how to handle the situation, in particular with respect to the northern regions, manifested itself as concern regarding the expediency of our plans to carry out social research in Kanem and Bahr el Ghazal. We received permission only on condition that we had our permits authorized both with the préfet of Mao and the sous-préfet in Mussoro[5]. Although pretty understandable under the circumstances, it caused us a great deal of extra travel and delays, the more so because the rainy season made travelling utterly difficult. At the time of our visit there were less than a 100 km of laterite roads and only about 10,000 km of dust roads in the country and these were largely in the South and under any circumstance mostly unusable in the rainy season. Motorized vehicles were few and far between. There were in fact but a mere 8,000 in the entire country at that time (1962 census) and we had no means to rent a landrover, even if this had been possible. Instead we relied on whatever kind of transport came our way to get to the field: planes, boats, landrovers, trucks – and, once we were there, camels, which we found at the market.

It started out the easy way: a French pilot who was going north to Faya-Largeau kindly squeezed us into a narrow seat behind him in a tiny military plan. He dropped us near Bol, a small town of about 1,800 souls and the seat of a sous-préfecture at the northeast shores of Lake Chad. We left in the morning of 16th July, and when the pilot took off to continue his mission we found ourselves in the midst of a sandy, deserted plain with nothing but a tiny backpack. The plane could carry no further freight, and our camp gear, though truly modest in size and weight, had to be sent by boat.

We placed our bags under a leafless acacia and waited. It seemed to me that we had landed in the middle of nowhere, a place of neither friend nor foe. A turtle dove cooed melancholically somewhere, but the burning heat of an approaching midday apparently discouraged other living creatures from giving any signs of life. Only the small desert flies buzzed happily at the sight or rather smell of our sweaty bodies. I looked around somewhat in despair yet noticed to my comfort that Johannes looked perfectly blissful. I should learn that there was no reason to worry. After a while a man approached us as out of the blue, and soon a tiny group of men and kids had gathered around us, obviously curious about our presence, not least mine. Few, if any European women had come their way, as the French military and administrative personnel were all male and rarely posted with wives. The pilot had circled over Bol after taking off, a signal that he had carried passengers, and after some time a young French extension officer, Mr Derier picked us up in his landrover and generously offered us a bed and board in his bungalow. He worked at Bol together with a Belgian colleague, Mr Van Aubel for the Agricultural Institute of Research to promote the local farming of polders (cf. Chapter 7), and the two of them kindly showed us various agricultural projects. They did also pick up our luggage when it finally arrived by ship from Fort-Lamy.

The 'airlift' was a leap forward, but from then on we proceeded in 'African time'. We had been advised at the Institut des Sciences Humaines to go to N'Guri, in and around which some Haddad were supposed to reside. We managed to do so but only at the speed of a tortoise. On July 19th we got a ride with Mr Van Aubel, but the landrover broke down, and after a night en route, we returned to Bol. The next few days were again spent here to familiarize ourselves with the local life of the Yedina, Kanembu and other ethnic groups living here. We walked the heavy sandy paths of the town, past neatly fenced family clusters of beehive huts adorned with ostrich eggs on the top of the pointed roofs. We watched Yedina families

swimming with their livestock to and from nearby islands, heads held high to keep their clothes, baskets and belongings dry. We did also establish contact with some Haddad, however. We spent time with Haddad smiths at the market and befriended Haddad hunters that made a living from fishing and hunting on Lake Chad. One memorable night we went crocodile hunting with three of them on the Lake. We stayed two days in Baga Sola west of Bol where we met other Haddad hunters and paid a visit to the Agricultural Research Institute. After yet another night in Bol we finally reached N'Guri on July 25th.[6]

We spent about one week in N'Guri where we were kindly hosted by the local administration and count Corard des Escarts, who had created a horse insemination centre to improve the local stock of horses with Arab thoroughbreds, primarily for sale for polo in Nigeria. Through this nobleman we soon established contact with some Haddad in the neighbourhood, but to our disappointment it turned out that hunting had become of little significance to them. A Haddad who had specialized in catching small animals primarily for the sake of their furs or to sell as pets took us along with him on several day-long expeditions. Due to the insignificance of hunting in the area we decided to proceed directly to Mussoro, where we had been told by Colonel Chapelle that the Haddad still relied on hunting for their livelihood. On the 1st of August we drove to Mao with Mr Van Aubel to get our research permit authorized. Mao is the administrative centre of the prefecture of Kanem. The town has a proud history as the residence of the Sultan of Kanem but is nowadays a somewhat sleepy place. It consists largely of single-storey adobe houses, all rectangular buildings sealed off from the streets by tall adobe walls, except for a door that opens onto the rectangular courtyard around which the family quarters are built. Mao reminds you of the small towns of North Africa and it would all be very quiet, were it not for a contingent of the Légion d'Honneur. The following day we were lucky to get a lift to Mussoro, where we arrived late at night on August 2nd.

Mussoro had about 8,000 inhabitants at the time and was hence by far the largest town in the northern part of Kanem and Bahr el Ghazal. It lies at the centre of an area dominated by Kreda pastoralists and we decided to use it as a base for our exploration of those Haddad whom we knew shared camps with Kreda pastoralists. We rented a few camels and found a local man, Ali, to assist us. Ali knew some

1,3. Ready to go. Johannes was an accomplished camel rider, who had traversed a good part of the Sahara on his own with five camels, while it was my very first experience with these animals. I soon found out that individual camels are quite different to ride. Some walk in a lovely gentle way, others have a bumpy fast trot. One of our rented camels was simply quite unpleasant to mount. In Kanem proper riding saddles are rarely used. Most make do with simple pack-saddles. Whatever the technicalities, it is a fantastic experience to travel on the back of these strange animals, due to the peace of mind it induces and the grand view of the scenery that you have from atop their backs. Photo J.N.

French, but it was only when Bogar Bechir joined us that we were able to communicate properly with the Haddad, as previously acknowledged.

We made two journeys on camelback. On the first one we went west. We left Mussoro on the 6th of August and returned late in the evening of 21st August, having completed the following route: Mussoro - Oual Tibin - Sasal - Hamatier Rémelé - Taigoni - Anizanihumoy - Bidenga - Dangaraba - Kyllinga - Michemille Kutu - Dugin - Méchimeré - N'Galu - Wanagal - Tigenej - Kolu - Adjaja - Sidigé Joroso - Mussoro. The areas furthest to the west proved to be beyond the grazing territory of the Kreda. The land around Méchimeré for example is inhabited by settled Kanembu farmers and in that region we also encountered some Haddad who subsist by tilling the soil but among whom hunting still plays both an economic and a cultural role.

On the second journey we chose a different route, initially venturing northwest and then turning south towards Chedra, a tiny village largely inhabited by Haddad agriculturalists. We left Mussoro on August 25th riding towards Kurei Iruso - and then on to Kulu Jesko - Gaba - Chakara - Andjalay - Joli Rémelé - Erémelé - Kinemanga - Wagag and Chedra, where we stayed from the 6th to the 14th of September. From here we continued towards Mussoro, camping with some Kreda on the way. We arrived on September 16th in Mussoro and spent a few days writing up notes and checking the translation of local texts with Bogar Bechir. I had devoted quite some time to the study of the material culture of the Haddad and collecting ethnographic specimen and was busy packing these and arranging for their transportation back to Fort-Lamy. On September 20th, we climbed on board an old lorry loaded with specimens for the museums in N'Djamena and Denmark. We had rented it to bring us to the capital, a chance which a good dozen other people immediately took advantage of, having milled around us for hours to get a free ride. The route went via Chedra and Massakory, but it took us a few days to reach our destination. We proceeded slowly due to the heavy load. A flat tyre in the middle of a large flooded area and no tube with any solution for mending it left us stranded in water to the ankles for some twenty hours, while someone walked the twenty kilometres there and back to acquire what was needed. The motor ran hot, the driver had business to attend to, a number of gendarmes posted in the midst of nowhere were busy playing cards

and took their time to inspect the vehicle - all in all the familiar trials and tribulations of travelling in this part of Africa. It takes time, yet is also an inseparable part of the charm of being there, because of the many unexpected experiences and funny situations that come as extra gifts and the warm feelings of togetherness that bond you with your fellow travellers. In N'Djamena we presented our findings to the staff of the Institute and offered them to take their pick from the ethnographic specimens to supplement the local museum collection. We left Chad on September 29th.

Our plan was to undertake a preliminary study in preparation for further long-term fieldwork. As it happened, we were never to resume work among the Haddad. Within a year of our return, Johannes was appointed the first professor of anthropology in Denmark, and the workload of building up the Institute of Anthropology at the University of Copenhagen did not permit fieldwork for a couple of years. In the long run, a more serious complication turned out to be the political development in Chad. The country became plagued by latent and at times open rebellion by the Tibu-dominated region to the North against the southern part of the country and the central government under president Tombalbaye. The seriousness of the situation was already noticeable during our stay, with curfews in the major cities, but the insurgency grew dramatically during the following years and resulted in harsh military intervention by Franco-Chadian forces. It is a sad fact that France left its former colony ill-prepared for self-determination and that the various ethnic groups were not accustomed to engaging in a democratic process. The educational, socioeconomic and religious discrepancies between the North and the South were staggering. The elite of the North, so recently the enslavers of the South, could not accept not holding the reins of power in an independent Chad, and far less the idea ever to be ruled by whom they saw as their former 'slaves', or their offspring. Although the state of open hostility in Kanem was curbed at times, because of collusion between the Kanembu Muslim potentate of Kanem, the *alifa* of Mao, and the government, in practice North Kanem and Bahr el Ghazal were off-limits for researchers. The political situation remained explosive, at times turning Kanem into an actual zone of combat, and for decades after our fieldwork it remained extremely repressive. It is well known that tens of thousands of people were killed and tortured during Hissene Habré's rule 1982-90. International estimates mention figures up to 200,000 out of a population of merely 6 million - the reason that Human Rights Watch has tried to prosecute Mr. Habré in Senegal, where he went into exile in 1990 (*The Herald Tribune*, January 26, 2000). A Truth Commision created by Habré's successor mentions a total of 40.000 political murders and tortures and accuses Habré of using the secret police to persecute ethnic and indigenous groups. A Belgian court has called for the extradition of Habré.

It is indisputable that researchers become part of the political scene where they work, although we often ignore or minimize this aspect of our work. It became painfully clear to the entire research community that this was the case, however, when the French archaeologists, Françoise and Pierre Claustre were taken hostage by the FROLINAT in 1974. On the order of general Habré they were held in captivity for close to three years as a strategic measure to bolster his attempts to obtain the means to equip an army that could expand the territory which FROLINAT controlled beyond Tibesti and bordering parts of Borku (cf. Buijtenhuijs 1987: 34-5). The political instability of Northern Chad put a damper on our enthusiasm to resume work in Kanem and the Bahr el Ghazal, the more so as a study of the Haddad required a long-term investment in our view. There were several reasons for this: The people that we were interested in studying were living in fairly small groups scattered over a vast territory and they were partly nomadic. The foraging Haddad sustained themselves by two entirely different subsistence strategies in different parts of the country and neighbouring Niger, and were living among or with different dominant ethnic groups whose language they spoke. Haddad artisans lived in the towns and posed a challenge of their own. This situation and the fact that an in-depth study of the Haddad would require quite some knowledge of their interaction with the dominant ethnic groups among whom they lived made it clear to us that the ideal would be to plan for long-term fieldwork. In view of the political developments in Chad that made it unlikely we could resume work among the Haddad in a foreseeable future, we both decided to work elsewhere: Johannes among the Negritos of Northern Luzon, a task that he unfortunately had to give up after some months due to a military decision to offer him the 'protection' of some young soldiers with automatic

weapons, not an ideal situation for fieldwork among timid foragers to say the least. He then turned to the Penan of Borneo, where he spent about a year before his untimely death. I 'nestled in' with the Punan Bah of Sarawak, with whom I have worked more or less continuously for the past thirty years.

THEORETICAL VICISSITUDES

Ever since the end of the 19th century when anthropology came of age, the profession has been deeply fascinated by the remaining hunting and foraging societies of this world. Data on these, once perceived as the most 'primitive' of human societies, were crucial to the construction of the grand evolutionary theories which engaged the minds of late 19th century scholars like Lewis Henry Morgan (cf. *Ancient Society* 1877) and through him Marx and Engels. The societies of the Australian aborigines were among the ones providing empirical data for subsequent theoretical works. Ethnographic data on the beliefs and rituals of these were critical to James Frazer's comparative analyses and attempts to reconstruct an inaccessible past as well as for his argument that magic preceded religious beliefs (cf. *Totemism* 1877; *The Golden Bough* 1890). The social and cultural characteristics of hunting and foraging societies were also significant for the theorizing by Viennese and German cultural historians in the early decades of the 20th century, be it Wilhelm Schmidt's giant effort to capture 'the origin of the idea of God', or the determination of scholars like Leo Frobenius, Graebner and Ankermann and later Hermann Baumann to set straight the world's cultural history by ascribing cultural traits to specific clusters such as Baumann's *Pygmy Culture, Eurafrican Steppe-Hunting Culture* and the *"Malhalbi" Culture* (1940) and ranking these in a temporal order. In order to provide a solid empirical base for culture historical theories, Father Martin Gusinde spent two and a half years among one of the remaining 'Urvölker', the hunting and foraging groups of the Tierra del Fuego Islands in 1919-23 and among the nomadic fishing communities of the Yámans and Halawúlup of Cape Horn. Also Franz Boas, the founding father of American ethnology, went into the field to explore societies still relying entirely on foraging at that time. In 1883 and 1884 he investigated the arctic habitat of the Baffin Island Eskimos and their knowledge

1,4. Johannes loved hunting, not the killing or the trophies, but because of the affinity with nature and the satisfaction of being able to provide one's own food. He was determined to pursue his hobby and decided to bring a rifle that he had 'organized' from the Germans during the war. He had neither a permit for the rifle in Denmark nor for bringing it into France and Chad and back. He was certain that this would cause no problems and happily wrapped the rifle in the two tartan blankets and tied the whole thing together with a cord, arguing that no one would notice. And Lord and behold no one did, although the bundle looked exactly what it was, a rifle wrapped in two blankets. Apart from the one gazelle, however, he only shot a few guinea fowl, but the Haddad were most happy to borrow the rifle all along.

of the area (Boas 1888). He later struggled to document the intricacies of the social organization, secret societies, complicated exchange systems, and totemistic beliefs of Northwest Coast Indians (Boas 1897, 1916). Boas was to be followed by scores of students and other scholars who described the cultural richness of North American Indian and Inuit foraging societies.

Also the pioneer of British structural-functionalism, A.R. Radcliffe-Brown chose a hunting-foraging society as the subject of his field research, namely that of the Andaman Islanders, subsequently providing us with his fine monograph on Andaman social organization and be-

haviour, including an intricate analysis of the custom of crying (*The Andaman Islanders* 1922). The bulk of his later theoretical contributions relied on data from societies like these, not the least the Australian aborigines (cf. *Structure and Function in Primitive Society* 1952).

In France, Émile Durkheim drew on the richness of religious beliefs among the very same Australian aborigines when writing his classical structural analysis: *The Elementary Forms of the Religious Life* (1912) as had Lucien Lévy-Bruhl in a publication two years earlier on collective representations and his repudiated idea of the pre-logical thinking of primitive man, explicated i.a. in a specific sec-

1,5. The small army plane that dropped us somewhere near the tiny city of Bol at the Lake Chad. Ida is sitting on the sparse equipment of the expedition. Photo J.N.

tion on beliefs related to hunting (cf. *Les fonctions mentales dans les sociétés inférieures* 1910). Claude Lévi-Strauss followed the main path in his key work on kinship systems, in which the Australian aborigines once again were subjected to analysis (cf. *Les structures élémentaires de la parenté* 1949), and later when writing *Le totémisme aujourd'hui* (1962). Lévi-Strauss' personal acquaintance with the ethnographic field was primarily with tribes in South America who all relied heavily on hunting for their subsistence, as described in *Tristes Tropiques* (1955).

The post-war period witnessed a surge in anthropological field studies and debates. New interests developed and an array of innovative theories saw the light of day. A milestone was the symposium published as *Man the Hunter* by Richard B. Lee and Irven DeVore (1968). It was to be followed by successive publications from later conferences, such as Åke Hulkrantz and Ørnulf Vorren (eds.): *The Hunters. Their Culture and Way of Life* (1982), which

was dedicated to Johannes, and publications from subsequent conferences such as Hunters and Gatherers, I-II, edited by Tim Ingold, David Riches and James Woodburn (1988). The development has escalated over the past decade, reflecting the diversification of anthropology on the threshold of the twenty-first century. The kaleidoscopic nature of studies over the past few decades that focus on hunting and foraging societies will not to be dealt with here. For an overview of the theoretical diversification, see e.g. Fred R. Myers: *Critical Trends in the Study of Hunter-Gatherers* (1988); Barbara Bender & Brian Morris: *Twenty Years of History, Evolution and Social Change in Gatherer-Hunter Studies* (1991); Richard B. Lee & Richard Daly: *The Cambridge Encyclopedia of Hunters and Gatherers* (1999). It is worth noticing, however, that empirical studies do not match this theoretical spread in the sense that scholarly interest in regions and ethnic groups appears somewhat unequally distributed. Some ethnic groups have of course been off limits to Western scholars for political reasons, as has been the case till recently of those living in Siberia. Other groups have failed to attract more than a few researchers, as is the case e.g. of the Penan of Central Borneo, although these people made headlines in the world press in the 1980s and 1990s due to their adamant protests over the logging of the rainforest.

At the time when Johannes and I were engaged in research among the Haddad, anthropological discussions were dominated by an interest in organizational forms and social exchange, as indicated by the title of the influential publication from the first ASA conference in 1963: *The Relevance of Models for Social Anthropology* (1965). There was little interest in historical analysis at that time, "... the emphasis was on cross-cultural systemics hinging upon notions of rationality and ecological adaptiveness", as Bender and Morris aptly formulated it (1992:4). A number of the more prominent topics within hunting-foraging studies were issues of territoriality, residence rules, and marriage preferences as a critical determinant of the character of the band as well as questions as to the basic socio-political structure of these societies. Elman Service argued, for example, that the patri-local band was 'the simplest, most rudimentary form of social structure' and that it preceded the composite band (Service 1962: 97). A budding field of interest was the economics of hunting-foraging societies, spurred on i.a. by Richard B. Lee's work among the 'Kung San and James Woodburn's among the Hadza. Lee's assessments of the subsistence pursuits and yields of the Dobe and his claim that albeit it is: "... impossible to define abundance" ... "one index of relative abundance is whether or not a population exhausts all the food available from a given area. By this criterion, the habitat of the Dobe-area Bushmen is abundant in naturally occuring food." (Lee 1969: 49) Woodburn's claim that the Hadza obtain sufficient food without undue effort, and that "Over the year as a whole probably an average of less than two hours a day is spent obtaining food" (1968: 54) sparked Marshall D. Sahlin's argument in *The Original Affluent Society* (1972; (1968)) about the nature of hunting gathering economics as characterized by an 'imminence of diminishing returns' and his claim that: "... the amount of work (per capita) increases with the evolution of culture, and the amount of leisure decreases" (1972: 35). This view was vividly debated i.a. by Johannes on the basis of his studies among the

Negritos and the Penan (cf. J. Nicolaisen 1975, 1976). The trend to read "modern hunters historically, as an evolutionary base line" (Sahlins 1972: 38) loomed in discussions despite warnings that data on contemporary geographically, politically and socio-economically marginalized groups of hunters and gatherers be considered a documentation of earlier, palaeolitic forms of social organization. The evolutionary/ecological interest was in part ignited by Leslie White's grandiose generalizations in *Evolution of Culture* (1959), but it became linked to the theoretical frameworks of cultural materialism and structural-marxism, which played a considerable role within the social sciences of the 1960s and 1970s. These were the heydays of heated debates about pre-capitalist modes of production, with combatants such as Godelier, Hirst & Hindess and Claude Meillassoux. The last-mentioned wrote, for example, about two co-existing modes of production among the Gouro: one based on complex co-operation (hunting) and a lineage mode based on simple co-operation (agriculture) (cf. Meillassoux 1972: 98).

The defining criteria of foragers did also give rise to theoretical debates. Woodburn proposed a classification of foragers into immediate-return systems and delayed-return or delayed-yield systems, the former being characterized by a strong orientation towards the present and lack of concern about the future (Woodburn 1980). Tim Ingold maintained that the socially important diagnostics of these communities were: "whether or not people are bound to one another by enduring relations in respect of the control and distribution of the means of subsistence." (Ingold 1987; Burch & Ellanna 1996) Other scholars argued that foragers should be perceived as marginalized classes or castes rather than as exemplars of a specific way of life. The proponents claimed that simple technologies and sharing of food among foragers in the late 20th century were spurred on by poverty rather than by a genuine hunting tradition. Camel Schrire and Wilmsen & Denbow argued, for example, that hunting-gathering societies often are merely shambles of a former past, cut to size by colonial and global forces (cf. Schrire 1984; Wilmsen & Denbow 1990). A good deal of the latter debate referred to the situation of the San in Southern Africa, but empirical cases from other parts of the world have also shed light on the discussion (Lee & Daly 1999: 6). The views of the foragers have been given less attention (Feit 1996: 433-36).

1,6. The sleepy town of Bol where our Kanem journey began. Photo K.M. Fig.4,1; 31.3.1954.

Data on current hunting and foraging societies have also played a prominent role in the feminist dissection of theories on the origin and evolution of 'primitive society' and anthropological theory in general. The feminists revealed that many of these were biased due to a male perspective, be it marxist or structuralist (cf. Sally Slocum, Gayle Rubin and Rohrlich-Leawitt; Sykes and Weatherford in Rayna R. Reiter (ed.): *Toward an Anthropology of Women* (1975); Martin and Voorhies: *Female of the Species* (1975). Men's and women's different roles in foraging societies became a hot topic, highlighted by Sally Slocum's article: *Woman the Gatherer: Male Bias in Anthropology* (1975), a provocative title that put into perspective the research agendas of previous studies.

Research carried out among hunting and foraging societies since the 1960s reflect the wide scope of theoretical interests that characterize modern anthropology. Empirical studies are unevenly distributed around the globe, however, leaving the social, economic and religious life of some groups fairly unexplored. Australian Aborigines, Inuit, North American Indians, the Orang Asli of Malaysia, the San of South Africa and Namibia, the Batwa of Zaire and Uganda and the Aka and Baka of Cameroun continue to attract a host of anthropologists. Other groups are almost consigned to oblivion, as is the case in West Africa, for instance. Peter Robertshaw may be right in arguing that hunter-gatherers in this area were submerged within farming societies during prehistoric times and/or adopted pastoralism. Hunting has been significant to some pastoral groups in the Sahara, for example the Tuareg (Nicolaisen & Nicolaisen 1997, I: 220; Lhote 1951: 108). Hunting is also economically significant to agro-pastoralists further to the south across the Sahel and among many agriculturalists in the bordering Savanna, not though among the Kanembu of Kanem. But Robertshaw is mistaken when stating that there were no hunting-foraging peoples left at the time of European contact (Robertshaw 1999: 187). They still existed although they were few in numbers and did not attract attention. One such people were the Nemadi of Mauretania, among whom Jean Gabus spent some two weeks in 1951 and 1976 respectively. Like the Haddad, they were traditionally discriminated against and relegated to an inferior position within the wider Maurish society. Traditionally, Nemadi men hunted on foot with lance and dogs for gazelles. As game became hard to come in the 20th century they ventured on ever longer hunting trips mounted on camels, which they borrowed from Maure pastoralists, to whom they were tied in an asymmetrical exchange relationship. Some borrowed guns as well, in which case as little as one quarter of the meat went to the hunter upon return (Gabus 1977: 61). The Nemadi were still nomadic in 1951, but had become sedentarized by 1976 on government incentive. By then they lived in straw huts near Walata with a few cows, and the kids went to school, where they performed extraordinarily well (Gabus: 1977: 64).

The reasons why hunting and foraging groups in West Africa have caught so little attention that they are not even listed in the *Cambridge Encyclopedia of Hunters and Gatherers* may be several. Not only are they few and far between. They have experienced dramatic declines in the fauna population over the past century due to ecological transformation, political unrest, and, as far as the Haddad are concerned, more recently also government regulations that directly prohibit their age-old occupation. Still, the main reason for the lack of studies of hunting and foraging in the Sahel region may be the one given by Murdock in his overview in *Man the Hunter.* Reminded by William Shack that there were half a dozen such groups in Central Ethiopia alone originally omitted from his survey of world cultures, Murdock explained that due to the "scanty references available to me, they seemed more like dispersed outcast groups than independent tribes. If they do in fact lead independent lives, they certainly deserve early and intensive study." (Murdock 1968: 16-7) This remark is indicative of the research attitude of the 1960s, a time when anthropologists still conceived of and analyzed societies as structurally, identifiable units and did not apply self-identification as the defining criteria, as is now widely approved following UN practice. The 1960s also experienced a growing awareness of the plight of indigenous peoples and the responsibility of researchers. This development was spurred on by and/or went hand in hand with academic interest in peasant movements, with cases of scientific malconduct

by researchers and increasing demands by indigenous peoples themselves to acquire a say over research carried out among them. Some researchers took these developments to heart and 'Action Anthropology' was born. To this day, concerned anthropologists speak up for underprivileged groups with whom they work. Examples that spring to mind are: Robert Knox Denton, Kirk Endicott, Alberto G. Gomes and M.B. Hooker's book on the situation of the Orang Asli of Malaysia (1997) and, not the least James Woodburn's adamant defence of Hadza rights to their land – advocacy which made these anthropologists highly unpopular among ruling politicians in the respective countries. A few of us have the privilege of raising our voices at the UN Permanent Forum on Indigenous Issues.

SOURCES

Little had been written about the Haddad of Kanem and Bahr el Ghazal in 1963, when we made our acquaintance with these people, as just intimated, and only few sources have been added. It is not because this part of North Africa constitutes a void in terms of historical chronicles. Kanem was linked to Tripoli via the Fezzan-Kawar-Chad trade routes, which flourished in Roman times and probably even during the Phoenician era and Lake Chad is supposed to have been known by report to Ptolomy (AD 150). He drew a big lake at about its position on his world atlas, the first of its kind, probably the very one known as the Kura Lake in the Middle Ages. At that time Kanem was the centre of the Kanem-Bornu state, which compares well with the great empires of western Sudan such as the Mossi states. Islam was introduced here in the eleventh century, and the Kanem-Bornu State does in fact have the longest Muslim dynastic tradition in Africa known to us due to its old written tradition (Lange 1977; Trimingham 1962: 110-26). Initially, information on this part of the world was passed on from traders to Arab geographers such as al-Ya'kūbī (late 9th century), al-Muhallabī (late 10th century) and later Ech-cherif-al-Edrīssī (d.1166) and Ibn Sa'id al Maghrībī (d.1274 or 1286). (H.F.C.A. Smith 1971: 169-70) These early sources deal largely with dynastic matters and offer little information on the social and cultural life of people. The writings of the Europeans who explored this part of North Africa during the 19th and early 20th centuries are somewhat more informative. Travellers like Capt. G. F. Lyon, Denham, Clapperton & Oudney, Heinrich Barth, Gustav Nachtigal and Boyd Alexander do offer insights into the geography, economy, cultures and general socio-political situation in Kanem and Bahr el Ghazal. Unfortunately these explorers faced extraordinary difficulties in reaching Kanem proper and hence give a first-hand ethnographic description of the people living here. Most of them never got that far, and those who did were faced with great hardships. The first of them, Captain Lyon reached only as far as Fezzan, somewhat north-east of the Tibesti massif in 1820, but he did gather some information from traders about the region south of his whereabouts and the prevailing socio-economic state of affairs there. In 1823, a British expedition headed by Dr. Walter R. N. Oudney, the other members being Captain Hugh Clapperton and Major Dixon Denham managed to get to the shores of Lake Chad, which they named Waterloo. There is little information in their travel account about the people of Kanem and the Bahr el Ghazal, however. In 1850, James Richardson, who had several years of experience of the Sahara already, was commissioned by the British to open up commercial links with the states of the western and central Sudan. Accompanied by Heinrich Barth and Adolf Overweg, he left for Sudan by way of Tripoli, as had Lyon and Oudney. His untimely death (1851), and soon afterwards that of Overweg (September 1852), forced Barth to carry out the mission single-handedly. He continued explorations of the Sudanese states and did not return to Europe until 1855. His detailed account of all that he experienced and learned was published in five volumes simultaneously in German and English, the title of the former being: *Reisen und Entdeckungen in Nord- und Central-Afrika in den Jahren 1849 bis 1855*. However, Heinrich Barth too was unable to get to the heartland of Kanem and the Bahr el Ghazal. Barth's and Overweg's attempt to reach the town of Mao in 1851 proved unsuccessful, for example. They were totally at the mercy of a looting and slave-hunting group of Awlad Sliman (Uëlad Sliman), with whom they travelled, and these people were constantly attacking or being attacked by surrounding tribes and the Tuareg. Suffering great hardships, Barth and Overweg had to return from the eastern shores of the Lake with few notes, for which Barth makes an excuse (ibid. II: 105). Barth was later accused by the British-Foreign Anti-slavery society of his participation

in this expedition (ibid. I: 27). Barth does provide a vivid eye-witness account of the northern parts of Kanem and the turmoil which reigned here at the time, however, and he offers a few paragraphs on the Haddad or Bungu, as he calls them (H. Barth 1857-58, II: 301; III: 106).[7]

Gustav Nachtigal, who travelled to the region two decades later, succeeded where Barth had failed. Commissioned by Bismarck to present gifts to the Sultan of Bornu, Nachtigal set out from Tripoli in 1869 on an expedition which was to last five years. His voyage brought him via Tibesti and Borku to Kanem and the Bahr el Ghazal which he crisscrossed in the following years. Nachtigal offers a broad spectrum of geographical and ethnographic data on the region and the first precise information on the Haddad Kanembu or Danoa (Nachtigal 1881, II: 258-64; 330-1). I shall return to his description in Chapter 4.

Then there is a span of almost three decades with hardly a hint as to the life and fate of Kanem and its people. In 1890-93, Lake Chad was divided by treaty between Great Britain, France and Germany. The first to make good its footing in the region was France. Communication between Algeria and Chad by way of the Sahara was established after repeated failures by the French explorer F. Foureau in 1899-1900. During the ensuing decades, a number of explorers and administrators familiarized themselves with the area: M.A. Landeroin, R. Gaillard & L. Poutrin, Henri Carbou, F.W.H. Migeod and Boyd Alexander, to mention just some. The last-mentioned offers a vivid picture of the socio-political turmoil in Kanem, which he crossed on his way from Niger to the Nile at the beginning of the century, a picture supported by Carbou (1912: 93, 141, 143). But neither he nor subsequent French expeditions exploring the Lake Chad region such as those of F.W.H. Migeod and Voulet & Chanoine mention the Haddad. The only source of significance is Henri Carbou, a trained physician who became an administrator in Chad during the first decade of the 20th century, a time when the French established their colonial regime. Carbou presents a useful survey of the ethnic groups, including the Haddad, based on his reading of Nachtigal and Barth, his own inquiries, and on data gathered by the French administration.

Post World War II publications include little more than a few paragraphs or pages on the Haddad, if any at all. One has to go through the sources with a tooth-comb to find little nuggets not already known from Carbou's sketch. French civil servants like Grall (1945) and Charles Le Coeur (1950) came in sporadic contact with the Haddad during an expedition in the Gouré region in 1942-3. Entries in the latter's *Dictionnaire Ethnographique Téda* offer useful comparative data i.a. on material culture, smiths and musicians, although there are no hunting and foraging groups or families among the Teda of Tibesti. Another civil servant, Colonel Chapelle, knew more about the Haddad through his study of the Tubu. He became intrigued by these pastoralists as early as 1930 and took up a proper study of them upon retirement in the 1950's. In his monograph on the various Tubu groups *Nomades noirs du Sahara* (1957), Jean Chapelle tells of Haddad hunting and attachment to the Kreda as part of his description of the role of hunting to the pastoral economy. Another civil servant who became intrigued by the ethnic

kaleidoscope of northern Chad is Albert le Rouvreur and one finds a short chapter on the Haddad in his book: *Sahariens et Sahéliens du Tchad (1962)*. Le Rouvreur not only lists a good number of Haddad clans or groups, but provides more general information about their name, numbers, whereabouts and modes of subsistence – and I shall draw on this source of information in some chapters.

In the 1950s, German scholars resumed an interest in Tibesti, Wadai, Borku and Kanem initiated by their famous compatriots Barth and Nachtigal. Ethnographic fieldwork was carried out by Peter Fuchs in various parts of Northern Chad. Apart from articles and books, he and W. Konrad produced eight short films (all between 5 and 17 minutes long) on Haddad crafts, circumcision, dance, natron production and the cutting up of a hippopotamus.[8]

1,7. Our ethnographic specimen have been transferred from camels to a lorry rented for the purpose to continue their long journey to museums in Fort-Lamy and Denmark. People were hanging around to get a free ride to the capital. Photo J.N.

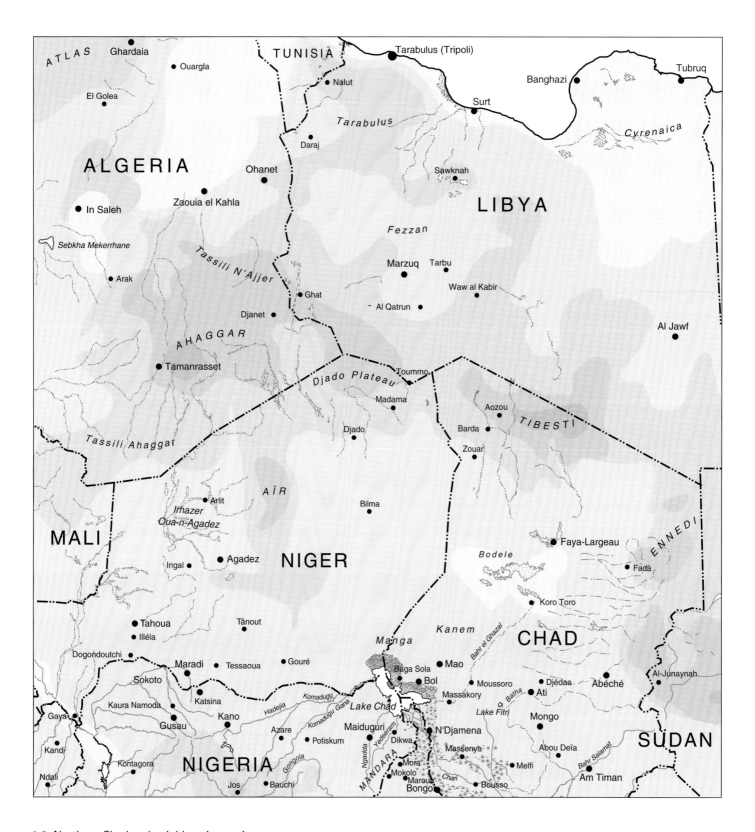

1,8. Northern Chad and neighbouring regions.

In 1972-73, ten years after our fieldwork in Kanem and Bahr el Ghazal, a French anthropologist, Edouard Conte took up a study of the Kanembu, the numerically and politically dominant ethnic group in Kanem.

He worked in the densely populated district of N'Guri district, and, as it happened, at the peak of the drought which ravaged the Sahel in those years. Due to health problems and shortage of food and petrol he spent "short stays of two to six weeks, totalling only 8 months" in the field and his mobility was restricted due to the security situation. (Conte 1983a: 20-24) Despite these obstacles, Conte has written a fine and thorough account of his findings entitled: *Marriage Patterns, Political Change and the Perpetuation of Social Inequality [in South Kanem (Chad)]* (ORSTOM 1983). Part of his work has been published in Paideuma, entitled *La dynamique de l'alliance parmi les chasseurs sédentarisés Duu Rea* (1986). Conte's study of Kanembu political and social organization follows the tenet of classical social anthropological monographs. As the title indicates, the theoretical focus is on inequality and political change. The analysis pursues a classical structuralist, one may say Lévi-Straussian approach, a trend still quite powerful in French anthropology at the time, rather than drawing on Pierre Bourdieu's concept of 'habitus' and a discussion of how dominant groups reproduce themselves (cf. P. Bourdieu 1977: 78 ff). Conte's treatise centres on clan organization and marriage alliances. It covers the Kanembu proper as well as the Duu, a category defined by Conte as constituting a specific social stratum within Kanembu. It includes sedentarized hunters, captives and artisans irrespective of their cultural affiliation and professional speciality, be they of blacksmith or hunter heritage (Conte 1983a: 167). The Duu of hunter heritage are the ones denoted Haddad Kanembu in this book. At the time of Conte's research, hunting had apparently come to a stand-still among the Duu. They subsisted largely by growing millet and keeping some livestock if not working as artisans. Conte states simply that: "Since the 1972-1973 drought, the hunting culture - still observed by J. Nicolaisen in 1967[9] (1968 and personal communication 1978) in both North and South Kanem - must be considered defunct" (1983a: 103). As Conte's focus is on social structure and social history, moreover, Duu economy is only treated in terms of its relation to the hierarchical social organization.

Another French anthropologist, Catherine Baroin, has worked in the region, but further to the north-east where she studied the Daza section of the Tibu. In 1969, she spent five months with Madame Marguerite Le Coeur among Tubu smiths in Niger (Le Coeur 1970: 40: 2: 160-8). Later, she spent a year among the Daza Kécherda in Niger, where the political situation then as now was more conducive to fieldwork. Her main contributions are on pastoral social organization, but she has also dealt briefly with Aza (Haddad) people who hunt with nets or bow and arrow and with Aza artisans. Catherine Baroin also works mainly within the theoretical framework of French structuralism, her thesis being on *Anarchie et cohésion sociale chez les Toubou (Les Daza Késerda (Niger)*, (1985). A short presentation of these findings was published in English in 1997. To my knowledge, professional anthropological work has not been carried out in recent years among the Haddad.

The overall aim of the ensuing treatise is to supplement the existing knowledge of social life in Kanem and Bahr el Ghazal in general, of the Haddad in particular and to offer further evidence on hunting and foraging groups in West Africa. The exposé relies on the ethnographic data we collected among the Haddad and accounts volunteered by Kreda and Kanembu acquaintances. To this day, our knowledge of Kanem and the Bahr el Ghazal and the people who live here is fragmental. In view of this, I have ventured far beyond traditional anthropological pastures and into those of naturalists, geologists, geographers, agronomists, historians, political scientists, archaeologists and linguists to place the Haddad within the broader historical and ethnic setting of which they are part.

DATA AND ANALYSIS

At the time when Johannes and I went into the field we had no specific theoretical agenda in mind. We looked upon the three months ahead of us as explorative, as a pilot study during which we would keep our minds open to the empirical reality of Haddad life, to what was culturally significant, in particular the issues to which the Haddad themselves attached importance. Johannes was determined to engage in long-term fieldwork among a foraging people, having just completed twelve years of work among the pastoral Tuareg. He had a long-standing interest in cultural history, yet it was not so much this field that provided the spur as a wish to study the worldview and beliefs of a foraging group. He had just written a long article on Tuareg religion and magic (cf. FOLK 1961: III: 113-62) and had become increasingly fascinated by pre-Islamic beliefs and symbolic expressions in North Africa, an interest which we shared. I was working on Poro and Sande secret societies in Liberia, Sierre Leone and Guinea Bissau at the time. I was looking at the properties of these gendered institutions and the ways in which their parallel organizational set-ups furthered economic and social ends, created political networks overarching tribal divisions, and lent symbolic expression to the activities in masks, dances and rituals. Although Islam was introduced in Kanem as early as in the Middle Ages, it did not get a firm grip on Kanem until the beginning of the 20th century. Capt. Lyon was told by traders whom he met in Murzuk that the Bahr el Ghazal "is inhabited by Negro tribes, of whom the greater part were Kaffirs, or at all events, not Moslems" (Lyon 1821:127). The Yedina or Buduma in the Lake Chad archipelago became Muslim only in the first half of the 20th century (Trimingham 1959: 17). The fact that Islam had not been adopted wholeheartedly in the region and might have but little impact on the world-view and beliefs of the Haddad contributed to our academic interest in doing fieldwork among these people.

Johannes was also keenly interested in kinship analysis at that time, a field that was a key subject of his ongoing Tuareg studies. He had been inspired by Lévi-Strauss' theory of fundamental kinship relations, his 'atom of kinship' and exchange theory (cf. *Les structures élémentaires de la parenté* 1949; *Structural Anthropology* 1967) as well as by the heated debates on structural implications of prescriptive and preferential marriages (cf. Barth 1954, Needham 1962, Schneider 1965). Due to the short time at our disposal, and the complicating factor of the prevalent linguistic diversity, we decided against a systematic collection of kinship data, and to defer such a study till later. This decision was made in view of the fact that a collection of data of sufficient depth and validity for solid theoretical analysis would take much more time than we had at our disposal. It would also require linguistic competence in Kreda and Kanembu. We chose to concentrate on fields that lent themselves more readily to observation such as Haddad subsistence activities, in particular their hunting and foraging endeavours, and those aspects of the culture which were related to these

activities. We went on hunting trips with the Haddad whenever we had a chance, studied the unfolding of daily life in camps and villages, in particular as it was enacted in front of us by the families we lived with. Johannes dealt in detail with the technical aspects of the hunting and foraging activities and with Haddad knowledge of botany and the animal world. We noted down myths and fables and songs about animals and whatever we could lay our hands on in respect to Haddad religious beliefs and magical practices. I concentrated on the daily life of women and children, and pursued on old interest in ethno-musicology. Finally, I collected some 200 ethnographic specimens from Haddad, Kanembu and pastoral Kreda for the National Museum and the Prehistoric Museum, Moesgaard in Denmark, as well as a smaller collection of specimens for the museum of IFAN, Fort-Lamy.

Upon our return from the field in 1963, Johannes wrote a preliminary report on our findings in Danish: *Haddad. Et jægerfolk i Kanem* (Unpubl. MS 1964). This was not intended for publication but conceived rather as a working tool for future research. He did also publish a short article entitled: "The Haddad - a Hunting People in Tchad. Preliminary report of an ethnographical reconnaissance" (*FOLK* 1968, 10: 91-109) and another in Danish about the pastoral Kreda entitled: "Kreda - et sudanesisk hyrdefolk" (Naturens Verden, April 1963: 97-128). In writing this book, I have of course made use not only of our field notes, ethnographic collections and photographs but also relied on Johannes' writings. I am beholden in particular to his work on Kreda pastoralism and sections in the unpublished manuscript about kinship and hunting techniques.

In keeping with the above mentioned premises of work and the nature of the available ethnographic data, the present analysis centres on Haddad technological knowhow and the widely different strategies of subsistence activities pursued by the Haddad Kreda and Haddad Kanembu respectively. Moreover, it describes the intricate interplay between the disparate hunting and foraging specializations and Haddad systems of knowledge, beliefs and magic. It attempts, finally, to place the ways of life of the Haddad within the larger socio-political setting of Kanem and the Bahr el Ghazal through time.

"The historian is not an eyewitness of the facts he desires to know," Collingwood observed (1961: 282) – anthropologists are. We create our own records, our field notes to document past occurrences. Yet, like the historian, we re-enact the past in our minds when analysing and writing up our observations and other data. The use that we make of our fieldnotes relies on a subtle interplay of the past and the present and the presence of memory. Perhaps because it was my very first experience of Africa and of doing fieldwork, my ability to recall landscapes and social situations so many years later has actually surprised me. I am acutely aware, however, that these memories have been filtered through the lens of time and experience.

The writing up of field notes after forty years raises particular problems. The notes themselves are by nature 'experiments in interpretation'. They are partial constructions of complex social and historical configurations, part of a negotiated and refracted reality, as George Bond has argued (1990: 276). Presenting these data so many years later invariably adds still another layer of interpretation and reconstruction. Research agendas have changed in the meantime and so have the perspectives, knowledge and interests of the author. The fact that a good part of the data was collected by Johannes has caused me particularly delicate methodological problems and ethical considerations. I can only hope that Johannes would have been satisfied with the use I have made of his observations and discussions with the Haddad.

EXISTENCE, HISTORY AND IDENTITY

Two thematic areas forced themselves upon us in the field. One was the overall difference in way of life and ethos of Haddad groups, in particular the modes in which this manifested itself between the nomadic, net-hunting Haddad and the settled, bow-and-arrow hunting Haddad. We became intrigued, not least, by the ways in which the two modes of subsistence went hand in hand with distinct world-views and differences in the role of magical beliefs and practices. Another major theme was the issue of Haddad marginalization within the wider social setting, the discrimination they experienced, and the cultural notions and explanations offered for this sad fate. Evidently, the socio-economic hierarchization and cultural complexity characterizing Kanem and Bahr el Ghazal is the result of a century-long history. It is the outcome not only of ecological adaptation, social migration and cultural processes

but of the insurgency, gruesome fighting, slave-raiding, robbery, arson, political domination and subordination which has characterized the area, at times closely associated with holy wars and the spread of Islam in an ever-changing cocktail. The violence of the past sets the stage for ethnic crystallization and identity formation, economic performance, socio-political privileges or disadvantages and for current politics in Chad. "Blest is that Nation whose silent course of happiness furnishes nothing for history to say", Thomas Jefferson wrote to John Adams in 1786. Sadly this is not the case with Kanem and Bahr el Ghazal, which rather confirms Gibbon's view that: "History is, indeed, little more than the register of the crimes, follies, and misfortunes of mankind" (*Decline and Fall of the Roman Empire* 1909, I: 84 (1776). As history unfolded across the subtle Sahelian plains and sandy dunes it created winners and losers still chiselled in the collective memory of the population. Gillis has argued that "The core meaning of individual and group identity, namely, a sense of sameness over time and space, is sustained by remembering; and what is remembered is defined by assumed identity" (Gillis1994). To the Haddad collective remembering of the past century is associated with continuous insecurity, fear and discrimination. At the time of our fieldwork, the vulnerable situation of the Haddad was endorsed by the State. The government had proclaimed the equality of all men, yet, at the same time, forbidden the Haddad to hunt, threatening not only their economic survival but leaving them in a cultural limbo. Deprived of their traditional means of subsistence their singular resource - the wealth of knowledge of the environment and animal behaviour on which their livelihood was founded - became residual. The exchanges which were tied up with hunting and formed major building blocks of Haddad sociality, as well as beliefs, magical acts and overall values associated with hunting could not be put into use and lost meaning. Kleinman et al. have argued that social suffering similar in kind to Haddad experiences both prior to and during our fieldwork enforce silence and that this very silence increases traumas (*Social Suffering* 1996). I cannot judge to what extent this was the case due to the briefness of our fieldwork. We registered not only widespread discrimination against the Haddad but also a sense of social despair among them, in particular among the Haddad Kreda, a despair which took the form of virtual muteness when it came to assessments about their situation and visions of a future. What struck us again and again was their genuine surprise that anyone from the outside would take an interest in their fate. They were unaccustomed to discuss their plight and found words only gradually and hesitantly to do so. I shall argue in this book, that the roots of the discrimination against the Haddad are linked to the turbulent history of Kanem and Bahr el Ghazal.

NOTES

1. Throughout this oeuvre I shall use the term Kanem in the sense of 'Kanem proper' which is a smaller geographical area within the much larger administrative préfecture denoted Kanem today. This is in line with the use of the term by Nachtigal, Le Coeur, Le Rouvreur, Sikes, Chapelle, Clanet, Conte and other explorers and early French administrators who have written about this part of Chad.

2. Fort-Lamy gained significance as a military stronghold of the French. In 1945 it had a mere 700 inhabitants, but by 1961 these had reached an estimated number of 58,179 and by 1995 the city, now called N'Djamena, has a good half million inhabitants. It carried the name Fort-Lamy from a commanding French officer, who lost his life fighting the Rabah (cf. *Encyclopedia Britannica*).

3. In 1995 the estimated population was 6.5 million according to EIU (cf. *EIU Country Report*, 4th Quarter 1997).

4. The cotton industry goes back to the colonial period. It is entirely dominated by the parastatal cotton company, Société Cotonnière du Tchad (Cotontchad), and France still exerts a virtual monopoly with respect to ginning and marketing of fibers and seeds (*EIU Country Report* 1997, 4: 34, 70).

5. To my amazement, Johannes had no problem in acquiring permission to hunt - 'permit de petite chasse'. He used to cater for himself in the Sahara and had insisted on bringing an old rifle - one he had 'organized' from the Germans as a resistance fighter during the German occupation of Denmark in World War II. I remember my protests, as he had no license to carry arms. But we got it in and out of Denmark, France and Chad wrapped in a tartan plaid without problems, although the parcel looked just what it was: a rifle wrapped in a plaid. It proved a valuable asset, as the Haddad were most happy to borrow it.

6. It was among the Haddad Kanembu in the N'Guri ares that Peter Fuchs worked in 1959 and Edouard Conte conducted fieldwork in the early 1970s.

7. Heinrich Barth writes e.g. that: "Ein eigenthümlicher Stamm wird von dem Imam Ahmed häufig als "el Kenaniyin" erwähnt, über den ich noch keine ganz feste Ansicht habe, obgleich ich glaube, dass er mit den sogenannten Haddada in Kanem identisch ist" (1857, II: 301).

8. Peter Fuchs's five documentaries are available through Institut für den wissenschaftlichen Film in Göttingen, the same is the case for W. Konrad's three films.

9. The year was 1963.

2:

2: KANEM AND THE BAHR EL GHAZAL

NATURE AND SURVIVAL

The rolling green grass and vibrant life of Kanem and the Bahr el Ghazal through which we led our camels in the summer of 1963 could not but cast us into a state of bliss: the flowering acacias, millet growths that all but hid the huts of the Haddad Kanembu from sight and not least the exuberant bird wildlife with flights of black storks, crowned cranes, plovers, bustards, guinea fowl, sand grouse, doves, bee-eaters, hoopoes, weaverbirds, warblers and yellow wagtails enriched our stay, bird-lovers as we were. Nature seemed generous. The seasonal rains had been sufficient for annual plants to cover the dunes and plains for several months, and for the perennial ones to bloom, set fruit and regenerate. The livestock was well-fed, hunting was good, the children not malnourished - no big tummies here. In short, food was, if not in abundance, at least sufficient to support the population at the time.

The lushness that we experienced is not given, however. Kanem and Bahr el Ghazal are periodically hit by hard times. This is a deceitful environment, mind you, one of major climatic oscillations which change living conditions from one year to the next and on in which the balance between profitable pastoral and agricultural activities fluctuates. Rains can be treacherously scarce, and throughout history some frightfully harsh periods with hunger and death have been in store for cultivators, pastoralists and hunters alike. This occurred in the 1980s, when it hardly rained for four years and an ensuing epidemic wiped out most of the small ruminants. It happened again in 1972-73, when a period of below average rainfall beginning in 1967 culminated in a dramatic dry season, with large-scale losses of livestock and wildlife, of crops and trees and a high rate of infant mortality (cf. Clanet 1977: 241; Gallais 1975). But also abundant rains and high levels of water in Lake Chad cause problems. Islands and the low-lying areas west and south of the lake become flooded, forcing the inhabitants to seek new homesteads and preventing the growing of crops on huge areas of otherwise fertile land.

Kanem and the Bahr el Ghazal are situated squarely within the Chad basin, a vast indentation which formerly marked the borders of the Paleo-Chad, an immense lake which existed some 55,000 years ago, its surface being some 380-400 metres above mean sea level. It was gradually replaced by the Mega-Chad, which after a period of regression and early dune formation between the years 22,000 and 12,000 reached its maximum size with a surface some 320 metres above sea level upon a period of more humid conditions 12,000 to 7,000 years ago. Since then, the lake has steadily regressed, reaching an average 282 metres above sea level in the early 1960s, the equivalent of an area of 9,700 sq. miles or 10,000 sq. kilometres (Sikes 1972: 60-4; *New York Times*, March 27, 2001). In fact, it has retreated by a shocking 95 percent, i.e. from covering an area of about 10,000 sq. kilometres to a mere 1,350 sq. kilometres in 2000[1] (Coe & Foley: *Journal of Geophysical Research - D: Atmosphere*, February 2001: 106(4): 3349-56). The fact that the size of the lake is one of considerable fluctuation seriously affects life around it. Barth describes, for example, how the inhabitants of Ngégimi (N'Guigmi) had to rebuild the town at a new higher location in 1853 due to high waters (Barth

2,1. Kanem was teeming with wildlife in the 19th and early 20th century according to explorers like Barth and Nachtigal, and so was the Bahr el Ghazal. Capt. Lyon writes that, "Elephants, rhinoceroses, lions, buffaloes, and the cameleopard, or giraffe, called Jimel Allah ... God's camel, by the Arabs, are in great numbers." He also notes that, "Great quantities of elephants' teeth are procured in the woods." (1821: 127-28). Elephant herd at Lake Chad. Heinrich Barth 1857, III: 45.

1857-58, III: 49). Tilho, who was the first to systematically investigate the hydrology of Lake Chad, found that it oscillates periodically between what he termed 'Little Chad', with a water surface of 9000 sq. kilometres (1905-8, 1916), 'Medium Chad', with a water surface between 15,000 and 20,000 sq. kilometres (1909-13; 1917-20, 1953-6, 1958-61, 1965-8) and 'Great Chad' with a surface level of between 20,000 and 25,000 sq. kilometres (19th century, 1957 and 1962-65 (Sikes 1972: 83-94). At that point in time, the northern basin of the lake had a depth of seven to eight metres, the southern of three to four metres. There is little doubt that in a distant past the wide 'river of the gazelle', Bahr el Ghazal has carried fresh water into Lake Chad. Local traditions suggest that during Noah's Flood, the wa-

ters from the Middle East flowed down this depression into the Mega Chad, whence the derivation of the word Bornu or Bahr el Nuhu, meaning the 'flood or river of Noah' (ibid. 1972: 71). A backflow from the lake up the Bahr el Ghazal also occurs. It happened e.g. in the years 1870, 1873, 1874, and 1900, and after a pause again in 1956 and in 1957-8 (Sikes 1972: 71-2). In 1870 the backflow reached more than a hundred km up the Bahr el Ghazal from the shore of the Lake, and Nachtigal could still observe remnants of this flooding in 1873 some 80 km up the valley (Nachtigal 1881, II: 358-9). Cf. *Fig. 2,3 & 2,4.*

The inundation of the Bahr el Ghazal is thus related to the lake level in any given year. According to local people, these backflows of water recur periodically. Our research in

2,2. The crocodiles and hippos of Lake Chad are hunted by the Haddad, but the animals are few and far between today and it is prohibited to kill them. Apart from the dangers that these animals pose to man, one must be careful with the Lake. As appealing as its cooling blue waters may seem to a passionate Nordic swimmer, its coastal stretches are, in fact infested with bilhiaziosis, which causes major health problems to the ethnic groups living along its shores. Heinrich Barth 1857: II: 44.

Kanem occurred during the rainy season and in a year when rains were plentiful and the surface of Lake Chad therefore above medium level, yet this was not sufficient to cause a backflow. The Bahr el Ghazal nowhere became a river in the proper sense of the word. In some places, water flowed gently and considerable parts of the valley had turned into ponds and soggy fields, but these floodings did not stem from Lake Chad but were exclusively due to local showers. What causes and regulates the overall climatic cycle of the Chad Basin and determines the oscillation of the Lake is still debated. The other unresolved problem is its low salinity, which despite considerable scientific effort still remains a mystery to the best of my knowledge. Whatever the causes of the oscillations, in any one year the size of Lake Chad and the related

backflow of water up the Bahr el Ghazal set the stage of the subsistence and hence the economic strategies pursued not only in Kanem but also in the surrounding tracts.

Today, most of the plains and dunes in Kanem lie about 320 metres above medium sea level and thus not much above the level of Lake Chad, which was about 282 metres in the 1960s. The highest parts are normally stable dunes formed in the past at a time when the desert stretched further south. The dunes run largely in a north-northwest to south-southeast direction, separated by interdunary depressions, pans and marshes. To the north and east of Lake Chad lies a stretch of dunes known as the Erg of Kanem. In the southern part of Kanem, the dunes are of an average height of between 14 and 20 metres, while the dunes

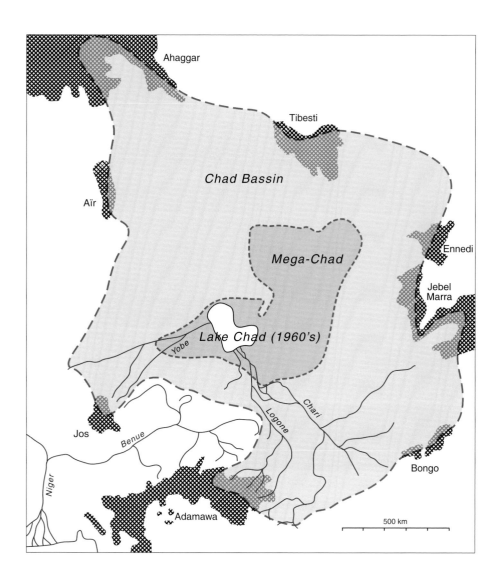

2,3. The extension of Lake Chad has varied considerably over time. Mega-Chad indicates the Lake's surface 12,000-7,000 years ago.

2,4. Lake Chad has shrunk to a fraction of its size in the 1960s, when we were in the area. NASA, satellite photo. ▶

between Mao and N'Guri attain heights of up to 50 metres. In between the dunes one finds plateaus covered by relatively sparse growths of *Andropogon* grass (cf. *Fig. 7,1*) and indentations with *dum* and other palms, which rarely grow so high that they are visible from the plateau. Most of Kanem is thus covered by sand, a fact which makes transportation by motor vehicles quite complicated. Stony ground is to be found nowhere, but near the lake at places like Bol there are fertile interdunary deposits of clay, which makes more intense polder farming a possibility.

The climate is tropical, with an average temperature of 20 to 25 degrees for January and around 30 degrees for July. This is not the hottest month, however, for the temperature is moderated by the rainy season, which begins in June

and ends only at the start of September. It falls considerably when the rains are at the highest only to go up again, once they have stopped. The warmest part of the summer are the months preceding the rains, i.e. from April into the beginning of June, while the coldest part of the year is between December and January. Even then, the temperature never drops below zero. The dry north-easterly trade winds prevail most of the year and only when these are replaced by the monsoon blowing from the Bay of Guinea does the rainy season begin. Rain usually falls as heavy showers, often accompanied by thunder and more often in the afternoon than in the morning. When it rains continuously for twenty-four hours, as occasionally happens, there is generally no thunder. Showers may occur during the

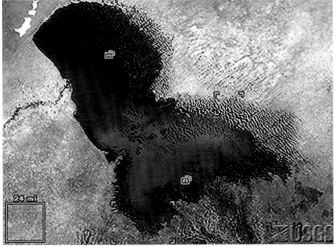

1963

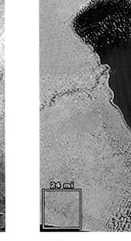

1973

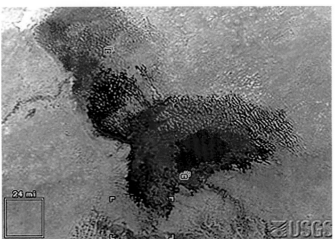

1997

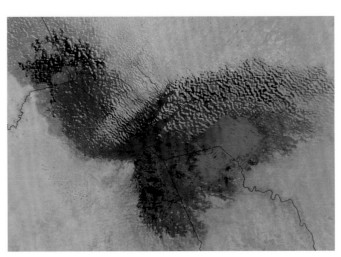

2009

night, but rarely in the morning.[2] The annual amount of rain in Kanem is thus fairly modest, considerably smaller than further west in Sudan, as a matter of fact, even at the same degree of latitude. A good amount is absorbed by the dunes, but a large part gets trapped by the interdunary depressions and forms temporary ponds and smaller or larger flooded areas during the rainy season. In some places one finds more permanent lakes, but they contain only a modest amount of water at the end of the dry season.

Differences in rainfall are reflected in the vegetational cover. South of the Bahr el Ghazal, one finds the rich coverage of the savanna while most of Kanem remains firmly within the Sahel spilling into a desert-like environment up north. The Sahel forms a sort of 'shore' (Ar. *sahil)* of the

great Saharan desert, as the Arabs say. It is the more subtle difference in rainfall between Kanem proper and the middle stretches of the Bahr el Ghazal beginning shortly above the latitude of Mussoro, however, that has an impact on Haddad subsistence activities and possibilities. The Bahr el Ghazal has on average a total of seven months with only one day of rain, as against Kanem's six months with one day of rain. This difference in precipitation determines the northern limit for the cultivation of millet, and to a certain extent the southern limit for the migration of the pastoralists and hence the overall agro-pastoral pattern of subsistence. It does also mark the border between the hunting grounds of the bow hunting Haddad Kanembu and the net hunting Haddad Kreda, respectively.

In Kanem and the south-western parts of the Bahr el Ghazal, the vegetation is open with trees rarely higher than 10 metres. In the fairly level landscape these generally grow in lower-lying areas where soil conditions are more favourable. Thorny acacia species are prominent, in particular *Acacia raddiana*, but there are also *Acacia albida, Acacia seyal,* and *Acacia senegal.* In the southern parts of Kanem one finds baobab trees, which are of use to the local population in several ways. In some areas near the lake each baobab is traditionally owned and cannot be utilized or cut down without the owner's permission (Sikes 1972: 106). The Kanuri name for the baobab tree is '*kuka*'. Oral tradition has it that when the second Sefuwa Dynasty was founded in the 19th century, the city that became its seat was named Kukawa. It so happened because the founder, Shehu Lamihu had been sitting under the canopy of a baobab reading the Koran when he decided to stay at the place (ibid. 1972: 108, 162). Kanem is also host to species such as *Balanites aegyptiaca,* the so-

called desert date, which produces a fruit that can be used for human and animal food. Its wood is widely used for handles; *Zizyphus species* such as *Zizyphus jujuba,* the fruit of which is edible and can also be made into a drink, and *Zizyphus Spina-Christi;* as well as species like *Maerua crassifolia, Commiphora africana, Salvadora persica* and *Boscia senegalensis.* In some areas there are large expanses of the humble but decorative Sodom apple, *Calotropis precera* used by the Haddad Kanembu as timber for their *djongo* huts (cf. Chapter 12) and among the Yedina as a source of fibres for the making of fishing nets (ibid. 1972: 183). Also the dum palm, *Hyphaene thebaica* is plentiful in some areas. It is of great use to local people, supplying them with leaves for mats, baskets, rope etc. Its fruit is a source of sugar. Between the trees grow perennial grasses and weeds, but the vegetation is dominated by growths of annual grasses i.e. by *Andropogon sp.* which the Haddad Kanembu use for thatching their huts. Other prominent plants include the prickly, devilishly

2,5. Getting stuck between two dunes east of Bol.

hooked grass "cram-cram", *Cenchrus biflorus,* which sticks to everything and make walking on bare feet both tricky and painful. The annual plants sprout immediately after the first rains, but most of them have already withered away before the rainy season has come to an end. Of particular use to the Haddad Kanembu and other ethnic groups living near Lake Chad is the papyrus plant, *Cyperus Papyrus,* which grows along the Lake's shores and islands (cf. *Fig. 8,9*). The stems are used for utensils, firewood, mats, rope and not least for the making of pirogues.

Haddad mode of subsistence depends evidently on the presence of wildlife. Game had become fairly scarce by the 1960s both in terms of species and actual numbers as compared to the pre-war situation. Commercial and trophy hunting and the introduction of automatic weapons had taken its heavy toll on many species. The situation has since become further aggravated due to droughts, the activities of the armies and most recently hunting parties that fly in from abroad to hunt with falcons, in particular from the Middle East and Pakistan. In Lake Chad, for example, there was previously a substantial population of hippopotami, *Hippopotamus amphibious.* In 1905, Boyd Alexander saw a herd of sixty hippopotami on one of the islands in the Lake near the mouth of the Yobe river (1907, II: 46). Even in 1942, Gentil refrains from taking a bath upon his arrival in N'Guigmi due to the prevalence of hippopotami, crocodiles and bilharzias (Gentil 1946: 199). There were also plenty of elephants, *Loxodonta africana africana.* Boyd mentions a herd of no less than 96 animals that enjoyed the aquatic habitat of the Lake almost as much as the hippopotamus (ibid.) Barth describes how huge elephant herds repeatedly crossed their paths (Barth 1857-58, III: 45). Around the turn of the 20th century, elephants were "... still to be found in considerable numbers in the south-east part of Hausa-land between the river Binué and Lake Chad", as were li-ons and leopards (Robinson 1897: 168). In the 1960s, these magnificent animals were only encountered in small herds that ventured north from Cameroun towards Chedra and the Bahr el Ghazal during the rainy season to dine on the young dum palm near the temporary ponds. The buffalo, *Syncerus sp.,* and big cats occur only rarely in Kanem today. The lion, *Panthera leo,* used to be plentiful in the region. Gentil mentions, for example, that they were seated on lion skins recently killed at N'Guigmi in 1942 (1946: 199). At the

time of our visit, lions still lived just southeast of Lake Chad, but we were told that years could pass between a lion be-ing registered in the Bahr el Ghazal. The leopard, *Panthera Pardus,* had its northern limit in Kanem and the cheetah, *Acinonyx jubatus,* existed but was rare. Small- to medium-sized carnivores were common. There were the long-legged African civets, *Viverra civetta,* the largest and most dog-like Viverrid with the greyish and black spotted coat of long, coarse and bristly hair; the common genet, *Genetta genetta,* an agile tree-climber weighing only around five lbs. It has a beautiful long tail and a spinal crest rising above the coarse greyish to fawn-coloured coat with blackish spots and is the only genet found in open dry savanna. When stalking, it crouches so low as to become completely flat on the ground. There were a number of mongooses moreover, both the white-tailed mongoose, *Ichneumia albicauda,* and the slender or lesser mongoose, *Herpestes sanguineus,* which is about 12-15 inches long and weighs but one and a half lbs. It lives singly or in pairs, is mostly diurnal and prob-ably the type of mongoose most frequently seen. Another inhabitant of Kanem and the Bahr el Ghazal is the Egyptian or greater grey mongoose, *Herpestes ichneumon*, the largest of the African mongooses, and in the southern parts of the area perhaps also the banded mongoose, *Mungus mungu.* The latter is a highly social animal that lives in packs of be-tween a dozen to fifty individuals. Not uncommon but rare-ly seen is the zorilla or striped polecat, *Ictonyx striatus,* as this is nocturnal and takes refuge during the day in crevices and burrows. Nor did we see the omnivorous ratel or honey badger, *Mellivora capensis.* More frequently encountered is the jackal, both the common jackal, *Canis aurerus,* and the side-striped species, *Canis adustus,* as well as two species of hyaena, both the striped, *Hyaena hyaena,* and the spotted, *Crocuta crocuta.* A fairly common species is the insectivo-rous fennec, known as the sand fox or the pale fox, *Vulpes pallida aertzeni,* a relative of the fennec *Fennecus zerda* that lives further to the north in the desert proper. The pale fox is larger and lives up to its name with a pale fawn coat, ex-cept for the black tip of its tail. It has proportionately small ears, unlike the enormous triangular ones of the fennec. The pale fox hunts on the shores of Lake Chad and does not venture into the country, we were told by the Haddad, who themselves hunted the animal.

The rarity of large predators in Kanem indicates that also species of graminivora are relatively few, as is the case. This is even so around the Lake according to Sikes, who states that: "... the mammalian fauna of Lake Chad has never been rich in species, and is today poor not only in species but also in numbers" (cf. Sikes 1972: 131). This, however, was not the case when early travellers like Denham traversed the region. At that time, flocks of the Nubian giraffe, *Giraffa camelopardalis,* browsed on the Kanem plains and large antelopes were not rare. Dama antelopes, *Damaliscus korrigum,* still graze in parts of Kanem, but are fairly common only during the rainy season. The scimitar or white Oryx, *Aegoryx algazel algazel,* is rarely found south of the 15° E northern latitude except towards the end of the dry season, when it ventures further south browsing in herds of between ten and twenty animals. Addax, *Addax nasomaculatus* were previously encountered in herds of up to several hundred individuals (Sikes 1972: 139). The Addax is the antelope that ventures furthest north. Johannes encountered it in Tasili-n-Ajjer in the 1950s, but by 1991 it had come close to extinction in Western Sahara according to a UICN report on the fauna of Air and Ténéré (Tiéga 1991: 16). The Addax were not tracked down by the Haddad families we stayed among in Kanem, but still pursued by Haddad groups further to the north, or so we were told, and we did see Addax hides in use. Equally well adapted to the desert is the large Dama, *Gazella dama,* which lives in the northernmost parts of Kanem and the white desert gazelle, *Gazella dorcas dorcas,* which frequently migrate into southern Kanem during the rainy season. Far more common in parts of Kanem and the Bahr el Ghazal is the somewhat larger Thompson's gazelle, also known simply as the red gazelle, *Gazella rufifrons.* Haddad Kanembu hunters told us also of encounters with species such as the impressive African buffalo, *Syncerus,* the eland, *Taurotragus derbianus,* the hartebeast, *Alcelaphus buselapsus Lelwel,* and the horse-like antelope, *Hippotraginae.* Finally, there were certain species of antelope living exclusively in the marshes around Lake Chad and the Chari delta such as the beautiful situtunga, *Limnotragus spekei,* the hides of which are popular as reclining mats among wealthy Kanembu, the Bohor reedbuck or *Redunca redunca nigeriensis,* and the kob, *Adenota cob.*

The wart hog, *Phacocherus aethiopicus,* thrives largely in more swampy locations, yet may occasionally venture into some fairly dry parts of Kanem if able to hide in thickets. Porcupines, *Hystrix cristatus senegalica,* occur all over the place. Hares, *Lepus ochropus chadensis,* are common as

well, while the true rabbit, *Oryctolagus,* does not exist south of the Sahara. There are other mammals as well, including the Anubis baboon, *Papio anubis,* and the red monkey or patas, *Erythrocebus patas,* the shy and elusive as well as fastest of the primates, but these species are not common any more. Smaller ones, such as the hedgehog, giant rat and squirrels also occur. Snakes, scorpions and other reptiles are found in abundance. Snake bites are common and

one comes across quite a number of individuals who suffer from paresis, normally in the legs, as a consequence.[3]

What makes any travelling in Kanem a delight is not the least the teeming birdlife. Weavers fly busily in and out of their intricately woven and hanging homes. Way up in the tops of acacias are emerald-coloured bee-eaters on the outlook for insects, hoopoes busily search the ground for ants and other edible creatures while warblers, waxbills,

2,6. On our way. Riding through green pastures of annual grasses and scattered acacias.

flycatchers and other minor tropical species add to the ambiance everywhere. Kites and various kinds of vultures circle the sky, as does occasionally an eagle, while a secretary bird, *Sagittarius serpentarius,* may catch one's attention, as it marches majestically through the shrubs on the lookout for reptiles and other dainty morsels. The birdlife is particularly rich during the rainy season, when migratory birds range on flooded areas. Flights of storks including the white-necked, *Ciconia episcopus,* Abdim's stork, *Ciconia abdinii,* and the marabou stork, *Leptoptilos crumeniferus,* ibises and numerous ducks feed side by side and in great numbers.

Much to our disappointment, we did not encounter any ground hornbill, *Bucorvus abyssinicus,* the looks and behaviour of which the Haddad Kanembu imitate when hunting. The bird propagates very slowly and is extremely rare. It is highly selective in respect to biotope and Kanem

provides optimal natural conditions for this extraordinary creature only where land has been cleared and burned (cf. Serle et al. 1983: 139).

Among the edible species that we came across and which the Haddad trap or hunt, were several species of doves and pigeons, whose monotonous voices are an inseparable part of the sound-picture of the African landscape. Only one of these does not end in the pot and that is the large speckled pigeon, *Columba guinea guinea.* Although common around villages in the southern part of Kanem, it is venerated as a holy bird or *marabou* and hence not eaten. We encountered numerous flocks of grey-breasted helmeted guinea fowl, *Numida meleagris strasseni,* which invariably got confused and ran hither and thither in front of our camels as we crossed their chosen land. We shot a few but not any of the other *Phasianidae* i.a. Butler's stone-partridge, *Ptilopachus petrosus butleri,* and Clapperton's

2,7. An inundation near the Haddad Kanembu hamlet of Chedra.

francolin, *Francolinus clappertoni clappertoni,* nor any of the species of sand-grouse or *'ganga', Pteroclididae,* which came our way. These species are all hunted by the Haddad, however. So are all the bustards, *Otididae,* including the Sudan bustard, *Choriotis arabs stieberi,* the fairly rare *Neotis cafra denhami* or Denham's bustard, a bird that is about 76 cm high and has a rufous-coloured neck, the somewhat smaller (61 cm), northern black-bellied bustard, *Lissotis melanogaster melanogaster,* the Nubian bustard, *Neotis nuba,* and the Senegal bustard, *Eupodotis senegalensis.* We got 'our' share of the ones the Haddad caught, nevertheless. They taste deliciously, I must confess.

We saw a few ostriches, *Struthio camelus,* but these great birds existed only in a few places at the time of our visit and they have since come near extinction. Ostriches have always been sought after for their plumage, but they became excessively exploited in the 19th century before ostrich farms could catch up with the European demand created by the fashion industry and some armies. The ostrich was of great economic importance to former generations of Haddad, not only as a great source of meat but because they could market its eggs and feathers. They used to hunt in a disguise of ostrich feathers, moreover, as did the prehistoric hunters of the Sahara known to us from rock paintings. Ostrich eggs are considered a delicacy by the Kanembu, who also adorn the top of their beehive huts with one or more of these as do people further to the north. Lyon notes that in southern Tripoli nearly all the graves were ornamented with one ostrich egg or more, as were the doors and corners of the mosques and other enclosures (Lyon 1821: 75). We came across small flocks around Méchimeré and witnessed how soldiers pursued them with automatic weapons from landrovers.

Finally, fish and game has been available in abundance in Lake Chad, creating the economic basis for or supplementing the livelihood of a number of ethnic groups that lives in the archipelago and along the shores, in particular the Yedina and the Haddad. Fish are not found in Kanem apart from in the Lake, where they are particularly abundant around the archipelago. The species have affinities with fish living both in the Nile and the Benue-Niger River systems, the former going both ways, the latter only from the Chad Basin into the Benue-Niger Basin, according to Sikes (1972: 119). Fish are not only used for personal consumption and sold at local markets but also dried for export. In the lagoons of Lake

2,8. Young Haddad with an Egyptian goose, *Alopochen aegyptiaca,* which he had shot with Johannes' rifle.

Chad there are tortoises, terrapins, swimming snakes and monitor lizards, *Varanus niloticus*, as well as crocodiles. The lake contains three species: *Crocodylus niloticus, Crocodylus calaphactus,* and *Osteoloemus tetraspis.* Both crocodiles and monitor lizards are subject to extensive commercial hunting. Sikes visited a warehouse in the old city of Yerwa stacked from floor to ceiling with crudely tanned skins of pythons, monitors and crocodiles, and she notes that there must be many similar warehouses in Maidugari (ibid. 1972:125). A French businessman in N'Djamena told us that he had founded his commercial enterprise by hunting and buying up the skins of crocodiles when he first came to Chad, estimating his toll alone to be about 40,000 skins over a twenty-year period. Full-grown crocodiles were so rare at the time of our research according to local Haddad hunters that it was difficult for them to make a living out of crocodile hunting any more.

THE ETHNIC PALETTE

What I found most overwhelming when I arrived in this part of the world for the first time was the multi-facetted, ever-changing human environment. Kanem is a sheer wonder of ethnic groups who carve out a living in a wide variety of ways in response to natural, cultural and socio-economic conditions and constantly re-invent themselves on the ever-fluctuating socio-political and economic arena. Linguists have identified no less than around 200 ethnic groups and some 110 languages in Chad, so far,[4] a tricky pursuit it must be stressed, in that the use of the term ethnic group is far from unequivocal. The issue is further complicated by the fact that although some societies are classified as ethnic groups, they may still not have a language of their own but speak that of a dominant or conquering society (Azevedo 1998: 9; Grimes 1992: 215-19).

In Kanem and the Bahr el Ghazal the various groups share significant cultural traits today. A unifying force is the Muslim faith, but this was not so a century ago. The Yedina, who lived in the archipelago of Lake Chad were still pagan

or 'fetishists' at the beginning of the 20th century (Carbou 1912: 109), and the Haddad probably embraced Islam only at about the same time. Another factor has been the unifying aspects of the Sultanate of Mao, which ruled the area for centuries. The many ethnic groups do also adhere to a largely patri-lineal system of social organization irrespective of their mode of subsistence. Marriages tend to favour patri-lateral relatives and for couples to settle patri-locally. The position as Sultan passed ideally from father to son within the royal Kanuri-Kanembu family, for example and rules of inheritance follow similar principles, as laid down by the Koran. By implication a daughter inherits only half of that of a son. Yet, the history and specifics of most of these groups, the nature of their relations, including those with specialized groups such as Haddad hunters and craftsmen, are fairly poorly documented to this day. This is due in part to a lack of research, as previously mentioned, and in part to the turbulent history of the region. Migrations, fighting, slave-raiding, the extensive practice of taking and incorporating captives as individuals or social categories in existing social entities lend sociality in Kanem and Bahr el Ghazal its special character of both permanence and flux.

Countless ethnic groups have entered Kanem and Bahr el Ghazal over the centuries, some to stay, others to fade into oblivion in the wake of the persistent warfare, and, until the beginning of the twentieth century, also slave-raiding, which characterizes the history of Central Sudan. Apparently, quite a proportion of those living in Kanem and Bahr el Ghazal today stem originally from the North, a point indirectly supported by the fact that Kanem means 'the land of the south'.[5] One of these groups is the Awlad Sliman, who caused a great deal of havoc in Kanem in the 19th century (cf. Carbou 1912: 85-103). Others migrated from either the East or the West. Over the past thirty years, for example, the Bororo have been able to assert themselves quite forcefully in Chad. Fleeing eastern Niger in response to the droughts of the 1970s and 1980s, they pushed eastwards into Chad, some even further into the Sudan. Other Bororo groups came in the 1990's, due to skirmishes with the Tuareg and dissatisfaction with the political situation in Niger to seek new pastures in Cameroun and as far south as close to the Central African Republic.[6] As of the spring of 2004, thousands of refugees from Dafur have poured into the Bahr el Ghazal in the wake of the gruesome killings in this area.

◄ 2,9. A Haddad Kreda hunting party en route with nets and other paraphernalia.

However, it is not least the recurrent and often devastating social unrest in northern Chad that has shaped and constantly re-shapes ethic composition and sociality. Historical sources bear this out. Several of these, notably Henri Carbou, devote space to the complex socio-political situation in Kanem during the late 19th and early 20t century. Carbou considers the constant warfare, in particular the raids conducted by the Awlad Sliman and the Sanussiya, as the driving forces in ethnic displacement and mingling at the time, and hence in social diffusion. He writes of the power balance at the time that: "Except for the Ngouri and Debenentchi regions inhabited by the Ḥaddâd and the district occupied by the Toundjour (Mondo) where the Wadai people come quite often, the rest of Kanem belongs to the Oulad Sliman" (Carbou 1912, I: 34; IN transl.). Yet,

some decades later, the 'wheel of fortune' had turned and the Awlad Sliman relegated to a marginal position while the Kanembu had risen to power once again with the aid of the new player in the field, the French colonial power. Considering the fighting, slave raids and robberies, it is easy to understand, Carbou says, that: "... blending of the various populations of Kanem must have been frequent. In addition, the natives have retained in most cases but a confused memory of their origin. It is difficult, therefore, to establish clear distinctions between the various populations," and even:"... more difficult to establish the differences which exist between various parts of each population" (Carbou 1912, I: 36-7; IN transl.). Carbou notes, for example, that one finds individuals of other ethnic backgrounds mixed together: "... the Nguedjem[7] with the Kanembu and

2,10. A Haddad Kreda camp. The small dwelling if inhabited by an elderly widow.

2,11. Haddad Kreda
women returning
from a foraging trip.

the Boulala; one sees the Maguemi and the Kreda, the Kreda and the Nguedjem, the Nguedjem and the Boulala, the Boulala and the Ḥaddâd claiming a shared origin" (Carbou 1912, I: 36-7; IN transl.). Conte claims, however, that:" ... in spite of constant population movements and political upheavals within Kanem before and after colonisation, the association between given group names and particular areas appears in most cases to have remained relatively constant over 100 years" (Conte 1983a: 33).

The complexity and turbulent history of Kanemese societies has been a major challenge to government officers and scientists who wanted unequivocal principles for the administration and scholarly description respectively. Diverse criteria have been in use over time to bring a seeming order to the diversity: linguistic, religious, environmental and socio-cultural. Among the more recent attempts one can mention S.P. Reyna, who divides the Chadian societies essentially according to ecological, subsistence and lifestyle criteria, explaining the intermingling of people as a result of largely environmental changes. He distinguishes between:" ... the pastoralists, the micro-environmental specialists, the cereal producers, and those who combine pastoralism with limited agriculture and fishing who could perhaps be called 'diversified survivalists'" (Azevedo 1998: 7; Reyna 1990: 18).

Modern social scientists are painfully aware of the methodological and theoretical problems of analysis when dealing with ethnically complex societies. In few instances is caution more called for than in the case of Kanem and the Bahr el Ghazal, where the social landscape has been and still is volatile. Kanemese complexity does not yield to simplistic scientific categorization and the application of 'objective' socio-cultural criteria. It cannot be analysed as a simple conglomerate of well-defined cultural units. However, the available literature predates current theoretical discourses on cultural complexity, fluidity and temporality. It throws but limited light on the ethno-historical processes, cultural negotiations and understandings and expressions of identity of the many social groups in Northern Chad. New research and methodological approaches are called to address these issues, such as Denis Cordell's effort to single out religion and conquest as major classifying tools in his study of the Dar al-Kuti. He introduces the concept of a 'frontier zone' to describe the perceptions of the intruding, predominantly Muslim inhabitants from the desert and Sahelian North of the pagan, indigenous populations

in the South, perceptions which served as a rationale for their expansion and power to acquire human resources here (Azevedo 1998: 6; Cordell 1985: 11-13).

In the light of the above mentioned problems, I shall limit myself to a sketch of the socio-cultural stage to introduce the groups that carved out a living for themselves in Kanem and Bahr el Ghazal at the time of our fieldwork and had an impact on the existence and fate of the Haddad. Social interaction is based on self-identification and on perceptions of others. Cultural and social distinctiveness is negotiated in social arenas and hence influenced by politically and economically dominant groups. The Haddad have not been able to set the rules of the game, yet they do not accept the perceptions of 'others' as socially and culturally marginalized and dependant. They claim a different social identity, pointing to their oral traditions which identify them as a people with a singular history and tradition, i.e. defining themselves in praxis as an 'indigenous people'. I shall apply this latter understanding as the working principle of the ensuing analysis in line with the United Nations' acceptance of self-identification as a criterion for recognition as an indigenous people within the UN system (cf. United Nations Permanent Forum on Indigenous Issues: DP1/2309 - May 2003).

The Haddad

The Haddad do not stand out on the grand ethnic palette of Chad. They are few in number, marginalized and mostly impoverished and they do generally lack political clout. They are scattered over a vast area in Northern Chad and the eastern parts of Niger, where they have carved out a living as hunters and gatherers from ancient times. By the mid 1960s there were still Haddad hunters in Kanem and the Bahr el Ghazal as well as to the north-west of Lake Chad and further west into the Dillo area of eastern Niger. We shall return to the issue of Haddad identity and the complexities of names for these people in Chapter 4. At this point it is enough to state that the Haddad of Kanem and Bahr el Ghazal identify themselves as being of three 'stocks': the Haddad Kreda, the Haddad Kanembu and the Haddad artisans.

One category of Haddad camp for most of the year with pastoral nomads, mostly Daza-speaking Kreda, hence the practice of identifying them as Haddad Kreda. They forage for most of the year on the edaphic grassland of the

Bahr el Ghazal, where also the pastoralists graze their cattle and migrate at times with these as far as to the Lake Fitri region. Traditionally, they went up north into the Sahara to hunt for antelope during the winter season. The foraging techniques of the Haddad Kreda are adapted to a fairly and/or totally open environment with only scattered growth of acacia, dum palm, Calotropis and thorny shrubs. Hunting is based on collective efforts, groups of men and children, sometimes also women that set out together to chase flocks of gazelle and antelope into nets that are set and made for each species specifically. The Haddad Kreda migrate in small groups with particular groups of pastoralists, mainly Kreda, for most of the year, pitching their tents at the very same campsites as these. Each family erects its domicile right behind that of a Kreda family

2,12. Kreda pastoralist.

with whom it has developed a close exchange relationship. The fact that a camp is inhabited by both Kreda pastoralists and Haddad hunters is revealed not only in the lay-out and pitching of the mat tents in two discrete rows, one behind the other, but also in the far more modest appearance of the domicile of the hunters. Haddad subsistence strategies are different from those of their Kreda hosts, centered largely on hunting and foraging and in part on assisting the Kreda in return for food, in particular milk and for protection. The Haddad were barred from possessing cattle until the later part of French colonial administration. Initially none of the Haddad had cattle or small ruminants (cf. Carbou 1912, I: 49-72). By the mid-1950s their situation was changing. Chapelle mentions Haddad families in Kanem, whom he characterizes as craftsmen and semi-nomadic pastoralists who on average possessed 10 cows, 5 sheep or goats and one donkey. This information does not correspond with the data we collected, however, and I wonder whether Chapelle's data in fact refer to agro-pastoral Haddad Kanembu of the N'Guri area (Chapelle 1957: 217). The Haddad Kreda whom we encountered and heard about had no cattle whatsoever.

The Haddad Kreda form part of a wider category of nomadic Haddad, all of whom speak a Teda-Daza language and hunt with nets. Carbou writes that these hunters are the most numerous and that one finds them a bit everywhere (Carbou 1912: 50, 210). Besides the Haddad living among the Kreda, there are net hunting, Teda-speaking groups staying with the pastoral Kecherda, the Murtcha, the Bornuans at Wadi Rima and the Maḥâmid. "Further to the south, one finds a village at Massaguet (on the road from Fort-Lamy to Massakory)," Carbou informs us (1912, I: 212; IN transl.). There are Haddad hunters even further to the south at this time but: "... these are not Gourân all of them [i.e. Teda-speaking; IN]; some of them claim to be Arabs. This is the case of the Arab-speaking Ḥaddâd from the Ourel region, the Maskéa (near Gouêno at Médogo), the Oulâd Ḥammad (at Tchalaga, near the Bédanga), the Ḥaddâd Cherek from Baguirmi and others," says Carbou [1912, I: 212; IN transl.]. Furthermore some Haddad still make a living from foraging and hunting with nets east of Rig-Rig in Chitati and in eastern Niger in the Dillia, which connects southern Termit with the north-western shores of Lake Chad, while a smaller contingent roams the plains southeast of Termit (Baroin 1991; Chapelle 1957: 163, 406, 450). Chapelle writes about

2,13. Young Haddad Kanembu women. Chedra.

these Azza [Haddad, IN] that they were more numerous than the Teda and Daza pastoralists to whom they were subservient as vassals. Officially, vassalage had been abolished, but in practice the old relations were still sustained by means of voluntary gifts, in particular of dried meat. In return, the Teda and Daza presented the Azza with animals and clothes. Still, the Azza were in fact the richer of the two parties, Chapelle observed. They had magnificent hunting grounds south of the Ténéré desert, where the pastures attracted numerous flocks of antelope and gazelle. As there were very few wells in the area, the wild game did not face competition from the herds of the pastoralists and could be hunted by the Azza (Chapelle 1957: 163). Apparently, Haddad foraging has continued to flourish in this area. E. Granry observed net hunting parties in a valley near Dillia,

east of N'Gurti in 1987 (personal communication to Baroin 1991: 342). In the spring of 2004, the Azza were still hunting here and successfully so, as game was plentiful, I learned from Ingrid Poulsen, a Danish anthropologist who had just returned from the area.

Apart from these Azza or Haddad one does or did also find an:" ... important group which nomadizes around Koutous, to the north of Gouré (chief: Taïba)," according to Carbou [1912: I: 212; IN transl.). In this part of Niger and eastern Chad they are known locally as Azza or Aza. Apparently, net-hunting Haddad do not coexist with the camel-breeding Tebu or with Arab pastoralists to the north of Kanem, but Haddad Kreda families venture or did venture periodically into the desert here to hunt antelope, as previously mentioned.

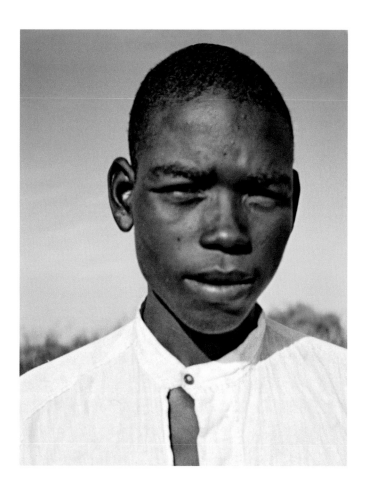

2,14. Young Haddad Kanembu man. Wanagal.

and simulates the movements of this peculiar animal as he approaches the game. According to the Haddad other forms of disguise, for example ostrich feathers were previously in use. Foraging activities are dwindling among the Haddad Kanembu, however, and nowadays they subsist largely on agriculture. Some families possess small ruminants.

Finally, there exists a contingent of largely urban Haddad, who make a living as smiths, craftsmen and musicians. Some supplement their income with a little farming and the breeding of a few small ruminants, as well as by hunting. Haddad artisans are found not only throughout Kanem and Bahr el Ghazal but way up north in Tibesti and Borku, to the east around Abéché and as far as Ennedi, as well as to the north and north-east of Lake Chad in Manga and the Dillo wadi. In some areas and among some ethnic groups the 'true' smiths supplement their income by hunting, among others not at all. The latter is the case in Tibesti. Le Coeur notes, for example, that: "The Téda craftsmen, unlike their brethren the Aza living among the Daza, do not constitute proper hunting tribes that are vassals to noble tribes whom they provide with dried meat, almost all bags, and a good portion of baskets and mats" (1950: 95; IN transl.). This point is confirmed by Peter Fuchs, who notes that in Tibesti, Borku and Ennedi smiths live in tiny groups of one to two families that apparently make a living from the craft only. Among the Baele of Ennedi these smiths are known as Mai or Bai, while they identify themselves by the term, *naver,* a word belonging to the so-called 'smith language' (Fuchs 1961: 184; 1970: 298). In Dillo in eastern Niger the smiths supplement their income by digging wells for pastoralists, a highly strenuous and extremely dangerous task (Chapelle 1957: 181). According to Grall, the wells belonging to the western Tibu had all been dug by these Haddad or Azza people (1945: 24). In the Gouré region smiths function in yet another capacity, interestingly enough, and that is as learned men or *marabout.* According to Baroin the literacy rate is higher among these Haddad than among the Daza-speaking pastoralists. The *marabou*s pray and bless their clients. They write stanzas from the Koran for amulets or in black ink on a plate to which they add water for the client to drink to get well or succeed in an enterprise (Baroin 1991: 339).

The Haddad are all Muslims today, but appear to have converted quite late compared to other ethnic groups in the area, turning to Islam only towards the end of the 19th

Another group of foraging or rather previously foraging Haddad lives in Kanem, primarily in the N'Guri area and further to the south, where their villages are found in between those of the Kanembu towards Massakory. They are widely known as the Haddad Kanembu, because they speak the tongue of the Kanembu. These Haddad forage in an environment with a denser cover of trees and bushes than the Bahr el Ghazal and their hunting technology and method is entirely different from that of the Haddad Kreda. Hunting is largely an individual pursuit except when large mammals like lions and formerly elephants are pursued and the prey is killed with bow and poisoned arrows. The prominent feature of Haddad Kanembu hunting, however, is the use of disguise. The hunter creeps up upon the game disguised as the ground hornbill, a stately black bird, covering his back with a black sheepskin. The hunter wears a mask in the shape of the head of the ground hornbill on the forehead

2,15. Haddad potters
selling their products
at the market at Bol,
Lake Chad.

2,16. A Haddad smithy at the market at Bol, Lake Chad.

century and at the beginning of the 20th century, as far as we can assess.[8] Haddad world-view, perceptions of themselves and artistic modes of expression are still intimately connected with the surrounding nature and animal world on which they depend for a living.

Characteristically, most of the existing sources mention the Haddad only briefly - if at all - and then only as an occupational category, caste or small tribe, as previously indicated. They can hardly be blamed for this. Few of the writers were scholars and none had set out to shed light on Haddad society and culture. Barth and Nachtigal would only accidentally have come upon Haddad hunters, moreover, and post World War I writers were largely government officers to whom the Haddad were fairly insignificant players. Liminal to the economy and too few and/or too marginalized to play a political role, they stirred little interest. Typically, we are offered but brief statements about the Haddad or Azza, as e.g. living "... in small tribes or as isolated families. They are hunters, smiths, tanners, while their wives work as potters or basket makers. They occupy an inferior position in Toubou society, even one of vassalage, but there is no racial distinction between them and the other Toubou, nor do they speak a different language" (Chapelle 1957: 7; IN transl.). There were many other ethnic players on the stage of Northern Chad, all more numerous and politically influential. Five of these shall be mentioned briefly in the following, namely the ones that primarily co-exist and interact with the Haddad in Kanem and the Bahr el Ghazal and/or have exerted an influence over them historically.

Arab pastoralists

Historically, the Arab-speaking Awlad Sliman or Suleyman have had a major impact on Haddad existence due to their aggressiveness and exertion of political power in the 19th century. They form part of larger contingent of Arab pastoralists or semi-pastoralists which also include the Djoheina (or Eastern Arabs), the Hassauna (or Western Arabs) and, according to some scholars, the Tunjur. Some raise camels, horses, goats others zebu cattle and they own in fact the largest herds in Chad. Some Arabs live as merchants in the cities, where they more or less control the retail business.

The Arabs count between 14 % and 20 % of the population of Chad, and are thus the second largest ethnic group after the Sara. The latter inhabit the south-western part of the country

and sustain themselves by growing the cotton and rice that forms the backbone of the Chadian farming economy.

According to oral tradition, the Awlad Sliman are named after an ancestor, who was assigned the task of bringing Islam to Tripolitania by the Prophet. During the early part of the 19th century they clashed with the Turks over the trans-Saharan caravan trade from Bornu to the Mediterranean and decided to migrate to northern Chad, where they were to cause havoc. It was with the Awlad Sliman, for instance, that Barth had such hair-raising experiences during his attempts to reach Mao and the eastern shores of Lake Chad (Barth 1857, III: 90-100). The Awlad Sliman have retained their way of life as 'grand nomads' with flocks of camels and by trading dates and salt from the Saharan oases of Borku and Kawar on the Kanemese markets. The majority live in Manga land, but some groups pitch their tents of mats or cloth in the Bahr el Ghazal (cf. Le Rouvreur 1962: 298-300). In 1928-30, another contingent of Awlad Sliman left Fezzan to pitch their white tents in the Eguei due to conflicts with the Italians. After some years they moved their grand herds of camels further south and forged asymmetrical marriage alliances - not with the other Awlad Sliman, as one might think - but with Hassauna and Daza pastoralists, a move which enabled them to maintain their claim to nobility (Le Rouvreur 1962: 437).

The Djoheina and Hassauna entered Chad from the Nile valley and Tripolitania, respectively, but at a much earlier time than the Awlad Sliman; some scholars believe as early as in the latter part of the 14th century, others are of the opinion that it took place only during the 17th century (ibid. 1962: 293). Today these nomads graze their cattle in Manga on each side of the 16th meridian, hence the name-tags, Eastern and Western Arabs respectively. The Hassauna do also venture further south into the northern parts of Kanem where they mingle and intermarry with Daza-speaking pastoralists. The northern Hassauna are pastoral nomads with herds of zebu, goats and sheep; the southern Hassauna or Choa sustain themselves not only by raising cattle and goats, but also by growing of millet (ibid. 1962: 296).

A similar subsistence strategy is pursued by the Tundjur, the descendants of an Arab population which fled Wadai in the 17th century due to decimation and discrimination, as they tried to evade Islamization (ibid. 1962: 105). They are now settled near Mondo in Kanem and around Massakory.[9] (Conte 1983a: 72-73).

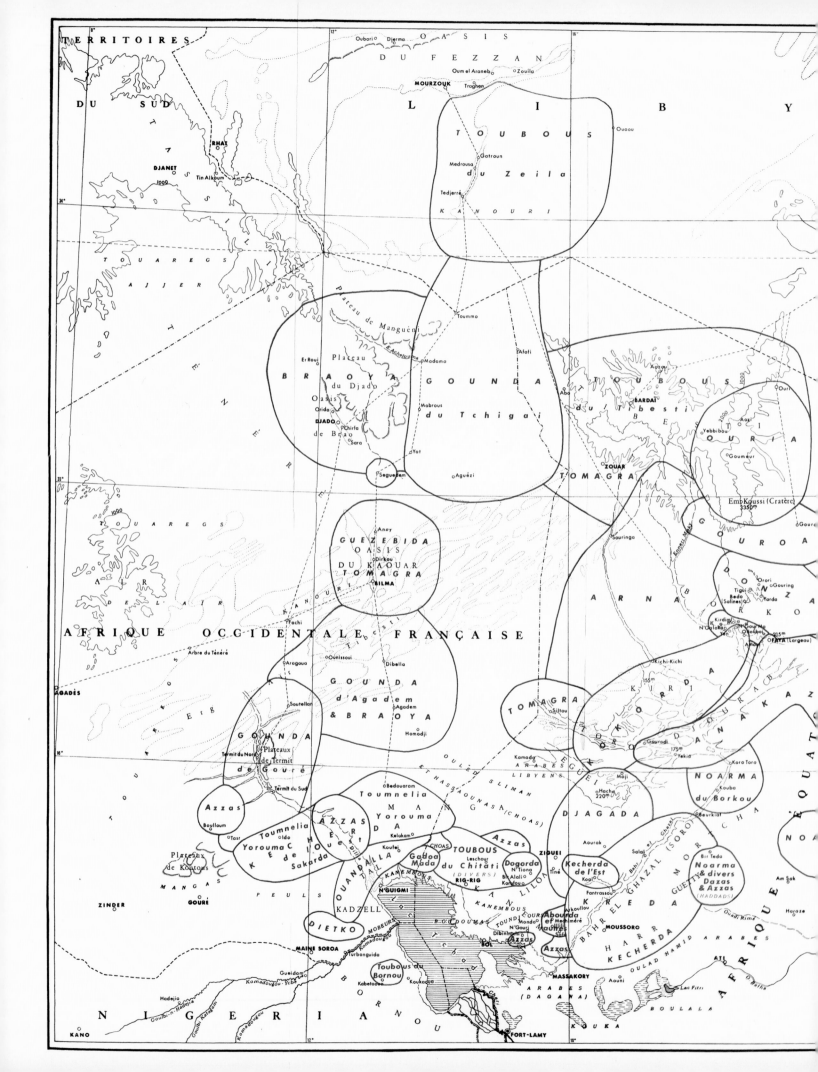

AIZERBO

E

O A S I S

E   K O U F R A

Bou Zeima

RIBIANA   DJORF
                 (Kebabo)

T O U B O U S -

d e   K o u f r a

Assenou

Tropique   du   Cancer

Djebel Aouenat
1934 m

Sarra

Takro

Erdi · Dji

Ouninga Serir   Dimi (Salines)

N I A   E r d i   M a

          M E R D I A

       M O U R D I
          & M O U R D I A

G O U R O   A
        TABIA
                    E r d è b è
   Oum el Adam

Baki   FADA   Basso
       Archei   1450 m

A E D A   B I D E Y A T

        B I l i   a

        Beskaré

        Aïn Djares

Oum Chalouba   Berdoba

              Hawar

        K o b e
              Orba
        IRIBA
ARADA   Kapka K a p k a
              Kapka
        GUEREDA
BILTINE   L. d'Oumdout

A   D   A   I

ABECHE

E G Y P T E

E G Y P T E

S O U D A N

CARTE DES
GROUPEMENTS TOUBOUS

0   100   200 Km.

The 'black nomads' or Tubu

To the south of the Arab pastoralists are the camps of the numerous cattle-owning Tubu, popularly known as the 'black nomads'. Tubu (Tibu) is a Kanuri term commonly used to designate a largely pastoral population of Northern Chad and adjacent areas in Libya, Sudan and Niger, an immense space of not less than 1,3000,000 sq. kilometres or approximately one quarter of the Sahara. There are only few studies of these people and no well-informed estimates of their numbers. Chapelle believes that there are about 195,000 Tubu (Chapelle 1957: 2). "Since that date the demographic growth may well have been significant, but the drought and the political conflict in Chad have also taken their toll, so that nowadays the only sound estimate which can be made - however imprecise - is that the Tubu population numbers more than 200,000 but probably less than 600,000," Baroin remarks (1987: 137-9).

The Tubu are divided into a large number of clans, but none of these form geographical units or have a common political leadership. Clan members are united by oral traditions of joint ancestry symbolically expressed through the use of the same camel brand, and "... the same sense of honour, which is of no little significance in this anarchic and feud-ridden society" (ibid. 1987: 139). It comes as no surprise therefore, that the Tubu possess no ethnic term to designate themselves as a group, contrary to the two other major pastoral groups in West Africa: the Tamachek (Tuareg) and the Maures. Linguists distinguish between a) the Teda-speaking groups of Tubu who live mostly in the North above the 18th parallel, i.e. in and around the Tibesti Massif, Kufra, Djado, Kawar, Borku, Erdi Ma, Murdi and Basso Erdé'bé, and b) the Daza-speaking groups, who graze their cattle to the south of the 18th parallel. The latter are found in Manga in Niger - where the Tumnelia, Kecherda, Wandalla and Dietko clans exploit the plains, in the Chitati

2,17. The ethnic scene is complex to the confusing, as the map indicates. Kanem and the Bahr el Ghazal sustain a variety of agricultural, agro-pastoral and pastoral groups besides the Haddad. A fair number are mobile, moreover. Some have followed a reasonably predictable pattern of migration over the past century, while others have expanded or subtracted territorially, notably the Fulani. Chapelle 1958, Pl. I.

region at the northern fringes of Kanem itself which hosts a range of Tubu clans, in Kanem proper, where the Kreda have their camps, and further to the east and north-east up the Bahr el Ghazal, where the Aburda, Anakarda, Norea and some eastern Kecherda have their grazing grounds. The most easterly of the Tubu, the Beri are found in Wadai, a group that comprises both the Zaghawa and the Bideyat.[10] The *Teda-ga* and *Daza-ga* languages or, according to some, dialects, belong to the so-called 'east-Saharan' category of languages. They are closely related to *Kanuri* as spoken in Bornu, north-eastern Nigeria (Baroin 1987: 139).

In Kanem and the Bahr el Ghazal the Haddad interact largely with two of the Daza groups: the Kecherda and the Kreda. The former numbered approximately 7,200 individuals within the Bahr district at the time of our visit, according to Le Rouvreur, while Chapelle lists 6,300 here plus 2,612 in N'Guigmi and 1,200 in Gouré. The Kecherda are considered the Daza par excellence. Oral traditions tell that they migrated from Borku in the 18th century. One group, the so-called eastern Kecherda went to Kanem and further on towards Manga, where they live between Arab pastoralists and the Kreda, with whom they used to be on very bad terms. The other group migrated directly to the Bahr el Ghazal. They still exploit these two distinct environments some 300 kilometres apart, a total area of some 12,000 square kilometres (Le Rouvreur 1962: 351). The Kecherda migrate seasonally with their livestock and camels venturing south into the Harr during the winter. They possess fewer animals than the Kreda, move less frequently, and do not migrate as far south at the time of the first rains owing to the considerable number of camels. But unlike the Kreda they maintain contact with the oasis to the North, supplementing their income by bringing camels to Borku to sell butter and buy dates and salt, which they then transport back to the market in Mussoro (ibid. 1962: 357).

The pastoral nomads with whom most of the net-hunting Haddad have developed close relations are the Kreda, however. According to oral tradition, the Kreda stem from the north or north-east, more precisely from Kéré i.e. the lowlands around the Manherté wells and Borku oasis some 200 kilometres from their present habitat. It is from Kéré that they have derived their name: Kéréda or Kreda, i.e. the inhabitants of Kére (ibid. 1962: 267-8). The apical Kreda ancestor, Kara, is said to have come from a place called Fôdi Tinemi, i.e. 'tiny river', and the Kecherda name for the Kreda

is Karra. Kreda migration to the Bahr el Ghazal took place some time during the 17th and 18th centuries. In the wake of this exodus they displaced the Dagana and Awled Hamid, two Arab clans who at that time were living in the central stretches of the Bahr el Ghazal (Chapelle 1957: 145).

Kreda society comprises nine major clans, administratively united under three chiefs by the French. One chiefdom comprises the Yiria, Dirguima and Bria clans another one the Bédula, Djarma, Gorda and Sunda clans and a third the Yorda and Djarwa. In the 1960s, the Kreda numbered an estimated total of 50,000 to 66,000 individuals. They grazed their herds in the Bahr el Ghazal, from Dagana all the way to Beurkiat (some 300 kilometres), as well as in the Harr, i.e. migrating within a territory of about 20,000 sq. kilometres. More precisely, the Kreda lived roughly within a rectangle marked by the cities of Chedra in the Bahr, Mussoro to the North, Salenga to the East and the Sayal Mountains to the South (Le Rouvreur 1962: 262-285; Chapelle 1957: 144-147, 405). Kreda economy is based primarily on herds of zebu and small livestock, but they also raise horses, possess some camels and engage increasingly in the growing of millet. Kreda subsistence strategies vary somewhat from clan to clan, however. Those living up North, as, for example, the Bria clan do not engage in agriculture at all, but base their existence largely on an extensive form of nomadism with their camels. The Yiria, Gorda, Béduala and Djarma clans, who migrate in the central stretches of the Bahr el Ghazal, support themselves by raising cattle and small livestock and supplementing their diet by the growing of millet. In the southern parts of Kreda territory the Yorda, Djarwa, Sunda and Dirguima rely on huge herds of zebu. They do not raise camels and possess only male animals, which they apply for transport. Despite this diversity in subsistence strategies, the Kreda are first and foremost famous for their large herds of zebu. They are in fact the most prosperous pastoralists in the Sahel, argues Le Rouvreur, with a registered 800 zebus per 100 individuals (cf. 1962: 272). Sedentarization occurs from time to time, usually in the wake of severe droughts or other hardships that for a while force these pastoralists to settle down. The moment they are able to acquire new animals and increase their herds, however, the semi-nomadic way of life is resumed (Carbou 1912, I: 178).

Kreda camps consist of from five to more than twenty tents usually inhabited by patri-laterally related kinsmen.

The residents may well belong to two, three or more clans. In fact, the pastoral way of life of the Kreda is not based solely on firmly organized kin-groups. Herding units or camps are established and dissolved in response to a mixture of kinship, marriage and personal considerations. In this sense the Kreda are much more flexible than any other of the pastoralists in Chad. The Kreda were perceived as hot-headed and belligerent by the French (Carbou 1912, I: 179-3). The Kreda are known for being easily agitated and on their guard as are other Tubu groups. At the time when we got to know them young Kreda men were still pursuing the age-old trade of pillaging although on a small scale, as far as we were informed. Chapelle has described them as the most devout Muslims among the Tubu (Chapelle 1957: 147).

The Kanembu

East of the Bahr el Ghazal and the Kreda lay the neat villages of the Kanembu. They form the majority of the population in Kanem proper, but also live in the Bahr el Ghazal south of Chedra, in particular between Massakory and Lake Chad and in Mussoro, the capital of the Bahr el Ghazal. All in all, the Kanembu number about 65,000, of which about 42,000 live in Kanem proper, while some 23,000 are located in a narrow strip on the western side of the lake, in colonies in Bornu and elsewhere (Le Rouvreur 1962: 76-7).

In the widest sense, the word Kanembu denotes people whose mother tongue is *Kanembu-Kanembu,* a dialect of Kanuri – a language spoken on both sides of Lake Chad. The language of the groups living on the western side of the lake, the Sugurti, Kuvuri and Temageri differ but little from Kanuri proper; those spoken by the eastern Kanembu form a separate category. According to Lukas, it can be divided into two forms: a) *Karkawù* spoken by the inhabitants of the south-east side of the Lake and the islands and b) *Kanembu* spoken around Mao, Mando and N'Guri. The *Mao* dialect must be separated from the other two being very similar to Kanuri proper; the *Mando* and *N'Guri* dialects are different, but mutually understandable (Lukas 1967 (1937): IX-X). Carbou writes that the Kanembu are known to the Arabs by the pejorative term *Ḥammej,* the name of the locally produced, greyish-black salt, presumably as a slighting reference to their complexion (Carbou 1912: 36). According to Conte the *Ḥammej* of North Kanem constitutes only one of the sedentary groups of the Kanembu.

2,18. Young Yedina from the island of Reria, Lake Chad. Photo K.M. Fig. 3,2; 10.10.1957.

2,19. The limited number of shops that we encountered in Kanem was a clear indication of the prevalent subsistence economy. A fair amount of the shop owners were Lebanese, like the man in the photo. On the death of his first wife, he had remarried a much younger woman, also Lebanese. The marriage of the two had been arranged by their families.

The Kanembu claim that their ancestral home is Yemen and/or Ethiopia and that they provided Kanem with different dynasties and over time mixed with other groups. They consider themselves closely related to the large Kanuri population, who live west of Lake Chad, and maintain close ties across the political border between Chad and Nigeria, both at family levels and through trading. Interaction between the Kanembu and the Kanuri has intensified during the 20th century as the crossing by boat of Lake Chad has increased. Until the early 20th century, the Lake posed a major obstacle due to piracy and the Yedina islanders, who prevented strangers from crossing their waters (Le Rouvreur 1962: 77). In those days, neither the Kanembu nor the Kanuri had boats or fished, but left the Lake to Haddad and Yedina exploitation. An expression of the close ties across the border is the fact that the Kanembu consider Maïduguri in Nigeria their capital, rather than N'Djamena.

Kanembu history has been turbulent and resulted in a good deal of displacement and intermarriage with other groups. Despite this legacy, the Kanembu have a distinct way of life and mode of organization, according to Le Rouvreur, who praises their tenacity and vigour (Le Rouvreur 1962: 80). Most Kanembu live in small conglomerates of beehive huts and sustain themselves by a mixture of agriculture and animal husbandry. The villages are placed on top of the dunes to avoid the humidity that plagues the depressions during the rainy season. Each village has a number of wells to provide water for man and beast. Here, as elsewhere in the world, the wells are also important social spaces where gossip is exchanged and young girls meet the young boys who come to water the herds (Le Rouvreur 1962: 84). Most fields can be reached from the villages, but if these lie too far off, the Kanembu build small huts for use during periods of intensive work. The main crop is millet *Pennisetum typhoideum,* which can grow without irrigation as far north as a little beyond the cities of Mao and Mussoro. It comes in two variants, one that is suitable for sandy soils and reaches some 2 metres when fully grown, and another, much smaller, which requires moister conditions. The latter is largely cultivated in the interdunary depressions and in the vicinity of Lake Chad, where the groundwater level is higher. Where irrigation is possible, cultivation takes place all year round and the Kanembu may harvest two or more annual crops of barley, maize, beans, tomatoes, onions and gourds. They also grow vegetables such as Spanish pepper, various kinds of melons and papaya. The French expanded irrigation through the building of dams and the development of so-called polder farming. In the early 1960s, the polders embraced approximately 6,750 ha in Kanem, yielding some 2000 to 3000 tons of wheat of fine quality. The fertility of the polders is high, and besides an annual crop the Kanembu harvest two crops of maize besides vegetables, sugarcane, manioc, sweet potato and tobacco (Fuchs 1966: 29). Wheat came to Kanem around 1830, introduced by Fezzanese emigrants who probably initiated its cultivation in polders. The cultivation of wheat has since been encouraged by the successive governments for export. It is normally grown with irrigation only. Dates are found here and there in northern Kanem, but are not of major significance to the Kanembu (Cf. Krarup Mogensen 1963: 5: 14). The Kanembu of the southern parts of Kanem are able to grow groundnuts because the rains are more abundant. They do so for cash purposes. Husbandry is also important to many Kanembu families. They breed zebu and some Chad cattle near the Lake, as well as small ruminants, largely sheep – except in the south, where goats take over (Le Rouvreur 1962: 86). The role of husbandry has apparently varied. The French noticed upon their arrival at the beginning of the 20th century that the Kanembu were practically without cattle. This was probably caused by the ravaging of the Awlad Sliman and the general insurgency at the time, and by cattle plague. The herds are guarded by young men. They get paid in livestock and are able, in this manner, to accumulate herds of their own. The Kanembu neither hunt nor fish, but leave these activities to the Yedina and the Haddad, according to Le Rouvreur (1962: 102).

The Yedina
Yet another habitat, the Lake Chad has traditionally been shared in part by the Haddad and other groups, primarily the Yedina. While some Haddad had their dwellings along its shores, the homeland of the Yedina was its vast archipelago. The Yedina or Yéténa are widely known among other ethnic groups by the derogatory name Buduma, a Kanuri term meaning 'people of the tall plants'. This is a reference to the extensive growth of the papyrus which they put to good use in their daily life, as well as to the myth that their ancestor was found in a basket made from papyrus, just like Moses (Le Rouvreur 1962: 221). Facing slave-raiders on the mainland and having a reputation for piracy themselves, the Yedina kept a distance

2,20. A Yedina family swimming from their homes at a nearby island in Lake Chad to the market at Bol with clothes and produce held high on their heads or tied to a wooden board or a bundle of papyrus.

from the shores of the Lake and built their huts on distant is-lands in the archipelago until well into the 20th century, when the French enforced law and order. Since then, they have set-tled on islands closer to the coast, along the upper reaches of the Chari and on the eastern shores of Lake Chad all the way to the Niger border - and perhaps beyond. The Yedina are fasci-nating people, but little is known about them. A vivid but brief sketch of their way of life is provided by Sylvia Sikes, who first came to Lake Chad in 1955. Intrigued, she decided to launch an expedition in 1969-70 to explore its waters with her sailing boat, the 'Jolly Hippo'. During her voyage she went ashore on the islands and met Yedina people. Sikes writes that there are: "... three recognised sections of the tribe called the *Guria,* the *Madjagodia (or Majagujia),* and the *Maibulua.*" The former live in the northern part of the Lake, while the *Majagujia* are

centred on the island of Kan and the Bulariga Kura Islands, and the Maibulua on Yiribu and Ngaloha Islands (1972: 172). She is also of the opinion that: "... the Yedina are indeed a very ancient people, originally completely isolated from the sur-rounding mainland tribes, essentially 'reed-orientated' if I may coin the expression, yet strongly pastoral, and above all proud, independent, and generally of outstanding physique (ibid. p. 174). In the early 1960s the Yedina numbered about 25,000 and they were all living in fairly small settlements. Their huts were simple constructions of dum palm covered by straw mats. They lived primarily from fishing, but supplemented this with seasonal farming and husbandry, primarily cattle. The latter are not the usual zebu but the special race found at Lake Chad. *(cf. Fig. 7,5).* The Yedina are semi-nomadic, one could say, in that they make use not only of the habitat on the islands but also on the coast, growing millet, beans, maize on the former and primarily wheat on the polders of the mainland. They migrate with their horses, cattle and goats between the two habitats as well as between the islands in the archipelago using simple pirogues made of bundles of papyrus or simply by swimming, sometimes with a bundle of papyrus stems for buoyancy (Le Rouvreur 1962: 225; Carbou 1912, I:

109). The Yedina were still pagan at the time of the French occupation although they had adopted some Islamic customs (Carbou 1912, I: 109). Sikes writes that at the time of her visit still: "At least one section of the Yedina tribe, if not all, worship the Spirit of the Lake, performing an annual rite during which a woman prepares grain, which as part of a ritual ceremony, is thrown into the lake" (Sikes 1972: 174).

NOTES

1. According to the hydrologists Dr Michael T. Coe and Jonathan Foley, who have carried out the research, the extraordinary shrinkage was caused by a drop in precipitation and expanding irrigation. The relative contributions of human activities and natural climate changes were determined using computer models simulating the natural water cycle in the region. Using 40 years of data on regional climate and water flows, the scientists found that the model closely replicated the actual changes measured in the lake level and extent up to the late 1970s. Between 1966 and 1975 the lake shrunk some 30 per cent first and foremost due to drier climatic conditions. From mid 1983 to 1994, however, the shrinkage far outpaced the climatic factors predicted. More than 50 per cent of the retraction was now due to human activities, not least major irrigation systems financed by international agencies which have diverted considerable amounts of water from the Chari and Logone rivers which carry 90 per cent of the runoff that enters into the lake (Coe & Foley 2001, 106(4): 3349-56; Revkin 2001).

2. During the period between 1931 and1945, the annual rainfall was an average 285 mm in Bol at Lake Chad, while Mao a bit further north got 270 mm, and Mussoro east of Bahr el Ghazal, 310 mm. The following decade the average rainfall in Bol was somewhat higher. Clanet states that Mao received an average rainfall of 316,7 mm and Mussoro 341,6 mm. In comparison, Zinder, which lies at about the same altitude as Bol received approximately 535 mm, while Niamey, also lying at about the same altitude but even further west got 538 mm. But the average rainfall varies. During the following decade, i.e. between 1946 and 1955, the average rainfall in Bol rose some 40 mm to 324 mm (Clanet 1977: 240; Krarup Mogensen 1963: 2: 9).

3. We treated several cases of fresh snakebites in Kreda camps. The condition of one woman was so serious that she was getting paralyzed but she recovered. The next morning she had left the camp, where she had sought refuge on her way to the market unhappy to stay among strangers.

4. Some twentyfive of these onehundredten languages are still in the initial stages of identification (Azevedo 1998: 9).

5. According to Nachtigal, the word Kanem stems from Tubu *anum*

or *anem* and the noun creating the prefix k (1881, II: 337), a view repeated by Carbou and subsequent authors (Carbou 1912, I: 4).

6. Personal communication by the French anthropologist Patrick Paris, November 1997, whose Bororo family was among those migrating from Niger to these new pastures.

7. The Nguedjem are said to be descendants of captives taken by the Bulala (Kanuri) at the time when these ruled Kanem. The Nguedjem did not join the Bulala exodus, however, but stayed at Dibinentchi according to Carbou (1912, I: 46).

8. Captain Lyon writes, for example, on the basis of information about Kanem that he got from traders he met in Murzuk, that the Bahr el Ghazal:"... is inhabited by Negro tribes, of whom the greater part are Kaffirs, or, at all events, not Moslems" (Lyon 1821: 127).

9. Conte classifies the Tunjur as Kanembu due to their assimilation to Kanembu way of life (Conte 1983a: 72-73).

10. Civil servants, historians and anthropologists have attempted to outline the history and socio-cultural relationships between the various Tubu groups and to classify these on the basis of a range of criteria (cf. Le Coeur 1950, Urvoy 1942, Chapelle 1957, Annie M.-D. Lebeuf 1959, Baroin 1985). In his book *Nomades noirs du Sahara* (1957) Chapelle categorizes the Tubu primarily according to differences in regional distribution and pattern of subsistence (1957: 141-67). He distinguishes between: 1) the Teda-speaking Tubu who populate the Tibesti Massif plus those who live scattered over the vast areas north, north-east and west of this Massif, including those staying in the oases as far apart as Kufra, Murzuk and Djado. They all rear camels and goats and make use of donkeys for transportation and/or for the cultivation of date palms and small gardens in the oases. 2) The Tubu of Borku, Ennedi, and Wadai, who comprise a number of groups including the Zaghawa (cf. Marie-Louise Tubiana 1964). These Tubu people subsist largely on cattle and on cultivating dates and growing millet, tomatoes and onions. 3) The Tubu of the Bahr el Ghazal and Kanem, who mostly breed cattle, as do for example the pastoral Kreda, and/or grow cereals. A few of them own camels. 4) The Tubu of the south-west, i.e. N'Guigmi, Gouré and Bornu. The latter category includes the Daza Kécherda of Niger studied by Catherine Baroin (1972, 1985 and 1991).

3:

3: THROUGH THE LOOKING GLASS OF TIME

Life in Kanem and Bahr el Ghazal has time and again been subject to insurgency. For centuries it has been the arena of fighting, slave raiding, murder, arson and robbery of the worst kind. Until well into the 20th century, strife was frequent between various ethnic groups and slave raiding was widespread. The latter reached an all-time high in Central Sudan and probably in Kanem and Bahr el Ghazal prior to the French colonization. Kanem has experienced intruders coming from the North, political dynasties to the West fighting local rulers and the Bornu state to the East and vice versa, people in power engaged in relentless slave raiding, not to speak of ethnic segments wrought by conflict on the home turf, and even clans of the same ethnic group stealing cattle from one another, risking casualties along the road.

Although the French brought political stability and gradually curbed the atrocities of slave raiding, they did not put a formal end to the slave trade until 1926. All the major kingdoms in the area, Bornu, Baguirmi and Wadai, mounted frequent expeditions to capture slaves, who were then promptly sent north and east on the various caravan trails. Throughout the early 1920s, large numbers of slaves were still captured and exported to the Maghrib, Turkey and Arabia (Decalo 1977: 260). Nor did the French wipe out robbery and cattle raids in Kanem and Bahr el Ghazal. Rather the colonial administration upheld control and pursued its own agenda of extracting profit and manpower in ways which were exceedingly gruesome and devoid of any respect of human rights. The French did not set a moral example, nor did they radically alter traditional Kanemese polity and prevailing cultural notions of inequality. If anything, French rule cemented the perception that power goes hand in hand with violence and justifies it.

This general pattern of violence and disrespect for human dignity and suffering went hand in hand with the glorification of fierceness and courage among a number of groups. The fearlessness, tenacity, and bravery of Tubu and Kreda men is renowned, for example, and glorified in numerous poems:

> *Have you seen the place where I fought*
> *The place where I was victorious*
> *A man did me harm*
> *His wife shall cry at that very hour,*
> *Lament her husband, whom I killed.*
> *I am Kosseye Abdallah*
> *I am the one who can do such a deed*
> *I am the most evil of men of the Bahr*
> *I am strong among the strongest.*

(Chapelle 1957: 335; IN transl.)

Cattle raiding and vendettas were commonplace among the Kreda, with whom the Haddad camp, as well as among some of the other pastoral groups at the time of our stay, although on a restricted scale compared to previous times, according to Kreda informants. The atmosphere of the camps was at the point boiling when cattle had been stolen. The men were extremely agitated, in particular the younger ones who were eager to seek revenge right away and get back what was theirs, preferably with interest. We

3,1. Foraging Haddad Kanembu women.

treated a number of casualties during our relatively short stay among these pastoralists, some quite serious, including a case of a fractured skull with exposed cerebral tissue. Armed attacks and the stealing of cattle from non-clan members were not publically condoned but it took place. Raids were discussed with enthusiasm and pride among both Kreda men and women. They were deeds endowing those who took part in the raiding not only with material gain but cultural acclaim. To steal cattle had the qualities of a 'rite of passage', one of coming of age for young men, a way for them to gain wealth and prestige just as it was a means to cement social standing. Raids were an acceptable means of accumulating the heads of cattle required for bride-wealth payments among the Kreda and the Tubu (cf. Chapelle 1957: 322). Stealing cattle seemed a kind of litmus test of young pastoralists, a kind of proof that they were to

be counted on, and stolen heads of cattle was part of many a herd. This was proven to us by the profits made by our travel companion, Ganai, an old man of no means. Given the opportunity of criss-crossing Kreda pastures with us and protected by his reputation as a fierce fighter (he had notoriously killed several men, a fact of which we learned only quite late as we did of his 'entrepreneurial activities') Ganai collected 'kickbacks' whenever possible. He blackmailed Kreda pastoralists in part by threats, intimating his intentions of informing the rightful owners of heads of cattle that he spotted, or by promising to be on the outlook for cattle lost during raids.

The fact that slave raiding, robbery and general insurgency has characterized life in this part of Africa for centuries, and that violence was systematically applied as a means of control by the French is of crucial significance to an analysis of the current socio-economic and political situation in Kanem and Bahr el Ghazal in general and to the existence of the Haddad in particular – in the view of this author. It is to the collective memory of the past as well as to the actual exercising of economic and political power that we have to look for an explanation, at least in part, of the caste-like bondage between Haddad-Kreda and Haddad-Kanembu families respectively. We must venture briefly into the past therefore - both the distant and the more recent - to gain an understanding of the forces which have been pivotal to the development of the existing socio-political and cultural reality.

PRE-HISTORICAL PERSPECTIVES: FORAGING AND AGRO-PASTORALISM

The habitat of Kanem and Bahr el Ghazal has changed dramatically over the past 11,000 years, a span of time during which also hunting and foraging groups have carved out an existence for themselves in the rolling plains. The Late Stone Age period (9th to 3rd millennia BC) had a more humid climate than today, with a higher water level in Lake Chad and in other African lakes. Lake Chad had the size of the Caspian Sea. Teeming with maritime life, it offered ample food and hence a possibility for those living at its northern and eastern shore-land of establishing permanent or semi-permanent settlements and facilitating food-production, or so it has been argued. Yet, little is known of these early foragers (Soper 1965: 176-94). Evidence of their existence is difficult to come by as much of the area would have been covered by water and archaeological field research in this area has been limited (Connah 1981: 76-7). However, there is no good reason why hunters and gatherers should not have been present in the region even at a much earlier time, as indicated by the 1994 find of Australopithecus bahrelghazali and the remnants of the skull of a possibly seven million-years-old Sahelanthropus tchadensis made public in 2002 (*The Herald Tribune,* January 26, 2000).

The middle of the fifth millennium BC marks the end of the wet period and the beginning of a dramatic change in Sahara and the Sahel, with seasonal rainfalls and increasing aridity accompanied by an extension of Mediterranean vegetation, grasslands, as well as a major fall in the water levels of the lakes in the region (cf. Chapter 2). Around 2500 BC,

the climate took still another turn towards the drier. Lake Chad gradually dried up, dense vegetation gave way to savanna and Sahelien plants and by 2000 BC the grand desert or *erg* of Air-Ténéré was a fact, effectively hampering communication between groups living east and west of these vast sandy plains. As Lake Chad receded, the now swampy land became an obstacle to human interaction (*Fig. 2,3*).

It has been convincingly argued that the grand *erg* imposed by the shift in climate posed a barrier to social contact. This is reflected in the persistence of two very different language systems: the so-called Chadic languages of the west and the Teda-Daza languages of the east[1] and in the different course of early state formation in historical times, manifest in the establishment of the Hausa states in the west and the first Kanuri Empire in the east (cf. H.F.C.A. Smith: 161-2). The cultural difference was temporarily bridged in the 15th century with the establishment of the Kanuri-Bornu Empire but it remains a fact.

Another consequence of the desiccation was a southbound migration - a movement still retained in legends told both among the Hausa and in Bornu and Kanem. The migration appears to have facilitated the emergence of state formation as well as proven a fertile source of conflict between immigrant groups - a conflict eventually solved by the Kanuri domination of Kanem and an assimilation or expulsion of the southern peoples, according to H.F.C.A. Smith (ibid. 1971: 161-3).

Pre-historians generally emphasize the importance of food production to population growth and socio-economic evolution. Permanent and larger settlements, social hierarchization, a specialization in crafts and in non-material endeavours have all been considered dependent upon agricultural production and the storage of food surpluses. The process was set in motion, it was long believed, by the domestication of cereals and development of dry-farming methods initiating the so-called Neolithic Revolution. However, the 'thick descriptions' of modern archaeological excavations offer a more varied picture of the transition from foraging economies to more complex forms of subsistence. They demonstrate that while early Neolithic subsistence in the Near East was based on a whole spectrum of agro-pastoral activities, in North Africa herding preceded agriculture by several millennia and foraging continued to play a highly significant role

3,2. Masks used by Haddad hunters. Cat. Nos. 6, 13, 12, 5 & 15. Photo J.K.

here. Pottery was made in Sahara at an early date - the first attempt to master ceramic technology may even predate 7500 BC[2] - and ceramics are consistently associated with seed-grinding equipment intimating that the harvesting, preparation and storage of edible grasses were an integral part of the subsistence practices then, as it is today. Tools found at the Neolithic sites are not linked to the development of agriculture or agro-pastoralism as in the Near East, but with pastoralism developed among foraging peoples. Herding economies with cattle and small stock developed in North Africa shortly after 5000 BC (Clark 1976; Barker 1981; Andrew B. Smith 1980b, 1984, 1992; Gautier 1987; Marshall 1994).[3] The skeletons of bovids and small livestock occur in a number of Neolithic deposits in the Sahara and the Sahel and pastoralism was practised

in the Tibesti massif soon after 6130 BP. It might already have taken place around 8065 BP. according to Gautier (1987: 174). One of the best known subsistence forms of this Neolithic era is that of the Ténéréan peoples from Ténéré and adjacent areas of Central Niger. Andrew B. Smith describes the Ténéréan peoples as "basically herdsmen, but wild animals such as antelopes, hippo, rhino, and warthog were hunted. The plants identified from impressions in pottery are predominantly hydrophiles that grew around the marches of Agorass-in-Tast" [4] (1980a: 455).[5] By the fourth millennium BC, pastoralism was widespread throughout the Sahara from the Nile Valley near Khartoum to Niger and Mali. Although it showed some regional variability, it still had strong similarities, especially in the over-all 'genre de vie' of herding com-

bined with hunting and, from the large number of grind-stones, the gathering and processing of wild grains (cf. Andrew B. Smith 1980b, 1984). Like the Kreda of our times, prehistoric pastoralists probably adjusted their migrations to coincide with the harvesting of these plants.

A drier environment exerted some pressure on the herdsmen already by the onset of the fifth millennium BC. One response to the increasingly seasonal rainfall may have been a stronger reliance on small stock at the expense of cattle (Gautier 1987: 173). At the same time, however, the Sahel became free from tsetse infestation, opening up new areas for pastoralists, and a widespread strategy appears to have bee to move south to these better pastures (Andrew B. Smith 1987: 1992; Street & Gasse 1981; McIntosh & McIntosh 1988; Petit-Maire et al. 1983; Nicholson & Flohn

1980). We know, that cattle was raised at Adrar Bous, Arlit and Karkarishinkat in the Sahel between the fourth and second millennium BC (Gautier 1987; Andrew B. Smith 1980b, 1984), and in the Sudan (Kadero) as early as 4500 BC (Gautier 1987; Haaland 1992). By the second millennium BC the Sahara was as dry as it is today, and grasslands had vanished; by 1000 BC much of it was deserted, as Marshall writes (1994: 20-21).

Food production did not occur at the time when pastoralists established themselves in the Sahel. The earliest evidence of food production in North Africa stems from Fayum and dates from the fifth millennium BC, although some manipulation of the environment to produce more food may be traced back much further, an example being the exploitation of geophytes around the Klasies River in

South Africa some 70,000 years ago (Deacon 1989: 557-89). The early Egyptian farmers cultivated barley and emmer wheat. The Fayum culture was based upon mixed farming, as pointed out by Caton-Thompson & Gardner as early as in 1934 and the same holds good for certain other prehistoric Egyptian cultures of about the same age (cf. Childe 1935: 49 ff.). Wheat and barley are undoubtedly introduced directly or indirectly from the Near East, as there is no evidence for any prototypes for these grains (cf. Phillipson & Phillipson 1981: 72). Many of the continent's most important food crops are indigenous, such as sorghum and most millets, probably first cultivated in the savanna country between the Senegal and the confluence of the Blue and the White Nile.[6] Although our insight into the initial cultivation of indigenous African plants is hampered by a lack of hard archaeological evidence and hence based largely on botanical arguments, such as the distribution of wild prototypes (ibid. 1981: 71-73), it seems reasonable to assume that Sub-Saharan agriculture was an essentially indigenous process.[7]

Various theories have been launched to explain the situation which led to an intensification of food-producing. It can be assumed that the ecological conditions pertaining during the early Holocene provided a suffiently large harvest from wild species (e.g. *Panicum, Echinochloa, Eragrostis, Cenchrus, Aristida, Pennisetum* and *Sorghum*) to have precluded the necessity of turning to cultivation before obliged to do so by the more rapid onset of desiccation. The single scene in the Tassili rock art, claimed to represent women harvesting grain (Lhote 1958), could equally well refer to wild as to cultivated species" Clark 1976:77 f.). During his extensive fieldwork among the Tuareg, Johannes regularly observed self-sown plots of millet and sorghum round deserted camps in the Ayr where many seeds are lost in the process of preparing them for food (Nicolaisen & Nicolaisen 1997, I: 251-2). These self-sown plots were not made use of by the Tuareg, "... but it is not difficult to see how a population living in an ever more impoverished environment would turn to harvesting such spontaneous yields and hence to intentionally sowing and reaping, if this could be done without great time and labour, especially since *Pennisetum* and *Sorghum* mature rapidly and two, sometimes three, crops a year can be obtained under favourable conditions," says Clark (1976: 83). In short, it seems that circumstances are favourable for collecting wild

seed in the Sahel zone and, under normal conditions, collecting would supply pastoral peoples with their necessary plant food, although today pastoralists of the Sahel zone also rely on cultivated grain.

Shaw sums up the main theories regarding the factors that led to an intensification of food production as follows: a) the pastoralists moving south from the Sahara adopted agriculture as a response to their dwindling food supplies. This seems a fairly simplistic model, but more reasonable if the pastoralists had already been accustomed to timing their transhumance patterns in such a way as to be able to reap the grain from stands of wild grasses (Oliver & Fagan 1975: 15-17); b) the pressure of the incoming pastoralists caused the hunter-gatherers already occupying the West African savannas to adopt agriculture (Clark 1972); c) the hunter-gatherer-fishers who had worked out a stable way of life based on aquatic resources during the Megachad period began to make use of stands of wild grain in their territory as the climate deteriorated (Shaw 1981: 104).

The change from a sole dependency on hunting, fishing and gathering to a livelihood relying on herding small ruminants and later growing millet and sorghum was the result of a cumulative number of small changes in emphasis of the various strategies employed to exploit the environment. Yet, it was a revolutionary step. Evidence from Neolithic times on groups who continued to rely predominantly on foraging is wanting. Little is known of their subsistence techniques and strategies or of their culture in general. We have few clues as to the nature of their social life, and it is unclear to what extent such groups relied upon and engaged in exchange relations with pastoralists. We have noted that pastoral groups made substantial use of wild resources, and there is evidence that some foraging groups were quite specialized wild-grain collectors, hunters or fishermen (McIntosh & McIntosh 1988; Petit-Maire et al. 1983; Sutton 1977), some perhaps semi-sedentary (Close 1980; Gautier & Van Neer 1982; McDonald 1991); thus, there must often have been competition for food, as pointed out by Marshall (1994: 20-21).

The Neolithic scene of North Africa is a reminder that the interpretation of archaeological findings of hunting equipment such as arrows and other projectile-points and specialized gear, in particular in sites which also contain findings of pottery and grind-stones is a delicate matter. Hunting implements may testify to the presence of groups relying predominantly on hunting and foraging activities, but may also be remains from temporary camps of neolithic agro-pastoralists or herders supplementing their livelihood by hunting, as pointed out by Roset (1987: 230). Just as pottery and grind-stones point to consumption of wild plants, obtained by gathering, as well as to subsistence, relying upon agriculture makes it, if not optional, at least possible to interpret the findings as either indicators of food-extraction and/or food-production. These are some of the very problems which future archaeologists must grapple with, if they are to make sense of findings from Haddad and Kreda camps.

What has not been taken sufficiently into account in theorizing about these early phases of human existence in this part of the world is a possible coexistence and cohabitation of professionally specialized groups, as is the case in our times of the Haddad and Kreda. What we do learn from the above exposé on human livelihood in Neolithic times, however, is that it was based on a wide range of economic pursuits, ranging from predominantly hunting-gathering and pastoral over agro-pastoral to largely agricultural activities. Presumably, foraging groups were players in this field down through the centuries, as are the Haddad of today, although hard core evidence to substantiate the claim is limited. What we do know, however, is that the conditions under which they pursued their trade varied greatly. The more recent history of Kanem and Bahr el Ghazal has been characterized by a similar variety in patterns of subsistence, still flourishing at the time of our fieldwork, but apparently dramatically changed since then due to the severe droughts, the spread of automatic weapons and civil war. These factors have contributed to a seriously diminished mammalian and bird fauna and to a general upheaval of social life. The depletion of game crucial to specialized hunters like the Haddad was already a fact in the 1960s. Not only were the large herds of elephants mentioned by Barth or of hippopotami, which Alexander Boyd came across in the beginning of the 20th century a thing of the past, so were the herds of Oryx, which had formed a cornerstone in Haddad Kreda economy. Gazelles, ostriches and bustards were few and far between compared to a generation ago, the Haddad complained to us. In line with the environmental degradation, foraging and hunting activities could only diminish in economic importance and the Haddad have had to adapt to the situation, as we shall see. In order to appreciate the characteristics of Haddad life, we shall look at another facet of the past.

THE KNOW-HOW OF IRON TECHNOLOGY: A PIECE OF THE HADDAD PUZZLE?

Metal Age in Africa beyond the Nile Valley is essentially an Iron Age. South of the equator, iron working began at about the same time as food production. Archaeologists have argued that in general there was a pronounced cultural contrast between early metal-using farming people and their immediate stone-tool-using hunter-gatherer neighbours and predecessors. Apart from Egypt (where copper was smelted early in the 4th millennium BC and bronze some two thousand years later), Nubia and the still obscure history of metallurgy of Ethiopia (which shows stylistic affinities to southern Arabia), iron melting is only preceded by proto-historic copper-working in West Africa (cf. Derricourt 1984: 95).[8] Iron melting dates back to approximately 1400 BC. It reached the Mediterranean and Egypt between the 10th and the 8th century BC. Until the mid-1960s many historians and archaeologists assumed that the craft was transmitted from here to Nubia, and that the cradle of East and West African iron technology was Meroe, the Napatan city founded by the 7th century BC at the upper Nile, and known to us from Herodotus, who travelled as far as to present-day Aswan. From here the iron technology was believed to have spread to Kanem along the Bahr el Ghazal, which since ancient times was renowned as an important trading route and a passage for hopeful migrants on the outlook for better livelihoods, although the furnaces found so far did not resemble the more primitive ones known from Meroe (cf. Treinen-Claustre 1982: 193). Some scholars argued that the process was spurred by the very fall of Meroe (cf. Forbes 1950: 35; Fuchs 1970: 328). Arkell suggested, for instance, that iron technology was brought to Kordofan and Darfur with the royal family as this fled westwards (Arkell 1961: 147).

Other scholars have looked towards North Africa as the source of origin of iron technology in the Sahel. It has been argued that the technology followed the trade routes from the North African coast, iron evidently being one of the most valuable goods that the Berber caravans could carry. According to Thomas "The pastoralists of dry rocky ranges and the Sahara edge were in contact with the Nile Valley to the east, and to the north-west with settled farmers of the coastal Maghrib. Some Greek colonies and the Phoenician settlements from Iron Age Asia on the Mediterranean coast, and especially at the Tunisian site of Carthage, influenced these indigenous societies. The mobile Libyan communities traded Saharan salt for West African gold, Mauritanian copper, slaves, ivory, skins, and other products and, in turn exchanged these for imported goods, notably cloth and beads" (Thomas 1984: 95). Iron was probably introduced in North Africa by Phoenician colonists in the eighth or perhaps ninth century BC, but there is no material evidence for early iron work here so far. This lack of evidence has led some scholars to support the theory of iron smelting being independently invented in sub-Saharan Africa. Iron smelting furnaces in Niger and Nigeria, radio-carbon dated to 500-1000 BC, indicate that iron-smelting in Sub-Saharan Africa may be as old as in Egypt. At Taruga, on the Bauchi Plateau of modern Nigeria, no less than thirteen iron-smelting furnaces produced the metal for the Nok society between the fifth and third centuries BC. The Nok made use of ground stone axes, exploited oil palms and made sub-Saharan Africa's oldest sculptures of human figures and other objects in terracotta (Iliffe 1995: 34). Early sites of iron smelting have also been located in the Zaire basin, all stemming from furnaces of the shaft-bowl type. Non-calibrated

3,3. Rock engraving showing masked hunters. Fezzan. Barth 1857-58, I: 210.

data from the lakes area place these in the period 2500 to 2300 BP, and according to Kriger more solidly at 1700 BP from Butare (Rwanda), while there are several dates from Gabon from 2200 to 200 BP (Kriger 1999: 36). A series of excavations in Chad, both at Koro-Toro to the North and at Mdaga to the South, though offering no definite answer to the puzzle, have led scholars to argue that these iron-age cultures developed without previous knowledge of copper and bronze technology (Childs & Killick 1993: 22, 321). Others find it difficult to believe that such a technology could develop without prior experience with high temperature pyro-technology, such as shaft kiln firing of ceramics or copper smelting, which happens at 1,083 degrees Celsius - iron needs between 1,100–1,200 degrees Celsius to rid the ore of most impurities (slag). Silver, gold and copper alloys can be melted at open hearths, but pure copper which melts at 1,084 degrees Celsius only, is difficult to produce without a blast furnace or kiln. The same holds for iron. Modern experiments have demonstrated, however, that one can reach temperatures of 1,200 degrees Celsius in a furnace by means of the wind alone. Bellows increase the temperature to 1,350 degrees Celsius (Kriger 1999: 34). Childs and Killick claim that the question of origin is still unanswered (1993: 22, 320-1).

Whatever it was, however, the making of iron metal out of iron ores has been a challenge then as it was well into the 20th century, when such metallurgical processes were still carried out in Chad. Kriger has pointed out that scholars have been mistaken in arguing that the extraction of metals in pre-colonial Africa were 'simple' technological processes to be analysed with other 'foraged or collected' commodities conflating altogether different types of resources and confusing mineral ores with metals. Iron metal is produced by people, not simply gathered or collected. "One must be taught to recognize which rocks are ores, for example, which only sets the stage for the rest of the technical and labour processes, all required if iron is to be successfully won from ore," she argues (Kriger 1999: 30). Iron smelting itself is a highly complicated process, as just indicated. Recent research has demonstrated that African smelters adapted their work to a wide variety of ore resources and designed highly specialized furnaces, developing along the way kinds of expertise that were unanticipated even by experienced geologists and metallurgists (ibid. 1999: 32).

3,4. Game was abundant in Kanem at time of Nachtigal's travels. Nachtigal 1879, I: 550.

Whatever the origin of iron technology in this part of Africa its arrival apparently did not alter the everyday way of life of the Saharan and Sahelien inhabitants as far as we can judge from the existing evidence. There is no difference, for example, in arrangement between the sites of habitation of the early Iron Age and those of the Neolithic in the Eghazer basin, no defensive constructions, and the economy continued to rely heavily upon pastoralism and hunting. According to Grébénart: "... it seems as if the use of metal was simply added to that of stone, bone and wood to round out the small tools and weapons of everyday life: pins, arrowheads, knives and so forth" (1987: 312-3). In Sahara the Neolithic and Iron Age were contemporaneous for a while, while the latter clearly succeeded the former in the Sahel region.[9] This general picture is in concordance with the archaeological excavations in the Koro-Toro area at the northern extremities of the Bahr el Ghazal. This dig

tells of groups relying on foraging and animal husbandry for their subsistence and of an increase in iron production between the fifth and tenth centuries AD (Treinen-Claustre 1982: 178-81; Conte 1991: 231).[10]

Gradually, however, the overall socio-political arena changed. Archaeological records indicate a broad trend toward increasing social and economic complexity, higher levels of wealth and social stratification. In writing the histories of some of the early dynasties of Central West Africa, historians sometimes assert that ironworking played a major role in the formation of centralized government. Kriger warns us not to jump at such conclusions, however. "At first glance, this might seem like a reasonable assertion to make. After all, ironworkers and iron imagery crop up in some oral traditions that tell of the founding of polities or ruling dynasties, and ritualized ironworking gestures were sometimes featured in the investiture ceremonies of leaders.

Logone plains south of Lake Chad. The Haddadien culture relied heavily on iron and Coppens believes that it reached the Bahr el Ghazal from the East and gradually proceeded towards Lake Chad (Coppens 1969: 132-44). Dierk Lange argues that the emergence of Haddadien culture coincides with the beginning of the dynastic history of Kanem known to us through a chronicle called the Dīwān of the sultans of Kanem-Bornu. Lange hypothesizes that the Haddadien are the precursor of the Zaghawa dynasty or perhaps their contemporaries and allies (Lange 1977: 151-3). He argues, moreover, that the Zaghawa are synonymous with the Banū Dūkū, whom Lange argues are the ancestors of present day Duu or Haddad (Kanembu), a point to which we shall return (Lange 1977: 151). Unfortunately, no systematic archaeological excavations have been carried out in Kanem itself, as previously mentioned, and it is impossible to assess whether the development just described corresponded with an expansion of iron production closer to Lake Chad. Further research is needed to assess the role of ironworking in the shaping of Kanemese society. In a fine analysis of ironworking in 19th century West Central Africa, Colleen Kriger has shown that the blacksmiths made a highly important contribution to agricultural production and to hunting. As among the Haddad essential weapons of the hunt were harpoons, lances, spears and arrows and distinctly different types of blades of the latter were applied in hunting various kinds of small game. Kriger argues that the development of special types of blades in pre-colonial Central West Africa was but one of the results of long-standing collaboration between hunters and blacksmiths here. The author demonstrates furthermore that in general the latter proved important agents of change. Ironworkers were founders and shapers of workshops, labour forces and communities in rural and urban settings, innovators in social and economic networks and a class of individuals deemed worthy of respect in pre-colonial Africa. In pursuing their careers, they persistently transcended local and family affiliations, crossed ethnic and language boundaries and generated a regional dimension to their work. The tools they produced became standardized in form and each recognized and prized for its particular efficacy. The blacksmiths sold them, not simply to hunters and fishers in the villages and towns where they lived, but to ready markets further a field that were known to merchants. By the 19th century, certain examples of these tools were widely available and traded over long distances (Kriger

3,5. Knife worn on the upper left arm by Tubu men. Such knives are also popular among the Kreda and other pastoralists. Cat. no. 95. Photo J.K.

But not only are these images and rituals very different in the kinds of references they make to ironworking, they are quite possibly anachronistic and not to be taken at face value. Rarely, however, are they examined critically, and with chronological issues in mind" (Kriger 1999: 40).

Kanem witnessed the emergence of what Y. Coppens called the Haddadien culture in the first millennium AD, a culture he considered a contemporary of the Sao culture at the Shari-

1999: 4, 5, 130). This situation is in line with Conte's description that: "The close social and ritual proximity of hunters and smiths observable in modern Kanem could reflect a very long-standing economic tradition in the north-eastern Chad basin" (1991: 231). A similar point of view has been aired by Peter Fuchs, who described a series of historical, cultural and social aspects of the relationship between smiths and hunters in an article on iron extraction and forging in Northern Chad (Fuchs 1970: 313). Conte learned from older blacksmiths in Central and South Kanem that ore extraction and smelting continued to prosper there, labour-intensive though these activities were, until the pre-colonial period" (Conte 1991: 232).[11] Fuchs claims that iron extraction took place as late as in 1953 in the Ennedi area, the reason being, in his view, that scrap iron was harder to come by because the area was untouched by the military operations of World War II (1979: 313). However, the fact that iron was produced a century ago does not prove a historical continuity of smelting in Kanem, of course.

Iron production and the craft of forging, currently done with such skills by Haddad smiths in Kanem played a role in the process of state formation and expansion in Kanem and elsewhere in Central Sudan in the 9th and 10th centuries like it had for the Phoenician expansion in the Mediterranean. In its wake it brought widespread deforestation[12] and hence ecological transformation throughout the Sahel as it had done around the Mediterranean a thousand years earlier, a factor often neglected when assessing the impact of iron technologies not only on local conditions but on the wider polity.

Material remains and artefacts are keys to an understanding of the specific constellations of foraging, agro-pastoral activities and iron production that has characterized the pre-history in this part of the world. It is through historical records, however, that we get a deeper perspective on the social, economic and political context that conditioned the existence of foraging peoples of the region, such as that of the Haddad. We shall turn, therefore to the more recent past for a brief moment.

EMERGING POLITY AND HADDAD ANCESTRY

It can be safely assessed in the rear-view mirror of history that the Sahel displays features favourable to the develop-

ment of complex, large-scale polities as the one emerging in Kanem during the second half of the first millennium AD. Comparatively rich in water, arable land and pastures, Kanem is and was attractive to pastoralists and agriculturalists alike and has proved a viable environment for hunters since ancient times. The area is relatively open to human movement and hence to trading, except for the hindrance posed to the north by the great *erg* which complicates east-west communication, as we have heard. Kanem has been able to produce a surplus of food necessary to feed both an elite of rulers, craftsmen and other specialists at urban centres, like the ones emerging during the twelfth century AD east of the Lake, described by Ech-cherif-al Edrīssī (ca. 1154). The existence of specialized crafts at earlier phases of Kanemi polity has not been verified, as Connah remarks, but there were probably potters, blacksmiths and leather-workers, cloth-workers, grindstone- and salt-makers, natron traders, builders, hunters, fishermen and priests (Connah 1981: 221). The upcoming of the Kanemese state in the first millennium AD and its subsequent development was due to a series of factors such as knowledge of iron technology mandatory to the making of weapons, military capacity backed by a fine cavalry, long-distance trade in goods and slaves, the forging of politically expedient marriage alliances and in due time the advent of Islam which brought with it an administrative structure, a code of new laws and behaviour, a new sense of commonality of values and purpose on earth and elevated the African ruler to a higher pedestal as a representative of Allah and the Prophet, as noted by Azevedo (1998: 22). It is within this complex environmental, socio-economic and cultural setting that the central Sudanese empires came into being and grew in power, including that of the Banu Duku of Kanem, which may have been the very first of the West African states. Systematic ethno-archaeological investigations covering the last one thousand years are still to be carried out. When we pool our knowledge of adjacent regions with linguistic reconstructions and the available written records, a fairly coherent picture of the socio-economic and political development in Kanem and the Bahr el Ghazal emerges however, and hence of the overall conditions for the existence of foraging peoples like the Haddad.

The earliest historical sources on the socio-economic history of Central Sudan are those of Arab scholars, as previously intimated. It was the expansion of trans-Saharan trade due to the Arab conquest of North Africa in the 7th and 8th centuries which eventually opened up the region to men like al-Yaʿqūbī (late 9th century) - the first to actually use the name Kanem, as well as al-Bakri (c. 1050) and al-Muhallabī (late 10th century). The latter offers information on the Zaghawa rulers of Kanem alias the Banū Dūkū mentioned in the Dīwān (Lange 1977: 5). We are also enlightened by Ech-cherif-al Edrīssī (c. 1154), Ibn Saʿīd al Maghrībī (c. 1240), who probably based his information on a manuscript by Ibn Fatima now lost (Lange 1977: 5), Ibn Khaldun (14th century), Ibn Battuta (c. 1356), al-Maqrīzī (15th century) and Leo Africanus (16th century) (cf. H.F.C.A. Smith 1971: 168; Lange 1977: 115). By the middle of the 19th century, the first Europeans penetrated the Sahara and reached Kanem itself, enabling a Western scholarly tradition to take root. But it is only from the middle of the 20th century that more consistent efforts to come to grips with the social history of Kanem get off the ground and an understanding of the formation and characteristics of the Kanem-Bornu state during the ninth and tenth centuries and the ensuing socio-cultural development takes shape.

The first generation of European scholars writing about Kanemese history were all interested in one aspect of this complicated story, namely in the origin and arrival on the scene of 'founding fathers', an issue which still occupies researchers like Connah (1981: 37-8). The initial spur to the formation of Kanemese polity is shrouded in myth and object of much speculation. Several scholars argue that it was set in motion through an influx from the Nilotic area of So, Sao or Saw people (cf. Palmer 1936, Urvoy 1949 and Trimingham 1962). The latter considers the role of these people seminal to Kanemese polity and argues that the So "had a well-defined civilization, which from the historical point of view is centered in the walled town state, divine kingship with ritual murder, and elaborate hierarchization of political organization." But he cautions that the term So belongs to the realm of myth and used by nomads for those inhabitants of the Chad region other than the paleo-nigritic 'little red men', known as the *gwaigwai* in Hausa folklore (Trimingham 1962: 104).[13] Migeod believes, in fact, that the So are the actual ancestors of the present Kanuri (Migeod 1924: 124, 207, 210), a point of view substantiated by oral traditions collected by Connah (1981: 37). Jean-Paul Lebeuf argues that the So (Sao) culture was developed by pre-Islamic herding and foraging groups who came from the region

east of Lake Chad and the Mandara mountains. They settled at Kanem from where they were dispersed only in the late 16th century by Idris Alawma (Alooma) of Borno[14]. Lebeuf ascribes the knowledge of iron technology of these herding and foraging people a determining role in the founding of So culture and polity (Jean-Paul Lebeuf 1962).

A number of scholars look in other directions for explanations of the emergence and growth of Kanemese polity. Some link the development of the Kanemese state with the Zaghawa; others argue that the founding fathers may well be the pastoral Sefawa, while Dierk Lange claim that the Banū Dūkū preceeded the Zaghawa (Trimingham 1962: 104-5, Lange 1977: 116 and Azevedo 1998: 24). Trimingham supports the view that the Zaghawa played a seminal role and that these Negroid Kuchites facilitated the diffusion of Nubian culture into central Sudan. He argues that the Zaghawa provided the dynasties for Kanem and certain Hausa states, for example Gobir: "... giving them a different outlook from that which characterized city-states, where the So civilization was relatively unmodified (Trimingham 1965: 105). However, the hypothesis is questioned by H. F. C. Smith[15] who believes that the founders of Kanem polity were the nomadic Sefawa and that they came into power sometime during the first millennium AD. The Sefawa dynasty had military clout and an effective cavalry, it is argued.[16] Two separate patterns of habitation had been formed in the region by then: one consisting of Teda-Daza-speaking pastoralists in Kanem north-east of Lake Chad[17] and one of Chadic-language-speaking groups in Hausa-land and Bornu to the east of the Lake. Smith writes, that the Sefawa were a product of the former and that these people developed and ruled a coalition of previously separate Teda-Daza pastoralists. He attributes major significance to Sefawa marriage alliances in creating the Kanuri state, to the ongoing sedentarization in cementing the unification of the Kanuri and, in that context, to the significance of the urban centers (H.F.C. Smith 1971: 166, 169). In due time the *mais* (lord) of the Sefawa was transformed from a purely nomadic sheikh encamped among tributary cultivators, to a divine king or despot exercising direct rule over people and country. It is possible that the institution of divine kingship, which implies the ritual seclusion of the ruler from his subjects, was adopted from settled peoples with whom the pastoral and foraging Sefawa came in contact in Kanem.[18] The court itself remained semi-nomadic moving between a number of towns that functioned as administrative and commercial centres, according to Smith (ibid. 1971: 167).[19]

Dierk Lange is also of the opinion that Kanem was ruled by the Zaghawa from the second half of the 9th until the first part of the 13th century. Initially, the Zaghawa were semi-nomadic but they took up a more nomadic way of life after their expulsion from Kanem. Al-Yākūt tells that the Zaghawa comprised a great many people. They lived in huts made of straw, subsisted on millet, barley, beans and on their cattle and small ruminants. The majority wore leather dresses or went around naked. The royalty had trousers of delicate wool and over these fine clothes of silk from Sousse and brocade. He tells us, more importantly, of the total devotion to the king. "Their religion consists of adoration of their kings; they believe that it is they who make for living or dying, who bring illness and health" (Lange 1977: 116-19). Lange notes that al-Yākūt describes the Zaghawa not only as rulers of Kanem but also of the Hausa, but argues that the latter probably were conquered at a later point in time than Kanem. The Zaghawa Empire was immense compared to the other kingdoms of Sudan, writes al-Muhallabī, but the dynasty was dethroned during the first part of the 13th century by the Sēfuwa, who stayed in power until the middle of the 19th century (Lange 1977: 124, 128).

However, the Kanemese kingdom came into existence much earlier than the 9th century, according to Lange, probably already during the second half of the 6th century (Lange 1977: 151). It was ruled at that time by the Banū Dūkū or Banī Dūgu, who are said to have 'exerted a certain authority over Kawar and other oases south of Fezzan during the 9th century'. This makes Kanem the oldest state in West Africa. The argument is founded upon a thorough reading of Arabic sources and of the Dīwān. The latter document was located by Barth and exists in two copies only, the original having disappeared. The Dīwān contains information on the history and chronology of 67 sultans of Kanem Empire from around 975 AD until 1808. Lange claims that the Banū Dūkū mentioned in the Dīwān and the Zaghawa known through the writings of al-Yākūt and al-Muhallabī are in fact one and the same dynasty (Lange 1977: 145, 150).

Of specific interest to us is Lange's argument that there is a continuing 'smith' tradition from those pre-Islamic times

to the present. In his view the Duu or Danoa [Haddad, IN], also described by Nachtigal as the oldest inhabitants of Kanem, are in fact the very descendants of the Banū Dūkū (Arabic) or Duguwa (Kanuri). He writes moreover, that the carriers of the Haddadien culture, whose relics stem from the fifth century AD, according to F. Treinen-Claustre, are the direct precursors of the first Zaghawa or Banū Dūkū rulers. At that time the two terms signified neither a 'dynasty', in the strict sense of the word, nor a nomadic people, even less a caste of smiths, but rather a dominating allogene group that was to rule Kanem until the end of the 11th century. Lange concludes that one may regard the Haddad of today as the very heirs of these early pre-Islamic potentates (Lange 1977: 151-3).

There is wide agreement among all scholars that by AD 1000 a fully fledged state had come into being in Kanem and that it exerted power for the ensuing eight centuries. The first the rulers seem to have consolidated themselves at Njimi east of Lake Chad. Their polity was constantly undermined by inter-dynastic rivalries, however, with ensuing poisoning, assassinations and blinding of family members considered threats in the power game. In the 1390s this enabled the Bulala of the Lake Fitri region, a branch of the ruling clan, to take over. The court was forced to flee and it re-established itself to the west of the Lake in the province of Bornu leaving the Bulala to rule Kanem. Throughout the 15th century petty states proliferated on the ruins of Kanem. Under Idris Katagarmabe (1503-26) Kanem was re-conquered, but the Bulala were allowed to remain as tributary independent rulers, and they continually threw off even that nominal recognition (Trimingham 1962: 122-42). The Bornu state established its capital in Birni Ngazargamu in 1484 and reached a second zenith under Alooma's rule in the 16th century, during which it exacted annual tribute from people as far away as Wadai and Darfur. Alooma or Alawma, who reigned from about 1572 to 1619, introduced Turkish musketeers and an Arab cavalry which gained his campaigns renown. He recaptured Kanem and is generally eulogized as a genuinely wise ruler and builder of the empire (Trimingham 1962: 122-3; Azevedo 1998: 23).

The political situation in Kanem and Bornu was nevertheless fluid throughout the centuries. There were no strict frontiers. Political dominance and influence varied through time and space. No important commercial towns developed in either Kanem or Bornu during this long peri-od, presumably because of the endemic state of insecurity. One thing did not vary, however, and that was the clear distinction between rulers, vassals and subjects. Political control was exerted over the latter through direct admin-istration by the court. Vassals both came within and were outside this jurisdiction, and many of these groups still re-main distinctive within the Kanuri today, says Trimingham (1962: 123-5).

TRADE, SLAVES, WARS AND THE ADVENT OF ISLAM

The development of states in the Sahel was spurred by a range of factors including long-distance trade. It is well known that the Arab conquest of North Africa boosted the existing long-distance trade and hence stimulated the creation of polities throughout the area. The trans-Saha-ran trade fed into the trade network of the Arabs, which reached from Spain through North Africa to Egypt, where it branched up through Syria to Iraq and down the Red Sea to India. The trade brought wealth to local communi-ties and empowered individuals and groups through con-trol over its distribution. It provided "… the *raison d'être* for the rise of numerous cities" in this part of the world as it did in Europe, Mabogunje argues (1968: 45). A spectacular case was the rise of the ancient realm of Ghana, but also Kanem profited from its trans-Saharan trade, although it lacked the gold of Bambuk. The trans-Saharan trade in gold dates back to the 3rd century AD. It picked up with the rising of gold as a medium of exchange in the economies of the Mediterranean and beyond, and the Roman practice of paying taxes in gold coins from the 4th century AD. It was facilitated by the introduction of the camel around the same time and more favourable climatic conditions which made the trans-Saharan journeys both a practical and prof-itable proposition[20] (Reader 1999: 285).

There is wide agreement, as we have seen, that by AD 1000 a fully fledged state had come into being in Kanem. It was to endure for eight centuries although in slightly var-ied forms over time. The ruler or *mais* (lord) held a strate-gic position vis-à-vis the trans-Saharan trade at that time. Kanem extended its powers along the trade routes towards the Fezzan at its peak controlling the Bilma trail, which led from Tripoli through different oases in the Fezzan, south

of Kawar, and on to Lake Chad, and hence the valuable salt trade from the deposits at Bilma (R. Cohen 1978a: 8; Thomas 1984: 132). Many different items found their way through the desert including horses, cotton, cloth, copper, kola nuts, ostrich feathers, ivory, hides, wax, perfumes, muskets and glass (Azevedo 1998: 25). The most coveted commodity, however, was slaves, and slave-raiding became an intrinsic element of Kanemese state policy and a major impetus to wage war on neighbouring groups (Cuoq 1975: 49). Azevedo argues along the same line that: "… beside ter-ritorial conquest as one of the reasons for violence, the ma-jor incentive for warring in Central Sudan was the acquisi-tion of slaves. There would have been fewer wars had slav-ery and the slave trade not been major features of Islamic societies in this part of Africa, which, in the name of Allah, authorized the faithful to enslave those of alien faiths or the idolatrous, as the Muslims called non-Muslims" (1998: 45). In his view, moreover, the control of trans-Saharan trade enhanced state revenues and hence made it possible for rulers to realize dynastic and personal ambitions and to transform acephalous societies into hierarchical and cen-tralized polities. It is beyond doubt that the Kanemese state profited from long distance trade and fed into the trans-Saharan trade routes. It bolstered this enterprise with an engagement in slave raiding which provided the highly prized human merchandise that subsequently trudged the long trails to markets in unbelievable misery.

Proficiency in iron technology and hence the ability to produce weapons was another key to the unfolding of polities, as it went hand in hand with the development of armies (Mabogunje 1968: 37). Some scholars have argued, in fact, that warfare was critical to the very emergence and expansion of states in Central Sudan. "War made the state, and the state made war" Tilly notes (1975: 42), a point of view that cannot be taken too literally, of course, as the ability to conduct warfare in itself does not guar-antee the organizational capability of holding together a state (R. Cohen 1984: 337; Azevedo 1998: 23). Still war-fare enabled the Kanemese rulers to expand and hold their own against other states in accordance with the strength and effectiveness of their armies and weaponry. Mai Idris Alooma (Alawma), for example, consolidated the Bornu state in the late sixteenth century by his command over a substantial army, including a regular force of musketeers, a quasi-regular cavalry and a probably non-regular infantry (Connah 1981: 222). The rulers used a cavalry to force groups into submission. "We do not know exactly whence they obtained their horses," says Smith, "but the valley of the Bahr al-Ghazal in which these developments are most likely to have taken place retains its reputation for horse-breeding down to the present day," (H.F.C.A. Smith 1971: 167), something to which I can personally testify. The regular use of the horse dates back to the ninth century in Central Sudan, but there is no conclusive evidence as to when horses reached this part of the Sahel from Northern Africa (Law 1980: 8-9, 14, 28-29).[21] The Kanemese rulers received tribute in exchange for protection against other marauders. They based their power not only on military superiority but also on intertribal alliances sealed by marriages producing offspring to whom the various tribes in turn pledged allegiance, as previously intimated. Smith argues that the influence of the so-called *maina* class, which was to be substantial in later times, may be sought in the fact that these rulers relied on delegating military powers to loyal subjects "... it is perhaps in the wars of the thirteenth century, in which the ascendancy of the Sefawa was extended beyond the tribal lands of the Kanuri, that the feudal system of later times has its origin. Newly conquered territory could, as elsewhere, be most easily organized by granting it as a fief to military commanders" says Smith (1971: 175).

3,6. The palace of the Sultan at Mao. Nachtigal writes about the town that 150 of the huts were inhabited by the Dalatoa [i.e. Haddad Kanembu]. Photo K.M. Fig. 4,17; 26.3.1954.

1. Ein Kanembo als Speerträger   2. Ein Bogenschütze
beide im Dienste des Scheik v. Bornu

3,7. A Kanembu with spears and an archer both in the service of the 'Sheik of Bornu', says the caption of these two etchings from Denham, Clapperton and Oudney's travels in North Africa. The archer could well be a Haddad as these were renowned for their skills with bow and arrow at that time. Denham, Clapperton & Oudney 1831, Pl. 2: 1.

Throughout history there as been an influx of people into Kanem and Bahr el Ghazal from the north just as groups have left these areas again. These were movements that often entailed fierce combats for control over land and resources. Oral traditions, Arab historians and the *Chronicle of the Sultans of (Kanem-) Bornu* tell of migrations from Tibesti to Kanem between the ninth and thirteenth centuries and beyond (cf. Chapelle 1957: 44-48), of pastoral Teda-speaking groups settling in Kanem during the thirteenth and fourteenth centuries and later of the

threat to the stability of the Kanemese state due to Tuareg expansion in the seventeenth century. The Tuareg forced the Teda to move eastwards where they "menaced the material security of all the northern Bornuan provinces, in the eighteenth century they harassed all the country north of the Yo, and in the nineteenth there was no power to arrest their inroads except their inability to combine," according to Trimingham (1962: 151).

To what extent warfare actually stimulated state formation in Kanem and elsewhere in Central Sudan is a

3,8. One of the Sultan of Begharmy's lancers. Denham, Clapperton & Oudney 1831, Pl. 2: 6.

6. *Lanzenreuter des Sultans von Begharmy*

topic of intense discussion. Azevedo has argued that: "... evidence seems to indicate that here states rose, shrank, expanded, and disappeared as their instruments of coercion and war oscillated between adequacy and superiority vis-à-vis those of their neighbors. Certainly ... the fall of Bagirmi, the rise of Wadai, and the successes of Rabah in Central Sudan at the turn of the century (19th) were primarily determined by the degree of strength and the effectiveness of their armies and their ability to wage successful warfare" (Azevedo 1998: 23). Turney-High has

attributed the apparent cause and effect relationship between warfare and state formation in this part of Africa to the fact that people were relatively well off relying on both agricultural production and husbandry, and that this economic potential together with open expanses of Sahel environment facilitated military operations. He argues that: "The threat of defeat united many communities in defence of their lives and property. Widespread war-chieftainships and confederacies arose which survived into peace times. When outside aggressions welded wide territories into defensive organizations, this added strength was used to the detriment of some still independent peoples." (Turney-High, H. 1971: 239)

A key factor in the formation of polity and social development in Sudan was the spread of Islam. It offered an administrative structure, a code of new laws and behaviour, a new sense of commonality of values and purpose on earth and elevated the African ruler to a higher pedestal as a representative of the Prophet (cf. Azevedo 1998: 22). Muslim faith was first adopted in Bornu and Kanem in the eleventh century. It probably spread along the northern trade route, but there were interludes of pagan chiefs. The rulers are said to have opposed widespread conversion out of fear that it would detract from their veneration as divine kings (H.F.C.A. Smith 1971: 177). By the thirteenth century, Islam was firmly established in Kanem and Kanemese pilgrims had a hostel in Cairo where they could dwell on their way to Mecca (Trimingham 1962: 115). It remained a minority faith for centuries, however, confined largely to royal courts, traders and towns, some of which became learned centres of scholarship. In Kanem as throughout Central Sudan its spread appears to have been closely associated with conquests and slave raiding. Alawma Idrīs (1581-1619) enforced Islam as a state religion and constructed brick mosques, but his wars were *jihads* only in the terminology of his imam. He did not liberate freemen among the captives, nor were these invited to embrace Islam (cf. Azevedo 1998: 24; Trimingham 1962: 123).

It was through the eastward migration of the Fulani from their homeland in the Senegal valley across the Sudan, however, that Islam eventually became a major force and local polities were reformed (Last 1978: 1-30).[22] Fulani pastoralists reached Bornu in the 16th century and were grazing their cattle on the hill slopes of northern Cameroun by the 18th century. Most of them were pagan, as far as we know, but they were accompanied by the *torodbe* i.e. 'those who pray to Allah', a Fulfulde-speaking group adhering to the pursuit of Islamic learning. Despite this influence some peoples converted to Islam only much later. This was the case, for example, of the populations of the Chad islands, the Yedina, who adopted the religion only in the late 19th century (Trimingham 1959: 17). It appears also to have been the case with the Haddad.

THE TURMOIL OF THE 19TH CENTURY

Kanem and the Bahr el Ghazal suffered massively from wars, marauding and slave-raiding throughout the 19th century, a state of affairs in which they themselves took active part. Towards the end of that period, the aggravations were intensified by the constant raids of the Awlad Sliman under the leadership of Rabah ibn Fadlallah and by the widespread lawlessness which reigned throughout Central Sudan. Sudanese states waged constant wars on one another and conducted military raids, especially to the south to procure slaves. They mustered substantial force, with armies ranging from a few thousand soldiers in Bornu to 15,000 men at Bagirmi, when this state was at its peak (Azevedo 1998: 48; Barth 1857-58, III: 527, 530, 560). The weapons consisted of spears and poisoned arrows, as was still the case during our stay in Kanem, but the arrival of explorers and colonial governments increased the availability of gunpowder and rifles in the region.[23] Denham writes of the war between Bornu and the sultan of Bagirmi at the time of his visit that, although he lost a beloved son, thirty thousand Bagirmese were killed or taken as slaves (Denham 1831: 461). Rabah ibn Fadlallah subdued several Muslim and non-Muslim societies, including the Sara of southern Chad between 1880 and 1890, but was defeated by the French at Kussuri on April 22 1900 (Carbou 1912, I: 28). Azevedo quotes Cordell, who notes that:" Rabah's presence in Oubangui-Shari and the Chad basin between 1878 and 1891 had dramatic demographic effects", the result of his taking with him perhaps as many as 40,000 people from the South (ibid. 35). Also the Dar Kuti and Bahr el Gazal states were viciously slave trading during the late 1890's, when parts of the south "...ran dry of anybody worth enslaving", according to Azevedo (ibid. 36). As late as in the early 1870's, Bagirmi just south of Kanem was once again invaded by Wadai resulting in the loss of an estimated 30,000 souls, and in addition the Wadaimese took "... weavers, dyers, tailors, saddlers, princes and princesses" (Cornet 1963: 22-23).

To what extent the slave-raiding in Kanem and surrounding parts of Central Sudan fed into the Atlantic slave trade is uncertain. It is estimated that about 11 million Africans were shipped to the New World between 1451 and 1870. The trade peaked in the late eighteenth century - the Bight of Biafra, especially the Niger Delta being a key source - and then declined slowly during the nineteenth century (Iliffe

1995: 131-2). But trading in slaves is age-old in North and West Africa. There were Africans in the Cathagese army when it invaded Sicily in the 5th century BC and, according to Pliny, Strabo slaves must have been a staple part of the north-bound caravans during Roman days, although these got most of such human merchandise from markets around the Mediterranean (Bovill 1958: 46-7). The same appears to have been the case throughout the Middle Ages, although gold was the key item of the trans-Saharan trade. Leo Africanus writes, for example, of a present given by the Sultan of Fez which consisted almost entirely of produce of the Sudan including: "Fifty men slaves and fifty women slaves brought out of the land of the Negroes, ten eunuchs, twelve camels, one giraffe, sixteen civet-cats, one pound of civet, a pound of amber and almost six hundred skins of a certain beast called by them elamt (addax gazelle) whereof they make their shields ..." (Bovill 1958: 124).

It is one of the ironies of history that, at a time when the Western world abolished slavery, the Sudanese sultanates increased the traffic in human beings on the pretext that Sharia allowed the enslavement of non-Muslims (cf. Azevedo 1998: 33). That trade in slaves was widespread and highly profitable in Kanem and neighbouring regions in the middle and late 19th century is a sad fact. Writing of the poverty of Bornu in 1827, Denham mentions that people can hardly sustain themselves, "... ihr Reichthum besteht nur in Sklaven, Rindern und Pferden" (Denham 1831: 449). Although detailed information on the situation in Kanem and western Bahr el Ghazal at that time is waning, the repercussions of the massive and widespread warfare must have been severe. It is well known from other parts of West Africa, moreover, that in general the significance of the slave trade lay less in the number of people lost than in the changed social patterns and reproductive capabilities of those who remained behind.

COLONIAL CONQUEST AND THE RULE OF THE FRENCH

The constant raiding and warfare were brought to a temporary halt by European intervention. However, French Colonial Rule was itself soon to prove a bloody affair. The French administered Chad with little respect for civil rights and human life, establishing a form of governance which

the past forty years of civil war and general insurgency have only prolonged.

The first Europeans crossed the Sahara and approached Kanem by the middle of the 19th century. The African Association (which later formed part of the Royal Geographical Society) had been formed in 1788 in London for the exploration of the interior of the continent and Mungo Park had entered Timbuktu in 1805. The Napoleonic wars put a brake on the exploration of Africa, but soon after the emperor had been deposed, the British government again turned its attention to West Africa to promote trade and establish Great Britain as a colonial power. In 1823, Lake Chad was reached by the way of Tripoli by Dr Walter Oudney and two other members of this British expedition: Captain Hugh Clapperton and Major Dixon Denham. They were able to report on the existence of the large and flourishing cities of the Bornu and Hausa states. In 1841, the British attempted to establish a white colony on the lower Niger, an expedition which ended in utter failure, but British traders remained in the area and their continued presence led ultimately to the acquisition by the British of political rights over the delta and the Hausa states.

From the middle of the 19th century, the British, French, Germans and Italians speeded up their efforts to secure markets and control over North and West Africa. In 1850, James Richardson was commissioned by the British to open up commercial links with the states of the western and central Sudan. But his untimely death soon after and that of his travel companion Adolf Overweg left it to the third member of the expedition, the German scholar Heinrich Barth, to carry out the mission. The five volumes he wrote about his travels provide us with useful information about the region, including Lake Chad and Kanem, as previously mentioned. The same can be said of Gustav Nachtigal's writings about his explorations in the years 1869–1874 of Tibesti and Borku, which at that time had still been visited only by a handful of Europeans, as well as of Bornu, Bagirmi, Wadai and Kordofan, which was terra incognita. Nachtigal had been commissioned by Prince Bismarck to collect information on the state of German commerce with the intent of making annexations on the coast. A net result of his efforts was a treaty signed on 5th July 1884 with the king of Togo, placing his country under German protection and one week later the proclamation of a German protectorate over the Cameroon district.

Rivalry between the European powers to assert sovereignty in Africa eventually affected the Lake Chad area including Kanem and Bahr el Ghazal - the homeland of the Haddad – which eventually was to come under French administration. France had occupied Algeria in 1830 and several French expeditions were launched from here to push south and southwest. Some went via Tripoli, still held by the Turks, while Darfur to the east was in the hands of Khedive Ismail of Egypt. Captain Lyon explored southern Libya as early as 1820, providing us with some information on the Tubu (Tiboo), but only after repeated failures was communication opened up between Algeria and Lake Chad by way of the Sahara by the French explorer F. Foureau in 1899-1900.[24] Lake Chad had attracted the attention of travellers for years, as previously indicated. The fact that the nature of this desert lake remained a puzzle, combined with the political interest in controlling the region, spurred on no less than three French expeditions. In 1898, they set out from the west, north and south respectively. Gentil, fighting against enormous difficulties, came from the west via the Congo and Ubanghi rivers. Foureau came down from Algiers through the Sahara and was not heard of for nearly a year. Voulet and Chanoine set out on their infamous expedition from Senegal, leaving behind a bloody trail of pillage, rape and murder, one of the darkest pages in the history of Africa. The survivors of the expedition eventually reached Lake Chad under Joalland and Meynier and joined with the forces of Gentil and Foureau (Boyd 1907: 3-4).

In the main, the Berlin Conference of 1885 defined the territorial borders of the possessions of various European powers in Africa. In the wake of the agreement, the Anglo-French declaration of 5th August 1890 recognized French influence in the Sahara, and British ditto between the Niger and Lake Chad. This did not mean, of course, that local rulers had necessarily accepted this new sovereignty, or would in decades to come. Kanem and the Bahr el Ghazal continued to be a highly volatile and troubled region, not only due to continuous grand-scale slave raiding and internal fighting but spurred on by the insurgency arising from the French intervention, which created new structures of violence to a large extent responsible for the post-colonial troubles and fighting, as Mario Azevedo has demonstrated.

In his interesting book *Roots of Violence: A History of War in Chad,* Azevedo offers a vivid account of the troubles the French encountered in conquering Chad and of the brutality or their rule. French colonial administration proved "intrinsically violent, enlisting the army, the police, and all other available means of coercion to impose control and elicit conformity," and, Azevedo argues, "It created, particularly in the south, conditions of permanent violence such as once existed in pre-colonial Central Sudan" (ibid. 1998: 65). In 1923, the Governor-General sarcastically remarked: "In ten years, the administration of the military territory (of Chad) inflicted twenty centuries [sic] and fifteen years of detention to a population that does not exceed 1,300,000" (ibid. 1998: 83).

French involvement in Chad was spurred on in part by nationalistic sentiments, inflamed by the defeat by the Prussians 1870 as well as by the need for raw materials and markets. Chad became the main producer of cotton in West Africa, but only through compulsory cultivation and the creation of horrendous socio-economic conditions for the growers. Last but not least, Chad was of strategic importance to the French in linking their positions in North and Central Africa. The conquest cost them dear, however, with heavy casualties in particular in northern Chad. The region, including Kanem and the Bahr el Ghazal was in turmoil at the time not the least due to the aggressive behaviour of the pastoral Awlad Sliman. At the beginning of the 19th century, these pastoralists had fought the Turks over the control of Fezzan. In 1842, upon the defeat and murder of their chief, Abd el Djelil, they moved south in search of 'greener pastures', causing widespread fighting and misery in Kanem and stirring up the Sanussiya in the wake (Carbou 1912, I: 31-35). Apart from the Haddad around N'Guri and Dibinentchi and the Tunjur of Mondo, who all succeeded in fighting off the Awlad Sliman, these expert warriors met no serious resistance and were soon rampaging throughout Kanem and the Bahr el Ghazal, pillaging wherever they came. Along with their allies, the Barka Halloui, they acted with unsurpassed brutality, treating the Kanemese population with utter spite for being both black and infidels, according to Carbou (1912, I: 31). Everyone was alternately ravaging and plundering everyone else, including the Haddad, the ones living around Dibinentchi pillaging those of N'Guri. The Haddad are also chronicled as offering resistance to the French, more specifically to the

3,9. Captain Lyon wrote of the Arabs that they:"... are good and bold horsemen, and though in general but poorly provided with food for their horses, they make them perform very long journeys." He continues: "The inducement to all exertion, however, is now nearly at an end, their wars having ceased; but in the time of the Waled Suliman, who infested the road from Tripoli to Fezzan, and committed every excess, journeys were made and difficulties overcome which equaled any of the stories of the Arabs of old." Capt. Lyon 1821: 54; Pl. p. 47.

Joalland-Meynier mission as this contingent pushed south in 1899 to join Foureau-Lamy, who was spearheading the French conquest (Carbou 1912, I: 33-35).

Kanem and Bahr el Ghazal were up for grabs and the French and the Awlad Sliman were not the only ones going for it. Others took advantage of the anarchy. First and foremost the French faced the Libyan Sanussiya, an orthodox Sufi fraternity established by the Algerian scholar, Mahammad bin 'Ali al-Sanusi in 1837, which exerted an influence on the sultans of Bagirmi, Wadai and in the Bahr el Ghazal (cf. Evans-Pritchard 1949: 11-12). The Sanussiya maintained its own arsenals of guns, ammunition and canons as well as repair shops of firearms and warehouses for the manufacture of gunpowder (Fisher and Rowland 1971: 223). The Order taxed commercial goods along the age-old trade routes, including slaves, and was fully in control of what was destined for Tripoli (Carbou 1912, I: 137). According to Azevedo, the Sanussiya opposed not only the 'white devils' (i.e. the French) but also Rabah ibn Fadlallah and his secularizing policies (Azevedo 1998: 73). The French were fearful of Rabah ibn Fadlallah, a 'warlord' who with an initial group of a mere 600 men had succeeded in suppressing Wadai, Ubangui and later Bornu. By 1890, Rabah, the Emir of the Faithful as he called himself,

3,10. A slave caravan or kafflé. "At the end of the month, a large kafflé of Arabs, Tripolines, and Tibboo, arrived from Bornou, bringing with them 1400 slaves of both sexes and of all ages, the greater part being females. Several smaller parties had preceded them many of whom also brought slaves. We rode out to meet the great kafflé, and to see them enter the town - it was indeed a piteous spectacle! These poor oppressed beings were, many of them, so exhausted as to be scarcely able to walk; their legs and feet were much swelled, and by their enormous size, formed a striking contrast with their emaciated bodies. They were all borne down with loads of fire-wood, and even poor little children, worn to skeletons by fatigue and hardships, were obliged to carry burdens, while many of their inhuman masters rode on camels, with the dreaded whip suspended form their wrists, with which they, from time to time, enforced obedience from these wretched captives." Capt. Lyon 1821: 120; etching p. 324.

was the most powerful person in Central Africa (Chapelle 1980: 219; Azevedo 1998: 68). The French went for Rabah in the year 1900 with a joint attack at Kusseri by their three expeditionary forces: Lamy & Foureau, who had come with their troops from Algiers, Voulet & Chanoine, who committed grave atrocities against the Africans along the way from Niger, as just mentioned, and Emile Gentil, who came up from the Moyen Congo. Led by Commander François Lamy, the French defeated Rabah. Lamy and nineteen of his men lost their lives as did about a thousand of Rabah's troops. The victory made the conquest of the rest of northern Chad possible, and two years later the Sanussiya were chased out of Kanem. Fighting continued and by 1912 the Sanussiya had been seriously weakened, their headquarters conquered and the Order's grip on the Chadian Muslims curbed. It continued nevertheless to support the Tubu, enabling these to pose a threat to the French until 1920. Tibesti became part of Chad only in 1929, but the population retained its contempt for everything French including the educational system, which they considered poison to their children (Azevedo 1998: 68-71). This resistance against the central government in the capital flared up at the time of our stay and flourishes to this day.

For the French, the most significant resource of Chad was manpower. The country became the main provider of recruits for the colonial army, which drafted some 181,000 soldiers in the colonies, mostly from Chad for World War I alone, few of whom ever returned. This pattern repeated itself during World War II and also with respect to the war in Indo-China. The French also used forced labour, letting people work under abominable conditions here as elsewhere in their African colonies. It is estimated e.g. that some 50,000 Africans died during the construction of the Congo-Brazzaville railroad (1924-1934) alone, many of whom were from Chad. Compulsory porterage took its heavy toll too. Taxation was at times met with violent resistance and ensuing retaliation. Azevedo mentions the macabre Bouna incident, which resulted in a massacre by the colonial administration of almost the entire population of the Canton of Bouna, numbering perhaps 20,000 individuals (Azevedo 1998: 82).

While the vision of French colonial rule in Africa had been to create a peaceful, multi-ethnic empire, the individuals responsible for the implementation of such a grandiose ideal, in Azevedo's words: "... took measures that would undermine the whole metropolitan plan. First, as they attempted to eliminate the vestiges of slavery and slave trade in the north (in which they did not succeed until 1917) the French made compromises that left the north, particularly after the introduction of cotton in the south, almost self-governing. French authorities in the north were satisfied as long as the sultans paid taxes on their herds, opened the trade routes to legitimate merchants, and provided unfettered access to the few colonial agents posted in the region" (ibid. 1998: 86). Although Kanem and Bahr el Ghazal are not part of the north in a geographical sense, the situation was similar and proved substantially unchanged at the time of our visit in the early 1960s, i.e. shortly after independence. Apart from an increase in polder farming near Lake

Chad, the area was left to its own devices as far as development support went. The power of the French was literally visible in the form of a huge camp of Foreign Legion soldiers in Mussoro.

THE CURSE OF HISTORY

It is evident from the above description as well as from the writings of Heinrich Barth, Nachtigal and Carbou that the late 19th and early 20th centuries were marred by social unrest and hardship for the population. The entire geographical region of Central Sudan experienced a general upsurge in slave raids and trafficking in slaves by Muslim merchants, prompted by the Anglo-Egyptian takeover of Sudan (1886–99), which restricted slavery and the slave trade within Sudan proper. This nasty situation escalated conflict in the region, particularly in Chad, and the 'impending and threatening arrival of the French, the British, and even that of the Germans heightened the regional frenzy for territorial conquest and the acquisition of slaves', according to Azevedo (1998: 34). This author mentions, for example, that Bagirmi raided on the left bank of the Sarh river, and in Oubangui-Chari, and it is believed that they snatched at least some 2,000 slaves from Lai each year, among whom the Sara were always prominent (ibid. 1998: 34).

One eyewitness account of the situation at that time is provided by the Englishman Boyd Alexander, who travelled from the mouth of the Niger via Lake Chad south and south-west to the Congo-Nile watershed and then finally homewards up the Nile, as previously mentioned. Alexander offers an unsentimental description of the social insecurity and lawlessness which governed the region. Like Gustav Nachtigal, he found himself involved in local fighting on his way towards Lake Chad and he provides a first-hand account of regular battle between the Tubu and local potentates in neighbouring Bornu, an event which he might equally well have witnessed in Kanem on the Chad side of the Lake. He writes of the Tubu: "... that whenever they appear upon the scene, it is always in connection with some characteristic act of lawlessness and brigandage. They are a nomad robber tribe, who live in the French Sahara beyond the River Yo, where they lead a camp life, and their only industry is rearing sheep and cattle, the wool and skins of which they bring to the markets to exchange for corn. No doubt their flocks and herds are raised from the animals they carry off on their raids across the river into Bornu. Also we have seen that they kidnap women and children when they get the chance, and sell them to the Budumas for slaves" (Alexander, II: 1). Boyd Alexander goes on to describe how the Tubu gang up with the Mobburs and make raids on people who come to markets. The entire district was in a most unsettled state and the natives were armed and travelled only at night for fear of the Tubu. These were on the war-path when Boyd Alexander was in the area and his presence coincided moreover with the passing through the country of the Mecca caravan "... and as this affords them a great opportunity for plunder, they were hovering like vultures all along the line of peaceful pilgrims and their flocks," Alexander writes (II: 2-3). He goes on to say that: "The pilgrims from the west go by way of Fort Lamy and Fitri to Wadai, and so on through Darfur to the Nile where they take a boat to Khartoum, through which place, I am told, 80,000 passed this year" (II: 3) ... "The caravan which now comes into my story had originally started from Timbuctoo, and, increasing its following as it went along from all the countries on the way, now numbered 700 souls and a thousand head of sheep and cattle. Its leaders were Hausa and Fulani mallams, who saw to the feeding of the pilgrims and were responsible for law and order in the caravan. ... It was a wonderful organization, this slowly moving community, with its population of varied races, and cattle and sheep, forming a column that stretched for miles along the way. Whole families were there, carrying all their belongings, and perched upon the backs of oxen were little children, some of whom had been brought forth upon the road. Cattle were their wealth to trade and pay their way with" (II: 4-5).

In 1905, when Boyd Alexander comes across the caravan, it is under the protection of the Kachella of Yo, who safeguarded its passage through his realm with some 150 horsemen. It was nevertheless ambushed just outside the town of Bulturi by Mobburs, who poured in a volley of poisoned arrows, killing some of the horses and one or two of the escort, soon after to meet an even more formidable enemy of 400 Tubu horsemen ready to launch an attack. Alexander describes how the Kachella bravely attacks these, although the Tubu outnumber his men by three to one, losing seven men and thirty horses, and of how he himself got no less than eight wounds. The Tubu then besiege the town for three days before a messenger asking for assistance reaches Alexander, who with the help of the king of Yo, immediately collects some six horsemen

and thirty arrow men and advances towards Bulturi to accompany the caravan. As he approaches he can hear the Tubu signalling to the beleaguered town, its message being: "Where are your big friends? We are coming to eat you up." As the caravan moves on they come by the Tubu, catching them by surprise and succeeding in killing some thirty men, including the leader, and wounding an equal number (Alexander 1907, II: 6-19).

The Tubu still organized major raids into the 1920s, primarily to steal camels and slaves to carry out menial agricultural labour. The raids were organized by men known for their audacity and good luck, tributes which enabled them to attract a gang of followers for the purpose. Armed with spears, they attacked Tuareg caravans carrying salt and dates from Kawar and Fashi, while slaves were captured south of Tubu territory - be it among settled groups in Kanem, Bahr el Ghazal and Mangaland or towards Borku. Unlike the Tuareg, who are much admired by the Tubu for the way in which they engage in combat, man against man, the Tubu themselves rely on surprise. Villages were rarely attacked openly, more often the robbers sneaked up upon their unsuspecting victims, capturing one by one, for instance as these were on the way to wells to water cattle. Loot was divided equally between participants, the leader was not granted special favours (Le Coeur 1950: 110, 198-9).

I have dwelled on these passages describing the insurgency in Northern Kanem at the beginning of the 20th century, because they so vividly convey the lawlessness governing everyday life and hence by implication the constant fear which must have been the state of mind of the people living here. Boyd Alexander's unsentimental testimony is confirmed by other sources and indirectly by evidence such as, for example, the fact that the Yedina had all withdrawn to live on the islands in Lake Chad, its shores being unsafe for man and beast. These people were so fearful, writes Boyd Alexander, that they fled instantaneously at the mere sight of foreigners (1907, II: 47; I: 322-3).

It takes little imagination to understand that fear of life and belongings mould collective memories in Northern Chad including those of the Haddad. Yet, the situation of the various Haddad groups differs in that respect. The Haddad Kanembu were numerous and widely feared by neighbouring groups because of their adept use of poisoned arrows. As reputable and fearless archers they had inspired respect in pre-colonial

3,11 The ostrich has been hunted in North Africa since prehistoric times for its meat and beautiful plumage. Its tasty and nourishing eggs are cherished, the shells used for decoration. Strabo writes that, "The natives hunt these birds in two ways. Some pursue and kill them with bow and arrow others disguise themselves in a suit of feathers of one of the birds with the right arm stuck in its long neck to imitate the movements that these birds make with their necks. With the other hand, they pick grain from a bag that hangs at their side, strewing it on the ground. With this bait, they entice the birds to ravines and depressions where other hunters lie in wait to kill the birds with clubs (Strabo 1886-90, III: 368). Previously, ostriches were pursued by pastoralists mounted on horses and camels. Rüppell writes of Arab pastoralists doing so in Sudan, but adding that it is only in dead calm weather or the horses will suffer and be unable to keep up with the birds (Rüppell 1829: 63). The trans-Saharan caravans brought slaves, ivory and ostrich feathers to the Mediterranean. These were the most costly of the merchandise from antiquity until the end of the 19th century. At that time, the surging demand for the plumage by fashion conscious women and European armies took a major toll on the ostrich population, not the least because French military and civil servants provided local people with firearms to kill the birds against small gratuities (Lhote 1951: 150, 152). This was a serious blow to Haddad subsistence. Watercolour, Buffon 1772: II.

days, when they had proven themselves against intruders. They had faced serious set-backs over time, however, probably from as early as the late seventeenth century, if we can trust Barth (1857, III: 301, 471-4), leaving them increasingly on the retreat. Still, at the time of Nachtigal they were holding their own. He tells of a village of 600 huts inhabited in part by the Haddad, "in part by Kanembu living with them" (1881, II: 259-260). The advent of the French would gradually change their social situation and fairly independent political standing to the worse, as we shall see (cf. Chapter 16). The Haddad Kreda were in a much more vulnerable situation. Being few and always on the move in small groups and slowly so on their donkeys, the Haddad Kreda were unable to defend themselves against raiders who came down upon them on the fast hoofs of camels or horses. They were in fact more or less forced to seek the protection of a stronger party to survive. I shall argue that the relationship between the Haddad Kreda and the Kreda pastoralists and Haddad acceptance of Kreda supremacy is rooted in this overall socio-political context of insurgency and violence, paired with the specificities of Haddad Kreda ways of subsistence. Kanem and the Bahr el Ghazal have always been a hard place to live - a land where men had to fend for their lives, their families and belongings. It is consequently a place where male endurance and fearlessness are highly valued, and where society expects its men folk to prove their worth. Courage is proven quite literally among the Kreda by the number of scars that men have on their bodies from fighting. These values are part and parcel of pastoral identity, but seem never to have caught on among the nomadic Haddad who live among them. The latter have no tradition for bravery or for engaging in raids. They were not allowed to possess cattle by the dominant groups, but may occasionally have looked for donkeys - an animal indispensable to their pursuit of a livelihood.

NOTES

1. According to J. H. Greenberg, the latter includes Teda, Daza, Kanembu, Kanuri and Zaghawa (1966: 45-8).

2. At Tagalagal in the northern Bagzanes massif pottery sheds, grindstones and stone tools found in situ have been dated to 9330 BP +/- 130 years and at Bir Kiseiba in the eastern Sahara the radio carbon date ranges from 8920 BP +/- 130 years to 9820 BP +/- 380 years (Wendorf & Schild 1984).

3. Skeletons of bovids and small livestock occur in a number of Neolitic deposits in Sahara and the Sahel. Clearly identifiable domestic stock in the form of ovicaprids appears at Haua Fteah in Cyrenaica ca. 4800 BC and at Fayum ca. 4400 BC (Smith 1992: 128). At Adrar Bous the ceremonial burial place of a bovid was unearthed in a deposit dated between 5260 and 3940 BC and at Chin Tafidet there is evidence that bovids were offerings to accompany human burials (Gautier 1987; Grébénart 1987: 292).

4. I should add that Smith mentions a single find of sorghum indicating that cultivated plants may have been known by these people. The interpretation of this and other findings of cereals are still hotly debated, however (cf. Smith 1980a: 455). A new site in the Ténéré desert reported in 2000 may offer new insights into this matter and the complex subsistence pattern and social life of these people 5000 years ago. The site is extraordinarily promising in that it contains two burial places with no less than 130 skeletons identified so far, as well as ceramics, grinding stones, harpoons, fishhooks, arrowheads and jewellery plus the bones of cattle and small ruminants. According to Dr Augustin F.C. Holl (Univ. of Michigan), these people maintained herds of domesticated cattle, goats and sheep. They did not grow crops but harvested the abundant wild grains that grew along lakes and streams. Dr Abdoulaye Maga (Institute of Research in the Human Sciences, Niamey) and Susan McIntosh (Rice Univ.) argue, however, that these people had cereals and that the settlement was probably permanent (B. Fowler: 2004).

5. The origins of pastoralism in this part of the world, however, are still a matter of controversy. There is some evidence from Egypt (Napta Playa and Bir Kiseiba) to suggest that local wild cattle, the large Bos, may have been domesticated in the eastern Sahara about 7000 BC (Gautier 1984a, 1987). But according to Fiona Marshall:"… little is known about the ecology and morphology of North African Bos primigenus, and archaeological samples are small, so this date is not widely accepted (Smith 1980b, 1986; but see Wendorf et al. 1987)" (Marshall 1994: 18). The conventional view is that domestic cattle in North Africa originated in the Near East and most scholars also look to this region for the origin of domesticated sheep and goats, as no suitable wild species existed in Africa (Gautier 1984a, 1987; Marshall 1994; Iliffe 1995).

6. According to Marshall: "It has been suggested that sorghum and millet were domesticated in a number of different places in the Sahelien zone at this period (Harlan 1976, 1982, 1989, 1992), but our knowledge is hampered by poor preservation and retrieval of botanical material. Seasonal use of domestic plants, however, was certainly adopted by many pastoral groups by 3000 B.P." (Marshall 1994: 21)

7. One may well ask why the mixed farming cultures of Ancient Egypt did not spread to the Sahel country at the same time as domesticated ani-

mals. It can be argued: Firstly, that it was easy enough for the ancient Sahel people to subsist on wild food plants. Secondly, that as the cereals cultivated by the early Fayum farmers were varieties of wheat and barley introduced from West Asia, it cannot be excluded that the mere taste of foreign grains may not have been to the liking of the Sahel people. More important, however, is the fact that wheat and barley could not be grown in the Sahel zone because of the short rainy season in summer, while this is a perfect climate for certain types of millet and sorghum. Under the prevailing climatic condition in the Sahel in Neolithic times, wheat and barley could only be introduced with the help of artificial irrigation in the winter. So we may postulate that, unlike domestic animals, these two grains were probably not brought to this area, and that experiments had to be made with other plant species from which millet and sorghum eventually evolved. Once these species had been domesticated, farming could spread throughout the Sahel and the role of collecting diminished as that of agriculture grew. Millet growing is easy because it demands little work apart from that of sowing and harvesting. Furthermore, it is said that millet and other grown cereals are more nourishing than wild seeds.

8. Small scale mining for copper took place in Mauretania (9th to 3rd century BC) and scores of bellows-assisted furnaces have been found at the Eghazer basin near Agadez in Niger. The excavator Grébénart initially dated these to a period between 2500 and 1000 BC, one furnace as far back in time as to 2800 BC. A subsequent and more thorough technical study of the residues from the furnaces found no definite proof of copper metallurgy in Niger before the early first millennium, however (cf. Killick, van der Merwe, Gordon and Grébénart 1988).

9. According to Robin M. Derricourt, "The gradual nature of much of the Iron Age transition is seen at Daima, south-west of Lake Chad. One level of a mound of continuous settlement shows that neolithic herders acquired iron in the first centuries AD. Certain traditions - in burial, huts and clay figurines - continued through the introduction of iron, with occupation maintained at the site until recent centuries." (Derricourt 1981: 96)

10. Treinen-Claustre indicates that farming only grew in significance during the Late Iron Age (11th to 16th century), a time when iron production fell presumably due to lack of wood for melting (1982: 181-3).

11. Conte claims that: "It has been a commonplace belief that Kanem is practically devoid of mineral resources. Indeed, no iron ore is of the quality of that to be found in Ennedi, in the northeast of Chad, whence Kanemi smiths claim to originate, nor is it available in Wadai, to the east of Kanem near the present-day Sudan. Nonetheless, the ferruginous soil accessible from 0 to - 2.5 m at certain *b'la* bottoms in Central Kanem contains a sufficient proportion of iron oxide to allow, granted adequate wood supplies, successful if painstaking reduction. Analyses of soil samples taken in 1974 at Koro *b'la*, 65 km west of Mao, sustain this assertion. Kanemi smiths affirmed that comparable ore was obtained at numerous other sites in Kanem. Smelting, as any traveler may observe, was common along the southern Bahr el-Ghazal, notably around Chedra. To the south of Lake Chad, the Haddad (Arab affiliated smiths) reduced iron-rich nodules collected on the surface." (1991: 232)

"Nonetheless, it is important to observe that founders did use locally obtained ores. This fact has been surprisingly neglected until now and would in itself warrant serious archaeological investigation of mining and smelting sites in central Kanem and along the southern Bahr el-Ghazal," as Conte argues (1991: 232-3). And to get systematic dating of smelting activities at a range of sites in order to see whether and when local resources would have been drawn upon to satisfy specific military and economic requirements, would be highly valuable if we want to get a more nuanced picture of Kanemese history (ibid.).

12. Accounts from 1785 at Ulefos Ironworks (Norway) demonstrate that about 6.6 kilogrammes of charcoal was needed to produce one kilo of iron in blast furnaces. Much larger amounts went into the melting production (Buchwald 1996).

13. According to Teda oral tradition, the So lived in the oases of Bilma, Tadjere and Fashi in the seventh century AD (Palmer 1936: 2-4). However, by the tenth century we find the So south of the Lake Chad in the Kotodo-Logon area where they have left behind them remains of their civilization and living tradition (Trimingham 1962: 105).

14. Scholars date Alooma's rule somewhat differently, but most commonly it it believed to have begun at the year 1570 or 1571.

15. According to H.F.C.A. Smith the Zaghawa appear in many Arabic works on the Sahara and Sudan, but to attribute the foundation of the Kanuri people and empire to them is unwarranted as the Kanuri sources make no mention of this people, nor do they live in Kanem any more but far to the east and north-western corner of the Sudanese Republic. Smith finds it more plausible that these people were driven out of Kanem by the emergent Kanuri and never incorporated in the latter (cf. Smith 1971: 168).

16. While Smith believes that the Kanuri initially founded their policy upon the conquest of desert dwellers in central Sahara, Cohen and Brenner claim that the Maguemi clan and within it particularly the Sefuwa lineage gained superiority over other clans in Kanem (Cohen & Brenner 1978: 93-4).

17. Nachtigal writes that this embraced the Ngalaga, the Kangu, the Kayi, the Kuburi, the Kaguqa, the Tomagra and the Tubu (1879-89, I: 415-8), a view which Smith finds likely, as the information is supported by another source (Smith, H.F.C.A. 1971: 165-8).

18. Notions of divine kingship apparently go way back in time in this region. Al-Muhallabī reported e.g. about Zaghawa attitudes towards their chief that: "They exalt and worship him instead of God. They imagine that he does not eat, for his food is introduced into this compound secretly, no one knowing whence it is brought. Should one of his subjects happen to meet the camel carrying his provisions he is killed instantly on the spot. He drinks with his intimates a beverage which is concocted from millet laced with honey. ... Most of his subjects are naked except for skin waist-wrappers. They subsist on the products of their cultivation and the stock they own. Their religion is king-worship, believing that it is they who bring life and death, sickness and health" (cf. Trimingham 1962: 111).

19. The Lake Chad region witnessed not only the rise of the Kanem-Bornu states, but these released forces that led, more or less directly, to the formation of a more southerly tier of states. According to Thomas, "The dynasties established over and partly assimilated with autoch-

thonous groups claim north-easterly origins. The cavalry states of the interrelated Mamprusi, Dagomba and Mossi (established in their modern location in northern Ghana and Upper Volta from the 15th century on) and the Borgawa (Borgu) may be direct offshoots of the Hausa/Bornu expansion. Alternatively, they may represent parallel developments, and longer-established states with these traditions, such as Nupe, the Yoruba states, Benin, the Aja states, and, perhaps, the small polities of the Ewe and Ga are perhaps best seen as parts of a wider process that includes the developments in Hausa-land and Kanem-Bornu (Thomas, Roger G. 1984: 133).

20. The discovery of a royal burial in the rainforest at Igbo-Ukwu (Nigeria) dating from the eight to tenth centuries AD was the first discovery which gave rise to heated debates as to whether social stratification and craft specialization was an indigenous phenomenon or due to external stimuli. Later, the excavations at Jenne-Jeno (Mali) proved, that a large walled city existed here around 800 AD and that its coming into being was unrelated to the trans-Saharan trade (Childs & Killick 1993, 22: 322-3).

21. The rulers took pride in their nomad origin and preserved customs of their pastoral life well into the 13th century, i.e. long after they had built their cities and become rulers of settled Kanemese, according to the Arab geographer al-Maqrīzī (H.F.C.A. Smith 1971: 166).

22 The Fulani tradition of *jihad* was a significant factor in the development of caliphates from Futa Jalon to Bornu, where they established themselves around 1800. They were eventually overpowered by Amin el Kanem, a Kanembu cleric whom the *mai* had called to assistance, but who in turn deprived the old dynasty of power and brought Bagirmi, Kanem and Wadai under his rule, and later that of his son Umar (1837–53). The Fulani exploited differences within the ruling classes in other pagan areas to superimpose their rule, as was the case in Adamawa. Barth visited Yola in 1851 and notes that the ruling Fulani families were no longer nomadic, but lived on the produce of slave-cultivated farms.

23. Azevedo quotes for example Cordell for the information that the Sanussi of Dar Kuti acquired a considerable number of weapons after the massacre in 1891 of Paul Campel's expedition, which had carried 175 flintlocks, 30,000 cartridges, some 60,000 percussion caps, hundreds of kilogrammes of powder and a small *caché* of revolvers (Azevedo 1998: 50).

24. Cf. Capt. Tilho: *La Géographie, March 1906;* E. Lenfant: *La Grande Route du Tchad.* Paris 1905; Freudenberg, H: *Étude sur le Tchad et le bassin du Chari.* Paris 1908.

4:

4: THE HADDAD – WHO ARE THEY?

HADDAD ELUSIVENESS

Our first meeting with foraging Haddad was with families who exploited the lacustine environment of Lake Chad. We had been dropped near the town of Bol by a small French military plane, as will be recalled, and began our enquiries as to the whereabouts of the Haddad as soon as an opportunity presented itself. Written information was scarce and we had obtained only scanty information at N'Djamena. We explained the purpose of our visit to the Belgian extension officer, Mr Derier, who kindly put us up in his house, but our host knew only of the Haddad smiths who worked and sold their products at the nearby market. Yet, Mr Derier's assistants and other local people had heard of the Haddad families near Baga Sola, and of others near N'Guri to the northeast of Bol, where Nachtigal had met them a hundred years earlier. No one in Bol could tell us anything further about the Haddad. No one had heard of people hunting with bow and arrow, or of foragers using nets to catch game.

We spend a few days with the Haddad smiths, and, eventually, met the Kanembu-speaking Haddad in the vicinity of Baga Sola, a sleepy little town on the shores of Lake Chad east of Bol. They exploited a highly specialized niche, supporting themselves by hunting crocodiles, which they sold in part for export in part at the local market. They fished, as did the other groups living at Lake Chad, and gathered wild rice, waterlily roots, locust beans, shea nuts, wild baobab and tamarind fruits. We spent two nights here and had fun going crocodile hunting with three men.

During the ensuing week in and around N'Guri we met other Haddad Kanembu families. They were all living in small hamlets and subsisted mainly on agriculture, as most of the Haddad Kanembu of the area. The families grew millet and some other crops and kept chickens and a few small ruminants. Some families supplemented their diet and income by hunting porcupine, rabbits and other small animals with nets. A couple of men brought us along on their hunting trips. Except for a Haddad man at N'Guri and a family near Chedra who used nets, animals were hunted primarily with bow and poisoned arrows.

Throughout the Bol or Massakory region, knowledge of the Haddad Kanembu, their way of life and whereabouts was strikingly wanting among the other ethnic groups. The Kanembu were genuinely taken aback, in fact, when learning that we intended to actually stay with and study the Haddad. Such information invariably prompted invitations to come and live with them instead, and, by implication, the view that this would not only be socially appropriate but also much more rewarding for us. Correspondingly, the reaction of the Haddad Kanembu we stayed among was one of genuine amazement that we would want to be with them.

From N'Guri we travelled to Mao (cf. Chapter 1) to present ourselves to the Chef du Préfecture in order to obtain local approval of our research plans. We proceeded to Mussoro with our credentials and upon acceptance rented three camels, employed a local assistant and embarked on our search for net-hunting Haddad Kreda families. We soon came to realize that these people were even more elusive than the Haddad Kanembu. In N'Djamena Colonel Chapelle had reassured us of their existence, yet at

Mussoro, be it at the prefect's office or when asking around at the market place, knowledge about the Haddad Kreda was almost non-existent. Constantly on the move and of little interest to other ethnic groups, the Haddad were in fact hard to track down. We had moments of despair at the beginning, thinking that we might fail entirely. Still, after some days traversing the seemingly endless Kanemese plains on our camels, we were able to settle in with the first batch of Haddad Kreda families. There were just a few of them, and they camped and migrated with Kreda pastoralists, but had no domestic animals themselves. They subsisted largely on foraging and hunting and by offering services to the pastoralists. Our troubles were not over, however. We encountered continuous problems in tracking down Haddad camps, and when we finally located one, the families would flatly deny that went hunting. The reason proved to be quite simple. The French had forbidden all hunting with traditional weapons: spear, bow and arrow, nets etc., a policy that was upheld by the new Chadian government. We learned after a while, that the Haddad had in fact experienced police officers confiscating their nets and spears, literally depriving them of their livelihood. At the time of our fieldwork, actual policing to enforce the law was lenient. To the consternation and despair of the Haddad, however, they had unexpected 'visits' from 'marauding' soldiers, who roamed the plains in army vehicles and came down upon the Haddad like vultures, burning their nets while lecturing them on the decree against hunting. Concurrently, the very same men chased all the game they spotted from their landrovers, mercilessly gunning it down with automatic weapons, as we ourselves were able to observe. It was no wonder therefore, that whenever the Haddad encountered foreigners, including a strange, camel-riding party like ours, that the air was vibrant with apprehension. Once we had explained the purpose of our visit and had settled down, however, their hospitality and generosity knew no bounds. We were thoroughly moved by their kindness which went far beyond the call of duty, but explainable, it would seem, by their humble joy that anyone would show a positive interest in them personally, their culture and plight.

◀ 4,1. Making a stop on the way.

There was a subtext to the elusiveness, however – even more clearly so here than among the Haddad Kanembu – a subtext of incomprehensibility on part of the surrounding society that anybody could take an interest in the Haddad, matched if not surpassed by the amazement these people felt at being the object of our attention. We took government officials by surprise, when explaining our research plans, and faced disbelief and dissatisfaction among Kreda pastoralists, when we chose to camp at the back of their spacious tents next to the modest dwellings of the Haddad. This was 'not done', we sensed. The Kreda felt directly slighted, because we stayed with families whom they considered no more than servants. They were offended that we did not prefer their civilized company and to be spoiled by their notorious hospitality, and, in return brought some change to a monotonous everyday life. Wherever we went, the Kreda made it no secret that we were violating unwritten laws of appropriate behaviour by letting the Haddad be our hosts. Perhaps the persons being taken most by surprise were the Haddad Kreda themselves. There is no doubt, that our visits astounded them to the brink of embarrassment, while at the same time pleasing them tremendously. They would soon overcome their initial shyness and the unusual situation of having to deal with our presence. We arrived seemingly out of the blue, a couple of Europeans, I the first white woman most of them had ever laid eyes on, and social and cultural preconceptions were cast in doubt for a brief time between them and us, and perhaps between the Haddad and the Kreda.

We also met Haddad smiths and other craftsmen on our way, as just indicated - men as well as women. They were all settled in the towns and carried out their trade either in their living-quarters or in the market-place. Neither the settled Haddad Kanembu, who subsisted mainly as agriculturalists, nor the foraging Haddad Kreda possessed any knowledge of iron extraction or forging. Rather, this trade is exclusively in the hands of professional Haddad smiths in the towns, who on their part have limited knowledge of collecting and hunting. Haddad smiths claim different origins and culture. Some are Kreda-speaking, while the language of the others is Kanembu. At the market in Mussoro, both groups practised their arts.

Both the Kreda- and the Kanembu-speaking smiths are divided into a number of clans, none of which overlap with those of the Haddad Kreda or Haddad Kanembu foragers, respectively. While none of the latter clans includes smiths, they do include people who support themselves by other crafts. All over Kanem and Bahr el Ghazal, for example, the Haddad Kreda are recognized as skilled tanners, with some supporting themselves exclusively by means of this trade, while some Haddad Kanembu make a living as weavers. I shall return to these crafts in chapters 7 and 11. We did not study the smiths in any detail, as their way of life was beyond the scope of our research agenda. In the following the term Haddad is used exclusively to denote the foraging or previously foraging Haddad Kanembu and Haddad Kreda, if not stated otherwise.

Our impression from reading the available sources and talking with colleagues and administrators in N'Djamena, that the Haddad were perceived by society at large as peripheral was amply confirmed as time went by. I believe it to be no coincidence or lack of systematic pursuit on our part that it proved difficult to locate their settlements, but rather an indicator of the lack of interest that befalls all disdained people, those who 'do not count' in the opinion of the ones with power and prestige. Haddad elusiveness is socially embedded, I would argue. Local people of whatever ethnic background had little if any knowledge about or interest in the Haddad, and why should they? The Haddad were not prominent. They were not known for their cattle or cattle raids as the Kreda and Kécherda, or for having ruled an empire as the Kanembu and Kanuri. Spatially dispersed except in the N'Guri area and economically marginalized, they were of negligible political significance. Whether they fared better in previous times is an open question. The annals of Kanem and Bahr el Ghazal lend them no prominence, but historical records are selective narratives, of course, more often than not, reflecting the interests, knowledge and viewpoints of the powerful or of the chronicler, as modern historians and feminist writers have made clear. In the case of Kanem, the historical sources offered by Arab scholars and European explorers and administrators dwell more on dynastic matters and the doings of the prominent, than on the livelihoods and culture of "The Wretched of the Earth", to paraphrase Frantz Fanon (1963). This should come as no surprise. However, Haddad ancestors may well have played a more significant role in Kanemese polity, as claimed by Dierk Lange (cf. Chapter 3). It can be assumed, however, that the fate of the Haddad has largely been one of subjugation. They have

suffered not only from widespread prejudice and discrimination but also from the prevalent warfare, robberies and raiding of the region. The social or political agenda has not been set by the Haddad but by groups that were more numerous and/or were able to move fast by means of horses and camels or, in recent times, by mechanized vehicles.

NAMES AND PLACES

It is not unusual for classical anthropological books and traveller's accounts to offer disparate names for one and the same ethnic group, a fact often derived from the very context of information gathering. Indigenous people are not necessarily called by a name of their own but identified by labels given to them by neighbouring groups or colonial powers, a classical example being the Eskimos, whose own term Inuit (i.e. human being) has gained common use only recently outside Inuit society. In a few cases the proliferation of names has been more pronounced, however, than in the case of the foraging or previously foraging Haddad. The existing sources on the Haddad illuminate the difficulties that scholars face in trying to define groups in polyethnic societies by means of 'objective' cultural attributes or social specificities, as pointed out years ago by Frederik Barth (Barth 1969: 11-15). We shall return to this topic later when analysing how Haddad identity is assessed through interaction with other ethnic groups.

The term Haddad derives from the Arab word for iron, ḥaddid, pl. ḥaddadin). In northern Chad the term denotes people who work this metal as smiths but also groups living entirely or in part by foraging activities or claiming a tradition of having done so. In such contexts the term ḥaddâd identifies a group or tribe (cf. Carbou 1912: I: 49). The term is also used to denote a range of other craftsmen and musicians. The picture is further complicated by the extension of different ethnic terms for the smith profession to cover a wider category of people. We shall dwell briefly on this prolific set of names offered by scholars over time to approach the issue of Haddad identification and identity.

The oldest European source on the Haddad, the account of the explorer Heinrich Barth, offers only scanty information about the Haddad or Haddāda, as he calls them. There is a short reference to them in his account on the peoples of Kanem, which Barth learned about during his stay in Bornu through the 'Dīwān' i.e. Imām Aḥmed ben Sofîya's account of King Edrīss Alaōma's wars against Bornu and Kanem. Using this as a source he notes that the Haddāda may be synonymous with" ... a strange tribe often mentioned by Imām Aḥmed as 'el Kenánīya ..." (Barth 1857, II: 301; IN transl.). Elsewhere it is intimated that the Haddāda may be identical with the Búngo or Búngu (ibid. 1857, III: 106, 433, 471-2), a point not confirmed by later sources.

There is more substance to Nachtigal's account of his expedition to Kanem with the Awlad Sliman in the early 1870s. In his view, the Haddad constitute a foraging group known by various ethnic terms throughout the region: "The Arabic name Haddâd (i.e. blacksmiths) is not an arbitrary denomination recently chosen by the Aulâd Solîmân, as one would be entitled to suppose due to the poor attention paid to ethnic appellations by the natives. It is, on the contrary, the correct translation of the name Âzoâ or Âzâ, the names by which these people are known to the Dâza. They themselves have no explanation whatsoever of their singular name. Moreover, one finds neither an unusually high number of ironworkers in the tribe, nor are they despised by the surrounding tribes like these, and they do not possess any property or custom that might link the two of them," i.e. the hunters and the smiths (1881, II: 259; IN transl.). Nachtigal explains that the Haddad themselves use the Kanuri name Dânoâ or Dânawa, but notes that this sheds no further light on the issue, as they are Kanuri-speaking. He describes the Haddâd as a tribe (Stamm in German) located around Bari (i.e. south of N'Guri), and claims that it has four divisions: the Darkaua, Arigimma or Arigîwa, Amedîja and Beqarŏ, and that members of these divisions live spread out in other localities in north Kanem (Nachtigal 1881, II: 345-6).

Henri Carbou, the French physician and administrator who traversed the same region some twenty years later, is somewhat more informative. Carbou is obviously intrigued by the Haddad, their way of life and the proliferation of names by which they are known. Carbou makes a distinction between three categories of Haddad, defined primarily by their different technological skills:

a) Ḥaddâd smiths, known in Arab as *ḥaddâd sandala*, in Kanembu as *dogoâ kakéla* and in Tubu as *azâ aguildâ (éguillâ)*, the three terms *sandal, kakéla* and *aguildâ*, all meaning anvil. These Haddad do not constitute a special group. Rather each population has its own smiths. It must

be noted, however, that most of the smiths in Kanem are of Tubu origin, says Carbou.

b) Ḥaddâd armed with bow and arrow, known in Arab as *ḥaddâd nichâb*, in Kanembu as *dogoâ battara* and in Tubu as *azâ battardâ*, the word *nichâb* meaning arrows while *battara* is the Kanembu term for quiver. Carbou tells us that: "At the beginning of the French occupation they were called 'Kanembu of the arrow' to distinguish them from the true Kanembu, whom one denoted 'Kanembu of

4,2. A Haddad Kanembu bee-hive hut. The family had recently taken up hunting with nets. The nets are stored outside.

the lance'. We have already stressed that although the two are physically similar and speak the same language, the Kanembu and the Ḥaddâd constitute two quite different populations" (1912, I: 50; IN transl.).

c) Ḥaddâd hunting with nets, known in Arab as the *ḥaddâd cherek,* in Kanembu as *dogoâ ssésséguéa* and in Tubu as *azâ séguidâ,* terms which all refer to nets. At the turn of the century, these Ḥaddâd hunters were found:"... a bit everywhere in Kanem, in Baḥr el Ghazal, in Fitri, in Ouadaï,

and who catch game in their nets" (1912, I: 50; IN transl.). They lived in great numbers among Kreda and Kécherda pastoralists, but also among the Bornuans of Wadi Rima and further south in a settlement in Massaguet on the road between Fort-Lamy and Massakory. Some of the net-hunting

4,3. Young Haddad girl pounding ogu seeds for porridge. The seeds of ogu, millet and certain other plants get treated in this way prior to cooking. Grinders are not in use, most probably because suitable stones do not occur in the region.

Haddad in the south stayed among Arab pastoralists and spoke Arabic. Among the Kreda the Ḥaddâd went by the names of their 'hosts' i.e. as Ḥaddâd Brokhara, Ḥaddâd Kodera and the Ḥaddâd Bedossa (Oulad Béchené) respectively. Carbou notes that not surprisingly the Nagalamiya denied any relationship with the Ḥaddad Nagalamiya, as did the pastoral Kreda we knew a hundred years later (Carbou 1912, I: 49-50; 209-12).

Carbou claims that he did not come across the use of the term *danoâ* as a synonym for Ḥaddâd, mentioned by Nachtigal. The natives whom Carbou and his people questioned on the subject pretended not even to know the term. He reports, however, that the Arabs and the Gourân (i.e. the Teda) sometimes apply the word *danâ,* meaning bow and arrow in expressions such as '*haddad siyâd danâ*' and '*azâ danâ*', respectively. Carbou mentions that in Teda the Ḥaddâd are sometimes called *noégué,* and says that while the latter syllable indicates plural, *noé* or *noa* sounds similar to *danoa* (Carbou 1912, I: 50). According to Le Coeur's ethnographic dictionary the word *noe* or *nai* denotes a small mammal popularly known as the mountain rat (Le Coeur 1950: 150). Carbou sums up the nomenclature in the three main languages:

a. Arabic: Ḥaddâd, to which can be added one of the ensuing signifiers: *nichâb* (of the quiver), *cherek* (of the net) or *sandala* (of the anvil);

b. Kanembu: Duu, to which can be added the ensuing signifiers: *batarda* (of the quiver), *seseya* (of the net) or *kakela* (of the anvil);

c. Dazaga: Aza, to which can be added the signifiers: *batarda* (of the quiver), *segida* (of the net), or *agilda* (of the anvil).

Writers on northern Chad tend to perceive the Haddad through the lens of the ethnic group at the focus of their work. The French administrator, Colonel Chapelle, for example, sticks to the Tubu term Azza in his monograph on the Tubu pastoralists, *Nomades Noirs du Sahara.* He identifies the Haddad Kreda of Kanem and the Bahr el Ghazal as part of Tubu society, although separately organized in small tribes or family groupings and of inferior social position (Chapelle 1957: 7). In his later book: *Le Peuple Tchadien, ses racines, sa vie quotidienne et ses combats,* however, Chapelle uses the term Haddad and or Azza in a wider sense. The Haddad are portrayed as tiny units of

people attached to various sedentary and nomadic tribes, whose language, behaviour, alliances and quarrels they have adopted, while retaining their own traditions, dances and specific prohibitions. In short: "The Haddad are classified by profession as they are not only smiths and smelters, but may also be hunters, fishermen, tanners, and leather workers and shoemakers. Their wives are very frequently potters."(Chapelle 1980: 117-8; IN transl.)

Le Rouvreur does also apply the Arab term Haddad in his general description of the Saharan and Sahelien peoples of Chad. (1962). Under the heading: 'autres peuplades', i.e. other peoples he offers an overview of a good many Haddad groups that supposedly are clans. Le Rouvreur distinguishes between two main categories: the sedentarized, Kanembu speaking *Haddad Nichab* characterized by the use of bow and arrow. He lists forty of these Haddad groups (i.e. clans) by name, location and subsistence activities and notes that two of these, the Kodia of Michiméré and the Séséya of Dibinitchi use nets as well. Most appear to be artisans who support themselves by a mixture of crafts and agriculture (Le Rouvreur 1962: 378-80). The other category are the nomadic, 'grand chasseurs', the great hunters known in Kanem as *Haddad Sézéguida* and in the central part of the Sahel as *Haddad Daramdé* (sing. *Daramoudi*). They are the most despised of all the Haddad he notes (ibid. 1962: 383).

The French anthropologist Annie M.-D. Lebeuf applies yet another terminology, using the term *Haddad* for those people only who are vassals of Daza pastoralists (i.a. the Haddad Kreda), while she reserves the term *Danoa* for the Haddad Kanembu, whom she describes as closely affiliated with the Haddad Kreda. Finally, the name tuna is used to identify the groups living at Gouré in Niger who pay tribute to a number of pastoral Kécherda groups such as the *Yorouma, Bugurda*, and *Gounda* to secure protection (Lebeuf, Annie M.-D. 1959: 9-10).

The German anthropologist Peter Fuchs, who has written on the peoples of Chad (1961, 1966) and on iron extraction and smiths in northern Chad (1970), distinguishes between the artisans found among the Kanembu, Yedina (Buduma) and Daza in Kanem and likewise among other peoples of northern Chad and 'the ethnic group called Haddad (smith) by the Arabs'. According to Fuchs, the latter call themselves Do, but are known by their Kanembu neighbours as Kalela and Dogo and by the semi-nomadic

Daza as Aza. Most Do clans trace their ancestry to a hunting past, we are told (Fuchs 1970: 299).

Catherine Baroin, who primarily worked among Tibu pastoralists in eastern Niger, applies the term *Aza* in her analyses of the Teda-Daza smiths. She regards these as an integrated part of the wider Teda-Daza society and notes that some *Aza* subsist as hunters, an occupation she describes as an *Aza* speciality on a par with tanning. Baroin follows the ethnic Teda-Daza categorization by differentiating between specialized net hunters, *Aza segide* (or *sagiri*) and hunters with bow and arrow *Aza firi* (*firi* meaning arrowhead). Those *Aza*, who support themselves as musicians are called *ézé kiride*, literally 'smiths with drums'. (Baroin 1991: 341-3)

Edouard Conte, who wrote on marriage patterns and inequality among the agro-pastoral Kanembu and the Haddad Kanembu, avoids the term Haddad, preferring the Kanembu term for smith, *Duu* or *Dou*. He applies the Kanembu distinction between *Duu* smiths on the one hand and 'northern' and 'southern' *Duu* hunters on the other. The latter distinction reflects the different hunting technologies used by the two groups respectively and, in fact, corresponds to the distinction between the Haddad Kreda and the Haddad Kanembu. In Kanembu language the former are called *seseya*, literally 'of the net', the latter, *batara*, literally 'of the quiver' (1983a: 92). Conte mentions elsewhere, that the word *duu* actually means 'poisoned arrow' and hence refers directly to the hunting technology used uniquely by the latter of these people. (1983b: 133). Conte does not consider the *Duu* a distinct ethnic group but a part of Kanembu society, in keeping with the overall theoretical agenda of his thesis (1983a: 1). The *Duu* are defined as"... a composite social stratum which includes all craftsmen and their kin in addition to the descendants of hunter groups and many non-craftsmen descended from or socially assimilated to the Kanembu" ... "Membership of the *Duu* stratum is both hereditary and perpetual, as is that of the Kanembu stratum" (Conte 1983a: 30; IN transl.).

The Kanembu make a distinction between blacksmiths qua craftsmen, *kagelma*, and members of a 'smith', *duu*, lineage, according to Conte. The term *kagelma*:"... derives from the noun *kagel* or *kakul*, meaning anvil, and the suffix *-ma* which here indicates the bearer of a profession. *Haddādī* renders the term *duu*, also pronounced *dugu* or

dughu." ... "A *kagelma* is always a member of a *duu* lineage and, in principle, a non-Duu who adopts the profession of blacksmith is thereafter, along with his descendants, considered *duu* with all the contempt this status entails. Even most non-smith *duu* would be very reticent to become *kagelma*," Conte argues (ibid. 1983a: 92; IN transl.).

The issue of names is complex, as just demonstrated. The existing evidence demonstrates that the net-hunting Haddad, who live among pastoral groups in Kanem and the Bahr el Ghazal, are identified and identify themselves by this Arab term for smith, *Ḥaddad*, just as the foragers in the Dillo region further to the west apply the equivalent Tubu term for these professionals, Aza/Azza. Thus Haddad foragers make use of ethnic markers, which do not refer to their way of life as hunters. This is not the case with the terms denoting the Haddad Kanembu. These people were previously known Dânawa or Dânoâ, according to several authors, a name that specifically refer to the use of bow and arrow, *dana*, as does the Kanembu term, *duu*, which is another name for the Haddad Kanembu, according to Conte. All of these terms appear to be giving way to the name Haddad, however, the name by which these people identify themselves and are known administratively. The different meaning of the traditional labels of the two groups, does underscore, however, that the Haddad comprise a diversified population with a different history. Some are still nomadic, others settled and they have different languages, modes of subsistence, social organization, world-view and values. The term could therefore appear somewhat problematic and liable to misunderstanding. Even so it is the very name currently used by the Haddad themselves throughout Kanem and the western Bahr el Ghazal, perhaps indicating their 'current' commitment to or need for an overarching identity associated with hunting-foraging and forging traditions that cut across linguistic and cultural differences, perhaps reflecting their silent acceptance of a terminology forced upon them by the dominant groups. There exists no other name, no 'genuine' indigenous term by which the Haddad in general identify themselves as a group to the exclusion of others. The sad fact is that the term Haddad identifies a stigmatized ethnic group. The label flashes denigration and the hardcore reality of Haddad segregation from and by the rest of the society. The latter is ensured through strict enforcement of endogamy, as we shall see.

HADDAD TONGUES

The Haddad have a great deal in common with surrounding societies, in particular with the Kanembu and the Kreda, the two groups with whom they primarily interact: the Muslim faith, basic building blocks of social organization, cultural perceptions, material expressions and behavioural codes. They do not possess a language of their own, but speak the tongues of the peoples among whom they live and/or are economically involved with: Haddad foragers of Dillia and Manga in eastern Niger use Daza, the Haddad living among pastoralists the Teda language of the group with whom they camp, while the Haddad Kanembu speak Kanembu, a language described by Lukas as a dialect of Kanuri. Haddad smiths speak both languages in Kanem and Bahr el Ghazal, Dazaga in Chitati and Manga, Tedaga in Tibesti, while those living in the area of Abéché speak Arabic. According to Carbou there were also Arabic-speaking Haddad at Ourel, Gouéno, Bédanga and Baguirmi, but we do not learn anything about the size of these groups (cf. Carbou 1912, I: 212).

Tedaga, which is spoken mainly in the Tibesti region, Dazaga and Kanuri form what Lukas has called the Kanuri group of languages. These are all tone languages and Dazaga and Kanuri, in particular, are closely related (Lukas 1936: 332-4). None of these tongues have been studied in any detail to this day, as far as I am aware, but what is known has been put to use by historically interested scholars.

Linguistic studies of language families have long been used to elucidate the African past, assessing relations between ethnic groups, the time depth of social units and to trace migrations. Scholars have studied loan words to delineate the diffusion of plants and animals, population movements, trade patterns and, most recently, to reconstruct the history of social institutions (cf. Tamari, T. 1995: 80). In a study reviewing the terms used for 'castes' in West Africa, although not including data east of Niger, Tamari reaches the conclusion that all West African languages (except, perhaps, Tuareg) have at least one native term for blacksmith or metal smith. "This implies," Tamari argues," either that West African peoples became familiar with ironworking before they acquired castes, or that they evolved blacksmith castes independently of one another. Non linguistic data show that the first interpretation is the

4,4. A Haddad Kreda man. Wanagal.

right one" (ibid. 1995: 68). There is not yet a similar study of the languages spoken in northern Chad, but it is not unlikely that a similar linguistic constellation existed here. If this proves to be the case, the early presence of iron technology among the foraging and agro-pastoral communities in northern Chad may point to an early development of segregated occupational groups and social hierarchies in the area.

4,5. A Haddad Kreda woman. Wanagal.

DEMOGRAPHY AND APPEARANCE

The lack of proper censuses and disparate nature of Haddad camps and settlements - both in Kanem and Bahr el Ghazal and on the limitless plains to the east and the west of the southern part of the Termit plateau in Niger - flaw estimates of the size of the Haddad population. The earliest assessment is found in Nachtigal, who writes that the Dânoâ

[i.e. Haddad] number about 6,000 individuals belonging to four groups (Nachtigal 1881, II: 345). Henri Carbou offers no numerical data from the first decade of the 20th century, but claims that the Ḥaddâd Gouran [Haddad Kreda] are 'numerous' (Carbou 1912, I: 209). Some forty years later, the former French administrator Jean Chapelle claimed that there were 7,600 Azza or Haddad in Kanem and about 1,500 (1080) Azza at Gouré in Niger (Chapelle 1957: 162, 406). His colleague Le Rouvreur, on the other hand, believed that there were no less than 100,000 Haddad in Chad north of 13 degrees North at the time of writing (Le Rouvreur 1962: 372), i.e. approximately at the time when we conducted our fieldwork – a figure which to us appeared exaggerated.

Johannes and I estimated that the total number of Haddad Kreda numbered no more than two to three thousand individuals organized in a limited number of clans. This assessment was reconfirmed by Conte, who wrote that: "In the predominantly Arab and Daza nomadic zones of North Kanem, the Haddad and Aza represent only one to five per cent of the population, living in small communities comprising no more than a few nuclear families, stationed behind the groups of tents of their masters or independently along the latters' routes of transhumance. (Conte 1983: 93)

The Kanembu-speaking Haddad were more numerous. This is in line with the general demographic distribution in Chad, which is thinly inhabited in the northern administrative units and more densely so in the central and southern parts of the country. Conte estimated, for instance, that the préfecture of Kanem had two individuals per square kilometre in its northern sous-préfectures as against some 20 persons per square kilometre in its southern administrative units in the early 1970s (Conte 1983a: 29). Le Rouvreur was of the opinion that the sedentarized Haddad in Kanem numbered some 25,000 Haddad distributed district-wise as follows: Mao: 8,000; Bol: 4,000; Massakory: 11,000; Nokou: 2,000 (Le Rouvreur 1962: 378). This figure is in keeping with the fact that the Haddad were organized in a great many clans. We noted down no fewer than 54 Haddad Kanembu clans, a list which we are sure was far from complete. Le Rouvreur lists about 40 clans, only ten of which occur among those recorded by us, and Conte enumerates 43 clans in the chiefdoms of South Kanem, some of which differ from both Le Rouvreur's list and ours. He argues that the Duu, 'when considering people of all heritages', as he puts it, form approximately 1/5 or 1/4 of the Kanembu population estimated at 100,000, but says that this proportion varies greatly from place to place. His estimate thus includes a good many others than the Haddad Kanembu (ibid. 1983a: 93). Conte does not present general statistical data in support of his estimate, except for eight cantons where he conducted surveys. He does say, however, that among the semi-sedentarized Kanembu around Mao, where many of the Duu are integrated into the 'noble' Kanembu villages, they form but small groups of ten to twenty persons. Among the Kanembu at large, the Duu may live separately in hamlets associated politically and economically with given neighbouring villages of Kanembu. In this area, he continues: "... where they constitute some 10 % to 15 % of the population, the number of actual craftsmen is quite reduced and the latter, it may be noted, are mostly of Daza rather than Kanembu origin." This is in agreement with other sources. Further south, the Duu are more numerous forming up to 20 % to 50 % of the population. Duu status in this region is highly variable, however, ranging from:"... that of 'slave' among certain riverine kanembu-kanembu speaking Kuri groups to that of politically independent 'tribes'," according to Conte (1983a: 93-4).

Then there are the Haddad or Azza of Gouré in eastern Niger, whom Carbou denotes Citons (Carbou 1912, I: 212). Chapelle notes that these form six fractions that roam and hunt particularly in Dillia, i.e the huge wadi occasionally flooded by water from the plateau of Termit and debouching into the northern shores of Lake Chad. Two of these Azza fractions are incorporated (Fr. inféodées) into Yoruma society, two others into the Tumnelia pastoral group. Compared to the 2020 Teda and Daza pastoralists, their former masters, the Azza number 1,080 out of which 660 were vassals of the Teda and 420 of the Daza (Chapelle 1957: 157).

There are no figures from the Arab-speaking Haddad.

Scholarly work on the genetical make-up of the populations of Kanem and the Bahr el Ghazal does not exist to my knowledge. Existing sources rely entirely on phenotypical characteristics. Carbou describes the Kanembu as having a darker complexion than the Tubu, but he finds no physical difference between the Ḥaddâd Nichâb (Haddad Kanembu) and the Kanembu proper (1912, I: 39, 50) and

Colonel Chapelle finds the looks of the Haddad living among the Teda in northern Chad no different from that of their masters (Chapelle 1957: 7, 343). Le Rouvreur describes the Haddad as "un Noir", but devoid negroid traits (1962: 378), and Baroin depicts the Aza of eastern Niger as generally smaller than the Daza among whom they live, many women being not even 150 cm tall (Baroin 1991: 356-7). While time may show whether the Haddad of Kanem and the Bahr el Ghazal do indeed constitute a distinct 'breed' or not – all that we can say at this point is that to us they were in fact distinguishable by appearance from the various peoples they lived among. This is not surprising in view of the fact that they are strictly endogamous. We had rarely any difficulty in identifying the Haddad and Kreda respectively, while living with both in the camps. Similarly, the Kanembu speaking Haddad looked differently than the Kanembu, not by complexion, as the skin colour of the two groups seemed more or less identical, but du to the finer features of the Kanembu, including the fact that generally they had relatively narrow noses and small mouths.

Such observations were made not only by us but more importantly in this context by the Kreda, the Kanembu and other ethnic groups in the area and by the Haddad themselves, all of whom used physical characteristics as ethnic markers. Both the Kreda and the Kanembu proper talked of Haddad as being 'black' in contrast to themselves. One should not jump to the conclusion that such comments necessarily reflect an objective 'truth', rather such utterances lend symbolic weight to the stigmatization of the Haddad. Still, in other contexts it became clear that the Kanembu do not consider the Haddad less attractive physically, on the contrary. Both parties stated freely, that beauty and ethnic affiliation do not necessarily coincide, and Haddad women were often praised for their great beauty. Modern genetic research is needed to reveal, whether the apparent difference in physical appearance of the Haddad does in fact mirror a specific genetic make-up. If this proves to be the case, it may shed further light on the demographic history of this part of Africa.

At the time of our fieldwork, anthropology was still dominated by structuralist or structure-functional paradigms and theory. Doubt was creeping in as to the applicability of these neat theories to explain dynamic social processes as well as to the usefulness of the categories that were applied

4,6. A foraging Haddad Kreda
woman.

to identify social groups, not least by scholars who worked with complex and more fluid societies. Critical questions were posed regarding static models of society and the notions of empirical properties on which these were based. Advocates of new paradigms and concepts argued for a shift i.a. towards a focus on:"... the ethnic boundary that defines the group, not the cultural stuff that it encloses" (Barth, F. 1969: 15; IN transl.). Barth's view was that ethnic groups are socially constructed and, consequently, that ethnic identification is the result of interaction between groups. Identity is constantly negotiated, Barth argues, it is defined and redefined through processes that mark distinctions between 'them' and 'us'. Membership of a specific group is therefore based on self-ascription as well as on ascription by others. Anthony Cohen pushed the argument further and defined ethnic boundaries as meanings shared by a community (or group) which illuminate important facts about its identity to outsiders. "Boundaries are marked because communities interact in some way or other with entities from which they are, or wish to be distinguished," he notes (Cohen, A. 1985: 12). Barth and Cohen have later been criticized for downplaying the impact of external constraints and power

in boundary assessing, an impact which definitely is crucial in understanding, for instance, the maintenance of Haddad identity and way of life (Donnan and Wilson 1999: 25). Barth's and Cohen's theoretical approaches had not yet seen the light of day when Johannes and I were trying to make sense of the complex socio-cultural situation in Kanem and the Bahr el Ghazal, nor had later refinements in the analyses of social interaction and identity, of course. I shall nevertheless introduce these views at this point to indicate why attempts to define and label the Haddad by means of 'cultural stuff' and/or social criteria alone posed problems to scholars who came both before and after us.

The ensuing analysis takes as it point of reference Haddad self-identification and categorization, in line with indigenous peoples' views on how to be portrayed. Throughout the book, a distinction will be maintained between the Haddad and the dominant groups among whom they live, as well as between Haddad sub-groups in tune with 'indigenous' labelling, and the linguistic, socio-cultural, spatial and economic markers applied by them to negotiate ethnic identity. Whenever reference is made to Haddad people supporting themselves by forging this will be made clear.

NOTES

1. In Kanuri *dúgd* signifies musician, while the word *dúgùram* means craftswoman or female musician and *dugún* means hatred or enmity, according to Lukas (1967: 195).

2. The many, at times interchangeable denominations for the foraging or previously foraging Haddad and Haddad smiths illustrate, in Conte's view:" ... that generic names, like the genealogical constructs of which they are elements, evolve from generation to generation." He mentions, for example, that:"My repeated questions concerning the Danoa elicited no reaction among my informants, until one day, when I was collecting different versions of the Rea (Nachtigal's *Ariqimma*) genealogical charter, an elderly man spontaneously continued beyond the Rea eponymous ancestor, Teu, to his father, the common ascendant of the Rea, Adia (*Amedîja*) and Bara (*Baqardâ*), and thence to *Dana* ... The only tradition known about *Dana* was that he was believed to be a hunter 'from the North' who had come to settle in North Kanem whence his descendants moved south to become the Duu of the Bari district" (Conte 1983a: 97). That denominations of ethnic groups can be contextually defined is a well-known fact. Unlike Conte, however, I am struck by

the apparent constancy of the labels used to identify the Haddad and not convinced by Conte's statement to the opposite.

3. Basically the current language distribution supports data indicating a general shift in the distribution and significance of languages that coincides with changing environmental conditions caused by the desiccation over the past seven millennia and later socio-political transformations, as described in Chapter 3. In short, the creation of the great erg cemented the existence of two language systems: the so-called Chadic languages of the West (cf. Greenberg 1966: 45-8), and the Tedaga-Dazaga languages of the East, including the Tedaga, Dazaga, Kanembu-Kanembu, Kanuri and Zaghawa. Smith is of the opinion that the Kanembu-Kanembu language presently spoken in Kanem is made up of a mixture of elements from various old Daza languages, occasioned by the political unification of a number of tribal groups in Kanem. Much later, around the fourteenth century AD, when large sections of the politically unified people speaking this language moved west of Lake Chad and cut their connection with the peoples remaining to the east of the lake, their language began to diverge from the speech of Kanem to produce what is now known as Kanuri. If there

is any truth in this, says Smith, then the Kanembu-Kanembu is really 'classical' Kanuri (H.F.C.A. Smith 1971: 162).

4. Tamari mentions, for example, that most Senufo terms for metal smiths are non-native. This is a proof in her view that endogamous artisan groups developed among the Senofo essentially under outside influence (ibid. 1995: 68).

5. According to Nachtigal the Danoa consisted of an estimated 2,000 Darkaua, 1,500 Arigimma or Arigiwa, 1,500 Amedija, and 1,000 Beqaroa (1881, II: 345).

6. The Aza have better teeth due to a healthier diet, according to Baroin. Although the subsistence of both groups is based on millet and milk, the Aza grow more millet, whereas the Daza often fall short of self-sufficiency in this staple as they dislike farming. Yet, the crucial factor in explaining the better nutritional condition of the Aza is rooted in cultural values, more specifically in taste and economic spending, Baroin argues. The Daza milk only cows while the Aza also milk their goats. Whereas the Daza drink almost all of the milk produced by theier cows, that Aza economize, drinking only some and churning the rest into butter. Moreover, if the Daza sell a cow, half the revenue will be spent on buying tea, while the other half has to cover both millet and other household necessities (Baroin 1991: 359-60). This is similar to the cultural attitudes of the Tuareg, who in their own words may become destitute from spending their income on tea and sugar. Again, the Aza prioritize differently, spending less on tea and sugar and nothing on tobacco.

5:

5: ORIGIN AND IDENTITY

The ancestry of the foraging Haddad and their relations to other groups in Kanem puzzle Europeans who meet these people. Apparently, this issue does not bother the Haddad themselves. Like the rest of us, they are perfectly able to live with contradictory perceptions and statements as well as contextually defined explanations of their past. The Haddad see themselves as clearly distinguishable on the multi-coloured palette of Chadian ethnic groups. They may hold no records of a glorious past, tales of hazardous raiding and profitable caravaneering as do Arab and Teda-Daza speaking pastoralists, nor of having created city states and held high office like the Kanuri and Kanembu - records applied by these other groups as prominent symbols of ethnicity. The past of the Haddad is largely clouded in oblivion, their oral traditions few, of limited time depth and relating different and incongruous tales of origin. The Haddad hold different views as to a common ancestry and how to contextually in- or exclude one another. Yet, we were never left to doubt that the Haddad perceived themselves as being just that, 'themselves', i.e. caretakers of traditions of their own, and hence in essence an indigenous people. Had that nomenclature been known to them, I am convinced that they would have described themselves as such. As outsiders, we noted that in line with indigenous peoples all over the world this sense of identity was taken for granted by the Haddad. They would point to their ancestral way of life, to the hunting technologies that they mastered, be it net or mask, bow and poisoned arrows as marks of identity that symbolically set them apart from other ethnic groups. The latter, for their part, stressed other cultural properties in the constant game of not only negotiating ethnic iden-

tity but also claiming superiority. It was to the 'European Others', those who came to Kanem and the Bahr el Ghazal as travellers, administrators and scholars that the ethnic complexity was disturbing, in the sense that the Haddad did not fit neatly into the categories with which they tried to make sense of the multifaceted social and cultural reality that they encountered.

IN THE EYES OF THE 'EUROPEAN OTHER'

Haddad groups are not easily, nor unequivocally distinguishable from other ethnic groups by 'objective' cultural and social features, as indicated, be it by language, beliefs, institutions, dwellings, dress codes, hairstyles or jewellery. Tools and other material objects are largely the same as those with which the Kreda and Kanembu surround themselves, although in the case of the Haddad Kreda generally of poorer quality and more worn than the corresponding belongings of the pastoralists. As the Kanembu proper, the Haddad Kanembu live in villages of various sizes, dwelling in beehive huts sometimes decorated with an ostrich egg at the pointed top of the thatched roof. They grow millet, sorghum and maize, keep some goats and poultry and a few own small livestock and cattle. The Haddad Kreda for their part move camp with the Kreda pastoralists, putting up and taking down the same kind of mat tents, but without cattle and few if any goats of their own.[1]

Basic building blocks of Haddad social organization are similar to those structuring Kanembu and Kreda society respectively. Social life is founded on patrilineal principles sustained by the Islamic doctrine which the Haddad have embraced, although fairly late. Despite these common traits, the Haddad nevertheless constitute and perceive themselves as distinct social units with specific modes of subsistence, distinct cultural perceptions and traditions, and, in the case of the Haddad Kanembu, also magical practices which set them apart from other peoples in Kanem.

To explorers, scholars and administrators, i.e. to 'the European Other', the origin and identity of the Haddad have generated a good deal of speculation. They have tried to make sense of the poly-ethnic setting in terms of an implicit or explicit agenda set by their profession and potential readers - be it fellow academics, the explorer's 'enlightened reader', or a government that relies on a well-defined categorization of the social universe to carry out its policies with efficiency. The implementation of the latter has in turn fed back into and influenced the ethnic landscape. Despite the distribution in time and interest, almost all existing sources touch upon the origin of the Haddad Kanembu. This is linked to various historical or pseudo-historical groups, to foraging groups living further to the south, to the craft of forging which points to the north and north-eastern origin among other explanations. Most of these relate to the Haddad Kanembu, while the ancestry of the Haddad Kreda has been less explored.

The prevalent view has been that the Haddad constitute the oldest segment of the Kanemese population - and that they have lived as nomadic foragers since prehistoric times. Subsistence in Kanem and Bahr el Ghazal has relied on complex agro-pastoral, foraging and smith adaptations to the natural and social environment for the past seven millennia, as previously described (cf. Chapter 3: 79-83). Livestock herding developed in North Africa shortly after 5000 BC and was widespread by the fourth millennium; domestic plants - millet and sorghum - some two millennia later. Foraging has been part of the subsistence activities throughout the millennia. Possibly, the social environment in Kanem and Bahr el Ghazal has encompassed specialized groups like the Haddad of the 1960s relying exclusively on foraging and forging. It is evident that certain specialized hunting techniques, such as the use of masks, date back to prehistoric times in North Africa. This has been documented by rock-engravings, for instance at Tasilé-en-Ajjer. The use of nets may well be ancient too. However, it is still to be seen whether these sophisticated methods of subsist-

ence can be tied in with other data, including hard-core genetic information to substantiate the view that the Haddad do indeed constitute an ancient element of the Kanemese social landscape. Also 'softer' historical data such as oral traditions, in line with the theoretical track outlined by Jan Vansina (1982), have yet to be mined. So far the writings on the origin and cultural specificity of Haddad society have been lightly wrapped in a culture-historical cloak, the more recent writers often leaning heavily on the shoulders of Heinrich Barth and Gustav Nachtigal. The descriptions of these early writers lend some depth to Haddad history and intimate that their situation has changed dramatically to the worse from the end of the 17th century till today. If Barth's suggestion, that the Haddad and the Kenánie were one and the same, then their numbers and political influence has subceded radically. But let us see what the available sources have to say about Haddad origin and specificity.

Much to his own regret, Heinrich Barth was not successful in reaching Kanem and the Bahr el Ghazal, being at the mercy of the looting and slave hunting Awlad Sliman, as previously mentioned. However, his fellow traveller Dr Overweg overcame the difficulties and Barth offers an annotated edition of parts of his dairies. On an excursion southwards from Mao that lasted five days, Overweg comes upon: "Mailo, a place next to a lake full of fish, inhabited by the Haddāda or Búngu, a peculiar Kanōri speaking people, who walk around quite naked apart from a leather apron and are armed with bow and arrow and a strange kind of iron chain, gólió. They are skilled archers, and if attacked they withdraw into the thick forests of their territory, which appears to be known by the common name Bāri, a term also rendered repeatedly by Imām Ahmed, [they] know very well how to defend their political and religious independence - they are pagans. To this group belongs the well-known tribe, known among the Oülād Slimān by the name of Duárda Hádjra. A well-known locality of the Haddāda is Dimāri, the place of Malá Dīma. ... In the year of 1853 the Uëlād Slimān ganged up with the Haddāda and defeated in this way the administration of Wádáï" (Barth 1857, III: 433-4; IN transl.). Barth has also a few entries on the Kenānīe or Haddāda in his summary of the Arab scholar, Imām Ahmed ben Sofiya's chronicle of King Edrīss Alaōma's campaigns against Bornu and Kanem, which Barth located on his expedition. Edrīss Alaōma ruled Bornu between 1572 and 1619, and his fifth campaign was

5,1. Haddad Kanembu hunter with mask displaying his skills as a 'marksman', the skills that made these people feared by neighbours and intruders alike.

directed against the Kenánīe. Barth remarks in this context that: "I must confess, that I doubt the indigenous origin of the name Kenánīe the more so as I hold this people identical to the Haddāda or Bongu, who seem once to have constituted a very numerous tribe and to have been, perhaps, the original inhabitants o Kānem. At that time the principle seat of this remarkable tribe was Ssúlú, a frequently mentioned place, the reason why the tribe was generally known under the name of 'the people of Ssúlú'. Fearing the Bórnu king, whose wrath they had provoked by their predatory habits, they left their settlement while he was returning to Kānem, and went to Kargha." As a result of this campaign the Kenánīe tribe, who until then had the most numerous in Kānem, was totally humiliated (Barth 1857, III: 471-4; IN transl.). The account places

Ssúlú or Suluwas between Beri and Mao on the shore of the Lake's northern basin, above the 14th parallel.[2] This indicates that Azza/Haddad groups have lived between the northern limits of Lake Chad and southern Manga in western Chitati for centuries. The possible historical link between the Kenánīe and the Haddad is later picked up by Palmer, who muses about the former's origin as Berber and Tuareg slaves (Ikli) claiming that at the time of Makrisi (ca. 1400): "... there were obviously communities of Ikli resident in Kanem, and it seems therefore highly probable that these Kananiya were Ikli who had remained in Kanem throughout the civil war between the Saifawa and Bulala" (Palmer 1928, I: 11). However, as Conte remarks that: "... until new evidence appears, if and when this happens, the putative Kenaniya-Duu link

5,2. Haddad quiver and arrows. Cat. no. 9. Photo J.K.

might best be removed from circulation." A view that I fully share (Conte 1983a: 99 - 100).

Nachtigal encounters the Haddad or Dânoâ/ Dânawa, as he learned they were called in western Chitati. He also paid a visit to N'Guri, the 'capital of the Dânoâ' on the 5th of December 1871, passing through an area densely dotted with Haddad Kanembu villages (1881, II: 259, 330-1). He found Haddad living along the eastern shores of Lake Chad and quite isolated further to the southwest of here in a number of densely wooded valleys rich in water as well as to the southeast in the Bahr el Ghazal. Nachtigal notes that widespread feuding was causing the Haddad normally living throughout the Bari district to rally and take refuge near N'Guri. He describes the Haddad as a tribe, 'Stamm' in their own right, but underlines that they have no language of their own but speak Kanuri, and that they only "distinguish themselves from the surrounding Kanembu in that they make use of bow and arrow" (1881, II: 331). Nachtigal ponders several times about Haddad origin (ibid. 336). He is doubtful at first, when learning from "the experienced Faqîh of Metalla", that the Haddad and

Manga are related, in part because the Manga do not live in Kanem, and, in part because the Faqîh himself was without first-hand knowledge of Bornu (ibid. 259). He returns to the subject later, however, contemplating the possibility. He notes e.g., that the Manga still speak a language of their own, and that distantly located Manga villages are surrounded by thick 'walls' of thorny branches, like those of the Haddad in Kanem. Nachtigal writes furthermore that they may have joint ancestors once pushed southwards by desert people, the Manga to Bornu, where they are numerous along the Joo, the Haddad to Kanem where they may have mixed with the Bulala (ibid. 331). Nachtigal's theory of a common Haddad-Manga ancestry is totally refuted by Henri Carbou, who is told by informants familiar with both groups that there are no similarities between the two groups whatsoever: their customs are not the same, neither their weapons, nor had the Haddad ever heard of the Manga (Carbou 1912, I: 52-3).

The origin and specificities of Haddad/Azza society are also discussed by French administrators who were in Kanem and the Bahr el Ghazal to rule and increase taxes, men such as Henri Carbou, Le Rouvreur and Colonel Jean-Paul Chapelle. Carbou deals with the Haddad Kanembu only, while Chapelle has is information primarily from working among the Tubu and hence concentrates on the origin of the Haddad Kreda. Carbou is of the opinion that the Haddad Kanembu are of the same 'blood' as the Bulala, who are part of the overall Kanembu family (Carbou 1912, I: 52). Carbou supports this view by referring to Kanembu explanations of the origin of these Haddad:

"At the time of Boulala domination in Kanem, a Boulala by the name of Abdou Doubouboul had a pagan slave called Kaoua. Taking advantage of the absence of her husband the mistress of the house tempted the loyalty of Kaoua, who certainly must have been happy with the new turn which his job as captive was taking. Later a child was born out of this illegitimate business. What astonished everyone was that this offspring, supposedly of pure Boulala race had entirely the facial traits and appearance of a captive. But what was even more surprising was to see him fabricate *gabag*, skin of killed game, dye clothes, etc. The Boulala were stupefied watching young Hanna Kouliaï engage in menial tasks so dishonourable and entirely reserved captives. One fine day he showed a bow and arrows which he had made. Someone asked him to tell what these peculiar objects were which he held in his hands and he answered that: *da harba hanaï* (these are my weapons). Completely exasperated the father vehemently reproached his wife that she had brought a child into the world with nothing in common with the Boulala, a child who brought him nothing but disgrace in the eyes of his fellows. Apparently she calmed down her husband avowing the fault she committed with Kaoua. To cut the story short, Hanna Kouliaï became one of the ancestors of the present Haddâd: the Bôgara, Regâ, Amadiâ, Darkoâ segments all descend from him" (Carbou 1912, I: 51).

The Kanembu have another take on the origin of the Haddad, according to Carbou:

"At the time when Drisi oueld Amsâ and the Maguemi [a Kameni clan, IN] suppressed the Boulala at Mondo, a Boulala grabbed his child and sent him fleeing on his galloping horse. Upon arriving at Dibinentchi [an area still inhabited by Haddad Kanembu IN] the animal collapsed, never to get on its feet again. The Boulala [father] who had followed after the child entrusted a Boulala smith of Dibinentchi with

the small boy and took flight. He was killed, apparently by the pursuing Maguemi engaged in the search for his son at the village of Dibinentchi. Having the child in his custody the smith painted its hands with indigo to make them look like those of his own young sons. When the Maguemi turned up at the smith's place, he showed them the three children, all with blue hands, and declared never to have laid eyes on the one they were looking for. The Maguemi believed him and searched in vain elsewhere. Having been saved in this way the young Boulala, Toumâgueri, became Haddâd like the two sons of his adopted father, Moloriou and Léguéréa and the three of them are the ancestors of the Haddâd carrying this name" (Carbou 1912, I: 52).

What shall we make of these tales, Carbou asks? That the Haddad and the Boulala share some blood? Most probably, he argues, pointing to the fact that the Sultan of Fitri, Gadaï at one point exchanged gifts with Milma Tchiloum, the chief of the Haddad Bogara, indicating that they had the same ancestor. It must also be remembered, Carbou says, that captives (Nguedjim) are found in Haddad society. Perhaps the very Boulala, claimed to constitute the ancestor of the Haddad population are in fact but a Boulala captive, Carbou speculates. In his view the Haddad Kanembu population most probably stem from a mixture of Boulala or Boulala captives and more or less pagan smiths and/or captives.

"If one acknowledges that the Kanembu Nguedjim as well as the Haddâd Nguedjim have the same ancestors as the Boulala Nguidjemi from Fitri one might explain the distinction between the two populations by saying that the Nguedjim allied with the Kanembou have become Kanembou, while the Nguedjim allied with the smiths and pagan captives were scorned as not equal to the latter and hence soon formed a separate population" (Carbou 1912, I: 53).

This is only speculation, Carbou admits, but he adds that it would explain the formation of a new but despised population out of Kanemese stock. Carbou ventures further into guesswork as to how this population became armed with bow and arrow, admitting the difficulties in doing so, as these weapons occur only as far away as among the Manga and the Haussa and Peul [Fulani; IN]. I have dealt at such length with Carbou's airy conjectures because they are representative of an earlier era's free-wheeling extrapolations of oral traditions.[3]

Also Le Rouvreur ponders briefly on the issue: "Who then are the Haddad? Do they merit to be called a separate race? Do they form but a caste, the most despised which exists?" but without delivering substantial answers. He observes that: "One is not only faced with the mystery of their origin, one is also astounded by their powerful personality, by the exceptional place they occupy among the peoples of Central Africa" (1962: 377; IN transl.). Still the Haddad get more or less lost in his overall description of the major ethnic groups in Chad.

Colonel Chapelle deals exclusively with the origin of those Haddad, who live among the pastoral Tubu and he links this with the craft of forging. According to him these Haddad claim descent from Ennedi and constitute a 'caste' within the otherwise egalitarian Chadian society. The latter is also a reflection of the fact that he has worked primarily among pastoralists. Chapelle believes that Haddad origin: "goes back to the invention of iron [and] the first production of high furnaces" and he has little to add beyond this view. (Chapelle 1980: 117) Annie M.-D. Lebeuf has equally little to say about the Haddad. She notes that the Haddad [Kreda] living among the Daza are of oriental origin (1959: 9), without explaining this any further, and describes the Danoa or Dogoa [i.e. the Haddad Kanembu] as "in every respect similar to the Aza" (1959: 35; IN transl.).

A culture-historical perspective on the Haddad and their origin is offered, not surprisingly, by a German ethnologist, Peter Fuchs who analyses the issue in the context of an 'afrikanischen Schmiedentums'. Fuchs conducted fieldwork among the Haddad of N'Guri in 1959 and went on a research expedition to Wadai in 1963 by way of Libya and northern Chad. Fuchs' theoretical approach is that of historical diffusionism, and his perspective on the 'ethnological position of the Haddad of the Chadian Sahel' is therefore regional, embracing the ecologically homogenous environment of Tibesti, Borku, Ennedi and Wadai (Fuchs 1970: 297). Fuchs claims that the Haddad constitute an extended cultural community throughout this vast geographical area whether they subsist as smiths, agro-pastoralists or by hunting-gathering. His argument is basically that all people known by the Arab term for smith, Haddad, may trace their ancestry to a hunting-gathering form of subsistence and culture. Fuchs argues, moreover,

that insufficient returns from hunting due to a declining population of game forced Haddad clans in Kanem to take up crafts to support themselves, first as smiths, later diversifying their trade as shoemakers, saddlers, weavers, and dyers. Only later, when the Haddad had settled among the Kanembu did they turn to agriculture, substituting the produce from hunting with those of farming.

Fuchs writes that each of the crafts has its own tale of origin in Kanem and that some appear to have been adopted quite recently, for example the trade of shoemaker (cf. Fuchs 1970: 299). Forging is said to have been learned from immigrated smiths from the north.[4] This is in accordance with the traditions of the Haddad Kanembu blacksmiths, we talked to. They did also believe that forging had come from the north, just as they claimed affiliation with the Aza living among Kreda and Teda groups. These statements are in line with Conte, who writes that: "... metalworkers are often descendants of immigrants from the Bahr el-Ghazal. Many continue to use the Dazaga language among themselves long after having settled in kanembu-kanembu-speaking areas" (Conte 1983a: 167).

Each of the crafts exercised by Kanembu-speaking Haddad artisans is carried out by members of a particular clan, moreover. According to Fuchs, the Darka are weavers - a few of them shoemakers, the Adjurubi are indigo dyers, the Kuri are saddlers and the Kokolia blacksmiths (Fuchs 1970: 299). The clans are not the same, however, as those which occur among the foraging Haddad, as far as our data go. They tally with Le Rouvreur's enumeration of forty Haddad Kanembu clans none of which contains both smiths and foragers (Le Rouvreur 1962: 379). Still, most artisans claimed that their ancestors at one point had made a living as foragers. Ultimately, Fuchs argues, one must explain the present marginalized social position of Kanemese smiths as well as of those of smiths in northern Chad and Wadai, a position which Fuchs defines as 'outside society' as stemming from the hunting past of these peoples (Fuchs 1970: 311).

The interest of the French scholar Edouard Conte is mainly on the social present of the early 1970s. In line with his structuralist approach, he deals with the Haddad Kanembu largely as a social category or strata of the overall Kanembu society. He notes that:"Since the 1972-1973 drought the hunting culture – still observed by J. Nicolaisen in 1967 (personal communication 1978) in both North and South Kanem – must be considered defunct. It is my opinion that a detailed reassessment of existing data and complementary ethnographic investigation throughout the Chad basin would reveal the existence of even more hunter and gatherer groups sharing many cultural premises which clearly distinguish them from both the Chad's islanders and mainland agro-pastoralists" (1983a: 103).

Still, in Conte's view a contemporary analysis would undoubtedly confirm that the Kanembu and the Duu Kanembu are in fact one and the same ethnic group, but he adds that the inherent relations between these must be viewed through time as a phenomenon parallel to the historical and ethnic genesis of the Kanembu people as a whole. "Oral tradition certainly does not argue for 'pure' descent of the Duu from the Magemi, Kubri or Dalatoa lineages of Bornuan and Kanem fame. At best, when lineage names of Kanembu and Duu groups are identical or similar, Duu apical ancestors may be qualified as younger sons or brother Kanembu apical ancestors. Their inferior status is often further justified by some form of 'original treason' toward the lineage, an insult to the Prophet Mohammed or birth by a second wife of lowly origin," Conte states (1983a: 94-95).

Conte's take on the Duu is in line with the understanding of the dominant Kanembu. He notes, for instance, that while artisans and other specialists are frequently grouped into endogamous, professionally-defined castes in Islamic Sahelian societies this is not the case among the Kanembu. Among these people artisans of all trades, as well as hunters, diviners, musicians, praise-singers, natron-miners,

5,3. Learning by doing. Boys are setting up nets to chase chickens for fun. The red parasol was a given to us by the préfet of Mao when we started out on our exploration. I was baffled, but it proved a great asset shielding our luggage from both sun and rain. A Haddad Kreda camp.

and other persons with expert knowledge are amalgamated into a single, endogamous and hereditary social stratum known as the Duu (1983a: 89). He argues, that the actual composition and economic role of this social category has varied over time:"... through (1) the integration of non-specialized immigrants of low status and (2) the abandoning of their trades by many artisans and their progressive conversion into agro-pastoralists hardly distinguishable from the Kanembu *maskin*" (1983a: 89). In line with his broad conceptualization of the Duu category, Conte declares that: "Whatever their demographic and political situations, the Duu today share the language, technology and, in a wider sense, the culture of the peoples among whom they live. At the present time, they can hardly be outwardly distinguished from the pure Kanembu. Nonetheless, the Kanembu and Duu Kanembu, freemen though they all are, may be differentiated by several important social and economic criteria" (ibid. 1983a: 94).

In support of his categorization of the Duu as a social stratum that has emerged over time, Conte dwells briefly on the issue of Duu origin in time and space. He collected oral traditions among the Duu and the Kanembu, respectively, but presents none of these in detail. Not surprisingly, the former offers multiple but non-contradictory statements of origins, most of which mention hunter ancestry. They include:" 1) descent from hunter and gatherer groups of North Kanem or Manga; 2) descent from lacustral hunter goups; 3) descent from vassal groups of the Bulala; 4) integration into Duu lineages of groups of captives acquired as late as the end of the 19th century by Kanembu raiding parties in Central Chad and Bagirmi; 5) incorporation of groups of political refugees of diverse origins, who, fleeing the repeated invations which have plagued the wider Kanem all through its recorded history, were forced to barter their autonomy of movement and economic independence against 'protection'; 6) assimilation of elements not necessarily distinct from those which formed the Kanembu people but relegated to subservience during the formative centuries of the Kanem kingdom or during subsequent upheavals of the political system" (1983a: 95).

In discussing the issue of origin, Duu hunters were most comfortable speaking about their ties to the Karbina or Kerebina, a group of hunters living to the south of the Shari delta, scattered from Lake Chad to Mandara in northern Cameroon, according to Conte. The informants told him that as young people they had been sent to the hunters of these southerly regions for long initiatory periods, during which they would perfect their skills at tracking, trapping, arms fabrication and poison making, as well as their knowledge of plants, healing, divination and other techniques. Lukas defines the Kanuri word Karbínà as a "caste of hunters who also sell medicines" and mentions as a synonym the work Kandírà, "the very title still used today in South Kanem to honour old hunter-diviner-healers of repute… as well as to designate sorcerers" (Lukas 1967 (1937); Conte 1983a: 101). Quoting Nachtigal and Carbou, Conte tells of the Karbina that they:

"… are rightly or wrongly considered to be distant and dispersed heirs of the Sao peoples. During the 1870s, they made their living by hunting. They led a wandering existence in the wooded districts of the Makari province. There, they trapped their game by closing off areas of bush with thorn scrub, making hedge-like straw barriers and wooden palisades. The ensnared prey could then be slain with the bows and arrows with which all Karbina men were armed. In Bornu, they sometimes formed villages of their own. Most Kerebina lived, as have some Duu *kindira* to date, preserving their mobility, isolated in the bush with their families, sometimes settling for a period on the periphery or in the villages of different ethnic groups to whom they would sell their skins, meat and medicines and lend their various talents. They spoke *Kotoko* (Logon-Sprache) around Makari and a dialect of Yedina in Bornu proper, while also being conversant in Kanuri. Their mode of livelihood was an object of scorn for surrounding populations, including the sedentary Kotoko. Much ambivalence surrounded their relations with sedentary populations who considered themselves staunch Muslims. The latter would reproach them for their large consumption of bush pig, an animal considered *haram,* while purchasing pig tusks from hunters to protect themselves against the evil eye and other dangers" (Conte 1983a: 102).

Conte refers to Nachtigal's characterization of Tubu blacksmiths as being exterior to the 'society of citizens' as parallel to the situation of these 'masters of the bush'. Over time the Karbina's mobile existence and cultural specificity came under threat aided by environmental degradation, ensuring their gradual integration into and subordination by the dynastic societies of Bagirmi, Bornu and Kanem (Conte 1983a: 101-2).

The oral traditions of the dominant Kanembu are also treated by Conte. These are political rather than ethnic in nature, he observes, in that one of their major functions is to account for changes in inter-clan allegiances and alliances. These are largely determined by each group's capacity to constitute and maintain itself as an office- and land-holding entity with specific tributary or fiscal rights and obligations in relation to other clans as well as to superior authorities. This focus on clan origins does not allow for a description of the Kanembu as an ethnic group at any historical period or define the various socio-cultural strata along 'ethnic boundaries', Conte notes (1983a: 73).

Duu origin is also considered by Conte from the vantage point of Imam Ahmed be Sofiya's cronicle of the Bornu kingdom. According to Barth this renders Dugu, the legendary grandson of Sef and Aisha, the apical ancestor of the early pagan branch of the Sefawa ruling house, also known as the Bani Dugu or Duguwa. He writes that Dugu probably reigned during the last part of the 9th century and suggests that he died at Yira (Yeri Arfasa) in Kanem. Eight generations later, purportedly in the AD 1080s, Selma or 'Abd el Jelil', claimed to be the last of the Duguwa dynasty died at Ghumzu. Selma is also said to have been succeeded by his son Hume or Ume, the first Kanemi sovereign to embrace Islam and to found the Beni Hume dynasty. The distinction between the two dynasties is thus one of creed, Barth observes. Whatever historical truth there might be to this tradition, Conte claims:

"...the denomination Duu, Do, Dugu, Dugua is today used to designate the so-called Haddad populations whose conversion to Islam is by any account or standard a recent one. The only 'proof' of the relevance of this legend which I can furnish is that elders of the Duu of Bari refer to a certain Dugu as being an ancestor, even remoter than Dana, of all 'Haddad'. More knowledgeable lineage genealogists also mentioned their Keyi ancestress. By invoking the Duu tradition, I think that these men wanted to say that the Duu heritage is somehow prior to that of the Kanembu, the people of the lance, whose Islamic ideology belittled the 'aboriginal' hunter heritage" (Conte 1983a: 98).

Conte's general take on Kanemese reality is largely in line with the clan-focused model of society held by the dominant Kanembu, representing the society as organized along ranked status criteria based on, or legitimized in terms of purported modes of integration into polity, as just indicated. It is a society cross-cut, moreover, by three major cleavages, separating slaves from freemen, commoners from nobles and Duu from non-Duu. These divisions do not imply the existence of discrete social classes as criteria for inclusion, in Conte's rendering, although hereditary do not prove perpetual, as a notable widening of the commoner category into a composite class of dependents has demonstrated. In Conte's prism, in short, the Duu form an endogamous, professionally and ritually distinct sub-group of Kanemese commoners – a category established through time by the confluence of not only groups of hunters but of people with highly varied cultural backgrounds and social histories.

HADDAD LEGACY

The interpretation of oral traditions is delicate. Oral traditions are multilayered conglomerates of information, narratives of cultural explanations of social conditions and events, which carry the imprints of time and context. New light has been shed on African history over the past few decades, spurred on by Ian Vansina's seminal work, which urged scholars to treat these narratives as valid sources (Vansina 1985). The information transmitted in oral traditions about Kanemese history in general and that of the Haddad in particular must be assessed in this perspective and cautiously analysed.

In view of this and the disputed nature of the origin and specificity of Haddad society in the existing literature, it would be valuable to possess a rich sample of oral traditions. Johannes and I were not able to collect such data, unfortunately. Not because we were uninterested in Haddad history, on the contrary. Like the travellers and administrators who had pondered over the issue such as Nachtigal, Barth, Carbou, Le Rouvreur, Colonel Chapelle or later Conte, we asked about Haddad traditions of origin and tried to collect myths and oral traditions with a bearing on the issue. Due to a shortage of time and difficulties in finding informants interested in and knowledgeable about

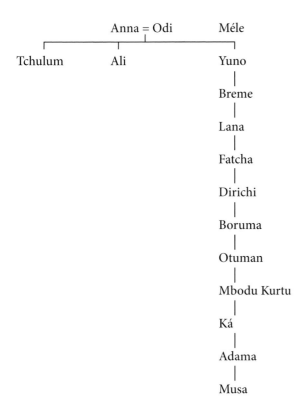

5,4. A genealogical chart showing that Kanembu and Haddad Kanembu ancestry is traced to the same founding fathers. The genealogy was told to us by Musa, an 85-year-old Haddad man.

the subject, however, we recorded only a few among the Haddad Kanembu and none among the Haddad Kreda. Some information volunteered to us referred to the immediate short-term history of clans or groups. Other narratives were of a more mythical nature, referring to an undefined past. All the information that was passed on to us was accompanied by comments and explanations for our benefit. These were more often than not cultural statements on the immediate, socially debased situation of the Haddad.

The Haddad Kanembu, with whom we discussed the more recent past, mentioned an exodus from N'Guri towards the Bahr el Ghazal and further to the south in Kanem. The stories told of an ongoing process of sedentarization, assessing the approximate time of foundation of the various Haddad villages, sometimes in 'real time', sometimes accounted for in genealogical terms. Some settlements had been established quite recently. The village of Wanagal, for example, was said to have been founded a generation prior

to our visit, i.e. in the mid 1930s. Chedra, a major Haddad Kanembu stronghold southwest of Mussoro was founded about forty-seven years prior to our visit it was explained to us, i.e. in 1916. The founders were six men from N'Guri, one of whom was still alive at the time. The six of them went to Chedra explicitly with the goal of establishing a new settlement, and when this had been achieved, they returned to N'Guri to fetch their wives and children. These oral traditions concur largely with written sources, which stress that N'Guri area was a Haddad stronghold towards the end of the 19th century. At that time it was dominated by the Darka clan and able to hold its stand against the marauding Ulad Sliman who were curbed by the French only in 1902. French policies facilitated the emigration, encouraging an expansion of the population beyond the large villages where it had concentrated for safety (cf. Conte 1983b: 133). It may well be, therefore, that there was an exodus from N'Guri induced by the window of opportunity to settle down on suitable agricultural land. According to an eighty-five-year old Haddad Kanembu by the name of Musa, many families had been farming already when he was a child, as they had been unable to support themselves by hunting alone. It was due to the 'miserable occupation of hunting' that the Kanembu did not want to marry them, he added.

When trying to pursue Haddad history further back in time, however, one runs into the obstacle of limited and conflicting oral traditions, as already intimated. One myth related to us about the origin of the Haddad Kanembu and typical as a statement of their current social situation was also told by Musa, himself a member of the influential Darkoa group. His narrative went as follows:

"The Haddad Kanembu and the Kanembu are all descendants of the Bulala people, who nowadays live around Lake Fitri. Originally the Bulala inhabited Kanem, and it is said that they lived here before the Kanembu.[5] At one point the Bulala left Kanem to wander southwards. One man stayed behind, however. This was a man by the name of Anna, and he became the forefather of the Kanembu as well as of the Haddad Kanembu. Anna was married to a woman by the name of Odi and the couple had three children - three sons called Tchulum, Ali and Méle. The two brothers, Tchulum and Ali adopted the spear, *sagai,* as their weapon and all the Kanembu proper descend from these two brothers. The third one, the brother by the name of Méle had a son by the name of Yuno. Yuno adopted the bow and arrow as his weapon and all the Haddad descend from Yuno. Since the time of Yono the Haddad have hunted with bow and arrow."

Similar myths about the fate of three brothers are found among other Haddad Kanembu clans. All bear testimony to the strong patrilineal bend of Kanemese society and illuminate how primogeniture ties in with the overall hierarchical organization. Considering what is known of the history of Kanem, however, the myth cannot be taken too literally. Rather than contributing to the general history of the Haddad Kanembu, the myth appears to be a statement on the prevailing asymmetrical relationship between the Kanembu and the Haddad Kanembu. In actual fact the Haddad are relegated to a lower step on the social ladder of the Kanemi community. It is a position which the Haddad negate by stressing the joint origin of the Kanembu and Haddad by locating their ancestry elsewhere i.e. with Bulala nobility and by claiming that they and the Kanembu descend from the very same forefather.[6]

Musa recalled another version of the origin of the Kanembu and Haddad respectively, telling us about the history of the well-known Dakoa clan to which he belonged. The subtext of this narrative paints a picture similar to the one mentioned above, indicating the sense of inferiority that prevails among the Haddad. This is what Musa told us:

"Three Kanembu brothers: Tchulum, Ali and Méle once found a baby boy lying far away in the savanna bush. They took the child with them and brought him up. But as they had found the boy together, they told him that he was to take turns and go from one brother to the other to have his meals. For that very reason the boy was called Darku, a name that stems from the Kanembu term *darkuyu,* meaning 'stop'."

Musa explained, that the very name entitled the boy to stop by and get a meal among the Kanembu wherever he pleased. One may wonder whether, at some point in time, this right to meals is an indication that the Haddad Kanembu and the Kanembu proper had developed exchange relations in line with those which still exist between the Haddad Kreda and the pastoralists among whom they settle. The myth says nothing of the boy's ancestry and origin, however, except that he was found in the savanna.

It offers no further clue to the legendary history of the Haddad *(cf. Table 5,4).*

Haddad Kanembu narratives of the past do also take the form of enumerations of genealogies, accompanied by comments. One such account was offered to explain that the Haddad Kanembu are of common ancestry with the Kanembu proper, an ancestry which the Haddad trace to the joint forefather Anna, some thirteen generations back in time, as previously mentioned.[7] (cf. *Table 5,4).*

We were not able to acquire any myths of origin among the Haddad Kreda, as previously mentioned. These people argued, however, that their history and origin differed from that of the Haddad Kanembu. They had come to the Bahr el Ghazal long ago, more specifically to the Mussoro area together with Kreda pastoralists, a view confirmed by the latter, but no one had any idea as to how long ago that happened. It may have taken place in the 17th or early 18th century, as previously argued, the period during which the Kreda most likely migrated to Bahr el Ghazal from their previous grazing grounds further north (cf. Chapelle 1957: 145).

SIGNATURES OF IDENTITY

The picture painted by existing sources on Haddad origin and history is far from simple, as is evident from the description just presented. The Haddad may rarely have captured the full attention of scholars and travellers, yet evidence of their past occurs in records of the past one-hundred-and-fifty years. These records testify to the existence of the Haddad as an identifiable and distinct group within the complex and highly volatile socio-cultural setting of northern Chad. The Haddad are known by numerous names in the region, reflecting the prisms through which they perceive themselves and/or are identified by others.

Towards the end of the 19th century, the Haddad lived basically a nomadic way of life as foragers and hunters, or as itinerant smiths. Portrayals gell in two clusters, one identity associated with those hunting with nets and living in close contact with the pastoral Kreda and Kecherda, the other with bow and arrow hunters living throughout the same region as the agro-pastoral Kanembu. Oral traditions depict the net-hunting Haddad as oriented towards the north with ties to Manga and Chitati, but without specifying these bonds in any detail. The more recent past of the net-hunting Haddad is linked to that of the pastoralists with whom they move. The majority bond with the Kreda, who migrate in the Bahr el Ghazal, but some live with the Kecherda who in the winter drive their cattle and camels further south into the Harr. In Chitati and Dillia, the fate of the Haddad is tied to the Daza groups. The same may well be the case of those camping among Arab pastoralists, be it the Maskéa, Ulad Ḥammad or the Ḥaddâd Cherek (cf. Carbou 1912, I: 212), but we know virtually nothing of the life of these people.

Oral sources on the origin and history of the Haddad Kanembu are richer and offer a more complex picture. Older sources identify these people as Bungu or Duarda Hadjra (Barth and Palmer) or Dânoâ, (Nachtigal and Carbou). Their origin is traced back in time to the fabled Sao people. Nachtigal links them historically with the south-western Manga, while some Haddad myths tell of descent from the Bulala, a branch of the Kameni nobility which ruled Kanem in the Middle Ages, inferring their ultimate noble heritage. While all sources agree that the epicentre of the Haddad Kanembu is Kanem, some indicate that they are affiliated with lacustral hunter groups at the Shari delta, known as the Karbina or Kerebina and may have ties as far afield as with foragers in northern Cameroon (cf. Lukas 1937: 208-209; Conte 1983a: 101).

Our discussions with Haddad individuals, who relied on hunting or claiming a hunting heritage left us in no doubt that, at the time of our study they perceived themselves as members of distinct ethnic units, as Haddad Kreda and Haddad Kanembu respectively, groups characterized by cultural traditions and livelihoods. The continuous use of the term Haddad in Kanem and Bahr el Ghazal does also reflect the hardcore social fact, however, that these people are set apart by neighbouring ethnic groups by rules of endogamy and stigma which brand them as culturally and socially inferior. Marriages between the Haddad and the Kreda or the Kanembu proper are socially unacceptable, for example. They do not occur, to the best of our knowledge, and sexual relations between men of the dominant groups and Haddad women do not lead to a social osmosis. This form of social exclusion is accompanied by other socio-economic and cultural barriers which curb social mobility as well as by outright stigmatization, issues to which we shall return.

NOTES

1. Le Rouvreur mentions a small group of Haddad near Chitati turned pastoralists like the Daza and Hassauna. These people have beautiful herds and, to his surprise, even camels – the symbol of an aristocratic heritage (Le Rouvreur 1962: 383).

2. According to Conte, the contemporary village of Sulu lies precisely in the Rig-Rig district of the northwestern part of the Lake Prefecture (Conte 1983a: 99).

3. The Haddad-Bulala 'connection' is discussed by Conte, who mentions that according to one of the myths of the Danoa [the Rea, Bara, Adia groups of Haddad Kanembu, IN] describes their ancestor Darka as the son of the Bulala (who is said to have ruled Kanem during 16th century) and hence by implication a descendant of the Bulala royalty of Metalla.

4. Tibesti blacksmiths maintain that they originate from Ennedi because the ancestor, Dudi, had to flee the area having committed a murder. He settled at Gubon, known for its rich iron ore. The area is the original clan land of the Guboda, indicating ancient relations with the smiths with whom they also share clan taboos. Another wave of emigrant smiths went from Ennedi by Unianga to Tibesti. Borku smiths are also said to stem from Ennedi, although they claim that Dafur and the southern part of Wadai is their ultimate land of origin. Fuchs points out that the reason why Ennedi was so significant to the spread of forging could be that Koro Toro was an ancient centre of iron production (Fuchs 1970: 297-9).

5. Regarding the relationship between the Bulala and the Kanembu cf. chapters 3 and 4; Nachtigal 1881, II: 185-6, 335-345; Conte 1983a: 71.

6. A similar myth was told to Conte by a member of the Rea clan. According to this, the ancestor of the Rea "...was a hunter who arrived from the North. He was armed with a bow and arrow and he came with his two younger brothers. The three of them settled in the Wai wadi (between Yalita and N'Guri). One of them was called Reu, the other Bar Woli, and the youngest Adu. They were all the offspring of the same father, Bar Kora, but Bar Woli and Adu had a different mother. In this case the ancestors is said to come from the North (Conte 1986: 138).

7. According to another informant, the ancestor of the Darkoa clan was Brahim, the ancestry of the clan can be traced back some ten generations. Brahim settled at Chedra in 1916.

6:

6: FATE AND INEQUALITY

CULTURAL BRANDING

Ethnic stereotypes seem a fact of life wherever you live on this tiny globe, Kanem and Bahr el Ghazal being no exception. Both the Haddad Kanembu and the Haddad Kreda experience cultural branding although not in equal measure, the difference being linked to their respective ways of subsistence, values and forms of interaction with the wider society. The ethnic composition of the region is kaleidoscopic, as already stated: a richly faceted texture of cultural traditions, socio-political arrangements and ecological adaptations in constant motion. It is a social environment, however, which - despite its plasticity, the upcoming and decline of states and political potentates and the ever ongoing spatial movement of ethnic groups and individuals - is deeply marked by asymmetries and permeated by notions of the inequality of man. People conceive of their social environment in terms of dichotomies, and apply these to sustain and recreate social inequalities. Johannes and I were immediately struck by the extent to which discourses and cultural concepts of social, occupational, physical or religious phenomena formed part of an underlying acceptance of inequality. Ranked dichotomies emerged in respect to social relations between and conceptions about freemen and slaves, patrons and clients, eligible marriage partners and non-suitable ones, hunters versus (cattle-owning) pastoralists, persons of black versus white skin colour, Muslims versus pagans and spear versus bow carriers. Closer scrutiny revealed the systematic ways in which cultural markers relegated both the Haddad Kanembu and the Haddad Kreda to the lower end of the social ladder.

A significant instrument of cultural branding is the oral traditions that circulate in Kanem and the Bahr el Ghazal. Several of these deal with the deplorable fate of the Haddad. The unfortunate fate of the Haddad Kreda, for example, is justified by the following myth:

"Once upon a time Nabi Djibrila [Archangel Gabriel]- the natives tell - gave two brothers an anvil and a net respectively, telling them that: Oh! You men of a despised race - go and earn yourself a living by means of what I am giving you. It is the descendants of these two siblings - it seems - who constitute the two main fractions of the Ḥaddâd Gourân: the Ḥaddâd Siyâd Sindala [the smiths, IN] and the Ḥaddâd Siyâd Cherek [the net-hunting, IN]" (Carbou 1912, I: 209; IN transl.).

The depreciation that clings to the Haddad Kanembu is linked by some people to the fact that they carry the name Haddad or smith. Carbou notes that the Haddad constitute "an extremely curious population" and proceeds:

"Not only are they the only ones in the region which we occupy who are armed with bow and arrow. On top of this they are despised, without exception, by all of the other indigenous peoples. Regarding this last point of view, by the way, the name *ḥaddâd* is significant in that it is held in such low esteem among all peoples of Central Africa as is the caste of the smiths: the *ḥaddâd* among the Arabs, *dogoâ* among the Kanembu, *azâ* among the Toubou, *noéguè* among the Boulala, *kabartou* among the Ouadaïens, all smiths that invaribaly are despised" (Carbou 1912, I: 49; IN transl.).

Carbou's suggestion that negative attitudes towards the Haddad are linked to the notion that these people are associated with iron and forging stands to reason. It is well known that smiths are set apart (though not necessarily despised) as a particular social category throughout North Africa, and that they are feared among some pastoralists. This is the case among the Tuareg, for example, who believe that work with iron lends the smiths special and potentially dangerous powers (cf. J. Nicolaisen 1964). This is in contrast to the general esteem in which smiths are held south of the Sahel. Yet, forging is not at the core of Kanemese depreciation the Haddad. Rather the widely held narrative among both the Kanembu and the Kreda on the deplorable fate of the Haddad is woven around their occupation as hunters. The ensuing story was told to us by our interpreter Bogar Béchir, a Kanembu himself:

"One day during his wandering in the desert, the Prophet Mohammed came upon a Haddad camp where a gazelle had just been caught in a net. The Prophet told the Haddad to let go of the gazelle to enable it to suckle its calf, as the little one was all alone and thirsty. Mohammed added that if the Haddad freed the gazelle, it would return to the Haddad and let itself be killed. The Haddad did not know that they were talking to the Prophet, as he had not identified himself, and they did not believe his words. Mohammed then told them to free the gazelle and withhold him instead, tying his hands and feet. If the gazelle did not return as he had foretold, they were allowed to do with him whatever they wanted. They could sell him as a slave, Mohammed said, or kill him. The Haddad listened to what was being said and decided to do as the Prophet suggested. They tied the hands and feet of the Prophet Mohammed and let the gazelle go, so that it could run and suckle its calf. When the gazelle had taken care of its calf it returned to the Haddad, as Mohammed had foretold, and the Prophet was released from capture. Then Mohammed told the Haddad that they were free to kill the gazelle, but he asked them to give him the hide when they had done so. The Haddad did as told. They killed the gazelle and offered the hide to Mohammed. The Prophet took this, knelt in prayer and threw the hide away. No sooner had he done so, than the hide turned into a live gazelle that took off. Ever since this event, however, the Haddad have lived as poor hunters in the desert. For although Mohammed's prayers had turned the hide of the gazelle into a live animal, he had also called upon God and asked that the Haddad forever should remain poor, wandering hunters. For this very reason no one wants to marry a Haddad to this day."

The myth is an illuminating example of how marginalization is culturally justified by mainstream society by relegating the despised from the protective canopy of religion. The Haddad did not believe in the Prophet, we are told. They even held him hostage in order to reclaim their prey. The Haddad sinned, in other words, and are subsequently punished. They are doomed by God himself and hence stigmatized, relegated from the pious, law-abiding society at large and rightfully so. In a Kanemese context the myth is lent further moral weight by the claim that it forms part of the holy scripture of the Koran itself. In combination with the fact that the Haddad are recent converts, who adopted the Muslim faith within living memory and hence by implication are but lightweights when it comes to solid faith, the myth serves as a powerful justification of social exclusion, of treating the Haddad as a disdained group within Kanemese sociality.

The fate of the Haddad of Kanem and the Bahr el Ghazal is replicated among the forging and hunting Aza of the Dillia region north of Lake Chad in eastern Niger. In her study of the historical development of roles and attitudes between these people and the pastoral Teda-Daza, Baroin describes the social, economic and cultural differences between the two groups and concludes that the significant distinctions are largely what she terms 'mental'. The Aza are described as an endogamous, occupationally distinct and socially inferior yet complementary group within Tubu society. Cultural conceptions make for significant differences moreover, in the way the Aza and the Daza perceive one another. The Daza hold the Aza in low esteem, while the Aza on their part despise the Daza. Daza pastoralists hold the Aza in contempt for a number of reasons. Their contempt extends both to Aza clans, which used to rely entirely on foraging and to those subsisting as smiths. In eastern Niger, where Baroin gathered her data, these foragers comprise the Karee, Togolele, Barabara, and Coea clans, who all used to hunt with nets and the Darkoa, Baara, Aadea, Rega, Yunoia, Yeeya, Moloroo, Tera, Gweioo, Keyi and Kafa clans, who make use of bow and arrow (Baroin 1991: 347). Daza pastoralists find the Aza ugly and spurn the manner in which they speak and dance. The Aza are also held in disrespect because they ride donkeys, something a true Daza would never dream of, horses and camels being the only proper means of transportation in their view. The Aza milk their goats unlike the Daza who only milk cows. But the Daza despise the Aza first and foremost for their presumed weakness. Aza men do not stand up and defend themselves and their kin, in the view of the Daza, to whom kinship solidarity is a must and the interests of kin must be guarded at all costs. The Daza, who easily take up arms, scorn the Aza for not doing the same. Any Daza man will take on raiders singlehandedly, they claim, and the Daza ridicule the Aza for their timidity, scorning the Aza that it takes at least seven of them even to go looking for stolen camels. In Baroin's view, however, the Aza are not fearful but inhibited in their relations with the Daza. Yet, Aza behaviour is interpreted as cowardice by the latter, into whom assertiveness and an obligation to stand up for one's right is distilled from an early age. We are confronted with two different mentalities, Baroin claims, the Daza being arrogant and fierce, the Aza humble and gentle (Baroin 1991: 359-81). The stereotypes that encapsulate Daza cultural interpretation of Dillia and Manga history are a negotiating instrument in the ongoing construction of identities. Daza values are attached to courage and the ability to fend for oneself, values crucial to pastoralists whose wealth - the cherished herds of cattle - are blatantly displayed and must be protected. This is so utterly different from the situation of Aza foragers, who by necessity live more or less from the hand to the mouth and are unable to accumulate capital.

The history of Kanem and Bahr el Ghazal is equally turbulent and open for discourse, interpretations of social relations and the creation of stereotypes by the various ethnic groups. The context is no less violent, suppressive and complex, yet there are other facets to the cultural and social institutionalization of Haddad inferiority within the wider Kanemese society than those which engulf the Aza of Dillia. Kanembu attitudes towards and views of the Haddad Kanembu are ambivalent, for instance. On the one hand, the Haddad command their respect due to the precision of their poisoned arrows. The Kanembu still talk in admiration, for example, of how the Haddad fought at their side against the warring Wadai in pre-colonial days. Unlike the Aza of eastern Niger, the Haddad Kanembu were able to defend themselves and their villages, and the Kanembu

are in awe of the fearlessness with which they stood up to marauders like the Awlad Sliman. The fact that they command respect does not protect them against social depreciation by the wider society, however. As Le Rouvreur remarks: "This is still a sign of the fate that befalls these people, who possess such superior arms compared to their neighbours yet remain in an inferior position and do not even try to rid themselves of this" (Le Rouvreur 1962: 383; IN transl.). Identification and stereotyping by weaponry is found throughout Kanem and Bahr el Ghazal. Not only do the various ethnic groups make use of different types of arms for hunting, war and defence, they identify with and are identified by whatever arms are carried. Arms are applied as cultural signifiers to mark ethnic identity and boundaries, in other terms. The bow and arrow which the Haddad Kanembu master so skilfully are thus held in general disregard by the Kanembu, who swear by and carry spears only. The Haddad Kanembu may be respected by the Kanembu proper in situations where they apply these weapons in defence of Kanemi individuals. Yet, bow and arrow is nevertheless a symbol of low status and used to label or rather brand the Haddad Kanembu.

Kreda attitudes towards "their Haddad" seemed similar to those of the Daza towards the Aza northeast of Lake Chad. The Kreda too are renowned for fearlessness and the eagerness and rapidity with which they take to arms to defend themselves or to go looting, and they cannot but look down upon the foragers who, according to them, are unwilling and unable to fend for themselves. The Haddad Kreda have no history of bravery, no codex of fierceness, no means to boost their standing among the Kreda and the wider society. On the contrary, they are said to turn to the pastoralists for protection in times of violence and conflict. This claim was forwarded by the pastoralists as the main reason why the Haddad Kreda were held in the lowest of esteem. Similar information was obtained by Le Rouvreur (cf. 1962: 383).

Haddad perceptions of themselves and their lot as compared to that of other ethnic groups, and of how they viewed the dominant groups, are not well documented. Our reading of the behaviour of the Haddad Kreda combined with our discussions with them on what was on their minds is in line, however, with Baroin's observations of the Aza of eastern Niger. We were struck by the friendly atmosphere in Haddad camps, by their easy-going behaviour and communication, and also by the apprehension and fear with which they watched Kreda aggravations and shunned Kreda space when the latter lost their tempers and violent incidents erupted. The difference in temperament was striking. We were present in Kreda camps that were ripe with tension. Shrill voices pierced the air, small groups of men moved restlessly around in the camp and agitated communication shot back and forth between the tents. It was in fact quite unpleasant. Meanwhile, the Haddad families stuck quietly to their tasks in and around their own tents, seemingly unaffected by the aggravation of their hosts. This is not to say that Haddad individuals are without temperament. They can definitely flare up, but this happens largely when game escapes the nets, in which case the hunters are searching for an explanation and someone to blame, a scapegoat, as we shall see.

Asymmetrical relations between ethnic groups, clans and lineages go back a long time in West Africa. It is well described how they characterize interaction between agricultural and pastoral groups throughout the region. Less attention has been paid to asymmetrical ties between foraging communities and pastoral and agro-pastoral societies throughout this vast region.[1] They are well described, however, from foraging societies in eastern Cameroun and from the Mbuti and other Batwa groups in Congo and Rwanda (Turnbull 1965). Asymmetrical relations between foragers and agricultural societies also colour relations in southern Chad, where the former are tied to dominant agricultural societies in much the same way as are the Mbuti pygmies of the Ituri forests to Bantu communities. This is the case, for instance, with the Nò-èy of the Ouham River, a tributary of the middle Shari in relation to the dominant Sara population. Like Haddad relations with surrounding groups, those of the Nò-èy with the Sara are marked by prejudice. The Nò-èy are both feared and despised, Matthey writes, and strict endogamy prevails, although the Nò-èy have adopted the Sara tongue and live right among these people (Matthey 1966: 38).

The apparently silent acceptance by foragers such as the Haddad Kreda of the pervasive social inequalities may be due to a range of factors. It is worth remembering that the deprived may well identify with the oppressor, and that deviant perceptions and opposition rarely find open expression but find other outlets, including that of social withdrawal, avoidance of controversy and silent obstruction,

as Scott has pointed out (Scott 1990). We did not become intimate enough with the Haddad Kreda to decode the subtleties of communication within this sensitive field. We noticed their uncertainty, however, and the difficulties they faced in assessing themselves as citizens with equal rights.

POLITY AND HIERARCHY

The inequality which permeates social life in Northern Chad and brands the Haddad as second-rate citizens has been constantly re-enacted over the past century in response to changing economic and political conditions. Haddad life and livelihood have been defined not only by the availability of game and access to other resources or cultural branding at any one point in time, but as much by socio-political agendas and administrative regulations that have crippled their opportunities and confined them to the margins of the wider society, be it the Caliphate of the Kanembu, the colonial rule of the French or modern Chad.

Until French colonization at the turn of the century, Kanem was a Caliphate under the leadership of the Sultan of Mao, a man of noble Kanembu descent. The Sultan had religious authority and exerted fiscal rights over the sedentary Kanemese population. It is doubtful, however, that he had much say over the pastoralists – or the foraging Haddad for that matter. Historically, the Caliphate of Kanem based its power on this hierarchical structure. The regime was dominated by the Kanembu and functioned on the premise that its cantonal territories largely reflected clan-vested land rights. (Le Rouvreur 1962: 90-1) Like other ethnic groups in the region, the Kanembu organize themselves in patrilateral kin groups of different depth. Ideally, the eldest son succeeds his deceased father, and succession to positions including that of Sultan is determined by patrilineal descent. This is highlighted at the ceremonies that mark the installation of a new Sultan or *alifa*, when dressed in a brightly coloured caftan he is crowned with a gorgeous turban and seated upon a carpet or bed, like similar ceremonies found in many places throughout the Sahelien West Africa.

The Sultan governed with a cabinet of ministers and a number of chiefs of major Kanembu clans, through whom he collected taxes. A private army with guns backed his political endeavours, curbed only by the Sultan of Bornu,

6,1. Amsakai, a Kanemese chief. Heinrich Barth 1857: III: 111.

to whom the Kanemese Sultan paid allegiance, as previously mentioned (cf. Chapter 3: 88-90). The very core of the Caliphate was the canton of Mao, the seat of the Sultan, which was administered by a number of noble families or clans. Vassal cantons were linked to the Caliphate, some closely with chiefs appointed by the Sultan, others more loosely. In the latter case, the chiefs were only installed not chosen by the Sultan. At the time of the arrival of the French, the southern part of Kanem was divided into five cantons: N'jigdada and Dibinenchi, predominantly inhabited and ruled by the Kanembu; Bari Kolum, which was inhabited by mixed population of Kanembu and Haddad but administered by the latter through an alternating leadership among the three main clans: the Rea, Adia and Bara; N'Guri also administered by the Haddad themselves, in this case by the Darka clan and finally Mondo, where the

inhabitants were ruled by the Tunjur (Le Rouvreur 1962: 91; Conte 1986: 133).

In principle, the Sultan held pre-eminent rights over all of the lands of Kanem, including the pastures where the pastoralists grazed their cattle. It was therefore necessary for any clan official appointed by his group's council of elders to obtain the investiture of the Sultan at Mao to validate his right to collect taxes from his clan members and others residing within the territory he administered. In turn, the clan leader passed on a share of the fiscal revenue due to the Sultan (cf. Conte 1983a: 34). These rights of investiture were taken over by the French colonial power and have since passed on to the Chadian State, as have certain of the fiscal prerogatives formerly vested in the Sultan. The Kanembu potentate, however, continues to exercise a certain 'moral' pre-eminence in the affairs of Kanem and can still exercise considerable influence over accession to office at the cantonal level, the distribution of land rights among clans and certain fiscal matters, according to Conte (1983a: 34).

At the arrival of the French, the Caliphate was in complete turmoil due to the marauding Awlad Sliman and the impact of the Sanussiya, yet an administrative system was in place for the French to build on. At first they relied on this, but in due time the administrative practices became increasingly centralized, in line with the way in which the French governed other of their colonies and France itself. The country was divided into a series of administrative units known in order of size and socio-political significance the *préfecture, sous-préfecture, canton* and *village*, each headed by a senior administrative leader. As was the case under the Caliphate, the *chef du canton* and *chef du village* were local clan and lineage leaders, whose duty it was to collect taxes.

At first the French did not realize that politics in Kanem is dominated by kinship, affiliation, solidarity and opposition. Clans were not recognized as key players in local politics, because the territorial dispersion of these did not necessarily coincide with a clear distribution along linguistic or ethnic lines. The Kanembu, Haddad, Kreda and other ethnic groups found themselves organized and later reorganized in spatially defined *canton,* administered by a *chef du canton.* In some cases the *canton* coincided with traditional political structures, in other cases not (cf. Chapelle 1957: 368-9). Still, the *chef du canton* was invariably head of a dominant clan, the *chef du village* a lineage leader. In practice, however, only certain clan chiefs got access to office in Kanem, because the division into and size of the *cantons* was regularly changed by the French during the period leading up to World War II. In due time, the administration became increasingly dominated by the Kanembu, although the power of the Sultan had been substantially curbed; and to this day the position is vested with religious and some political authority.

The administrative set-up with *chefs du canton* and *chefs du village* worked differently for the Haddad Kreda and the Haddad Kanembu. Among the Kreda and other pastoralists, the clan and lineage structures were accepted as the backbone of the new administrative units (cf. Chapelle 1957: 369), a policy that indirectly sustained traditional ties of dependency between Haddad Kreda families and their pastoral 'hosts', rather than integrating them as equal citizens of the colony. Being numerically few and moreover highly

dispersed throughout the Bahr el Ghazal, the Haddad Kreda were not in a position to assert themselves as separate units with their own *chef du village* or *chef du canton,* but remained stifled as a subordinate stratum among the pastoralists at the bottom of the social hierarchy.

The situation was different for the Haddad Kanembu. For one thing, they were far more numerous than the Haddad Kreda. They were settled, moreover, and hence able to form geo-political units that in some cases were accepted by the French for the establishment of self-government. Still, Haddad Kanembu clans were more dispersed than their Kanembu counterparts. The distribution of the offices of *chef du village* and *chef du canton* in eight cantons in Kanem conducted by Edouard Conte in the early 1970s revealed that although the Haddad were elected as village chiefs, few apparently reached the higher office of *chef du canton.* The study lists 314 villages administered by Kanembu clans, as opposed to 214 villages administered by 43 Duu clans, [read largely Haddad, IN].[2] Only nine of these Duu clans embraced more than ten villages and Duu local communities were smaller on average than those of the Kanembu. Cantonal offices were vested in four Duu clans only, namely the Darka, Bara, Dieri and Rea. These chieftancies were located at N'Guri and Dokara (both administered by the Darka clan), and at Yalia, Am Dobak and Molimari administered by the three other clans respectively. Taken in the above order, the four clans controlled 25, 17, 15 and 12 villages respectively, settlements that had a total population in excess of 1,300 persons and sufficient adjacent fertile lands to remain economically as well as politically autonomous, according to Conte (1983a: 38). Other Haddad clans are relatively large but dispersed. The twelve villages controlled by headmen of the Kei clan, for example, were dispersed in five different cantons over which other clans either Kanembu or Duu, had pre-eminent fiscal rights (ibid.). Some Haddad clans were never even close to achieving any form of say over their own affairs. The same applies to most of the blacksmith clans. The Kakuluru blacksmith clan, for instance, lived in eleven villages spread through five cantons, according to Conte (ibid.). How many Duu villages were in fact inhabited by Haddad Kanembu cannot be deduced from Conte's material, as will be recalled, due to his broad definition of the Duu category. It is safe to infer, however, that a fair part of the 44 villages listed by Conte as Duu in the N'Guri canton were in fact inhabited by the Haddad Kanembu. In fact, he labels them Danoa in a later article, indicating that they are foraging people (1983a: 133-5).

The French set up their first administrative post in Kanem at N'Guri, i.e. right in the heartland of Haddad Kanembu country. At that time, i.e. at the turn of the 20th century, N'Guri was dominated by the Haddad Kanembu, more specifically by the Darka clan. But the chiefdom was soon split up and reorganized administratively by the French in a way that catered solely for the interests of the Kanembu nobility and put an end to the precedence of the Haddad. As late as in 1933, the French contemplated the creation of a Haddad dominated canton through a re-grouping of the Am Dobak, Bir Bulo, Dokora and Kiwa chiefdoms, all Haddad Kanembu strongholds, but the plans were never carried out. Instead, N'Guri was incorporated into the chiefdom of Mao the following year further curbing Haddad Kanembu influence over matters of concern to them. Similar changes took place elsewhere, sometimes spurred on by local ethnic rivalries, internal Haddad conflicts, or the policies of Sultan of Mao, according to R. Catala's studies (quoted by Conte, 1983b: 134-5).

Over time, the changing administrative practices of the French entailed increasing centralization, as just mentioned. Local control over revenues from land was curbed by the transference of these means to cantonal chiefs, ultimately placing them in the hands of the French and subsequently Chadian authorities. The administrative set-up and practice were upheld by the Chadian government after independence with few changes. We encountered a number of people who argued that the chiefs ought to be ousted from their positions because of their incompetence and embezzlement of public funds.

The Haddad were never able to rally successfully and influence French policies in their favour, nor have they been able to do so later. The fiscal authority that Haddad chiefs had enjoyed under the rule of the Sultan of Mao was gradually abolished. Haddad Kanembu authority and say over their own affairs dwindled as time went by. Some groups shrunk in size, others suffered from time to time from incompetent leaders.[3] In some cases, the Haddad simply blew their chances. French policies and administrative practices exerted considerable influence over the Haddad way of life and their relations with the dominant groups, in particular the Kanembu proper, tipping the balance of power in favour of the latter. It is fair to say that the Haddad were probably influenced more profoundly by French colonialism in South Kanem than any other group. That at least is the conclusion that Conte draws (Conte 1983a: 28-29; 38). I can only subscribe to this assessment. At the time of our visit, i.e. the early years of Chadian independence, the political invisibility of the Haddad was striking.

SLAVES AND DEPENDANTS

The stigmatization and economic deprivation that the Haddad suffer is overtly similar to the situation of the affranchised slaves. It is culturally clothed in a different rationality, however, and more importantly, slaves were integrated into Kanembu economy and households in a way that was radically different from the nature of the relationship between the Kanembu and the Haddad Kanembu. Slavery was in fact an integral and significant part of Kameni society until the French brought a halt to slave-raiding and gradually curbed its formal existence.

In the first part of the 20th century, slavery was widespread among a great many sedentary and pastoral societies throughout North Africa. It was still pervasive among the Tuareg when Johannes and I stayed with these people in 1963, as was the case among the Tubu at that time. Traditionally, the latter distinguished between *boder,* who were first generation slaves and hence persons with whom the masters had no deep personal ties, which is why these slaves were freely sold, and *tiyeni,* slaves who had been born into captivity (Le Coeur 1950: 76). A defining characteristic of slavery is the deprivation of judicial rights. Slaves are not 'judicial persons' in their own right, and cannot retain the usufruct of their own labour nor, in principle, possess means of production such as land, wells or livestock. The master has 'jus in personam', as Radcliffe-Brown pointed out years ago (Radcliffe-Brown 1952: 32 ff.), and these rights are exclusive and different from the restricted rights that, say, a father may hold over his son. In other words, a slave is judicially a person without kin, an individual tied to society through his or her personal relationship to a valid member of society. This situation allows for the selling and purchasing of individuals as slaves (cf. M.G. Smith 1965: 120).

General insurgency prevailed in northern Chad well into the 20th century, as did slavery and even the miserable trade in human merchandise. At the turn of the 19th century, an estimated 5,000 slaves were still exported annually from the Bagirmi region alone to Bornu, Kanem and further north, according to Chevalier (1907: 357). Slavery was still widespread at that time in Kanem. The majority of the slaves were owned by the Kanembu proper, but all freemen were entitled in principle to possess slaves, and richer Duu families were able to exercise this privilege, according to Conte (1983a: 76-7). Kanembu noble families could have between 15 and 20 captives in the household, mostly captured on raid (Bouillié 1937: 150). However, a good number were purchased at markets such as that at Massenia, the capital of Bagirmi, either through sale of cattle or barter with salt cakes produced from *Salvadora persica* and natron. In 1903, the prices of slaves were as follows in Maria Theresia thalers: Male, 5-8 years of age: 20 thaler: male 8-13 years of age: 10 thaler, male 14-19 years of age: 20 thaler, male 20-25 years of age 25 thaler; male 30-50 years of age: little trade. Female slaves fetched lower prices, and children under the age of 5 were sold with their mothers only. By comparison, a good horse, an animal that the Kanembu value highly, was sold for about 50 thaler (Chevalier 1907: 300-400). It is difficult to assess the demographic weight of slaves in Kameni society at any one time, as Conte observes, but he estimates that their numbers were lower than that of the Duu population (Conte 1983a: 77). The Kanembu depend-

ed indirectly on the Haddad Kanembu for the very upkeep of the institution, he argues, as both salt and natron were manufactured by these people at the shores of Lake Chad and exchanged with the Kanembu proper for goods or as tribute(ibid. 1983a: 75).

The purchased slaves were largely pagans, while captives could be Muslims. Some people like the Lake Chad Islanders raided pagan and believers indiscriminately.[4] The majority of able-bodied male slaves were assigned to agricultural tasks like tiling and irrigation work, they herded domestic animals and served as messengers for their masters. Female slaves carried water, pounded millet and other grains, cooked and served meals. Male slaves could marry other female slaves only, and were hence unable to establish their own domestic unit. The children belonged to the mother's master, as among the Tuareg (Conte 1983a: 75; Nicolaisen and Nicolaisen 1997, II: 609). Female slaves were in principle allowed to marry freemen and the offspring of such unions considered members of the husbands' patrilineage and henceforth eligible to inherit. These marriage practices and the fact that male slaves and their descendants could not form politically and socially recognized patrilineages explains in Conte's view the later disappearance and 'assimilation' of the slave stratum as against the continued existence of the Duu stratum (1983a: 78). I fully agree with Conte that the endogamous marriage practices of the

6,2. Spears, the weapon par excellence of Kreda men. At marriage, spears are offered by the Haddad groom to the 'host' of his wife to be. Spears are carried in a leather pouch over the shoulder. Cat. no. 28. Photo J.K.

Duu/Haddad Kanembu are highly significant in perpetu-
ating the Haddad as a closed group and, I would add, indigenous people. We shall return to the marriage practices
of the Haddad Kanembu shortly.

Although French colonial intervention eventually
stopped slave raiding and trade, the formal abolition of
slavery and servitude was only made law in 1956, i.e. a few
years prior to Chadian independence. In the early 1960s
these institutions had not yet fully vanished. The process of
enfranchisement took its time. It could be bought by payment in currency, but was often bargained against a contract
of servitude or dependence that entailed servile labour, that
in many ways was similar to those found among Duu farmers and specific Kanembu lineages or communities, according to Conte (1983a: 79). Asymmetrical relations and certain forms of political and economic dependence between
former slaves and their masters probably prevail to this very
day in Kanem as they do e.g. among the Tuareg. The enfran-
chised slaves may be attributed unused lands for colonization, usually at a certain distance from existing settlements,
Conte writes, but they remain attached to their former master's lineage by links of political and tributary dependence.
A Kanembu man told Conte that although the slaves of the
Sultan of Mao were free: "they respect their master; they
will never forget. Even if one of them becomes a civil servant, he respects his master or his master's son when they
meet" (ibid. 80). A similar situation prevails in other North
African societies. Among the Tuareg, master-slave relations
are reactivated in the wake of the grave strains on their
way of life over the past decades. Thus impoverished noble
families are known to have taken up residence with their
former slaves in some regions, when experiencing hardship
and loss of cattle, letting themselves be sustained by their
former slaves. The latter accept this as a matter of obligation
and take a certain pride in feeding their old masters. Conte
has argued that the socio-economic situation of the Duu
[read Haddad Kanembu, IN] in many respects was similar to that of the slaves. The impact on Kanemese society
of the formal abolition of slavery was notable, in his view,
in that it led to a widening of the commoner category into
a composite class of dependents but without eliminating
all the forms of socio-economic subordination it entailed.
However, this did not result in a parallel transformation of
the norms that defined the jural and social position of the
Duu (Conte 1983a: 74).

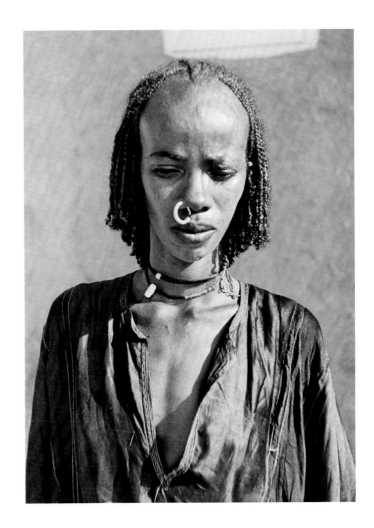

6,3. A Kreda woman with a neat hairdo. The forehead is shaved
to enhance her beauty. The woman wears a ring in her right
nostril as do most adult pastoral women.

SEX AND MARRIAGE BARRIERS

That socio-cultural barriers are 'for real' proves true in societies around the world in terms of prohibitions against
sexual and marriage relations between social groups and
categories. Such barriers also mark Haddad relations with
other ethnic groups. They manifest themselves in a 'clas-
sic', asymmetrical form, namely that it is socially accepted,
though not condoned, if men of the dominant groups engage in sexual liaisons with Haddad women, but strongly
condemned if Haddad men court Kanembu and Kreda
women. Nevertheless, it seemed that sexual relationships
between Haddad women and Kreda men proved to be not

that rare after all, and we heard about similar liaisons between Kanembu men and Haddad Kanembu women of both shorter and longer duration. The strength of the norm against such unions is underscored by the widespread belief that such liaisons cannot result in pregnancies. If a Haddad woman got pregnant, nevertheless, she and her family would do their best to hide the identity of her lover. Children born from illegitimate unions were invariably considered Haddad. To what extent, if any, women of the dominant groups have Haddad lovers, is difficult to ascertain. Everybody said of course, that such relations were unheard of, as was to be expected. Yet, public condemnation is never a guarantee that men and women do not get attracted to one another across ethnic divides and are able to find ways to have intercourse.

While sexual relations between individuals from different social strata, although problematic, can be handled with discretion, marriage cannot. Marriages are social contracts of implication not only for the man and woman involved but for their kin and future offspring. The Haddad marry only other Haddad, and almost always a person from the same category of Haddad, be it another Haddad Kreda or Haddad Kanembu. Marriages between these two groups are not prohibited, but we learned of no examples. Marriages between the Haddad and Kreda or the Kanembu are off limits. Informants claimed, that such marriages were possible in theory but considered unfortunate. They were bound to run into trouble. Baroin writes that in Ayer and Dillia in eastern Niger the avoidance of similar marital unions was due to the fear and contempt in which the hunters and smiths were held by the surrounding Daza and Kreda pastoralists. Even marriages between Aza (Haddad) men, who had given up their foraging occupation for husbandry, and at times so successfully that they were richer than the pastoralists, would not be eligible for marriage with pastoral women (Baroin 1985: 178).

The same attitudes prevail throughout Kanem and the Bahr el Ghazal. An Arab from the town of Mussoro, who contemplated marriage with a Haddad woman, had to call

6,4. Approaching a camp. The pale colour of the tents blends in beautifully with the dunes making it very hard to discern the camp from a distance.

6,5. A young Kreda pastoralist wearing a light cotton caftan, a dress that is widely used in the Sahel and Sahara where summer temperatures are beastly.

this off when his family learned of his plans and his older brother swore in public that he would kill him if he did so. Interethnic marriages are rare not only between the Haddad and 'their betters', but it must be said that endogamy prevails. The pastoral Kreda and the agro-pastoral Kanembu marry largely within their own ethnic group, the preference of the former being cousin marriages, probably under influence by the Kanembu (Clanet 1975: 50, 100). This is unlike other Tibu pastoralists, who in general avoid marriages with kinsmen that are not removed by four generations. To what extent the various groups actually live up to these preferences is another matter. Their 'relatives', the Daza of Ayer and Dillia proclaim similar marriage preferences, yet no less than 41 per cent do in fact marry non-kin (Baroin 1985: 190). This contrasts with the Aza (Haddad) of the same region, who turn out to be strictly endogamous. They not only

marry relatives but, unlike the pastoralists, frequently forge unions with matrilateral cousins. Out of a total of 41 Aza marriages that Baroin presents, 27 per cent were contracted with a patrilateral first cousin, 24 per cent with a patrilateral cousin further removed and not less than 44 per cent with a matrilateral first cousin, and a mere 2 per cent with another matrilateral kinswoman (ibid. 190).

The marriage patterns of both the Kanembu and the Duu, in particular of the Rea clan, have been documented by Conte. On the basis a fine quantitative material, it is argued that marriage practices are intimately linked to the prevailing hierarchical organization of Kanemese society. Conte is of the opinion, moreover, that the very pinion of pre-colonial Kanemese economy was a rigid hierarchical system, which allowed for very little vertical mobility. Chapelle, Fuchs and Le Rouvreur believe that this was enforced i.a. through Haddad endogamy, implicitly opposing this to Kanembu exogamy and free choice in marriage. Conte's findings do not contest that social stratification was maintained through the prevalent endogamy among the Kreda and Haddad respectively. They suggest that:" … in the pre-colonial period, endogamy was not the monopoly of any professional caste but rather a boundary-enforcing function in both main social strata as well as clan-based status groups within these strata" (Conte 1983a: 396).

Conte has looked closely at endogamy and lineage affiliation in his sample of some 311 Kanembu and 1,289 Haddad Kanembu marriages. He demonstrates how a strict prohibition on marriages between the Kanembu and the Haddad has been enforced throughout the 20th century concomitant with structural changes in marriage patterns and strategies and the waning of major political functions of the lineage and, foremost, the exercise of force. The comparison illuminates that endogamy was not, and is not a monopoly of professional castes or the lower strata of society in Kanem. Among the Kanembu, a greater solidarity of dominant lineages prevails to the extent that marriages, where lineage affiliation to the exclusion of traceable cousin links is an essential component are more than twice as frequent as among the Haddad. Unions where geographical proximity in the origin of spouses is the salient variable to the exclusion of lineage or genealogical links are today more common among the Haddad, who are attempting to break stratum barriers by inter-lineage marriage alliance but whose freedom of movement is greatly restricted in the Kanembu chieftaincies which surround them. Among both the Kanembu and the Haddad the issue of power account for as many or more marriages than those in which kinship – itself a partly political variable – is the most apparent determinant, says Conte (1979: 277). I shall not deal in further detail with this issue but refer the reader to Conte's study.

The antagonism against inter-ethnic sexual intimacy with Haddad foragers may well be bolstered by the fact that they carry the same name-tag as the smiths. Throughout North Africa, ethnic and professional groups avoid sexual liaisons with smiths, not to mention marriage, which is strongly discouraged. Chapelle writes, for example, that only an utterly destitute Teda pastoralist will contemplate marriage with a

daughter of a smith and only as a last resort, but, no matter how poor and disgraced, he will never give his own daughter away to a smith (Chapelle 1957: 274). Brandily claims that adulterous sexual relations between the Tubu and the smiths are unheard of both in Tibesti and Borku. The author tells a story of a Tubu woman who fell in love with an Aza man. In this exceptional case, the couple decided to defy their respective families and flee. To that end, however, they had to seek the protection of the French administration to avoid being killed (Brandily 1988: 132). Cultural explanations for this avoidance of marriages with smiths are generally rooted in beliefs regarding the special and presumably dangerous powers of these people, powers associated with

6,6. A joint Haddad and Kreda camp. Camps are very quiet at mid-day because of the burning sun, which makes people look for shade under the trees or stay indoors and also because cattle and goats are mostly grazing elsewhere.

their profession and work with iron, as previously intimated (J. Nicolaisen 1964; Baroin 1991). We did not register similar beliefs in respect to the foraging Haddad, but the very name, 'smith', may well signal a 'no go'. In any case, Haddad smiths in Kanem are strictly endogamous, like those living among the Tubu further to the north and other North African pastoralists. The same is the case for smiths living among many an agricultural society in Central Sudan.

The preceding two sections of this chapter illustrate that politics is a major player in the institutionalization of inequality and ethnic identity. In fact, the rule of the Kanemi and the French relied on an asymmetrical distribution of power and favours among ethnic groups that sustained traditional hierarchical structures and the dominance of some ethnic groups over others. The prevalent custom of endogamy curbed social mobility and ensured that the Haddad remained a self-contained social unit, moreover. Despite these structural barriers, day-to-day contacts between the Haddad and the two dominant groups, the Kreda and the Kanembu respectively, appeared to be relaxed. Daily communication between pastoral and foraging families was free and uncomplicated, for example. Children played all day long with one another in the shared Haddad Kreda camps and Haddad women worked together and danced at festive occasions with Kreda and Kanembu women. Informants told us, however, that the ease with which people interacted across ethnic borders had come only in the wake of the political change of 1960 and the imposed curb on the exploitation of the Haddad and other marginalized groups.

The overall socio-economic situation and the relations of the Haddad Kreda and the Haddad Kanembu with the dominant groups differ, however, because the foraging technology, economic strategies and socio-cultural 'make-up' of the two groups are distinctly different, as previously stated. For this reason we shall deal separately with the Haddad Kreda and the Haddad Kanembu in the following.

those who live among the Kreda, as they were the ones we stayed among. The Kreda numbered an estimated 50,000 to 65,000 at that time. They roamed primarily in the central parts of the Bahr el Ghazal and the northern parts of the Harr, an area of some 20,000 square kilometres between the 13th and 15th parallel and the 16th and 17th meridian. However, migrations bring some clans as far south as to Kharmé and Moïto during the dry winter season, eastwards to Challuf and Am Sugur, and north to Aurak and Salal during the rainy season between July and September.

The Haddad do not follow their Kreda hosts all year round, but stay put in the camp of a Kreda chief during the dry season. Nor do Haddad families or groups change camps to take up residence with different Kreda clans or families during the year. Each Haddad family has developed a close relationship with a particular Kreda family and this is maintained for years under normal circumstances. These ties between the foragers and the pastoralists are advantageous to both parties and no Haddad family had replaced their 'host family' with another one that we heard of. The relationship is asymmetrical, however, in the sense that the Kreda may well do without the Haddad, but the opposite is not necessarily the case.

One easily discerns if a camp is inhabited exclusively by pastoralists or shared by Kreda and Haddad families. The Kreda live in barrel-vaulted tents and pitch these in a long row with the entrance facing due west or west-north-west (cf. Chapter 12). The Haddad do likewise, but their row of tents is placed behind that of the pastoralists. Each Haddad tent is pitched right behind that of the pastoral family to whom the Haddad family has special ties. Between the two rows of tents is an open 'no man's land', a space of some eight to fifteen metres, a playfield for kids, dogs and stray chickens. We stayed in a number of such joint camps, and I shall use my data on one of these to illustrate the nature of Haddad-Kreda relations.

LIVING WITH THE KREDA

The Haddad Kreda share camp sites with pastoral nomads for a good part of the year. They stay primarily with the Kreda, hence the name-tag, but some do camp with the Kecherda, a much smaller Daza-speaking group, others with Arab nomads (cf. Chapter 2). I shall deal only with

6,7. Joint efforts. Three little girls, two Kreda and one Haddad pounding an ox hide belonging to the parents of the Kreda girls as part of the tanning process. The hide has been placed in small depression in the ground and covered with a mixture of cattle urine and plants called lifin to rid it of hair. The girls wear only coloured beads, the elder one also a 'g-string'.

6,8. Tents and belongings are loaded on oxen whenever Kreda pastoralists move camp. The oxen stand quietly, almost indifferent, it seems, while women pile heavy burdens on their backs, or, for that matter when relieving them of the loads, as is the case on this photo.

The camp in question was inhabited by a group of patrilineally related Kreda men of the *Yiria Etama* clan, its core being seven Kreda families who lived together throughout the year. During part of the dry season, these families camped with a number of similar patrilineally related groups. The social 'glue' of these larger camps is invariably kinship, in this case between patrilineally related clan members. The seven tents of the camp in which we stayed were pitched in the usual north-south direction, tent openings facing west. Behind the Kreda tents was a row of four Haddad tents, similarly facing west. The Haddad occupying these stayed with the Kreda for the major part of the year, as their parents and grandparents had done before them. During the dry season, when herds yield little milk and Kreda families get together in large clan-based camps, these Haddad stay with the chief of the *Yiria Etama clan*. The latter lived a settled life at a place called Chakara and functioned as the 'chef du canton'.

The fact that Haddad Kreda families camp with pastoral hosts beg questions as to what interests the two parties have in engaging in these arrangements. When raising this issue with the Haddad, the answer was invariably that they camped with the pastoralists for protection. In view of the historical insurgency in Kanem and the Bahr el Ghazal, including the havoc caused by the Awlad Sliman for decades at the beginning of the 20th century,

6,9. Women moving camp. The Haddad Kreda load tents and belongings on their tiny donkeys, while their Kreda hosts pack their tents on oxen right next to them.

and the ongoing banditry still caused by some pastoralists at the time of our visit, this explanation seemed perfectly understandable. We heard endless stories of Kreda and Tubu cattle thieves, and stayed once in a camp that was raided. We learned of encroachments on Haddad property, in particular of the loss of donkeys, which are vital to hunting. It is evident that the Haddad felt and probably were much less vulnerable to robbery when living with pastoralists, who are both eager to and capable of settling scores in their favour. The frequent migrations offered the Haddad some protection, moreover, against another economic threat, namely government confiscation of their hunting gear. Uncertainty of their whereabouts and the

presence of 'tough' patrons apparently discouraged local law enforcement.

Another benefit of joint camps, in particular for the Haddad was exchanges in kind and labour. The key substance of these can be summarized as follows: A Haddad family usually receives a daily quota of milk from its Kreda 'host', a supplement to the diet that is crucial during the rainy season. At this time of the year, cows yield a good deal of milk, while hunting is rendered difficult and offers the Haddad insufficient returns on their exertions. Most Haddad families own few if any goats or cows. They had been barred from doing so by local custom, a tradition which had been sanctioned by the French administration.

6,10. Haddad families who camp with the Kreda place their tents in a row behind those of pastoralists, each Haddad family pitching its dwelling right behind that of its particular host family.

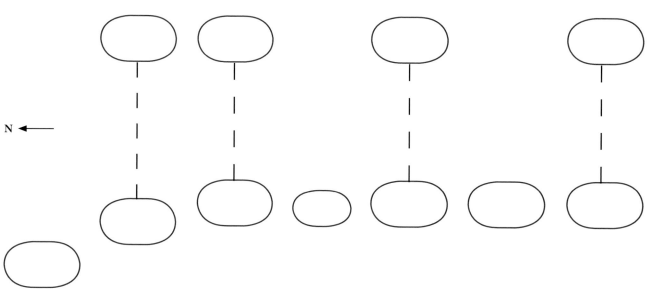

6,11. Diagram showing the lay-out of a joint Haddad and Kreda camp.

Only after Chad had declared its independence and new policies had been introduced, were the Haddad able to acquire livestock. All of the Haddad families staying with the *Yiria Etama* clan declared openly, that they were unable to get through the rainy season without milk from the pastoralists. They had hardly any goats, no cattle and did not grow millet. At that time of the year their subsistence was based solely on milk, the collection of seeds from the *ogu* grass and a rare catch of game. Hunting is severely hampered by the rains, because nets are made from sinew. Most hunters are reluctant to go hunting during the rainy season for this very reason, so as not to ruin their hunting gear.

Every morning and evening we observed young Haddad women or girls pick up bowls of the lukewarm, frothy, slightly smoky milk from their Kreda 'hosts'. Cows are milked by Kreda women only, not by the Haddad, who know little if anything about breeding and milking according to the Kreda. The amount is at the discretion of the Kreda. It is determined by the family's wealth in cattle and may vary, moreover, according to the yield and general needs of the pastoralists. If fodder is plentiful and the cattle yields generously, the Haddad may receive milk from as many as three cows. Is it in short supply and/or the economic situation of the Kreda family strained for one reason or another, the milk will flow less generously. The pastoralists may cut back on the supply for a number of reasons, as experienced by our host family. This Haddad family was simply told by the Kreda to give us their daily ration, as long as we stayed in the camp, a decision of which we learned only after some days and over which we had no say. Luckily we had been sharing the milk with our hosts all along and did of course make up for their hospitality at our departure. The Kreda decree is indicative of the asymmetry of Haddad-Kreda relations, underscoring their uneven economic situation and the authority and higher social status of the Kreda. Moreover, in a not too subtle way, it underscored Kreda dissatisfaction with our decision to camp with the Haddad. This was a blow to their social prerogatives and to their pride, one they did not take lightly and rectified unilaterally by redirecting the flow of milk. The 'gift' put us in a receiver's position of expected gratitude with the added twist of stressing our dependence on their generosity, without which we were barred from getting milk, a basic source of nutrition for us as for the others. To me it was a most illuminating example of how inequality is played out and cemented in subtle ways.

A Kreda pastoral family rarely offers its Haddad counterpart material support apart from milk. Kreda wealth is vested in herds of cattle, small ruminants, horses and sometimes camels. As other pastoralist they slaughter largely on ritual occasions, in dire need of cash or if an animal falls seriously ill and is about to die. When the latter happens and the Kreda are camping too far from the market to get the meat sold, it will be eaten and the Haddad given a share. Both parties claim, however, that neither party is under obligation to present the other with meat. The pastoralists need not share the meat of their goats or cattle if they slaughter, nor do the Haddad feel obliged to present their 'hosts' with game or other kinds of food that they collect. We noticed, nevertheless, that Haddad families made gifts of the tasty *ogu* grass to the Kreda.

In return for the regular supply of milk and an occasional lump of meat, a Haddad family offers its Kreda counterpart a number of services. These are largely performed by Haddad women, not the men. Firstly the Haddad undertake the tanning of hides (cf. Chapter 15: 357-61). This work is highly valued by the Kreda, who do not measure up to the skills of the Haddad in this respect. Moreover, Haddad women do the hair of the Kreda women and teenage girls without any payment. Mending the many fine braids, the female coiffure in this part of the world, is a time-consuming task, and one which calls for dexterity. Occasionally Haddad women do the hair of Kreda women other than those of 'their family' in return of a small gift, perhaps some tea, a luxury rarely available to the Haddad. In fact, Kreda women travel quite a distance to find a Haddad woman who can do their hair and the subsequent payments are highly welcome additions to the household economies of the Haddad.

Relations between Haddad and Kreda families are characterized by a series of material exchanges, as we have seen. The nature of these falls largely within the category characterized by Service as 'balanced reciprocity' (1966: 15). It manifests itself in terms of economic transactions, in physical and political protection of the Haddad by the Kreda, as well as in other forms of social interaction. When a Haddad girl or woman marries, for example, her husband presents the Kreda family to whom the woman and her family are tied with a gift of four spears. Spears

6,12. Donkeys, the hardy beasts without which Haddad hunting would be impossible. A Kreda family is obliged to give a donkey to the man, who marries into the Haddad family with which the Kreda family has a formalized relationship.

are the arms par excellence of Kreda men, as previously mentioned, and the gift can be interpreted as a symbolic acknowledgement by the Haddad of Kreda supremacy and role as protectors. The exchange is reversed when a Kreda girl marries. In that case, her husband presents the Haddad family who lives behind his bride's tent with a donkey, an animal crucial to Haddad hunting for transport. Symbolically, the exchange can also be seen as a symbolic statement on the subordinate social position of the Haddad vis-à-vis the Kreda, who mount grand, expensive and highly valued horses and camels.

The Haddad Kreda engage in the above-mentioned exchanges with the Kreda by choice, a fact they underscored. They are not tied to Kreda households as slaves or in a slave-like position, relegated to a jural position of dependents. The French had declared all Chadian citizens free and equal in 1956, relinquishing restrictions on economic pursuits, such as the traditional ban on Haddad ownership of horses, cattle and small ruminants. Still, the Haddad Kreda, with whom we talked, declared that they were unable to sustain themselves economically without a close symbiotic relationship with Kreda pastoralists. The French colonial power brought general peace and order to Chad, yet was unable to fully control or punish robberies and encroachments in the vast territory under its jurisdiction. The Haddad Kreda were an easy prey and experienced encroachments and economic losses from time to time. Kreda pastoralists offered them protection and hence economic security, as we have seen, a good reason for the Haddad to maintain traditional bonds with their respective Kreda families.

THE HADDAD AND THE KANEMBU

It was far more difficult for us to get an informed picture of relations between the Haddad Kanembu and the agro-pastoral Kanembu due to the more subtle and complex nature of the interaction between the two groups. In spite of the considerable size of the Kanembu, some 65,000 all in all (Le Rouvreur 1962: 77), these people were largely un-studied in 1963, and there was little information available about these people apart from Le Rouvreur's general description in *Sahariens et Sahéliens du Tchad*. It was only natural therefore that we collected data about Kanembu society where ever we went. During long hours on camel back we talked at length with our Kanembu interpreter Bogar Béchir about Kanembu relations with and perceptions of the Haddad. Since then, Conte's PhD thesis, *Marriage Patterns, Political Change and the Perpetuation of Social Inequality [in South Kanem (Chad)]* has become available. I shall draw on this fine dissertation, although I do not share the overall theoretical approach of Conte's structural analysis, which subsumes the Haddad Kanembu - as part and parcel of a composite social stratum called Duu - under an overarching Kanembu sociality in keeping with the political dominance and worldview of the latter.[5]

The way of life of the Kanembu and the Haddad Kanembu displayed many similarities in the 1960s, yet there were major differences in respect to political roles and influence, to subsistence possibilities and strategies, and last but not least terms of relative position within the overall social setting. Socio-cultural and economic barriers such as the strict prohibition against inter-marriage and Kanembu monopoly of cattle sustained the ethnic boundary between the two. Haddad-Kanembu relations were not coloured by symbiosis like Haddad-Kreda interaction, but by separation and usurpation of the Haddad on the part

of the Kanembu, and this state of affairs was sanctioned by and interfaced with the cultural depreciation of the Haddad, as already described.

The Haddad Kanembu and the Kanembu proper do not live together in the same villages or get together on a daily basis, as do the Kreda and Haddad Kreda in their joint camps. Personal interaction between the Kanembu and the Haddad Kanembu is largely confined to neutral ground, so to speak, such as markets or other public spaces. Some relations are sporadic and short-term, as when Haddad products are sold or bartered, be it those of the artisans, foragers or salt extracted by Haddad men from Kanembu owned pits. Beyond these kinds of relations, however, more fundamental bonds exist that are asymmetrical and of long duration. They doom the Haddad to a state of dependency, due to the unequal rights to valuable natural resources such as land and natron pits.

Relations between the Kanembu and the Haddad are, and have always been marked by Kanembu efforts to exert power and extract services, labour and taxes from the Haddad. In this undertaking they have generally been pretty successful, although their dominating role was curbed during the twentieth century. I have already dealt at some length with the historical transformation of polity in Kanem, the abolition of slavery, alterations in the system of taxation and the impact these transformations on relations between the Kanembu and the Haddad. In the following, I shall touch upon other aspects of Kanembu-Haddad sociality, namely the way in which this is shaped by differences in access to resources, by the pervasive hierarchical order and the marriage practices which support the former.

Inequality between the two groups extends to demography. The Kanembu is the largest of the ethnic groups in Kanem proper, totalling some 42,000 souls, while the Haddad number a mere 7,600. Other Kanembu settlements are found in the Bahr el Ghazal and south of Chedra. In some areas the Kanembu are totally dominant, in others the villages of the two peoples are placed in between one another and the Kanembu do not necessarily make up the majority of the population. At N'Guri, for example, the Haddad have held their ground. The Kanembu were still politically dominant in Kanem in the 1960s, however, as they had been during the Caliphate (cf. Chapter 3).

The villages of the Kanembu are located on top of dunes that run in a south-westerly direction, in order to profit from the predominantly north-easterly winds. A village consists on average of some thirty huts that are built in a circle around a public area, each hut at a distance of some 10 to 20 metres to the next one. The Kanembu are devout Muslims and space is set aside in the circular central area for a 'mosque', usually consisting of a simple roof of mats for shade and a fence of thorny branches to keep out livestock. Haddad Kanembu villages have much less of a structure. The huts are spread out and situated at quite some distance from one another. It struck me that even from the height of the camel's back villages were often hard to locate and demarcate for this very reason, in particular if the maize was growing well. I did not come across places for worship in Haddad Kanembu villages, although they may well exist. Prayers were said within the private family space, i.e. on a mat placed in a corner of the courtyard.

The Kanembu support themselves by a mixture of agriculture and animal husbandry. They grow millet and sorghum as well as a number of other crops, and they raise cattle and small ruminants. The Kanembu are also famous horse-breeders, and they own camels and donkeys as well as chickens. The contribution of the latter to their diet is minimal, however. Being truly French, Le Rouvreur observes that: "... these animals are better adapted to running than to the cooking pot" (Le Rouvreur 1962: 100). The size of Kanembu herds of cattle, goats and sheep is difficult to assess. Taxes are levied according to the number of heads, and families are therefore eager to avoid any counting of their herds, as are pastoralists.[6] The Kanembu neither hunt nor fish, but leave these subsistence activities to the Haddad, and, in the latter case also to the Yedina, from whom the Kanembu purchase these food items (Le Rouvreur 1962: 102).

In the 1960s, the Haddad Kanembu relied on many of the same subsistence activities as the Kanembu proper, as described in chapter seven. This had not been the case at the beginning of the 20th century, when game was abundant in numbers and species, as vividly described by Boyd Alexander 1907: 298). The ensuing reduction in wildlife forced the Haddad Kanembu to engage ever more actively in agriculture, however. What distinguished Haddad Kanembu economy from that of the Kanembu proper at the time of our fieldwork was the lack of access of the Haddad to land suitable for water-fed agriculture, ownership of cattle and rights in natron fields. These unequal conditions were intimately linked to the overall hierarchical nature of Kanemese sociality.

Natural resources are fairly favourable in Kanem compared to those available to Sahelien groups elsewhere in West Africa. There is suitable soil for the growing of millet, wadis that lend themselves to water-fed cultivation for most of the year and extended pastures for the raising of cattle and small ruminants. Yet, the resources were and are not equally distributed, and the economic situation of most agriculturalists is generally precarious (Le Rouvreur 1962: 95-6). In fact, approximately three quarters of the Kanembu population and an even larger proportion of the Haddad Kanembu are poor, dependent agriculturalists who succeed in accumulating little if any surplus as a result of their labour. This is due to systematic expropriation of labour and produce in the framework of institutionalised hierarchical relationships (cf. Conte 1983a: 38-9).

Land rights are largely held collectively in Kanem. A man's right to usage of land is determined by patrilineal descent and on an effective cultivation of the plots he is allotted, or these revert to the lineage after a two-year lapse. A group's wealth in land is not necessarily proportional to its population, however (ibid. 107). All clans, including those of the Haddad Kanembu, generally have adequate access to land for growing millet, but only few clans possess wadi land suitable for water-fed cultivation and these stretches are largely in the hands of the Kanembu. Agriculturalists rely on the latter and on complementary husbandry to secure economic autonomy, however, and in both respects the Haddad are at a loss. Haddad groups with inadequate resources in land are forced, if possible, to engage in collective or, subsidiarily, individual share-cropping arrangements with more powerful clans, and these are largely Kanembu. The share-cropping arrangements were formalized under a *morfei* or share-cropping contract, whereby the dependent handed over half of his harvest, exclusive of personal and other taxes to be taken from the remaining produce. Such arrangements were not considered appropriate among members of the same patrilineage, Conte claims, yet the provision: "... did not exclude unequal redistribution of tax revenues and levies

6,13. Haddad woman churning butter for her Kreda hosts. The milk is stored for the night before churning in a huge calabash suspended from the bough of an acacia tree.

6,14. Haddad woman braiding the hair of a relative late one afternoon. Coiffure is a specialty of Haddad women and one they extend to Kreda women as part of the exchanges that bind Kreda and Haddad families together.

in kind between household heads of lineages presumed to exercise collective control over all lineage lands including those rented out to non-members of the patrilineage" (ibid. 39).[7][8]

The unequal economic opportunities for groups and individuals are closely interwoven with the overall hierarchical organization of Kanembu society, as just intimated. In pre-colonial times this was founded upon distinctions between nobles and commoners as well as between freemen and slaves. According to Conte, however, a third division was one between the Kanembu proper and the

Duu. He defines the latter as a composite and hereditary social stratum that includes all craftsmen and their kin in addition to the descendants of hunter groups and many non-craftsmen descended from or socially assimilated into the Kanembu. Also 'captive elements' were traditionally included in the stratum. The craftsmen are integrated into the Duu stratum, irrespective of their cultural affiliations, in such a way that all professional groups are organized as specialised subordinate lineages practising subsistence agriculture and one or more trades but excluded from cattle husbandry. The artisanal functions of the greater part of the small and dispersed Duu lineage groups waned during the colonial period and these people were subsequently integrated economically but not socially into a proportionately expanding mass of poor dependent cultivators, which constituted the majority of Kanem's population (ibid. 167-8;). The formation of the Duu stratum is thus quite complex, ethnographically speaking. It is not defined in ethnic terms as a distinction between the Haddad Kanembu and the Kanembu proper, but as far more encompassing.

Each of the above-mentioned categories included both masters and dependents, Conte claims. The Kanembu proper were and remain all freemen. A minority were masters or collectors of tribute, a status largely determined by genealogical position. The vast majority of the Kanembu proper were tributaries, however. The Duu were also freemen, a minority even 'masters', but only unto their own 'kind' and a few very lowly Kanembu (Conte 1983a: 42). However, although the Duu were all freemen both in the 19th century and at the arrival of the French, in practice they shared in their majority the socio-economic status of the slaves. Slavery was hereditary, but not necessarily perpetual, whereas the status of Duu or Kanembu noble or commoner was both hereditary and perpetual (ibid. pp. 73-4). The composition and economic role of the Duu has varied over time inter alia due to the integration of non-specialised immigrants of low status and the abandoning of their trades by many artisans and their progressive turn to agro-pastoralism, which makes them hardly distinguishable from the Kanembu *maskin,* Conte argues. The distinction between the Kanembu proper and the Duu has been maintained by a strict prohibition against intermarriage (ibid. p. 89).

With the partial exception of four politically autonomous Haddad lineages of the N'Guri and Yalita area, the Haddad are largely political and economic vassals of the Kanembu. This state of affairs manifest itself in terms of tribute levying and relative standard of living, Conte argues (1979:281). Duu clans and lineages are generally smaller and weaker than those of the Kanembu. In the 1960s, the majority of them comprised but two or three small local communities and few of them exercised corporate control over sufficient land resources to be economically autonomous (ibid. 1983a: 168). Prior to the statuary order of 1956, the majority of the Duu/Haddad Kanembu were under obligation to part with half their agricultural produce

to Kanembu chiefs and/or heads of aristocratic lineages, we were told. Conte argues that: "... the socio-economic advances they could realise were bound by the fact that their status was not only hereditary but perpetual. The economic handicaps attached to their condition precluded under many circumstances, the possession and bequest of, or access to important capital resources including reproductive cattle stock" (1983a: 40). In Conte's view, this exclusion from ownership or access to adequate means of production for the pursuit of a complementary agro-pastoral way of life appears to be the main reason for the perpetuation of Duu/Haddad Kanembu subordination in spite of the high economic value and the indispensable nature of their production and services. Kanembu discourse justifies this unequal access to and distribution of economic goods, as we have heard. It postulates: "... a difference of 'nature' and quality between Duu and non-Duu, despite linguistic and cultural similarities" (Conte 1983a: 43).

In his analysis of Kanemi society Conte has looked into the structural features which sustain the social discrepancy between the Kanembu proper and the Duu. He argues convincingly that: " ... the *absolute* character of the Duu/Kanembu opposition, as contrasted with the *relative* character of the former division between slave and freeman suggests that the historical persistence of the Duu condition beyond that of slavery ideologically and economically guarantees against the disappearance of the concept of 'natural' inequality upon which the Kanembu political and social stratification systems are founded. The relegation of certain categories of subordinate immigrants into the widening Duu stratum and other low status groups preserves Kanembu 'purity' while offering a road for political expansion through the maintenance and extension of tributary relationships" (1983a: 90-1).

The social and cultural distinctions by means of which the Kanembu create their identity were discussed already by Carbou. He looked for an explanation in their violent past: "They have been conquered by different rulers: Boulala, Toundjour, Dalatoua, Ouadaïs and Oulad Sliman. They have been pressured and looted without mercy for centuries. Yet, in spite of this they have retained a memory of a role once played as successors of the king of Sêf. They considered themselves a superior race which counts among its ancestors illustrious warriors. This idea enables them to maintain a prejudice quite strangely against all oc-

6,15. Kanembu women arrive at the market at Baga Sola with goods for sale. They have mounted oxen of the special Lake Chad breed, the so-called kuri cattle. Photo K.M. Fig. 12,1; 3.4.1954.

cupations more or less which are not genuinely Kanembu, and this, just as with the difference in armament, allows them to set apart the Ḥaddâd, as it is impossible in other ways to distinguish between the two populations, as they have the same appearance and language. This is why it is considered disgraceful for a Kanembu to carry out dyeing, to weave gabag (i.e. the six by eight centimetre-long bands which serve as a medium of exchange in the country), to skin animals which have had their throats cut, to be armed

with bow and arrow, etc" (Carbou 1912, I: 40; IN transl.).

The Haddad know all too well the low esteem in which they are held by the dominant Kanembu. They continue to be stigmatized, set apart by prohibitions on intermarriage and relegated to a marginal political position. They have seen their mode of life curbed by a drastic decrease in game over the past century and their economic possibilities curbed by the Kanembu and the French colonial power. All of this they share with most indigenous peoples.

NOTES

1. This is at the very core of the organization of the prominent pastoral societies in West Africa, from the Maures and Tuareg to the west of Kanem and the Bahr el Ghazal, the Tubu to the north and the Zaghawa to the east. Tuareg society, for one, encompasses both nobility, vassals and a slave or former slave population, and all of these pastoral groups exploit and or attempt to ensure dependants to cultivate the Saharan oases and work at salt mines at Bilma, Amadror, Taoudeni and other pits, as already described.

2. It will be recalled that the Duu are defined by Conte as: "a composite social stratum which includes all craftsmen and their kin in addition to the descendants of hunter groups [read Haddad Kanembu - IN] and many non-craftsmen descended from or socially assimilated to the Kanembu" (Conte 1983a: 30).

3. At Teteya, the chief of the Rea, M'bodu Bugar was accused of theft by the French and had to be replaced by his nephew (Conte 1983b: 136).

4. Conte tells that he:"... met several Duu *kindira* (hunter-diviners) who were affranchised descendants of Bornuan Muslims, some of whom had passed through pagan hands at the close of the 19th century," adding that:"... Duu status here represents a form of partial emancipation for 'worthy' dependants" (Conte 1983a: 76).

5 Conte's thesis is a comparative study of marriage patterns and lineage organization among the Kanembu with particular reference to the way in which endogamy and exogamy are linked to mechanisms of economic and political domination (Conte 1983a: 1). Kanembu-Haddad relations are analyzed within this frame. Empirical data on the latter stem primarily from the Rea, a Duu clan of 1,314 members controlling 23 small villages concentrated in South Kanem's political centre, just south of N'Guri (Conte 1983a: 26). In explaining his methodological considerations for selecting the Rea for quantitative data collection to the exclusion of four major Duu clans, Conte writes that the Darka, the most powerful of the pre-colonial Duu groups were entangled in sub-clan hostilities at the time of his fieldwork, a fact that he found would render data collection difficult; the Adia and Bara clans were geographically dispersed throughout the Bahr el Ghazal and *'distanced from the political process in Kanem's core'* [italics IN]; similarly "...the Dieri,

a former semi-nomadic hunter group, presented the *disadvantage of residing in the periphery and being somewhat marginal to the political life of Kanembu society* [italics IN]. The Rea clan, on the other hand was concentrated in South Kanem's political centre, had a manageable and sufficient size for basic statistical analysis and was constantly interacting with the most powerful Kanembu clans (Conte 1983a: 220). This choice clearly cements Conte's theoretical vantage point that the Duu per definition, so to say, constituted but a stratum of Kanembu society. Ethnographic data on groups that were peripheral to Kanembu polity and hence by implication led 'a life on their own' were not central to the study. Elsewhere these very clans are identified as 'auchtotones', i.e. indigenous and described as semi-nomadic hunters (Conte 1986: 133). Conte's focus on the Rea clan through some light on why his view of the Haddad Kanembu/Duu offer a different but complementary picture of the Haddad to the one adopted in this expose.

Conte presents a wealth of ethnographic information and insights into the overall historical changes of Kanemi sociality, largely built on his wide-based survey technique. He deals with the Haddad Kanembu in an article entitled *La dynamique de l'alliance parmi les chasseurs sédentarisés Duu Rea du Sud-Kanem (Tchad)*, 1986. In this the sedentarized Duu [read Haddad, IN] are described as an indigenous group, traditionally supporting itself by hunting and known by the name of Danoa, referring to the bow and arrow by means of which they made a living, as already mentioned. But let us take a closer look at the Kanembu and Conte's description of Haddad-Kanembu relations.

6. Le Rouvreur estimates that the Kanembu of the Mao, Bol, Massakory and Mussoro districts, with a total population of some 71,000, had no less than 175,000 zebu, 15,000 donkeys, 4,000 horses, 3,350 camels and 102,000 goats and sheep (Le Rouvreur 1962: 98).

7. Conte distinguishes between:"... a) autonomous clans and lineages which are territorially based in spite of differing degrees of geographical dispersion, and b) named, genealogically defined groups which lack autonomous control over a territorial basis." According to him, the Duu stratum [read Haddad Kanembu, IN]

includes groups of both types, but that of the Kanembu comprise larger clans which again exhibit complex forms of internal stratification. It is possible, therefore to distinguish:" ... autonomous from dependent lineages within wider clans, as well as aristocrats and dependents, within each constituent segment, whether autonomous or not" (Conte 1983a: 43). Still, rules of prescribed marriage prevent unions between Duu and Kanembu and this perpetuates cultural and social differentiation between the two groups. "Thus, while political integration of the Duu into Kanembu society is total thanks to the extension of the Kanembu lineage system, the social resolution of the Duu/non-Duu opposition, in contrast to that of the freeman-slave division, has been rendered impossible", Conte argues (1983a: 45). The Kanembu ideology of hierarchization of social strata and of clans and lineages within each stratum, masks the structural opposition between autonomous and dependent Duu groups while instituting a socio-economically fallacious but politically advantageous distinction between autonomous Duu and Kanembu of all classes," Conte claims (1983a: 44).

8. These factors did also prevent an effective unification of poor, landless Kanembu and the poor Duu, in Conte's view (1983b: 159-60).

7:

7: MAKING A LIVING

Adaptable subsistence strategies have been critical in Kanem and Bahr el Ghazal over time as well as in response to micro-climatic conditions and differences in the soil quality. Considerable variance in rainfall between the northern and southern parts and hence in vegetation sets the stage for pastoralists, agro-pastoralists and foragers alike, imposing flexibility and adaptability that has to go hand in hand with fluctuating socio-political conditions. Although camel and livestock breeding dominate in the north and the growing of millet, durra and maize in the south, most of the ethnic groups rely on both farming and livestock – but to a varying degree. In the northern parts of Kanem, one finds people who do little if any farming such as, for example, the three Kecherda clans: the Medema, Sakerda and Sannakora. They graze their camels north of the 15th parallel on the sandy Solia plateau from October to June, moving their camps to the Bahr el Ghazal only during the rainy season. A similar mode of existence prevails among the eastern Kecherda and the Hassauna Arabs in the sparsely populated plains of Manga land. But most ethnic groups in Kanem and Bahr el Ghazal apply a more diversified subsistence strategy. This is the case for the two dominant groups, the Kreda, who migrate with their herds of cattle for most of the year yet also engage in some farming, and the sedentary Kanembu, who apply the opposite strategy in relying primarily on the growing of millet and durra while also, if at all possible, keeping some cattle and herds of small ruminants. Also the Haddad gain a living by applying various economic strategies, both those who camp with Kreda pastoralists and hunt with nets and those who live in beehive huts in hamlets like the Kanembu and supplement their diet and income by hunting in disguise with bow and arrow.

Kanem and Bahr el Ghazal repeatedly face shorter and longer periods of drought, as previously noted. These affect the ecosystem, killing game and livestock, laying barren millet and durra fields and pitching pastoralists and sedentary peoples against one another. At times the droughts uproot people, forcing them from their homelands and/or to abandon established migratory patterns. North-western Kanem prospered from long-distance transhumance and intensive livestock breeding in 1851, when Heinrich Barth in vain tried to reach Mao and the eastern shores of Lake Chad. This was at the onset of what was going to be four decades of abundant rains, and Barth saw flocks of about a thousand heads of cattle and estimated that the Kanembu herds of the neighbourhood numbered some 11,000 head (cf. Barth 1857, II: 416-17). Yet, at the time of the French arrival at the turn of the century there was virtually no cattle in the region due to ten years of rapid decrease in precipitation and added periods of civil strife, the devastating effects of cattle plague and near the Lake also trypanosomiasis (Le Rouvreur 1962: 88, 89, 92; Conte 1991: 229). The situation improved only to deteriorate once again. The below-average rainfall which began in 1967 reached an all-time low in 1972-73. It continued to be at the low end from 1975 up to the early 1980s causing a severe toll on man and beast in Kanem, desiccating wells and ponds, decimating herds and wildlife and damaging the vegetation.

However, factors other than precipitation shape the subsistence strategies of the people of Kanem. Colonial policies, economic incentives and/or the lack of these are major players as well. To the Haddad, the presence of game has evidently been particularly pertinent. After World War II the wildlife came under increased pressure, however, due to the hunting of the French military, increased access to guns in the region and the general political instability - if not outright civil war. That war and the availability of automatic weapons is a deadly cocktail for game is well known – one needs only to think of Mozambique, where the war in the beginning of the 1990s seriously decimated and/or caused the complete extinction of a large number of species throughout the country. A reduction in wildlife happens the more easily in an open landscape like the Kanemese, which offers few hideouts for gazelle and antelope, the most important game of the Haddad. Both species are the more vulnerable, because they show little fear of motor vehicles. The most serious threat to the continued existence of Haddad foraging, however, was the ban on indigenous hunting introduced by the French shortly after World War II and maintained by the Chadian government. In fact, game was so scarce in the 1960s, that it was becoming difficult for Haddad families to rely solely on hunting and foraging. Although we lack information about the current state of affairs, it is likely that the situation of Haddad families has grown only more precarious and that it may become impossible for them to continue their age-old trade in the 21st century.

At the time of our visit, however, the Haddad Kreda were still largely relying on hunting with nets, but agriculture was gaining ground, in particular the growing of millet. None of the families we encountered had livestock. There seem to be several reasons for this, apart from lack of skills in husbandry and insufficient capital for investment, one being a tacit acceptance of the French policy, which had prohibited the Haddad from owning livestock. None of the Haddad living among pastoralists seems to have engaged in husbandry prior to World War II. Carbou offers no documentation that this should have been the case, for example.[1] Whether the ban on ownership of livestock was ever rigorously maintained by the French or the Chadian authorities is difficult to assess, of course, but the existence of the policy was never questioned by pastoralists or by the Haddad themselves. Rather, it was tacitly endorsed by a local norm that allowed non-Haddad to appropriate livestock freely from the Haddad were cattle or small ruminants found in their possession. We met a few Haddad families, who had purchased goats, but the only domestic

animals of true significance for the Haddad Kreda were donkeys. These were used not only for the transport of tents and belongings when moving camp and in daily life to carry water, but most importantly to transport men and children and their nets on hunting expeditions.

The decimation of wildlife during the first part of the 20th century, the prohibition on ownership by the Haddad of livestock and the ban on hunting imposed by the French and, later, the Chadian government had also a major impact on Haddad Kanembu subsistence strategies. Pressure on the wildlife was generally heavier in Kanem as this region was more densely populated than the Bahr el Ghazal. The Haddad Kanembu were also more susceptible to government control than the nomadic Haddad Kreda, as they were settled in hamlets. In spite of its illegality, however, hunting was still pursued, in particular by those Haddad who lived in the more remote hamlets. Yet, fear of the Gendarmerie and the confiscation of hunting implements had put a damper on hunting pursuits, also among the Haddad Kanembu families who had turned recently to the use of nets. Even so, we encountered families, in particular around Chedra, to whom hunting with bow and arrow was economically significant. At N'Guri, the core area of most Haddad Kanembu, hunting had dwindled on the other hand. Families were deploring this fact and blaming the government for its ban on their age-old trade. Game was a welcome and necessary supplement to an otherwise largely vegetarian diet, they claimed, and dried meat and hides an important source of cash income which they increasingly had to do without.

Most Haddad Kanembu families relied heavily on agriculture, primarily the growing of millet and sorghum. Some kept a few goats and sheep and/or heads of cattle. The latter does not hold cultural value as among the Kanembu, where it is intimately linked to the customary payment of bridewealth, a tradition not shared by the Haddad Kanembu. The possession of herds is for the privileged only, due in part to the fact that French colonialism favoured this state of affairs through its taxation policy.

7,1. Young Kreda woman milking a cow. Its hind leg has been tied with a rope to prevent it from kicking away flies while being milked. Some of the milk will be offered to the Haddad family living behind her tent.

This discriminated against small herders, who had no income from other sources and, moreover, paid their taxes through local notables or their at times corrupt representatives (cf. Conte 1983a: 167). Still, husbandry appeared to be on a limited rise among the Haddad Kanembu, but so were agricultural activities.

But let us take a closer view at the prevalent subsistence activities of the Kreda with whom the Haddad coexist and/or are closely linked economically and politically. We shall examine the activities of the Kreda and the economic niches made available to the Haddad Kreda by the pastoralists. Then we shall turn to the agricultural endeavours of the Haddad Kanembu which resemble the Kanembu practice, although the subsistence systems of the two groups are at variance due i.a. to the unequal access to fertile land. Subsequently, the very hunting and foraging activities of the two Haddad groups will be described.

KREDA PASTORALISM AND HADDAD NICHES

The middle ranges of the Bahr el Ghazal and adjacent plains, which we criss-crossed on camel-back in 1963, are the grazing grounds of immense herds of cattle and small ruminants and the home of thousands of donkeys, fine riding horses and some camels. Most of these belong to pastoralists, like the Kreda, the largest of Kanem's many pastoral groups. We had not set out to study these proud people, as already mentioned, the aim of our endeavours being to prepare ourselves for future research among the Haddad. As it happened, however, we ended up spending quite some time with these pastoralists. We spent nights in pure Kreda camps and lived next to them when staying with the Haddad. Yet, the unwritten ethical code of not grazing another anthropologist's pasture made us refrain from collecting systematic data about the Kreda, because

7,2. Annual pastures at the Bahr el Ghazal in the summer of 1966.

Colonel Chapelle had intimated that he intended to pursue studies among these people. However, we could not help but observe daily life, learn about their society and values, while profiting from their hospitality.

As we tracked down Haddad Kreda families, we found that they all lived and migrated with Kreda pastoralists. This implied that decisions regarding the location of camps and the routes and duration of migration were decided upon by the Kreda. They did not take into account the trade of the Haddad, i.e. the presence, availability and accessibility of game. Rather, the Haddad had to carry out their trade wherever the pastoralists chose to camp. By implication, the hunting grounds were dotted with grazing cattle in many places. The Haddad expressed no concern that cattle and game were competing about the same ecological niches, however. Modern research in East Africa has also demonstrated that this is need not be the case, as the domestic and wild species may well browse on different plant and tree species. I am not able to say whether this is the case in Kanem and Bahr el Ghazal, but only remark that the very number of people and cattle did disturb the game, according to the Haddad.

The Haddad and the Kreda have developed a symbiotic relationship of economic and political significance to both parties, and they share certain cultural values and customs. The socio-economic, political and cultural situation of the Haddad cannot be understood, in fact, without taking the Kreda way of life into consideration. Relations between the two groups are primarily forged between individual families, in such a way that closely related Haddad families migrate with the same group of Kreda pastoralists, each Haddad family serving and cooperating with a specific Kreda ditto for most of the year. The social bond between families manifests itself in the spatial lay-out of camps, Haddad families pitching their tents directly behind those of their Kreda 'masters', as already mentioned. Due to this intimate relationship, it is necessary to look briefly into the livelihood of the Kreda to understand the economic niches available to the Haddad. At a later point, we shall return to the specific services offered by the Haddad to their 'host' families.

In the 1960s there were still Kreda families who did not engage in any form of cultivation but relied entirely on their large herds of zebu and small ruminants for their subsistence. Families who had begun to grow millet in the 1950s were changing their pattern of migration to accom-

7,3. Young Kreda woman with her child. Hadad nets in the background.

modate this new economic activity. During sowing and harvesting time they had also begun to stay in conical huts similar to those of the Kanembu *(cf. Figs. 12,15)*. This major change in the subsistence pattern of the Kreda had not involved the Haddad Kreda, in the sense that we heard of no Haddad family engaged in the cultivation of the fields of their 'hosts'. Rather, the Kreda relied on work parties consisting of fellow Kreda for major work loads, in particular sowing. When the owner has cleared and burned the plot, he calls upon relatives and passes the word that whoever is interested will be most welcome to join in. In return for the labour devoted to the task, the owner provides solid meals that even entail slaughtering a goat or sheep. Harvesting, on the other hand, is considered a relatively easy load that does not necessitate work parties but can be carried out by the owner and his family.

The Kreda are among the most mobile of the pastoralists of the Bahr el Ghazal. What keeps them on the move is a wish to cut short the hardships of the dry season - when they are forced to be near wells to draw water for the herds. For this reason they migrate southwards in the beginning of June to meet the rains. Just north of Kanem at the fringes of the desert a proper rainy season does not occur, while the monsoon is of longer duration just south of Kanem, extending a good four months. In the heartland of Kreda country, the lower and middle ranges of the Bahr el Ghazal and adjacent areas the rainy season lasts about three months, the dry one almost nine. The economic strategies of the Kreda are constrained by this overall environmental setting. In fact, their way of life oscillates in tune with the length and nature of the five seasons categorized by the Kreda. These are: *boro,* the dry season, during which the Kreda live in large tents, rarely move camp and graze their cattle in the vicinity. This is the time when cows yield very little milk and the Haddad are forced to find other means to survive. Most of them will leave their host families during this period to take up residence with a settled Kreda chief; *archat i.e.* the time of tornadoes, which precedes the actual monsoon rains. During this period unmarried men and young couples move south at a rapid pace with the cattle, only being en route for two to six days, and taking shelter in small tents. Meanwhile adult couples look after the goats, sheep and camels; then at the beginning of *n'guélé,* the rainy season, the cattle is driven north again to the areas where families grow millet. Towards *aoulai,* the end of the rainy season, the livestock is brought to graze in areas rich in ponds until the millet can be harvested. This is a time of bounty, leisure and festivity, of young people getting married. The large tents are pitched again by the women, milk is plentiful, the landscape covered by annual grasses for the cattle to browse and the herds can be guarded by only a few herders. Gradually, as *douso* sets in, i.e. the three cold months of the winter, the camps are slowly but surely moved towards the traditional grazing grounds of the dry season (Clanet 1977: 250, 253).

The Bahr el Ghazal is well suited for livestock-breeding, as already intimated. If one takes a look at Le Rouvreur's

map over the distribution of livestock in northern Chad, it becomes clear that nowhere is the livestock-man ratio higher than here, in particular for cows and horses. At the time of our fieldwork, the number of cows in Bahr el Ghazal was said to be 182,000 head, the population about 61,000 (Le Rouvreur 1962: 67-71, maps 17-21; Chapelle 1957: 408). Chapelle estimates further that a Kreda household of five persons (comprising a couple with two children and a senior family member) has an average of seventeen cows, twelve goats or sheep, one horse or camel and a donkey (Chapelle 1957: 217). However, our findings indicate that Le Rouvreur's and Chapelle's estimates were on the low side, as is often the case with statistics on ownership of stock, not least when the collector of information is a government officer. No pastoralist in his right mind discloses freely the size of his herd to administrators, suspecting that such data will be used for taxation purposes. Our estimate was 30-50 head of cattle for most households, and we met a few individuals who owned some hundred heads – indeed, it was said about very rich Kreda that they owned more than a thousand. Statistics published for the Kanem and Lake Chad préfectures, which prior to the 1969-73 drought had a combined population of some 323,000 individuals, records approximately 1,370,000 head of cattle, 900,000 sheep and goats, 80,000 donkeys, 62,000 camels, and 25,000 horses (Conte 1991: 229), implying a human-cattle ratio of 1:40. According to Decalo, Chad had the biggest herds of cattle in Africa until the droughts set in, with an estimated 4.7 million head in 1972 (Decalo 1977: 74). The Chadian veterinary service estimated the 1969 cattle population in the Kanem préfecture alone to be 1,250,000 head. In 1974, after the onset of the droughts, the World Bank report estimates that there were 1,100,000 bovines (Conte 1991: 245).[2]

Kreda economy is based on the sale of butter, cattle, small ruminants and some millet. The income is used largely to buy grain, tea, salt and clothes. One does not find numerous, small markets to serve these purposes, due to the fact that the Bahr el Ghazal is inhabited largely by pastoralists. There is no shortage of beasts of burden among these: oxen, donkeys and camels and as there are few agriculturalists in the area, there is no possibility for the exchange of produce between pastoral and sedentary people. The market that primarily serves the Kreda is the one at Mussoro, but this is sizeable and can be compared to the huge one at Abéché to the east, which they also frequent. Likewise they trade at Am Djéména, Méchiméré and Massakory. The former two are far from any government administration and hence control, and therefore wide open to the theft of cattle, something which the Kreda appreciate, according to Le Rouvreur. "Where is the Kreda who has not stolen at least one cow," as he remarks (Le Rouvreur 1962: 281-2). Kreda trading expeditions usually last about two weeks. They will take three to four oxen, sell one and purchase whatever they need. One should not be deceived by the look of hundreds of oxen at the market place, however, for, as Le Rouvreur reminds us, a family may well own a hundred head, but they still sell only about one nice ox, an old cow and bull calf and, as a rare exception, a heifer per year. The animals are either slaughtered on the spot and the meat sent to Fort-Lamy, or the oxen are herded by middlemen to markets in Nigeria.

Cattle

The Kreda breed a variety of domestic stock: cattle, goats, sheep, camels, donkeys and horses, but also dogs, cats and fowl are found in the camps. Although many families grow millet during the rainy season, it is the herds that are of value to them. The Kreda are cattle-breeders by inclination and heart. To possess a huge herd is the ultimate goal in life for a Kreda, not only for the wealth and the social prestige that comes with it but because cattle occupy a unique and singular place in Kreda culture. Cattle are the passion of the Kreda - it is a simple as that. Our interpreter, a Kanembu,

7,4. Joint Haddad and Kreda camp. Horses are highly valued by the pastoralists. The Kreda breed very fine horses and export a good deal of these to northern Nigeria, where they are used for polo.

7,5. Ox of the humpless *Kuri* breed. The rein has a cord that goes through the ox's pierced nostrils. The rein is tied behind the horns of the animal.

sometimes commented on the love the Kreda had for their cows, remarking that 'all the Kreda think about is cattle', or that 'a Kreda values his cattle even higher than his wife'. We were reminded again and again of E.E. Evans-Pritchard's fine description of the relationship between the Nuer and their cattle, and there can be little doubt that a very similar bond existed between the Kreda and their beloved cows (Evans-Pritchard 1949: 16-50). Husbandry was of particular interest to Johannes, one kindled during his studies of Tuareg pastoralism. It did not leave him in Kanem, and the ensuing description draws on his notes and writings (Nicolaisen 1964, 1978).

Cattle are of significance to Kreda subsistence in multiple ways. They use oxen when migrating, loading the bulky mat tents, household utensils etc. on their backs. Donkeys may take their place if a household is short of oxen, i.e. castrated bulls. The animals are guided by means of a rein attached to their pierced nostrils. Riding saddles are not in use. If a Kreda wants to mount an ox, a piece of skin or a blanket is placed across the animal's back. When tents and other items are to be transported, the pastoralists make use of a simple cushion-saddle consisting of two 'cylinders' made of rags or grass that are placed on each side of the back of the animal and held together by cords running across this. Cattle are rarely slaughtered even by families with large herds. As a rule, animals are killed only if suffering from incurable diseases or if they are victims of an accident. Cattle may be sold to professional butchers at village markets, if a family needs a substantial amount of money, for example to pay taxes, buy costly items and/or

7,6. *Kuri* cattle, a breed mainly kept by the Yedina and other settled people near lake Chad, but also found occasionally among the Kreda. Fig. 6,2; 20.4.1954.

stock up provisions. It is said, however, that if a Kreda has to sell some of his cattle to meet expenses, he will make an effort to purchase an equal number of calves, so as not to diminish the size of his herd.

There are three distinct breeds of cattle in Kanem and the Bahr el Ghazal, according to Le Rouvreur: a) a breed named the 'Arab Zebu', which is the one found among the Kreda. It resembles the breed widespread among other Sahelien pastoralists including the southern Tuareg, with its fairly short horns and a hump which is not always developed as in other types of Zebu cattle; b) the Fulani breed also known as the M'Bororo Sebu which is widespread among the Fulani of western Africa;[3] c) the so-called *Kuri* cattle, which are endemic to northern Chad.[4] We find a similar constellation of coexisting cattle breeds in East Africa, where the hump-

less long-horned species of cattle characteristic e.g. of the 'Lowland Savanna Pastoral Neolitic 3000 BC', preceded the Asiatic humped Zebu and the so-called Sanja cattle (cf. Lamphear 1986: 229; David 1983: 72, 76, 94).

Cattle-breeding is not governed by economic considerations in a narrow sense among the Kreda. The possession of a large herd lends prestige to its owner, as just mentioned and barren cows are not necessarily disposed of for that reason. The same holds for old and excess bulls. Decisions to keep such animals may well cause problems, apart from tying up 'capital'. It may happen that bulls fight over cows in heat, with the result that a combatant may get so badly wounded that it has to be slaughtered. Under normal circumstances, however, bulls are gentle and do not attack humans. I have been sitting at a camp

7,7. Haddad boy milking a cow for his Kreda hosts. The plaited milch bowl is held between the knees. Note the rope around the hind legs of the cow to prevent it from moving during the milking.

7,8. Plaited bowl used for milking. Cat. no. 69. Photo J.K.

7,9. A halter with acacia thorns inserted into a nose-rope. The device is used by the Kreda to prevent calves and foals from suckling. Cat. no. 91. Photo J.K.

fire many an evening with one or more of these impressive animals leaning above me, because bonfires keep insects and flies at bay and, presumably, because they like company. Being such keen breeders of cattle, perhaps the most eager ones among all of the pastoralists of Chad, we were surprised to find few 'rational' stock-breeding practices such as systematic regulation of the copulation of cattle, goats or sheep. Castration, for example, seems to be rare and done only to obtain strong and docile animals for transportation and riding. Stallions are rarely gelded, nor are jackasses, rams or he-goats. When performed, the scrotum is opened with a knife to extract the spermatic cords. Although some old and excess bulls may be kept, the herds nevertheless largely consist of milch-cows and young animals.

A considerable number of milk-yielding cows are the alpha and omega of Kreda existence. If pastures are plentiful, families may be able to subsist largely on milk, although vegetables invariably form part of the daily diet. It is possible to live on milk for weeks and months on end, but 'the stomach gets tired' if you get only milk, as the pastoralists sometimes say. During the dry season and, in particular, towards the end of this when the weather is very hot, cows yield little or no milk at all and vegetable food attains a correspondingly greater significance. Because milk is crucial to Kreda nutrition, young animals are not allowed to suckle mother animals unrestrictedly, but are kept in the camps, those of cows, sheep and goats tethered to poles by a cord around their necks, those of camels and mares by a cord attached to a foreleg. When calves are allowed to roam with the mother cows, they are equipped with a muzzle of fibres or made from wood, string and acacia thorns that will hurt the udder of the mother cow should the calf attempt to suckle (cf. Cat. Nos. 89, 90 & 91). This device is also used for camel calves (cf. Baroin 1972: 8) and sometimes for weaning foals that are a nuisance to the mares. There may be other weaning devices, but we failed to register methods other than those mentioned (for further details on Kreda breeding practices and veterinary methods, cf. Nicolaisen, J. 1978.)

Milking is women's work, but may occasionally be done by boys or young men. It is never left to the Haddad, either women or men. It is carried out twice a day - early in the morning and late in the evening - when the cows come back to the camp to be with their calves. Cows are sometimes milked in the middle of the day if they are grazing nearby, as is the case when pastures are plentiful during the rainy season. Herds may even return to camp at midday at that time of the year. Calves are tethered to poles whenever the cows return from grazing and are not let loose again until the mother cows are to be milked. The calf is allowed to suckle a little before the milking begins, after which it is tethered once again to a tree or to one of the forelegs of its mother cow. If a cow is difficult to milk after it has calved, the Kreda will blow into the animal's vagina through their folded hands. In case a milch-cow has lost its calf, a dummy calf is made out of the skin, or the calf of another cow is made to suckle before milking. Special treatment of the udder to facilitate milking seems to be unknown to the Kreda (cf. Nicolaisen & Nicolaisen 1997: 102). Milking is done in a squatting position. The milkmaid holds the milk-bowl between her legs to be able to squeeze the udder with both hands. Normally a short rope is tied around the hind legs of the cow to prevent it from kicking during the milking. Kreda women make beautiful milch bowls of coiled basketry. These are plaited so neatly that even new ones are impervious to milk (cf. Cat. No. 69). After some use, the inside of the milk-bowl becomes covered by a black membrane due to repeated smoking over a fire, which women do to cleanse the bowl whenever it has been in use. This black layer makes the milk-bowls impervious even to water.

In a fine rainy season, the Kreda may obtain a considerable surplus of milk. Among the Tuareg, where Johannes lived solely on milk for long periods, a fine milch-cow of the 'Arab' Zebu breed yielded up to seven litres per day when grazing on a good annual pasture - some of this yield being consumed by the calf, however. In contrast, a cow rarely gives two litres of milk – more often only a mere one and a half litres during droughts (Clanet 1975). These figures appear to hold good for Kreda cows as well. A household may therefore basically cover its daily nutrition with milk from a limited number of milch-yielding cows. A surplus can be disposed of in different ways. Some of it will be given to the Haddad, if there are such foragers living with the Kreda family in question, another part may be sold at the market, if any is located within walking distance of the camp. However, most of the surplus of milk generated during the rainy season is churned into butter. This is easy to sell either at markets or to the Libyan merchants who still trade in Bahr el Ghazal, sending this and other local produce to

Faya Largeau and other towns in northern Chad. There is usually a need for imported butter in the desert regions and in dry years the commodity fetches high prices here. In 1963, the price of milk at Mussoro was 10 Francs C.F.A. per litre, while butter cost about 90 Francs a litre. Yet, when resold in the north by the Libyan merchants, butter fetched a price of 200-250 Francs C.F.A. per litre.

Butter is made from cow's milk that is churned in huge calabashes which the women hang up in trees (cf. Cat. No. 92; *Fig. 7,10)*. Churning is a female responsibility among the Kreda, as among so many pastoralists. Unlike milk-

ing, this task may be done by Haddad women. In fact, if a Haddad family is attached to a Kreda household, the task of churning is bound to fall upon Haddad women or girls. It is carried out early in the morning when the heat is not too oppressive. The milk should be from the day before, the bulk of it preferably from the previous morning, as this allows for the settling of the milk for an optimal twenty-four hours before it is churned. When the calabash has been shaken for a while, the butter clots and water is added to facilitate the removal of the butter from the container. Then the butter is heated in a pot over a fire, a

7,10. Haddad women churning butter for their Kreda 'hosts'.

process that lends it a light yellowish colour. Except during cold winter nights, butter remains liquid and is kept and sold in bottles or larger metal cans. Traditionally, the Kreda used butter containers made from camel hide, fairly similar to those in use among the Tuareg (cf. Nicolaisen and Nicolaisen 1997: 302, *fig. 10,13*). However, these containers have largely been replaced by handier, industrially produced bottles and cans. Neither the Kreda nor the Kanembu make cheese, as is the case with most ethnic groups south of the Sahara apart from the Tuareg and Arabs. During the season of fresh annual pasture, the Kreda eat little butter, but they do make some use of it. Butter forms part of certain dishes and is applied when cooking sauce for porridge and other dishes. Butter is also used for greasing women's hair, the numerous tiny braids and larger whip which make up their coiffure. The task of dressing this also falls upon Haddad women (cf. Chapter 13; *Figs. 13,2*).

Goats and sheep

While the Haddad Kreda had not (yet) acquired cattle, some of them did possess a few goats. As far as we could assess, these were still of very limited economic significance to the Haddad economy, but they represent capital. To the Kreda, goats and sheep are economically significant, though less so than the cows. Small ruminants are slaughtered whenever a family needs meat for a social or ritual occasion. A single goat or sheep does not go far, of course. It is easily consumed by a household, yet the Kreda prefer to slaughter several small ruminants to one of their beloved cows. This is not only due to economic considerations but as much to the esteem, one is tempted to say love in which the Kreda hold cattle. When milk is plentiful, the Kreda eat but little meat, and like other African pastoralists they do not consume much meat on the whole. However, a certain number of goats and sheep are sold or killed annually to raise capital and meet domestic needs. The hides of goats are used for bags of various kinds, covers and sleeping blankets.

The goats reared by the Kreda are of relatively high stature and of a short-haired type resembling that of the Sahelien Tuareg further to the west. A few tiny goats that we saw at Mussoro resembled the pygmy goats of western and central Africa, and we assume that they have been introduced from the south. The common breed of sheep in

7,11. Young Kreda herder carrying a meal in a small basket and a spear for protection. The latter is made from an acacia root and the horn of a gazelle (cf. Cat. no. 29).

Kanem and Bahr el Ghazal does not seem to belong to the hairy type widespread in the western parts of the Sahel. Rather, the Kreda sheep resembles the *Ovis longipes* breed common among the Tuareg, with its long tail and the shape of its horns, but they have a different, light dark-brown or black coat. We have found no reference to this breed in the literature. The milking of goats and sheep is done from behind and the milk is drunk without any preparation. Goat and sheep milk are not used for churning butter, as previously intimated.

Donkeys, horses and camels

The Haddad Kreda way of life would not be possible without the donkey – it is as simple as that. Donkeys are used for riding and transportation. Without this hardy and te-

nacious beast to carry huge bundles of nets, the Haddad would not be able to search far and wide for game and round up herds of antelope and gazelle. The donkeys supply families with their daily rations of water or loads of firewood. They are indispensable whenever families move camps. Tent poles, mats, household utensils etc. are also loaded on the backs of these tiny, but incredibly strong animals, to the point where they almost disappear under the heavy burdens with only their heads and stalk legs still visible. The donkeys are also of considerable importance to other inhabitants of Kanem and Bahr el Ghazal, be it the Haddad Kanembu, agriculturalists or agro-pastoralists like the Kanembu or the pastoral Kreda.

Donkeys vary somewhat in colour. Most animals are greyish with a faint zebra-striped pattern on the lower part of the

7,12. Goats with their
newly born kids.

7,13. Donkeys are indispensable to the Haddad Kreda for transportation. These two animals carry a simple saddle of basketry covered by a goatskin. Such saddles are widely used in Northern Chad. The donkeys are carrying the hunting equipment, i.e. nets and strips of goatskin for an upcoming expedition.

legs, much like the wild asses of Northeast Africa. Asses do not live in Kanem and the Bahr el Ghazal, however, but only further north in and around the mountain massifs of the desert. As far as we could ascertain, neither the Haddad nor the Kreda make concerted effort to effectively breed donkeys. They leave this to nature, a tactic that suffices because donkeys are allowed to roam freely with just a rope tethered between either their forelegs or between one fore- and one hind-leg.

Neither the Haddad nor the Kreda make use of head-gear when riding their donkeys, as a clip or actually a series of clips with a stick is what it takes to control the pace of the animal. Saddles are rarely made use of either, although special donkey saddles are in use in Kanem and the Bahr el Ghazal, in particular among the Haddad Kanembu. Donkey saddles are simple. They consist of a piece of dum palm mat that covers a wooden structure of two sticks connected by a pommel in front, sometimes also by a cantle or hind-bow. The Haddad Kreda and Kreda pastoralists may also use two long pads when mounting their donkeys that are similar but shorter than the ones used as saddles when mounting oxen. A plaited double basket is used for carrying a variety of loads including the heavy earthenware jars for water (cf. Cat. Nos. 80 & 81).

The Haddad Kreda do not possess horses, but the Kreda certainly do, and we were told that some Haddad Kanembu

7,14. My favorite riding camel. It was by far the largest and most beautiful of the animals we rented in Mussoro. When Bogar Béchir joined us, he made it clear that this was the animal he wanted to mount. Sensitive to his wish and male pride, I gave up my fine camel, of course. I could not help but feeling a little 'schadenfreude', however, when it threw him off a few hours later. I never had that problem. The camel has an iron headgear decorated with leather strips of the Tebu type for decoration.

owned horses as well. Just as desert nomads gain prestige on the possession of fine riding camels, the horse is cherished in Kanem and the Bahr el Ghazal, where it is the riding animal par excellence. The region is famous for its fine breeds and has quite an export of horses to Nigeria, where the popularity of polo still makes for a profitable market. At the time of our stay in Chad, Le Rouvreur estimated that there were fifty to one hundred horses per one thousand people (Le Rouvreur 1962: 70). Considering that horses cannot live on natural vegetation alone but must be given supplementary fodder, which is a costly affair, this is quite an impressive figure. Among sedentary people like the Kanembu, horses are fed on millet and other cultivated crops while the pastoral Kreda let their horses drink butter-milk.

The horses of northern Chad appear to be of the Dougolaw breed believed to have been introduced from northern Egypt along with Arabian immigrations during the 12th and 13th centuries (Doutressoulle 1947: 287; Mauny 1961: 283). This is in agreement with the fact that the riding gear - bit and saddle - is similar to that used by Arabs, except that the saddle has a somewhat lower cantle. The stirrups are also of the large square type typical of northern Arabs. They are used for spurring the horse by pressing the pointed edges against the animal's side. When horses are let loose to graze, a hobble is tied between the forelegs and/or between one fore- and one hind leg. The latter furthers ambling and, a great number of the horses in Kanem and Bahr el Ghazal are amblers, in fact. At camp, horses are tethered to a pole with a rope tied to one of their forelegs. This is also the procedure with foals and the young of other domestic animals.

Neither the Haddad Kreda nor the Haddad Kanembu own or deal with camels. These strange and persevering creatures have no role in their way of life. Haddad men do not assist their Kreda 'hosts' with the breeding, keep or use of camels. It may well have been the very first and only time that camels formed part of Haddad hunting expeditions when we were allowed to come along mounted on these animals. Camels reach their southernmost distribution in Chad along the 13 degree N. Lat., although camel caravans may venture further south. We met small caravans near Fort-Lamy, almost 200 km south of camel territory, but the number of camels in Kanem is as low as 0-10 animals per one hundred people. It is somewhat higher in the Bahr el Ghazal (Le Rouvreur 1962: 68, *fig. 18*).

All Kreda families own one or more camels, it is claimed by Le Rouvreur, yet that did not hold for the Kreda that we encountered (Le Rouvreur 1962: 277). The main reason that families keep camels is that these are well suited for the transportation of heavy loads and long journeys and hence enable the Kreda to reach distant markets. The Kreda are not engaged in long-distance trade as the Kecherda and Hassauna Arabs, who service oases to the north. The Kreda use markets usually located at quite a distance from the camps. They are not used for riding, however, but only for transporting goods. Camels are of little further use to the Kreda. The meat is inferior to that of cattle, goat and sheep, it is hard to prepare and badly suited for drying. The hide is unfit for tanning, although it can be used without preparation for lashing and for the manufacture of butter containers. The milk differs from that of cattle, goat and sheep as regards the chemical composition and although it can be churned, the butter yielded is scanty and of poor quality and taste. So when camels are not needed for transport and trade, not much speaks in favour of breeding these animals. Some Kreda do perfectly well without them, as we observed. The men prefer to mount horses, while women ride oxen or donkeys, and the transport of tents and other burdens falls upon the oxen and the donkeys. What speaks for camels, however, is that they can do without water for long periods and that they find their own food during the night, while horses have to be fed subsidiary fodder such as millet, barley and even milk most of the year.

All work with camels falls upon men, as already mentioned. Milking takes two men standing on each side of the animal milking simultaneously. Unlike many camel-owning peoples, the Kreda do not apply a dummy calf in case a she-camel has lost her calf and hence is unwilling to give milk. They sew the nostrils of the calf-less camel firmly together for a few days, and argue that this enables them to milk the animal. Property marks are burned into the skin of the animal with a red-hot iron. Earmarks cut with a knife are also in use to indicate ownership.

The camels are short-haired with no proper wool, and of grey or greyish-brown colour. We never saw white or piebald camels in Kanem and Bahr el Ghazal. The Kreda do not breed camels on any major scale, as intimated, a limiting factor being the rather high humidity during the rainy season. One does see camels with newly born calves, however, when annual pastures are plentiful. Kreda camel-

7,15. A camel covered with a net of plaited strings made of strips of dum palm leaves. The net protects the animal from flies, a true pest in Kanem. Johannes had not seen such a net in use elsewhere in North Africa.

breeding techniques seem influenced by those of the Arabs, a fact that appears obvious considering the presence of Arab tribes and the general impact of Arab culture in northern Chad. Both pack- and riding saddles are known among the Kreda by the Arab word *basur*. Similar saddles are in use all over northern Chad and western Niger among the Daza and Teda (cf. Grall 1945: 25 ff.; Chapelle 1957: 251, fig. 10) and they are classified by Bulliet as 'North Arabian Saddles' (Bulliet 1975: 87 ff.). The headgear used for riding camels is two iron shackles tightened around the camel's nostrils and lower jaw by means of a single rein. This type of headgear is also used by the Tuareg, who apply a nostril ring to steer the animal by a double rein (Nicolaisen & Nicolaisen 1997, I: 121, fig. 3,35a). This is practiced by the Kreda, although they generally do without such nostril rings. Actually we came across only one single camel bull equipped with a nostril ring, probably because it was difficult to control. As for pack camels, the rein is simply a piece of cord attached around the animal's lower jaw. When grazing, camels are usually hobbled with a short rope between the forelegs preventing the animals from wandering too far during the night. In order to keep a camel in a couched position - e.g. a pack camel during loading - a short rope connected with a little stick may be attached around the animal's left bent foreleg, a technique typical of the North African and also Arab camel-breeding tradition (Nicolaisen & Nicolasien 1997, I: 121, fig. 3,35a-e & 45a). All of these utensils are made by Haddad smiths.

Dogs, cats and chicken

One might expect dogs to be widely used for hunting by the Haddad, trained to round up game either to keep it occupied and hence facilitate the task of hunters to set in their spears, or, in case of the Haddad Kreda, to chase gazelles and antelopes towards the nets. At the time of our visit, however, the Haddad Kreda did not breed or train dogs systematically for hunting, and there were not that many dogs around. Not all Haddad families owned dogs, in fact. This was an indication that Haddad families were finding it harder to feed their dogs and increasingly forced to give up large-scale hunting for antelopes.

Chapelle offers a vivid description of this was conducted and how every man brought not only his nets but also his dogs for the hunt. The dogs were on leash until the very moment when the antelopes were going to be driven towards the nets. Then the dogs were set free to do their part of work and secure that the antelopes ran in the right direction and did not escape the nets (Chapelle 1957: 202-6). Grall mentions that antelope hunting was done at Gouré by individual hunters with the assistance of a pack of dogs (Grall 1945: 32). We took only part in a single hunting expedition which brought a trained dog, but teenage boys and young men were still hunting for fowl with dogs trained to track down and make the birds take flight.

The Kreda had more dogs in fact than the Haddad families with whom they shared camps. The pastoralists keep these to guard goats and sheep against jackals and as watch dogs. Little effort is put into the training of these dogs, Kreda men claimed, yet we came across one capable of guarding goats and sheep all by itself. It left camp with the flock in the morning and returned with it again late in the afternoon. If visitors arrived at the camp during the day, as we did, the dog herded the entire flock back right away in expectation of a possible share of bones from the goat or sheep that invariably is killed in honour of the guests. The Kreda thought that was great fun. To what extent dogs in general assist in herding I do not know.

Quite a number of Haddad and Kreda families also had one or two cats to kill small rodents, insects and scorpions. Chicken are reared and move camp in a cage that is tied to the back of an oxen or donkey (Cat. No. 103).

HADDAD KANEMBU AGRO-PASTORALISM

The Haddad Kanembu, we met were primarily cultivators, but agriculture had not always played that role. It will be recalled that the environmental conditions had changed considerably during the last few generations. At the beginning of the 20th century, game was abundant, not only on land where huge flocks of elephants shared the surroundings of Lake Chad with a wide variety of other game, and giraffes, antelopes and gazelles grazed in fine numbers in the Bahr el Ghazal and further up north. The drastic reduction in game had put a substantial brake on the outcome of hunting and increasingly forced the Haddad to turn to the cultivation of millet and other crops. Some families supplemented their income and diet by raising a few goats and rearing chicken and some ducks, but hunting

7,16. A small Haddad Kanembu settlement near Méchimeré surrounded by fields of sorghum.

and collecting was still of economic significance to most households. None of the families we stayed with had any cattle, but we learned that others did. Haddad Kanembu agricultural activities resemble those of the Kanembu, but the economies of the two groups differ in that the latter for the most part are eager cattle breeders. Cattle are so plentiful among many of these people that it must be herded far from the villages for a good part of the year to get sufficient fodder. Some Kanembu families live a semi-nomadic life for that reason.

The agricultural potential of Kanem and the Bahr el Ghazal has generally been favourable to man, as previously indicated, but it fluctuates from north to south due to a considerable variation in annual rainfall and soil condi-

tions between the sandy dunes, the fertile interdunary depressions and more soggy soils of the wadis, where the level of the groundwater lies much higher. There is a close correspondence between prevalence of the fertile tracts and population density. The fertile interdunary depressions are found in a broad belt off Lake Chad towards the northeast and again around Mao, as well as in south-eastern Kanem from Bol towards Liwa. It is no wonder that the Haddad Kanembu have done better in this area than elsewhere. Salinity is a problem, however, which significantly influences the nature and distribution of vegetation and people. Where the concentration is high, the vegetation becomes sparse with growths of *Phragmites* reeds in the marshes while *Sporobolus spicatus* clump on the dunes. Yet, due to the high ground water level vast, low-lying stretches of land are able to support a fairly numerous population. The joker of the game is rain, as throughout the Sahel. The rainy season begins in June and ends only at the start of September, the time when agricultural activities are at their highest and animal herds stock up their body weight, devouring the fresh green plants that sprout everywhere. But there are years when the rains do not come or only insufficiently so and man and beast suffer. Poor families in particular get hit, as they face grave difficulties in replacing seed and domestic animals, be it goats or sheep.

The main crop in Kanem and the Bahr el Ghazal is millet, which can grow without irrigation as far north as a little beyond the cities of Mao and Mussoro. It comes in two variants, one suited for sandy soils which grows to a height of almost two metres and can be harvested after a period of 60-70 days. The other requires more the muddy soil of the depressions and grows to a height of one and a half metre, and it provides a higher yield (Krarup Mogensen 1963, 5: 12). In the interdunary depressions and the vicinity of Lake Chad where the watershed is often easily accessible, the Haddad and other local farmers may take two or more annual crops of cereals, beans and other crops. Where irrigation is possible, cultivation takes place all year round and the Haddad also grow vegetables. The French expanded the building of tiny dams and developed so-called polder farming in these areas. In the early 1960s, the polders covered some 6750 ha and yielded between 2,000 and 3,000 tons of wheat, as previously described (Fuchs 1966: 29). This type of farming was encouraged by the Chadian government,

7,17. Haddad Kanembu grow some vegetables near their huts, such as gourds and chili pepper.

but few if any Haddad were involved in the schemes, as far as we could ascertain.

Most of the families we got to know only had access to soils that enabled them to get one annual crop. But families near Chedra and N'Guri had fields in depressions that got flooded during the rainy season. They would first grow wheat and then, immediately after harvesting this crop in April-May prepare the fields and sow a second crop of maize. This was ready for harvesting after another two or two and a half months, i.e. at the beginning of July, just before the rains set in. At N'Guri the millet was 30-40 cm high at the time of our visit (25th July-1st August): in Chedra the same crop was almost ripe during the second week of September.

By far the most significant crop for the Haddad Kanembu is the variety of millet that is suitable for sandy soils, (*Pennisetum typhoideum*). If a family can cultivate but one crop of millet it has little economic leeway, even when the rains are reasonably good. At the Kanembu village of Reria, in which Krarup Mogensen spent some time, the size of the millet fields was between one and a half and two hectares. A family consisting of a married couple and one child could not subsist on the millet from such a plot alone, but had to rely on produce from husbandry or some other source of income, according to Krarup Mogensen's assessment. The economic situation was quite different for Kanembu families who had access to irrigation or flooded land and hence could take two crops a year. At the village of Tandan, for example, a field the size of two hectares could yield up to four tons of maize and two tons of wheat under optimal conditions. A harvest this size would support some fifteen to twenty people. Some families subsisted on lesser yields and were even able to sell some of the harvest to get cash (Krarup Mogensen 1963, 5: 20).

Haddad men and women share the work of growing millet. The main agricultural implement is the hoe (Cat. No. 38) but men also use a machete to cut branches and smaller trees to clear the fields. Most of the work can be done with the hoe, however, including the removal of shrubs and general preparation of the soil. All this must be completed before the rains set in to get a good burn.[5] Husband and wife usually work jointly on this task, the man cuts and rakes the field, the wife cleans up and prepares the soil with the hoe. When the weeds and shrubs have dried for a few days the man sets fire to them. The hoe is also used for sowing,

7,**18**. A cranium of a horse has been put up in a garden to protect the crops against the evil eye. We only came across this one near Chedra, but the custom is common throughout North Africa.

7,19. Fields on terraces near Chedra. The two wooden structures are wells with counter-poised sweeps made from dum palm trunks.

7,20. The hoe is an indispensable tool of agriculturalists in Kanem. Cat. no. 38. Photo J.K.

a task likewise entailing a division of labour between man and wife, in that the man makes the holes with the hoe some 60 to 80 cm apart while the wife follows him, putting five to ten seeds into each of these and afterwards covering each hole with soil, using her bare feet. When the millet is about 40 cm high, it is weeded and thinned out (Krarup Mogensen 1963, 5: 13). The Haddad also loosen the soil around each growth of millet. This part of the agricultural work is also done jointly by husband and wife, but the burden of the ensuing work of tending to the millet field falls upon the latter. Guarding the field is no small job. Birds may spoil a harvest if they are not kept at bay, so women and children keep the fields under surveillance from scaffolds that are put up for this very purpose and scare away predators with rattles and by shouting. The Haddad Kanembu

7,21. Some Haddad tend small gardens with papaya and vegetables which need constant care and water.

do not make use of any fertilizer. Unlike the Kanembu they possess next to no cattle and cannot therefore collect any manure. Millet can be harvested about two months after sowing. Harvesting is done largely by women and children with an ordinary knife, the cobs being cut one by one as they ripen. The stalks are left as fodder for the small ruminants. Despite efforts to secure a good harvest, an average 20-25% is bound to be lost, even when the rains are sufficient. Krarup Mogensen estimates that the average yield of millet in Kanem is about five hectokilo/ha, although variations are considerable (Krarup Mogensen 1963, 5: 13-14).

The Haddad Kanembu grow a variety of crops apart from millet, the more common being durra, wheat, maize, sweet potatoes, melons, onions, tomatoes and beans. Some families own a few date palms, but apart from the area around Mao where dates are plentiful, these palms are not common.[6]

Durra (*sorghum*) thrives on sandy soils only. It plays but a limited part in the diet of the Haddad, but is of considerable economic significance further to the south. One does find tiny plots of durra in between Haddad huts, however.

Wheat (*Triticum durum)* is also cultivated by the Haddad Kanembu, but only in small quantities as it requires irrigation. It is grown in the winter and primarily in the polders though occasionally in depressions where the height of the ground water makes for relatively easy access to water. This is, for example, the case around Chedra and N'Guri. Water is drawn from wells with sweeps of a type shown in *fig. 7,19*. The ones we saw had a shaft lined with stems of dum palm, the same material which is

used to construct the case above ground level. The latter consisted of some vertical forked stems with cross-bars to support a counterpoised sweep. The container is often a simple hemispherical basket some 60 cm in diameter with a tin or jar, while the balance weight is made from a similar basket or two filled with soil (stones are difficult or almost impossible to come by in Kanem). Other methods of getting water for irrigation do not occur. Wheat is not harvested with a knife or sickle but by pulling up the straw while simultaneously loosening the soil around the root of the plant by means of strokes with a knotty stick. Wheat was introduced into Kanem in the middle of the 19th century, and the French encouraged its cultivation. Higher yielding varieties of *Triticum vulgare* were introduced in the 1950s to replace *Triticum durum,* according to Krarup Mogensen (ibid. 5, 14). However, wheat has not

7,22. Donkeys find their own fodder near the hamlets. When fields are ripe with crops, however, the Haddad make sure that the animals are prevented from munching by a muzzle made from twisted dum palm leaves, much like the ones used to prevent calves from suckling.

7,23. Muzzle to prevent donkeys from eating crops. Cat. no. 89. Photo J.K.

yet become a fully integrated part of the local diet and it was our impression that only few Haddad engaged in the cultivation of this crop.

Maize is another crop that thrives on the silty soils of the depressions, where it is grown in rotation with wheat. Although maize is the highest yielding of the crops and plays a significant role in local nutrition, it fetches lower prices than millet. In 1957 one had to pay 30 CFA for one *zaka* millet, as against 25 CFA for maize and 55 CFA for wheat - one *zaka* corresponding more or less to one kg (ibid. 5, 17).

The Haddad Kanembu also grow vegetables, largely right next to their huts or on small plots in between these, preferably with silty soils. They plant red onions, *Allium cepa,* and garlic, *Allium sativum,* both highly appreciated as ingredients for sauces, as are Guinea pepper, *Capsicum frutescens* as well as *Hibiscus esculentus and Hibiscus sab-dariffa.* Spicy sauces are an important part of Haddad meals, an almost necessary addition to the fairly bland porridge of millet and durra that constitutes their stable diet. The Haddad do also grow gourds, *lagenaria vulgaris,* tomatoes, *Solanum incanum,* water melons, *Citrullus vul-garis,* melons, *Cucumis melo* of which there are two va-rieties, and gourds, *Cucurbita sp.* We noticed, moreover, that they had sweet potato, *Ipomaea batatas,* and manioc, *Manihot utilissima.*

URBAN ARTISANS AND MUSICIANS

Groups of artisans and musicians are found throughout Saharan and Sahelien Africa, among agricultural Soninke, Wolof, Toukoulor, Dogon, Senufo and Songhay as well as among the pastoral Maures, Fulani and Tuareg. There is significant ethnic and regional variation as to the precise social, religious and occupational roles attributed to these people. Some of them farm, herd or trade apart from con-ducting their primary trade which can be metal- and/or leatherwork, woodcarving, weaving or as musicians – the most frequent of these specialities. Usually, the artisans hold the same rights as other members of the wider society which they serve. However, as a rule, they never achieve political office (Tamari 1995: 61).

This general picture holds for the specialized craftsmen of northern Chad as well, all of whom are known by the Arab word for smith, *haddad.* One finds these gifted ar-tisans throughout Kanem and the Bahr el Ghazal. They make a living at the markets in towns and major villages as blacksmiths, potters, leatherworkers, tanners, basket and mat makers and wood carvers. The various ethnic groups may engage in some of these trades as well such as wood-carving, basketry and tanning, but they rarely trade their produce and do not work as professional artisans. Forging and pottery are the trade par excellence of Haddad artisans and their expertise in these fields will be discussed further in Chapter 15.

Most of the Haddad artisans in Kanem are Kanembu speaking. They live in beehive huts or adobe houses like the Kanembu proper. As they have not been properly stud-ied, it is unclear to what extent they are socially and cul-turally similar to these agro-pastoral people. In the Bahr el Ghazal a good number of artisans are Kreda speaking, as is the case in the town of Mussoro. These Haddad ar-tisans may well share cultural values and customs with the Kreda pastoralists, whose tongue they speak, but this too need to be properly documented. (For further data on these people and their crafts see Chapter 15 and the Catalogue).

A number of Haddad men make a living as travelling musicians, but like musicians in Tibesti most of them do so only part-time working as smiths the rest of the year. Tibesti musicians accompany their songs by beating a drum, known as a *kidi* (dog), and a popular saying has it that 'Tibesti smiths travel around with their drums in search of food just like dogs'(Kronenberg 1958: 88; IN transl.). We came across these musicians and singers in Haddad and Kreda camps. One turned out to stem from Faya Largeau in Tibesti, from where he had migrated to Kanem. His only instrument was therefore an oblong drum, which he played on skilfully with both hands, beating the skin at each end of the drum simultaneously. He used the drum to accompany the hymns in praise of first one, then another person in the audience, in the hope of being rewarded materially for his exertions. We met this musician several times and realized that he was a great success and earned handsomely, taking local earnings into consideration. Le Coeur lets us know that: "Among the Tubu the musicians play a role as town-criers and in particular as presidents of public dances, dur-ing which they play a specific kind of tambour and sing like women, for which they are paid in silver. The musicians

7,24. A young Haddad
smith working the
bellows at the market
at Bol.

are also compensated by those in whose honour they make songs of praise." (Le Coeur 1950: 95; IN transl.)

The favourite instrument of the Haddad musicians is not the drum but the mandolin (for a description of the instrument (cf. Chapter 17). They either play the instrument solo or make use of it to accompany songs about women and hunting – the two favourite themes - songs which at the same time may well refer or hint to current socio-political events. Lyrics are created on the spot for the occasion, in line with the age-old art forms of West African poets, who in recent years have commanded international interest due to their poetic ability and refined styles. The poetic creativity of Haddad musicians and the fact that they travel from camp to camp and from hamlet to hamlet make them important sources of general information to societies where mass media were - supposedly still are - largely unheard of. There was next to no public radio service in the mid sixties and no other 'artistic competition' in the villages and pastoral camps. This enabled the musicians to achieve singular popularity as well as a certain influence on public opinion. The music was cherished by Kanembu and Kreda people alike, in particular by the women, who enjoyed dancing to the tunes together with Haddad women. Musicians are not paid up front for the entertainment, but meals and gifts may be bestowed upon the performers.

Haddad smiths constitute endogamous units wherever they live, as do the foraging Haddad. Locally, this is explained with reference to their profession, i.e. the fact that the smiths handle fire. Haddad smiths are held in higher esteem in Kanem and the Bahr el Ghazal than the Haddad, who support themselves by hunting, foraging and farming. Still, the agro-pastoral Kanembu do look down upon these people while the various pastoral groups hold conflicting views. On the one hand the smiths are respected because their skills are in demand and highly appreciated. Knives, spears and lances are indispensable to men both for practical usage and for protection. Weapons are intrinsically associated with maleness and personal identity in these highly competitive and formerly war prone societies. Men do always carry weapons of one kind or the other, and a fine knife, lance or sword lends its owner status. Haddad smiths are indispensable to pastoralists as providers of these valued specimens. They are also feared, however, due to the specific and mystical powers that enable them to deal with fire and exercise their trade. Peter Fuchs writes that

in Northern Chad and Kanem:"... one hesitates to eat together with smiths, basically one excludes marriages with smiths, to call somebody a 'smith' is considered a deadly insult, and one is careful not to affront smiths, nobody will attack, injure or kill a smith, and in cases where everyone else is bound to lose his or her life by swearing, smiths go unpunished. Nor will smiths antagonize non-smiths. They may accompany warriors in combat, but they do not take part in the actual fighting, not out of fear, but due to the 'taboo' of engaging in arbitration with non smiths (1970: 304). Similar views are held by the Teda-Daza speaking pastoralists of eastern Niger and the Gouré region north-east of Lake Chad, according to Baroin (1991: 348). Similar conceptions and fears of the mystical powers of the smiths do also prevail among the Tuareg. No one in his or hers right mind will oppose or quarrel with a smith, as such an act is bound to backfire and potentially prove fatal to the contender (Nicolaisen & Nicolaisen 1996, II: 60-61). Johannes and I had the impression that similar fears and attitudes as those described by the above mentioned authors characterized interaction between Haddad smiths and the various ethnic groups in Kanem and the Bahr el Ghazal.

HADDAD MINERS

The extraction of natron has been an important economic activity in the Lake Chad region way back in time. Barth mentions its significance to the local economy several times (cf. Barth 1857, I: 426 & II: 151-2, 180, 188-9). When he passed through the Kano in 1851, for instance, trade centred on cotton-cloth, kola nuts, slaves and natron. The last-named commodity passed through Kano in great quantities in transit between Bornu (and hence Chad) to the east and Nupe land to the southwest. Barth writes of the latter that:" ... natron constantly passes from one hand to the other, leaving in its wake a considerable surplus in the town. The commodity is cheap, but its quantity sizeable; it offers work to a great many hands ... I assess the quantity of natron handled in Kano in this way to be no less than 20,000 burdens, i.e. burdens of oxen, horses and donkeys" (Barth 1857, II: 151-2; IN transl.).

Natron is used for medical purposes and as a dietary supplement for domestic animals. Cattle and, in particular, camels suffer widely from salt deficiency. Natron is

7,25. Haddad searching for natron at the quarry at Liwa. Photo K.M. Fig. 9,4; 5.11.1957.

extracted mainly in the cantons of Liwa and N'Guéla and the workers are almost exclusively Haddad. We never met any of these, but as the mining is of considerable economic significance to Haddad Kanembu families, I shall dwell briefly on the trade relying on the data of other authors. Natron occurs in two forms. One is generated by evaporation and crystallization in flooded areas. It forms thin layers that can be collected every two months during the dry season. Work has to be suspended during the rains. The natron is shaped for transport and sale in 'slates', some 80x40x10 cm in size (Le Rouvreur 1962: 100-01). The qual-

ity is somewhat impure, as the chemical invariably gets mixed with soil at the surface. Natron is also extracted at a depth of between one to two metres. It occurs in layers that are between five to fifteen centimetres thick and of varying purity. The size of annual production in Kanem was not known at the time of our visit. Krarup Mogensen believes that it was around 5,000 tons in the 1950s, the official export from Baga Sola alone being 4,102 tons (Krarup Mogensen 1963, 9: 1-2).

The quarries at Liwa and N'Guéla are controlled by local chiefs. They can be mined every year from October, when the inundations dry up. The chiefs decide where and when the extraction can take place and also the amount that can be taken. The mining itself is left entirely to workers, all of whom are Haddad. In return for the right to mine, the Sultan claims a part of the production. In pre-colonial times this was one fifth, the usual payment throughout North Africa for the utilization of land belonging to others. At one point in time, the French cut the share of the chiefs to one tenth, only to abolish it formerly in 1950 (Krarup Mogensen 1963, 9: 2). What the nature of the contract between the worker and the Kanembu owner is today is hard to assess, says Le Rouvreur, but the profit of the latter is considerable (Le Rouvreur 1962: 102).

Once the permission to mine an area has been announced by the chief, each of the workers decides where to try his luck. He is free to do so as long as he does not get in the way of others (cf. Krarup Mogensen 1963, 9: 2). The procedure is the same everywhere. The miner searches for the natron with a wooden stick with a flattened iron head at the one end. He bores this into the ground and can feel the natron as hard lumps. The actual excavation is done with a used pot or other suitable tool, even with bare hands, and that which flows in water is scooped up with a calabash. Minor lumps are sold without further ado, while larger ones may be cut into oval slabs. The actual mining usually takes place in the coolness of the morning, the cutting of natron slabs in the afternoon, after which these are left to dry in the shadow of trees to avoid the surface turning into dust (Krarup Mogensen 1963, 9: 3).

The natron business involves several ethnic groups: Kanembu owners, Haddad workers, Yedina and Teda transporters and Kanuri merchants. In Baga Sola there were about fifty buyers, half of whom were locals. They would

7,26. Natron slabs at Baga Sola with the marks of the owner. A pastoralist, perhaps the owner of the camels, has brought the slabs. A fully loaded papyrus canoe is moored in the background, ready for departure. Photo K.M. Fig. 9,6; 3.4.1954.

see to the distribution of the natron to Fort-Lamy, from where it was sent further south. Other loads went to Baga Kauwa in Bornu, where the merchants had struck business deals with Nigerian importers (Krarup Mogensen 1963: 9: 4). At Liwa two bags of natron slabs fetched 150 CFA. The packing for further transportation costs 50 CFA and the Teda charged 300 CFA to transport the bags on camel to the harbours at Baga Keskéra. The Buduma (Yedina, IN) demanded 500 CFA for taking the load on a pirogue to Kawa, where the Kanuri merchants sold it at a profit of 1,000 CFA (Le Rouvreur 1962: 101).

The Haddad come from afar to do the hard work of mining. Krarup Mogensen mentions that apart from local Haddad from Liwa itself, he met Haddad diggers from Kaya, Mayala, Kemekemé and Dumilla. He estimates that several hundred Haddad families were dependent on the trade and that natron was their most important source of income. The trade generates income for the other ethnic groups as well, be it Teda or Yedina, stimulating local demands for food as well as crafts. In that sense natron has a positive effect on the trade of Haddad artisans (Krarup Mogensen 1963, 9: 7).

NOTES

1. Chapelle indicates that one finds cattle among Azza craftsmen in the 1950's. He lists in one table that families have herds of ten cows, three goats and one donkey, and in another that Azza families (now defined as artisans and hunters) get an annual increment of three cows and two goats, equivalent of an estimated purchasing power of 14 goats (cf. Chapelle 1957: 219-20).

2. Even these figures must be taken with a grain of salt, as previously indicated. It is most difficult to get solid data on the size of herds of livestock, not only because these are moved about, but also because the owners usually have hidden agendas influencing the information they are willing to share. This is made painfully clear by Clanet, who as part of the project "contact paysans-éleveurs et mobilité au Sahel," studied the effects on the bovine population of the droughts 1969-1973 (Clanet 1975; 1977: 242).

3. The M'Bororo Sebu is of impressive stature and has extremely long horns often in the shape of a lyre. According to Le Rouvreur, this breed is found mainly around and towards the south-east of Lake Chad. This, no doubt, is a correct observation, but one may also meet the breed further north. We did not meet any cattle-breeding Fulani in Kanem and Bahr el Ghazal during our stay there, but only a few Fulani who had specialized in sheep-breeding. That the Fulani have migrated into the area later has already been mentioned.

4. The *Kuri* cattle are hump-less *Bos primogenus* with very heavy and long horns. It is found along the northern beaches and in the archipelago of Lake Chad, where it is the only breed. Occasionally, however, one may come across *Kuri* cattle around Mao, and some Kreda raise a cross-breed between the *Kuri* cattle and the Arab Zebu. The *Kuri* cattle are probably the biggest of the West African breeds and said to possess excellent qualities. The Kreda claim e.g. that they are a much better milk-yielder than the Sebu.

5. The hoe is also used by those engaged in irrigated agriculture to heap up soil on each side of the tiny canals.

6. According to Krarup Mogensen no less than twenty-six species of plants are cultivated in southern Kanem, mostly on silty soils (1963, 12).

8:

8: FORAGING

PLANTS, FRUITS AND BIRDS

Foraging is significant in Kanem and the Bahr el Ghazal, not only to the Haddad, but also to some extent to the agriculturalists, agro-pastoralists, pastoralists and craftsmen who live in northern Chad. Environmental conditions make for a rich variation in resources that can be tapped. Ethnic groups around Lake Chad, for example, profit from a variety of plants feeding on its water and the lush vegetation along its shores and islands that enable them to gather wild rice and water-lily roots, locust beans, shea nuts, wild baobab and tamarind fruits. Of particular use is the papyrus, so well known from Ancient Egypt, where it was cultivated first by the Egyptians themselves and later by the Arabs, and its many uses described by Theophrastus. As in Antiquity, the Haddad use the roots of the papyrus plant for utensils, its stems for boats, mats, baskets and cords. I cannot say for sure whether the pith is eaten cooked or raw, but only that the plant is extremely important to the Haddad Kanembu living near the Lake.

Wild plants are essential to the nutrition of all Haddad. Most of these foods are for immediate consumption. The collection of edible plants, seeds, fruit and nuts in the wilds rarely enables a family to stock up supplies that can sustain it for any major period of time. Most families do in fact face shortages of food at regular intervals, sometimes quite seriously. Plants and trees are also of value in other respect, providing material for tools, dwellings - tents or huts - mats, baskets and other household utensils both for a family's own consumption and at times for sale at markets.

The collection of edible wild plants is generally the task of women all over the world – their trademark one is tempted to say. The crucial significance of foraging to the economies of hunting-gathering societies was not given full recognition in anthropological theory till the second part of the 20th century, however, when it was highlighted by feminist writings. One need only to recall Sally Slocum's contribution: 'Woman the Gatherer: Male Bias in Anthropology', to get a feel of the debate (Slocum 1975). These scholars challenged the predominant focus on men's hunting activities and pointed to women's crucial foraging contribution in time and substance to the nutrition and economy of these societies, and at times also to hunting.

Foraging activities are also in women's hands among the Haddad, except, interestingly enough, for the gathering of the nutritionally significant grass, *ogu*. These seeds are invariably harvested by men, both among the Haddad Kreda and the Haddad Kanembu. Of all the plants gathered by the Haddad none surpasses this grass in nutritional importance. Both the plant itself and its seeds are known as *ogu*, or by the Arab name, *kreb*. In the rainy season, *ogu* is plentiful on periodically flooded meadows between the dunes, and the Haddad harvest considerable quantities every year. The seeds must be gathered while the plant is still green, yet at the point when the seeds are fully developed, i.e. during the latter part of the rainy season and for some time thereafter. Haddad Kreda men mount their donkeys almost daily in search for *ogu* when the time is ripe. The seeds make for a truly tasty porridge, the stable in this part of the world. It is much preferred to porridge

8,1. The wild seeds of the ogu grass form a cherished part of Haddad Kanembu nutrition. It is men only, who collect these seeds. They do so by swinging a basket through growths of the grass. In the process, the grass is threshed and the seeds collected in the bottom of the basket as they pass through a grid that keeps out the straw.

made from millet both by the Haddad and the Kanembu and Kreda. As *ogu* is appreciated not only by man but also by cattle and other animals grazing on the plains, the men are compelled to venture far and wide.

The seeds are collected in baskets specifically made for the task. They come in different sizes and are known in Kreda as *sumpu* (pl. *sumpa*). Although these baskets are used by men only, they are made jointly by men and women: the plaiting of the container being carried out by women, while the frame and finish is taken care of by men. This work entails an aggrandizement of the brim with a wooden frame made from a thin branch of the *kolu* tree and the adding of a handle of rope of twisted strips of dum palm leaves. Finally a cobweb-like grid of thin rope is tied to the basket just below its rim. This serves as a threshing device, separating the edible seed from a medley of straw and unedible stuff that gets into the basket when in use (cf. Cat. Nos. 62 & 63).

8,3. Plaited container for the storing of ogu. Cat. no. 68. Photo J.K.

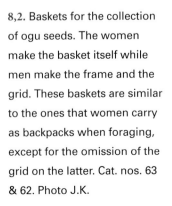

8,2. Baskets for the collection of ogu seeds. The women make the basket itself while men make the frame and the grid. These baskets are similar to the ones that women carry as backpacks when foraging, except for the omission of the grid on the latter. Cat. nos. 63 & 62. Photo J.K.

8,4. Haddad women an
a foraging trip.

8,5. Freshly collected ogu grass placed in a tray to dry in the sun.

Haddad men collect *ogu* walking systematically through stands of the grass holding a basket in the right hand. They swing the baskets back and forth through the grass as they carry on - the sheer force of the movement threshing the ripe seeds from the ear and separating these from the straw in the process. The seeds are collected in the basket - the straw being stopped by the grid. It is quite a strenuous task, evidently, and our Haddad friends claimed that this was the reason that it was men's work both among the Haddad Kreda and the Haddad Kanembu. It is a task that yields visible results, however. Considerable portions of *ogu* seed are collected in this manner every year. During the second half of our fieldwork, we registered mats with large heaps of *ogu* laid out to dry next to Haddad tents and huts or placed on the circular trays known as *afray*

(pl. *afra*) (cf. Cat. No. 64). These come in various sizes, all in coiled basketry, and are used both for drying and - the smaller ones - for winnowing *ogu* and millet. Women do so by flipping the seeds into the air with tiny, but firm and precise movements, enabling the wind to carry off chaff and other debris.

Ogu is eaten as porridge, as already mentioned. It constitutes not only the most important, but to many families also the one and only form of nutrition during a time when stocks of millet are at their lowest and the new crop not yet ready for harvesting. For this reason and because *ogu* porridge is delicious and appreciated throughout Kanem, the Haddad are able to sell part of the collected seeds to settled people who are unable to collect the grass themselves. We learned that recently some Kreda pastoralists had taken to the collection of *ogu*, conferring the task on women, in line with the general division of labour among these pastoralists. Kreda men hold little interest in anything else but their riding horses and the raising of cattle, and the tasks they carry out are all related to these passions, such as the making of ropes, slaughtering of animals and roasting of meat. It falls on women and children to do all other mandatory tasks in the camps, including organizing the practical tasks of migration.

We were not able to follow Haddad foraging efforts and use of plants or detail dietary habits during a full annual circle, but inquired into these matters wherever we went. The ensuing list of edible plants does not lay claim to being complete for that very reason, but it certainly includes the most important species, the names being stated in Kreda:

Arken (*Maerua crassifolia*). Its fruits, *arkima, are* collected during the dry season and eaten right away.

Feri, a tree with reddish trunk and branches. It is not an acacia species, but the Haddad eat its resin, *nogo,* as they find it, just as they do with that of true acacia species. The resin is collected during the dry season.

Kaazom, a tree with fruits, *kaazom tjola,* which the Haddad collect during the dry season. They are eaten raw.

Olo (*Balanites aegyptiaca*). The fruits, *oloa,* are eaten raw during the dry season. The bark is used as a substitute for soap.

Tefi is the Kreda term for the defoliating, summer-green *Acacia raddiana,* a tree of great significance to the Haddad and other ethnic groups in region, as it is throughout the Sahel and Sahara. The roots of *Acacia raddiana* are used for the construction of the tent (cf. Chapter 12: 446; Fig. 17,65) and its foliage makes great fodder for camels and small ruminants. The Haddad collect the resin, *nogo,* during the dry season and eat it without further ado.

Tjorogu (*Zizyphus sp.*) alias the jujubier tree. The berries, known by the same name, are collected and pounded in a mortar producing a substance that the Haddad eat mixed with milk. Occasionally the berries are eaten whole with milk. They are never cooked, according to our informants.

Tugey (*Acacia sp.*). As in the case of *Acacia raddiana* the Haddad also collect and eat the resin, *nogo,* of this acacia species. The resin is not prepared in any way prior to its consumption. *Nogo* is considered healthy and to hold curative properties, hence its use as a remedy against stomach pains.

Uyi (*Salvadora persica*) is an evergreen tree or bush known for its sweet berries, *udela.* These are collected during the rainy season and consumed with milk without further ado.

Yogur is another tree with fruit, *nerga,* which the Haddad collect during the rainy season, pound in mortars and mix with milk.

Diger is a species of grass. The seeds, *digera,* are collected during the rainy season by Haddad women to be pounded and cooked as porridge similarly to *ogu.*

Eri, a plant which sprouts on temporarily flooded land during the rainy season. Its fruit is collected by Haddad women for the making of porridge, *runku.*

Kiri, a plant with some likeness to millet but it grows in the wild. It is treated, cooked and eaten like millet, i.e. generally with a thick, vegetable sauce or kind of ragout.

Kulu, a plant with red berries that are collected and eaten during the dry season.

Molu is a term used for two different plants. Haddad Kreda women collect the berries of both to make the vegetable sauce that is eaten with porridge. One of these two plants grows on the low-lying stretches or valleys between the dunes. The fruit is chopped, dried in the sun and then pounded in a mortar. The fine flour is used as the basic ingredient for a sauce. The other plant is found in the dunes themselves. The Haddad dry its leaves, pound or roll these between the fingers to a kind of flour that is used to make sauce.

Mu, a plant with seeds resembling those of the *ontul* grass (see below). The grain is pounded in a mortar and cooked for porridge.

Ola is a species of melon with sizeable fruits. These are eaten without any preparation.

Olu (*Citrullus colocyntis*), the wild coloquintida known in Arabic as *beter*. It is eaten raw, roasted in fire or cooked.

Ontul (*Spirobolus spicatus*), a species of grass with a star-shaped ear. The Haddad acquire this in a manner similar to the one described by Foucault for Tuareg collection of *Aristida pungens* (Foucauld 1922: 29; Nicolaisen & Nicolaisen 1997, I: 240). The Haddad capitalize on the fact that ants store these seeds in quite impressive quantities. Haddad women exploit this and dig out these supplies from anthills during the rainy season. Apart from this method of acquiring *ontul*, the seed is not collected. In due time, the seed is pounded in a mortar and used for making porridge.

Tere (*Cenchrus* species) is an annual plant with prickly fruit generally known as *cram-cram*, a plant that is a nuisance when walking bare-feet. The fruits are collected during the rainy season, pounded in a mortar and cooked for porridge.

A palm of singular significance throughout Kanem and Bahr el Ghazal is the dum, *Hyphaene thebaica*. The Haddad make use of its leaves and nuts in various ways. The leaves are dried and used for plaiting or coiling baskets and mats for the tents (cf. *Figs. 4,1; 12,9i*). The fruit is eaten in two ways: Young nuts are cut open with a knife to get at the kernels, which the Haddad munch; ripe nuts have an outer, edible coating which is scraped off and consumed.

Another source of nutrition is birds and the eggs of birds. Birds are of significance to the diet in particular during the rainy season i.e. at the time of nesting. The Haddad collect the eggs of a series of species nesting on the ground such as the grey-breasted helmeted guinea fowl, and the various species of partridge, francolins, sand-grouse and duck (cf. Chapter 2; Fig. 2,8). The Haddad are not the only people to do so - no one who comes upon a nesting guinea fowl will leave it alone. Neither the Haddad nor members of the other ethnic groups in Kanem and the Bahr el Ghazal seem interested in or collect grasshoppers, rodents, reptiles as common in many places elsewhere in the Sahel. They may bag a tortoise, *testudinidae,* if they come across one, not for their own consumption that is, but to sell it to Europeans in the towns – administrators, development workers or the military.

HARVESTING LAKE CHAD

The Haddad Kanembu living along the shores of Lake Chad do of course take advantage of unique aquatic environment, as do the Yedina, who also inhabit the islands. The lake harbours both mammals and a rich variety of fish, including the highly priced Nile perch, which already at the time of our visit was exported for the tables in fashionable restaurants in Paris, where it went by the name of 'Prince du Shari'. If not immediately consumed, fish are dried or

8,6. Papyrus it not only used for canoes but also for making huts and other things. Children learn from early on to contribute to the daily chores of their family.

8,7. Some Haddad Kanembu have specialized in harvesting the aquatic environment of Lake Chad. They live in small settlements along its southern shores, here in bee-hive huts near Baga Sola.

smoked and then sold at local markets along the shore or exported to inland markets.

The Haddad use several methods of fishing. The common and age-old ways are by netting, setting traps and using fishing spears. Modern nets of nylon were in use, we observed. Traditionally, however, the Haddad made their own nets from fibres of the *Calotropis* plants. The Buduma applied papyrus stems to hold these up, cutting the stems short to serve as floats, according to Sikes (1972: 183). The Haddad may have done likewise. The Yedina do also set lines laden with imported hooks, something they had not done before, having no hooks, Sikes writes (ibid. 183). I do not know if the Haddad did that too. We were not able to study fish trapping, but saw spears in use. Haddad fishing spears, *alasa,* consist of a barbed iron head, some 18 to 22 cm long. The point is tied to a wooden shaft with a cord that runs through two holes in this (cf. Cat. Nos. 2 & 3). Some Haddad use hooks imported from Nigeria, as the method traditionally is foreign to this part of Africa. Large fish are taken with a harpoon, *tjagal,* a tool mainly used for the hunting of crocodiles and hippopotami.

It was to the mammals in Lake Chad, however, that the Haddad looked for the bulk of their subsistence. It is quite appropriate, in fact, to characterize them as aquatic hunters, for it was the hunting of crocodiles and, the protected hippos which, till recently, provided the main source of income and still did to some families.

The hippopotamus is pursued with harpoon and spear. Our Haddad informants were somewhat reluctant to tell us

8,8. At the lake side, the Haddad make use of several types of huts, including cylindrical huts with roofs of a bee-hive shape. The photo is from Baga Sola.

in detail about how they hunted hippos, as this is strictly prohibited, yet it was intimated that they still targeted these huge aquatic mammals. The hunters kill hippos with long lances and harpoons that all have to be coated with poison to finish off a hippo (cf. Cat. No. 1). Hippos come ashore at night to graze or, if they are staying among the floating islands they eat while standing in the shallows. The Haddad hunt them only while they swim, however. It is a dangerous undertaking and hunters must succeed in setting in five to six harpoons and later get at such close range that they can lend the animal the coup de grace with a lance. Getting too close to a wounded hippopotamus has cost the life of many a hunter. Sikes writes, that it occurred quite often that hippos overturned a canoe, sometimes biting it in two and mauling the occupants. She mentions that hippos may

get entangled in gill-nets or foul-hook lines in which case they may drown or be speared to death by fishermen (Sikes 1972: 144-5).

Crocodile hunting is another specialized and quite dangerous trade. Apart from hunting skills, it requires investments in time and cash to make and/or purchase the necessary hunting equipment, the harpoon and above all a means of transportation, either a papyrus or dug-out canoe. The latter are not made locally, due to a lack of the appropriate wood, but imported from down the Shari River. Wooden canoes are pretty costly, the prize ranging about 20-25,000 CFA, a considerable sum in the local economy and beyond the means of most Haddad families. The papyrus canoes, on the other hand, can be made of local material and by the Haddad hunter himself. He will need to set aside the

8,9. The Haddad use canoes made of papyrus for fishing, foraging and crocodile hunting. We had no opportunity to observe the actual construction of a canoe, unfortunately. Sikes offers a short description of how a Yedina fisher sets about the task, which is similar to the way the Haddad do it, noting that, "He starts with the prow, which he makes of a simple bundle of papyrus. Then he inserts extra papyrus stems and binds these into the primary bundle. The prow is then curved upwards and wedged in a forked stick planted in the ground. Additional bundles are bound into the sides of the prow, and then extended backwards by the addition of more stems to form the gunwales. Palm fibre rope is used, the knots being secured with the teeth. The canoe is widened and extended backwards." Sikes notes finally that, "... the prow is secured by means of a stay to the floor, knots are tied off, and the kadai is now ready for immediate launching. It must never be allowed to dry out, and will always be kept on the water of the lake." Sikes, S. 1972: 141.

time for collecting the necessary amount of papyrus and rib the stems of leaves. Moreover he has to collect leaves of the dum palm, and dry and braid these into ropes. The papyrus stems are tied together in firm bundles and the boat is constructed by simply tying a number of these together with the above mentioned ropes of dum palm leaves *(Fig. 8,9)*. We were told that a canoe could be constructed in a day by three men, once the material had been gathered. The canoes are simple yet perfectly suitable for transportation along the shores and between the islands and the papyrus and rush vegetation floating in the lake. They may carry four to five persons, but are not durable and must be replaced after a month or so.

Crocodile hunting has been an important source of income during the past century for those Haddad who exploit the aquatic environment of Lake Chad. Crocodiles have not only made a significant contribution to the nutrition,

8,10. A Haddad aquatic hunter.

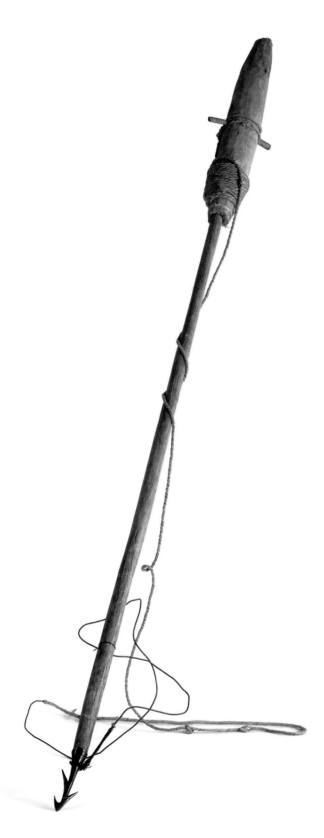

8,11. A harpoon for the hunting of crocodiles. Cat. no. 4.
Photo J.K.

the tasty meat being highly appreciated, but also provided a cash income. Crocodiles were still quite common in Lake Chad at the time of our fieldwork. Larger animals had become rare due to excessive hunting, but specimen of one meter or one meter and a half in length were quite plentiful. The strong demand for crocodile skin by the fashion industry of Europe during the first part of the 20th century had taken its toll. Prices went up, and so did the income for a period of time. The skin of a fairly small crocodile fetched 4,000 to 5,000 CFA, making crocodile hunting a lucrative business – perhaps less for the first link in the chain, the Haddad than for middlemen at various levels. There were Europeans who bagged their share and earned handsomely. We met a Frenchman in Fort-Lamy who had made crocodile hunting his main business in his younger years, killing some 4000 - 5000 crocodiles along the southern shores of Lake Chad and the lower parts of the river Shari. He

8,12. Lake Chad looks tempting, but its blue waters are infected with bilharzias. The Haddad rarely wash clothes. Both water and soap is in short supply in the Sahel.

used his earnings to found an import-export business and bought a cargo ship from the spoils. The Haddad hunt all three species of crocodiles for commercial purposes, as far as we could assess, i.e. the *Crocodylus niloticus, Crocodylus calaphactus* and the *Osteoloemus tetraspis*. We became friendly with some young crocodile hunters who lived with their families in a small hamlet at some distance from Baga Sola. They went hunting on a regular basis, using a harpoon as their only weapon. Apart from crocodile hunting, which provided them with the bulk of their income, they made a living from hunting fish with spears and harpoons.

We were invited along one night with four of them, each of us sharing a canoe with two hunters. Unfortunately, we had no luck, because it turned very windy. Crocodile hunting is largely a nightly undertaking and the water has to be calm. Normally, men hunt with a companion, each man being armed with a harpoon, as was the case the night we were along. One man stood upright in the stern polling the boat through the shallow water with the shaft of his harpoon. While he steered the boat almost noiselessly along narrow channels lined with thrush and papyrus vegetation, the other hunter searched the thickets with a bright cone of light from a powerful torch to catch the reflecting eyes of crocodiles resting on banks or lurking in the shoals. Every now and then, one of the hunters imitated the wail of baby crocodiles, a peculiarly enticing sound which is very hard to describe, or they tried to decoy an animal by imitating the crocodile way of swimming, moving a hand swiftly through the surface of the lake, concluding the performance with a few firm claps on the side of the boat to simulate the forceful beat of the tail, as a crocodile speeds up its movement. To my great disappointment, we found no crocodiles, as just mentioned, nor did the hunters get any of the large fish attracted by the bright torchlight, although they repeatedly tried to spear them with their harpoons. We did not learn of the hunting of the varan, *Varanus niloticus* or the large water tortoise, *Trionyx triunguis,* which the Yedina pursue for their delicate meat, but the Haddad Kanembu probably go for these species as well. Both are caught by means of a long line, after which they are killed with a stick, Krarup Mogensen writes (1963, 7: 2-6).

Our Haddad acquaintances near Bol and Baga Sola did not live from fishing and hunting alone, however, but supplemented their nutrition with foraging and some agriculture. I have already mentioned the fact that Haddad families living near the shores of Lake Chad gather wild rice and waterlily roots, as well as locust beans, shea nuts and wild baobab and tamarind fruits, which are plentiful in this area. They would also pursue hares and porcupines, species that are quite common on land just beyond the shore. Occasionally, they were able to kill a pale fox, a hyena, a jackal or a ground squirrel, species that they characterized

8,13. Haddad women selling fish at the market at Bol.

as un-edible pests but apparently cooked anyhow. Apart from the above-mentioned species, the snaring of birds, an occasional encounter with a python, however, hunting was largely confined to aquatic animals, in part because large game had become virtually extinct in the dunes and sandy plains beyond the shores of the lake. Very rarely, a hunter might come across a stray Damalisque antelope during the rainy season, perhaps a gazelle – the reddish *Gazella rufif-rons,* or a bit further to the north the smaller, white *Gazella dorcas dorcas*, but this was not to be counted on.

9:

9: HUNTING

Kanem and Bahr el Ghazal are rich in game - or were so well into the 20th century before commercial demands, automatic weapons, population growth and droughts severely diminished the populations of large mammals including antelopes and gazelles. Although we do not have quantitative data on this change or on its effects on the subsistence patterns, it is certain that the significance of hunting for local subsistence and economic exchange have shrunk considerably over the past century. However, hunting is still part and parcel of Haddad existence, in terms of physical survival, nutrition and way of life as well as in respect to how they see themselves and their role within the larger scheme of things. The Haddad have an extensive knowledge of the natural world and of the nature and behaviour of animals. This is part of a wider system of understandings and explanations of the forces and rules that recreate and regulate nature, man's place in the world and his and her relations with natural species. These insights and perceptions govern Haddad behaviour, and they find expression in magical practices and artistic creations. They feed into Haddad hunting practices, be it as a prohibition against mentioning game by its proper name, as is the case among a range of indigenous hunting and foraging societies, or in finding outlet in magical precautions and practices, as for example Haddad Kanembu treatment of their masks. Haddad fascination with the natural world finds cultural expression in poems and music (cf. Chapter 11), but also in great animal fables, all set in a mythical past when the animals could speak. Let me just relate one of these:

Once upon a time the lion did not know how to roar. That was a time when the animals could talk with one another. The lion could also speak, but it could not roar. This made the lion very sad. So one day it sent for the ostrich, for the ostrich knew very well how to roar. The ostrich promised the lion that it would teach it how to do so. Some days later, the ostrich visited the lion. It told the lion to open its large mouth. When the lion had done as told and its jaws were wide open, the ostrich put its head and long, long neck deep inside the gap. It told the lion to close its mouth and roar Uuh! Uuh! down its throat. Ever since then, the lion has roared like this, almost like an ostrich.

In a fundamental way, Haddad knowledge systems and cultural perceptions of nature set them apart from other ethnic groups in the area, as previously stated, lending them an identity of their own. At the same time, the social and cultural ways of the Haddad Kanembu and the Haddad Kreda vary in a range of ways, including their hunting techniques and understandings of the natural world, its animals and the forces at work. In this chapter we shall look closer at the applied technologies and the methods and organization of hunting used by the two Haddad groups, respectively. We shall do so while bearing in mind the environmental conditions under which the Haddad Kreda and the Haddad Kanembu exercise their trade. The different climatic and soil conditions in the Bahr el Ghazal and Kanem respectively implies that the vegetational cover varies, leaving the former with wide-open plains with few patches of acacia and thorny bushes and Calotropis, while Kanem has far more trees and becomes increasingly covered by bushes and trees as one moves south. These environmental facts set the stage for entirely different hunting methods: the use of nets in the more open country, and bow hunting when the cover is denser. The Haddad Kreda and the Haddad Kanembu have perfected these two hunting methods, as we shall see.

In the vast literature on hunting and hunting methods, one sometimes encounters a distinction between active and passive hunting, as originally stated by the Finnish ethnologist U.T. Sirelius (cf. Lagercrantz 1974: 19). This categorization tried to capture a major difference in hunting technology and method: active hunting engaging the hunter directly with the game with bow and arrow, spear, lance, boomerang or gun to kill; passive hunting relying on traps, snares, nets and the like to enclose, arrest or kill the animal. The distinction points to a major difference in hunting technology and methods between the Haddad Kreda and the Haddad Kanembu: the former relying on nets, the latter predominantly bow and arrow. Even so, it does not fit entirely. For Haddad Kreda hunters are not passive spectators waiting silently for the game to be caught but active participants who yell and chase the animal to its fate. I shall not pursue the active-passive distinction much further; other examples will easily illuminate its inherent problems.[1]

There are other, significant features that distinguish Haddad Kreda and Haddad Kanembu hunting, some closely intertwined with organizational aspects, others with the spiritual and magico-religious conceptualization and contextualization of the animal world. But let us first take a look at the hunting technologies.

TECHNOLOGY AND KNOW-HOW

Hunting is largely a male undertaking in Kanem and the Bahr el Ghazal, as is the case among most foragers around the world. Haddad Kreda women partake occasionally in the communal hunts, joining those who drive the game towards the nets. Haddad Kanembu women never hunt. Hunting is pursued as a main source of nutrition and/or for the income that hides, antlers, meat, sinew brings the hunter. Game is also killed for medical use and a few species are hunted for sale as pets. This is the case with monkeys and sometimes the cheetah, which were popular among French

colonial officers, military personnel and private businessmen. To young men and big boys, hunting also represents entertainment and sport, as well as a training exercise and a means to assess themselves as persons and, if successful, achieve fame. Hunting with dogs is not used on a substantial scale today by the net-hunting Haddad Kreda. There is little doubt that it played a much greater role as long as these people made regular expeditions up north to hunt herds of *Oryx* antelopes. Some dogs are trained to hunt down guinea fowl, some even to retrieve. When the dogs scent, track down and make the birds take flight, the young men set off in pursuit to kill the guinea fowl as soon as the birds try to settle. This is possible because guinea fowl rarely make long flights, and dogs are trained not to devour game. Men engage largely in such hunting to divert themselves – in fact they pursue their hunting luck at the slightest chance. A nesting guinea fowl will be bagged if spotted, a gazelle dozing in the heat of the midday sun killed with whatever weapon is at hand if discovered. If several men are out together, hares, gazelles, antelopes and other species, which come their way, are certain to be pursued.

Men and older boys of all ethnic groups are armed wherever they go in Kanem and Bahr el Ghazal. They carry weapons for personal protection, but use these for hunting as well, so as to take advantage of a chance prey or to pursue game for the pot more systematically. Depending on ethnic affiliation and location, men's weapons are spears, a lance, throwing knives and/or a boomerang and a knife. The principal weapon among the Haddad Kreda and the pastoral Kreda is a barbed spear known as *aedi* in both Kreda and Kanembu. Spears normally 'come' in sets of four and these are carried over the shoulder in a leather pouch, *karaga* (cf. Cat. No. 28). The spears are about 132 cm long, the spear-heads alone about 32 cm. The latter are forged by Haddad smiths and are bought from them at local markets. The iron blade has two rows of barbs and a socket into which the shaft is fitted. Blades are finely incised with geometrical designs. Haddad smiths do sell spears with shafts, but most Haddad men fit up the spear-heads with shafts and balancing devices themselves. Shafts are made from roots of *Acacia raddiana,* or *tefi,* the balancing device of an iron or more commonly a copper thread wound neatly around the shaft's end. Weapons are frequently furnished with a copper ring because the metal is believed to hold magical properties and hence protective forces.

Another weapon of protection used occasionally for hunting among Kanembu, Kreda and the Haddad is a lance known as *aedi* in both languages (cf. Cat. Nos. 30, 58 & 59). These lances are about 215 cm long, the iron blades 48 cm. The Haddad Kanembu carry the lance largely as a weapon of protection nowadays, while the Haddad Kreda still make use of it when hunting antelope. In Europe, the deadly efficiency of the lance in expert hands has been known from Cossack regiments and it was demonstrated at Waterloo by Napoleon's cavalry, leading to a boost of lancer regiments in Britain in the 19th century. In Kanem as well as in many parts of western Africa the lance has been in use by cavalry way back in time. It was the weapon par excellence of the cavalry of the Kameni kingdom *(cf. Fig. 3,8)*. To the Haddad, the lance was previously indispensable and the ultimate weapon when in risky pursuit of dangerous game such as elephants, large antelopes and, not least, lions, undertakings that have become extremely rare.

Lions used to be common in Kanem and the Bahr el Ghazal but had become rare by the time of our fieldwork, so rare in fact that people kept track of every specimen coming to their attention. We learned of a few lions that had been spotted in the Bahr el Ghazal a few months prior to our stay, and of one specimen that had appeared in the late 1950s. One of the former had been tracked down by four Kreda, two or three of whom got seriously injured by the beast in trying to kill it with their lances. The Haddad used to organize communal hunts in which forty to fifty lancers would track down a lion, surround and chase it out of hiding by means of shouting and by throwing pieces of wood into the thickets where these animals typically take refuge. Chapelle mentions that despite the fact that lion hunting was extremely dangerous, the hunters were supposed to show no sign of fear (1957: 206). Our informants painted a slightly different picture of traditional lion hunting. We were told that only the very brave would go lion hunting, but also that the key exercise was the trapping of the animal in huge nets prior to any attempt by the hunters to thrust their lances into the big cat.

Ethnic groups in Kanem also use a spear with a conical iron spear-head called *kulai* (cf. Cat. No. 56). The name refers to the tip of the antler of antelopes, a material previously in common use for these heads and a template for the iron ones, we were told. We saw a number of *kulai* in use among the Kreda and were able to purchase one with

a.   b.   c.   d.

9,1. Spears. Photo J.K.

a. Spear with blade of a horn of a damalisque antelope and a shaft made from the root of a tefi acacia. By nature, damalisque antlers are curved and have an undulated surface. The Haddad transform this by heating the horn in embers, after which the horn can be straightened out. These spears are used by teenage boys. Cat. no. 34.

b & c. Two out of an original set of four barbed, iron spears, aedi, with shafts of the root of the tefi acacia. Cat. no. 28.

d. Small spear, kulai, with a conically shaped blade of iron. Used by boys to enhance their throwing skills. Cat. no. 56.

9,2. Boomerangs, safarok, made from wood. Cat. nos. 61 & 60. Photo J.K.

9,3. Throwing knives are used by the Haddad Kreda and also some Haddad Kanembu. Around N'Guri, however, this was not the case according to our informants. Cat. nos. 31 & 65. Photo J.K.

the head made from the tip of the horn of the scimitar. It is sharply pointed and not curved as is its normal shape, because it has been artificially straightened out. This is done by rubbing it with butter and placing it under glowing embers until it softens and can be given the desired shape (cf. Cat. No. 34). *Kulai* with antelope spear-heads are used by teenage boys, who make these weapons themselves. Younger boys are given spears with heads of gazelle or goat antlers to enhance their throwing skills. These are also known as *kulai* (cf. Cat. No. 29).

Another weapon in use throughout Kanem and Bahr el Ghazal both for hunting and as weapons of defence and/ or aggression is the throwing knife, *ngili* (cf. Cat. No. 32). It gained prominence during the rule of the French, who armed local policemen with these knives, the common weapon of the Sara people of southern Chad who formed the main stock of the force. Police officers carried three to

four knives when patrolling until 1963, when these were replaced by revolvers. Still, throwing knives were not common in Kanem and Bahr el Ghazal, when we lived there. They were rarely used for hunting, although they may effectively cut the legs of a fleeing gazelle. We found only small Haddad boys playing with these knives (cf. Cat. No. 31).

Yet another, quite rare weapon in Kanem and the Bahr el Ghazal is the boomerang, known as *sofrok* or *safarok*. We learned from the Haddad that boomerangs of wood and iron were commonly used by previous generations, not only as a regular weapon of defence, which in the hand of an expert could be a deadly, but also for hunting. A boomerang is a missile weapon. It comes in two types: the return boomerang well known from its use by Australian Aborigines for hunting and ritual use, and the non-return boomerang normally used for defence. The Haddad boomerang is of the latter kind. It is made of wood of the savonier tree and lightly sickle-shaped. We purchased a heavy, slightly curved specimen from a man in Chedra, whose place of origin was Wadai, where boomerangs apparently are common (cf. Cat. Nos. 33 & 60). According to this informant, Wadai men generally carry several boomerangs at the time, using them not only as a means of defence but also for hunting gazelles and guinea fowl. What was still in use was a smaller wooden version made for children as part toy part a means of practising their skills of throwing and aiming (cf. Cat. No. 61).

Ethnic groups of Kanem and Bahr el Ghazal also attract and kill animals and birds with ingenious devices such as snares, traps and pitfalls. We found only little evidence of these methods among the Haddad, however. We were told by some Haddad Kanembu that they used to put up snares for some species of birds, but not guinea fowl. They rarely took the trouble anymore, they said, and we did not come across anyone who actually did so. People explained that snares were made from hair, each noose being tied to a long string or rope to be placed on the ground at a carefully selected spot. The string would be hidden with sand, the nooses left in the open for catching birds by their feet. Some Haddad Kreda said that they made snares from the hair of horses and cows; others told that they did not even know how to use a snare. The fact, that we did not meet any trappers does not necessarily imply that traps are not set. Kanembu and related groups to the west of Lake Chad are reported to do so, not only for small animals but also to trap larger ones (Meek 1931: 415-16).

The most significant of Haddad hunting technologies, however, are either nets or bow and arrow, the one generally excluding the other, apparently. The Haddad Kreda hunt solely with nets, while the Haddad Kanembu of the N'Guri region are archers. Some Kanembu-speaking Haddad living at the fringes of the Bahr el Ghazal turned to nets during the early part of the 20th century, as far as we could assess, yet were forced to abandon the technique again a few years prior to our arrival. The French gendarmerie had come down hard on them for doing so, confiscating and/or burning their nets and imposing heavy fines on anyone caught with one. The ban on net-hunting had proved much simpler to enforce among the Haddad Kanembu than the Haddad Kreda, because the former were sedentary and hence easy to locate. We were not able to assess how wide-

9,4. The ground hornbill (Bucorvus abyssinicus) is by far the largest of the hornbills, measuring an impressive 90-100 cm tall bird. It weighs a good four kilos. The bird's look and movements are imitated by hunters not only among the Haddad Kanembu but also a number of other indigenous groups in northern Nigeria, Cameroun and Sudan. Little is known about the ground hornbill in the wild. It has been described by Buffon and Levaillant, the latter observing that the bird has very big eyes, an observation which is reflected in Haddad masks (Levaillant 1806, V:111). It inhabits savanna and sub-desert scrub and nests in big trees, preferably the baobab. The bird is sedentary and forages in pairs with one or two offspring, feeding on vertebrates, including tortoises, lizards, spiders and beetles. Fruits, seeds and groundnuts are also eaten, according to Delhoyo. Delhoyo, J. 1992-2005, VI; Levaillant, F. 1806, V: Fig. 230.

9,5. Hunter demonstrating how he creeps up on game. He wears a mask cut to the liking of the ground hornbill tied to his forehead (cf. Cat. no. 13), simulating the movements of the bird on the outlook for fodder. The hunter holds the bow in the left hand, the arrows in the right. ▶

9,6. Bow with a case to protect it from moisture. This is important, in particular during the rainy season, as the twined sinew string is ruined if it gets wet. Cat. nos. 16 & 17. Photo J.K.

9,7. Haddad hunters carry quivers with between 10-20 arrows when they go hunting. Quivers are made from the roots of tefi acacia and covered with hide. Cat. nos. 11 & 18. Photo J.K.

9,8. When a bow is not in use, the string is wound up at the one end. Cat. no. 17. Photo J.K.

9,9. Hunter demonstrating how to shoot. The bow is held horizontally with the left hand while the arrows rest on the index finger.

spread the use of nets was among the Haddad Kanembu, but there is no doubt that the hunting method par excellence among these people is and was archery, the art to which we now turn.

DISGUISE – HUNTING THE HADDAD KANEMBU WAY

Hunting was of dwindling significance to the subsistence of the Haddad Kanembu at the time of our study, as previously stated, yet still pursued systematically by some men. As long as buffaloes, elephants and other mammals were plentiful in Kanem, i.e. well into the 20th century, game formed a crucial part of the nutrition and communal hunting had its place in the economy. An older hunter

at N'Guri told us, for example, how he had killed buffalo in his younger years. With the considerable decrease in the populations of large game, hunting not only decreased in economic significance, it became more individualized. The hunters we became acquainted with around N'Guri and Chedra were relatively few in number. They primarily hunted gazelles, in particular *Gazella rufifrons,* but a Dama antelope was killed shortly before our visit just north of Chedra. Other species were also bagged, but the hunters did not chase all of the species in the area. Some Haddad Kanembu men claimed, for instance, that they did not eat jackals, as do the Haddad Kreda. Nor would they go bow hunting for guinea fowl, some argued, claiming that even when wounded by an arrow these birds could fly too far away to be retrieved.

9,10. On the hunt. The masks were purchased for the Moesgaard Museum. Cat. nos. 5 & 6.

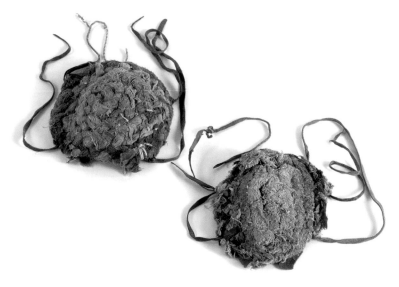

9,11. Hunters wear protective pads on their knees when creeping up on the game as the ground is often full of thorns and sometimes gravel that is hurtful. Cat. no. 19. Photo J.K.

9,12. Hunters use different kinds of arrows, depending on the species they want to kill. The shafts are all from reed, but the arrowheads are of different size and form. This particular hunter carried specific arrows for guinea fowl as well as for buffalo, which he had killed several times. Cat. no. 9. Photo J.K.

The Haddad Kanembu hunt with bow and arrows, as previously indicated, the plural 'arrows' being the proper description as most Haddad Kanembu hunters shoot two arrows at a time. Other characteristics are the use of poison and the application of magic, the latter being considered absolutely indispensable to secure hunting luck and bag game. Poison is crucial to the successful bagging of game and invariably used when the Haddad hunt larger animals like gazelle or antelope not to speak of the buffalos, lions and occasionally elephants which were killed historically. Smaller species can be bagged more easily without a poisonous remedy. Still, the hunters of Chedra maintained that they used poison without exception. Only porcupines and foxes are hunted without further ado, as they are taken in the den.

The most striking feature of Haddad Kanembu hunting, however, is the use of disguise and emulation of animal behaviour to approach the game. The common form of disguise nowadays is to emulate the Abyssinian ground hornbill, *Bucorvus abyssinicus,* a majestic bird some 107 cm tall. It has an almost black plumage and a curious casque which is truncated and open at the front. The head and neck are without plumage and largely of a blue-grey or red and grey colour. The bird utters a deep and far-carrying grunting sound. This hornbill species seeks food on the ground, as the name indicates, walking slowly and gracefully while picking up food items with its long beak. It is the looks and behaviour of this grand creature that Haddad hunters try to copy. They use a black sheep-skin to cover the chest and obscure the fact that there is a man behind it, and attach a mask to the forehead that is made to look like the neck and head of the ground hornbill itself, sometimes by applying the cranium and beak of a dead specimen (cf. Cat. No. 12). When game has been spotted, the attire is put on and the hunter crawls towards the animal, moving in the same way as the live ground hornbill, bending his head first to one side and then to the other, emulating the bird's search for food. The Haddad have used other forms of disguise as well, the most spectacular being the application of complete slough of ostrich feathers, as depicted on rock paintings in the Sahara. This was commonly used as long as these grand birds were numerous on the Sahelian plains. This is not the case anymore nor is the grand flocks of antelope which the Haddad approached in this disguise. The Haddad are not unique in emulating animal behaviour when hunting. It is an age old technique used by hunters all over the world in various forms. Hunters in Nigeria and Sudan are also known to have sneaked up upon game emulating the Abyssinian ground hornbill as do the Haddad Kanembu. We shall return to this issue and the use of disguise and magic in Chapter 10.

The equipment of a Haddad hunter consists in short of the following items: Bow and arrows, a quiver, a pair of cotton pads to protect the knees when creeping up upon the game and a disguise consisting of a black sheepskin and a mask that represents the ground hornbill, a knife to cut the throat of the animal, as prescribed by Islam, and finally a spear or lance for protection and/or eventual hunting.

The bows are all of a kind - a type more similar to the longbow than to the recurve bow, except that it is not 'as tall as a man', measuring only some 125 cm to 127 cm. It is a simple bow, reflexed and incurved at the middle, and consisting basically of just a bow leg and a string. Like the longbow, it has no handle section or winding, nor an arrow or a notching point at the place where arrows shoot most smoothly and consistently. Haddad hunters are experts and make do with basics. Their simple bow allows for optimal speed. The bow leg is made of a single stave from a branch of *Acacia raddiana* or the jujubier, *Zizyphus sp.,* known locally as *solu* or *solo* (cf. Cat. Nos. 8, 10 & 16). The central part of the bow leg, where the hunter takes his grip, is stiff and resisting, tapering off gradually towards the ends, to which the string is fitted. Some bows are furnished with amulets to improve their performance (cf. Cat. No. 8).

A bow is only stringed when in use. The string is somewhat longer than the bow, the spare part being wound around the upper horn of the bow, as is the rest of the string when the hunting is over. When strung, it runs longitudinally along the middle of the belly. The Haddad do not string the bow very tightly and therefore the string runs pretty close to this. The string is twined from strands of sinew (ox). It is round, smooth and not frayed, as a defect string may result in a broken bow. Some hunters make use of a 'cat's-whisker', one or two tufts of cotton thread or fine leather strips to reduce the vibrations, the noise of which may give away the hunter when the arrow is released. Neither bows nor the sinew strings fare well in rain and most hunters make cases for their bows to protect these (cf. Cat. No. 17).

The arrows, *kini,* are of a type widely used throughout the Sudan. The head is of iron and purchased from Haddad smiths at local markets. It measures some fourteen to fifteen centimetres when including the iron stem, the end of which is inserted in the shaft and fastened with resin. The shaft is made of reed, in rare cases of wood. Sinew threads are wound around the joints of the reed to reinforce the shaft, as well as around the notch at the back of the arrow to prevent it from splintering. The Haddad do not fletch their arrows. The head measures between 13 cm to 14 cm including the stem, the head itself some 3 cm. It is razor-sharp and has two pointed barbs. Arrows weigh a mere 14 to 16 grams and are hence light enough to fly with a flat trajectory to the animal, yet still heavy enough to be precise and penetrate the skin. This is different from the arrows used by European bow-hunters, which aims at killing the animal by penetrating deeply into its body and hence weighs considerably more than the arrows of the Haddad which only needs to penetrate the skin in order for the poison to work.[2] Arrows are regularly given a coating of poison, except those used for hunting guinea fowl, pigeons and other birds. Instead, these are furnished with special arrowheads (cf. Cat. No. 9).

Ten or more arrows are usually carried in a quiver, *kara.* Typically, quivers are made of the root of the *tefi,* alias *Acacia raddiana,* as are so many of Haddad implements, and then covered entirely or partly by ox-hide. Other sorts of wood are applied too (cf. Cat. Nos. 9, 11 & 18). The quiver is carried in a leather or bast strap over the left shoulder, this being the most expedient if the hunter is right-handed and must be able swiftly to pick an arrow. Despite the poisonous coating, experienced hunters carry their arrows heads upward because they can be seized faster this way, as the barbs do not entangle so easily. The arrows are wrapped in a piece of cotton cloth to prevent them from rattling when carried, as this is potentially damaging to the arrows and may alert the game.

Shooting is almost always done from a kneeling position. Most hunters shoot two arrows a time when hunting gazelle and other mammals. The bow is held horizontally with the left hand - arrow or arrows resting on the index finger *(cf. Fig. 9,9).* The bow string is pulled by the three middle fingers of the right hand, the notch located between the index and the middle finger. The Haddad bow is not always pulled the full length of the arrow. We did

9,13. Mask made to resemble the head and neck of the ground hornbill; cf. *Fig 9,10*. Cat. no. 5. Photo J.K.

not measure the drawing-power of the bows while in the field, and cannot make up for this with museum specimens, as the strings of these since long have lost their elasticity.

The Haddad Kanembu are highly skilled archers, as previously mentioned. Our informants claimed that they never missed their target. Whether such statements reflect wishful thinking or merciful forgetfulness, I cannot say. Hunters seem keen to keep up skills, training on various targets. They possess one or more arrows with a blunt head for that purpose, made, for example, from an empty cartridge. The hunters we observed were fine marksmen, easily hitting a 15x15 cm target at twenty metres. This is

a normal shooting distance for gazelle and antelope, we were told, as is the case of bow-hunting in Europe, where training at distances up to thirty metres is recommended to achieve the necessary skills for targeting game at a distance of 20 metres (Richter Nielsen et. al. 1999: 23).

Like a bow-hunting sportsman, the Haddad Kanembu also aim to hurt the animal fatally by shooting the arrow into its vital organs, i.e. right into the zone of the major vessels that carry blood to all parts of the body. The art of a Western bow-hunter is to make the animal bleed swiftly to death. Generally, animals have to lose about one third or thirty-five per cent of their total blood volume in order to succumb. A fine shot causes maximum blood loss in the shortest possible time. If an animal is only superficially wounded, the chances that it may escape and recover are very good (Barnhart, J. (ed.): 1994: 35-6). Haddad Kanembu hunters target the heart, liver and blood-carrying vessels in this part of the body to make the poison work most effectively. But the death of the animal depends not on bleeding, but rather on the contrary, that the poison flows with the blood to paralyse the animal. Strong poison is the alpha and omega of successful archery, yet the animal does not die instantly. Hunters do spend time trailing game, but claim that they are always able to successfully recover downed game. Due to their intimate knowledge of the environment and the animals' habits, they can 'read nature' and locate wounded or killed game.

Hunting is basically a one-man venture among the Haddad Kanembu today. Historically, large mammals and predators such as lions and leopards called for communal efforts, but such hunting parties had come to a stop in the 1960s' and the hunters set out on their pursuit alone or in the company of one or two men at most. In fact, hunting is perceived as an individual undertaking among these Haddad. In their view, hunting entails the ultimate encounter between man and beast, and we found that the hunting equipment including bow and arrow was highly personalized. Each man made his own gear, except for arrowheads which were bought from smiths at local markets. Bows are for sale here, but it appeared that these were purchased largely by non-Haddad. A Haddad hunter makes his own bow and hafts the arrows. He does also endow these with supernatural power by means of magical formula, amulets and poison smeared on the arrowheads.

Poison, secrecy and success

Technical skill not withstanding, Haddad Kanembu hunters consider strong poison crucial to their success at hunting. The alpha and omega, however, is magic, as we shall see. The potency of the poison depends both on the ingredients and on the very way it is produced, a skill that hunters not willingly share with one another. Some hunters know how to make strong poison others are not that good at it, the Haddad say.

Most hunters make their own poison and keep the recipes to themselves. They have to purchase the necessary ingredients, however, as none of these are locally available. The most potent poison, according to our informants, is made of the bones of snakes imported from the Bornu region. The bones are pounded to flour in a mortar, but we learned no more about the process of fabrication. The poison was said to be extremely venomous and to have been dispensed with lately, as it spoiled too much of the meat.

Instead, the Haddad Kanembu use a vegetable poison, which only affects meat around the wound itself. The distinguishing factor is that two plants are required to make it effective. The major ingredient is the chopped fruits of a tree known as *djo,* which grows in the mountainous parts of northern Nigeria. The fruits are purchased by middlemen at large markets, for example in Fort-Lamy, and then sold to the hunters at local markets such as those at Chedra and N'Guri. The price was 75 CFA for the contents of a small tin equivalent of about 10 centilitres (cf. Cat. No. 20). We bought four of these in Chedra - the usual portion purchased by a hunter who wants to make fresh poison - and had one of the hunters make the substance near the hut where we stayed in order to register the process in its entirety. Our friend started the process on the evening of the 7th September and finished it on the following day.

The very first rule when making poison, the hunter stressed, was to exert great care when handling the substances. A scratch or small wound on the hand could prove fatal if it came in contact with the toxicant. The following implements were used: a big earthenware pot, part of a chipped earthenware pot, an old basket of dum palm (used as sieve), a pear-shaped spoon of calabash provided with a half-metre-long wooden shaft, the blade of a knife with a bent point, a wooden mortar with a chisel-shaped iron

pestle, a piece of mat of dum palm leaves, a tripod (which actually only had two legs) to support the pots during the cooking. The modus operandi was as follows:

1. The hunter poured four measures of chopped *djo* fruit (four decilitres) and a corresponding four measures of cold water into the large earthenware pot and left it there for the night. Early the following morning, the water was filtered from the fruit substance through the shabby basket over the chipped earthenware pot.

2. Next the steeped fruit was poured back into the big pot with eight measures of water and put on the fire. The contents cooked for about two hours. Once again the brownish substance was filtered, the impure water passing through the shabby basket over the chipped pot.

9,14. Haddad Kanembu hunters are renowned for their ability to make effective poison. The main ingredient is seeds from the djo tree. The seeds are imported from Nigeria and bought by the hunters at local markets. The mortar and iron pestle are used to pound a lump of the finished poison into very fine grains. These are diluted with water and applied to the arrows. Cat. no. 20a-e. Photo L.L.

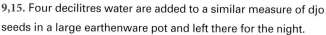

9,15. Four decilitres water are added to a similar measure of djo seeds in a large earthenware pot and left there for the night.

9,16. The steeped and cooked poisonous substance is poured from the cracked pot, where it has been cooking into an earthenware pot through a filter made of a piece of a dum palm mat.

3. Then the steeped and cooked fruit substance was mixed once again with fresh water in the big pot, this time with five measures of water only, i.e. approximately 5 decilitres, to be cooked for another hour, after which the contents were filtered once more, as previously.

4. The fruity substance was then removed from the big jar by means of the calabash spoon and put on a mat made of dum palm leaves. Fruit that accidentally had been poured out with the water during the filtering but had been retained by the sieve was placed next to the mass already placed here. The fruity leftovers in the big jar, which could not be removed with the spoon, were cleaned out as follows: The largely empty jar was put on the fire once again, but only for a short while. Being al-

most empty it dried up quickly, and the fruit substance that had stuck to it could be removed quite easily. It was placed with the bulk of the fruit substance on the mat.

5. The brownish liquid contained in the chipped pot from the previous filtering, was poured into the big pot and put on the fire to cook for three to four hours.

6. Then the brownish liquid was once again poured back into the chipped pot and put on the fire.

7. After another few hours a tiny bit of pounded plant material, twice what could be held between two fingers was added to the poisonous liquid. The powder was made from the roots of a tree called *barkawada* - a species which grows in the region of Chedra but appears to be quite rare. The plant's powder is said to make the poi-

9,17. The brownish, poisonous substance is once again put on the fire to boil on the chipped pot, which rests on three conical, earthenware 'legs'.

9,18. The finished, finely pounded poison is placed on a piece of an old wooden container and stirred with a little water, after which the substance is ready for application.

son 'strong'. Without the *barkawada* powder the poison would not be efficacious.

8. When the brownish poisonous liquid had boiled about twenty minutes, it turned glutinous and blackish and was taken off the fire. By then the substance had boiled down substantially and the hunter proceeded by meticulously scraping off that which had coagulated on the side of the chipped pot during the process. Using his bent knife as well as the blade of an axe, he worked his way all around the rim of the pot, taking care that the scrapings mixed with the main substance. Then the tripod was removed from the fireplace and the chipped pot placed directly in the embers to heat up the poison to very high temperatures.

9. After about an hour of constant heating in the embers and continuous scraping the sides of the pot to mix what was drying up here with the rest of the poison, the substance had condensed into a thick mass, no more than a tin in volume, the very same measure the hunter had used for the initial ingredients of chopped fruit.

10. Then the hunter raked the embers aside and put the chipped pot directly on top of the warm ashes for a few minutes.

11. Finally the pot was removed completely from the heat, its sides cleaned of whatever poisonous mass was still sticking to its sides, after which all of the vicious substance was shaped like a sausage, some 15cm long and three to four centimetres thick. The hunter kept the

9,19. The arrows are carefully inspected before the poison is smeared on them.

9,20. Arrows with fresh poison.

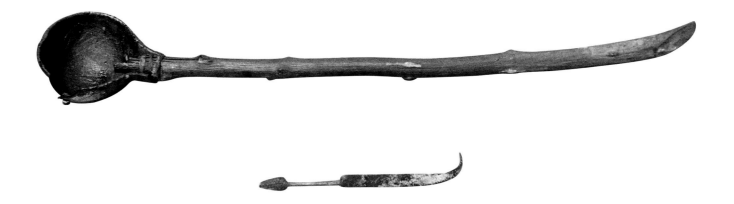

9,21. Tools used during the production of the poison: a) a ladle made from a calabash and furnished with a long shaft which is used to remove the chopped djo seeds, and b) a small knife with a bent blade which the hunter used to scrape the sides of the pot while the substance is boiling.

poison wrapped for a few days before he showed us how to apply it to his arrows. He went by this as follows:

a) Firstly a tiny piece of the poisonous 'sausage' is cut off the main substance with a knife and placed in the tiny wooden mortar.

b) After pounding the substance for some time with the iron pestle most of the poison will be pulverized, although still mixed with some harder grains of poison.

c) Then the content is poured into a fragment of an old wooden container. A little water is added and the hunter stirs the mass with his knife or the pestle until almost all of the grains have dissolved.

d) Then the poison is placed in the sun for about twenty minutes, after which the hunter again stirs the substance with a stick adding a little more water.

e) By now the consistency of the dark poison is fairly thin and ready for application.

However, before doing so, the hunter carefully inspected all of his arrows, checking if the notches were fine, the arrowheads firmly fixed in the shafts and the two parts perfectly aligned. Being satisfied with the result, the poison was smeared on the arrowheads with a spare arrowhead. Each arrowhead was turned around to ensure that the coating covered all parts while taking care that the poison did not drip. When the arrowheads had been coated with poison, they were placed vertically for drying - each shaft stuck carefully into the sandy ground.

The poison used by Haddad hunters is not only easily soluble but also said to be highly potent. We were told that if a poisonous arrow hits an animal and has contact with the blood the animal is bound to die, sooner or later. This will be the case with a gazelle, for example, even if this has been grazed only slightly on one of its forelegs. How fast an animal succumbs depends on a variety of factors, one being the nature and place of the wound but also the seriousness of bleeding and whether or not the animal gets stressed.

Despite the deadly effect of poison on game, the meat can be safely eaten except for a small lump right around the wound, an area say of five to six centimetres. This part must be cut away but the rest can be eaten without discomfort. The meat does not have an unpleasant after-taste. Arrows can be used several times without recoating if they have hit the ani-mal only superficially. If the arrowhead has gotten deeper into the animal, however, new poison has to be applied.

Masks and disguise

Hunting takes great skill. It requires an intimate knowledge of the environment, the fauna, its properties and behaviour and of how to adapt the hunting method to existing conditions. It goes without saying that a hunter must know how to track down and creep up upon wild animals without alerting them. Hunting with bow and arrow presupposes that the hunter gets as close to the game as about twenty metres, as previously mentioned. Haddad Kanembu hunters live in locally varied environments and have developed different hunting techniques adapted to these. In the southern part of Kanem, where the vegetation is pretty dense as the Sahelien sparseness give way for a more lush savannah, there is sufficient cover for the hunter to steal up on his target without further ado. This is not the case further to the north, where trees and bushes such as the decorative Sodom apple are few and far between. When Haddad Kanembu hunters cannot find cover in nature, they apply the age-old trick of disguise to get up close to the animals. They disguise themselves differently depending on what kind of game they are after. An economically significant form of hunting, widely practised by the Haddad Kanembu of Chedra in former days was for ostrich. The great flocks were drastically diminished during the later part of the nineteenth and early decades of the twentieth century, as we have learned, but up till World War I Haddad hunters would still sneak up to these huge birds in a disguise of - yes, ostrich feathers. Some hunters told that they sometimes simulated the marabou stork, *Ciconia abdinii,* but the most commonly used method was to creep up on game like gazelle, antelope and other large animals disguised as and emulating the movements of the ground hornbill, *Bucorvus abyssinicus.* To do so successfully the hunters cover their chests and sometimes back with black sheepskin and wear a mask on the head in shape of the head and neck of the bird, as previously mentioned. Each hunter makes his own mask, just as he creates most of his hunting gear and the masks look somewhat differently (cf. Cat. Nos. 5, 6, 12, 13 & 15). Some are carved of simple wood and not embellished with a leather cover, while others are. The beak of one of the masks that I purchased was made of the horn of a buffalo (cf. Cat. No. 6), while the head of another was decorated with small ostrich feathers inserted under the leather cover on top of the bird's head (cf. Cat. No. 15). One mask incorporated the cranium of the ground hornbill itself as its main component. The 'head' is part of – or tied to – a 'neck' carved in the likeness of a bird's neck with a tightly fitting bandage. The mask's head may be entirely or partly covered by leather. It is invariably adorned with eyes, made from cowries and beads glued onto the 'face' with resin. The eyes are highly important, one hunter told us, as it is they which 'fool' the game. This reminds me of the fact that when the Inuit of Greenland hunt grouse they look for the eyes of the bird. The grouse is so well camouflaged that it is betrayed only by its dark eyes. The lower part of the 'neck' ends in a rectangular or disc-shaped wooden piece which is placed against the hunter's forehead. A leather strap inserted in a hole in the flat end-piece keeps this in position when tied firmly behind the head. Another leather string, also tied to the 'neck' of the mask is held between the teeth of the hunter to stabilize the mask when approaching the game.

Technical skills, knowledge of animal behaviour and clever disguise do not make for the bagging of game alone. In the view of Haddad hunters, this depends ultimately on potent magic. For this reason, the bows are treated with magic, just as the very making of poison involves magic precautions. Last but not least, the effectiveness of masks and hence of the hunters in fooling the animals is believed to rely utterly on the effectiveness of such forces. A bird mask treated with truly potent magic enables its owner to crawl up close to any kind of game, so close, hunters would say, that the two of them may share the coolness of the very same shadowy tree. Any use of magic is highly personal and knowledge hereof should under no circumstance be shared with other hunters or the magic will loose its power. We were only told about magic under tight secrecy. Beyond securing that his hunting equipment is endowed with magic, a hunter may take other magical precautions to ensure luck in hunting (cf. Cat. No. 20).

However this may be, an accomplished hunter must possess the patience, sensitivity and the ability to get close to wild animals, the marksmanship to set in a poisoned arrow or lance and the skills to track down wounded game, as previously indicated. The Haddad are experts in these fields. They can move noiselessly through the vegetation, do not scare off wounded animals and know how to 'read' traces, however miniscule, marking the trail of flight. Haddad hunters put on their disguise only when game has been spotted. A sheep-skin is tied with a string to cover the chest, another to cover the back whereupon the mask is tied firmly to the forehead. When ready, the hunter will slowly and cautiously approach his quarry, first in an upright position. Later, as he gets closer to the game, he crawls forward on his knees and bends his head with the bird-mask first to one side then to the other, simulating the movements of a ground hornbill picking seeds and other edible stuff from the ground. Now and then he pauses, as do all birds and animals, being always on the alert, only to proceed a few moments later peacefully 'eating' his way towards the game. To crawl up on game in this way is both strenuous and often highly uncomfortable due to thorns and other prickly vegetation on the ground, in particular at places where the "cram-cram" has favourable conditions of growth. Hunting in the midday heat, when game doze lightly in the shimmering heat means that the hunters must crawl on burning sand. To take some of the strain and ease their path hunters cover the knees with pads made from old rags. The disguise and gestures simulating a slowly moving bird are applied with great ingenuity. For obvious reasons, we could not follow hunters actually crawling up close to the game but had to base our appraisal on 'performances' which hunters 'staged' for us. These were remarkable.

HUNTING PORCUPINE IN THE DEN

One of the animals hunted regularly both for its meat and quills, is the porcupine, *Hystrix cristatus senegalica*. We had hoped to participate in a hunting expedition ourselves during our stay in N'Guri. Due to a misunderstanding, the hunters went off on their own, however, returning with a live porcupine for us, a kind gesture but not at all what we had had in mind. The hunters told us afterwards how they catch porcupines in their dens without weapons of any kind except for a burning torch. It requires specific skills, we learned, possessed by a few Haddad only in any given village.

Porcupines are stout, heavily built rodents that feed on roots, bark, tubers and other vegetable food. Their meat is highly sought after, and I can only confirm that it tastes delicious. For this reason they are hunted regularly. Porcupines are nocturnal creatures that sleep during the day in subterranean dens, which they generally dig out themselves. They run pretty fast but do not gain such speed that they

9,22. After a successful hunt for porcupine. The feet of the animal are tied together in order that it can be hung on a long stick for transportation.

can avoid being hunted down if encountered in the early morning or at dusk. They are easily killed with one blow. As they are nocturnal, the Haddad largely hunt them in their dens. Porcupine hunting requires collaboration between a few men sometimes with the participation of a teenage boy or two as well, as these can make their way through the galleries of the den more easily due to their smaller size. This task is not without danger. Porcupines place their dens up to four metres below ground and the galleries leading to and fro may be as long as ten metres. Some sections of the galleries are wide enough for a man to pass through, but now and again they narrow down and must be enlarged by digging before the hunter can proceed. A gallery may even be so cramped and/or make one or more bends, in which case shafts must be dug to make a passage. Encountering such hindrances on his way, the hunter signals his posi-

tion to his fellow hunters by knocking on the ceiling of the gallery, enabling these to commence the arduous work of digging the shaft. The same procedure is repeated when the den itself has been located, after which the hunter backs out into the free. The entrance is subsequently blocked and a shaft dug to get to the den and the porcupine alive. An extra incentive to engage in porcupine hunting is the not infrequent chance of killing hyenas, as these animals frequently take refuge in the dens. It should be added, however, that this seldom poses a danger to the hunter, as hyenas rarely attack in the dark. It reveals a lot about Haddad livelihood and efforts to subsist that they will spend so much energy on getting a porcupine. A reminder, once again, to take simplified theories on the low energy spent by hunting and gathering societies with a grain of salt (Barnard & Woodburn 1988: 11).

9,23. Chari with a pale fox, vulpes pallida aertzeni, completely entangled in a net.

HUNTING WITH CHARI

Only few Haddad Kanembu who hunted with nets, as previously indicated. We met some families east of Méchimeré who had picked up the occupation fairly recently from the Haddad Kreda. They caught gazelle, jackal and other small animals, but not antelope. They made their nets from sinew, either from domesticated animals, cows, goats or sheep, or from the bark of an acacia (*Acacia raddiana*) - never from cotton thread, as was the habit of our friend Chari, whom we got to know quite well. He was a fairly young man, probably in his thirties. He lived near N'Guri and supported his family largely by hunting with nets. He applied his skills to relatively small animals, in particular to the pale fox and to hares. The pale fox is said to have very fine and tasty meat, somewhat similar to rabbit. It feeds largely on small lizards but also on plants and roots. Another animal hunted by Chari for its meat was the genet, which occurs in quite large numbers. It is related to the civet and somewhat larger than a normal European cat. The genet is quite fierce but Chari would still bag it alive, as he did the other animals he pursued. Another part of the diet of Chari and his family was the ever-noisy guinea fowl and, in lesser numbers, partridge, francolin and sand-grouse. I do not know whether Chari went for bustards as well, probably so, but he did not hunt gazelle, antelope or any other large animal. He had learned the trade from his father, he told us. Hunting with nets was alien to the Haddad Kanembu, he declared, and no one besides him used these in the N'Guri area, nor did he know of any oral traditions indicating that the Haddad Kanembu had ever done so.

Chari hunted alone. His nets were tiny. He made them himself: the sticks from branches of a tree he called *bolokor* (Kanembu) or *chaw* (Arabic), the meshes from cotton thread bought at the local market. The sticks were approximately 65-70 cm long, the length of the net between 70 to 80 centimetres, the width of a mesh about 4-6 cm (cf. Cat. No. 22). We joined Chari on his hunting expeditions for several days, exploring first one then another part of the Sahelien landscape surrounding N'Guri. We were not particularly successful, but this is by no means an indication of Chari's general ability to bag game.

The pale fox is one of the most common mammals of Kanem. Dunes are dotted with fox holes in many places, even when these do not rise steeply. Dens are also found in gently rolling countryside and even in places which rise but slightly above ground level. Wherever the foxes choose to live, they dig their way into the dune through some ten to fifteen holes, all entries to an overall system interconnected by subterranean galleries. As soon as Chari had spotted one of these complexes, he looked for indications that the den was inhabited. Kneeling in front of various entries he searched the sand for fresh tracks and put his head as far into the gallery as possible to hear whether the foxes were at home. If concluding that this was the case, he prepared for the hunt. The overall strategy for putting up the nets depended on the distribution of the holes. If these were located fairly close to one another, the nets were put up in a semi-circle in front of these, all twenty-one of them, encircling one part of the entire complex (*cf. Fig. 9,27*) - the one planned to be the escape route of the fox. Chari placed the nets so closely that one slightly overlapped the next, and also in such a way that they leant towards the fox holes. The sticks were stuck so lightly into the ground that a catapulting animal could easily knock over the net in its flight, hopefully getting itself entangled in the process. Normally the 'battue' proceeds with the wind, which is why nets are put up on the 'lee side' of the complex. This is not always the case, however – not, for example, if the den is located on a fairly steep slope, in which case the foxes are beaten from cover from the windward side.

Once the available nets are in place, the holes at odd angles are blocked with material at hand: pieces of clothing, the hunting bag or whatever, and those most peripheral to the nets filled with sand to prevent the escape of the fox via these. Only then would Chari start to actually chase the fox out of the den. Success depends on whether or not the fox runs out of an entrance in front of the nets. To make that happen the hunter must pester the animal in such a way that it chooses to take flight using a gallery facing the nets. Chari jammed his stick in and out of the entrance holes at each end of the 'back' side of the complex, treating first one then, in turn, the other holes initially blocked with sand. In each case the sand was removed and then put back again to prevent the fox from escaping through these 'back doors'. As soon as all of these holes had been covered his efforts centred on those loosely blocked with cloth or a basket. Whenever the fox had been 'teased' by his stick the hole was blocked again, this time thoroughly with sand. Finally Chari turned his attention to the last

9,24. Pestering foxes to make them leave the den and run into the twenty-one nets that have been placed in a semi-circle.

9,25. Dry weeds are set on fire to smoke out the fox.

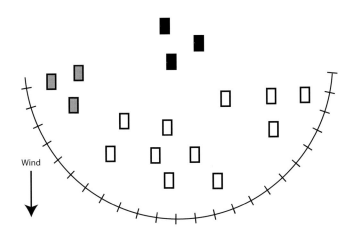

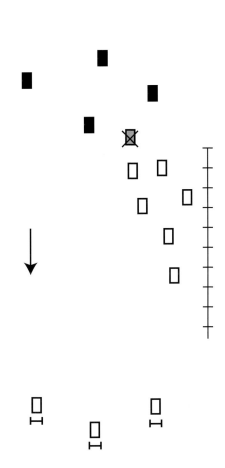

9,26. Diagram showing the most common way of setting nets for foxes. The black spots indicate those entrances to the den blocked with soil; the hatched spots entrances blocked by some other material. Drawing Jens Kirkeby.

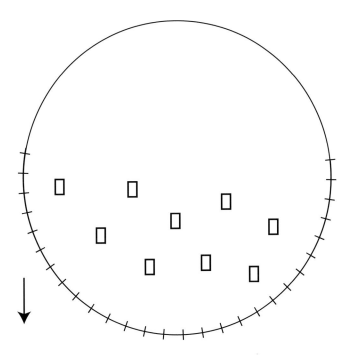

9,28. Eighteen nets set in a row for a fox. The black spots indicate entrances to the den blocked with earth. The hunter began pestering the fox with his stick at the entrance marked with a cross. As this did not work out, he tried to smoke out the fox from the same entrance. Drawing Jens Kirkeby.

9,27. Nets set in a semi-circle to catch a fox. The hunter marks a full circle in the ground, drawing a thin furrow in the ground with his iron knife as a magical precaution to prevent the fox from running in that direction. Drawing Jens Kirkeby.

9,29. Assessing whether the fox is in the den or not.

holes, i.e. those located centrally at the 'back side' of the complex. When inhabited the foxes normally leave the den only when all of the entrance holes have been meddled with. They do so with great speed, and if unlucky right into the nets, where they get entangled in their desperate efforts to escape. However, this is not always the case. Foxes may orient themselves swiftly and avoid the nets by running so that they bypass these, or they may knock down a net and pass right by without getting entangled.

If the entries to the den are widely dispersed, other hunting strategies have to be adopted and the nets placed differently. In one case, eighteen out of the twenty-one nets were placed together, as previously described while three nets were placed at the more distant entries to the den *(cf. Fig. 9,28)*. Chari's attempts to make the fox to leave the den by jamming the stick in and out of the various holes proved unsuccessful, in this case, and he decided to give it another try by using fire. Bonfires were lit at several of the entry holes from grass, twigs and dry manure which Chari collected nearby. Our friend then turned his attention first to one and then another of these, fanning the flames with his empty bag to increase the smoke in the galleries. Despite

these efforts and the fact that smoke soon oozed out of all the entries, demonstrating that the galleries formed one huge, interconnected system, no fox left this particular den. Despite careful examination, Chari had apparently misinterpreted the tracks. In fact, out of the five dens where he tried his luck, only one gave any result. Out of this particular one catapulted first a female fox with a tiny cub in its mouth. Assessing that there might be another fox or two in the den, Chari resumed jamming his stick in and out of a few more holes, and still another female shot out of an entry. Both were bagged alive and carried back home, the bag securely laced up with strips of dum palm leaves.

Hares are hunted in and near their preferred environment: clumps of young dum palm not tall enough to hide a man. Hares take shelter here during the day, finding shade and protection from the sharp eyes of birds of prey. These surroundings required a different hunting strategy than the one used for fox hunting. We witnessed how Chari went about this task on one of our excursions with him. His first step was to track down the hares through the growth until he spotted tracks leading to and not from an insular part of the overall vegetation. Then the nets were put up in such

9,30. Hunting hares in a dum palm growth.

9,31. Nets are set for hares in a dense dum palm growth.

9,32. Chari with his nets.

9,33. Securing his hunting bag and the live catch of the day. The bag was fabricated by the hunter himself from twisted rope of strips of dum palm leaves. The making of ropes and baskets from twisted ropes is men's work as opposed to the making of other kinds of baskets. The bag is carried over the shoulder on a stick, kari. It is the very same stick, which the hunter uses to drive the foxes out of the den. If this stick is not sufficiently long, Chari makes longer ones on the spot. Cat. nos. 23 & 24.

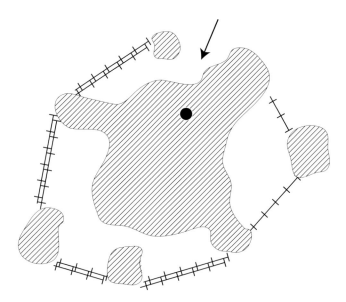

9,34. Nets set in a growth of young dum palm to catch a hare (the dark spot). The arrow shows the direction of the drive. Drawing Jens Kirkeby.

a manner that they covered all the openings, after which Chari beat the leaves until the hare leapt out. In one case, the hare came out all right, but succeeded in bypassing the net and escaping, as we watched (cf. *Fig. 9,30*).

CATCHING BIRDS

Snaring birds is apparently a technique that plays a minor role in Haddad Kanembu subsistence, but birds are caught this way, both smaller ones and doves, in addition to such fowl as partridge, sand-grouse or francolin. The Kanembu eat many species of birds. Most of these are caught with a specific kind of net, the so-called *mburu*. The most common birds that our friend Chari would bring back having used this net were various species of doves, turtle doves and blue starlings – apart from a range of smaller species. He had caught guinea fowl and partridges in his net, and occasionally a thirsty hare, he told us, but this seemed an exception. A hunter may bring back quite a considerable catch from a day's work during the dry season, and as the preparation may take up to two hours, it goes without saying that it is most profitable when birds can be lured to the net by water. The Haddad Kanembu also catch guinea fowl and bustards by means of a single, long net, however I do not know how common this practice is among these people, but it is widespread among the Haddad Kreda.

Nets are set for small birds during the dry season only, i.e. when water is in such short supply that even a tiny man-made puddle is alluring to winged creatures. We were in Kanem at the end of the rainy season, but Chari agreed to demonstrate how he caught birds with the *mburu,* a net made from cotton that measures about 230 cm times 150 cm. Apart from the net itself, it consists of a long rod bent into an oval shape and a good piece of rope. The nets are manufactured by the hunters themselves. Cotton thread is bought at the market, and Chari had made the meshes a mere 1.5 cm in diameter. The net is fastened to the oval or rather bow-like frame with cotton cord and the net is pulled over the birds with a long rope, for further description of the manufacture of these nets (cf. Cat. No. 25).

Chari tried his luck at a place next to a small acacia bush some forty to fifty metres from a minor inundation, reasoning that there would be birds in the vicinity. His very first step was to place the net where he intended to trap the birds. Then he marked where the bow-shaped rods would fall on the ground when the net was released. A small furrow was dug on top of the demarcated circle with an axe, deep enough to harbour the bow-shaped rod. The next preparation entailed the nailing of each end of the frame to the ground with wooden pegs. The latter were hammered into the ground, after which the wooden frame was tied to the pegs with pieces of cord. Chari proceeded by locating the centre of the net, using as measurement the length of his arm from elbow to fingertips, after which he coloured the spot green with some sap from a plant. Meanwhile, the rope had been soaking in water. It was tied to the centre of the bow-shaped frame and the effectiveness of the trap was tested several times as Chari pulled the rope and made the net come up and then down and over the very centre of the marked circle. Satisfied with the result, the net was put in place and covered with a thin layer of earth, as was the rope all the way from the rod to the hide-out from where Chari conducted the operation. His next step was to build his hide-out behind a tiny acacia bush. Branches were collected and rammed down in three pre-prepared holes, which Chari had made with his axe. As a final touch, the entire hiding place was covered with fresh dum palm leaves. He then returned to finish his work on the trap itself, making the puddle that was to attract the birds. He removed a good deal of soil with his hoe and made a shallow inundation at that part of the encircled area not already taken up by the net. Water was fetched from the nearby water hole, and poured into the puddle, after which Chari carefully smoothed out the mud. More water was added and the smoothening resumed until a fine little artificial puddle, a few centimetres deep had been made. As a finishing touch to make the puddle look completely natural Chari placed a few leaves of a rush-like plant on the surface. A few acacia branches were rammed into the ground at the 'back' of the net and the puddle was ready to receive the birds.

With everything in place and to his satisfaction, Chari took cover in his hide-out and we in a thicket under a big tree at a nearby waterhole entrusted with the work of scaring away birds that intended to drink here instead of at Chari's 'pond'. The birds were not long in approaching and soon a turtle-dove, *Oena capensis,* was caught under the net. Chari did not push his luck. He put the live dove in his bag, as he did with other game, having tied its feet with a strip of dum palm leaf and pulled out its quills. It was surprising to us that the birds were so easily attracted to the puddle, considering the nearness of the water hole.

9,35. Chari with a bird-net over his shoulder and an ax, the only tools needed. Birds are hunted mainly during the dry season, as described in the text. Cat. no. 25.

9,36. The bird-net has been spread out on the ground to outline its location. A small furrow replicating the net's wooden frame has been dug in the sand to accommodate the frame itself once the net has been released over the birds.

9,37. The net is placed in such a way that a hide-out can be erected at a suitable distance for the hunter to release the net. Photo J.N.

9,38. Fastening the net to the ground with six pegs. The net is placed along the curved furrow.

9,39. Digging a small inundation to make a puddle to attract the birds.

9,40. Mud and water from a nearby waterhole complete the puddle together with tufts of weed to lure the birds. Behind the net the hunter put up two acacia branches for the birds to sit on when they come to drink.

9,41. Setting the net with a supporting stick.

We did not observe other Haddad Kanembu netting smaller birds in the same way as Chari, nor how they hunted for guinea fowl, partridge, sand-grouse or francolin. But Chari explained that to do so the nets are placed between existing vegetation at some distance from the birds and these are then gently driven towards the nets.

Bustards, a favourite game of the Haddad Kreda were not hunted for by Chari. These huge birds are caught in a special net and Chari did not possess one. The Haddad Kreda, on the other hand, are eager hunters of bustards, particularly young men. Bustards are large, some of them in fact very large, terrestrial birds with three-toed feet and long necks. There are several species of these great birds in Kanem and the Bahr el Ghazal. Bustards are quite common, but exceedingly shy. One needs luck to come across a buff-coloured Sudan bustard strutting slowly and majestically through the scrub on the outlook for food. It is an impressive bird, some 74 cm to 90 cm tall with fine neck vermiculations and wind-covers tipped all white, or to meet the slightly smaller (76 cm) and much less common Denham's bustard with the rufous-coloured neck. Other species are more common, as far as we could observe: the northern black-bellied bustard, the Nubian bustard and the Senegal bustard, all some 61 cm in size. The Haddad themselves distinguish between two categories of bustards, probably reflecting the differences in 'pheno-type' between the 'larger', *Ardeotis* and 'smaller', *Eupodotis* species.

Haddad Kreda men hunt singly for bustards, as they do when out to catch smaller birds. The technique applied, however, is quite different, being one of 'battue'. Only a single net is applied, but this must be fairly long and high to catch these great birds. I purchased two nets, one from a Haddad Kanembu, another from a young Haddad smith. The former, known as *sarada* among the Haddad Kanembu, measured some 530 cm, but would be even a little longer when put up between the two tall sticks, measuring 188 cm and 151 cm respectively. When set for hunting the net is as high as a man. The nets are made from a thread of twisted sinew, the meshes measuring some 8 cm (cf. Cat. No. 26). The other net was lower and shorter, measuring 260 cm, the sticks around one metre (cf. Cat. No. 48). Younger men in particular pursue this form of hunting, walking slowly, all eyes and ears, through the Savannah. When a bird or two

have been spotted, the hunter places his long net at a suitable distance from the prey, circumvents the bird and drives it towards the net. First, at a very slow pace, but when the birds are very close to the net the hunter speeds up and attempts to scare the birds and make them run headlong into his net. We saw quite a number of bustards on our travels, having a great view over the fairly open plains which they favour from the backs of our camels, but not the luck to go hunting for these birds with nets. It happened more than once, however, that Haddad hunters shared their bag with us. Roasted bustard is a delicacy, as I have already confessed.

The Haddad Kreda use a similar technique for guinea fowl and, if the chance arises, other species of fowl. They seem to do so quite regularly, and birds are a by no means insignificant part of their subsistence. The net used to catch guinea fowl, *segia goulaya*, is somewhat smaller and lower than the ones used for bustards. The one I purchased at Sidige Joroso measured some 125 cm in length, the sticks between which it was suspended some 85 cm and 86 cm respectively (cf. Cat. No. 47).

NETTING MAMMALS
– THE TRADE OF THE HADDAD KREDA

The trademark of Haddad Kreda hunting for mammals is the use of nets, although all Haddad men make do with a throwing stick, pick up a stone at the spot or use a spear if game is encountered by chance. Hunting with nets is practised throughout Kanem and the Bahr el Ghazal, also by the Haddad who live among the Kecherda. The Haddad Kreda venture up north into the fringes of the Sahel and a little beyond moreover to hunt for the scimitar-horned Oryx antelope. The same do Aza [Haddad] hunters in the eastern part of Nigeria. Catherine Baroin met a family with nets near the Chadian border in 1969, but was never able to take part in an actual hunting expedition. She notes that hunting is strongly on the decline, but also that E. Granry observed net-hunting parties in a valley near Dillia, east of N'Gurti in eastern Nigeria in 1987 (personal com. to Baroin, cf. 1991: 342). In the spring of 2004, the Aza were still hunting with nets in the area and game was fairly plentiful, according to Ingrid Poulsen, a Danish anthropologist who had just come back from a stay in the area (personal com. to IN).

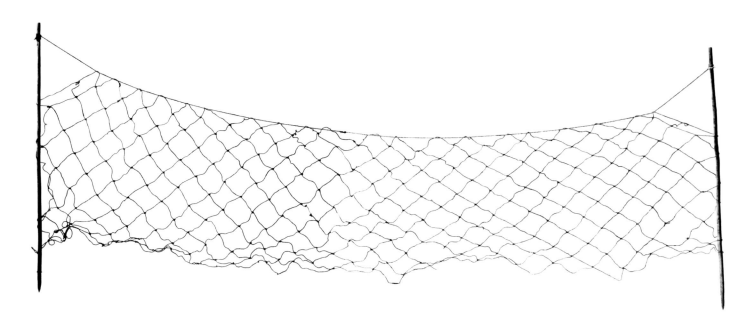

9,42. Fairly long nets are necessary for catching bustards, by slowly driving them in the right direction. This one is 530 cm. Cat. no. 26. Photo L.L.

9,43. A black-bellied bustard, Otis melanogaster. Rüppell 1835-40; Fig. 7.

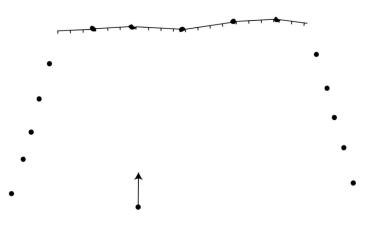

9,44. Diagram showing location of nets and Haddad Kreda engaged in hunting a hare. Drawing Jens Kirkeby.

Haddad Kreda hunting is a communal affair, moreover, except for the hunting of bustards, guinea fowl and other birds, as described above. While hunting in disguise with bow and arrow is a highly individual undertaking among the Haddad Kanembu, basically an encounter between man and beast, the successful outcome of which relies on the technical skills, environmental knowledge and intimate understanding of animal nature and the behaviour of the hunter, as well as of the possession of proper magic, Haddad Kreda hunting is a collective undertaking dependent on a similar knowledge of environment and animals. The Haddad Kreda use a technique that relies on more equipment, than is at the disposal of the individual hunter and necessitates collaboration between households. The hunting of antelope, in particular, requires considerable manpower and the collaboration of a great many persons.

We shall return to the socio-economic characteristics and implications of Kreda hunting in Chapter 10. At this point we shall look a little closer at the technology and at how the hunters execute the hunt of various species.

Haddad Kreda make their hunting implements, the nets, in various sizes. Each is produced for the hunt for a specific animal, and hence based on detailed insight into the nature and behaviour of each species. Nets are knotted from sinew, in particular from gazelle and antelope, although sinew from cattle or small ruminants is used from time to time. Only nets for the hunting of hares are made occasionally from fibres of *Acacia raddiana*. The latter are produced mostly by boys, the very persons who hunt these most eagerly. The animals which the Haddad Kreda pursue most frequently are: hares, jackals, various species of gazelle and antelope – as well as ostriches, bustards and guinea fowl, mentioned above.

9,45. Haddad Kreda men and boys setting nets for a hare that was spotted in a den next to the camp.

Hare and jackal

Hare hunting is done in the same way as did the ancient Greeks, according to Xenophon's *Cynegenicus*. The hunters look for the hare in its form. When found it is either driven into nets previously set in its runs or run down in the open. Haddad Kreda boys engage happily in this form of hunting. Hardly a day goes by in a camp without boys exercising their skills, and, if there are no hares in the vicinity, then the poor chicken are doomed to be chased and caught over and over again. The hunt for hares is a communal undertaking, as are other forms of Haddad hunting with nets, although some Haddad Kreda claim that it is possible for a single man to be successful if the terrain is accommodating and nets can be put up in a suitable semicircle. The nets, *segi tioro,* are the smallest of all the nets used by the Haddad. Out of a set of four purchased for museums, two were made of sinew, the other two of twines of bark of the *tefi* acacia, *Acacia raddiana*. The Haddad say

that hares are eaten by boys only, but this may not hold up, although some may object to the meat, as in other parts of North Africa.

We participated in a hare hunt once along with not only boys but also five to six adult men and a woman, because the animal was spotted in its form quite close to the camp. The adult men set the nets, thirty-four in all, some 50 metres away from the camp itself, while the rest of us made ourselves useful as beaters. The nets were placed in a single line between bushy perennials in an otherwise quite barren depression between dunes. A fairly rich growth of plants allowed for fine coverage. When the nets had been placed in the thicket, a younger man crouched down behind these, somewhere near the centre of the line of nets, his job being to fly at the animal once it got itself entangled in the meshes. Five people took a stand at each side of the row of nets, creating a kind of 'human funnel' towards these and hence enhancing the chances of mak-

9,46 The chase. The hare ran for its life - and successfully so - while some chicken got entangled in the nets in the heat of the hunt.

ing the hare race against the nets and not bypass them. As soon as everyone was ready, one of the men shouted: *heit! heit!* and beat a stick against the bushy perennials where the hare had taken cover. The efforts proved successful. The hare shot out of its cover in the direction of the nets. Unfortunately for the Haddad, however, it ran against one of the small sticks holding a net, knocked it over and escaped unharmed on the other side.

Another species frequently hunted is the jackal. The Haddad have also a specific size of net to catch these animals, known as *sarta turka*, or just *mofuin*, meaning 'neither too big nor too small'. The nets are made from twine of sinew. Some Haddad Kanembu use nets made of fibres of *Acacia raddiana*. Jackal hunting has become increasingly important because the population must be kept down to protect small ruminants. For this reason it is tolerated by the administration unlike hunting for gazelle, antelope and other big game. Jackal meat is favoured by all Haddad and the furs make a good profit. Covers, sewn together from nine to twelve furs, are popular among towns-people and Europeans (cf. Cat. No. 84).

Jackals are hunted during the daytime as well as at night, but preferably when it is dark. The hunt takes place almost exclusively during the dry season, when animals are searching for drinking water and hence seek out the few existing waterholes. A man may go hunting alone, but men usually gang up to kill these animals. One or more nets are put up near a waterhole, barring the tracks which both cattle and wild animals use to get to the water. The hunter takes cover on the far side of the nets, choosing his hide so that he can observe any movement on the track. Once a jackal is approaching the net, he jumps up and screams, hopefully sending the bewildered and scared jackal headlong into the net to be clubbed. We were told that on a good night three to five jackals may be caught in this manner. At the time of our visit, however, jackal hunting was on the decline around Mussoro, because a French veterinary doctor had put out poisoned mutton to disseminate the population.

Gazelle

The most reliable source of meat all year round is the gazelle. The Haddad Kreda hunt several species, first and foremost the red-fronted gazelle, known to these people as *wedene meru*. It is the most common of the gazelle in the Bahr el Ghazal and the only one to venture south of Kanem. It is a rather stockily built animal of medium size, weighing some 25 to 30 kilos.[3] The red-fronted gazelle lives singly, in pairs or in small herds, averaging five to six head and never exceeding fifteen (Dorst and Dandelot 1972: 245). The Haddad also bag the somewhat smaller white or dorcas gazelle or *wedene tchauma,* which wanders long distances in search of nutritious pastures and migrates to the northern parts of Kanem during the rainy season. This gazelle is less shy than the red-fronted gazelle but holds much less venison, weighing only some 20 to 23 kilos. The white gazelle used to live in small herds of up to twenty head in the area. It has been severely hunted down all over North Africa and can hardly be found in larger herds anymore (ibid: 242). Both species are caught with nets called *segia duska,* the name of the two sticks upholding the net being *muska*. The Haddad may use the same nets to pursue a third species, the red-necked gazelle. However, they prefer the larger nets used for hunting antelopes because the red-necked gazelle is a much larger animal than the other gazelles, weighing an average of 73 kilos. It lives mainly in the desert or the fringes of these barren areas, browsing singly or in small herds of up to 10 to 15 head, often together with the white gazelle. Large herds were still observed in the middle of the twentieth century - reports mention herds numbering up to 600 head during the seasonal exodus from the desert into the Sahel during the driest part of the year, according to authoritative sources on African mammals (cf. Dorst and Dandelot 1972: 237).

A gazelle net is approximately 135-145 cm wide, its meshes 10-15 cm and the sticks about 184-187 cm high. When not in use, the Haddad place the nets way above ground on forked sticks to be out of reach of termites and animals. During the rainy season, the nets must be protected from the moisture, which ruins sinew. For that very reason and because hunting is more profitable during the dry season and no milk is available from the cows of the pastoralists, some Haddad Kreda hunt only during the dry season, according to our informants. We found, nevertheless, that the Haddad Kreda organized shorter hunting expeditions on a regular basis, i.e. at least a few times a week in most of the camps we visited during that time, bagging at an average one gazelle a week. The most successful of the hunting expeditions in which we took part brought home

three gazelles. It was not common to bag that many on a single hunt at that time of the year, we were told. We were not able to obtain reliable data as to the number of gazelle that Haddad Kreda had bagged during extended periods of time, however. We noticed that the five families, who hunted regularly in Kurei Iruso, had killed four gazelles during the three-week period between our two visits. They had not done a lot of hunting during our absence, we were told, but had stayed put in the camp except when game had actually been spotted in a particular place, in these cases by children and by a man.

Hunting with nets for gazelle is always a communal affair, as previously stated, because the game has to be driven into these. It requires the participation of at least six to seven persons, i.e. more than any single family can muster, as well as a good deal of nets. The families we hunted with owned between ten and twenty nets each, a sufficient amount given that a good number of beaters come along for the hunt, but the larger the number of nets the better coverage evidently of the hunting ground. The key factor, however, is always the available manpower. To compensate for the inherent shortage of this the Haddad Kreda use a great number of forked sticks, *eba,* on which they hang bundles of strips of skin, *tari.* These are lined up in the terrain as a tromphe-l'æil for beaters, either in the shape of a 'funnel' that guides the animals towards the nets or in a line in between trees and bushes. At a distance they function amazingly well as a substitute for living human beings. It is possible with these devices to 'close off' a vast area, the larger of course the more families that participate with their gear.

Hunting with nets is not possible without a means of transportation, in casu donkeys. These animals are well suited for hunting. They can be kept at a steady pace over long stretches while carrying both people and the bulky and quite heavy hunting equipment - and along the way also game that has been bagged. Moreover, they hardly ever make sounds that could betray the hunting party and scare off the game. Haddad Kreda families possess no other beast of burden, no oxen, no horses, no camels, but donkeys make up for them

▶ 9,47. A hunting party taking a rest. Two youngsters accompany the two men, one girl and one boy. The three donkeys carry nets, sticks and hides for the hunting of gazelle.

all. It is amazing what these tiny beasts can carry, and they blend nicely into the landscape with their greyish colour and calm demeanour. This is in stark contrast to the camel, which roars loudly and complains whenever mounted or brought to lie down and hence is unfit for hunting. A small hunting party normally brings five to seven donkeys, all without headgear or saddles but controlled just with a simple stick. These are frequently mounted by more than one person. Most Haddad Kreda were not accompanied by hunting dogs on such trips. Only on one of our hunts did a dog come along. It kept pace with the party and was trained not to interfere with the hunt except at a signal from its owner, directing it to act if a gazelle were about to escape from the nets. Dogs played a much more significant role in former days when game was more plentiful and there were lots of left-over bones to gnaw. I have witnessed a similar development in Central Borneo, where the reduction in wild boar hunting led to a drastic decline in the population of dogs in the longhouses.

Hunting expeditions set out in joyful anticipation. Participants chat loudly as they leave camp, discussing particulars of the hunting grounds, the likely whereabouts of the gazelle etc. After a while, as the party approaches areas where game can be expected to linger, the pitch of the voices goes down and an occasional exchange of words turns into a murmur. An adult man walks ahead to scout, keeping a distance from the donkeys and the rest of the party of some 100 to 200 metres. When a gazelle has been spotted, his fellow hunters are told by the call of the guinea fowl, the only kind of signal Haddad hunters apply to communicate with one another during hunting. The Haddad Kreda prefer to go for a flock of gazelle rather than put up their nets for a single animal, not only because it may yield a better return on the effort, but because a single animal is harder to chase into the nets. When grazing together, gazelles are much calmer and hence easier to drive slowly towards the nets.

As soon as game has been spotted, the hunting party makes a halt to work out a strategy for the hunt, which takes into consideration not only the specifics of the environment, the actual position and number of the gazelle and the direction of the wind, but also the number of nets and persons, who take part in the hunt. Hunting in open territory with little or no vegetation is difficult, for example, as the game may spot the hunters from afar. If a hunting party nevertheless decides to try its luck under such

9,48. Nets set between trees for a gazelle hunt. The game browse on the open plains.

9,49. Nets set between stands of leptadenia bushes. Behind the bushes stand some acacia trees.

9,50. Posts set for a gazelle hunt. The sticks and hides create the illusion of a row of human beings.

circumstances, efforts are made first to drive the animals gently towards an area with acacia or other trees and bushes. If this plan does not bear fruit, the Haddad may well give up hunting for these particular animals, because the nets must be placed where the hunters can find some cover both while they are setting up the gear and, later, near these, when the gazelles are being chased towards the nets. However, the nets must be placed in a fairly open environment, one not overgrown by trees and bushes, because gazelle seek the open when hunted.

Each net-owning household puts up its nets and forked sticks at a separate site, eliminating any discussion as to whom the animal belongs in the first place. If a hunting party comprises members and nets of two households, the nets are placed at two separate sites; if there are three households represented with nets, the strategy will incor-

porate three sites for the putting up of the nets – and so on and so forth as the ensuing three examples from hunts in which we participated will illustrate:

1. The party consisted of members from two households. Gazelles were spotted on a vast, open plain. The hunters decided to put up their nets at two sites between scattered bushes. The two sets of nets were put up at a distance from one another of almost 200 metres. Each household had ten to twelve nets at its disposal and placed these in a single row at the chosen spots. The two sets of nets were 'united' with a row of forked sticks with bundles of strips of skin, that functioned as a kind of 'fence' linking the nets of the two households. The remaining part of the sticks were placed in a V-shape with a spacing of five to twenty metres between each stick - each 'leg of sticks' leading from the

nets towards the gazelle so that an overall U-shaped 'trap' was established. Whereas the nets were partly hidden by some bushes and low trees, the sticks would be clearly visible to the gazelles once these had been set in motion.

On this particular hunt, the Haddad attempted to chase three gazelle into their nets, but failed. The beaters, who had walked round the grazing animals and at a signal scared these to take flight were outsmarted when two of the gazelle turned around and escaped through the line of the beaters themselves, while the third got off between the nets and the forked sticks. A similar arrangement of the nets a few days later proved more successful. One gazelle was caught, as it was chased from a shady wooded area towards more open land.

2. Another hunting party in which we took part consisted of four adult men and three boys from three different households camping together at Gaba. They brought along twelve, fourteen and eighteen nets respectively. The scout in front of the party spotted first three red-fronted gazelles. After some discussion the nets were put up in a kind of semi-circle interspersed with lines of forked sticks with bundles of strips of skin, again in such a way that the latter formed an extension towards the gazelle. The hunting party had a relatively large number of forked sticks at its disposal. These were spaced with quite some distance between them so that the final setting covered a considerable terrain – so large in fact that we were unable to get a complete overview over the set up from our point of vantage. The attempt proved unsuccessful, however, as the gazelle ran through the row of sticks, an accident which caused a major row. Later that day, when the party was joined by still another man and his daughter, the combined four sets of nets were put up in a similar way to catch three white gazelles, but again without result, as the animals escaped to the rear, shooting through the line of beaters.

Any net-hunting endeavour relies on a definite division of labour, which is put into action once the strategy of the hunt has been agreed upon. Each net-owner puts up his set of nets without the help from other members of the hunting party. He does so at the spot already decided upon, while the other participants place the forked sticks and hang up the strips of skin. The task is carried out as fast as possible not to alert the game. One man runs ahead with the forked sticks

swiftly putting these up along the way, while a younger man or child tries to keep up with him while placing each bundle of skin in the fork of a stick as best he can. Once the nets and the 'trompe-l'œil' of forked sticks are in place, the owners of the nets hide behind in the scrub near their respective nets, while the other participants, adults and children alike, position themselves in a row on the opposite side of the game. At a given they start the drive. Children shriek at the top of their voices, some of the men beat wooden sticks against one another and shout in a peculiar manner resembling the bark of dogs to make the gazelles take flight and run in the direction of the nets. If the animals head towards these and come quite close, the owner may jump up from his hide-out yelling at the top of his voice to further frighten the quarry out of

9,51. Young hunter ready to set up a drive with bundles of goat hides over his shoulder.

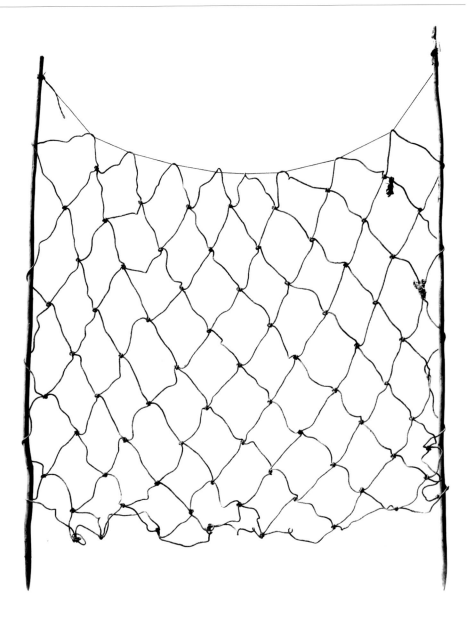

9,52. Net of solid, twisted sinew strings for hunting antelope. When erected, the net is about 2 metres high and 175 cm wide. Cat. no. 57. Photo L.L.

its wits and make it run headlong into the nets. Gazelles hit the nets at very high speed. The 'collision' is so violent that the animals and nets hit the ground some ten to twelve metres ahead of the site where they were first caught by the net (*cf. Fig. 9,53*). When the flustered gazelle has been trapped, the owner jumps at the animal, breaks its neck with a heavy stick and subsequently cuts its throat in reverence to Muslim custom. Once the chase and killing of the prey has been accomplished and excitement is over, the party gets together to

rejoice and chat happily about the challenges they have faced and the successful outcome, highlighting details of the hunt over and over again and each person underscoring his or her crucial contribution to the outcome. If the hunt proves unsuccessful, on the other hand, a major row is doomed to begin (cf. Chapter 10: 270). After some time when the party has rested up, the donkeys are mounted once again and head back to the camp, trotting patiently under the heavy burden of the participants, their gear and the game that was bagged. The Haddad always bring back their kill to the camps for flaying, cutting up and the apportionment of the meat.

9,53. A gazelle has been netted, clubbed and then had its throat cut in accordance with Islamic law. Erected nets can be seen in the background.

Antelope

The Haddad Kreda hunt several species of antelope and fabricate specifically large nets to catch these animals. The

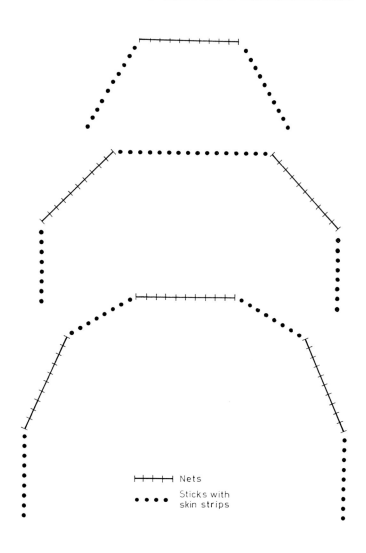

9,54. The author demonstrates how the Haddad beat pairs of wooden sticks together at a given signal to scare game towards the nets. Cat. no. 54. Photo J.K.

⊢⊢⊢⊣ Nets
•••• Sticks with skin strips

9,55. Diagram showing the 'game plans' of some of the hunts that we witnessed. Drawing by T.O.S.

9,56. Nets are in need of repair whenever game has been caught.

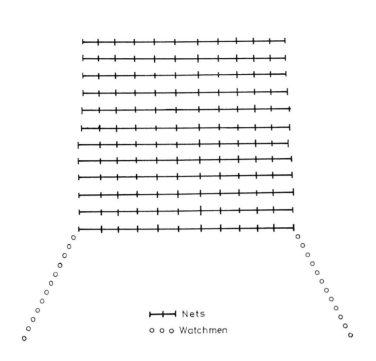

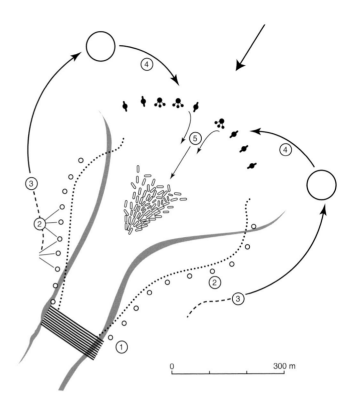

9.57. The nets are placed at the 'mouth' of the drive. They are put up in rows, one after the other.

9,58. The conduction of a hunt for oryx antelopes. 1. Placing the nets; 2. Putting up the scarecrows; 3. Encircling the antelopes; 4. Coordination of hunters on foot, dogs and horsemen; 5. The final chase. After Chapelle 1957: 203.

nutritional and economic significance of antelope hunting declined after World War II, however, as the population diminished due to environmental changes and excessive hunting with firearms. The government ban on the traditional hunting with nets did not stop the decline but had a further negative impact on Haddad subsistence. As it requires a major communal effort to hunt antelope with nets, one that cannot easily be hidden for the authorities, Haddad Kreda pursuits were hampered and did in fact decrease dramatically, we were told. Still, antelopes were hunted at the time of our visit, albeit at a diminished scale. Unfortunately, we had no opportunity to participate in an expedition as it was the wrong time of the year.

The technique of antelope hunting is slightly different from the one applied to the gazelle. Firstly, antelope are grander animals and it is necessary to use higher and stronger nets known as *segia urula*. The predominantly white, scimitar-

horned Oryx is 190–220 cm tall and weighs around 140 kg. An animal of this size with horns that are more than a metre long is not easy to stop in the flight. Like other nets, those made for Oryx hunting consist of two wooden posts of the *kolu* tree between which the net is suspended when in use and around which it is rolled during transportation and for storage. The net we purchased measured approximately 165 cm in height, the posts 228 cm, and the meshes were about 20 cm wide. The net itself is made from sinew, either from domestic animals or from gazelle and antelope, but with more solid and thicker meshes. It is kept in suspension by a string twisted from the hair of oxtail that is tied to the upper part of the two sticks (cf. Cat. No. 57). Antelope, in particular a herd of Oryx antelope, are not easily fooled by 'scarecrows'. Unlike the gazelle, they do not take the forked sticks with strips of skin for people. To take on a herd of Oryx therefore, considerable manpower must be mustered, not only as beaters and guardians of the nets, but to function as live 'scarecrows', lining the path or 'corridor' to the location of the nets. The Oryx antelope gallop with such speed and force when set in motion by the beaters that many rows of nets are needed to stop any one animal, let alone a herd. For this reason, a Haddad Kreda family cannot hunt Oryx antelope on its own, nor can a few families joining forces. Traditionally, therefore, Oryx hunting was organized and undertaken by clans.

Antelopes rest during the midday heat preferably in the shade of acacias, scrub or growths of perennials, and that is the time when the Haddad will go hunting. Where and precisely how the nets are put up depends on the terrain, the vegetation and the direction of the wind, as the drive must go with the latter. Hunting strategies vary slightly, moreover,

9,59. The hide of a damalisque antelope, Damaliscus korrigum, an impressive 150-230 long animal, weighing up to 160 kg. It is glossy purplish red in color, apart from dark patches on face and upper limbs. On top of the hide is the lance with which it was killed. Cat. no. 59. Photo J.K.

depending on the species of antelope, but the nets are put up in much the same way for all three of them. The nets are placed in a manner that offers equal opportunities for each household. There are strict rules in regard to the division of the kill to secure that all participants get their rightful share, with due consideration to the special rights of the owner of the net in which the antelope was trapped.

Three species of antelope are of particular economic importance to the Haddad Kreda. One is the Damalisque or Topi antelope, *Damaliscus korrigum,* known to these people as *n'ghanran.* The Damalisque is highly gregarious and lives in herds of between fifteen and thirty head. It is known to have formed herds of up to several hundred head and assemblages of up to even 12,000 individuals have been encountered in the eastern part of the distribution area of this species (Dorst and Dandelot 1972: 236). The Damalisque antelope is a precious supplier of meat to the Haddad, as each animal weighs between 100 kg and 150 kg. It is hunted when encountered in Kanem and the Bahr el Ghazal, and we were told by a European that he had witnessed the kill of eleven Damalisque antelopes in nets by some Haddad Kreda near Mussoro a few years prior to our visit.

The fiercest of the antelopes, the scimitar-horned Oryx, *algazel algazel,* known as *trua,* is hunted in much the same way and with the same technology as the Damalisque. The Oryx is a large, pale coloured and rather heavily built antelope that weighs a good 200 kilos. It browses on the Sahelien plains and ventures into the semi-desert but never into the truly arid zone, usually in flocks of between twelve to sixty head. In previous times it has been seen in enormous herds numbering thousands when rain had fallen in particular districts (Dorst and Dandelot 1972: 201).

The hunt takes place during the winter season. The Oryx do not migrate as far south as Kanem and the lower stretches of the Bahr el Ghazal. The Haddad have to travel northwards for days to locate the herds. Because of the distance and the serious decline in the Oryx population quite a number of clans gave up hunting this antelope quite some time ago. According to our informants, the *Tchatchauma Mada* clan stopped doing so about 'one century ago' i.e. in the mid 19th century, but other clans still set out to get Oryx. This is the case, for example, of the *Bichia Yunnussia.* During the winter of 1962-1963 some twenty-nine men and a number a children, all of the *Bichia Yunnussia* clan, went north to try their luck. The reward was not huge, only two antelope got entan-

9,60. The scimitar-horned Oryx, fabled for its slender and arched horns, which can reach the length of 100-120 cm. The animal itself measures an impressive 190-220 cm. It feeds on woody plants growing in moisture-retaining troughs between dunes and outcroppings providing some cover and shade, but it is flushes of grass that draw these nomadic animals back and forth across unknown distances. It is reluctant to remain solitary and generally seen in flocks, according to Jonathan Kingdon. He writes that it probably is extinct in the wild (2004: 254). Initially the antelope was called Oryx Leucoryx by the earliest travelers to meet the animal in the wild, the German naturalists Hemprick and Ehrenburg, who explored Nubia and Arabia from 1820 to 1825. Buffon coined the term l'Algazel and Pallas the term Oryx now in common use. Sclater & Thomas 1894-1900, Vol. IV: Pl. LXXXI.

The Leucoryx.

9,61. Addax, addaz nasomaculatus, is a stocky, 120 to 175 cm tall animal. It is quite fair and has long, annulated horns following loose spirals. The sexes differ very little. The addax lives in sand dune habitats. It is probably extinct except for small pockets in Niger and possibly Chad. Sclater & Thomas 1894-1900, Vol. IV: Pl. LXXXVI.

gled in the nets, but a hunting party may bag a considerably larger number. No less than twelve net owners participated in this expedition, each with fourteen to sixteen nets. The clan decided to place the nets in twelve rows successively one behind the other, each row belonging to a particular man. The distance behind each row of nets is the length of a lance, *aedi,* i.e. between 225 cm and three metres (cf. Cat. No. 58). An Oryx knocks down several rows of nets before it is stopped, usually about four, we were told. As they come in herds, a great many nets are needed. An Oryx antelope is not caught in the net by its fine, scimitar-shaped horns getting the backward curvature entangled in the meshes, as one might think rather it gets stuck with its body and hind legs. A female can be held with bare hands while entangled to have its throat slit, as it is somewhat smaller and has less dangerous, more slender horns. The male, on the other hand, is extremely dangerous and must be killed with the lance, before one can cut its throat. It is the only antelope against which the Haddad use the long lance. This is not mandatory even when facing the grand Damalisque, as this may be killed with a stick, as can gazelle.

The Addax is a third species of antelope, but one that is hunted quite rarely by the Haddad Kreda. This rather heavy and clumsy animal with its long and spirally twisted horns has been hunted almost to extinction throughout its habitat, the Saharan desert. It weighs between 82 kilos and 122 kilos. Previously, the Haddad around Termit and Dillia went on seasonal hunting expeditions of several months' duration into the arid and uninhabited areas to the north to chase the Addax. Hunting parties are said to have killed up to several hundred head on such tours (cf. Grall 1945: 33 f.; Brouin 1950: 450 ff.; Chapelle 1957: 202 ff.).

The hunting of Addax antelopes has been described by Colonel Chapelle. He writes that the Haddad choose a narrow valley or basin in the landscape or perhaps a depression between the dunes for the formation of the nets, which they put up in rows of two to three hundred metres in length. There may be up to ten rows all in all, making a barrier of 15 to 50 metres in depth. Right and left of the nets, the Haddad set up 'scarecrows' made of sticks with strips of skin or old pieces of cloth before they take cover. Chapelle estimates that about a dozen men are positioned on each side of the trapezoid-shaped drive at these hunts. When everything is ready, the hunters position themselves in two groups on either side of the herd, no man ever getting between the animals and the direction of the wind. Some mount donkeys, others are on foot with their dogs, a few may be on horseback or on camel. At a given signal, the two groups set in motion, closing in slowly on one another. As they join ranks a loud, piercing hunting call is heard from the hunters, setting the herd in a wild gallop towards the nets pursued by screaming hunters and baying dogs. Any Addax attempting to break away from the herd to escape will be pursued with spears and lances; others are attacked by the dogs. Chapelle writes furthermore that most of the herd will be caught and killed, and that every hunt results in wounded hunters and dogs. "One understands the usefulness of the skin clothing, which when made of the hide of the Addax, resists the long and pointed horns which offer such powerful blows," he adds, referring to the traditional clothing of the Haddad (Chapelle 1957: 205).

NOTES

1. To give another example: Active hunting in its simplest can be a hunter picking up a stone to kill an animal with a precise throw, a common method for example of the Inuit of Greenland to get grouse. If the hunter supports the stone with a stick, ties a cord around the stone which he pulls if an animal eats of the fodder placed under it, then Sirelius considers it a case of passive hunting (Lagercrantz 1974: 19).

2. Arrows used by European bow-hunters must weigh a minimum of 25 grams for deer and geese, 20 grams for smaller game, the pull of the bow being some 50 pounds.

3. This species has been divided into a number of races, i.e. Heuglin's gazelle in Ethiopia, Senaar and the Bahr el Ghazal, considered by some a full species (Dorst & Dandelot 1972: 245).

10:

10: SHARING, MAGIC AND MISTRUST

Animals, their characteristics and behaviour are quintessential in how the Haddad view the world, identify themselves and maintain social relations. We talked at some length about these matters with some Haddad men and our data all testify to the significance of game to social and ideational construction. One source of insight into the role of game to Haddad perceptions of nature and themselves turned out to be poetry. Kanem and the Bahr el Ghazal have been rich in wildlife through extended periods of time. The lake and backflows of water from here into the 'river of the gazelle' offered ideal conditions for hippopotami, elephants, herbivores and their predators as well as for birds. This earthly 'garden of Eden' provided the Haddad great hunting opportunities up to the second part of the 20th century, when droughts and commercial and excessive hunting drastically curbed their livelihood, as previously described. Haddad poetry reflects the former richness in animal life and the significance of game to their very existence. Haddad hunters compose poems about elephants, ostriches and lions. They praise the addax and gazelle, idolize the scimitar or white Oryx and tell of the magnificent Dama antelope. They chant of jackals and wart hogs and poke fun at the hyena, and they sing of the hunter who offers his true love a fine and fat guinea fowl only to be betrayed, as we shall see. However, let us first look at the social context of Haddad hunting: the ways in which they organize hunting and dispose of game, as this is done in dramatically different ways among the Kreda and Kanembu-speaking groups respectively. Hunting among the former is essentially a collective enterprise involving men, adolescents and children - sometimes even women,

while men and men only pursue game among the Haddad Kanembu. Moreover, Haddad Kanembu men usually hunt alone, occasionally in parties of just a few men. The two Haddad groups also vary in respect to how they partition and distribute game.

HADDAD KREDA COLLECTIVITY

Hunting with nets is largely a collective enterprise, as we have seen. Haddad Kreda hunters, who set out to catch game like gazelle and antelope are in need of partners. Even hares, the species on which boys practice their hunting skills, guinea fowl and jackals are sometimes hunted jointly by adult men. However, different rules are brought to bear when bags are to be partitioned, rules which are closely associated with the species of game being pursued, the way in which the nets are placed, the overall organization of the hunt and, not least, Haddad Kreda values.

Haddad Kreda sociality is lent flavour and tenacity by various kinds of exchanges among which the sharing of game is the most significant. Haddad exchanges of meat does not fully comply with the widely applied anthropological categories of 'generalized' and 'balanced' reciprocity, two concepts supposed to reflect the tacit understanding by both the giver and receiver that while a 'generalized' exchange need not to be repaid in either kind or amount within a specific time frame, 'balanced' exchange requires such reciprocity (cf. Service 1966: 15). Among the Haddad Kreda most partitions of game encompass both forms. Some members of a camp or clan, typically the elderly, re-

10,1. A Haddad Kreda hunting party dividing the spoils.

ceive a share although they take no part in the hunt and presumably never will. They are treated as partners in a 'generalized' exchange that covers a lifetime. They are entirely at the receiving end and not expected ever to reciprocate. Able-bodied adults and children, on the other hand, get a part only if they have joined the hunting party. What the individuals do with the part they get is in principle up to them. In praxis, they may feel bound to share with others than the immediate household, perhaps to reciprocate a gift previously received, out of the kindness of their heart or for some other reason. The overall principle of Haddad partition of game is that individuals must be actively engaged

in hunting to receive a share of the bag, and moreover that this is shared equally between all participants irrespective of gender, age and the part they had played in a given hunt. How the game is actually divided up depends on the species of animal bagged and the ways in which the hunt is organized and carried out.

Hare hunting is largely a recreational diversion, as we have heard, more than a serious subsistence activity. Men chase hares with children because it breaks the uniformity of the day. To boys it is a joyful and competitive play, yet also training in assessing the likely movements of the hare and in transforming these insights into strategic planning.

Hares are tiny animals, however, and this determines the way in which a bag is delt with. If the kill is the result of men and boys having chased the animal together, the prey is simply given to the latter and they will feast and roast the prey over an open fire. Should a group of men for some reason or the other decide to chase hares on their own, these will belong to the man, in whose nets the animals get entangled.

Nets are usually placed in a long row when the Haddad Kreda hunt guinea fowl, and, as with hares, the catch will belong to the hunter in whose nets the bird(s) were caught. Guinea fowl is never partitioned, we were told.

If a group of hunters bags a jackal, on the other hand, the fur will be given to the man in whose net the animal was caught, while the meat is parceled out in equal amounts to all of the participants in the hunt.

Apart from the seasonal hunt for the scimitar or white Oryx, it is the pursuit of gazelle which dominates Haddad Kreda hunting activities. It cannot surprise, therefore, that the division of a bag of gazelle is strictly regulated. The basic principle of partitioning relies on ownership of the hunting gear. The man in whose net a gazelle is caught holds the right to the animal's head, neck, skin and to all four legs up to the knees - i.e. to those parts of the legs from which the Haddad Kreda get sinew, the very material of which the nets themselves are made. This rule applies even if the owner of the net has not participated personally in the hunt but only lent his nets to others. The meat, on the other hand, is divided equally between all of the members of the hunting party including the net owner irrespective of age, gender or family membership. Even small children who are unable to make a significant contribution to the outcome will be handed a share. But the meat is divided even more extensively. Old people - men as well as women - who no longer are capable of participating in hunting expeditions but forced to remain in the camp will be given a share equaling those of the ones who brought back the spoil. This applies also when partitioning game such as the white Oryx or scimitar, the Damalisque and the addax antelope.

A specific proviso is applied to the partitioning of gazelle, whether *Gazella rufifrons* or *Gazella dorcas dorcas*, if a hunting party succeeds in bagging three or more animals. In such cases, the meat of an entire animal must be given to the chief of the clan, whether he has participated in the actual hunt or not. The head, neck, skin and sinews, however, will still be the property of the owner of the net in which the animal found its death. If more than three gazelles are caught, the chief of the clan will receive an even larger portion. If he participates in the actual hunt, he will get his share of the remaining spoil on a par with the other hunters.

By far the most challenging of Haddad Kreda hunting expeditions are those for antelope. These hunts are major undertakings, involving a considerable number of related hunters from each and every camp of a specific clan under the leadership of its chief, as I have mentioned. If the clan chief is not able to participate, the hunt will be led by the senior clansman. After discussions with the adult participants, the chief decides on a strategy, taking into consideration the number and location of the animals, the general terrain, the direction of the wind, the number and age of the participants, the number of nets available, etc. The setting up of the nets follows specific rules, however, and this has an impact on how game is partitioned. If the Haddad are out to hunt the scimitar or white Oryx, the nets will be placed in rows, one behind the other, according to a fixed system reflecting the age of the participants. On the first of the hunts, the first row of nets will be those owned by the most senior of the hunters. On the second hunt, the nets of the youngest of the participants are placed as the front row followed by those of the most senior of the hunters. On the third hunt, the nets of the second youngest of the participants are placed as number one, followed by those of the youngest participants and after his again, those of the oldest hunter and so on until every hunter has had his nets placed up in front of everyone else's. If the clan leader is also the eldest among the hunters, his nets will be placed as the first row on the first *battue*. If this is not the case, his nets are placed as are those of the other participants, i.e. in order of succession according to his actual age. Ownership of nets is thus of major significance to the kind and size of the share of game allotted the hunter. We were told that some hunters mark their nets, either with a piece of cotton cloth or a cowrie shell tied to a mesh to be sure to get their part, although our informants claimed that such measures were unnecessary.

Game is cut up and parceled out upon the return to the camp. Joy is unconfined if the meat is plentiful. Children

and women scuttle back and forth, pots are put on the fire and one can feel the anticipation of a good meal. No discussions here, no grumbling. The practical handling of the partition follows a fixed pattern. The bag is usually cut up and divided by the man in whose net it was caught. He will set aside the portion which falls to him as owner of the gear and then parcel out the rest of the carcass. The meat is divided into portions equaling the number of participants in the hunt and of old and incapacitated persons in the camp. The Haddad Kreda do not differentiate between various kinds of meat, whether filet, hind quarters or intestines. The man who does the partitioning tries his best to make portions of equal size. When ready the portions are allotted by means of a draw. Every person entitled to a portion will bring a small stick, known only to him or her. These are placed in a tiny heap, and a man with no knowledge of 'ownership' to the sticks and usually with no personal claim to the meat, places one on each of the meat portions. The portion can then be picked up by the various stakeholders. We noticed that meat was parceled out in a slightly more detailed manner if the bag was plentiful. In such cases the bag was divided with an eye to the kind of meat, and intestines were shared.

As far as we could assess, the Haddad Kreda adhere to the above-mentioned rules fairly strictly. One time, Johannes and I made for a break of the custom, however. We had taken part in a hunt which turned out a total failure. No gazelle had been caught in the nets despite a number of attempts. The only bag brought back to the camp was a gazelle that Johannes had shot with his rifle. It was decided by the hunters that the meat should be portioned out according to the number of families who had taken part in the hunt, not the number of individuals. The argument was that as this particular gazelle had not been caught through joint efforts but shot, the usual right to meat could not be upheld.

Our data indicate that the ways in which the Haddad Kreda divide their bags are more intricate than previously suggested by existing sources. Rouvreur writes, for example, that all of the meat is divided up between the participants, except for the head, intestines and skin of the animal, which are given to the owner of the net (Le Rouvreur 1962: 3-4). Bruel claims that throughout (former) French Equatorial Africa bags which are the result of communal hunts always belong to the owner of the nets (Bruel 1935: 226). This information is not in concurrence with the situation among the Haddad Kreda, as we have seen.

Hunting with the Haddad Kreda turned out to be not only interesting but also at times quite a surprising experience. This was due, not the least to the great variation in 'atmosphere'. Graciousness and constraint, were not necessarily the prevailing behaviour on the expeditions, certainly not if something went wrong. An opportunity that is missed, game that escapes – and fierce discussions are bound to follow. Voices are raised; blame and loud outbursts bounce back and forth. Individuals are blamed for not having yelled enough, for not having beaten their sticks hard and repeatedly during the battue, or for having driven too hard as the game approached the nets, making the animals panic and take flight. Insults and abusive language otherwise unthinkable suddenly fill the air. Restraint is not on the agenda. Brothers curse one another, even fathers and sons engage in arguments. Angry discussions may last for hours on end, continue all the way back and perhaps continue at night in the camp itself. I recall altercations after more than one hunt for gazelle, and one miserable hunt in particular, when three gazelle had taking flight and run to the rear between the beaters instead of straight into the nets. The beaters were largely children, yet that did not deter an adult man from blaming them loudly on the failure. After another abortive hunt, where three gazelle had escaped their fate by a hair's breath we heard a man shout at his brother: "If the Lord has nothing else to do today, He may think it fit to kill you!" The fact that the Haddad Kreda quarrel and take another to task if a hunt fails to give results does not breed permanent ill feelings among them and we never heard of corporal outlets of anger. Fights and bodily injuries seem unheard of among the Haddad Kreda, unlike among their pastoral hosts.

HADDAD KANEMBU: SELF-RELIANCE AND SHARING

Unlike the Haddad Kreda, a Haddad Kanembu hunter is usually on his own when hunting and whatever bagged is for him to dispose of: skin, meat, sinews and all. A hunter is under no specific obligation to share the meat in particular ways, but he may honour and reinforce social ties of his own choice, be these family or other relations. In former days, when game was plentiful, however, and once in a rare while today several men may set out to hunt together.

10,2. The Haddad usually grill meat whether from gazelles and antelopes or smaller animals and birds. Meat from sheep and goats is also prepared in this way - in fact all the meat we were served was grilled. If the Haddad get a major catch, i.e. an antelope or several gazelles some of the meat will be dried and probably sold. The meat is cut in strips hung on trees and bushes way above the reach of dogs and goats until it has dried. Dried meat is a significant source of income for many hunters, who have few other ways of getting a cash income and hence of purchasing necessities such as clothes, household utensils and millet. The Haddad do not take the dried meat to the markets themselves out of fear of the police, but trade it through middlemen and hence at a much lower price than they might otherwise have obtained.

When this is case, the bag is partitioned according to the following set of rules:

a) If the animal is injured and killed by the arrow(s) of one hunter only, he will be the one to get the skin, head and lower part of the back of the animal. The remaining parts are distributed equally among the participants, including the one who brought down the animal.

b) If more than one hunter wounds an animal, its skin, head and lower back belong to the first man who hit the beast.

c) A man who has killed an animal all alone, but finds that this has already been injured by the arrow of somebody else is obliged to bring back the arrow, identify the owner and offer this man not only the skin, head and lower back of the animal but also a share of the rest of the meat, as if the man had been along on the hunting expedition. This rule should be complied with even though the game has lived with the arrow for an extended period of time, the Haddad claimed. Identification of the owner is facilitated by the fact that each hunter marks his arrows in a particular way. Every man has his brand, so to speak, a specific sign enchased somewhere on the iron point.

Finally, there are a few Haddad Kanembu who have taken up collective hunting with nets, as already mentioned. Unfortunately, we were not able to obtain any data as to how these people organized their hunts, set up their nets or divided up the catch. It is likely, however, that they go about the partition of the game in much the same way as the Haddad Kreda, from whom they adopted this form of hunting.

HUNTING, BELIEFS AND THE USE OF MAGIC

The differences in organization, technology and social behaviour which characterize Haddad Kreda and Haddad Kanembu hunting respectively are accompanied by distinctions in respect to worldview, in particular to perceptions of man's possibility of influencing the invisible constituents of this. The overall worldview of the Haddad is shaped by Islam, as are the belief systems of other ethnic groups in Kanem and the Bahr el Ghazal. The Haddad embraced Islam as late as in the beginning of the 20th century, as previously mentioned. Johannes and I had hoped in fact that we would encounter Haddad families who would still rely more fully on beliefs linked to their intimate dependence on the animal world. This proved not to be the case, however, although some fundamental pre-Islamic conceptions and magical practices were adhered to, in particular among the Haddad Kanembu. They believed that the animal world mirrored that of human society. Not only did animal species form discrete clans as did human beings, the animals had been able to speak in former days just like man. More elaborate ideas about the animal world, linking animal species with specific clans as totems, for instance, seemed not to be of part of Haddad Kanembu worldview at this point in time. Magic beliefs, however, were still at the core of their understanding of how the world works. They relied thoroughly on magical practices as part of their hunting activities, as against the Haddad Kreda who

went about their business in a quite secular way. The fact that there were few if any specific religious or magical beliefs linked with net-hunting concur with the practice of Haddad groups hunting with nets north-east of lake Chad. Brouin observes, for example, that: "Il ne semble pas qu'il y ait chez les Azzas une préparation spéciale magique ou religieuse, dans la conduite de la chasse et la confection des filets" (Brouin, 1950: 450).

The Haddad perceive themselves as Muslims and they comply by and large with the fundamental Islamic prescriptions for believers: the Five Pillars. If asked, the Haddad declare that they perform the prescribed ablutions and prayers five times a day, for instance, although the families we lived among were somewhat lenient in that respect, in particular the Haddad Kreda and their women. One prescription which is impossible for the Haddad to follow is to go on a pilgrimage to Mecca. The Haddad are poor, also by local standards, and we learned of no Haddad person who had been able to undertake the pilgrimage to Mecca. In theory, the Haddad comply with other Islamic prescriptions and laws as well, but in practice this is not necessarily the case.

The worldview of the Haddad encompasses beliefs in the existence of spirits, including a range of evil ones, the djinn. Protection against these is sought through prayers to the Prophet and by means of magic. The Haddad believe that the djinn may have evil intentions and also that their plots can be averted by amulets, as may evil emanating from fellow human beings, be it an evil mouth, an evil eye or the like. Amulets are purchased from the local marabout who are quite numerous among the pastoral Kreda. The marabout writes a protective formula in Arabic and this is then carried in a leather pouch around the neck or in some other way. The Haddad try to protect themselves against evil spirits in other ways as well. Like a great many people throughout the Sahel the Haddad believe, for example, that evil spirits are the masters of both animals and human beings and that these spirits dwell in the canopy of the *Maerua crassifolia* tree. Before they seek shade under this particular tree, therefore, as many marks must be cut in the bark of the stem as the number of persons going to rest under the canopy, a custom which none of our informants had any explanation for, however. A Haddad will also utter a *bismillah* as a precaution against the spirits in case he or she cuts a branch from the

Maerua crassifolia, because the canopy may shake during the process and hence upset the spirits. Haddad Kreda hunters claimed that these very spirits, the evil djinn are the true 'owners' or masters of wild animals. As far as we could assess, however, the belief was not deeply encoded in their spiritual life, at least not any more. We learned of no major ritual or sacrifice linked to this belief, nor did we notice any special measures taken in respect to the djinn when out hunting with these people.

It was a different matter with the Haddad Kanembu. Our friend Chari, whom we accompanied on several hunting trips, invariably took the djinn into account when pursuing his luck. He said a *bismillah* before he began to chase the animals out of their dens and also took certain magical precautions. We noticed how he made a protective semi-circle with his knife in the sand from one end of the row of nets he had put up to catch a fox to the other. This was done, he explained, to prevent the fox from escaping its fate by running behind the nets. He did so because of snakes but also because of the spirits which reside with and are the masters of the foxes in the den, are said to be afraid of iron. They were deterred by the semi-circle, he explained, as this had been drawn with his iron knife. By implication it would also guide the movements of the foxes. Chari communicated with the spirits in other ways as well. Having successfully bagged a fox and its pup, for example, he ate two succulent, green shoots from the *kayo* tree known as *chaou* in Arabic as a precaution against evil spirits, who might disturb him in his sleep at night. Chari was not able or willing to explain his beliefs in this regard any further. He had been told to eat the shoots by his father, he said, and it was his father who had taught him the art of hunting with nets.

I have already mentioned the fact that both Haddad groups believe that metals are associated with special powers due to the link to fire and forging. These powers can be activated in various ways. Like peoples elsewhere in North Africa they are convinced that iron prevents assaults by evil spirits, djinn. One may do as Chari and draw a circle in the sand with an iron knife to prevent the spirits and animals from entering this. A knife or other iron weapon is often placed next to small children for protection against the very same evil forces. The potency of iron arms, de facto and spiritual, calls for precaution and counter measures. The Haddad try to guard themselves against the poten-

tially mortal force of other peoples' arms and/or increase the force of their own by means of other metals such as copper and brass. Both copper and brass are said to attract and host benevolent spirits that may act both as protective forces and empower the arms. For this very reason, the Haddad wind copper and brass wire around the stems of lance heads and knives, at the point where these are fastened to the shafts or handles to make these penetrate their targets more efficiently. Armrings and other jewellery of copper and brass are worn for the very same reason, i.e. not only for embellishment but as a means of protection against stabs and other evils.

Despite Haddad Kreda beliefs in the djinn and the fact that they consider spirits the 'owners' of animals, we found no trace of rituals or magical practices addressing animal spirits, as just mentioned. Nor did we come across magical precautions or activities to block the potential damage or avert the lack of hunting luck that the djinn might cause. The Haddad Kanembu on the other hand, translated their beliefs and concerns into concrete ritual actions, took magical precautions, and communicated actively with the djinn. Some hunters tied Islamic amulets to their bows, for example, to counter bad luck sent by these powers (cf. Cat. No. 8). The magical beliefs proved fairly similar to those described by Evans-Pritchard from Azande in Sudan. These people rely on the use of magical plants believed to possess homoeopathic properties. The plants are placed on glowing embers to release and transfer these powers to the hunting equipment by means of the smoke that develops. The Azande believe that the souls of the plants are set free through this process. Haddad Kanembu explanations of their own magical rites with plants follow a similar path and all of the hunters, whom we knew, used magic to enhance their luck. They treated both weapons and other hunting gear with magical plants to ensure a positive outcome of a hunt. Many of the plants were quite rare species. One of these was known as *konuwai* but called *kaebua*, i.e. red blood by the hunters.[1] The roots of this plant contain a reddish sap which hunters smear on the inside of their bows on each side of the grip before they go off to hunt. The sap lends the bow the colour of blood, the very fluid which the hunter hopes to provoke with his arrows. Basically, the use of *kaebua* is believed to secure the shedding of blood from game. Some hunters told us that when *kaebua* had been properly applied, the hunt could not fail.

10,3. A Haddad Kreda man praying in front of his tent while two others look on. While Kreda pastoralists and the Kanembu are devoted Muslims, religion appeared to play a less significant role among the Haddad. We saw very few Haddad pray and it is known that they converted to Islam only in the late 19th and early 20th century.

The Haddad Kanembu possess other kinds of magical know-how as well, knowledge that is individually 'owned' and handed down from one generation to the other, normally from father to son. One of the most important of these individually held insights and practices concerns the treatment of the masks which the hunters use as disguise to lure game. We were initiated into some of this secret knowledge by hunters at Chedra, but always under circumstances where we were alone with the hunter.

The importance of this esoteric knowledge and practice was underscored by the constant concern of our 'teachers' that other hunters would sneak up secretly behind the place where we were and listen to our conversation to 'steal the magic'. Once in a while when we were receiving secret knowledge, the informant would jump up and run out to scout for fellow hunters that might be eavesdropping behind the mats that fenced in the compound. This is indicative, I believe, of the significance which the hunters ascribe to magic as a means of success in hunting. We learned most about this esoteric knowledge at Chedra, in particular from hunters from whom we purchased masks for the museums. Let us therefore turn to the magical treatment of the masks, which the hunters use to fool the game they are hunting, pretending that they are ground hornbills and not deadly killers.

The masks, *ngudontul,* i.e. ground hornbill, are made from wood and sometimes the cranium of this strange bird to look like its head and neck, as previously described. They are carried on the forehead and the hunter simulates the movements of the bird as he creeps up upon the game. We purchased five masks in all (Cat. Nos. 5, 6, 12, 13 & 15) and shall look closer at the magic that had been applied to the last two numbers.

The owner of one of the masks (Cat. No. 13) had treated this with three plants, each said to possess different magical properties. He had used one perennial plant, *ngeremi* that he described merely as being between ten to thirty centimetres high. The plant and its root had been dried and then pounded in a mortar. Subsequently, the substance was placed on embers and the mask turned carefully in the smoke that it would penetrate the mask. Another plant, *mauru,*[2] described by the owner as being about ten centimetres high, having a long thin root and growing all year round in the savanna was handled exactly as the former, i.e. dried, pounded, and put on embers in order that the mask could be treated in the smoke from the plant. The third plant was treated in a similar way. It is called *kumbo,* can be found all year round and has a ligneous root.[3]

The smoke, and hence by implication the smell is thus perceived as the very agent that can fool the animals. It may have this effect whether the game actually spots the mask or smells it. In either case it is bound to approach the hunter or stand absolutely still, thus enabling him to get within shooting range. The owner of the mask told us that when he had treated the mask with the smoke from all three of the plants it did not matter whether he approached the game to windward or not, the game would not move upon having smelled the smoke. He might use the plants individually, but the strongest effect was accomplished if their forces were combined. When the treatment over the embers is completed the mask is wrapped in a piece of cotton cloth or some other material in order to prevent it from being seen by cocks, in which case the magic would lose its

power, our friend explained without being able to provide further detail.

The owner of another mask (Cat. No. 15) proceeded in a somewhat different way to ensure his hunting luck. He used not only smoke but inserted seeds of a plant believed to hold magical properties inside the mask itself. His knowledge stemmed from his father, who again had learned the trick from his father. The magical properties would bar the game from talking flight, in some case even induce this to move towards the hunter rather than away from its potential slayer, the hunter explained. He made use of two different sources of magic. One was the hairy seeds of a perennial plant, about thirty-five centimetres high, known as *beitap* (cf. note 4). Some of these had been put inside the cranium of the hornbill and covered by the skin of its neck already when the mask was made. One part of the seeds was put on glowing embers, whereupon the mask had been turned carefully in the smoke for some time. His other magical secret was the use of feathers from a tiny bird identified as *paké* only. The bird need not to be shot with particular care, a specimen found dead in the brousse can also do the trick.

A third hunter used also a mixture of no less than three plants to treat his mask, a combination that was necessary to achieve maximum strength. The plants were: a) the perennial plant *beitap,*[4] b) an annual plant, known by the same name, *beitap,*[5] but described as being a different species and a more delicate one but with hard, hairy seeds as the former, and finally a fine annual plant by the name of *dungudo*[6] which grows only during the rainy season.

Other plants believed to hold magical properties are also widely used by hunters and by society as such. One such plant is called *koromai.*[7] Hunters bring along this perennial on their expeditions, root and all wrapped in a piece of skin or cotton cloth. Another plant with magical properties is a wild onion known as *kailku* in Kanembu or *birete* in Arabic. It grows only in the savannah and is quite rare, but other plant species of similar appearances are common and may be used as substitutes, although they hold less potency. The Haddad Kanembu grow specimens of the *kailku* in their compounds and try, sometimes with success, to keep them alive by watering them carefully. It is believed that the *kailku* bring plenty to its owner and enough to eat for the family. To make this happen, however, a man has to strip and rub his torso all over with the sap of a large bulb.

10,4. A dum palm leaf used for magic purposes. Photo L.L.

The Haddad Kanembu claim that if a person has done so, no one will be able to resist a request by him, including animals which he pursues. They are bound to let themselves be killed.

Even the dum palm can hold such magical properties. If a hunter is out of luck on an expedition, he may try to alter the situation for the better by cutting a young leaf of the dum palm, tie a strip of bass around its stalk, place the tiny leaf on the ground and then jump over it one time. Our informants did not develop their thoughts about why this action was able to facilitate the spotting of game.

Plants are also used to obtain fertility, in particular one known as *kari dubu* or 'thousand root', *kari* meaning root, *dubu* a thousand. This too is a perennial, some 25 cm high. The roots are dried, pounded into flour and mixed with milk from a goat with many kids. The liquid is consumed not only by women to avert sterility but also by those who want many children. The Haddad Kanembu may also give it to domestic animals to further their productivity.

The latter usages of plants are not part of the magical universe specifically tuned to serve hunters, as we have seen but more widely applied. It is evident that the men who spend a good deal of time in the wilderness generally have a sophisticated knowledge of plants and wildlife. They know about rare species and may locate even those that are extremely difficult to come by. They can tell of *ngeremi* - a plant that wanders about due to the devil, *schatan*, taking root first in one place then another and is hence almost impossible to find. No wonder that this plant plays a specific role in Haddad understanding of magic. The plant was applied by a number of specialists at Chedra, at the time when game was plentiful and hunting economically significant. We learned this from a younger man who had been taught this form of

magic by his father who had been a famous hunter. A precondition to make use of *ngeremi* was not only the possession of the rare plant itself, but also of a specimen of the horn of a specific antelope, most probably a female Eland. These horns are some 60 cm to 70 cm long. Our informant did not use this form of magic himself, he assured us, but he treasured the horn still in his possession and believed, obviously, that this very fact brought him luck. His father, however, had used the horn actively to promote his own cause. To make the magic work the horn had to be held over embers and treated with smoke just as the masks. The father had used a mixture of flour made from scrapings from the antelope horn and material from the *ngeremi* plant to create the potent smoke. He had also been able to produce magical effects by simply placing the horn in an upright position, we learned. If positioned vertically, the horn could prevent the killing of game by all other hunters. However, if these promised to share their spoils with him game could be bagged again. Renowned hunters never made use of their horns in this way, as they invariably received shares from other hunters, or so the saying goes, our informant added. It was obvious that he felt very special himself, having such a potent tool at hand.

Haddad Kanembu hunters may also turn to prayers to obtain hunting luck. These are created, recited and owned by individual hunters, but may be passed on from father to son just as magic knowledge. The above-mentioned informant told us about a prayer that he recited to Allah upon leaving the compound to go hunting, a prayer that both his father and grandfather had used before him. He would pray as follows: "*Djida, babuna, assalamata, monna, yata, yawahabu!*" The meaning was the following, according to our interpreter:" Grandfather *(djida),* grandmother

10,5. Haddad masks collected
near N'Guri by Krarup-Mogensen.
Moesgaard Museum. Photo J.K.

(*babuna),* I am prepared for the savanna, (*assalamata),* I may bag game or not (*monna),* I shall be happy (if I get some), (*yata),* (I shall think in my heart): how lucky (*yawahabu), (*if all goes as I think and hope). The informant's father had also instructed him never to kill pregnant game or dams with offspring. I should add that this prohibition seems to be complied with by both Haddad Kanembu and Haddad Kreda hunters.

Hunting in disguise has been widespread in the Sahel, as previously stated, and there may well have been a good deal of shared beliefs among the people who sustained themselves by this trade. One hint of this can be found in Meek's work on the Jukun of the Benue in Nigeria. Like the Haddad Kanembu the Jukun hunters disguise themselves as hornbills and use various kinds of secret medicines to secure success. Meek writes that the hunter:" … is fumigated with a secret medicine which is believed to have the power of drawing bush-animals towards him. He also arms himself with charms designed to protect him from the evil spirits which are believed to accompany the larger game-animals. He has charms which render him invisible, or prevent him from losing his way. He washes his hands in a medicine which ensures that arrows, on hitting a target, shall not fall to the ground without effect. He offers rites to Kenjo the day before he sets out, and he must avoid sexual relations that night. He leaves his compound at early dawn in order, apart from other reasons, that he may avoid meeting or speaking to anyone; for he is in a condition of taboo, and contact with things profane would cause the disturbance and disappearance of the spiritual forces which surround him" (Meek 1931: 414-15). The Jukun do also believe that certain animals have a powerful soul-substance or *bwi,* and if a hunter kills any of these animals he must protect himself by special rites. If these are not performed the hunter will be pursued by the ghost and killed (Meek 1931: 418). The Haddad Kanembu may well have had a similar complex view of the world and of interaction between animals and human beings prior to their conversion to Islam. Hunters use the horn of the dama antelope to signal to one another during hunting expeditions, for instance, but this is a totally secular activity. Among other hunting groups between Lake Chad and the Niger, however, these horns are intimately associated with magic to ensure the hunting luck of the hunters (Frobenius 1933: 70ff). Similar notions may well have occurred among the Haddad Kanembu some generations ago.

Scholars have wondered why some peoples use magic while others do not. Johannes mentions this issue very briefly in his short article on the Haddad, suggesting that in case of hunter-gatherers these practices could be linked to the organization and methods of hunting. We discussed this question at length in the field. The two Haddad groups proved to be socially similar in many ways. They were organized in patrilineal clans, for example, and both groups professed Islam. Still, the use of magic turned out to be prominent among the Haddad Kanembu and totally absent among the Haddad Kreda. Magic beliefs flourished among the Haddad Kanembu hunters, who were largely on their own in tracking down and killing game. They were all deeply occupied with the question of hunting luck and its explanation: why would game be plentiful one day yet impossible to bag, while scarce but approachable on another; why was luck in hunting bestowed upon some men but failing others. In their view, the answer to these riddles was ultimately linked to the agency of spiritual forces. Facing the unpredictability of hunting luck, the Haddad Kanembu turned to the supernatural world and attempted to forge ties with its powers by means of magical practices. The situation and perceptions of the Haddad Kreda were entirely different. Hunting was not an individual but a collective effort among these people. Not only did the Haddad Kreda hunt together, in their view the very outcome relied on the efforts of every single member taking part in the hunt, old as well as young, male as well as female. If the hunt proved unsuccessful it was generally agreed to be somebody's fault and the person held responsible for the failure was blamed both loudly and rudely, as previously told. The Haddad Kreda did not explain the outcome of a hunting expedition in simple terms of good or bad luck, deferring the responsibility to third party. Rather the failure became instantaneously the object of a heated debate and the blame placed on one or more of the participants, who in retrospect had misjudged the distance to the game, not run fast enough to drive it in the right direction or shouted sufficiently loud to scare it into the nets. Game would be bagged, in the view of the Haddad Kreda, if a party cooperated and each individual was on his or her toes – the opportunity lost when mistakes were made. There was no place for magic in their view of the natural world and its species.

NOTES

1. The *Kaebua* is a Boraginaceae, probably the species of *Heliotropium,* perhaps *Arnebia* or *Coldenia.*
2. Leguminosae, sub-family Papilionoideae, a species of *Rhynchosia, Eriosema* or perhaps *Moghania.*
3. Leguminosae, sub-family Papilionoideae, a single foliate species of *Crotalaria.*
4. Amaranthaceae, probably *Pupalia lappacea* (L.) Juss.
5. Leguminosae, subfamily Papilionoideae, species of the genus *Zornia.*
6. Brassicaceae, member of the genus *Farsetia.*
7. Convolvulaceae, a small species of the genus *Maerua.*

11:

11: POETRY AND PERFORMANCE

"Poetry is the breath and finer spirit of all knowledge; it is the impassioned expression which is in the countenance of all science," William Wordsworth writes in the preface to his *Lyrical Ballads*. Wordsworth's view captures the quintessence of Haddad poetry. Haddad creativity and artistic ability find their finest expression in this artistic form. Poetry captures their emotions and sentiments. Songs and the accompanying music and dancing lend meaning to Haddad insights into and knowledge about nature. The preoccupation of Kreda men with their beloved cattle, a passion shared with other pastoralists, finds no resonance among the Haddad. Men's imagination is spurred on by wild animals only, by the behaviour and nature of the game they pursue, by game as the key to survival and to a woman's heart or bed, or so it is hoped. What the Haddad men share with their Kreda fellows is this love of women, feelings which men of both groups express in poems too.

The poems composed by Haddad Kreda women describe male-female relations, turning on topics such as why a young woman should be for one man only, the feeling of despair of a middle-aged woman because her husband is looking for a younger, second wife, the allure of young men. The songs idolize specific persons, describing their attractions, their manliness, beauty and fortunes. One song was composed in honour, of a particular woman whose husband had gone travelling for a long period of time. In the song the woman was pitied, because she was forced to stay back home alone. Haddad women are not expected to follow their menfolk on travels and the song described the many localities that her husband was supposed to visit: Kano, Fort-Lamy, Abecher etc. and hence by implication

his loneliness and longings. But women may also make songs about the animals that their menfolk hunt: the character and behaviour of the jackal and its wanderings from one named locality to the other, where it stops to drink and how it is to be blamed for the killing of goats and sheep.

Haddad poetry is rich and influenced by their hunting experiences and way of life. It deals with animals more than any other topic. This preoccupation with animal species is reflected in Haddad thinking about and categorization of social units. Like many other foraging groups around the globe, the Haddad use animal species as emblems of social units – in this case of the clans, which they name after specific species. In fact, the Haddad perceive the animal world as being divided into clans, in the sense that each species constitutes a specific clan. The animal clans are united in larger units, super clans, one could say, each again with one species as the chief and emblem. The clans of all the four-legged animals, for example, are headed by the frog, *koko*. This animal is so powerful in Haddad understanding that it is the respected chief even of the largest of animals, the elephant. The various clans of birds are likewise united into a super clan headed by a tiny bird known as *ntchulokili*. Poems about animals are not therefore necessarily about the various species only, but may entail a subtext that tells of social categories, of power and social behaviour, rights and obligations.

When performed, each line of the poem is repeated one or more times at the choice of the performer. The accompanying music underscores the tone and content of the poem, changing subtly with each new stanza. It accentuates the content by sound imitation or onomatopoeia that grasps

11,1. A three-stringed spike luke. Cat. no. 78a. Photo J.K.   11,2. A three-stringed spike lute, reverse. Cat. no. 78b. Photo J.K.

the movements or behaviour of the animals portrayed in the poem. Certain compositorial traits are characteristic of Haddad poetry. Poems lend voices to both humans and animals, for example, as in the ensuing song of the jackal. Another characteristic trait is that the songs appear not to call mammals that are hunted by their proper name. That the very name of the more important species of game should be avoided while on a hunting expedition, in rituals invoking the spirits of the animals or in poetry composed at their praise is quite common among foragers. Haddad poets and musicians, for example, either refrain from mentioning the names entirely or use synonyms such as mouse or goat for the gazelle. There are no restrictions on naming birds, such as guinea fowl. Interestingly, the wart hog appears to be perceived as in a kind of in-between category, possibly because of its changing role in Haddad subsistence, from being a highly sought-after species in pre-Islamic times to being

prohibited by that very religion much to the regret of the Haddad. This intermediate position reveals itself in the last line of the song of the wart hog, which states explicitly: you must not be called wart hog but goat.

HADDAD KREDA SONGS

We noted down two poems about the guinea fowl and Oryx antelope as well as one love poem. The Haddad Kreda have quite an impressive repertoire of songs, however, and quite a number of poems are shared heritage with the Haddad Kanembu. The text is rendered in the language of the Haddad Kreda.[1]

The guinea fowl

The song tells of a Haddad Kreda hunter returning to the camp with his bag of guinea fowl. A Kreda woman asks him to give her the guinea fowl, hinting delicately that he may share her bed at night in return. The hunter gives her the fowl, but finds himself deceived as the night falls.

11,3. Young Haddad Kreda playing his three-stringed spike lute while waiting for his hunting companions.

Gouleï nou-urou wé, gouleï nou-urou wé
Tchatchaji-jou, tchatchaji-jou
Siri gountou dine, siri gountou dine
Filetidine, filetidine
Goumartchi-jou, goumartchi-jou
Yini tcheli-jou, yini tcheli-jou
Soura toou-jou, soura toou-jou
Impi koultcha-doou, impi koultcha-doou
Tchatchaji-jou, tchatchaji-jou

My guinea fowl where are you, my guinea fowl
Where are you
The woman is deceitful, the woman is deceitful
I smelled her scent, I smelled her scent
I was seduced by her incense, I was seduced by her
incense*)
Is she amorous to everyone, is she amorous to everyone
Strangely she deceived me, strangely she deceived me
Her bag is filled with meat, her bag is filled with meat
Her jar enriched with fat, her jar enriched wit fat
The woman is deceitful, the woman is deceitful

*) Smoke is a central force in Haddad worldview and magic. The smoke from special plants may induce game to stand still or even approach a hunter if his mask has been properly treated with it, as we have heard. Smoke is also a woman's weapon to lure a man to her bed. Haddad Kreda women use smoke from burning twigs of a tree called *tjorogou, (Zizyphus sp.),* as an incense believed to have a magical properties. Their pastoral companions do the same. Most women in the childbearing age keep a tiny heap of twigs from this tree ready for use in front of their tents. When a woman wants to 'bathe herself in smoke' to become irresistible to her husband, she will set fire to some twigs in a cylindrical hole that has been dug next to the tent. This is done at dusk when the food has been prepared and the shadows are getting long and full of promises of intimacy. She will place herself in a squatting position over the smoldering incense, usually on a tiny stool, cover her head with a piece of cloth and let the smoke ooze up under her dress and lend her the coveted, alluring smell. Some women treat themselves with this form of incense every night, and women joke among themselves about such frequent invitations to the husbands.

The Oryx

An absolute favourite song, one that is heard repeatedly in the camps of the Haddad Kreda, is the one about the Oryx. It tells of this grand antelope, that offers the Haddad meat in abundance once a flock is caught, but also is an adversary of great force, a dangerous challenge to the hunters. Only the Haddad Kreda sing in praise of this great animal. The Haddad Kanembu have no poems about this species, probably because they do not venture north to hunt it and hence have limited knowledge about and interest in this antelope.

Ngara ho, ngara ho, ngara ho
Ezeï koréga, ezeï koréga, ezeï koréga
Azza gadanga, Azza gadanga, Azza gadanga
Aka boudinga, aka boudinga, aka boudinga
Chelouf tchirida, Chelouf tchirida
Issilé tchirida, Issilé tchirida
Tchekir tchirida, Tchekir tchirida
Abal tchirida, Abal tchirida
Outouk tchirida, Outouk tchirida
Oguirdé tchirida, Oguirdé tchirida
Foroumounga tchirida, Foroumounga tchirida
Ngara ho, ngara ho, ngara ho
Kichidro gouli tama, kichidro gouli tama
Yosko Abokoriga, Hamid Sougou Younnoussi
Hamide Younnoussinga

Fair beauty where are you, fair beauty where are you, fair beauty where are you
Trophy of runners, trophy of runners, trophy of runners
Property of the ancient Azza, property of the ancient Azza, property of the ancient Azza
Relishing forest and desert, relishing forest and desert, relishing forest and desert
Near Chelouf, near Chelouf
Near Issilé, near Issilé
Near Tchekir, near Tchekir
Near Abal, near Abal
Near Outouk, near Outouk
Near Oguirdé, near Oguirdé
Near Foroumounga, near Foroumounga
Fair beauty where are you, fair beauty where are you, fair beauty where are you

11,4. Drinking tea and relaxing around the camp fire to the subtle tunes of the lute.

Belly filled and fatty, belly filled and fatty
[Killed previously by] Yosko Abokoriga, Hamid Sougou
Younnoussi, [and by] Hamide Younnoussinga

We were only able to write down a single love song among the
Haddad Kreda, but listened quite often to the music accompanying these. The following poem is a eulogy of Merambeina,
a renowned belle, claimed to be the most beautiful woman of
the entire Bahr el Ghazal. At the time of our visit, Merambeina
lived in Mussoro. Although elderly, her praise was still being
sung, also among the Haddad Kanembu.

The 'belle' of Mussoro

Kellibinga, Kellibinga, Kellibinga
Merambeina, Merambeina, Merambeina
Choukou dédé, jerou Choukou dédé
Merambeina Youssouf dédé
Sousoumi Merambeina, Sousoumi Merambeina
Wayayo Kellibinga wayayo Kellibinga

11,5. Professional Haddad musician playing a double drum. This man originated from Faya Largeau, but had married a Haddad Kreda woman and settled with her people. The Haddad Kreda do not play drums.

Kellibinga, Kellibinga, Kellibinga
Merambeina, Merambeina, Merambeina
Choukou the brother, Choukou, the younger brother
Merambeina, [her] younger brother [is] Youssouf
Sousoumi, [the daughter of] Merambeina, Sousoumi,
[the daughter of] Merambeina
The love of Kellibinga, the love of Kellibinga

HADDAD KANEMBU SONGS

The Haddad Kanembu are also extremely fond of poetry. Although hunting is on the decline, they still revel in songs about wild animals. These are generally performed to the accompaniment of the three-stringed spike lute, the *tuluru*.

The hyena

The song about the hyena is one of the most popular both among the Haddad Kreda and the Haddad Kanembu. The melody is identical but the text slightly different among the two groups. What distinguishes this song from other songs is first and foremost that the singer acts while he recites the poem, imitating the characteristic postures, movements and behaviour of the hyena. He is also disguised as a hyena with a black sheepskin over his back and a mask from leaves of *Calotropis precera*. The text pretends to render the thoughts and words of the hyena itself. It tells of the animal's intent to sneak up upon the goats, of how it mistakenly ends up among the camels instead, where it receives a good number of kicks before it escapes. In the last line it warns other hyenas not to make a similar error. The text is rendered in the Kanembu language.

Afi soudo biri goljaro
Chatan soudo biri goljaro
Yalni kola da manikou biri goljaro
Souana biri goljaro

Who has lured me into the pen of the camels?
The devil has tricked me into the pen of the camels
My children were hungry, I searched for meat for my
young ones in the pen of the camels
Be careful in a pen of camels

The gazelle

This is a poem sung by elderly hunters, as the text indicates. The men address the gazelle tenderly as the tiny clear-eyed mouse and as their goat. They claim the gazelle for themselves, urging young men to hunt for their 'own mothers', i.e. other species instead of chasing the gazelle. The melody itself is in praise of the gazelle, and the strings are plucked in a particular way to simulate its swiftly ticking tail.

Ntchokollombé soumgou kantam
Kani Dalhi Kellimbé
Djibrine Mbodimbé
Mbodou Choukoumbé
Ali Kellimbé
Kindira bilimi yengou tchéyi

Little mouse with the clear eyes
The goat of Ali Kellimbé
Djibrine Mbodimbé
Mbodou Choukoumbé
Ali Kellimbé
Young hunter pursue your own mother

The wart hog

The poem praises the meat of the wart hog, although this is considered unclean by Islam. Muslims should not touch the meat or that of any other pig. Nevertheless, the Haddad Kanembu expressed regret that they could no longer relish a dish of wart hog due to their adoption of the Muslim faith. Still, wart hogs are hunted by the Haddad Kanembu. It is generally maintained, that the hunting is only carried out to cater for the market provided by Europeans, Christians and pagan Africans from the South, who have no such food taboos. In reality, however, the situation was more delicate in that quite a number of Haddad from both groups appeared to enjoy and eat wart hog, according to Kreda and Kanembu informants. These would repeat over and over again that the Haddad were very sorry that the wart hog had been declared unclean by Islam.

Letou toura, keloyé toura
Na keline boro ti dotchibo
Na intchiboro to dotchibo
Ti ngodoudi goultou ténou
Nasara yé siraou, maï yé siraou, kindira yé siraou
Tiro kani miniga, ngdou goultou ténou

Great wanderer, producer of such fine sauce
You dislike the desert and favour thickets
You do not like places with a scarcity of water
To utter you name wart hog is prohibited
[Yet] you are loved by Europeans, by great chiefs, by hunters
One must say goat, not use your name wart hog

The Damalisque

The Dama antelope is important to Haddad Kreda subsistence, more so in former days that at the time of our fieldwork, and it plays still a significant role in their worldview and artistic expression. Like other game it cannot be mentioned by its proper name. In some poems an animals name is replaced by a metaphor such as 'little mouse' or 'goat' for the gazelle or 'great wanderer' for the wart hog. In the case of the Dama, the poem simply avoids the name. The animal is not mentioned once by name, nor has the poet used any other means to characterize the object of his praise.

Kindira souwayé tcheyou kida
Npram sagaïro tachou kida
Kore kokoï, ngalaro donkou tchika tchourti, adiyéï, kargoum manji
Koua karifi mooumbé, jouandia koulinga dahan kida

The Arabian hunter has killed it already
He has a granary filled with its bones
[A hunter] tiny as a frog*, unable to jump across a bean plant, contemplates to go hunting for it.
The tall and mighty hunter, who ties an elephant's hide around his loins, loves the hunt for it

*) Literally speaking, *kore kokoï* means 'tiny as a frog'. As mentioned, the frog is believed to be the most potent of animals.

The elephant

In the 1960s, elephants were no more browsing regularly in Kanem. Occasionally some animals wandered north up through the Bahr el Ghazal during the rainy season and a small flock was still living in the area of N'Guigmi, on the northwest shores of Lake Chad. Still, these grand animals were vividly present in Haddad memories and they sing of the elephants and of brave hunters successfully killing the giants. This song praises the elephant and caution people against the 'frog' or 'bull', the metaphors used by the poet to describe this formidable creature.

Koko Boula Mourdiliyé
Dalou Youssoua Moussaïbé
Ali Kala Kerimayebé
Djibrin Mbodoumbé
Tendi ngayo mooum toulo maïyéï
Roumia, Allah soutiléro malloum dangoui

The frog at Ouadi Mourdilyé:
The bull of Youssoua Moussaïbé
The bull of Ali Kala Kerimamayebé
The bull of Djibrin Mbodoumbé
All of these men loved to hunt [it]
If spotted, a man should ask the Lord for protection not to be killed

The ostrich

Ostriches were formerly abundant in Kanem and the Bahr el Ghazal. The bird was hunted persistently by the Haddad, who praise its meat, sold its feathers, and applied its plumage to disguise themselves when hunting, not only for the ostrich itself but also other animals. The song tells of the joy of hunting ostriches and the abundance of meat that it provides, so much in fact that the stomach is left for carnivores and vultures.

Tchouloumi ti roumia ngouri
Roumou kiri gonia ngouri
Ti yeyimia ngouri
Ti king-gai sounia dilaï yoloutchiki
Boltou tenguilé rogaï
Koou samélane, toumbol jarou-joutchi
Kadaou katéne diptchi

The black one if you spot it, what a pleasure
If you have spotted it and pulled out the arrows,
what a pleasure
If you have had the luck to kill it, what a pleasure
If it dies one day the jackal howls youlou
The hyena circles around it like a gazelle
Vultures descend from heaven beating the drum
The hawk circles above the dead bird

The rhinoceros

The rhino is also praised by poets although few if any Haddad have encountered this great mammal. Both the black rhino and the white rhino range pretty far from Haddad Kanembu homeland. The species most familiar to the Haddad is the smaller, black or hook-lipped rhino which grazes in thorn scrub covered parts of south-eastern Chad, northern Central African Republic and western Sudan, while the white rhino lives even further away in the Western Nile area. The Haddad nevertheless possess a song about Garba, a Haddad hunter who sings about his rhinoceros hunting. Garba sings of two other hunters, Mali Momo Kourana and Guiljami, of how Guiljami pursued a rhinoceros but had to return as he got frightened. The second time he went hunting, however, he was successful and Garba asks himself how that was possible, wondering what kind of magic he might have applied to kill the rhino. Garba himself has also killed a rhino, and the song tells of how he goes hunting once again for this grand animal, and is able to capture a rhino alive and drag it back home by the nose as if it had been a goat tied to a rope due to his extraordinarily potent magic.

The Kanembu term for rhino is *bourka*. However, throughout the song the rhino is termed *kodombour*, because wild animals must not be called by their proper names unless they will not let themselves be killed. The deeper meaning of this metaphor is not known to me.

Mali Momo Kourana kodombour mani
Guiljami kodombour mani
Kodombour roumi dounoum kodomo
Guiljami kodombour janoukoudé
Garba kodombour janoukoudé
Garba kodombour jayi koudo
Tchikaï faïdé ten-tenoune
Yeyoundo janou koudo

Mali Momo Kourana scouts for *kodombour*
Guiljami scouts for *kodombour*
The *kodombour* is spotted what a scare
Guiljami killed the *kodombour*
Garba killed the *kodombour* once
Garba snares the *kodombour* alive this time
Listen carefully, is the magic potent or not
I pulled it along as a goat this time

The lion

In this poem the lion is described metaphorically by the name of a dog, *kiri*. The song tells of the danger that lions pose to humans. However, the animal can be tamed like dogs and was kept by some great African chiefs, Haile Selassie being one who comes to mind as well as by some Europeans in colonial times. The sub-text of the poem is that lions were kept by certain chiefs of the South for passing sentence. If suspected of crime a person might be shut up with the chief's lions. Innocence was proven, if the animals left the person unscathed.

Kiri tagour, kiri tagour, kiri tagour
Roumou nguenégou janoum koudoumia
Salka nguenén rotibo
Ti kirido wassa kotta
Ti roumia deliline nagouro timi
Kiri nassaraï yé sirau

The dog cannot be trusted, the dog cannot be trusted,
the dog cannot be trusted
If you come upon its cubs watch out do not touch
A rope cannot tie its cubs, only chains
Never poke fun of the dog
Once spotted have patience or you will never get close
Dog of Europeans and great chiefs

The monkey

The poem tells of Abdou, a monkey that marries a bitch. Abdou promises to cultivate the field of his mother-in-law together with his male friends. Instead of doing a proper job, however the monkeys destroy all the plants leaving but sand behind. Realizing what has happened, the mother-in-law sends for her ninety brothers and declares war against the monkeys, a war that has lasted ever since. The word for monkey, Abdou is also used as a personal name for boys/men.

Abdou ndranoum jowa, Abdou ndranoum jowa
Doumdoum tchouroni jowa bis
Yanké douro tchoukou kadi daham douno
Nounouli-nouli, nounouli-nouli*)
Koulo kissaïngé baréro tiki-njou
Yamagou tchatchou koulo baréro
Koulo nanatchou douno
Kissa ngou sotina wou-yi-yi tchoukou
Kiri filigar tchatchou
Dolloun kiri noko kilkono

Abdou where does it hurt, Abdou where does it hurt
Listen I have a headache
Dressed in trousers with the tail sticking out
Nounouli-nouli, nounouli-nouli
The millet of the mother-in-law shall be cultivated
His friends are rounded up to cultivate the field
The millet is destroyed, nothing but sand remains
When the mother-in-law sees the destruction she yells
wou-yi-yi
She calls upon her dogs [brethren] ninety of them
Since then dogs and monkeys have disliked one another

*) onomatopoeic expression, indicating the way monkeys move and communicate.

The jackal

This poem lends voice both to man (first and second line) and the jackal (third to fifth lines), as is common in Haddad poetry. In the poem the jackal argues that if a person intends to kill it, the jackal invariably looks him straight in the eyes. This refers to the fact that jackals always stand still and stare at people.

Assa yolongana kani boula ndé traounou
Kamga bonou ouarou daaro touliki
Kay seciga ounou seci
Nguené kaké tchoudou ngoron tchiralibo
Tchiralié ép touli

Assa yolongana not loved by the white goat
It has controversies with man
If anyone tries to kill me I invariably observe him
Taming my cubs is difficult
Tame they pose problems to the owner

DANCE AND MUSIC

Poetry is generally performed to the accompaniment of a lute and sometimes dancing. Poems are composed, recited and sung by men and women alike, but if they are accompanied by dancing, the performers are usually women. This is not to say that a hunter may not sing to himself, but poems are as much part of public life, of evenings when the Haddad get together and relax around a bonfire, either in the camps of the Haddad Kreda or the homesteads of the Haddad Kanembu. On such joyful occasions, a man will bring out his three-stringed spike lute or *tuluru*, and one or more women may get up to dance to the melodies. Performers and spectators alike welcome these festive moments as a change to the monotony of the daily grind.

Haddad men dance mostly alone both among the Haddad Kreda and the Haddad Kanembu, except when they perform the dance of the hyena and the jackal. Few Haddad Kreda men dance at all, however. We saw one doing so once and were taken by the strangely jumping movements as the dancer simulated the behaviour of various animals. Haddad women hardly ever dance alone but always as a group, often three to five at a time, sometimes a few more. They form a line or semi- or full circles, but dance more or less on the spot, taking only tiny steps back and forth, while shifting the balance from one foot to the other and bending the upper part of their bodies forward in time with the rhythm of the music and the clapping of their hands. They accompany their respective performances by singing and/or a peculiar form of coarse humming. This humming is a speciality of women, produced while breathing both in and out.

11,6. Young Haddad Kanembu women dance at dusk.

11,7. Young Haddad man disguised as a hyena for his performance of the dance about the rivalry between this animal and the jackal. The mask was made of leaves of Calotropis. Haddad Kanembu, Chedra.

A popular dance among both Haddad groups is *ajewibarie*, since it can be performed jointly by men and women. The dancers stand in a row, swaying their bodies and arms as they clap in time with the song, which is performed by a solo dancer. He or she dances in front of the row improvising the steps, alternating between high stamping leaps, both legs at a time, and other forms of leaping.

Haddad women perform another appreciated dance called *moidanga* by the Haddad Kanembu. In this dance, women form a circle and hold on to each other by the little fingers while making swaying movements with the arms and trotting slowly in one direction. The dance is accompanied by song, the text of which is improvised on the spot by the lead dancer and then repeated, stanza by stanza by the other dancers. The lead dancer enters the circle to dance solo at the start of each new stanza, after which she returns to take her place in the circle of dancers while they repeat her song. The pitch of the lead dancer is higher when she introduces a new stanza than when it is repeated by the chorus. The steps themselves are quite simple: The dancers move with their left side turned towards the centre of the circle in a continuous slow trot, now and then stamping with their right foot to accentuate the rhythm. A variation is introduced when the lead dancer breaks out of the circle to dance at the centre, while she introduces a new stanza. She takes a long, firm step, shifts her weight to the left foot and proceeds by stepping backwards with her right foot towards the circle of trotting women, whereupon she does likewise with the left foot, upon which she stamps with her right foot, takes a step backwards and join the circle of slowly trotting women.

The lead dancer composes her songs around a variety of topics. Often the songs praise her male relatives: the virtues, merits and fearlessness of a younger brother, her father's braveness etc. The text is not always audible to the other dancers or the spectators, who are doomed to repeat the text the best they can. Among Kreda pastoralists the *moidanga* are often poetic descriptions of migrations, camps and herds. At Kurei Joroso we saw Haddad and Kreda women dance together, something which had been unthinkable, we were told, prior to the newly passed laws affirming the equality all citizens of independent Chad.

The 'standard' repertoire of the Haddad Kanembu and, probably, also the Haddad Kreda includes a highly popular song and dance about the hyena and the jackal. It is per-formed by two men, one representing a hyena, the other a jackal. The performers disguise themselves as the two animals, the hyena dancer covering his back with the skin of a black sheep and his face with a mask made out of the fresh green leaves of the *Calotropis procera,* one leaf covering the face except for holes for the eyes and mouth, and two folded leaves simulating the ears, each pinned on the upper edge of the 'face' with tiny twigs or thorns. The mask is fixed to the dancer's head with a string tied at the back of the head (cf. *Fig. 11,6*). The dancer playing the jackal had no disguise at the performance we saw at Chedra, except for a sheep's skin over his back. The dancers are capable of vividly conjuring up the movements and behaviour of the two animals and portray the jackals as for ever following the hyenas to steal part of the spoil. The hyena dancer came out first from behind a hut, leaping at full speed on 'all fours' into the semi-circle of spectators, but stopping abruptly as he spotted 'humans', turning his head from one side to the other, now aslant, now and then sniffing in the air or snorting as he moved around on the outlook for 'prey'. Soon the 'jackal' turned up, a teenage boy moving sometimes in jumps on 'all fours', following the track of the hyena but keeping a slight distance or stopping in a squatting position so as not to get so close to the hyena that it risked an attack. A 'goat' in the shape of a piece of white cotton-cloth was thrown in the sand, but whenever the hyena sneaked up on its prey, the jackal started howling and making a noise as is the custom of this animal – all to the great delight of the spectators. The Haddad believe that the jackal is jealous of the hyena, and that it howls to spoil the hunting luck of the hyena whenever it is out to kill goats.

Song and dance is usually accompanied by the lute, the *tuluru,* the musical instrument par excellence of all Haddad groups, whether foragers or artisans. The *tuluru* is not played by other ethnic groups in Kanem and the Bahr el Ghazal. It is a three-stringed spike instrument. The resonator is a bowl of wood from the *erei* tree made by Haddad artisans. It is generally decorated on the outside with simple incisions including a 3 cm broad band just below its rim, from which pyramidal designs extend towards the bottom. To obtain the desired shiny, blackish surface, the bowl has been charred and then rubbed in butter. Resonators are not produced specifically for the lutes, but made of the same bowls that the Haddad use for eating. A Haddad man who feels like playing music but has no instrument at hand, may well take an eating bowl and turn this into a lute just for the occasion. He covers the opening of the bowl with a piece of hide of ox skin in such a way that it stretches beyond the rim and down the bowl's outer side. It is tied and held firmly stretched with strips of leather put through holes in the hide itself. The spike is made from a stick of soft wood. It is about 50 cm long and will be fastened at the one end some 2.5 cm from the rim of the bowl by means of a leather string which also holds in place the bridge of the instrument. This is furnished with three incisions to stabilize the strings, all made of twisted sinew from gazelles, antelopes, cows or goats.

The instrument is played in the same way among the two Haddad groups, i.e. with the thumb and index-finger of the right hand. Certain melodies are accentuated by a beat or drumming on the hide with the middle finger.

Most of the songs that we heard were the same among the Haddad Kanembu and the Haddad Kreda, but it seemed that music played a slightly different role among the two groups. Music was eagerly performed among the more active Haddad Kreda hunters. Young men played the lute quite frequently, enjoying themselves with or without an audience in the lazy afternoons and coolness of the early evening. In Haddad Kanembu hamlets, music seems to serve more as general entertainment, often performed in connection with the dancing of women. When this happened a lute would be played in most cases. Each melody is associated with a poem. Even if this is not sung the text will be well known to the participants. Some praise a beautiful woman of the community or are love songs composed by the musician to his beloved, as we have heard. Many tell of wild animals and of the hunting of these.

NOTES

1. I have spelled the poems and their translations in accordance with French orthography to be faithful to the notations and original translation from Kreda and Kanembu into French by our interpreter Bogar Bechir.

12:

12: SPACE AND PLACE

HADDAD KREDA

Haddad family life is anchored in the dwelling, whether it is the mat covered tent or the thatched beehive hut. The spatial lay-out of the temporary camps of the Haddad Kreda or more permanent hamlets of the Haddad Kanembu create different physical frameworks and daily routines. These are culturally coded spaces with a matrix of meanings and social implications. The distinctive nature of the spatial layout is intimately associated with the subsistence strategies and socio-political situation of the Haddad Kreda and the Haddad Kanembu respectively. The location of tents and huts in the landscape and vis-à-vis neighbouring families opens up to radically different forms of social interaction and aesthetic perception. The Haddad Kreda place their camps on top of dunes in the vast landscape. The oval, yellowish-white tents are pitched next to one another in a row, each wide open to inspection by fellow camp mates and Kreda patrons. The thatched, greyish-looking beehive huts of Haddad Kanembu families, on the other hand, lie scattered in between millet fields, shielded from inquisitive glances by tall mats or fences of other straw materials. These differences set the stage for Haddad sociality and reflect in part the cultural baggage which they share with the Kreda and Kanembu respectively.

CAMPS AND CAMP LIFE

Your first impression of a joint Haddad and Kreda camp depends utterly on the time of the day or night that you arrive, much more so than on the weather. My favourite time is the late afternoon, when the burning heat subsides and the camp revives to a buzz of life. The low, reddish sun glows through clouds of dust whirled up by thousands of hoofs as the cattle and herds of goats head back from the pastures. The air reverberates from bleating goats and sheep, tethered calves calling desperately for their mother cows as they seek one another after a long day of separation, the hollow sounds from mortars as the millet is pounded in preparation of the evening meal and the soft voices of playing children. Young girls and women hurry back and forth to milk cows and goats, a man grooms his beloved riding horse, another is busy unloading a camel. Soon the camp exudes nothing but peace as animals and people come to rest and settle down at the bonfires. Throughout the day, on the other hand, the camp is largely deserted. Cattle and goats are out on the pastures except for the calves tethered in front of the owners' tents to prevent them from suckling, and perhaps some mother goat with her newborn kids. Young Kreda boys and men are with the herds, older men and some of the women may be at the markets. Both the pastoralists and the Haddad must walk long distances to sell their produce, as must so many other Africans. Most of the Haddad have also left camp, women and men to forage and hunt, leaving behind the elderly, the sick and small children. At midday camps ooze sleepiness. Hardly a sound is heard and there are few present to receive visitors, to welcome these inside a tent and show hospitality – a core value of these communities. It is immediately apparent from the spatial lay-out of a camp if this is inhabited by both pastoralists and foragers. The tents will be pitched in two rows,

12,1. When the Haddad camp with the pastoralists, the tents are pitched behind those of their Kreda 'hosts'. We met only one camp where the two groups pitched their tents in one long row and were told that the change had come about only after Chad had gained independence.

the larger Kreda tents in front, the more modest Haddad ones placed right behind those of their individual 'hosts'. In between is a kind of no man's land, an open space which the Haddad cross to assist their Kreda 'hosts' and traverse lengthwise to visit Haddad families at the other end of the camp. Young girls carefully pass carrying bowls with fresh milk and children use it as a playground in between stray donkeys and a few lazy dogs. The herds of the Kreda are often kept in front of the tents to enable the owners to keep a vigilant eye on them. The herds are always at the camp at night: Calves tethered to prevent them from suckling except for short periods, the mother cows lingering nearby guarded by dogs. Goats are sometimes kept within thorny enclosures, but they may also be left to their own devices. Riding horses are also fed and kept right next to the tents. Donkeys and camels, on the other hand, are let loose with a tight rope either between their two forelegs or between one

of these and a hind leg to prevent them from roaming too far away from the camp in search of fodder.

The tent and its immediate surroundings are the focal point of Haddad domestic life, more so perhaps for women and small children than for men. The latter spend a good deal of their time hunting and foraging or going to markets. When at home, the men lie idle on mats under a shadowy canopy, chat with one another or repair nets and tools. An older man may be pontificating with a small boy on his lap, a young man perhaps breaking the monotony with his lute. At a tent a man is patiently repairing his nets. Occasionally tea is served and a happy murmur of lively discussions fills the air for a while until the voices give in to the buzzing of flies. Like all Sahelien peoples, the Haddad enjoy drinking hot sweet tea, which they make in tiny teapots and drink out of small glasses. The economy seldom allows them the luxury of this stimulant, however, because sugar is too

12,2. A Haddad camp.

costly, and tea is largely drunk if it is offered to them by the pastoralists.

Men stay inside the tents during the night if they are ill, or when entertaining guests. They take their meal or meals here and sleep on the platform with their wives covered by the piece of cloth that they wear around the waist during the day, or if it is chilly by a hide. Women, on the other hand, are busy in or near the tent when not fetching water and firewood or on foraging expeditions. They are the first to get up in the morning and the last to go to bed. You hardly notice their silent shadows against the dawning sky when they disappear to complete their toilet before lighting the fire and preparing the first meal of the day. All day long they plait mats and baskets, repair household utensils and look after children.

Adults normally do with two meals a day, in the morning and the evening, but children are fed titbits of lefto-vers during the day. The staple of Haddad diet is porridge made from wild grass, *ogu,* or from millet that they barter or increasingly buy at markets. The grass seeds or the millet is pounded to remove the outer shell, then winnowed to remove the chaff and finally cooked in boiling water till this is more or less absorbed and the dish has become quite solid. Porridge is eaten with melted butter or a piquant sauce, made from vegetables and spices. It may comprise a variety of wild plants – and also nuts find their way into the sauce. The main meal is eaten in the evening. Leftovers are kept in a pot on top of a wooden stand out of reach of dogs and relatively safe from ants and other insects, and they will often make do for breakfast. The Haddad also feed on a wide variety of plants, berries and nuts that they gather and eat raw, roasted or pounded and cooked. Last but not least, they live on the game that men and children bring back from their hunting expeditions. The meat is cooked or roasted, innards such as liver preferably in embers. If the catch has been considerable, some of the meat will be dried for keep or sale. During the rainy season, when hunting is hampered by the rain, the pastures are green. Cows yield a lot of milk and this becomes an important nutrient for the Haddad. The milk is drunk as it comes or as buttermilk, both in the morning and in the evening, if provided by their patrons. Sometimes the milk is mixed with cold water to better quench thirst and prevent diarrhoea.

WOMEN AND THEIR TENTS

The Haddad and their Kreda 'hosts' live in tents all year round, unlike the Daza and Teda further to the north, who stay in straw dwellings during the rainy season and in the autumn (Baroin 1985: 51, 60). We met a few Haddad families who had recently begun to grow millet and had set up huts next to their fields. As hunting recedes, this may become a more common practice. The tent is the personal property of the married woman, as are most of the household utensils. A young Haddad woman is provided with the tent by her family at the time of her marriage. She retains control over this throughout her life. It is she who pitches and takes down the tent whenever the family moves camp, she who loads it on the backs of the donkeys when there is a decision to look for new hunting grounds, follow the migration of the Kreda 'hosts', or to grow millet. Kreda women also own and pitch tents and do the packing and unloading of mats, sticks and all the other belongings of the family on oxen whenever the camp is on the move in search for new pastures (cf. Baroin 1987: 305, Chapelle 1957: 273).

The tent and its immediate surroundings are kept extremely neat by the women. A small area right in front of each tent is perceived as within the domestic sphere, so to speak. It is carefully cleaned every day with a brush and utilized both for tasks such as pounding millet or *ogu* seeds, plaiting mats, coiffure, and for relaxation and the reception

12,3. Moving camp. A young Haddad plays his lute while the woman dismantles the tent. The other youngsters are just hanging around, as it is solely up to women to take care of the tent.

12,4. Old people and widows have only modest dwellings.
An elderly woman assisted by her relative.

of visitors in the morning and late afternoon, when it is still cool. This is also where small children play. The back side of the tent has no such space but opens out onto the 'wilderness'. The distance between the tents of the Kreda and those of the Haddad vary, but some ten metres seems to be normal. If there is a tree or two next to the tent, these are made use of as well. The nets may be placed up against them and leather bags for churning hung from a branch.

The Haddad tent is called *yegé* (pl. *yega)*, the name of the yellow-greyish mats that strike the eye from afar when

approaching a camp.[1] It is a barrel-vaulted structure made from the roots of the *tefi* acacia, *Acacia raddiana*, and covered by mats plaited from strips of dum palm leaves. The Haddad Kreda use the same type of tents as their pastoral hosts, but theirs are generally somewhat smaller and also in poorer condition. They bear a certain resemblance to the barrel-vaulted tents found among the Teda, some southern Tuareg and other pastoralists in West Africa, as well as those of the Beja in Sudan and northern Ethiopia. A closer look at the tents reveals, however, that they are structurally different from the other mat-covered tents of arch construction both with respect to the wooden structure and the kind of mats applied as cover, as we shall see.

When the Haddad and Kreda camp together, the tents are put up in two rows, as already mentioned, those of the Haddad being pitched right behind the tents of their Kreda 'hosts'. The two rows are oriented in the same north-southerly direction, the entrance facing west or west-north-west. A similar practice is followed by the Daza (Baroin 1985: 51), while the Teda appear to change the orientation according to the prevailing winds, the entrance being always on the lee side. During the dry season these are positioned in such a way that the shorter end, heavily weighted down and anchored by means of the bed, screens, baggage etc., provides a bulwark against the north-easterly wind. During the rainy season, the tent is rotated so that the entrance, still on the lee side, is now in the northwest corner and the bed and baggage in the southwest (Chapelle 1957: 233; Prussin 1995: 112). We were not able to observe whether the Haddad Kreda and the Kreda turn the direction of their tents in the same way, but our data did not indicate any such practice. We stayed with the Haddad during the rainy season, as will be recalled, a time when the prevalent wind is the monsoon blowing from the Bay of Guinea i.e. from the south-west. In the camps which we visited, the tents were pitched in a north-southerly direction, their openings facing west, i.e. to the windward side, not placed on the leeward side as among the Tubu. If the wind was strong and carried sand and debris into the tent, an extra mat was put up at the open front side of the tent for protection, just as it invariably is at night, when the family goes to sleep (cf. *Fig. 12,9i*). In some cases the Haddad put up a sheet made of antelope skin instead of a mat.

12,5. A Haddad woman
winnowing ogu seed that
has been pounded.

12,6. A Kreda woman
is being helped by her
Haddad affiliate making
a mat for the sleeping
platform of her tent.

12,7. A Haddad Kreda woman pitching a tent.

PITCHING A *YEGÉ*

Women and women only pitch tents, as previously indicated. On our travels we passed quite a number of camps being pitched or dismantled. As it happened, we were unable to follow the process of putting up a tent from beginning to end except once, and that was of a Kreda tent. The ensuing description is based on this event and on the detailed notes of the dismantling of another tent purchased at Gaba from a Kreda woman for the National Museum in Copenhagen (cf. Catalogue). To ease the understanding of how a tent is put up, I shall insert key measurements of the tent I bought, including relevant distances between posts, poles and arches, as well as catalogue numbers. I also refer the reader to *Figs.* 12,12a-12,12i for an exposé of the location

of the various poles. The tent measures approximately 440 cm x 265 cm and has a height of between a good 200 cm at the centre, slanting to 150 cm at the rear and a mere 80 to 143 cm at the entrance side, measured from the ground up to the prongs of the vertical poles.

Preparing the site

As soon as a camp site has been decided upon, the beasts of burden are relieved of their heavy loads. It takes four oxen to bring along a Kreda tent and all the belongings of the family. The Kreda may do with fewer oxen, but then the packing and unloading becomes much more of a hassle, I was told. The donkeys used by the Haddad are unable to carry as much as oxen, but they are strong and almost disappear under the loads that are put on their backs when a Haddad family moves camp. Tent poles, arches and mats and all the household utensils and belongings are unloaded right next to the site, where the tent is to be pitched. Bags and baskets with food and valuable possessions are hung in nearby trees and bushes to prevent termites, snakes, scorpions, goats, dogs or other animals from causing any damage. Depending on the time of arrival, the woman may cook a meal before she begins to pitch the tent, but she will make sure that at least part of the tent is pitched before nightfall, as neither the Haddad nor the Kreda wish to sleep in the open. If the family is migrating and only going to stay briefly at a given location, the women may decide to pitch the tents in a simpler way, as we shall see later, even if it takes only a few hours to pitch it properly. It is difficult for one person to fasten the arches that support the mats, and, if possible, women help one another with this part of the work.

Prior to the actual pitching, the ground is cleared of small bushes, plants and dung from animals with a hoe, *bon* (cf. Cat. No. 38) or a digging stick also known as *bon* (cf. Cat. No. 97). The latter is used again later for the digging of holes for the tent poles. Once the space has been cleared of growth, the woman works it over with a small scraper, *kerfe*,[2] meticulously removing twigs, thorns and other rubbish still to be found. Only when the place is spick-and-span does the actual pitching begin. Baroin has described the aesthetic significance which the tent and its surroundings hold for the Daza, their appreciation of the whiteness of the tent, of new mats, and of clean sand inside the tent (Baroin 1985: 60-1). One finds a similar aesthetics among the Teda (Chapelle 1957: 283), the Kreda and the Haddad, although the last-named seem less meticulous about the daily cleaning of the sand in- and outside the tent, as far as I could judge. Like the pastoralists, the Haddad remove their sandals before they enter a tent that is if they have any footwear at all, which was far from always the case.

The sleeping platform, *kiri*

An aesthetically pleasing and functionally successful pitching of the tent relies on careful planning and the right decision as to the position of the vertical posts that support the rest of the structure and the mats. Haddad women take great trouble in marking precisely where the bedposts are to be erected, as these constitute the very core of a well-pitched tent. If these posts are properly erected, women say, the rest of the tent can be pitched without much trouble in

a few hours. The sleeping platform takes up a good part of the central space of the tent. It is placed in the same north-south direction as the tent, but somewhat nearer to the back wall of the tent than to the entrance, leaving some free space between the latter and the platform for the daily use of the family and for the reception of guests. The sleeping platform is elevated approximately 85 cm above the ground. It is not used for sitting, but for resting and sleeping by the married couple and their small children. Older children and adolescents sleep with a grandmother or aunt in another tent if possible. A mat is spread out on the platform at night to sleep on, and animal skins – jackal, antelope, or goat skins – are used as covers. Visitors are offered a mat and sleep on the ground just inside the tent or outside this, depending on the nature of the relationship.

A woman begins the work of pitching her tent by meticulously marking the exact position of the vertical posts that support of the sleeping platform. If done with precision, the subsequent pitching of the tent causes few problems. In fact, if the bedposts are properly erected, the subsequent pitching of tent posts can be done in almost any order, one woman explained to me. A woman applies various measuring devices when marking exactly where she wants the posts. Firstly, the full length of the platform is measured out in the sand by means of one of the many slender poles that in due turn are used for the bed-board, known as *eriri* (pl. *erara*). Then she takes one of the four cross-bars, *kalafou* (pl. *kalafa*), on which the slender poles that constitute the board of the platform are going to rest, in order to measure the width of the platform. Finally the exact position of each of the eight pronged posts, *kidichi* (pl. *kidicha)* that actually support the platform are marked in the sand, with particular attention being given to the position of the corner posts. Only then will the actual erection of the platform begin.

The construction starts with the digging of holes for the eight vertical, pronged posts that support the platform. Those of the tent that I bought are 102-135 cm long, with a decorative, black meandering band burned into the plain wood. These *kidicha* are placed at a distance of one metre, another of between 79 cm and 85 cm, the two rows being erected some 107-112 cm apart from one another (cf. Cat. Nos. 115 & 16). The holes are made with a digging stick, *bon* (cf. Cat. No. 97). At the pitching which I registered from beginning to end, the digging of holes for the sleeping platform and for the storage facility was done at one go. At the outset,

12,8. Fetching water is a time-consuming task for Haddad women as for so many other women in the developing world.

the woman dug holes for the southern corner posts of the sleeping platform, each some 40 cm deep. Then she erected the remaining posts for the sleeping platform and the three pronged posts supporting the storage 'bag' to the north of this (cf. Cat. No. 125). Every time a post had been put up, the earth was stamped tightly around it to keep it firmly positioned. After the eight posts for the platform had been erected, the four cross-bars, *kalafu* (pl. *kalafa*) (Cat. No. 117) were placed in the prongs of these and then tied to them with a rope of twisted strips of dum palm leaves. Lastly, the board of the platform is put up. This consists of a number of long sticks, all very smooth and with cut incisions some 3 cm from each end to facilitate the tying of these to the platform. The Haddad Kreda and the Kreda call these sticks *eriri* (sing.) or *erara* (pl.). They are spread evenly across the cross-bars and then tied to these with two plaited leather strings. This is done as follows: The strings have a noose at one end. This is tied firmly around one of the corner posts of the platform's front side. The woman proceeds from here by winding the string half around each stick and tie each one consecutively to the next all across the platform. Once this has been done at one end of the platform, she does likewise at the other end. Two of the sticks are placed on the cross-bars, but in front of the four posts that constitute the front edge of the platform, while the others constitute the main board of the sleeping platform. The platform of the purchased tent is made up of fifteen of these sticks (cf. Cat. No. 118).

The sleeping platform is now ready for use except for the unrolling of mats for the family to sleep on. The woman who sold her tent to me used two mats as cover, an older and smaller mat that she placed underneath a newer and larger one. The mats were made of one centimetre thick sticks held together with fine leather strings in decorative bands and edged with red leather (Cat. Nos. 123 & 124). The mats can also be of a different kind, like the ones described as Cat. Nos. 120 & 121.

The storage facility or 'bag', *dela*

The next task is the setting up of the huge storage facility or 'bag' that is placed at the northern end of the tent parallel to the bed. It is made from an antelope's or sometimes a cow's hide that is suspended between four or five posts. These stand in two rows some 50 cm apart, the length of the structure being about or a little shorter than the width of the sleeping platform i.e. about 130 cm to 160 cm, its upper edge reaching 95 cm to 100 cm above the ground. Storage bags are quite roomy. They are used for storing grain and sugar as well as other edible items and family belongings: milk bowls, butter containers, riding gear and sometimes clothes.

The construction of the storage facility involves the erection of a number of posts to support the cross-bars between which the hide is placed. The vertical posts are known as *kidichi laru* (sing.) or *kidicha larua* (pl.) by the Haddad Kreda and Kreda alike. The number varies, as do the exact location of the storage facility, in part in accordance with the size of the tent. The purchased tent had a supportive structure of three poles at one side, the other being formed by the poles of the northern side of the tent. It was different with the tent I chronicled the erection of. Here the woman made use of the northern end posts of the bed for the southern side of the storage facility. She made her storage facility as follows: Firstly, two pronged posts were raised to support the northern side of the storage 'bag'. Then one cross-bar was placed in and tied to the prongs of these two *kidicha larua* posts, after which another cross-bar was tied to the northern corner posts of the platform in such a way that the two were level and ran parallel with the short side of the platform. Finally, the third cross-bar was tightly tied to the same vertical posts some 40 cm above ground level. This last cross-bar lent support to the bottom of the storage 'bag', a support that is crucial if a lot of heavy items are to be stored within it. The cross-bars are known as *larungudé* (pl. *larunguda)* (cf. Cat. No. 126). Then a large hide, *dela,* was brought to rest between the two sets of posts by means of a solid leather string, *agar* (pl. *agara).* This was wound around the cross-bars, running from one of the top bars down and around the bottom bar, then up and around the cross-bar at the other side of the facility, and then up and down again all the way from one end of the bars to the other, forming a kind of loose net of loops. On the inner side of this 'net' one will first put an old mat, (cf. Cat. No. 128) but often one places only the large hide, which functions as the storage 'bag'. This is done in such a way that it rests on the inside of the device of leather ropes between the two cross-bars. The storage facility can be closed with three leather strings that are tied to the hide, one at each end and one in the middle.

The tent structure

Only when the sleeping platform and the storage bag are in place can the overall wooden structure of the tent be put up. This consists of four rows of vertical pronged poles which support arches that run the full length of the tent, i.e. from north to south. The prongs are not necessarily naturally grown, but made by cleaving the top part of the post and then by the means of fire to make the wood expand. The cleft is prevented from splitting further than intended by a leather binding, a method generally applied in the region (cf. Chapelle 1957: 230). On top of the longitudinal arches a great many cross-arches are tied. The tent I purchased had twenty-six such arches. These are eventually covered by mats.

Each of the four supporting rows consists of six vertical posts. Each row has a specific name: *chini kude (*pl. *china kuda), dual* (pl. *duala), dede* (pl. *deda)* and *chini theréde* (pl. *chini theréda)* designated consecutively from the west, i.e. the entrance side, towards east or the back side of the tent. The names are partly metonyms in that *kude* means front and *theréde,* behind. The Haddad Kreda and the Kreda may also categorize the posts in a different manner, however, using a special term, *china kula,* for the posts at the southern and northern ends of the two central rows and the one at the rear.

Having completed the work of putting up the sleeping platform and the storage facility, a woman continues with the erection of the two rows of pronged posts that support the arches and mats of the central part of the tent. First, she digs holes for and puts in place the most westerly row of central posts, the *duala* (Cat. No. 130). The posts are placed parallel with those of the sleeping platform, but somewhat in front of these. In the purchased tent, they were placed some 20 - 30 cm in front and somewhat to one or other side (cf. *Fig. 12,12d).* The posts are not equally high. The pair in the middle measure 200 cm from ground to top, the two posts at each side of these 182-3 cm, while the two placed at each end of the tent only measure 125 cm and 130 cm, respectively.

When the first row has been put up, it is the turn of the rear row of central, vertical poles, all pronged as those of the front row. These poles are called *dede* (pl. *deda)* (Cat. No. 131). They are also placed more or less parallel to those supporting the bed, but in between the latter and some 10 to 20 cm further to the east of these. Furthermore, these will be

12,9a. Tents are pitched in the same way by Haddad and Kreda women. Once a woman has cleared the site of shrub, she can begin the task of putting up the sleeping-platform and subsequently the storage facility.

12,9b. Storage facilities are made from antelope hide among the Haddad and from cowhide among the Kreda. Families store household utensils and certain kinds of food in the bags.

12,9c. A hide making up sides and bottom of the storage facility, is placed inside loops of a long rope.

12,9d. Next step is the erection of the vertical forked poles supporting the longitudinal arches of the tent, *era*. The photo shows the south end of the tent.

12,9e. Women help one another in placing and tying the cross-arches to the longitudinal arches once these are in place. View of the tent from the north end.

12,9f. The mats are placed on top of the arches. Firstly, the one at the rear, *yegé tcheredé*, and secondly the one covering the western front row of tent poles called *yegé daudé*. The photo shows the tent from the north end.

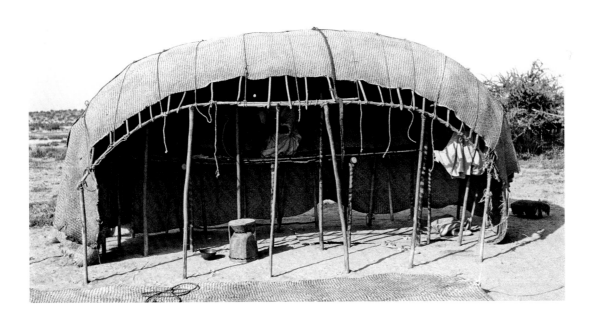

12,9g. The third tent mat, *yegé daudé*, that a woman puts in place when erecting her tent covers the central rear part of the tent.

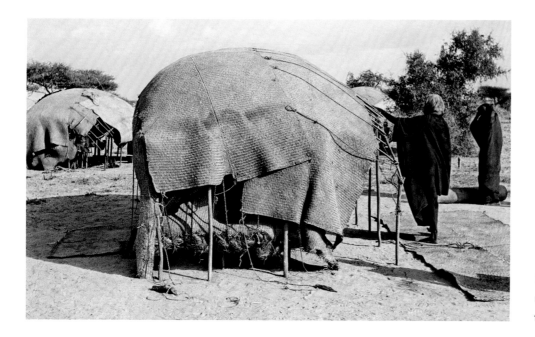

12,9h. The ropes of the central rear mat are tied to the wooden structure of the tent.

12,9i. The last mat to be put up when a tent is erected will be the one in front, *furgul kudé*. The photo shows the tent seen from the south-west.

erected diagonally to the western central row of tent poles. The height of the poles, measured from the ground to the top of the prongs, varies somewhat, the pair in the middle of the row being higher than those towards the end. In the tent involved, the former were 152 cm and 153 cm long, respectively, while the two to the sides of each of these measured 143 cm and 146 cm, respectively, and those at the rear of the tent only 125 cm and 81 cm. The four posts in the middle of the row are slightly tilted, so that the height from the ground

to the top is less than the 152 cm, making the roof slope gently from the rear central posts towards the back of the tent. The tilting of the poles lends strength to the structure against the prevailing wind, a measure that is taken a step further when it comes to the positioning of the poles at the rear, eastern side of the tent, as we shall see.

Having completed the pitching of the two central rows of poles, the woman will proceed by tying the slightly arched bars that run the length of the tent to the erected poles

12,10. A provisional Kreda tent, *chili-chili*, used during migration. It is made of only three pairs of forked poles and cross-bars to which three longitudinal semi-arches are attached.

(Cat. No. 136). These are known as *erem* (pl. *era*). They do not come in one piece, but are constructed from two of the slender bars that are used for cross-arches. When used for the longitudinal arches they are tied together two and two, as the work proceeds. The woman placed the bars in the prongs of the four vertical poles of the front central row, tied them together and then to the poles with a rope made from twisted fibre of the *tefi* acacia. Then she did likewise with the bars that formed the arches uniting the rear central row of vertical posts.

Up to this point the work is carried out solely by the female owner of the tent. The ensuing task of placing the cross-arches – one next to the other across the full length of the tent and of tying these to the two central rows of posts – is difficult to handle for a single person. If possible, women will call upon a relative or another woman to assist them with these tasks, and that is what my friend did. The two women worked their way from one end of the tent to the other, tying the arches, one by one, to the longitudinal, arched bars with ropes made from *tefi* acacia (Cf. *Fig. 12,11;* Cat. No. 138). The Haddad Kreda and the Kreda name the cross-arches *zewé* (pl. *zewa*). The purchased tent has twenty-six such arches (Cat. No. 137).

The woman proceeded on her own when the arches had been placed by digging holes for and pitching the six pronged posts that make up the front of the tent structure

(Cat. No. 132). These posts are denoted *chini kude* (pl. *china kuda*), *kude* meaning 'in front'. The posts are placed at a distance of about one metre from the front row of the central posts, and in such a way that the longest are at the centre of the tent, the shortest at each end. When solidly planted in the ground, the four posts in the middle measure 143 cm and 132 cm above ground, the two at the ends 80 cm and 84 cm, respectively. The posts are connected with slender, arching bars, *era*, as were the two central rows. The bars are tied to the posts with strings of acacia fibre.

The woman proceeded with the pitching of a single pronged post at each end of the tent right in between and in line with the two posts already put up as part of the rows of central posts. Raising these vertical posts, *chini kulu* (pl. *china kula)*, connecting them with bars and fastening these with rope to the posts at the northern and southern corners of the tent respectively is done only after the last row of vertical pronged posts, namely those at the rear back of the tent, have been put up. The Haddad Kreda and the Kreda use two different terms for the posts at these posts at the south end of the tent, as previously indicated. Designated from a position outside the tent, where the posts stand out as part of the tent structure, these are called *chini kula*. Looking at the same posts from the inside of the tent, the defining criteria is that they form part of the storage facility or 'bag' and they are hence called *kidicha larua*.

There are only three vertical pronged posts at the back of the tent, and these are known as *chini teréde*, (pl. *china teréda), terede* meaning 'hind' (cf. Cat. No. 133). They are quite high when pitched: the one in the middle measuring 208 cm, the two to each side of it, 198 cm and 200 cm respectively from ground to top. The posts are tilted so that the height of the posts is actually lower than that of the middle posts of the rear row of vertical central posts. This makes the roof of the tent slope gently from the top of the four vertical posts standing in the middle of the front row of the central posts towards the rear of the tent as well as in the other three directions, as already intimated. The pronged posts of the rear back row are raised with an approximately equal distance between them, and subsequently connected with bars, *era*, as were the other rows of vertical posts. The rear row of posts, however, more than any of the others lend support to the tent. By tilting the posts slightly one obtains maximum enforcement of the entire structure against prevailing winds. According to both Haddad Kreda and Kreda women, there is no definite way of putting up this particular row of posts.

The key elements of the structure of the tent are now in place. What remains to be done is the tying of the many cross arches, *zewé*, (pl. *zewa)* to the longitudinal arches, *era*, where this has not been done so far, including to both the front and back row of posts and to the bars at each end of the tent. The cross-arches are not evenly dispersed across the structure. Fewer were put up at the middle section of the tent, the actual distribution between the vertical posts of the central rows of posts being the following from south to north: eight, five, three, three and seven. With the cross-bars securely fastened the structure of the tent is in place and all that remains to be done is to cover it with mats.

Placing the tent mats, *yegé*

The Haddad Kreda and the Kreda apply four mats in all as cover for their tents, but one of these, the front one, is not always put up. The mats are plaited from strips of dum palm leaves in a herring-bone pattern without any ado. Three of them are longer than the tent structure, enabling the ends of the mats to cover the sides of the tent as well and hence offer the household adequate protection against wind, dust and the outside world in general. Only the front mat is somewhat shorter, allowing the inhabitants to look out from inside the tent. The mats are rectangular. The

ones of the purchased tent measure 420 cm to 600 cm in length and between 135 cm and 154 cm in width, sufficient to overlap when put in place. The mats are tied either to cross-bars or to the vertical posts by means of strings or thin ropes of *tefi* acacia. A piece of rope is used at each corner of a mat to tie this to the front and rear posts of the tent structure. A number of strings tied to the edges of the long sides of the mat serve to fasten this to posts diagonally to the tent's direction. The mats are generally at different stages of their 'life-cycle'. Some are fairly new, others, like the mat in front of the tent here described, are marked by the wear and tear of weather and of long days dangling on the backs of oxen on the move with the family.

The first mat to be put up is the one at the rear end of the tent. The woman tied it with thirteen pieces of rope to the cross-bars of the rear central row of vertical posts, *deda,* and with eleven pieces of rope to the lower part of the posts of the rear row. This mat is called *yegé tcheredé*, the meaning of *yegé* being synonymous with tent while *tcheredé* means 'hind'. It was a fairly new mat, some 600 cm long and 161/175 cm wide (Cat. No. 139). Then the mat covering the western front row of tent poles was placed in position. This mat is called *yegé daudé* (pl. *yega dauda*) and it measured 585 cm x 160 cm (Cat. No. 140). It is placed right behind the front mat and tied to the cross-bars of the rear central row of vertical posts, *deda,* as was the first mat that covered the rear, eastern side of the tent. In this case, however, the woman applied only half the number of strings to fasten the mat, namely six in all. Then the third mat was rolled out over the tent structure, the one to cover the central rear part of the roof. This mat too is called *yegé daudé* (pl. *yega dauda),* a fitting name as it covers the central part of the tent together with its namesake. This latter mat was tied to the cross-bars of the front row of vertical posts, *chini kude, kude* denoting 'front, as will be recalled, and with six long pieces of rope also to the hind row of vertical posts quite close to the ground. The size of this mat is 595 cm x 162 cm (cf. Cat. No. 141). The last mat to be attached to the wooden structure is the one that covers the front part of the tent. This is called *furgul kudé* (pl. *furgula kuda), kuda* meaning 'front'. This mat is not always in use, but often put up in day-time only to provide shade. It was not only the oldest but also the smallest of the four mats measuring a mere 420 cm x 168 cm (Cat. No. 142). The woman secured it with six pieces of rope in such a way that these ran over the two central mats and were tied to the cross-bars of the rear row of central posts. The Haddad occasionally put up a cover of antelope skin instead of this mat as protection against the wind.

Once the tent is pitched, the woman devotes herself to the arrangement of her household utensils. She erects a stand for the storing of food next to the bed at the south end of the tent. One end is dug into the ground, while the top, a bowl-shaped rack made of fine roots of acacia, is used for pots with cooked leftovers, meat, onions and other food items to

be kept out of reach of scavenging dogs, goats and insects. The stand belonging to the purchased tent is some 148 centimetres long before it is dug into the ground (Cat. No. 143).

TEMPORARY TENTS, *CHILICHILI*

Under certain circumstances the Haddad Kreda and the Kreda pastoralists make do with provisional tents structurally similar to certain mat tents among the southern

12,11. A shed for an insane Kreda woman has been erected at some distance from the main camp, because the woman was violent. An insane man lived in a similar way in another camp. Insanity seems rare. Johannes told me, that he had never met insane people before during his many years among pastoralists in North Africa.

12,12. A Haddad woman and child outside her tent. Ogu seeds in a large coiled tray placed in the sun to dry.

Tuareg. Apart from being smaller, the structure is simpler. The height of a provisional tent that I measured was a mere 120 cm to 130 cm at the centre, from where it rapidly decreased towards the ends of the tent. Space inside the tent was limited to an area of about 250 cm x 150 cm. Temporary tents are put up if a family plans to camp for a short time only. Some Kreda households use this simple mat tent during the rainy season, when they are constantly on the move, but it is not common among either the Haddad or the Kreda.

The provisional tent is constructed with the same posts as those used for the normal tent, except that these are put to a different use. The core structure consists of two rows of vertical forked posts only, instead of four, each row having the highest of the posts in the middle and two lower ones on each side of this. The tent has no platform bed, moreover, so the family sleeps on the ground. The two rows of forked tent poles are raised first, whereupon some of the curved *zewe* arches are tied to these. The basic structure of the tent consists of nothing more than these two "arches' raised parallel to and at a distance of about 150 cm from one another. Each of the vertical posts is placed directly opposite a post of the opposite arch. The two arches are subsequently connected with cross arches, the *era* of the ordinary tent. These 'diagonal arches' lend support to the two mats that make up the tent cover. The storage bag is put in place but in a less careful manner than when the tent is properly erected. A sheet of goat- or sheep-skin sewn together is sometimes placed under the mats of such a tent to offer better protection against the rain. A similar type of structure, but on even much smaller scale, is sometimes used as shelter for the very old and for persons who are insane. We came across one such diminutive tent inhabited by a mentally ill woman. It was placed at quite some distance from the other tents (cf. *Fig. 12,11).*

MAT-COVERED TENTS

Mat-covered tents are found among a great many pastoralists in West Africa, from the Atlantic Ocean to the Red Sea. Some authors attribute the wide distribution to the presence of the dum palm (cf. Chapelle 1957: 227; Baroin 1985: 51; Prussin 1995: 112). A closer analysis reveals a variation in the wooden structure of the tent across this vast region, and also that the one used by the Haddad Kreda and the Kreda is structurally different from other mat-covered tents, including those of arch construction. The characteristic feature of the wooden structure of the Haddad Kreda and Kreda tent is the fact that the long arches follow the longitudinal direction of the tent, resting in rows of forked poles, and that these support shorter arches placed at a right angle to the long ones. One might expect an almost identical tent structure among the Daza and Teda north and north-west of the habitat of the Kreda, as these pastoral groups share many other cultural traits. Yet, exactly similar dwellings are not reported from these peoples. The Teda of Ayer or Daza distinguish between five types of mat-covered tents, according to Baroin. Among these the so-called *yage hayire,* which is used during winter and the hot season is structurally similar to the fairly flat-roofed mat tent of the northern Teda described by Le Coeur and Chapelle. According to these authors, the tents of the Teda and Daza consist of three rows of forked posts erected the length of the tent: one row of posts in the centre and two rows of finer, somewhat shorter posts along the walls. The posts of the two outer rows are con-

nected by horizontally placed laths made of light sticks of acacia root, one tied to the other in the longitudinal direction. Crosswise on top of these laths the Tebu place bundles of long fine ribs of date or dum palm, tying the one rib after the other with a long rope. Finally, the mats are placed on top of the wooden structure: two mats to cover the roof and hence running the full length of the tent and reaching the ground at each end of this, while two others are tied vertically to the tent posts to cover the sides of the dwelling (cf. Grall 1945: 43 f.; Le Coeur 1950: 192; Chapelle 1957: 228-34; Baroin 1985: 50-2)). Another tent type among the Daza, called *yage jorro,* is composed of the same elements as the *yage hayire* according to Baroin, but it has a different shape. It consists of three rows of central posts that make up the longitudinal direction of the tent, but these are placed in 'groups of three' in such a way that only the central post stands up vertically, while the two others are placed on each side of this in an oblique position, lending the tent its barrel-vaulted shape (Baroin 1985: 52). The bed is not an integrated part of the structure of the Daza and Teda tent either. It is made separately and only after the wooden structure of the tent has been erected. The sticks used to construct the sleeping platform are not brought from camp to camp except by wealthy pastoralists who possess finely decorated bed posts (Chapelle 1957: 229-30). It should be noted that the mats of the Daza tent are made by Azza women, who either offer these as a gift of allegiance or sell them to the pastoralists (Baroin: 1985: 51).

The wooden structure of the Haddad Kreda and Kreda tent with its four rows of vertical pronged posts carrying arches running the full length of the tent is thus a variant form of the many types of barrel-vaulted tents found in West Africa. Its defining feature is the four long arches stretching the full length of the tent, lending support to the many shorter arches placed at a right angle to these. Other barrel-vaulted tent structures in Africa and Asia rely on a few arches raised at a right angle to the longitudinal direction of the tent, arches which then support some slender semi-arches that follow the longitudinal direction. Why the Kreda and Haddad Kreda do otherwise and build their tents in the above mentioned way we do not know.

THE HADDAD KANEMBU

HAMLETS

The settlements and dwellings of Haddad Kanembu families are quite distinct from those of the Haddad Kreda. The Haddad Kanembu are said to live in hamlets or tiny villages, a description that is somewhat misleading. For hamlets and villages are conceived as groups of people in African terms, rather than groups of buildings as noted, for instance, by Susan Denyer (1978: 19). Haddad Kanembu villages are certainly not a conglomerate of neatly laid-out buildings, as are Kanembu villages; it can be difficult to locate them even when on camel back with a wide view of the landscape. The huts lie fairly scattered, but a closer investigation reveals that they form loose conglomerates of family compounds, as just intimated. Some are miniscule settlements of but a few huts hidden behind millet growths, others are larger, spatially more condensed with family compounds surrounded by fences made of straw or straw mats. Many of these hamlets and small villages are inhabited solely by Haddad Kanembu, but there are Haddad families who stay in predominantly Kanembu villages. When this is the case, the Haddad inhabit a certain quarter, often recognizable by being less well maintained that those of the Kanembu. Haddad Kanembu villages never attain the size of the larger Kanembu settlements, which have several hundred inhabitants, not even in the N'Guri area. Villages had an average size of about forty people in one of the areas studied by Conte, and between fifty and sixty in another (Conte 1983: 251). Depending on the nature of the soil, agro-pastoral practices and socio-political constraints, the Haddad Kanembu move their villages more or less frequently. The availability of land is a determining factor. Villagers may resettle if the soil of their millet farms is exhausted, but such moves may well collide with pastoral interests in the very same land or face restrictions if codified land rights to the area exists (Conte 1983: 251).

The hamlet which Johannes and I got to know the best was Chedra, where we spent some ten days towards the end of our travels. Chedra seemed a typical Haddad Kanembu habitation to us. According to an elderly Haddad man, it had been founded around 1915 by six men. They had come from N'Guri, he himself being the only survivor. Like other hamlets of a certain age, Chedra had left its mark on the landscape, enabling you to identify its outer range when approaching, even if the huts themselves were still out of sight. An unmistakable sign was the increasingly tight web of paths winding towards and between fields towards the scattered huts, the fine old trees, mostly *Balanites aegyptiaca* or *Zizyphus* species that lent character to the hamlet and much appreciated shadow in the daytime and finally a few ruminants and a single stray dog indicating that people were not far away.

The lay-out of Chedra was fairly open. There was no centre in a traditional sense. The homesteads lay hidden in between small millet plots, yet in such a way that closely related families lived near one another. The majority of the huts were of the beehive type, but there were also round huts with a diameter equal to the height, walls of straw mats and thatched conical roofs. We registered a few huts with a framework of slightly bent sticks that were thatched with mats and some rectangular huts with a thatched saddleback roof, but no walls at all. Some households had two of more huts at their disposal: A large residential beehive hut, a hut with saddleback roof for cooking and perhaps yet another beehive hut for guests. A tiny, meticulously kept space functioned as a place for praying. Sometimes this was marked by a few plants or at times by a fence of straw-mats. A family compound often included a tiny fenced plot for growing vegetables, in particular chilli pepper that is indispensable for the sauce that goes with the millet porridge, and another one for a few goats.

The hut, its immediate surroundings and interior constitute the culturally coded setting of daily life. Depending on age and gender family members make use of, move between or avoid spatial sections during the day and night. Men spend relatively little time inside the compound, especially within the hut. They are mostly occupied elsewhere, either with the collection of wild seeds or other edible and useful products, on hunting trips or in the fields. They can be off to help family members with major tasks such as the building of a hut or simple relax in the company of fellow men somewhere. At home, men usually stay outside whether busy with chores or taking a rest on a mat or a bed in the shadow. Inside the hut, they stay at 'their' side visiting the woman's bed only at night. As in most other societies, women are the ones to do the household chores and take care of the children, tasks that inevitably tie them to the hut and its immediate vicinity for a considerable part of the day.

12,13. A Haddad Kanembu bee-hive hut with a kitchen tent. Chedra.

During our stay I spent time registering the various types of dwellings and noting down building practices. We saw only one hut under construction, and we arrived when it had been almost completed, but the men were most patient in explaining how they went about building it.

CONSTRUCTING A BEEHIVE HUT, *FADA GENI*

The Haddad Kanembu beehive hut is a greyish looking, circular, thatched building with an entrance that faces west. It is generally some 4.5 to 5 metres tall, those of

headmen being somewhat roomier, up to 7 to 8 metres in diameter. The hut has a framework of flexible poles dug into the ground at its base and tied together at the top. The thatch is usually made of straw known as *sidige* (*Andropogon sp.*), or of millet, the latter being less durable. Those Kanembu who cultivate wheat, also apply the straw of this crop. The thatch is placed on top of a mat likewise plaited from *sidige* straw, plain or stepped. The hut is slightly convex, as many beehive constructions in West Africa (cf. Denyer 1978: 135). Like the Kanembu and Kanuri the Haddad Kanembu often decorate the pinnacle of the roof with one or several ostrich eggs. The lay-

12,14. The Haddad Kanembu hamlet of Chedra.

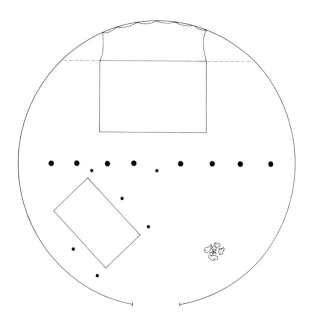

12,15. Diagram of the interior of a Haddad bee-hive hut; cf. Fig. 12,19. Drawing by T.O.S.

12,16. The compound of the village chief of Chedra. The hut was fairly big and meticulously kept by his wife. The interior of this Haddad Kreda hut is depicted in diagram 12,17. Chedra.

out of the interior follows some key principles: Opposite of the entrance is a large bedstead placed under a mat tent, to the left one finds the bed of the man and to the right the heath.

The building is done solely by men apart from the tent-like installation inside the hut, which is put up by women only. Elaborate and time-consuming preparations precede the actual construction of a new hut, a workload that falls upon both sexes. This is especially the case if the building material has to be amassed from scratch, but even when some of it can be taken from an older, dilapidated hut, the work is considerable. The building material consists of the following major categories:

a. long sticks made of wood from any of the following five species of trees: *kululi, kayo, sulu, kaula* and *sehete*;
b. a large mat made of a perennial grass, *so (Andropogon sp.)*;
c. ropes made of twisted dum palm fibre;
d. thatching material of a perennial grass, *so (Andropogon sp.)*.

The hut described below belonged to the village chief. It was a little larger than average sized huts with a circumference of 19.25 metres and a diameter of 6 metres. The point of the roof was close to five metres above ground level, the inside a good four metres. The door was 125 cm high and 40 cm wide at the top, about the double near the ground. A tent-like construction took up a good deal of the interior, its front row of vertical posts was placed about 360 cm from the entrance of the hut, its roof 220 cm above the ground measured at the highest point, i.e. at the rear row of central tent poles.

Structure and thatching

The size of a new hut is decided upon well in advance, to enable the family to bring together the necessary and right kinds of building materials. The actual construction can begin when the selected plot has been cleared of growth and debris. As the very first step, the exact position and circumference of the hut is determined. Depending on experience and inclination, the owner may do so himself, or he may call upon a more experienced person to assist him in this and possibly also in the actual construction as well. The unit of measurement is a pace, a long pace of a man that is, and the person in charge of the lay-out begins

by pacing out the diameter in one direction, whereupon he makes a second measurement along a line diagonally to the first. At the point where the two lines cross one another a post is put up. With the help of a string attached at the one end to this and the other reaching to one of the end points of one of the diagonal lines, the circumference of the hut is drawn in the sand and the actual construction work can commence.

Firstly, the structure of the wall is put up. It is made from scores of from 2.5 to 5 cm thick sticks, *agar*.[3] The sticks are dug some ten to fifty cm into the sandy ground along the fully drawn circle indicating the circumference of the hut, except for a space left open for the entrance, *kingumbe*. The sticks are placed vertically at a rate of nine to ten per metre. Later, when the roofing has been put in place, the sticks will bend towards the centre at the top, lending the hut its beehive shape. The Haddad try to find sufficiently long sticks for the vertical framework, but as they do not always succeed, the ones they have must be prolonged with other sticks, known as *yu*, to obtain the necessary length. The prolongation of the *agar* sticks are not done from the outset, but only as the upper parts of the hut is being thatched.

When the vertical framework has been raised, the entire structure is wrapped in a large mat all around the outer side. The mat is made of *so* grass (*Andropogon sp.*), like the mats that families put up around their domestic quarters. The mat in this case was about three times 18.75 metres, having been made in advance to measure the circumference of the hut minus the opening for the door. It was not tied to the vertical framework, but just placed loosely around this in preparation of the thatching. This work is normally undertaken by two men, one man working from the inside and out, the other conversely. The men work from ground level and upwards, proceeding gradually towards the top of the hut. Thatching is also done with the perennial grass, *so,* and the process is similar to practices in northern Europe, where reeds are tied to laths with thin strings. The laths, *babar,* are put in place one by one as the thatching proceeds. The first lath is placed just above ground level to run horizontally all around the inside of the vertical sticks, *agar,* that form the very framework of the wall. At the doorway, each end of the lath is inserted behind the two vertical doorposts, *kurtchum.* These are dug into the ground about five centimetres inside the circle of *agar* sticks. The tying of the laths and the thatching is thus part and parcel of the same work process, the laths providing the necessary texture and stability to the cover of perennial grass. The men start out by tying one end of a lath to the left side of the door-post, *kurtchum,* as seen from the outside. This is done with a string of twisted dum palm leaves. The string is then passed through the mat, covering the vertical sticks by means of a large needle to tie a tuft of the perennial grass to the mat, after which the needle and string are stuck through the mat again and around the lath once more. And so the work proceeds full circle till the men reach the right doorpost, to which the other end of the lath is secured, and a new round of thatching can begin above the one just completed, one row of horizontal laths being tied to the vertical framework above the other on the inside while one layer of perennial grass after the other is fastened on the outside of the wall in ever smaller circles, gradually lending the hut its particular beehive shape.

The thatching of the upper part of the hut requires scaffolding to enable the men to reach the top. A number of poles are tied vertically to the outer side of the wall for one of the men, while a proper scaffolding of sticks is made for the other at the inside. As the large mat, *suru,* reaches no further than up to about three metres above ground level, another, smaller mat is stitched to it to cover the upper part of the inside. When the men have thatched the hut all the way to the top, they lash the ends of the vertical sticks together with a rope, causing them to taper off to a point. This is covered by a big tuft, known as *toli.* It is made of perennial grass in such a way that it tapers off to a point. The tuft is secured by a lashing around the top of the *agar* sticks, lending the finishing touch to the roof – unless the family decorates the very top with one or more ostrich eggs. Then the scaffolding can be taken down and the men finish the work by placing the door in position. During the thatching, five thin sticks, *kalum,* have been put up at each side of the entrance next to the door-posts. When the thatching has reached as far up as the planned upper reach of the entrance, a lintel is put in place, after which the thatching proceeds. The door, *bab,* is made of simple, raw planks. It is fastened to the doorpost at three places with iron bands and opens inwards to the right.

12,17. Haddad homes usually have simple outside beds next to the hut. One may also find traditional Kanembu beds, such as the one depicted. The bed is made of branches of *Sesbania punctata.* It is covered with a mat of leaf stalks of *Hyphena.* Length: 2m; width: 1m; height: 0,7m. Bol. Photo K.M. Fig. 4,19; 22.11.1957.

Spatial lay-out

The men have now completed their part of the new hut and the women can take over. They fetch the household utensils, put these in their right place and initiate the elaborate interior decoration so characteristic of Haddad Kanembu and Kanembu huts. If the hut is used as a dwelling for a married couple, the hearth is placed to the right of the door. A four-poster bed for the man stands to the left of this, and a large tent-like construction with a bed for the woman is pitched right opposite the entrance against the back wall of the hut, as previously intimated (cf. *Fig. 12,15*). This is not a minuscule replica of a tent, a mere symbolic representation but a full-size construction that takes up a good third of the interior space. Inside this is the woman's bed along with an elaborate display of heirloom and containers for storing her belongings. Such 'tent' or tent-like structures are not unique to Haddad Kanembu and

12,18. Basic structure of a simple bee-hive hut with only one supporting circular wooden structure. To the left one can glimpse the skeleton of a larger hut under construction. Bol. Photo K.M. Fig. 4,8; 21.11.1957.

12,19. The wooden skeleton of a bee-hive hut seen from the inside. On the outside of the branches is a mat, *ségidi* (Kanembu), upon which there is the thatch material. Ngarangu. Photo K.M. Fig. 4,9; 27.9.1957.

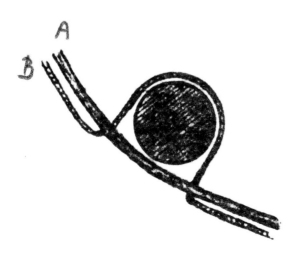

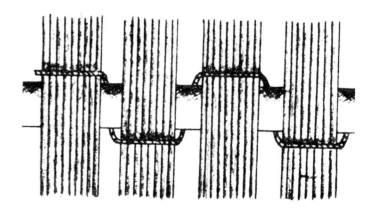

12,20a. Diagram showing how the mat made of so grass is tied to the branches. Photo K.M. Fig. 4,12.

12,20b. Diagram showing how the mat made of so grass is tied to the branches. Photo K.M. Fig. 4,12.

12,21. The thatching of the top part of a bee-hive hut requires a kind of scaffolding consisting of a circle made of wooden branches and a wooden platform erected inside the hut. The uppermost part of the so mats is still visible at the top of the hut. Ngarangu. Photo K.M. Fig. 4,6; 27.9.1957.

Kanembu huts. One comes across this intriguing design among other ethnic groups in West Africa. I have seen it, for instance, among Zerma and Sonray people along the Niger upriver from Niamey. The common type of dwelling among these people is also a large beehive hut inside which there is a mat-covered barrel-vaulted 'tent' erected above a bed. Interestingly, the Sonray and Zerma erect proper barrel-vaulted mat-tents as part of their marriage ceremonies, even though they live in beehive huts. In Mauretania, the common dwelling of Western Moors is a black tent of a peculiar pyramidal form, brought to the region by the Arabs. It is likely that the traditional inhabitants here, the Berber-speaking Tuareg made use of barrel-vaulted tents covered with mats and/or skin prior to the Arab invasions. Today the pastoral Maures use a barrel-vaulted tents inside their black tents and during the dry season they make do with the barrel-vaulted structure only, as I have also observed (cf. Urvoy 1942: 33 f. fig. 2; pl.I, figs. 3-4). There are other ethnic groups of North Africa who build one dwelling within the other, usually in such a way that the inner serve to shield the sleeping place from the rest of the living space. The northern Beja provide one such case. By analogy it is possible that the mat tent, which the Kanembu and the Haddad Kanembu use for bed-shelter is an ancient type of dwelling among them (Nicolaisen, J. & I. Nicolaisen 1997: 484). To the Haddad, the tent is simply an expression of a customary practice, but some of them argued that it is raised to offer protection against "dirt". We came across a similar argument regarding the shelter surrounding men's four-poster bed. That too was said to offer protection against "dirt".

Pitching the 'tent'

The Haddad Kanembu and the Kanembu put up mat tents inside their beehive huts in much the same way as the Haddad Kreda and Kreda pitch their proper tents, a key difference being that the tent of a beehive hut is not constructed around a sleeping platform, as is the case of the Haddad Kreda tent. The bed of the Haddad Kanembu is put in place only when the tent-poles of the front and rear row have been erected. The bed-boards are elevated some 40 cm above ground, as against the much higher sleeping platform of the Haddad Kreda tent. The large storage bag is not put up before the tent poles or invariably placed to the left of the bed as is the case in the Haddad Kreda tent.

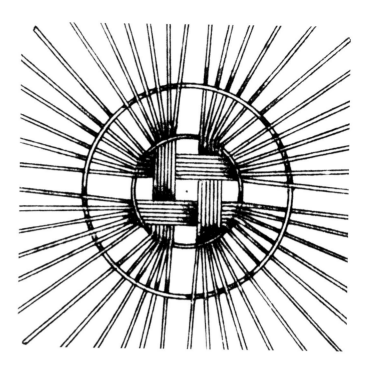

12,22. Diagram showing the inside structure of the top of the bee-hive hut. Photo K.M. Fig.4,7.

The main storage facility is behind the bed, at the rear back of the tent, but a much smaller bag can be found next to the bed in some huts. The pitching of the tent is solely the responsibility of the woman, and she goes about the task as follows:

The basic structure of the tent of the hut is also four rows of vertical posts, but these are erected in a slightly different order than those of a Haddad Kreda tent. While a Haddad Kreda woman first pitches the two rows of central vertical pronged posts and then proceeds to fasten the arched bars connecting these, her Haddad Kanembu counterpart puts up the front row of vertical pronged posts as the very first. There are eight, approximately 158 cm tall posts in all, and they are placed with a distance of 55-68 cm, except for the two central posts of the middle of the row which are placed at a distance of one another of 110 cm, allowing for a free passage to and fro to the bed and the belongings and valuables stored next to it. After the first row of vertical pronged posts has been put in place, the one to the rear back is erected.

The next task at hand is the putting up of the bed, which measures some 230 x 150 cm with its front edge located approximately 30 cm behind the front row of vertical posts

12,23. A spectacular feature of Haddad and Kanembu huts is a complete tent placed opposite the entrance against the back wall. Inside the tent again, one finds a huge bed and up against the back wall a display of the wife's wealth and heirloom: wooden bowls and enamel jars and trays.

(cf. Fig. 2,23). The bed consists of a grid of vertical and horizontal posts. It is supported by fifteen vertical pronged posts, *sua dengilé (sua* meaning ear, *dengil* meaning bed) dug into the ground in three parallel rows of five each. These posts support five cross-bars, *dui dengilé,* and on top of these again rest some twenty long sticks, *dra,* which form the actual board of the bed. The latter is covered with a mat, *kasar,* made of strips of dum palm leaves. When the bed has been put up the woman continues by pitching two rows of vertical tent posts running longitudinally at the centre of the tent. The front one of these measures 200 cm above the ground, the row behind it 220 cm, the maximum height of the interior of the tent. Then the bars connecting the pronged poles of each of the four rows are pitched, followed by the many cross-arches and finally the mats. These are tied to the wooden skeleton in a definite order: firstly the mat to the rear hind, then the mat

second to the front one, then the mat covering the roof between the two, i.e. the one placed next to the rear one, and finally the one at the front. The latter was replaced by two smaller mats, in this case because the woman had no suitable long mat.

Finally, a large storage bag was put up. This had almost the length of the bed. It was elevated some 40 cm above the ground and placed at the hind side of a grid that is put up at the back wall for the display of trays. It was constructed in the same manner as the ones found in Haddad Kreda tents: A long string hung in loops - the size of the depth or vertical side of the bag - to support the full length of the bag, each loop being tied alternately to a vertical post of the rear row of the tent and the wall of the hut. A mat inside the loops made up the sides and bottom. Some Haddad Kanembu and Kanembu women in need of more storage room will place an additional bag

12,24. Wooden bowls with lids of coiled basketry known as bordoa, are highly cherished by both the Haddad Kanembu and the Kanembu. Some of them are heirloom, others purchased more recently by the owner. Cat. no. 36; Photo J.K.

at the left, north end of the bed, as was the case in the dwelling described here. This however, was quite simple. It had neither a fine hide nor a mat to protect the objects that were stored. These were simply supported by the loops of the rope. The Haddad Kanembu call these storage facilities for *digedige*.

Interior design and cultural meaning

Haddad Kanembu women need not pitch the tent as solidly as their Haddad Kreda sisters, who must safeguard their dwellings against strong winds, and make sure that they offer appropriate protection against rain and sun. Strings and ropes of dum palm bast are not used to the same extent for this reason and the mats are merely tied to the structural framework with strips of dum palm leaves. The tent of the beehive hut is rather a cultural marker, a construction of considerable social significance. Not

only does it signify the forging of marriage ties and procreation, providing a protective canopy over the couple and possible offspring. It bespeaks the social standing of the couple through its lavish content of elaborately carved wooden bowls covered by coiled basketry lids and brightly coloured basins and trays of sheet metal that are exhibited at the back of the tent. The objects are hung on a wooden grid or piled up on top of one another as testimonies of the wealth and heritage of the inhabitants. The more the items, the more convincingly they testify to the economic status and social heritage of the woman of the house. The grand wooden bowls are mostly precious heirlooms, which pass from mother to daughter, while the brightly covered basins and trays come not only as gifts but are also purchased by the women themselves at nearby markets. The interior tent is pitched very neatly to add to the overall impression of orderliness and wealth.

Strangely enough, this was not the case with the tent described above. Unlike the tents of all the other beehive huts we visited, the one of the wife of the village chief looked less carefully pitched, perhaps because the woman was getting on in years and did not have the energy to keep everything spick and span. Her trays were displayed on a wooden grid at the tent's back wall, fashioned by the rear row of vertical tent poles and six long vertical sticks. On this she had placed a large mirror, fourteen sizeable basins and trays, and three smaller ones. Below the grid

she had piled up her treasures of large, decorated wooden bowls covered by lids of coiled basketry.

The tent and bed is the sleeping place of the woman and her small children. The Haddad Kanembu use very little bedding. Most make do with a few pillows with cotton covers and a filling of wild seeds.[4] Leather pillows are used only by the Haddad Kreda. On cold nights they cover themselves with an extra piece of cotton cloth and blankets of jackal or goat skin. A few families owned mosquito nets. The husband uses a bed placed to the left of the door, if he

12,25. Cylindrical huts, gone *ginane*, and bee-hive huts are often built next to one another by the Haddad Kanembu. Chedra.

is not spending the night or part of it with his wife. This bed is also placed beneath a shelter, not a tent in this case but rather a simple roof like a kind of four-poster. The most common type of bed is the one called *zuzum*. In the case described here the bed measured 165x100 cm. The bed-boards consisted of eleven, 165 cm long, wooden sticks that alternated with an equal number of short ones, building up the bed in layers. First, three long ones were placed in such a way that two formed the sides of the bed to be, while one ran down the middle. Then a layer of the short ones were placed on top of these, two at each end of the bed and one in the middle and so forth till the airy bed was completed. The sticks are tied together in each corner and a structure consisting of five vertical posts is raised around this, one post at each corner and the fifth erected right at the middle of the 'back' side of the bed. To this are tied two laths, one at each end of the bedstead and a third one at the middle. Five long sticks are put up on top of these three cross-bars, and the canopy over the bedstead is completed with a mat at the very top as cover.

THE CYLINDRICAL HUT, *GONE GINANE*

Beehive huts are by far the most common of Haddad Kanembu and also Kanembu dwellings, yet one does encounter cylindrical huts with conical roofs (*cf. Fig. 12,25*). These are used throughout Kanem and the Lake Chad region and found to the north in Fezzan and Tripoli, to the east in Sudan, and westwards all along to Dakar both among Sudanese agriculturalists and some Tuareg groups. A common trait of most of these huts is a central post, but apart from this the huts vary slightly in structure and in materials used for walls and roofs. Cylindrical huts with conical roofs are probably ancient to the region (cf. Nicolaisen & Nicolaisen 1997, I: 416-24). The huts we saw had mat walls and thatched roofs. I observed one under construction in Chedra. Its entrance faced west and it had a diameter of 335 cm. The necessary material had already been amassed, and the men in charge proceeded as follows:

They started out with the roof and completed this task before they went on with the wall. The roof was made next to the site of the hut and left on the ground until it could be lifted up and placed upon the wooden structure of the

wall. The men began by making a cylindrically shaped coil of branches and twigs, tying the material together with dum palm rope. The coil was made full circle cut to the intended size of the hut, which was about 335 cm. Then the rafters, *agar,* were tied to the branches all along the outer side whereupon they were tied together in a coil at the top, but in one that was smaller than the foundation of the roof but similarly made of branches and twigs. This completed the structural framework of the roof. Then the men turned to the thatching using bundles of perennial grass, *so.* This piece of work was carried out in a similar way to the one used by the Haddad when thatching their beehive huts: one man worked from the outside attaching bundles of grass with a string to a mat, which ran the full circle of the roof to be, another man lashing the mat to horizontal sticks, *barar,* at the inside, the two passing a large wooden needle with the string back and forth between them. The men gradually worked their way from the base of the roof i.e. the coil of branches and twigs, until they reached the top, where they tied the thatching material into a tuft.

Only at this point do the Haddad put up the wall. The structure of this is based on a circle of twelve pronged sticks measuring about a metre above ground level. These are known as *sua* and are the first to be put in place, leaving an opening of some 110 x 75 cm for the entrance. One may come across conical huts with a central post, however, which has normally been put up at a later stage to support the roof in case this should give in. Then three long thin sticks are tied to the vertical posts with a rope, so that they run vertically - parallel to one another - the full circle of the hut except for the entrance. This completes the structure and when a mat has been tied around it, the wall is finished. The final task is to unite the wall with the rooftop lying next to it. The latter is lifted up and placed on top of the pronged vertical sticks of the wall and then securely fastened with ropes and the hut is ready for habitation.

THE RECTANGULAR HUT, *DJONGO*

Another common type of hut throughout Kanem and the Bahr el Ghazal is the so-called *djongo,* a rectangular construction with a purlin roof. Unlike beehive and cy-

12,26. Rectangular, saddle-roofed houses are also found among the Kanembu and Haddad Kanembu. Chedra.

lindrical huts, the *djongo* is seldom used for habitation. It is largely a thatched roof, built for kitchens, stables for horses and, occasionally, as a kind of guesthouse and a place used for afternoon naps for the men-folk. Some *djongo* are provided with a wall or partially so, as was the case of the hut to be described, where a thatching covered the upper part of the sides.

Djongo huts are used widely by the Haddad Kanembu. We saw them in Bol and also elsewhere. One was part of the compound of the village chief in Chedra, where it was used for cooking. The entrance faced west and was placed at the centre of the west wall with the hearth to the right of it. The ground plan measured 350 x 300 cm and the entrance was 150 cm high and 80 cm wide.

The walls were 120 cm high, and the roof began some 200 cm from ground level, when measured at the centre of the hut. Most of the building material was of dum palm, i.e. posts and sticks and strings and ropes, while Calotropis, *calotropis precera,* was used for laths and the doorstep, and perennial grass, *so,* for thatching.[5] Huts like these are built by men, and even the straw mats are made by them.

The basic structure consists of six vertical pronged posts known as *sua,* some 15 to 18 cm in diameter. Four of these posts are raised at each corner, measuring about 120 cm from the ground to the end of the post. They are joined two and two with 300 cm long sticks, *dui,* also of dum palm. The two longer of the six vertical posts, meas-

12,27. A sun-shade in the shape of a thatched, saddle-roofed structure. Chedra.

uring 200 cm, are raised at the middle of the short sides of the hut and a 300 cm long stick, *dui,* is placed in their prongs and tied to these with dum palm rope as were the two other *dui.* Then the laths, *dra,* are tied to the *dui.* There are six of these on each side of the roof, and they are all of Calotropis wood. A mat is tied to the inner side of the laths and the thatching is done in the same manner as used for the beehive and the cylindrical hut with the conical roof. The Haddad Kanembu also cover the inside of the walls of the hut with mats, but only the upper part of the walls are thatched with perennial grass, *so.* Finally the doorstep, *takallum,* is put in its right place and the hut is completed, ready for the woman to take over and make use of it as her kitchen.

TENTS

On a few occasions we observed that households made use of a tiny mat tent of a quite simple structure as a kitchen facility. The ones we noticed had vertical pronged posts carrying horizontal cross-bars at a right angle to the longitudinal direction. Whether the women in case were of pastoral heritage, or this was an age-old Haddad Kanembu and/or Kanembu custom, I dare not say. We learned also that such simple tent constructions are used occasionally by Kanembu herders guarding flocks of cattle and small ruminants far away from the hamlet (cf. *Fig. 12,10*).

NOTES

1. Among the Teda the word designating the mat tent *yaobi* is also used for the stone houses used by the northern Teda, according to Le Coeur (1950: 190).
2. Scrapers are made from the *Alou* tree by Haddad smiths and sold at local markets (cf. Cat. no. 71).
3. These sticks are generally made from *Leptadenia pyrotechnica* or *Sesbania punctata*, in rare cases from *Calotropis procera* according to Krarup Mogensen (1963, 4 note 5).

4. The Kanembu use the seeds of *Aerva persica*. (Krarup Mogensen 1963, 4: 10)
5. The Kanuri make use of the straw of wheat and millet, according to Krarup Mogensen (1963, 4: 7).

13:

13: PERSONAL EXPRESSION AND IDENTITY

Haddad men and women seem to place less weight on personal appearance than do Kreda pastoralists and the Kanembu. This may be due in part to the fact that they are much poorer, generally, than the pastoralists and agro-pastoralists they live among. However, culture may also be involved, a more modest appearance being one of those hardly perceptible, and tacitly accepted markers of their caste-like position, in compliance with Ovid's words: "He has lived well who has lived obscurely" (*Tristia,* B III, Eleg. 4, 1: 25).

Identity, social standing and self-esteem are expressed in numerous ways among the ethnic groups in Kanem and the Bahr el Ghazal, one being in the hairdo of women. The difference expresses itself in women's coiffure. Women's hair-do is a means of enhancing beauty as well as an expression of orderliness and of having the time and economic means to care for one's look. Thus, in one sense women's coiffure reflects wealth and indicates social status. Women of well-to-do Kreda and Kanembu families may have their hair combed as often as every two to three weeks and they may pay Haddad women to do the task. Haddad women, on the other hand will rarely have their hair done more than every second or third month if that often. The female coiffure is also a social marker in another sense, flagging the marital status of women. Girls and young unmarried women have three braids running from their forehead towards the neck, married women only two.

COIFFURE

Haddad women are known as expert hairdressers and women of other ethnic groups may come from afar to have their

hair done by a particular Haddad woman. It takes up no less that a full day to get a coiffure and a beautiful hair-do is highly appreciated, as just mentioned. It has already been indicated that coiffure is part of the obligatory exchanges which characterize the formalised system of balanced reciprocity between the Haddad and their pastoral hosts. Haddad women do the hair of the women of the pastoral families with whom they share camp and are tied in formal ways. This is part and parcel of the 'obligatory exchanges' that characterize the balanced reciprocity which exists between the two families. But Haddad women will also comb the hair of other Kreda women and these may come even from far away camps to put themselves in the hands of a Haddad expert. In such cases a small fee will change hands. The pay consists in most cases of butter (among the Haddad Kreda) or oil (among the Haddad Kanembu), cash being scarce in these communities. But I was told that the price in cash would be some 100-200 CFS at the time of our visit.

Hair is known as *difinu* to the Haddad Kreda. Long hair is considered a beauty asset for women, and Haddad women prepare pomade to make their hair grow. Hair is not allowed to grow freely, but removed from various parts of the body on all Haddad, young and old. Women shave their foreheads and armpits or remove the hair growing here by pulling it out, one hair by one, now and then smearing their fingers in ashes so that they will not slip when pulling hard. Men shave their heads clean. They may also shave the face or pull out hair here with tweezers.

Only small children grow hair on their heads until the age of two to three years, i.e. to the age when they speak then most of it will be shaven off. The first haircut is a ritual event

13,1. Plaiting the tiny braids that make up the coiffure of all Haddad women. The photo shows a Haddad Kreda woman having her hair done. Haddad Kreda.

during which the parents bring an offering, *sadaga*. Each clan has its particular hairdo, and one child may therefore have a tuft high on the forehead, another at the back of the head, a whole brim standing like a cock's comb, or a wealth of other hairdos. The same is the case of the Kreda. Boys and girls have the same hairdo in younger years, except for a tiny braid on the rear back of the girls' head towards the neck. As Haddad Kreda society relies on a patrilateral concept of kinship, the hairdo follows the custom of the paternal clan. We were told, interestingly enough, that the custom had been changing over the past few years so that some children were given the clan hairdo of their mothers.

Young men get their hair shaved off at circumcision, i.e. some time between the age of twelve and twenty, after which they shave their heads at regular intervals. Girls on the other hand change coiffure at the age of eight to ten having different kinds of hairdos until they get the formal coiffure of young women. This happens at about the time of their first menstruation, at which point they get their hair done more in the style of adult married women.

The coiffure of women is called *kachera* among the Haddad Kreda. The coiffure starts high up on the forehead, as the lower part of this is shaven clean. It consists of a profusion of small braids, one next to the other from ear to ear,

and two braids plaited from a point high on the forehead and running back across the crown and down the back of the head. The number and thickness of braids marks the social identity of the woman. Adult married women carry two fairly thick braids while a single, thick braid running from the centre of the forehead down the neck indicates that a woman is a spinster. Unmarried young girls have two braids like married women, but much thinner ones. A young girl will have her braids changed to the thicker version just after marriage, rightly the day after the wedding night, when she will be carefully combed and also begin to wear a particular leather string, that is another mark of marriage. The thin, flat string is tied to the first four braids and then behind the neck to keep these tightly into the head and not 'free wheeling'.

The hairdo of Haddad Kanembu women is slightly different, in that they too have the forehead shaven clean and wear a wealth of small braids. Two central braids indicate that the woman is married, while unmarried women have three braids. A single braid is not used.

It is a laborious task to comb a woman's hair, as intimated above. The hairdresser does one side of the head at a time using a comb, a small iron awl known as *asun* by the Haddad Kreda and as *kantan* by the Haddad Kanembu (cf. Cat. No. 39), and having a tiny calabash at hand containing a kind of brilliantine. The latter is made from a mixture of pounded seeds known as *argumi* in Haddad Kanembu or

13,2. Hair is oiled with scented butter. To prevent the fingers from getting too greasy, a hairdresser occasionally dip these in a pot with ashes. The grease is stored in a cow's horn with a lid. Cat. no. 110. Photo J.K.

teba in Haddad Kreda, butter or oil, and sometimes some 'eau-de-Cologne' called *itir. Teba* seeds and leaves are imported from Nigeria, but we were unable to determine their botanical origin. They are the key ingredients in the pomade with which women smear the hair on their heads in order to make it grow and smell nice. *Teba* seeds and leaves are bought at the market as a mixture. Prior to their use the seed and leaves are separated from one another. The seeds are roasted on a dry frying pan and then pounded in a tiny mortar (cf. Cat. No. 46; *Fig. 13,11*). Then the leaves are treated likewise. They are roasted lightly on a pan and pounded in the mortar. Then the pounded leaves and seeds are cooked in a pot with butter and some eau de cologne is added. The pounded seeds and leaves can also been used in another way. They are placed on a tray. A lump of butter is gently rolled in the pounded mass and the mixture is then worked together. The substance is then rubbed into the hair, where it remains for two days, after which the woman will get her hair combed. The hairdresser unties a number of braids at a time, combs and oils them with the above mentioned pomade, whereupon they are plaited again. The procedure is the same all over Kanem and the one also applied among the Haddad Kanembu.

CLOTHES AND JEWELLERY

At the time of our fieldwork the Haddad were all wearing clothes made from cotton purchased at markets and dresses made from hides and skin which older sources describe as commonplace had largely gone our of use except for the occasional use of a hide worn by men over the shoulders. Previously hides of gazelle had been cut to fit as loincloths for men, skirts for women and caftans for both sexes. These clothes had been replaced by white cotton trousers and caftans for men while women's dresses were made from either black or dark blue cotton. Some Haddad Kanembu women used prints. Until the advent of industrial dye all dark blue cloth was dyed in indigo and hence expensive. Barth notes, for example that only rich people would wear black (Barth 1857-58, III: 69).

Babies are carried on their mother's back wherever they go, either in the same piece of cloth which the mother wears or in a separate one that she wraps around the child and ties above her breasts. The babies are naked apart

13,3. Normally Haddad women wear but a cloth tied around the waist or above the breasts. Our young hostess covered her body more than other Haddad women we met, whether it was due to our presence or because she had married and settled in the camp of her husband only a few years back in time, I dare not say.

13,4. A brass bell that was the only piece of clothing of a two-year-old girl. Strings of pearls worn by Haddad and Kreda girls; cf. *Fig. 17,37.* Cat. nos. 74 & 107. Photo J.K.

from a tiny piece of cloth that functions as a nappy and is cleaned with sand whenever soiled. Small children do also run naked most of the time. Baby girls had a string of beads around their bellies and nothing more, but at the age of about six they were given a pubic cover, *eri,* a tiny skirt made of strings of beads (cf. Cat. No. 104). This is also all that Haddad Kreda girls wear through their teens and often as young married women until they give birth. Haddad Kanembu girls began to cover themselves with clothes at a somewhat earlier stage, as far as I could observe. Small girls may wear simple necklaces with a tiny pearl, but most of them have bracelets and/or rings around the ankles of brass as a protection against evil forces. Small boys do also wear such brass jewellery for the same reason.

The dress of adult women is a simple rectangular piece of cloth, *algi,* wrapped around the body either at the waist or above the breast. In the latter case the cloth is draped once around the body and fastened at the right side with a knot. The remaining part is wrapped around the back and eventually up over the head as a protection against a burning sun or hard winds (cf. Cat. No. 112). Some women apply another piece of cloth as head-cover. One may also

wrap the end of the cloth around the head as a tiny turban. Most women wear black clothing only, but more colourful cloth including flowery designs are worn by younger women. We met only a few women wearing dresses and long trousers, presumably bought ready-made at a market place. On festive occasions, young Haddad Kanembu women and girls drape white or flowery shawls around their bodies, shawls which they set in graciously flowing movement when dancing. Women sometimes wear a leather headband. This is not to look dressy but as a means against headache. Underwear is not applied.

Most Haddad women wear some jewellery in everyday life, simple pieces generally, but a necklace, arm- and earrings as well as rings on the fingers adorn even the poorest of the lot, and many of them also wear a silver ring in one of their nostrils, as already mentioned (cf. Cat. No. 106). Young women are the more prone to use jewellery, just as they are more careful with their looks in general, while elderly women gradually scale down the use of finery so as not to be laughable, limiting themselves to a few simple pearls and nothing of silver. The modest use of jewellery is done away with on festive occasions, when women bring out and wear more costly pieces and heirlooms, if they have any. Although Haddad women have far less jewellery than their Kreda and Kanembu sisters, some of them do possess valuable and treasured pieces. I came across several women who owned strings of large, yellow beads of amber, so highly appreciated not only in Kanem but also by collectors in Europe and the US (cf. Cat. No. 75). They also wear beautiful rectangular silver pendants with finely incised patterns and pairs of black stone rings for the upper arms (cf. Cat. Nos. 42 & 111). Jewellery is not exchanged when young men court young women, nor is it a part of marriage exchanges. It is only later, when a marriage proves stable, that a man may give his wife a piece of silver jewellery. Rather, women purchase jewellery on their own, and let it pass on to their daughters or, should they have none, to other close female relatives. Some elder women sell their jewellery at the market if in need of money.

Haddad Kreda women have far less finery than the wives of their pastoral 'hosts, however. At a festive occasion, in which we took part a young woman wore a black velvet kaftan, three pairs of silver bracelets, two pairs of rings above the elbow, three pairs of silver rings, a necklace with a silver pendant and a pair of heavy silver rings around her ankles. None of her Haddad sisters would be able to show off in such a manner.

Haddad men wear wide cotton trousers which are tied with a string around the waist and reach somewhat below the knees. Very often Haddad Kreda men wear no other clothes. They do have loose, sleeveless shirts, however, and perhaps also long-sleeved ones, although we did not come across anyone wearing these. Haddad Kanembu men wore also the wide trousers worn by most men in the region together with long, loose shirts often with long sleeves that can be folded on the shoulder to leave the arms free.

CICATRISATION

The Haddad decorate their faces with scars like so many peoples in Africa but they have not turned the making of scars into an elaborate body art. The Haddad say that they make scars for the beauty of it and for health reasons. It is believed to be conducive to health to let one's blood flow. Scars are made at childhood, already at about the age of one month, but if a baby is sickly, the operation may take place at an even earlier stage.

Piercing of ears and the wing of the nose is also done at an early age. The Haddad say that it is carried out when the child is old enough to call for its mother or father, or at the time when it has got all its teeth. Women have the wing of their right nose pierced as well as both ears. In both cases the operation is done with thorns of an acacia tree when a girl has reached the age of about one year. Thorns are kept in the sores till these have healed. Only then are they pulled out and replaced with a piece of jewellery. While a girl only gets a single hole in the right nostril, her ears are pierced in three to four places: one hole being made in the lobe, three or four up the edge of the ear for tiny rings of iron, brass, silver or plastic.

SCENT AND MAKE-UP

Body scent holds particular cultural significance among the Haddad and other peoples in Kanem and the Bahr el Ghazal. Women especially the young and newly married, take great trouble to ensure that their bodies have a pleasant smell. This is a signal to husbands that they are avail-

13,5. Haddad and Kreda girls usually wear a string of pearls around the waist and a tiny g-string until they reach the age of about seven. They may have a simple dress as well. The photo is of a Kreda teenager.

13,6. Haddad men wear a pair of shorts tied around the waist with a cord and sometimes a shirt. They are rarely dressed up as our Haddad Kreda host, who wore an open kaftan over his shirt when posing for the photo. Boys wear no clothes or a pair of shorts until they reach their teens. Haddad Kreda.

13,7. Haddad Kanembu woman from Chedra. I noticed that Haddad women more often wore flowery and coloured dresses than their pastoralist sisters, who invariably dressed themselves in unicoloured indigo cotton as did this young Haddad Kanembu from Chedra.

able for nightly pleasures but also to the wider community that they are attractive and dutiful wives, prepared to do their outmost to please. To this end they use sweet-scented pomades, fluid butter and perfumes – if they can afford this at all – but most importantly flavoured smoke to scent their bodies and clothes. Among the Haddad Kreda a good wife finds time in between the daily chores to prepare for a 'smoke-bath' in the late afternoon to achieve the desired smell. This is done outside the tent and in plain sight of the wider society. The smoke is produced from bark of the jujube tree, *tjorogu*. Women scout the plains themselves in search of these trees and bring the bark back on their backs. When it is time for the bath, a small hollow is made

in the sand near or inside the tent, if one is not already there. Some of the bark is set on fire, and, when reduced to ember the woman places herself on a small stool above these for about a quarter of an hour. She has first oiled her entire body in sweet-scented butter, *empi tugortide*, which she keeps in a special container usually made from a horn of an antler. She then sits stark naked but shielded from view, wrapped in hides from top to toe, in order that the smoke from the embers can enwrap her body and leave its scent.

Women who have scented themselves are a delight to sleep with, we were told, and it is little wonder that young and newly married women in particular use 'smoke baths'.

13,8. Young Kreda pastoralist with embroidered west and a felt hat, an outfit that is common among urban dwellers but found only rarely among the nomads.

13,9. Young Kreda woman with jewellry.

Haddad Kanembu women do not take 'smoke baths' but scent their clothes instead. They make a tiny cupola-shaped rack from branches, place a tiny pot with glowing embers inside it and spread some fragrant seeds upon these. Then the clothes are hung on the rounded vault to absorb the aromatic smoke.

Another way to embellish the female body is by using henna. Like other women throughout North Africa and the Middle East, Haddad women colour their hands and feet to beautify themselves. I noticed, however, that the use of henna was far less common among Haddad women than among women belonging to the other ethnic groups of the region, perhaps because it is both costly and time-consuming, and

because Haddad women rarely come to markets where they can purchase henna. The colour is extracted from the leaves of the white-flowering scrub (*Lawsonia inermis)*, which Kanembu and other women farmers grow and sell at the market, either as powder or dry leaves. The latter must be pounded in a mortar before it can be mixed with water and applied. A woman pours about four small glasses of henna powder into a slim, long calabash, adds the double amount of water and sticks her hand into the container. She will have to keep it there for at least two to three hours. During this period she must constantly knead the mixture with her hand and fingers for the colour to do a proper job. When the hand is properly coloured, the skin is softened with fluid butter

13,10. Small calabash with herbs for personal hygiene and iron awl used for a variety of tasks (cf. Cat. no. 39). Haddad Kreda. Cat. no. 113. Photo J.K.

13,11. Little Kreda girl with pierced ears. Haddad girls normally wear fewer rings in the ears than Kreda girls.

and allowed to dry while the other hand is treated. When this has had a first colouring, the treatment is repeated for the first hand and so on, the entire procedure taking up the major part of a day. The feet are decorated in a similar way, but the treatment of these requires a larger quantity of henna. Feet are coloured at one go. The woman takes a piece of cloth, covers it with a layer of fresh leaves from the Calotropis tree upon which she places the henna. Then she smears her feet with a thick layer of henna paste and ties the cloth firmly around these. As in the case of the hands, the process takes up a full day or night.

Haddad women also use eye make-up, applying kohl or *sozerum,* the black powder of antimony sulphide on the upper and lower eyelid with a tiny iron awl-like stick, known as *murkat golei* (cf. Cat. No. 45). Kohl is not unduly expensive, yet applied only on festive occasions and when women go to markets where they meet other people and want to look their best.

NOTES

1. Krarup Mogensen mentions that the process can be speeded up by mixing the paste with a few pods of the Tamarind tree. The colour stands wear and tear much better, moreover, if the hands are held over glowing cottonseeds during the process (Krarup Mogensen, 1963: 11: 9). These practices are not used by the Haddad Kreda.

14:

14: SOCIAL LIFE AND CULTURAL PERCEPTIONS

RITES OF PASSAGE

Haddad social life and cultural expression underscore male prerogatives and the significance of paternal kin, as is the case among all ethnic groups throughout Kanem and the Bahr el Ghazal. This cultural construct goes hand in hand with Islam, the religion professed by Haddad Kreda and Haddad Kanembu alike and the rules of the Hadith. The Haddad turned to Islam only a few generations ago, as previously mentioned, and the inclination of Haddad social organization towards the paternal side dates back, undoubtedly, to pre-Islamic times. This is the case, for instance, for the patrilineal clans that form the grid of Haddad social organization and of their perception of belonging. Still, Islam has an impact on the ways in which the Haddad regulate marriages, divorce, inheritance and succession as well as on social highlights in the life of the individual. Rules, symbolic expressions and rituals performed at various stages of a person's life – name-giving, circumcision, marriage contracts and funeral rituals – are all intimately associated with Islam and performed under the eyes of or by a marabout. There is considerable consistency and similarities between these institutions throughout the region and hence also between the Haddad Kreda and the Haddad Kanembu for this very reason.

Pregnancy and birth

Haddad perceptions of conception, pregnancy and beliefs regarding birth are expressed in a series of precautions taken by women during pregnancy. The Haddad link the mother's state of mind and general well-being to the fu-
ture capabilities of her child. If a woman has a wish during pregnancy, if she sees an object, for instance, which she would like to possess, then one must offer it to her, the Haddad argue or the child will be born with a strawberry mark. The presence of such a mark is considered an imperfection, a sign that the child has not had all it needed. We were present at the Haddad camp at Gaba when a pregnant woman expressed a craving for meat from a gazelle which we had brought along. She was immediately given a piece in order to prevent her child from being born with an imperfection. Both Haddad and Kreda women may function as midwives in the joint camps of foragers and pastoralists, but they deliver babies of their own group only. In the camp at Kurei Ioroso, for instance, there were two Kreda and one Haddad midwife, but they did not work together when women were giving birth. When a woman is giving birth, her husband will absent himself and take up residence elsewhere. He returns to the marital tent after a week. I did not witness a birth, but was told by Haddad women that the new-born child is wrapped in a piece of cloth and placed on the platform that serves as the marital bed. Immediately afterwards, a knife is placed next to the child in order to chase away evil spirits, as is customary among a wide range of peoples in West Africa. Among the Kreda the placenta is buried at some distance from the camp. It is placed under three stones, in case it is a girl and four, if it is a boy. This is done by an old woman who also makes a small sacrifice of millet on the spot while mumbling wishes for the good fortune of the newly born such as: 'May God let you grow', 'May God give you as long a life as mine', 'May God let you become like your grandfather' (cf. Le Coeur 1950: 104-5).

Small children are normally carried on the back of their mothers in an algi. This is the piece of cotton cloth in which women also cover themselves. They may also be carried in a separate shawl which the mother ties with knots above her breasts and at the waist.

Naming

A Haddad child gets a personal name within a week of its birth, an event marked by a sacrifice. Among the Kreda and Kanembu a goat or sheep will let its life, if the family can afford it. I suspect that this is rarely if ever the case among the Haddad and probably never was, for the simple reason that the Haddad did not raise small ruminants. Even in the 1960s, Haddad families rarely possessed goats nor did they have cash at their disposal to pay for one to be sacrificed. The service of a marabout is not readily available to them either. Not surprisingly, some Haddad Kreda claimed that they followed the practice of their pastoral hosts. Among the Teda and Daza one name is given to the child by the marabout, and if an Aza smith is present, he will cry out the name three times, if not this will be done by a healthy man. Another name will be chosen by the mother. She will choose one from the father's side if it is a boy, from the mother's side if it is a girl, according to Chapelle (1957: 266). Charles Le Coeur tells us that it is the old woman in charge of burying the placenta who asks the mother, grandmother and other elderly female relatives gathered for the occasion what the child's name is to be, and then announces the choice that is made by the mother or grandmother (Le Coeur 1950: 105).

I have found next to no information on Kanembu naming practices. Conte states simply that it takes place seven days after the birth and that it is accompanied by gifts if it is a boy, gifts that constitute the nucleus of his personal patrimony. The most important is a bull contributed by his mother's brother if material circumstances so allow (cf. Conte 1983a: 225). He offers no hint as to the practice of the Haddad Kanembu and we learned only of the 'ideal naming ceremony' of the Kanembu from our Haddad hosts and their perception does not necessarily correspond to common practice.

Cutting the hair

The first cutting of the hair is a social and ritual event among the Haddad as among the Kreda and Kanembu. It takes place at about the age of two or, as the Haddad explain, when the child is able to speak and knows how to identify things around it. The cutting does not necessitate the blessings of a marabout, but it is a festive occasion accompanied by a sacrifice. Among the Haddad Kreda the nature of the sacrifice is 'decided upon' by the child itself, or so it is claimed. A knife and a ladle are placed in front of the child. If he or she picks up the knife, a goat or sheep will have its throat cut and the meat will be partitioned and shared with all the households of the camp. If the child picks the ladle, the one with which one stirs porridge, bule, when cooking, then a huge portion of this dish is cooked and given away to the other households of the camp. The cutting itself is largely a clean-shaven except for a few tufts left growing on the head indicating the child's clan identity. Haddad families follow this practice but not all children are given the coiffure of their fathers but sometimes that of their mother's clan. Baby sisters and brothers have the same hair-do except for a tiny braid worn by the girls running down the back of the head. This could be an indication that the paternal clan did not play the same role among the Haddad in former days.

Circumcision

For boys throughout Kanem and the Bahr el Ghazal circumcision is a most important event. This is also the case among the Haddad. Whether Haddad practice deviated from circumcision rituals among the Kreda and Kanembu respectively, we did not learn. Among Teda groups the circumcision was formerly done at the age of seven to eight, according to Le Coeur, but in the 1950s it was carried out somewhat later, i.e. at the age of twelve. He writes that the man who performs the circumcision begins his task by shouting: "Small boy! Look up!" Then he utters a bismilla while doing the cut and concludes by crying out: "Man! Look down" (1950: 117; IN transl.). Le Coeur also tells us that the boy recuperates in a separate tiny tent. On the seventh day the father performs a ritual in the presence of the entire camp. The boy is anointed in butter, given a silver earring, a new dress and headscarf, and a range of gifts. The ceremony concludes with dancing by the women (Le Coeur 1950: 117). Among the Kanembu the boy is offered even more lavish gifts than he was at the naming ceremony, according to Conte. In fact, circumcision represents:" ... the most important rite de passage in the life of a Kanembu man. Ideally, the gifts then received form a substantial capital composed of cattle, important sums of money and camels. These items often revert temporarily to the custody of the young man's parents. At the time of his first marriage they may be used to pay bride-wealth. Circumcision gifts frequently exceed in value that of required marital prestations, and, in such circumstances, are a guarantee of material viability of a new domestic unit" (Conte 1983a: 225). These rites are on the decline among the Kanembu, however, and Conte has no first-hand data on the circumcision itself, nor does he specify what the situation is among the Duu or Haddad. Considering their foraging past and the fact that their subsistence activities provide most of them with a limited surplus and hence a possibility of investment in cattle and small ruminants, it is unlikely that major exchanges take place at Haddad circumcisions. The Haddad practice neither clitoridectomy nor infibulation and apparently there is no initiation ceremony for girls with formal exchanges.[1]

MARRIAGE PARTNERS AND EXCHANGE

The Haddad choose brides and grooms largely within their own groups. Marriages across ethnic boundaries or unions, which imply a negation of the 'caste like' status of the Haddad, are few and far between. Endogamy is enforced to the extent that: "A union between a Haddad Kanembu and a Kanembu is considered legally void and, in certain instances, criminal in local jurisprudence. A Kanembu having unknowingly married a Duu is entitled to immediate divorce and appropriate compensation, " says Conte (1983a: 239).

Despite socio-economic and cultural differences, the Haddad Kanembu and Haddad Kreda share cultural conceptions of marriage and certain practices, as they do with the ethnic groups among whom they live. One of these is polygamy, which is widespread throughout the Muslim world. Yet, it seems to be more in theory among the Haddad, who appear to be largely monogamous, although a substantial number of them marry more than twice in a lifetime.[2] It is an unwritten rule that a man should not marry before his elder brothers, a woman not before her older sisters. We were told that a violation of this custom invariably gave rise to confrontations between brothers and that no one could remember marriages that had not complied with the tradition. In order to avoid complications and ensure that all passes smoothly, a man will do his utmost to arrange

for the marriages of his older siblings and hence work hard to amass the necessary means to make this possible. The maintenance of the custom may be linked to the authority of older siblings and the respect in which their younger siblings are supposed to hold them. As a married person has more prestige than an unmarried one, moreover, it seems desirable for the older to marry first.

Another custom practised by the Haddad as well as by the Kanembu and Kreda is the levirate. This implies that a man has the right to take over the widow and children of an elder deceased brother. In the event of a dead man having no younger sibling, his elder brother may take on the sexual, economic and social responsibilities vis-à-vis the wife and children. This becomes a duty if the deceased leaves behind offspring. The Haddad consider it highly important that these children remain part of the paternal descent group. That the levirate is perceived as a right rather than a duty is supported by the fact that the parents of the widow have to formally ask their deceased son-in-law's brother if he is willing to marry her even if there is no offspring. The sororate, on the other hand, i.e. the custom that a man has the right to marry the younger sister of his deceased wife is not found in Kanem. It is customary among all Haddad that small children follow their mother in the event of divorce and stay with her for as long as they need maternal care, only to return to the father and his family at a later stage.

The two Haddad groups vary in respect to choice of marriage partners, however. The Haddad Kanembu told us that they prefer marriages with kinsmen, in particular father's brother's daughter. In practice, however, marriage partners do not necessarily live up to this preference. The Haddad Kreda, on the other hand prefer marriages with non-kin, as we shall see. While the Kanembu require chastity of the woman until marriage, this is not the case among the Kreda, and similar differences in attitude to chastity are found among the two Haddad groups respectively.

Both the Haddad Kanembu and the Haddad Kreda legitimize marriages by exchanging bride-wealth. The marriage ceremonies are similar in the sense that the couple spends seven days in a particular hut or tent made for the occasion. Immediately after the ceremony, a Haddad Kanembu couple moves to the location of the man's family. The Haddad Kreda follow a quite different path. Among these people the bride remains in the camp of her parents for two years before she takes up residence with her husband and his family. During these years the man pay visits to his wife. He camps, eats and sleeps regularly with her but invariably returns to his father's camp. During the visits he is not expected to work for his in-laws in the sense of performing some kind of bridal service. If the woman gets pregnant within the two years, however, she will move to her husband's camp in order for the child to be born there and assume its rightful membership of the agnatic descent group, following the widespread rule that 'the child is not where the bride-wealth is.' Some Haddad Kreda explained to us that the reason why the wife stayed with her kinsmen for two years after the marriage had to do with the practicalities of getting the dowry ready, as this includes the future tent of the couple and its furnishings.

Haddad marriage contraction is marked by fewer and in general less conspicuous exchanges than those found among the dominant ethnic groups. In any particular case, the bride-wealth is up for negotiation between the families of the groom and bride in case, and determined in accordance with the wealth and status of the families. We were told very little about bride-wealth, probably because the Haddad are poor and exchanges less glamorous than the ones legitimizing marriage contraction among the Kreda and Kanembu proper, who flash their material wealth when exchanging cattle, small ruminants and other visual valuables. The Haddad largely exchange money, ideally Marie Theresia thalers having no possession of cattle and very few if any ruminants at all.

Kanembu and Haddad Kanembu marriage practices

Marriage patterns are at the very core of Edouard Conte's study of the Kanembu and the Duu, a category that includes the Haddad Kanembu in his analysis, which aims at explaining the structural basis and transformation of social stratification in Kanem. I shall briefly draw on some of his data to throw further light on the marriage practices of the Haddad Kanembu with the qualification that the ensuing data deal with a broader social segment than the Haddad Kanembu proper albeit most of the information stems from these people.

According to Conte, the ideology of marriage contraction and the wider socio-political organization has a strong patrilineal bias. The most frequently expressed marriage ideal is that of union that is 'close to home' in terms of both spatial and genealogical distance. The Duu not only subscribe to this view, in fact at the ideological level

they "declare themselves to be 'more patrilineal' than the Kanembu, claiming 55 % as compared to 44 % patrilateral parallel cousin marriages" (Conte 1983a: 389).

The Kanembu stress unilineal descent and encourage patrilateral and patrilocal unions in harmony with Arabo-Islamic norms and discourage marriages with uterine relatives and condemn outright mother's sister's daughter and mother's sister's son marriages. The Duu follow these norms in that real or classificatory patrilateral parallel cousin marriage is the predominant form of marriage. In fact, the frequency of patrilateral cousin marriage (parallel and cross-cousin combined) is comparable for the Kanembu and the Haddad (69 % and 75 % respectively), while matrilateral cousin marriages are somewhat more frequent among the Kanembu (31 % as against 24 % for the Duu) (ibid. 1983a: 388). All forms of cousin marriage are practised on a regular basis and considered more durable than marriages with non-kin. Still, only two out of 1,289 Duu marriages proved to be with true mother's sister's daughters, while marriages between classificatory matrilateral parallel cousins were statistically too frequent to be subsumed as 'exceptions'. Among the Duu Rea, who are Haddad, this pattern co-occured with clan exogamy and the emigration from the clan territory of at least 15 % of the people. Half of the first marriages were contracted between genealogically related persons. Conte concludes on the basis of his quantitative survey of Duu marriages that all categories of cousins, as well as kin of different generations who are not related in direct line of descent, may be considered as potential spouses. The major formal difference between the Kanembu and the Duu resides in the frequency of cross-cousin marriage. Among the Kanembu this made up 24 % of patrilateral and 28 % of matrilateral unions, among the Duu the respective incidence was 20 % and 13 % for matrilateral cross-cousin unions (ibid. 1983a: 239-40, 388). He found also that due to the low average settlement population and dispersed habitat of the Duu there was a high proportion of village out-marriage, even more so for women than for men. Yet, the great majority of men and women chose partners living no farther from their village than 10 kilometres.

Kanembu marriage exchanges are quite elaborate, as intimated above. They entail an exchange, which symbolically assesses the initiation of formal ties or betrothal of the parties, tabasqi, as well as other exchanges of which the bride-wealth in cattle, yara, is the most significant. The tabasqi consists of gifts from the suitor's family, such as a roll of cotton fabric, gabak, and a pair of sandals to the fiancée and some loaves of sugar, perfume and pomades to members of her immediate family. Ideally, the suitor should also give his future bride presents at religious festivals throughout the period of betrothal. These gifts are known as n'qurirom or 'share of the feast'. The major prestation is the bride-wealth, yara, offered by the groom's mother to the mother of the bride. At a second marriage its equivalent is called fida. "These prestations consist of a negotiable sum of money, preferably to be paid in thalers or other silver coins. Among the poorest, the yara and fida may amount to less than a thaler or its 1973 equivalent of 500 CFA. On average 3 to 10 thalers are given. In certain chiefly families, the sum may attain 200 thalers representing a fortune of some 20 prime head of cattle," Conte explains (ibid. 1983a: 228). The bride-wealth should be fully paid or the marriage will be postponed until the agreed wealth has changed hands. In the event of divorce, the bride-wealth should be returned, but if cousins intermarry it may be totally foregone or reduced. Another traditional exchange at marriage is the niarom, lit. 'share of the marriage'. This is a gift from the fiancée to his future wife's paternal uncle to be handed over on the day of the wedding. This is in the range of 500 to 2000 CFA, often higher than the fida, and can never be waived. Finally, the Kanembu exchange the sadau, a gift offered by the groom to the bride in the presence of her parents on the very day of their wedding. The sadau is usually cattle or goats, one to two cows being the normal amount, head that become the personal property of the bride at the time of cohabitation. In the event of this being exchanged by the Haddad, they will make do with one or two goats or a small sum of money (ibid. 1983a: 229). Conte explains the function of the sadau as a means of consolidating "the personal link between husband and wife", whereas an exchange known as the rabitina: "seals the new relationship established between their respective families." This is given in various kinds, e.g. a gold coin, cattle, a horse or dates (1983a: 229). The wife's kin also offers a trousseau that includes the furnishings and utensils that the young couple needs to set up their new household. These prestations to the groom's relatives are not formalized, but well-to-do people are expected to give their new son-in-law a horse as well.

Kanembu marriage exchanges are difficult to characterize normatively, in particular the role of cattle, as the bovine population varies greatly over time due to recurrent droughts, Conte writes. The exchanges vary with social status and are indispensable for the maintenance of the contracting parties' self-respect, but marriage is not a basic mechanism of capital transfer between generations or lineages. Still, marriage prestations tend to reinforce and perpetuate class boundaries, whatever the nominal 'value', according to Conte. A comparison between marriage prestations among Kanembu nobles, well-off people, richer Duu and poor people confirms that: "... what represents a 'moderate' marriage payment for a rich father constitutes an absolute impediment to hypergamy for a poor family of the same or a different social stratum." However that may be, it is also a fact that "The possession of even a few head of cattle can allow a nobleman or common dignitary to exercise considerable, often determining, influence over the marital destinies of his dependants, whether they are free Kanembu or Duu or of captive descent", Conte concludes (1983a: 233, 384).

Among the Kanembu marriage festivities may last for as long as a week and involve several dozen guests, including a marabout, witnesses, the fathers and uncles of the couple as well as a crowd of family and village elders. The groom's family carries the expenses of the marriage ceremony itself, often at great cost. During the celebrations the Kanembu slaughter goats and consume substantial amounts of millet and maize, tea, oils, sugar and cola nuts. The husband's witness enumerates the exchanges in kind, but as these promises often are somewhat exaggerated, it is customary to give the groom a six-month lapse to comply, in order to reduce possible consequent embarrassment. When the bride's witness has finished proclaiming the gifts offered by the groom, the officiating mallam seals the union by reciting the opening sura of the Koran. "The bride, concealed under a dark shawl, is then conducted on the back of a mare, ox or donkey, according to means, to her new home. Along the way she is cheered by the guests and accompanied by the shrill cries of her women friends and kin. On arrival, the tip of the head-rope of the bride's mount is buried in the sand. The groom then approaches and, before drawing the rope from the sand, remits a gift known as the jarm'but to his wife or one of her kin." This generally consists of a sum of money. The nomadic, pastoral origin of this cus-

14,1. Some Haddad Kanembu own cattle, among them the Darkoa clan, however, its members neither eat nor kill cows.

tom is apparent, says Conte, referring to a similar custom among the Teda and Daza (cf. Chapelle 1957: 281). If the bride is a virgin, the nuptial mat is exposed in front of her hut following the consummation of the marriage, an event that gives rise to a small celebration (Conte 1983a: 230-31).

The social and economic conditions of the Duu vary greatly, as previously mentioned:" ... some are effectively freemen, though generally poor, and others are virtually slaves and serfs," as Conte puts it (1983a: 234). This difference and not least the pervasive 'caste-like' distinction between the Kanembu proper and the Duu and/or Haddad Kanembu materialize poignantly in differences in marriage exchanges both in terms of size and kind. Among the Kanembu proper the core of marital exchanges is cattle, the larger the number the higher the status of the families involved. As the Haddad Kanembu have been barred from

possessing herds of cattle until Chad gained independence, their marriage prestations have necessarily been different in kind, in principle that is. In practice they have varied widely among various segments of Haddad society.

Haddad Kanembu, who are not subservient to Kanembu masters negotiate and contract marriages without interference from members of the dominant ethnic group within the overall ramification of ethnic endogamy. While those who are subordinated Kanembu masters face a series of ramifications both in terms of freedom to contract marriage and to exchange bride-wealth and other marriage prestations (ibid. 1983a: 234). These ramifications are similar to those under which slaves can marry among the Kanembu and resemble those governing slave marriages among the Tuareg (cf. Nicolaisen & Nicolaisen 1997, II: 606-7). Conte's Kanembu informants explained the restrictions as follows:

"A Duu did not have the right to own cattle. When the time had come for him to take a wife, he went to see his Kanembu. The Kanembu alone was allowed to make those payments which had to consist of cattle. Millet and maize were good only for the marriage feast. This meant one or two or at very most three head of cattle changed hands. They were given to the Duu's future parents-in-law. But these also did not have the right to keep the cattle. They passed them on to their own Kanembu with whose herd they would remain. The girl's parents gave the groom an azizi (gift, token of friendship) of some item of clothing and a little gabak" (1983a: 234). Conte concludes that: "In blunt economic terms, the master of the Duu groom thus acquired extensive rights over the labour of the in-marrying Duu woman and of her eventual offspring at the price of 'one or two or at the very most three head of cattle.' In the 19th century, this was cheaper than purchasing a slave woman. Furthermore, there was little risk at the new wife escaping, being captured by brigands or becoming ill on the road from Kuka market at Bagirmi. As opposed to the slave, the Duu did have the right to found a socially recognized domestic unit. However, in so doing the Duu man became indebted to his patron for the animals required to take a wife. This could represent several years' revenue in kind, considering the heavy taxes and levies to which he was submitted. As a result, he became or remained an indentured serf of his master for a very long term" (ibid. 1983a: 234-5).

Conte mentions also that comparable arrangements were implemented among the Duu and Kanembu maskin, i.a. resident on lands that were controlled by the Khalifa of Mao, but that those who resided in the former chieftaincies of Dibinenchi, N'Guri and Beri Kolom did not subscribe to these practices (ibid. 1983a: 235).

Generally, then, the marriage prestations of Haddad families dependent on Kanembu 'hosts' vary in accordance with the wealth of the latter, although it is impossible to discern from Conte's description whether differences exist between the Haddad Kanembu and other groups of the Duu category. He mentions, for example, a rather high level of marriage prestations among the Duu staying among the noble Kogona Sharu, while such prestations are dispensed with by those living among only averagely wealthy Kanembu. Some Duu communities appear to do almost entirely without marriage exchanges, except for the offer-

ing of a small jarm'buta, says Conte (ibid. 1983a: 386) and one may speculate whether these are synonymous with the foraging Haddad. The jarm'buta is the gift presented to the wife when her 'head rope is removed from the sand', a symbolic statement of her change of locality, the fact that she literally strikes camp to move in with her husband and in-laws. Conte does not dwell on the extent to which the Duu actually follow the normative prescriptions of marriage exchanges set by the dominant Kanembu. It is an open question to what extent bride-wealth, yara is exchanged by different segments of Haddad society. Conte mentions at one point, for example, that the yara prestations among the Kanembu poor are comparable to those of poor Duu (ibid. 1983a: 382). In view of the foraging tradition of the Haddad and the curbing of the economic assets of those who settled on Kanembu lands, it is likely that marriage exchanges have played a limited role in the overall set-up of Haddad communality, although marriage is a social crank among these people as elsewhere. Indirectly, Conte appears to confirm this point when writing for example about the exchange of sadau that it has a rather 'evolué' connotation among the Duu (ibid. 1983a: 231).

Kreda and Haddad Kreda marriage practices

The ethos of Kreda marriage is quite different from that of the Kanembu as well as from most pastoral societies. The Kreda prefer to forge marriage ties outside the immediate community. Marriages with relatives are rarities and prohibited outright between cousins by blood and even beyond.[3] The Kreda do not require the bride to be a virgin and the same holds for the Haddad living among them. There is no display of nuptial mats after the wedding nights. Young Teda marry at the age of about twenty, while girls may be married off from the age of twelve. In principle there is no age limit, according to Chapelle, who writes of marriages of girls from the age of only five years. In such cases, the life of a little girl will continue as before, except for her coiffure, which will be changed to the one befitting married women. The girl continues to live with her parents until she comes of age. Only then will she move to her husband's camp.

Marriage contraction is a delicate affair among Teda pastoralists, as young people are prohibited from marrying any of those with whom they have grown up but have to seek a partner from outside the clan. Chapelle does not dwell on Kreda or Haddad Kreda marriages, but writes in general about Tibu practices which in his view more or less cover the customs of the former. Marriages are arranged among the Tibu, he informs us, the initiative being on part of the man's family. It is up to the future groom's relatives to demonstrate their family responsibility for getting him married not only by selecting a girl but also sending a gift to her parents pledging the commitment, a custom known as 'the tying of the bead'. Then they have to wait to see whether the gift is accepted or sent back. If the former is the case and the groom's family maintains its interest in the girl, further gifts must be sent to her family. These are considerable in the sense that they can amount to several years' income. They are far beyond the economic means of the groom himself, but he will contribute to the best of his ability. A common way to amass funds for young grooms to be is to pursue the age-old craft of cattle raiding. Several suitors may try their luck with the girl at the same time, but none of them will know till the last moment whether he is to be the chosen one. The rejected suitors may try to get their 'investments' back, but this is an extremely delicate issue and most difficult to obtain. When the girl and her family have finally made up their minds, they will reciprocate, offering a series of gifts to members of the groom's family, the most important being the dowry offered on the day of the wedding. During the engagement period, the young man visits the camp of his bride to be, but he stays largely away from the camp of his future parents-in-law (Chapelle 1957: 277).

The marriage-exchanges of the Haddad Kreda are similar to those exchanged among their Kreda hosts. They comprise a bride-wealth exchange of cattle and gifts from the man of clothes and jewellery to his future wife, or so some informants claimed obviously not to loose face. As the Haddad are foraging people and moreover barred, traditionally, from actually possessing cattle and small ruminants, bride-wealth is de facto offered in donkeys, the only domestic animal that they owned traditionally. However, the donkey is an animal of pivotal significance to the existence of these people as a beast of burden during hunting expeditions and migration. The actual size of the bride-wealth is negotiable in each case. Whatever the size and composition, however, it should ideally be exchanged prior to the actual wedding ceremony. The usual number of don-

keys offered as bride-wealth was between three and four, we were told, on top of which the groom's family may add money, an amount of 4000 to 5000 CFA was the sum mentioned in this respect.

In view of both the Haddad Kreda and the Haddad Kanembu the bride-wealth is offered to compensate the bride's father for the cost of the dowry. It can be argued, that symbolically the exchange legitimates the future relationship between the offspring of the couple and their paternal relatives. Ideally, the bride-wealth should be exchanged on the day of the wedding among both groups. On the very same day the bride should also receive the dowry. This consists of eight hunting nets, four for the hunting of gazelle (cf. Cat. No. 51) and four nets for the hunting of the Oryx antelope (cf. Cat. No. 57), nets that she immediately hands over to her husband. The dowry remains the property of the wife and she will take them with her in the case of divorce, when she returns to her parents' camp.

The Haddad Kreda will not look for marriage partners among close kin, as previously mentioned. They hardly ever marry their cousins but prefer unions with persons who are distantly related or not relatives at all. Due to the prevalent prohibitions against marriage with the Haddad throughout Kanem and the Bahr el Ghazal, they are forced to find spouses within their community. Haddad Kreda families cannot arrange marriages as they please. Any liaison must be approved by the Kreda 'hosts' or masters of the bride's family. The acceptance of the Kreda is formally acknowledged through an exchange of four spears offered by the groom's family to the Kreda masters of the bride's family. The spear is the weapon par excellence of Kreda men, as previously mentioned. Spears are carried over the shoulder in a leather pouch, four at a time for protection and fighting, for example during cattle raids (cf. Cat. no. 93). Symbolically, the gift of the four spears underscores the obligation of the Kreda to defend and protect the Haddad. Symbolically, assertion of Haddad-Kreda ties is reversed at Kreda marriage contraction. The marriage of a Kreda woman entails a corresponding obligation on the part of her future husband and his family. In this case, the latter presents a donkey to the Haddad family, who 'gets milk from the bride's family', as a Haddad explained. These marriage exchanges seem to indicate that relations between the Haddad Kreda and their host families are of a solid and long-term nature. We found no evidence, on the other hand, that the exchanges were combined with fictitious kinship relationships between the parties, like those existing between the Kreda pastoralists and their slaves in previous times, i.e. the kind of ties prevalent in many other North African societies, e.g. between the noble Tuareg and their slaves.

KINSHIP AND CLANS

The social and cultural fabric of the Haddad contains many similarities with those of the ethnic groups among whom they live, as we have seen. Basically, there is a correspondence in respect to the way in which they all perceive kinship and classify relatives. Formally, their lot is cast on the paternal kin in line with the Arabo-Islamic ideology that permeates Kanem and the Bahr el Ghazal. It manifests itself in kinship terminologies, the pre-eminence of paternal kin-groups and clans, and formal rules of succession and inheritance. In principle, the Haddad comply with the general Islamic practice according to which a son is allotted double the amount of that given to the daughter. Children, siblings and parental relatives receive assets consecutively. They do not, however, abide by the code of offering blood-money in case of murder, as do the Kanembu and the Kreda.[4] Murder is not uncommon among the Kreda, who are easily aroused and fairly bellicose. The main causes are infidelity and cattle raiding. Among the Haddad, on the other hand, murder appears to be unknown. Both Haddad groups are familiar with the custom of blood-money, as it is practised by their 'hosts' or 'protectors', but we met no one with recollections of murder or the payment of blood-money within their ranks. In any case the Haddad would have no cattle to offer as compensation, the informants added with a smile.

The Haddad appear to comply with the patrilateral ideology at least as strictly as do the Kanembu and Kreda. They use the very same terminologies for kin as the dominant groups: the Haddad Kanembu those used by the Kanembu proper, the Haddad Kreda the very same as their pastoral hosts. In line with the overall cultural stress on the paternal kin, terms for father and brother are extended to a range of patrilateral relatives. A man talks, for example, of both his first and his more distant paternal cousins as 'younger brother' and 'older brother'. In line with the terminology,

the behavioural code stresses respect vis-à-vis older paternal relatives. Parents-in-law and sons- and daughters-in-law are expected to avoid one another, though not totally as among the pastoral Tuareg. It is acceptable for them to talk to one another, for example, but while doing so the younger person must look away and not confront his or her parents-in-law. Joking does not occur between Haddad relatives or between kin among other ethnic groups in Kanem and the Bahr el Ghazal. I shall not dwell further on the kinship system of the Haddad. Johannes and I had decided to delve into this subject upon our planned return and collected few data during our trip, as previously said. I refer to Conte's appendix 4 for a detailed description of Kanembu kinship terminology (Conte 1983a: 491-506).

The Haddad do not adhere as strictly to the principle of patrilocality as do the Kreda or the Kanembu. Upon marriage the Kreda settle patrilocally almost without exception with the result that sons live in the very same camps as their fathers. The Haddad Kreda are more flexible in that respect in that some men lived in the camps of their wives. Haddad Kreda families that camp together do not, therefore, necessarily make up a paternal kin group. A similar flexibility governs Haddad Kanembu choice of residence. Some married couples do not stay with the man's father but choose other options, as shown by Conte. The fact that the patrilocal principle is not strictly adhered to imply that kinship solidarity within the camp and hamlet is fragile. Grievances are quite frequent and occur far more often than among the Kreda and Kanembu respectively, according to our informants. The skirmishes are rarely grave, however, and apparently also more easily resolved than among the Kreda and Kanembu, the Haddad argue.

The impetus towards agnatic principles in line with Islam is embodied in the organization of clans. Among the Kanembu and the Kreda patrilineal clans constitute the very grid of the social set-up, determining and the foundation of its hierarchical structures: the distinction between aristocrats, commoners and slaves among the Kanembu and between ruling and non-ruling segments of the pastoral society of the Kreda. Once again the situation is slightly different among the Haddad. Haddad Kanembu society was not hierarchical but patri-groups including clans had recognized territorial rights and ruled two out of the five chiefdoms that existed prior to the French colonization. These were later dispersed over a vast area and according to Conte's detailed study in the early 1970', members of a particular clan live between those of other clans. Even hamlets may contain men from a number of clans. Thus Conte found that Duu clans were present in 214 villages throughout South Kanem (Conte 1983a: 32: table 2). Haddad Kreda clans did never attain political influence comparable to that of Haddad Kanembu clans. Haddad Kreda clans do also live scattered over a vast territory, but members of any one clan hold a notion of a core area identifiable by the presence of the chief of the clan. At Wanagal, for instance, a tiny place of only six huts, we located men from four different clans: Mada, Baraza, Karda, Baragara. Haddad clans play a minor role in respect to the succession of chiefs, a position which is of limited significance to the Haddad compared to the role of chiefs among the dominant ethnic groups.

ANIMALS AND IDENTIFICATION

Animals play a significant part in the cosmology and myths of the Haddad albeit Islam has achieved a hold on their beliefs. Like many other foraging people, we learned that Haddad clans are identified by reference to the animal world which they depend on and exploit. The nature and significance of animals as social markers spurred vivid debates among the early crop of professional anthropologists. Theoretical giants like Tylor, Durkheim, Radcliffe-Brown and Levi-Strauss all contributed significantly to the development of our understanding of the complex phenomena. It is widely acknowledged today that animals 'are good to think with' as Levi-Strauss argued and that imputed relations between animals and men must be understood not only as religious phenomena and/or linked to the symbolic identification of groups and marriage systems, but as intellectual endeavours, aimed at classifying objects of experience (Levi-Strauss 1963).

As it happened, although the Haddad were eager to share their knowledge and perception of animals and also of stories of how relationships between clans and specific animal species were established, few proved knowledgeable about these issues. Typically, the origin of relations between clans and animal species is linked to the fate of the clan ancestor and to a specific event in his life. The animal in case may at one point have saved the life of the

ancestor or intervened to the benefit of his family. The animals which become clan emblems are not object of specific religious attention, however. Haddad clans do not make sacrifices to the animals nor do the latter bear similarities to totems, as known among foraging societies such as for example the Australian aborigines, a point to which I shall return. It is generally believed, however, that the killing of the emblem of one's clan will cause death or severe illness to the culprit. The following examples, from clans among the Haddad Kreda and the Haddad Kanembu respectively, may serve as examples of Haddad traditions of the particular link between clans and animals:

The Haddad Kreda are divided into three major clans: the Tchatchauma, the Ossa and the Bichia. The former is split in two main sections. One is the Tchatchauma Mada clan who applies a gazelle species called tiguidim as its clan emblem. It is probably an Ourebia species, as the Haddad characterized the male as having tiny antlers and the female as having none at all. The other main section is the Tchatchauma Yeska who holds the black-bellied bustard, Lissotis melanogaster melanogaster as its emblem. The Tchatchauma Yeska relate the following story of the origin of their particular relationship with the bustard: Once upon a time their clan ancestor was close to dying from thirst and would have done so had the black-bellied bustard not come to his rescue. Seeing his condition, the bustard flew to the closest water hole. It dipped its feathers in water and flew back to the dying man and saved his life by sprinkling water all over him. Ever since, his descendants have abstained from killing and eating the black-bellied bustard.

One of the well-known clans among the Haddad Kanembu is the Darkoa, who owe their name to an ancestor called Darku. The Darkoa own cattle and hold cows with a red back, white belly and ears and a white cornea as an emblem. The Darkoa relate that their ancestor, Darku once upon a time had such a cow. It had a tiny calf that was tied to a post in his hut. Darku had a baby son as well, so young that he was still a toddler. One day when Darku was away and his baby son and the calf had been left alone in the hut this caught fire. The cow rushed into the burning home but rather than rescuing its own calf it brought Darku's son into safety. Ever since, the Darkoa have neither killed nor eaten cows with hides of that colour combination.

All Haddad clans possess emblems, we were told, although the origin of these proved to be unknown to some of

14,2. Hunter's mask made from the cranium of the ground hornbill. Cat. no. 12.

the clans and the role of the clan animals in the overall cosmology less significant than among the dominant groups in the area. A reason for this lack of interest and knowledge about the clan emblem may be due to the fact that clans and clan organization had limited social significance among the Haddad at the time of our fieldwork. Contrary to our surmise that clans and notions of specific symbolic relations between clan members and selected animal species might carry particular significance to the Haddad as foraging or previously foraging people in comparison with the agro-pastoral Kanembu or the pastoral Kreda who also

organize themselves along patrilineal descent principles and make use of clan emblems, the opposite proved to be the case. We found that knowledge about clan traditions and symbolism was far more profound and alive among the latter. We noted that clan emblems among the Kanembu, Kreda and Arab pastoralists were largely animals, but plant species occurred as well. Two Kreda clans claimed the very same species of tree, the yayanga as emblem. The yayanga was said to be able to make an entire Kreda camp invisible to enemies and to have saved one in this way from a murderous assault. Normally, however, animals are chosen as emblems among these ethnic groups. Members of the ostrich clan can narrate, for instance, how the ostrich saved a forefather by taking him on its back and carrying him away from his enemies, while those honouring the muflon tell of how this animal once led their desperately thirsty forefather to a spring. Generally speaking, both the Haddad and the other ethnic groups perceive the relationship between the clan and the species that functions as its emblem as an asymmetrical one, with clan members as the receivers, rather than as one of kinship or as characterized by kinship-like bonds. There are exceptions, however. A large group of clans among the pastoral Kreda known as Yorda are traditionally related to the leguan, which they never kill or eat. The relationship with the leguan dates back to the birth of the stem forefather of the clans, at a time when the animals were still able to speak. The clan tradition has it that the leguan turned up at the birth of the forefather claiming that it too was of Yorda stock. Another group of clans, the Yiria say that they are related to the chameleon. They forged ties with the reptile in the same way as did the Yorda with the leguan, the animal simply turned up at the birth of the ancestor, claiming that it was of Yiria stock. For this reason the Yiria never kill the animal, fearing that it may retaliate and strike down the aggressor. That these clans perceive their relations with the chameleon and leguan respectively as one similar to kinship relations is borne out by the fact that if a Yorda kills the clan emblem of the Yiria, i.e. the chameleon, the Yiria will demand a cow as compensation from the Yorda, while the opposite will happen if the Yorda kills a leguan. These rules of restitution are parallel to those regarding restitution in the case of manslaughter and murder, and indicate that ethnic groups in Kanem and the Bahr el Ghazal at times perceive relations between clans and emblems in the idiom of kinship.

NOTES

1. In this they are like the Teda and thus unlike the Arab pastoralists in the area (Chapelle 1957: 272).
2. Among the Duu Rea clan, which is a Haddad Kanembu clan, the rate of polygamy reaches 116.3, according to Conte (1983a: 248).
3. In Tibesti the Tubu say that there has to be a generational distance of three grandparents: "le marriage est interdit lorsqu'il y a trois grand-pères" (Chapelle 1957: 274).
4. The Kreda maintain that they offer one hundred head of cattle in compensation if the victim is a man, fifty in case of a woman.

These are claimed without specifications as to the colours, looks and age of the animals as is often the case among North African pastoralists. The actual number of cattle that changes hands is in any case much smaller than publicly claimed. The custom is supported by the administration as a means of avoiding revenge. Its success in doing so, however, depends on whether the two parties avoid meeting one another in the future.

15:

15: CRAFTS AND TRADE

Haddad foragers are fine craftsmen. They surround them-selves with simple and functional, yet delicate and aes-thetically pleasing things that testify to their ingenuity and skills. The Haddad, in particular the Haddad Kreda are skilled in basketry, not the least in the technique of coiling. The women make exquisite trays, bottle-shaped containers for flour and milk bowls of such quality that they hold both milk and water. The baskets are largely plain, not decorated with any colours though embellished at times with leather edgings that also protect the work against wear, and, on rare occasions with tufts of skin. It is in basketry that Haddad women give rein to their artistic vein.

Both the foraging Haddad Kreda and the foraging and agricultural Haddad Kanembu produce most of the material items that they need in daily life themselves. Besides dwellings - be it beehive huts or tents - men and women make uten-sils, mats, ropes, tools and the hunting implements they need from nature's provision of animal hides, wood, dum palm leaf, acacia root and other plant material. The Haddad Kreda are acknowledged throughout the Bahr el Ghazal as highly skilled mat makers and as expert tanners. They perform the tanning of the hides of cows, horses and goats of their Kreda hosts and other pastoralists, a service that constitutes a cornerstone of the exchange relationship between the two groups, as we have heard. The Haddad Kanembu also produce what they need in the way of material objects and tools, but I did not come across specimens or skills that set them apart.

Neither the Haddad Kanembu nor the Haddad Kreda hunters forge, weave, dye cloth, carve wood for mortars, stools or bowls, nor do they make pots, however. These crafts are all in the hands of urban artisans who sell their products at the markets. These Haddad craftsmen make a living as smiths and wood carvers, potters and dyers. They also work as tanners and leatherworkers, making saddles for horses, purses, sheaths for knives and small covers for amu-lets, shoes and boots. Each of these crafts is carried on from generation to generation within the same families. A few of urban Haddad supplement their income as musicians. Haddad smiths and other urban artisans are both Kreda and Kanembu speaking. In Mussoro, for example, the balance was about fifty-fifty between the two. The existence of an ur-ban contingent of Haddad artisans is not peculiar to Kanem and the Bahr el Ghazal. These specialists are found all over northern Chad, as previously mentioned.

The Haddad or Azza of the Guré region north-east of Lake Chad sustain themselves in a similar way either by foraging and net-hunting or as craftsmen. However, in this area the Azza also dig wells for the Daza and Teda pastoral-ists. This is a highly strenuous and dangerous task that they monopolize (cf. Chapelle 1957: 187). In Tibesti the Haddad or Duudi support themselves exclusively by forging weap-ons, iron utensils, silver jewellery, wooden mortars and the like and/or as public announcers and musicians playing the drum at marriages and other festivities. They do not hunt, nor do men work in leather or the women in tanning anymore (cf. Le Coeur 1950: 95).

TANNING AND LEATHERWORK

Game supplies the Haddad with food, in the case of the Haddad Kreda a substantial part of their nutrition in fact,

15,1. Two young Haddad men cleaning and softening the inner side of a hide that has been treated with a tanning substance. They use an iron scraper furnished with a long wooden handle. One man presses the scraper firmly against the hide while the other pulls the instrument over its surface. Haddad Kreda.

but the wild animals that they bag serve other purposes as well. Game provides all of the Haddad with hides for dwellings and previously clothing, sinew and bones, raw materials for utensils, nets, water skins, strings and cords. The nomadic Haddad Kreda make extensive use of hides, however, more so than the settled Haddad Kanembu to whom hunting is of less significance. Hides are valuable to all the Haddad, yet leather specimens are not the object of artistic elaboration as is the case among pastoral groups in West Africa such as the Tubu, Tuareg, Maures or Fulani, among whom leather work is a distinctive and highly appreciated form of cultural expression – a brand, one might say.

The Haddad make use of skins of most of the animals they hunt down, in particular antelopes, gazelles and jackals. The few who own goats use these as well. Tanned and dressed hides are stitched together with finely cut leather cords to make sheets used by both the Haddad Kreda and the pastoralists during the rainy season. The sheets are put up under the tent mats to provide extra protection against torrential rains. Sheets of hide without hair are also used for storing purposes in the tent. Water skins are typically made from the skin of the *Gazella dama* and so was clothing. Clothes were also made from hides of the smaller red gazelle, *Gazella rufifrons*. Animal skins were gradually replaced by industrially produced cotton cloth during the first part of 20th century. Since World War II this has wiped out the local production of homespun and woven cotton cloth of the Yedina and Kanembu as material for both men's and women's dresses. Hides are used moreover for straps, thongs and finely plaited strings and ropes. Tanned skins are sold to urban dwellers.

The Haddad also use skins of smaller animals without removing the hair of these. They make water skins out of these and pieces of skin are sometimes used for simple ornamentation of baskets. The skins of jackals, sheep and goats are stitched together to form large rectangular covers for chilly nights. These are used by the Haddad Kreda and the Kreda alike, but more often sold at markets to urbanites, including Europeans as 'duvets' and decorative bed-spreads (cf. *Fig. 15,4*). In colonial and post-colonial times the hides of gazelle, antelope and other game also found ready customers among European civil servants and military personnel, including soldiers of the Foreign Legion, who used them for decoration as they did with the antlers and other trophies that the Haddad got them.

The tanning treatment depends on the future use of a particular skin. The Haddad Kreda make use of two kinds of tanning processes, one that removes the hair of the skin and another that retains the hair. The latter method is used for treating skins of gazelles, jackals and other smaller animals. It is also commonly used for hides of goats and sheep, while those of antelopes and cattle go through a tanning process that removes the hair.

The tanning of hides of smaller animals like gazelles, goats and sheep is exclusively the work of women, while the treatment of hides from antelopes and cattle is carried out jointly by women and men, the first and last part of the process being the work of the former, the in-between pounding and scraping of the hides that of men. The ensuing description of tanning methods is based on data from a Haddad Kreda camp where I was able to follow an entire process, supplemented by information gathered in other Haddad Kreda camps.

Removing the hair
At the time of our visit the Haddad did only treat hides of cows and antelopes in a manner that removed the hair on the skins. As long as animal hides were used for clothing, however, the same tanning process was to hides of gazelle. The tanning of an antelope hide takes several days. It involves women and men at various stages of the process, but does not require the full attention of the tanners all the time. The tannin acid is extracted from various plants by the Haddad Kreda, one being a bushy one known as *lifin*. The acid is found in both its leaves and stems, but is

15,2. Haddad women rubbing a hide between their hands to make it supple before it is finally washed and ready for use. Haddad Kreda.

most easily extracted from the former. The plant defoliates during winter. For this reason the Haddad Kreda prefer to treat their hides at a different time of the year. The acid is activated by pounding the leaves and fine stems in a mortar and by mixing the substance with cattle urine. Another effective tannin acid is extracted from a plant with milky stems known as *amlebener* that can be picked during the rainy season only. *Amlebener* is treated like the *lifin* plant, i.e. pounded and then mixed with urine.[1]

Tanning is done in a hole or pit in the ground made with a digging stick and just big enough to hold one hide. The Haddad will work on one hide at a time. The first phase of the process is carried out by women. When the tannin acid is ready, the hide is placed in the pit with the hairy side upwards and in such a way that the middle part of the hide sticks fairly tightly to the bottom and sides of the pit. The rest of the hide spreads out beyond this. Then the tannin acid is added, the sides of the hide folded on top of this and covered with a mat. The hide is left for the night in the pit in order for the acid to do its work. The next step of the treatment begins the following day. This entails the laborious task of 'beating' the hide with a pestle, usually the one used for pounding the wild *ogu* grass and millet. Two or three women may join forces to ease the task if the hide is large, 'beating' the hide simultaneously in a specific rhythmic stroke. They will do so on and off for two to three days, adding cattle urine in the process. During the night, when the beating stops, the hide is covered by a mat, as already mentioned, never by soil the Haddad volunteered. Once this part of the process is completed, the hair being sufficiently

loosened from the follicles, the hide is spread out with the hairy side upwards, ready for the next step, the actual removal of the hair. This task is also performed by women, who scrape off the hair with knives. When completely clean, the hide is stretched, pegged to the ground with wooden pegs and left to dry in the sun for two more days.

Once the hair has been removed from the skin, however, men take over and do the work that softens the hide, scraping away remaining pellicles and other impurities. I deliberately use the plural here, because this task requires the concerted effort of two men at a time. The softening is done with an iron scraper fitted to a long wooden shaft (cf. *Fig. 15,1*). One man presses the scraper against the hide while the other pulls the tool across it. It takes a full day of hard labour to complete the scraping of an antelope hide.

15,3. An elderly Haddad woman plaiting leather strings. The Haddad make use of a wide variety of leather ropes, strings and cords in daily life, round and flat, thin and heavy - for the lining of mats, tying or decoration. Haddad Kreda.

15,4. Blanket of twelve, finely tanned jackal skins lined with red leather. Haddad Kreda use these blankets during cold nights or they sell them. Cat. no. 84. Photo J.K.

Men rarely take part in the tanning process of other than antelope and cow hides, however, leaving the scraping of gazelle and goat hides to women.

Once the men have completed their part, the women take over again. The hide is put back into the pit, this time to be treated with another tannin acid made from acacia pods of a species known as *gor*. The pods are collected during the dry season and kept for future use. Water is added to the pounded pods and the substance is poured over the hide. Then this is placed in the pit with the new acid for the night whereupon it is 'beaten' by women with heavy pestles for a good part of the following day. Then the hide is stretched across the bottom of a large mortar and scraped once again with a knife, after which it is placed for the last time in the pit with the 'hairy' side facing upwards. Pounded acacia pods and water is once again poured over the hide before this is put back into the pit. The last phase of the treatment takes up the major part of yet another day, during which the women alternately pound and rub the hide between their hands until it is considered sufficiently supple to be washed in water and be done with.

Retaining the hair

Hides of gazelles, jackals and sheep that the Haddad intend to use with the hair retained are treated differently. Firstly, the hides undergo a thorough scraping of the inner side to remove pellicles and leftover scraps of meat. Then the skin is placed in a pit - a large wooden container may also do - but this time with the hairy side of the skin turned towards the bottom and sides of the pit. It is left here to soak in a tannin substance made of finely pounded acacia pods and water. Now and then the skin is pounded with a pestle to speed up the process. To secure supple hides – of sheep for example – the Haddad refrain from the use of pestles. Instead, they rub the skins gently by hand from time to time to further the penetration of the tannin into the pit. As the process proceeds, the inner side of the hide is scraped carefully, usually with a particular iron tool known as *koni* (cf. *Fig. 15,1*). A simple piece of wood or other tool may also do. This process takes up the major part of a day. Then the skin can be removed from the pit and washed thoroughly with water. Some women rub the skins with butter to make them supple.

Leatherwork

Once the skins have been tanned they are ready for use. The Haddad are capable leather workers, but not leather artists, as previously stated. Among the foraging Haddad it is largely women who work with leather. They produce most of the specimens needed in the household: stitch tanned hides together to make sheets and containers, plait straps and cords for all kinds of usage, make strips to reinforce baskets and edge mats, small purses and strings for jewellery and other simple decorative purposes. Women were also the ones who made the traditional leather clothes for both men and women in pre-war times. Among the urban Haddad artisans, however, leatherwork is all done by men, whether it is sandals and shoes, sheaths for spears, lances and knives, tiny purses for amulets or objects for personal hygiene and trinkets.

BASKETRY

The Haddad produce a variety of baskets, containers and boxes for transport, storing and milking – and to meet other needs – using the age-old techniques of coiling, plaiting, twisting and knotting. They twine and plait palm leaves and acacia fibres, moreover, to make thongs and ropes to fasten, carry and store objects out of reach of animals and termites, to reinforce baskets and mats and to produce nets for hunting, bridles for domestic animals and a variety of other things. They move camp with their chickens in plaited hen-houses and make mats to cover tents, to sit and sleep on and to wrap and store household utensils. The bulk of these specimens are produced by women. Men may lend a hand with some – for example, the baskets used to harvest wild grasses. Among the Haddad Kreda the weaving of mats is done exclusively by women, while it is Haddad Kanembu men who produce a considerable part of the mats that their family needs. The most important species for the fabrication of the above-mentioned objects is the dum palm, *Hyphaena thebaica*, which, with its slender stem and slightly tousled fan, is an eye-catcher throughout Kanem and the Bahr el Ghazal. The dum grows along the slopes of wadis and thrives in indentations and depressions throughout the Sahel from the Atlantic to the Nile Valley and as far north as the Tibesti mountains. Its fruit is part of the local diet, but the Haddad mainly make use of the leaves for basketry, ropes and mats. The Haddad make use of both the stalks of the leaves and of the leaves themselves. The latter must be fairly fresh in order for the fibres not to break when plaited or coiled. In the Gouré region, the harvesting of dum palm leaves is an Aza speciality and their major source of income, as they make mats for the tents of the pastoralists (Baroin 1991: 340). But other plant material is also made use of. The Haddad use the roots of acacia, which has surprisingly long and flexible as well as strong and resilient fibres. Savannah grasses, for example *Andropogon sp.* are twined, moreover, and put to use, through rarely for basketry, as it is among the Fulani for example. To the Haddad at or near Lake Chad, the papyrus is an inexhaustible source not only for materials for basketry and mats but also for making boats and other things, as we have seen. Other materials such as small branches are occasionally used for the production of particular specimens or to make baskets more durable.

15,5. Delicate container of coiled basketry for the storage of *ogu* seeds - the highly appreciated grass that makes for a wonderful porridge. The container is made of strips of dum palm leaves. Haddad women are able to produce baskets plaited so finely that they can hold milk and water. Haddad Kreda. Cat. no. 67. Photo J.K.

15,6. Two young Haddad Kreda women plaiting a tent mat of strips of dum palm leaves.

Coiling

The art of basketry is ancient – just how old is impossible to know, due to the perishable nature of the objects. It has been argued that basketry developed at the time of early agriculture i.e. about 12,000 years ago (Sentance 2001: 11), but it may well be much older. The earliest remains, interestingly enough, are fragments of coiled basketry used for the lining of grain stores at Fayum in Egypt some 5,600 years old, the very same culture from which the art of forging spread to Kanem and further westwards in North Africa. Whether coiling goes back that far in Kanem is uncertain, but that it is a widespread and highly developed technique here is a fact. The Haddad produce exquisite coiled basketry, sometimes embellished and/or reinforced with leather plaiting. The technique is used to make containers for seeds (cf. Cat. No. 68), boxes for personal items (cf. Cat. No. 109), lids for calabashes, as well as for making the large, almost flat trays used for drying and cleaning the wild seed of the *ogu* of the debris from other plants (cf. Cat. No. 64;

Fig. 17,32). The Haddad Kreda in particular are skilled at this work and able to make objects so meticulously made that they can hold milk or be used as containers for water, as previously mentioned (cf. Cat. No. 69; *Fig. 7,8*).

To make coiled basketry, the raw materials must come in long lengths and/or be joined to achieve the necessary length. The material used to stitch the coils together must be tough but flexible (Sentance 2001: 61). Dum palm leaves meet these requirements. The Haddad use finely twisted cords of palm leaf fibres as coil and split other leaves into fine strips, no more than 0.2 cm or even less in width, for stitching when producing delicate baskets or trays. The basket-maker begins with a flat spiral at the base or centre of the future object. Each turn is secured by stitching to cord to the previous one. Using a bodkin to make holes for the strip to pass through, the basket-maker gradually interlocks the coils into a solid structure, stitching coil upon coil. This technique produces a

15,7. A Haddad Kreda woman repairing an old tent mat.

slightly uneven surface, with a thickening where the coil is covered by strips. It is characteristic of Haddad coiling that the stitches split or bifurcate the one below. This produces a delicate, slightly differently coloured surface due to the natural variation in colour of the leaves. Haddad basket-makers never attempt to embellish this any further by introducing coloured strips to make distinctive patterns of one sort or another.

Plaiting

Another technique for the making of basketry is that of plaiting. This requires flat strands of material of even width, and,

again, the dum palm is able to supply these. The leaves are split into suitable strips, the width depending on the object to be plaited. For cruder items such as hen-houses (cf. Cat. No. 103) and coarse baskets such as those used to gather *ogu* seeds (cf. Cat. Nos. 62 & 63) or hold cooking pots (cf. Cat. No. 99) the Haddad use split strips that are one centimetre wide or wider. For mats and finer baskets the strips will be only be 0.3 cm to 0.5 cm, at times even less. At its simplest, plaiting involves laying out two sets of strips, one at right angles to the other and interlacing them so that each strip passes alternately over and under to produce a pattern of squares. By bending the work in progress vertically, adjacent surfaces can be interlaced to form three-dimensional shapes such as baskets and hen-houses. The Haddad make certain objects in this way, but most of their basketry is produced by twilling, i.e. a technique that in its simplest form implies that the basket-maker lets one strip pass over two or more other strips. Haddad basket-makers prefer to make basketry with a zigzag pattern, using two times three split strips of dum palm leaf and plaiting them alternately: three under, three over. But other patterns and methods are in use as well. Mats that are used to sit on are often adorned with a border of a different plait than the mat itself, for example simple twilling. The Haddad Kanembu make some very coarse straw mats that they use as fences to shield their homesteads in this technique as well. This, I believe, is a Kanembu custom that they have adopted.

Mats

Haddad women are extremely dab hands at making mats both for tents, walls in huts and for sleeping – in particular the Haddad Kreda women. The latter plait mats for their tents twilling strips of dum palm leaves, as described above. These are similar to those made by the women of the pastoralists. In camps where the two groups stay together, Haddad women regularly assist their Kreda 'hostesses' in plaiting these mats, or they carry out the work on their own as a service to the pastoralists. Both rural and urban Haddad women are renowned for a special kind of mat that they alone make for sleeping. This is made out of the stalks of dum palm leaves by plaiting these together with a double leather string. Similar mats are made by Kreda pastoralists. We came across two old women - one Haddad and one Kreda - who worked together on such a mat (cf. *Fig. 12,6*). Neither the Haddad nor the Kreda pastoralists have developed the technique of combining plant material and leather strips in the artistic way characteristic of

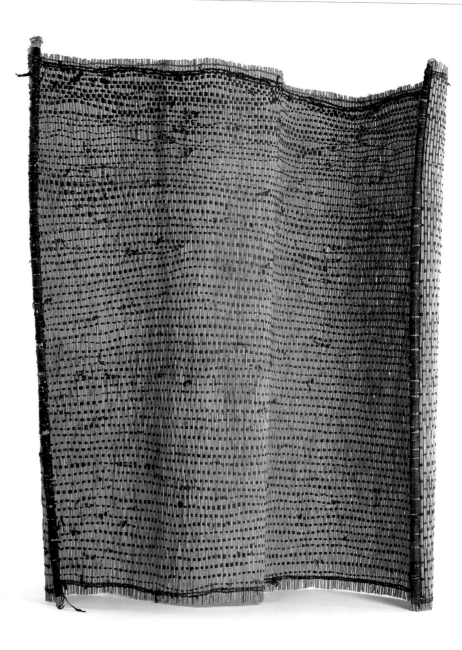

15,8. A sleeping mat made from reeds. The stems are tied together with leather bands. Cat. no. 124. Photo J.K.

North African pastoral peoples, be it the work of the Baggara of Darfur to the east or the exquisite reed and leather mats of the Tuareg and the Maures to the west.

URBAN ARTISANS

The town-dwelling Haddad are skilled craftsmen. The men work iron, silver, wood and hide for a living, while the women are potters, as just noted. A few make a living as dyers and weavers. Until the French colonization, Haddad artisans were the sole manufacturers and suppliers of weapons, tools, har-

nesses and saddles, pots and pans for Kanem and the Bahr el Ghazal as well as for the northern parts of the country. Despite changes and competition from European merchandise, Haddad products were still in considerable demand in the 1960s. Certain trades were facing difficulties, however. Local iron production had given in to European scrap metal and imported textiles had all but killed the products of Haddad weavers. Brightly coloured enamel basins, buckets and pots hit the eye and lured consumers to replace traditional earthenware pots and jars. While European footwear had not yet entered the market, it seemed bound to do so and replace the simple shoes the leather workers made for urban people.

The Haddad work and/or trade from tiny open sheds that provide shelter from the burning sun and in the rainy season the occasional shower. At times, they stay under the canopy of a large tree. Typically, the sheds consist of four posts supporting a few laths and a simple 'roof' of a mat or two. In these modest surroundings they produce merchandise that caters to the needs of their customers, urban as well as rural, pastoralists and farmers alike, and to the Haddad who make a living by hunting. Haddad artisans are found at the marketplace. In villages and towns with an all-week market most artisans carry out their craft at the marketplace. In areas where market days rotate between different locations the craftsmen may follow suit or work at their respective homesteads. Only potters come to the market exclusively to sell their products, as they produce and are compelled to carry out the firing elsewhere. Each craft is located at a specific section of the marketplace but next to other Haddad craftsmen. Here the artisans spend the day producing and/or selling their products, only to return in the afternoon to their respective dwellings. The number of Haddad craftsmen varies from town to town depending on the size and importance of the market and on whether or not they share their trades with other ethnic groups. In Mussoro, for example, half of the smiths identified themselves as Haddad, the other half as Kreda.

We had limited time to associate with and get to know urban Haddad artisans during our fieldwork - a visit that we thought was only the first in a series to come. We did collect data in the Bahr el Ghazal and also in the Kanemese town of Bol, where also the Danish geographer Krarup Mogensen had made some inquiries six years earlier. I shall draw on some of his data in the following to supplement our own, in particular on his description of pottery, dyeing methods and Kanembu terms for the tools these artisans use.

Smiths and Woodcarvers

The trade of Haddad smiths is age-old in Kanem and the Bahr el Ghazal. Knowledge of forging reached the area from Meroe in Egypt some 1,400 years ago, as far as we know, following the Bahr el Ghazal and then spreading further west (cf. Chapter 3: 83). The technological know-how of iron extraction from naturally occurring ore is complex. "The ore must be broken up, heated to a temperature of at least 1,100°C under carefully controlled conditions. To achieve such a temperature, aided only by the natural draught of a clay-built furnace and, usually, by hand-operated bellows,

is a major task in itself. Once smelted, the usable metal has to be separated from the waste products - the slag - and brought to its desired shape by repeated heating and hammering," David Phillipson notes (1985: 148-49).

The use of local iron extracted in Kanem and its immediate surroundings had become a thing of the past when we were there. Krarup Mogensen learned that melting had taken place in high ovens in the villages of Tchedadi near Mao in the previous generation. The ore had come from Brali, Kondou and Youmbou – the very same locations that produce ochre. Krarup Mogensen believes that it was in fact ochre that was used (1963, 10: 1). We came across no locally produced iron in the markets or elsewhere. The smiths all used scrap metal from European products, in particular from oil drums and cars.

The number of smith families varies from location to location. Many villages have no resident smiths, but are serviced by one on a rotational basis. Haddad smiths travel on their donkeys from village to village to cater to the needs of their customers, setting up their smithy wherever their skills are in demand. There were six smith families in Bol and Ngarangu, at least two in Dibinintchi and a single family at work in the villages of Isseirom, Njigidda and Sawa, respectively, at the time of Krarup Mogensen's study (ibid. 10: 1). N'Guigmi had more than twenty smiths around 1970 (Baroin 1991: 333). We encountered four to five families in Bol. Here and at Ngarangu, the smiths form cooperative groups, two at each location, one of them being in charge of the overall planning of the work of each group.

The tools that the smiths use are a double bag-bellow, *njefé* in Kanembu, of the type widely used in North Africa, the Sahara, among many Sudanese peoples and in East and South Africa (cf. J. Nicolaisen 1962: 73). The bellows are of goatskin, each with an attached earthenware mouthpiece partly covered by the embers placed in a hollow in the sand. The mouthpieces are tied to one another with a chain to keep them in position when in use. At the other end, the goatskins are furnished each with two pieces of wood. The bellows are operated by opening up and squeezing together the wooden pieces and subsequently filling and emptying the bag with air.

The red-hot iron is treated on a club-shaped anvil of iron, *kekíl*, a 40 cm long plug driven into the ground and stabilized by a piece of wood. Other tools are a pair of tongs, *bíti*, large and smaller hammers, *mánderaka*, a file, *jért*, a chisel, *njáltren*, a mandrel, *sútrem*, a whetstone, *kor*

15,9. Two Haddad smiths at work, one at the bellows the other embellishing calabashes with fine incisions using a red-hot tool. Split calabashes like these are used as cups and spoons. Tea is made in the tiny blue teapot on the embers. In front of the anvil are knives and hoes on display for potential customers. Bol.

koéyrem, and an adze, *sádaw.* All of these tools are similar to Europeans ones. This is not the case, however, with a flat, solid iron piece, known as *kâ kekílye,* which the smiths use to hammer out red-hot metal. Krarup Mogensen found this tool in two sizes in Ngarangu, but in one only at Bol. Peculiar to the Haddad craft is also a small pointed spear, *gengánjerem* or *kâda* that the smiths use to surface and engrave specimens. Smith apply the broad, flat side of the spear to do the smoothing, while ornamentation is done with the point. Characteristic is also a short wooden stick with a hole at one end, *sémam,* which is used to stabilize the hot item being forged. Lastly, the use of a tool known as *céwrem,* a wooden shaft with an iron point, that is used to tend to embers and rake out slag (Krarup Mogensen 1963, 10: 2-3).

On market days the smiths move their smithies to the marketplace to cater for the many buyers. They sell prefabricated products, receive commissions and do repairs. Haddad smiths make quite an assortment of products. The most prominent are heads for arrows, spears, lances and harpoons, throwing and sheath knives.[2] They produce riding equipment for horses such as caves sons and stirrups, simple bridles for camels as well as hoes and other agricul-

15,10. Haddad smiths work and sell their produce at markets. The stalls are put up next to one another, generally at the outskirts of markets. Bol. ▶

tural implements. A variety of household utensils are for sale: tripods for cooking pots, scrapers for preparing hides (Cat. No. 71), double-edged kitchen knives (Cat. No. 70), hammers for chopping pieces off sugar cones, etc. Braziers, pans, ladles and spoons are probably more recent additions to the repertoire of the smiths and due to European influence (Krarup Mogensen 1963, 10: 4). Smiths also cater to vanity. They make objects for personal hygiene and beauty care such as tweezers and the iron pins that women use for smearing antimony around the eyes.

Haddad smiths also work in wood, primarily with an adze and red-hot or at least very hot knives, which they use for engraving some of their products. They shaft weapons and agricultural implements and make handles for hammers, axes and adzes, knives and other tools that they forge. Smiths produce the wooden frames for saddles, and they make mortars and pestles, stools, bedposts, bedsteads, cupboards and other kinds of furniture as well as clubs for leatherworkers and dyers. Decorated pieces of wood are usually further embellished by charring, using a red-hot iron tool. The Haddad beautify stools, pestles and mortars this way, but most of the woodwork done by the smiths is simple. There is no traceable influence from the great woodcarving traditions to the south or from Wadai, from where there is an import of the elaborate and highly prized bowls found among the Kanembu. Smiths also take on repairs and work on commission. Finished products are piled up in front of the workplace to attract customers.

15,11. A Haddad smith handles the double bag-bellow. The other smiths heats the tool he is working on in the glowing embers. Behind the embers stands the club-like anvil. Bol

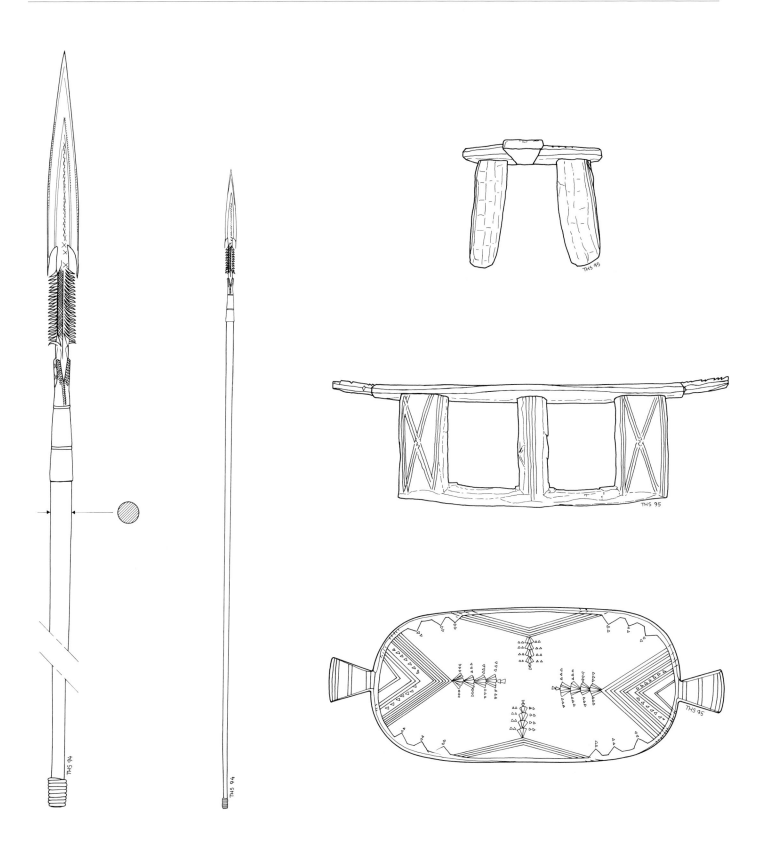

15,12. Spear of the kind carried by Kreda pastoralists.
The drawing shows the fine workmanship of Haddad smiths.
Cat. no. 93. Drawing by T.O.S.

15,13. Woodcarving is also a specialty of Haddad smiths. They
produce handles for tools, bedposts, bowls and stools like the
one shown here. Drawing by T.O.S.

Jewellers

Some Haddad smiths make silver jewellery: bracelets, necklaces and the rings that, for example, Kreda women carry in one nostril. Silver still comes from melting Marie Theresia thalers and the five Franc coin. Especially the Marie Theresia thaler enjoyed wide usage and popularity due to its high silver content. Minted by the Italians with the portrait of the German-Roman empress of the Habsburg Empire (1717-80), the thaler was the only currency in Kanem and Bahr el Ghazal as in most of North Africa until World War I. It was used not only as a means of exchange but also as jewellery, either hung in a leather string around the neck or sewn unto garments. Most silver jewellery at the markets at the time of our visit was of mixed origin, however, and generally of quite a low silver content. Jewellery of 'white iron' or aluminium was widespread. The tools of the silversmiths were a tiny ladle, *kesángerem* or *léla* (i.e. silver) for melting the metal and eventually a tiny, earthenware mould (Krarup Mogensen 1963, 10: 3). Haddad smiths also work in copper and brass, making bracelets, ankle rings and small rings for lances and spears for magical protection. Krarup Mogensen writes about the fabrication of a silver bracelet that he witnessed in Ngarangu in 1957. It was made from an old one, too small for the customer, and an additional Maria Theresia thaler:

"The old bracelet was broken in pieces with a hammer and melted in a crucible in the embers in front of the bellows. Then the melted silver was poured in a furrow in the sand into which there had first been poured some melted butter. More butter was poured over the silver and then this was covered by sand. After a few minutes the solidified mass was pulled out with tongs. It looked like a cigar but was of a golden-red colour. It was then beaten till twice the original length with the flat iron instrument, *kâ kekilye* through a process where the silver was repeatedly heated in the embers to get the right temperature. Using the flat instrument and a small hammer, the one end was turned into threads, while the other ended in a point. The entire object was now about 45 cm long, about one half constituted by the silver threads. The smith held the thick end with tongs, the threads with *seman,* i.e. the wooden stick with a hole that was mentioned above. He folded the silver threads over the thicker part of the object while at the same time twisting

this to a spiral form with the tongs and a hammer. The item was heated up once again in the embers in order to beat this to a ring over a hole in the piece of wood of the anvil. The bracelet now had its proper form but was only given to the customer after the smith had boiled it for five minutes in a pot with leaves of *Hibiscus sabdariffa.* Then it was dried and polished with sand." (Ibid. 1963, 10: 6; IN transl.)

Saddlers and shoemakers

Another age-old profession in Kanem and the Bahr el Ghazal is saddlery and the making of sandals. Historically, the Kanuri were famous horsemen and warriors (cf. Chapter 3) who not only required saddles and harnesses but also leather coats of mail (cf. *Fig. 3,8).* While the latter is a thing of the past, riding is still the most common means of transportation and saddles and harnesses are still in great demand. Most people walk barefoot. We saw no footwear among the Haddad and very little among the Kreda pastoralists, but wooden slippers are in use in villages as are leather sandals and shoes. The latter are of a simple, sock-shaped type or of the North-African style with a high counter and long flap. Imported European style shoes were used by some officials in towns. Shoemakers also fabricate simple leather boots without heels (cf. Cat. No. 85) and, more rarely, European-style riding boots. Generally, both boots and shoes are made on commission. Finally, the saddlers make sheaths for knives and swords, purses and amulet covers.

Haddad saddlers work in the open air under a tree or a simple open shed. Like the smiths they set up their workplace at markets to sell their produce and receive commissions. They will usually carry out the tanning process of the hides themselves using the methods described above, but Krarup Mogensen notes that the saddler mentioned below bought his hides from a colleague. These urban artisans colour the hides in white, black, red, green and yellow. The saddler produces the first two himself, the white by soaking the leather for a day in a mixture of milk and salt (one handful of salt to two litres of milk), the black by mixing slag from the forge with water, a little millet porridge and a bit of sugar. Colouring with red, green and yellow is usually done with European products that are bought at the market, although red can be made from the hollow stems of red millet (Krarup Mogensen 1963, 10: 8). Saddlers do not make their own tools except those of wood but acquire

15,14. Wooden bowl used for storage and display among the Kanembu and Haddad Kanembu. I was told that these bowls are made around Ati, Kororo and Lake Fitri and sold at the market at Masakory. We did not see any of them on display at the smiths' shops at Bol, Mussoro or N'Guri. Cat. no. 36a. Photo J.K.

15,15. Haddad saddlers and shoemakers are fine artisans. Johannes and I had a pair of boots of delicate goatskin made to measure in a few hours. They proved very useful, in particular as protection against the prickly cram-cram and snakes when walking at night. Cat. no. 85. Photo J.K.

these from smiths. The division of labour is such that few saddlers make the woodwork of saddles either, but turn to the smiths for this too. The tools are mostly traditional to North Africa but some are of European or Arabian origin although forged locally. In 1957, there were four saddlers and shoemakers in Bol. One of them, Boukar Baremi used the following tools: A piece of wood some 30 x 50 cm called *barám* in Kanembu, that functions a 'bed' when hammering in nails; a last, *kóli;* scissors in two sizes, *máso;* a bodkin, *kentám;* a hammer, *mándera-* ka; a knife for cutting out the leather, *gyâna kéra;* a knife for engraving, *gyâna corderòm;* a wooden club, *kantúl* or *kelkól;* a shoehorn, *kapún;* a pair of pincers, *swiy kúltu;* a pointed almond-shaped instrument for smoothing out straightening edges, *askílerem;* a slightly curved wooden stick, *kâ ngenjìye,* some 30 cm long that is used to insert temporarily a piece of leather, *jáda ngenjíye,* in the toe of the shoe while the shoe itself is made on the last; a corresponding piece that is placed at the counter of the shoe, *jáda ngówye;* a file, *jért;* a brush, *bros* and a needle, *líbera.*

The hammer, pincers, file and brush are all European products. Other tools are made by local smiths, as already mentioned, except for brushes which have recently been introduced from Europe (ibid. 10: 7).

Dyers and weavers

Dyeing cotton materials for clothing was also in the professional hands of the Haddad, interestingly enough for Carbou notes that: "while dyeing is a highly respected and significant profession in Bornu, it is looked down upon among the Kanembu and hence left to the Haddad" (Carbou 1912, I: 39). There is little doubt that dyeing was a major trade in Kanem and the Bahr el Ghazal in the early 20th century, but it gradually lost economic significance. Indigo died clothes were fashionable here as elsewhere in the Sahel region, but in the decades after World War II men's clothes were increasingly made of un-dyed cotton material. The indigo plant, *Indigo tinotonia,* is grown locally but dyeing is mostly done with chemically produced pigment to enhance the colour or using this as an addendum to natural produce. Johannes and I were not in contact with Haddad dyers, but Krarup Mogensen observed some of these at work: "Usually the preparation of the pigment is undertaken by the dyer personally, but it can also be bought at markets in cake-shaped pieces, each 6 cm long and 3-4 cm thick. These consist of a mixture of green indigo leaves that have been pounded in a mortar and then mixed with some pigment and a little water (one spoonful pigment to two litres of leaves) to be dried in the sun. "Normally the dyeing is undertaken in huge earthenware pots, *kawyé alímbo* (Kanembu), that have been dug into the ground and hold some 15 to 20 litres. The pot is filled with water, 200 to 300 pieces of the dyeing material and a similar amount of natron (burnt in the embers), as well as with a tea glass full of pigment. The mixture is left in the pot for two to three days and is then ready for use. The cloth is put in the dyeing liquid for about ten minutes, during which one turns it with a stick to make sure that all of the material gets soaked in the colour. Then the cloth is wrung and dried. If a deeper colour is required, the process will be repeated. A single bath in the pot colours the cloth light blue, three times gives a deep indigo. When the dyeing process is almost complete but the cloth not yet entirely dry, it is washed. After still more drying, the cloth is beaten on a piece of wood with a wooden hammer, *kantúl,* (Kanembu). This final treat-ment smoothes the material in much the same way as does ironing. The colour can be used continuously for about two months if applied regularly and occasionally adding some new pigment. If left unused, the dye will spoil in about two weeks." (Krarup Mogensen 1963, 10: 10; IN transl.)

Also the craft of weaving is rapidly disappearing in Kanem and the Bahr el Ghazal, as industrially produced cotton cloth conquers the market. We met no Haddad weavers, but a few weavers of other ethnic affiliation in Fort-Lamy. They were all in the business of producing blankets, both of cotton and goat's hair, predominantly white with black and red stripes and occasionally more elaborated, geometrical designs. However, Krarup Mogensen came across a few Haddad weavers still carrying out their trade using locally grown and spun cotton by Yedina and Kanembu women. They worked their tablet-looms with pedals, producing eight-centimetre-broad pieces of cloth in various lengths. Later, the fabric would be sewn together by the purchaser into a piece of cloth of suitable breadth and length for clothing and eventually sent for dyeing (ibid. 10: 9).

Pottery - the craft of women

While forging is an all-male profession pottery is made exclusively by women. In fact, most of the pottery in use among the various ethnic groups of Kanem and Bahr el Ghazal comes from the kilns of Haddad women. These female artisans do not work in a social vacuum. The ones with whom we were in contact were all sisters and in some way the relatives of Haddad smiths and leather workers.

Pottery is sold at market places, where Haddad women line up their stalls and products: the heavy jars used for water, cooking pots of various sizes, small jars, bottles, buckets, braziers etc. The profession is under pressure, however, as imported cooking pots, brightly decorated enamelled tin basins and trays and also the first plastic buckets and jars become available and catch the eye of the consumer. Still, the huge but heavy earthenware jars and cooking pots were the ones in use among both the settled Kanembu and the pastoralists at the time of our visit. Haddad potters make quite good money. A skilled potter can produce some five water jars or nine to ten pots a day at an average prize of 100-150

15,16. Haddad women selling their pots at the market at Bol.

15,17. Haddad women use various techniques when making pots. The bottoms of water jars are made by hand. The potter uses a slightly curved earthenware piece and the rib-bone of a cow to beat the clay into the desired shape and thickness. To the right of the woman are three finished pieces. Ngarangu. Photo K.M. Fig. 10,26; 24.9.1957.

15,18. The upper part of the water jar is coiled up with sausage-shaped pieces of clay. Ngarangu. Photo K.M. Fig. 10,27; 24.9.1957.

15,19. When the pot has been coiled up the inner and outer surface is smoothened by hand. Ngarangu. Photo K.M. Fig. 10,29; 24.9.1957.

15,20. Some potters decorate their cooking pots and the smaller ones that are used as braziers: cooking pots with a simple pattern made with a cord prior to firing; braziers with geometrical patterns with chalk after firing. Ngarangu. Photo K.M. Fig. 10,28; 24.9.1957.

15,21. Two Haddad potters prepare for the firing of their pots. The firing takes place in a circular pit in the ground. The pit was lined with straw before the pots were placed and covered with potsherds and donkey dung. The firing takes one night. Ngarangu. Photo K.M. 10,30; 24.9.1957.

CFA apiece. There is of course some loss, either in production and transport, or for other reasons, including the time that the potters must set aside to sell their produce at the market. However, potters may earn as much as about 400 CFA a week, according to Krarup Mogensen (1963, 10: 14).

Haddad potters are at work all over Kanem and Bahr el Ghazal except for Baga Sola, where earthenware is produced by the Kotoko.[3] Important centres of production are Dibinintchi and Ngarangu, where no less than 25 and 11 potters were at work in 1957. The same type of earthenware is made in a number of small towns and villages in this part of Kanem including Moun, Sawa, Yiló, Y'wla, Isseirom and Bol. We saw them at the market in Bol, where potters had them for sale, but the variety of Haddad produce is considerable in the vast region that they serve. The quality of the pots of the Ngarangu potters is unsurpassed in that part of Kanem, according to Krarup Mogensen who observed potters at work at Bol, Moun and Ngarangu and found that the overall technique was similar in all three places, but that different clays were used by the potters. The ensuing description of Haddad pottery relies on his observations.

The Ngarangu potters prefer and use imported clay from a place called Tuiy. Clay is available locally in many places but of inferior quality. Before the potter begins to form the material, the clay is mixed with dried donkey dung. For water jars the proportions will be 1:1, while other pots are made of a mixture of clay, dried donkey dung and finely crushed ceramics in the proportions 2:1:1. Both the dry dung and the ceramic material are pounded into a very fine powder before being mixed with the clay. The tools of the potters are simple: a tray of basketry on which the pots are made; a mushroom-shaped tool, known in Kanembu as *tutûdo,* that is applied when making larger pots; calabash pieces and/or a sea-shell for scraping; the pealed ear of maize to smooth the pot's surface; a *Calotropis* leaf in use when shaping the rim of the pot and a piece of dum palm cord to make decorative imprints (Krarup Mogensen 1963, 10: 11).

Haddad potters build up some pots freely by hand, others are made by coiling. The former of these two basic techniques is applied for smaller pots, the latter for the big water jars. For some pots both techniques are made us of. Furthermore, the bottoms of water jars are made in different ways. At Bol the potters moulded the bottom of the jar on top of an existing one, while the potters of Ngarangu built up every jar anew. Some of the potters here created the bottom of the jar using the *tutûdo* to stamp the clay into the intended thickness, after which they let this dry for half a day before resuming work on the upper part of the jar. Other potters made the jar at one go. Firstly, they shaped the bottom with their bare hands, then this was placed on the basket tray, *kwêrê keléye,* and turning this gently from time to time the potter continued her work from the bottom up to the rim without pausing. Krarup Mogensen is of the opinion, that the two techniques reflect two different cultural traditions, the use of the *tutûdo* stemming from Daza pastoralists, the simpler one of building up the jar without any tools being the local Kanembu tradition. The wheel is unknown throughout the region. Krarup Mogensen describes the production of a water jar and a pot respectively as follows:

"Clay and dung are pugged thoroughly on a mat, after which the mass is turned into 12 to 15 cm large balls. This is done in a hole in the ground lined with dung and covered by a mat. Using the mushroom-shaped *tutûdo,* one of the balls is gradually stamped into the shape of a pot, some 25 cm in diameter. Later the sides of the pot are stamped even thinner by holding the concave side of the *tutûdo* on the inner side of the pot and beating the clay lightly from the other side with a flat rib-bone of a cow. The pot is then left to dry for half a day, after which work is resumed, clay coils being added twice to the rim of the pot and smoothed by hand until the right shape is acquired while the pot is turned around in the sand. The potter made use of the ear of maize, pieces of calabash and the sea-shell in this process. Finally, the neck of the pot was made using a leaf of the *Calotropis* while turning the pot and then the handles were added. After a few days, the pot was ornamented with a pattern. The colour pigment was ochre purchased from Mao. The colour is dissolved in water and applied by means of a rug or the fingers. The firing took place three days later" (ibid. 10: 12; IN transl.).

The creation of the cooking pot went as follows:

"Clay, dung and ceramic powder were pugged thoroughly and shaped by hand into balls with a diameter of about 10 cm. A ball crudely bowl-shaped by hand was placed on the basket tray. Here the ensuing work took place. When the base had been created, the remaining part of the pot was made by a coiling process similar to the one used to make the water jar. The pot was placed on the tray basket to enable the potter to rotate it more easily than had been the case with the jar [which had been placed in the sand - IN]. The ornamentation of this pot was similar to other pots, the pattern being stamped into the clay with a piece of cord soon after the completion of the pot" (ibid. 10: 12; IN transl.).

The firing takes place in a hole about 2 metres in diameter and 50 cm deep and lined with straw. The pots are placed with the base turning upwards and covered with a layer of potsherds on top of which one strews donkey dung and some ash. The fire is lit by a girl (to ensure success) and burns throughout the night. It is rarely so successful, however, that all of the pots can be used. Some 10 % at an average are lost (ibid. 10: 11-12). Haddad potters at Ngarangu produced the following kinds of pots, according to Krarup Mogensen, who noted down their respective names in Kanembu:

a. *Njóro,* a large pear-shaped pot for transporting water. Newly made specimens can be used for storage of cold water, but as the pores gradually close due to the secretion of salt and continuous transport on peoples' heads and backs the porosity is lost and the cooling property disappears. Normally therefore, cold water is stored in another type of jar, known as *kélo-kélo.* The ornamentation depends on the size of the pot. It consists of band- and finger imprints. Jars of this type come in five different sizes all with lips.

b. *Kélo-kélo,* a jar for water storage and, occasionally for soaking millet prior to cooking. It comes in two sizes and is decorated with a pattern made with a twisted cord or a broad band in ochre around the neck.

c. *Kélo,* a pot made in at least six sizes. The smallest, *kelomá,* is used for melting butter and for keeping food and hot water for children. Food is usually cooked in a *kélo* and then poured into a *kelomá,* covered with a lid, and placed near the fireplace to keep warm. The *kelomá* is also used when milking goats. The ornamentation is always a pattern made with a twisted cord.

d. *Bêlé,* a pot that comes in three versions: One with two handles that is used as a bucket to bring food for work and/ or for carrying milk and water from the well. The second type is used for eating and drinking and the third to store holy, cleansed water for ritual use.

e. *Tulú,* a bottle-shaped earthenware used by men as a container for holy water. It is painted in ochre all over and comes in one size and shape only.

f. *Sindal,* a pot for holy water used for rituals by women. It is always fitted with a lip and decorated with an ochre coloured pattern similar to the *njóro.*

g. *Kongíy dowskerón,* an undecorated pan that comes in two sizes.

h. *Kawyó alímbo,* a jar, about 50 cm high that is used for dyeing. It comes in one size only and is always without ornamentation.

i. *Wonaróm,* a bowl used for burning incense and fetching embers [women collect these from one another's fireplaces to save the trouble of making a fire themselves when going to cook, perhaps for ritual reasons too - IN]. It comes in one size only and is coloured by ochre except for the base.

j. *Fúgo sháye,* a brazier with a hollow base from which a tiny opening leads up to the plate itself. It is furnished with 3 x 3 holes decorated with ochre and made in one size only.

k. *Kólo kesaróm,* a pot with lip for pouring melted butter into the nose. This remedy is applied in the rainy season to cure a range of ailments. The pot is normally without ornamentation, but sometimes coloured with ochre. It comes in one size only.

l. *Gwiy,* a support for pots in the shape of an 'upside-down' cup. It is usually without decoration, except for an occasional colouring with ochre. The production of these supports is dwindling (ibid. 10: 12-14).

MARKETS AND MERCHANDISE

The Haddad are largely self-sufficient. They cover basic needs by foraging, hunting and agro-pastoral activities, make their own huts and tents from material that they cut in the surrounding nature and they produce a good deal of the tools, utensils and other material objects needed in daily life. Yet, both Haddad groups depend on economic exchanges with other ethnic groups as well as with Haddad smiths. We may recall that the Haddad Kreda offer labour and game in exchange for milk and protection from Kreda pastoralists, and that the Haddad Kanembu offer services to the Kanembu in exchange for rights to cultivate on Kanembu land. Both groups rely on the market to trade for salt, cloth, iron tools, utensils and weapons, certain wooden objects and luxury items like butter and perfume. The Haddad Kreda occasionally go to the market to pur-

15,22. Spices for sale at the market at Bol.

chase millet, as may the Haddad Kanembu if their harvest is poor. Both groups may come to trade small ruminants. It is mostly the Haddad Kanembu who own a few goats, but some Haddad Kreda are picking up animal husbandry after the ending of the ban on their possession of domestic animals, apart from donkeys, as previously mentioned. Haddad artisans, on the other hand, base their existence on trading and produce for the market.

The environment of Kanem and the Bahr el Ghazal offers fine economic conditions for both agriculture and agro-pastoralism, as we have seen, and the market reflects this rural inclination. There is lively activity at the local marketplaces, where farmers, pastoralists and artisans buy and sell their produce. Professional traders, in particular from Nigeria, turn up at some of these to buy cattle, sheep and goats, camels, horses, hides and near the lake also dried sodium and

fish. They bring with them various goods, especially textiles. At the market sugar and tea and kerosene are also sold.

Markets are weekly events, held on specific days in various towns in Kanem, i.e. N'Guri, Ngarangu, Liwa, Baga Sola, Bol, Rig-Rig, Isseirom, Ngélea, Waydula, Nyideko and Dibinintchi, the last-named being by far the largest of them all. It was frequented by some 800 to 1000 people on market days, while markets in N'Guri, Baga Sola and Bol had only half that number in 1957, according to Krarup Mogensen (1963, 10: 5). We visited the markets of the last-named town three times as well as those in Mussoro and Mao. The population of these cities was so large that a small number of Lebanese and Arab merchants were able to make a living, conducting their businesses from tiny shops near the marketplace on a daily basis. Occasionally, Lebanese merchants are found in some of the minor towns

15,23. Haddad female potters with their wares. Bol.

as well. We got quite familiar with the marketplace at Bol. Our observations are in concordance with those of Krarup Mogensen and I shall draw on some of his data to offer a fuller picture than provided by our material alone.

Bol is a small town with a few scattered government buildings and quarters for officers. The local population consists mainly of Yedina and Kanembu families, whose roomy compounds behind tall straw mats deprive the place of any sense of city. The town is built on dunes that make driving hard and walking quite fatiguing. The marketplace is in the west end of the town. It is quite small, some 55 x 45 metres, and fenced in with straw mats. Behind it one finds a three-winged adobe hall built by the administration, the only one, as a matter of fact, in any Kanemese city. This is where firewood, meat and textiles are sold, each commodity in its section of the hall. A few stalls are put up at the mouth of each of the four streets that lead into the marketplace. At the centre are 'the permanent structures': five rows of stalls, simple constructions of poles with a torn mat or two as roof to provide shade from the burning sun. These belong to the Kanembu traders of the town and to Haddad artisans, while other traders that come to Bol on market days do their business in the open.

The marketplace is divided along ethnic lines that coincide with differences in livelihood and hence the produce that the groups bring for sale and are interested in buying. Haddad smiths, potters and craftsmen conduct their business to the north and east of the market building. Furthest to the east are the smiths and shoemakers with their goods. To the west of these are female potters from Bol and Moun selling their earthenware and still further to the west of them are Haddad women selling mats and baskets. The potters from Ngarangu sell their merchandise in another section of the marketplace, namely at the south-eastern corner north of the stalls of the Yedina. The pastoral Fulani, take up the north-eastern corner, from where they sell their main products. They bring fresh butter, which the women melt and bottle, while the men bring and sell firewood and fodder for horses, cattle and goats. To the south of the Fulani are some former slaves, trading their only produce: salt. To the east of these one finds Daza pastoralists, selling dates which they have brought in part from Mao in part from Borku, the place where they also get salt. The Daza also sell fodder for horses and various food items that they collect, such as the skin of dum palm fruit, which is used

15,24. Storing earnings safely in a tin. Bol.

as a sweetener, the spicy leaves from a bush known as *mbu-lubúl* in Kanembu, another spicy plant known as *katafé*, as well as the beets of *Cyperus esculentus*, which can be eaten raw or roasted. The roasted beets are pounded and kneaded with butter and lukewarm water. The south-eastern corner of the place and the streets leading into this are occupied by the Yedina. Most of the traders here are women who sell millet, wheat, milk, butter, chicken and fish (both fresh, dried and smoked) as well as the oval mats for which they are rightly famous in the region. Further to the south, one finds the men selling cattle and goats at the section that constitutes the cattle fair. Here one also finds Kanembu men selling their cattle, goats and sheep.

At the centre are the colourful stalls of the Kanembu as their merchandise is much more varied than that of the other ethnic groups, reflecting a fan of their agro-pastoral subsistence activities. At the stalls one can buy millet, wheat and maize, the last-named both as kernels and cobs from huge, brightly decorated enamel basins. There are red onions, garlic and beans for sale as well as tomatoes (dried and fresh), manioc and sweet potatoes. Some stalls have *Hibiscus esculentus* (both whole and in piecemeal), *Solanum incanum*, fresh mint, gourds and papayas, all from their own plots and vegetable gardens. From these also come spices like Spanish pepper and coriander. A few sell green and black tea and sugar, both granulated and cones. Some bring sugar cane to be chewed as a sweet. This is a widely used stimulant, especially among the Kanembu themselves. Cola nuts and tobacco is also provided by these market women. The dried tobacco leaves are chewed, never smoked. Smoking is not considered appropriate among the Kanembu and Yedina, Krarup Mogensen writes, but quite a number of men do smoke nevertheless, and cigarettes are on sale at the market. Kanembu women also offer prepared food, either couscous or various kinds of cakes, the favourite being made from peanuts or onions. The pastoral part of Kanembu economy produces live animals, which are for sale at the outskirts of the marketplace – horses, cattle, sheep, goats or donkeys – as is meat. Chickens are usually sold by the women at the stalls, as are eggs and sometimes fermented milk. Sale of fish is economically important to some Kanembu as it is to the Yedina – fresh, smoked or dried. Occasionally, a Kanembu brings crocodile or hippopotamus meat or vegetable products from a foraging expedition. Krarup Mogensen mentions pods of the tamarind tree (*Tamarindus indica*), a kind of butter made from *Butyrospermum parkii*, berries from a nightshade plant and kernels from the *Balinites*. The Kanembu sell medicinal plants and seeds, moreover, some cultivated others wildgrowing. The most common medicine is one called trona that appears to be used against almost any ailment.[4]

Textiles occupy still another section of the marketplace. Here one can purchase fabrics and the homespun cotton thread for weaving on the narrow tablet weaves on which all textiles were made traditionally. Almost all clothing in Kanem and the Bahr el Ghazal is made from industrially produced textiles from Nigeria, either cotton or rayon or other artificial fibres. All ethnic groups prefer white or indigo coloured clothes, but vivid colours do occur. Textiles are relatively expensive and a considerable drain on the household budget. Krarup Mogensen claims

15,25. Corn for sale. Bol.

that thin white cotton cloth cost as much as 100 CFA per metre in 1957.

Pomades, incense and a range of other perfumed and coloured articles for personal hygiene and the smartening up of oneself loom prominently as well. Krarup Mogensen counted more than a score of these products, the most popular being henna, which is used by women for the decoration of hands and feet (cf. Chapter 14). One can buy other imported goods which cater to basic needs such as vividly coloured enamel trays, basins, bowls and plates that one finds in all Haddad Kanembu but not all Haddad Kreda households, teapots and glasses for the highly appreciated drinking of tea, and spoons. Knives and forks are not used for eating. One can also buy safety-pins, needles, shaving blades, mirrors, combs, soap and blue for washing and personal hygiene, as well as sun-glasses and ordinary glasses. The latter are not on the market to cater to poor eyesight but simply as finery, as the spectacles are made from simple glass. For sale are also matches and torches, pencils, writing pads and envelopes, empty bottles and naphtalin (Krarup Mogensen 1963, 10: 6-9).

The Haddad Kreda and the Haddad Kanembu frequent the local markets, largely to buy millet and other necessities like clothes and salt, as we have heard but also, occasionally, to sell produce from their hunting and foraging activities like hides or basketry. However, it is the urban artisans that dominate local markets, selling the products that have been described above.

NOTES

1. A slightly different tanning procedure of a hide that preserved the hair was observed in a purely pastoral Kreda camp. Here the women were in charge of the entire process. They did not use wooden pegs, but stretched the hide with strings between four poles with the inner side upwards. Then they poured a tannin substance of pounded acacia pods and water directly on top of the hide and continued by scraping the hide with knives, irons and occasionally the iron blade of a hoe. I was told, however, that they followed the tanning procedure of the Haddad when hides were undergoing the complete tanning process of removing the hair.

2. Krarup Mogensen mentions that smiths also make swords. We did not hear of this. He believes that the forging of swords is a consequence of Tuareg and European influence (1963, 10: 4).

3. The ceramic forms produced here are also found in Limboy and Nglidou near Liwa (Krarup Mogensen 1963, 10: 10).

4. Plants used both as a spice and as medicine are mentioned by their Kanembu name by Krarup Mogensen: lévan kadiá, lévan oílan, kásebar and wúlwa, but also Melegueta-pepper is applied as medicine in particular against headaches and stomach pains. A plant called fisú is used against fatigue. It is pounded, mixed with butter and smeared on the body (1963, 11: 7).

16:

16: PERSPECTIVES

Foraging peoples have carved a living for themselves throughout the Sahel region since ancient times, first as the only inhabitants of these vast stretches, later in coexistence with pastoral nomads, semi-settled agro-pastoral groups and settled agriculturalists. A number of foragers have pursued their age-old trade into the 20th century, at which point commercial hunting, population pressure, colonial policies and other kinds of man-made impacts on the habitat caught up with them and put such curbs on hunting that they were forced to seek other means of subsistence. In general, little is known about these hunting societies, so little in fact that scholars have claimed that they had ceased to exist as autonomous hunters and gatherers in this part of Africa at the time of European contact (cf. Robertshaw 1999: 187). Still, written sources confirm that a number of hunting societies from the Nemadi of Mauretania to the Haddad of Chad continued their way of life well into the 20th century.

Haddad subsistence is intimately associated with the habitat of Kanem and the Bahr el Ghazal, as we have seen. It is based on two different hunting strategies adapted to the slightly different ecological conditions of Kanem proper and the middle ranges of the Bahr el Ghazal, respectively. The Haddad Kreda have used nets to gain a living, a hunting technique that is age-old in Africa. It still sustains foraging groups in the rainforests of Congo but no other foraging communities on the Sahelien plains to the best of my knowledge. The Haddad Kanembu have relied on hunting in disguise with bow and arrows, as did hunters in the region in pre-historic times. Whether the two Haddad groups have a common past is questionable. Oral traditions point to the north for the net-hunting Haddad Kreda with ties to Manga and Chitati and to a possible migration to the Bahr el Ghazal with pastoral groups. The history of the bow hunting Haddad Kanembu has Kanem as the historical epicentre and offers traces to the fabled Sao people and a branch of the noble Bulala at Lake Fitri. Over time both Haddad groups adapted to changing environmental, economic and social conditions and reinvented their modes of subsistence, cosmologies, religious beliefs and values in tune with externally imposed changes. The latter prompted them to redefine relations with other groups as well. The transformations have been massive. During the 19th and the early part of the 20th century the Haddad came under pressure, in particular due to commercial hunting, extreme social insurgency and the spread of Islam. Commercial ostrich hunting exploded to satisfy the needs of fashion-conscious women in Europe and the Americas and of European armies. The hunt took a devastating toll on the population of the bird and brought a halt to a trade which had flourished since antiquity and one on which the Haddad had thrived (Lhote 1951: 148, 150, 152). Another blow to Haddad existence was a drastic decrease in the stock of Oryx, Damalisque and Addax antelopes partly due to the introduction of automatic weapons. Other significant factors were the widespread social unrest caused by marauding Awlad Sliman and Tubu, and the introduction of colonial rule by the French. At the time of Johannes' and my fieldwork in the 1960s the combined effects of these factors and not the least the government's decree against indigenous hunting threatened the very foundation of Haddad existence. In fact, the prohibition against hunting amounted to no less than cultural genocide in my view.

The environmental and turbulent socio-political conditions in Kanem and the Bahr el Ghazal are crucial to a general understanding of Haddad existence at the time of our study, but do not suffice when seeking insight into the dissimilarities in Haddad Kreda and Haddad Kanembu ways of life, more specifically their different hunting methods, social organization and cultural perceptions of hunting and its premises and the ways in which these issues are interlinked. To gain some perspective on these issues, let us for a moment turn to discussions and theories which address some of these problems drawing on data from other foraging groups in Africa.

NET HUNTERS AND ARCHERS

The hunting technologies used by the Haddad Kreda and the Haddad Kanembu are ancient in Africa, as just intimated. The old Egyptians placed nets across minor valleys to catch wildlife with the assistance of dogs, for example, and hunting with bow and arrow and the use of disguise is also known from pre-historic times. In the 19th and the beginning of the 20th century nets were still in use throughout Africa. Certain clans among the pastoral Bahima went hunting with nets, for example (Lindblom 1926, II: 115), and the Dor living up the tributaries of the Bahr el Ghazal in Sudan chased game against convergent gates of nets with pits at each end (Heuglin 1869: 201). The Acholi east of Lake Albert in Uganda organized communal hunts with about a thousand participants at the time of Baker's expedition there in 1871-73. We are told that the hunters were all dressed up in "ostrich feathers, leopard skin mantles, and their faces painted a frightful colour with fresh cowdung," that one or to oxen were slaughtered, according to the wealth of the person who gave the festivity, and that a sorcerer was at work ... "to assure good luck by a variety of magic ceremonies, that would not only protect the hunters from accidents, but would bring the wild animals direct into their nets" (Baker, 1890: 436). In the latter respect they differ from the Haddad Kreda who never invoke magic to further their hunting luck. Baker describes a hunt with numerous men, women and children, some of the women carrying babies strapped to their back, protected from the

sun with gourd-shells. The Acholi placed their nets in a line of about a mile and a half.

"Each man had lashed his net to that of his neighbour and supported it with bamboos, which were secured with ropes fastened to twisted grass. Thus the entire net resembled a fence that would be invisible to the game in the high grass, until when driven, they should burst suddenly upon it." Fire was lit to make the game flee and run into the nets. At this particular hunt the participants caught a great many antelopes, while several buffaloes broke out in different directions, lions passed by and a rhinoceros went "though their nets like a cobweb" (ibid. 437).

The use of fire as a 'hunting weapon' appears to have been widespread among people living on savannas as was the use of dogs. Apparently, the Haddad Kreda did not use fire probably because they either hunted in the barren desert or desert-like county to the north or on land that provided pastures for the herds of the pastoral groups they lived among. But they too relied on dogs in particular in their hunts for antelope. Collective hunting with nets and dogs is not limited to foragers living on the African savanna or Sahelien plains. It is also used by foragers in the rainforests of Central Africa, for instance the Bakele of Gabon (Roscoe 1990, 3: 691) and the Babongo of Congo. Among the latter this form of hunting has been described by Anderson as a newer and exclusively male method of hunting (Anderson 1939: 89-99). The most well known of the foragers still applying nets are some of the Pygmy groups. Some of these make use of a single, long net, as do the Batwa; others put up series of shorter nets at a time. Only few foragers seem to combine the use of nets with the setting up of sticks with bundles of skin to create the illusion of human beings, as do the Haddad Kreda. Lindblom notes, for example, that as far as he knows the Bushmen are the only ones to do so in Africa (1925, II: 130-33). Stow offers the following description of how they carry on:

"When the Bushmen wished to prevent the game from passing a certain line, and yet were not numerous enough to form a cordon along it, they employed the device of planting stout wands about their own height, dressed with ostrich feathers, and a tuft of them fastened to the top. These were planted at short distances from one another

16,1. Antelope occurred in great flocks in the Sahel and the desert at the time of Nachtigal's travels. Nachtigal 1879, I: 550.

along the line they wished to mark out. The game appeared more terrified at the sight of these than of the Bushmen themselves and generally rushed from them in the greatest alarm. Even the lion himself very rarely approached them, but would skulk away whenever possible" (Stow 1905: 84).

Although the use of nets combined with the setting up of mock fences to create the illusion of people is rare in Africa, the method has been widely used by hunters in particular among North American Indians, the Inuit of Greenland and the Same people of northern Scandinavia.

The hunting method of the Haddad Kanembu - that of bow and arrow combined with the use of disguise of

various kinds - is widely applied in Africa. The Nupe of northern Nigeria, for example, hunt in exactly the same way using masks of the ground hornbill (Buschan, G. 1914-16, III: 26; Meek 1931: 414-15). Livingstone came across Mambowe hunters at the upper Zambesi who carried masks that looked like a kind of crane. These, he observed, enabled the hunters to sneak up upon wildlife and occasionally look out for this without being noticed when crawling through the grass (Lindblom 1925, I: 40). Other forms of disguise are in use as well. Some Bushmen crawl up upon game hidden behind a simple bundle of grass or some branches, other groups use masks made from the wings and head of vultures. Stow tells that some of the

San applied the feathers and simulated the movements of the ostrich when hunting this large bird. He also recounts how they would hide amidst a flock of live ostriches when hunting other animals. The technique is probably similar to that applied by prehistoric hunters of the Sahara just as it was to the Haddad in the 19th century, when ostrich hunting was of peak economic significance. Similarly, some San groups used hides of hartebeest to sneak up upon antelopes, hippos, elephants and apparently also rhinoceros with their spears and bow and arrows (Stow 1905: 82, 88; Holub 1881, I: 432).

A similar division in hunting methods, as those applied by the Haddad Kreda and Haddad Kanembu respectively, also occurs among other hunting societies.[1] In one of the most thoroughly studied foraging societies, the Batwa of Central Africa, one finds a corresponding specialization between and within the four main groups: the Aka apply nets, the Efe bow and arrow, the Baka spears and the Mbuti either nets or bow and arrow. Like the Haddad Kreda, the Mbuti and Aka organize communal hunts in which women routinely take part as beaters driving the quarry into the nets whereas, similar to the Haddad Kanembu, Efe archers venture more on their own with rare participation of women. Various theories have been proposed to explain specialization in hunting methods in fairly similar environments. Based on his extended fieldwork among the Mbuti, who are either net-hunters or archers and the Ik, who either use nets or bow and arrow, Turnbull argues, for example, that the distribution between net hunters and archers among these people is fortuitous because environmental conditions provide sufficient food sources to permit alternative hunting techniques (Turnbull 1968: 134-5). This explanation has been countered by Abruzzi who argues that if the environment is truly permissive, then the distribution of net-hunting and archer groups would be randomly scattered rather than constituting a broad continuum, as is the case (Abruzzi 1980: 12). Roscoe also reflects on the link between the nature of the environment and the choice of hunting technology. Unlike Turnbull, he finds this is by no means fortuitous. Roscoe argues that the Mbuti who make use of spread-nets do so in a densely forested environment and consequently capture terrestrial prey in visually obscured surroundings. By contrast, the Mbuti archers hunt in more a more open ambiance, as bow and arrow allow for the killing of animals over considerable horizontal or verti-

cal distances so long as the prey it not visually obscured and the passage of the arrow not impeded. Archery is therefore a technology of choice for taking arboreal and avian as well as terrestrial fauna in uncluttered environments. Thus, to the extent that the environment approximates one or other of these types, hunters will prefer the one technology over the other, Roscoe argues. He finds a corresponding correlation in the distribution of archery and net hunting in the Sepik region (Roscoe 1990, 3: 694-5). Katharine Milton also plays the ecological card, but she argues that the two hunting techniques have arisen in response to differences in wild food availability in different parts of the Ituri forest. Net hunting is favoured by Mbuti in the south-west because it offers a more dependable subsistence through exchanges with villagers of agricultural products in return for meat (Milton 1985: 77).

Other theories link the choice of hunting technology to changes in the environment due to the encroachment of agriculture, plantations and mining and to considerations on food security. Abruzzi maintains, for example, that expanding economic activities linked to population pressure induced a shift from archery to net hunting among the southern and western Mbuti. It required more labor but created a surplus of meat that could be traded with neighbouring agriculturalists for a steady supply of crop foods. The eastern Mbuti, by contrast, had no need of the net because they already received crop foods for keeping destructive animals away from the gardens of agriculturalists (Abruzzi 1980). Milton's and Abruzzi's theories have been challenged by Bailey and Aunger who argue that the two scholars base their theories on selective readings of the available literature and not on direct observations of the natural environment. Bailey and Aunger found no significant difference in the composition or diversity of the forests exploited by net hunters and archers, respectively. They claim instead that, while a large range of factors contribute to the present spatial distribution of hunting techniques, ultimately the returns that individuals earn per unit of effort will dictate their choice of subsistence strategy. Some Mbuti women engage in hunting as their primary subsistence strategy, they say, others in exchanging their labour for food working in the gardens of villagers (Bailey and Aunger 1989). Finally, some researchers have turned to culture-historical explanations and/or theories of diffusion to account for the distribution of Batwa hunting technologies. Harako favours the latter, arguing that net-hunting was adopted relatively recently by the Mbuti and that it happened through contact with Bantu-speaking horticulturalists (Harako 1976). However, conclusive evidence supporting this view is still lacking, according to Bailey and Aunger (1989: 275).

I have introduced these debates to throw further light on the use and distribution of the similar hunting technologies among the Haddad. As described, the debates revolve on the ensuing core elements: fortuity, visibility of game, food security, yield on effort and cultural diffusion.

To consider the relevance of these factors in a Haddad context it must be remembered, that the environment of Bahr el Ghazal and Kanem differs from that of the Mbuti. The Haddad Kreda apply their nets in fairly or completely open land whereas the net-hunting Mbuti chase game in a dense tropical rainforest. Similarly, the issue for the Haddad Kanembu is not whether vegetation is open enough to allow for an undisturbed view of the game as is the case among the bow-hunting Mbuti, according to Roscoe, but rather whether they can find ways to get within shooting distance of the animals.

With this in mind, let us first take a look at the Haddad habitat to discuss whether the choice of hunting methods can be considered fortuitous and/or whether it is related to the visibility of the game. The natural environment of the two Haddad groups varies, as described in Chapter 2. The heartland of the Haddad Kanembu habitat gets slightly more rain and has subsequently a denser vegetation than the middle stretches of the Bahr el Ghazal, where the Haddad Kreda forage and migrate with pastoralists for a good part of the year. Gazelle and antelope are found throughout Haddad territory, but they are particularly numerous when they can browse on annual and perennial grasses as on the open plains of the Bahr el Ghazal or, as in the case of the Addax and Oryx, further north in the true desert. The central and southern parts of Kanem accommodate species in need of denser vegetation and great mammals like giraffes and elephants were numerous in earlier days. Gazelle and antelope still live here, but the species tend to browse individually, in pairs or small numbers only. In the 19th century the difference in the habitat of the two Haddad groups was more pronounced. Kanem was fairly densely forested with huge trees when Nachtigal passed through

its valleys and game was available in abundance for the Haddad Kanembu. The Haddad Kreda, on the other hand, ventured more often into the northern fringes of the Bahr el Ghazal and the desert in pursuit of the huge flocks of antelope. Is the choice of hunting methods of the two Haddad groups fortuitous under these somewhat different ecological conditions, we may ask? Could the Haddad Kreda use bow and arrow and the Haddad Kanembu apply nets with equally good results? While an answer to this question is difficult to substantiate, it appears that each technique has a comparative advantage over the other within the specific environment where it is applied. Nets are well suited to open spaces with limited cover for the hunters and for hunting animals in flocks as long as the hunting expeditions are communally organized. The technique has served the Haddad Kreda well, as we have seen, enabling them to bag large numbers of gazelle and antelope at a time. Cover for the hunters is sparse or non existent, except when provided by geological formations. Could bow and arrow be applied in this environment? Certainly, but probably not with a return that is sufficient to sustain a foraging group. Although Saharan rock engravings do show prehistoric hunters using bow and arrow and approaching the game in disguise, it must be remembered that these engravings were made at a time when the vegetation was richer and wildlife more plentiful. Generally, the habitat of the Haddad Kanembu offers better, if far from complete cover for game and hunters alike. For this reason it is less suited for large scale battue with nets for antelope and gazelle, as it is difficult to control the chase of few and scattered animals, but well suited for hunting with bow and arrow as it enables the hunter to find cover and creep up upon the game in disguise. Haddad Kanembu hunters do so either individually or in small groups, mimicking the behavioural pattern of the game itself as we have heard. Larger hunting parties were formed from time to time in the 19th century but mainly to eliminate predators like lions and apparently also to pursue the African buffalo, giraffes and elephants. In such cases the Haddad used not only bow and poisoned arrows but also traps.

Haddad choice of hunting technology can be understood only in part with reference to the natural environment, however. The use of the two different methods begs an understanding of other issues raised by the Batwa debate, namely those of food security, yield on effort and population pressure respectively. According to Milton, nets offer a more dependable hunting strategy among the Mbuti than bow and arrow. The eastern and western Mbuti turned from archery to net hunting when natural resources declined due to population pressure. The Mbuti did so to kill more game even though nets demand a greater labour input, she argues (Milton 1985: 77; Abruzzi 1980). The Haddad faced a similar problem towards the end of the 19th century as population pressure increased and game became less abundant. The two groups responded differently to the challenge, however, partly in consequence of the applicability of their hunting method in a changing environment. The Haddad Kreda continued to put up their nets although the yield diminished. Still, a sufficient amount of game was bagged to sustain this foraging community but only if supplemented with milk and other foods obtained through exchanges with pastoralists. The Haddad Kanembu, on the other hand, were unable to support themselves by hunting and foraging alone in the face of a diminishing stock of game and increased population pressure. Their solution was to turn to food production. The argument that nets offer a greater return than archery may hold true, however, also in the Haddad case. It is validated by the fact that in the 1950s some Haddad Kanembu families gave up archery in favour of nets to meet the deteriorating subsistence conditions. These families did not organize large-scale expeditions to venture up north for antelope like the Haddad Kreda, but sustained themselves by hunting antelope, gazelle, jackal and other smaller species in Kanem proper.

Finally, the Batwa debate raises the question of cultural diffusion as an explanation of the choice of hunting technology. Oral traditions offer no indication that hunting technologies spread from one group of Haddad to the other and I found little evidence in support of a culture-historical explanation of the distribution of the different hunting methods between the two groups. We heard only of Haddad Kanembu families who had turned to nets a few years prior to our fieldwork, as just mentioned. Our Haddad Kanembu friend Chari and his father did also hunt small animals with nets for fur and to provide pets, but these few instances do not suffice as an indication of a major cultural diffusion from one group to the other (cf. Chapter 9).

The use of nets as well as of bow and arrow is ancient in North Africa, as previously stated, and Haddad spe-cialization in either of these hunting techniques probably goes way back in time, the more so as these are differently embedded, both socially and culturally. The Haddad Kreda base their existence on communally organized hunting expeditions, the Haddad Kanembu largely on individual pursuit. The two groups diverge considerably, moreover, in their perceptions of nature and of man's relations with animals. The Haddad Kreda hold a largely 'secular' view of the environment and trade. A failed battue is blamed on the behaviour of specific individuals, not explained in terms of cosmological forces or lack of magical precaution. The Haddad Kanembu, on the other hand, consider magical forces an alpha and omega to luck in hunting. These socio-cultural differences between the two groups do not point to a historical transformation from one method of hunting to the other. There is no indication that Haddad Kreda have taken to the use of bow and arrow, and only a few Haddad Kanembu families had recently begun to make use of nets, as we have seen. The difference in mode of hunting between the two Haddad groups flags the problem of a scholarly definition of the Haddad as an ethnic group, however, albeit not, as I have argued, as an indigenous people, as the latter relies on self-identification.

INSURGENCY AND SURVIVAL

The history of Kanem and the Bahr el Ghazal is a long and bloody tale of usurpation, violence, and the coming and goings of potentates, as previously intimated. Towards the end of the 19th century the social landscape was as fluid and turbulent as ever due to the aggressive politics and raiding of the Awlad Sliman, Tubu, Fulani and Arab slave traders. Alexander Boyd and other writers describe how the caravans of pilgrims were looted on their way to Mecca and villages and families preyed upon by these marauding and bellicose groups into the early 20th century. Add to this the widespread resistance against the French occupation and the subsequent insecurity as the colonizers craved forced labor and initiated a massive drafting of soldiers. No wonder that Haddad society was affected. The turbulence did not have the same impact on the two groups, however, due in part to the different ways in which they sustained themselves, in part to the variation in population size and in part the ability to confront intruders in their respective environments.

Let us first take a look at the impact of the insurgency on the Haddad Kreda. Generally, foraging groups are small in size and rely on a nomadic lifestyle to maximize their harvesting efforts, as has been the case with these people. Being just that, i.e. nomadic and relatively few in number as compared to other ethnic groups in the region made it utterly difficult for the Haddad Kreda to fend for themselves, gain social recognition and political influence. In fact, they have gotten nothing of the sort. At times of armed conflict, the Haddad Kreda have been highly vulnerable. There are no retreats or ways of hiding on the open plains of the Bahr el Ghazal, where they hunt most of the time, nor in the desert further north where the Awlad Sliman and the Tubu are in control. Haddad Kreda vulnerability was further exacerbated because their only means of transportation are donkeys whereas raiding pastoralists and Arab slave traders move on the rapid hoofs of fine horses and camels.

The Haddad Kreda themselves tell of the situation in the early 20th century as one of hardship. There is little doubt that widespread raiding and violence paired with the socially induced decline in game posed a threat to their very existence and forced them to seek physical protection and alternative sources of income. They obtained both by forging stronger ties with pastoral groups, accepting an inferior social position as the silent part of the bargain. Exchanges of labour for milk and protection between the Haddad Kreda and various pastoral groups probably go further back in time. Such ties are beneficial to both parties but evidently were crucial to the Haddad during the havoc created by Awlad Sliman and other raiders at the time. They are not the only group of hunters forging exchange relations with pastoralists as a strategy of survival. The Aza or Azza Gouran living to the northwest of Lake Chad in eastern Niger were in the same quandary according to Carbou. He notes that the Aza"…at times were manhandled and looted by the other indigenous peoples. All that they would then possess would be a hide around the loins." (Carbou 1912, I: 211; IN transl.) As families or clans they teamed up with Daza pastoralists and, according to Grall, accepted voluntarily a vassal-like position and the obligation to furnish their protectors with dried meat and tanned hides of antelopes that they hunted, and not the least to maintain the wells of the pastoralists.

Haddad Kreda existence was also made difficult during the first half of the 20th century by the socially provoked decline in the population of ostriches and Oryx and Addax antelopes which brought the large-scale communal hunting of these species close to an end and reduced the surplus of meat that the Haddad used to market in exchange for agricultural produce and other necessities. In response they took up residence, periodically, with pastoral chiefs to get by seasonal shortages of food. The pressure on their way of life never eased, however. At the time of our visit, population growth increased competition on access to natural resources in the Bahr el Ghazal leading to further diversification of subsistence activities primarily through the acquisition of small ruminants. This had neither been necessary nor an option for the Haddad Kreda during the first part of the 20th century when the Haddad were barred by custom from possessing livestock. This situation did not change during French rule but only with the ordinance of 1956 passed by the new Chadian government.

The Haddad Kreda faced greater obstacles in this respect than the Azza at Chitati and in eastern Niger. Some of these groups already acquired livestock during the first half of the 20th century and took up a pastoral way of life similar to that of the Daza and Hassauna whom they were living among, according to Rouvreur. They had beautiful herds and, to his surprise, even camels – the symbol of an aristocratic heritage (Rouvreur: 1962: 383).

The transition from hunting and foraging to a pastoral way of life, however, is neither common nor is it well documented by scholarly work. Still, it has taken place, for instance among Siberian and some African groups. Eric Ten Raa's study of the Sandawe, an East-African, Khoi-san speaking group of hunters provides one example. Sandawe foragers used to retreat when preyed upon, leaving their shelters and few belongings behind and remained invisible as long as necessary. Ten Raa describes how intruding pastoral groups managed to suppress the Sandawe with the assistance of the colonial power, which recognized the former as the 'chiefs' of the traditionally chief-less Sandawe society. The Sandawe gradually turned to herding, but their oral history shows a pattern of repeated loss not only of cattle but also of people during their attempts to become pastoralists. The Sandawe themselves explain these events as caused by the strong medicine of groups who raided them. Superior numbers, or better weapons or training is never mentioned, says Ten Raa (1986: 371).

Whether the Haddad Kreda will be able to succeed in taking up a pastoral way of life remains to be seen. Pastoralism requires not only capital to purchase livestock but also thorough veterinary and botanical knowledge to ensure that the herds are properly fed and that each kind of livestock gets the right mixture of fodder in order to stay healthy. Skills are needed of cures and precautionary methods to avoid some of these sicknesses. Pastoral economies depend on social collaboration, moreover, both in regard to practical work with the herds and as a safeguard in times of economic strain. All in all, this complex set of requirements makes for a problematic transition from a foraging to a pastoral way of life.

The ultimate threat to the hunting existence of the Haddad Kreda occurred after Chad gained independence, as the new government enforced its ban on their traditional hunting method with nets. It cracked down on every family who possessed nets, citing the need for protection of wildlife. The situation was paradoxical, as the very same gendarmes and soldiers who confiscated and burned the nets of the Haddad would kill whatever animal came their way with automatic weapons on their patrols from camp to camp. We may hence conclude that, while the nature of insurgency changed upon the arrival of the French and assaults and marauding gradually quelled, the hunting way of life of the Haddad Kreda came under new threats. Apart from the volatility in the availability of game, the most serious was the ban on hunting with nets introduced by the French and upheld by the Chadian government. This forced the Haddad Kreda into a form of hiding and put them even further at the mercy of the pastoralists. They were able to uphold their hunting way of life only at great risk of having their nets confiscated and destroyed and other government sanctions. In my view, the prohibition on hunting with nets amounts to no less than cultural genocide. It is not only in blatant violation of the human rights of the Haddad Kreda but also disgraceful in view of the fact that the authorities continue to issue permits to rich foreigners enabling these to hunt and even kill endangered species in the very same areas that are barred to the Haddad.

Insurgency and increasingly the scarcity of game as of the end of the 19th century changed the way of life not only of

the Haddad but also of other foraging groups living on the southern fringes of the Sahel, as previously intimated. Most turned to food production and settled among agricultural groups. This was the case of the Gow and Katté, for example, foraging peoples who at that time lived among the Djerma and Songhai along the Niger - the Gow being renowned for hunting ostriches on horseback. Another group giving up its nomadic way of life was the Kallé, who settled among the Hausa in Nigeria; also the Kerétina of Bornu became farmers. Social and environmental pressures had a similar impact on and consequences for specialized hunting castes such as those existing among the Mossi and Guruni (cf. Bauman & Westermann 1948: 329, 414).

The Haddad Kanembu chose a similar path and turned increasingly to food production. Like the Haddad Kreda they were hurt by the widespread insurgency but in contrast to these, they were able to effectively fend off encroachers partly because they were more numerous. Nachtigal tells from his visit to the N'Guri area in 1871 that the Haddad successfully withstood attacks by the Wadaï and the Awlad Sliman for more than thirty years. He writes about their tactics that: "When an enemy is approaching they leave their huts and climb the natural fortress wall of tall trees to shower poisoned arrows upon these people" (Nachtigal 1881, II: 259). At that point in time, most of the Haddad Kanembu were still semi-nomadic and this too proved a strategic advantage in fending off hostile groups. They subsisted on hunting and foraging but were increasingly forced to supplement the diet with food production. Upon the French conquest the Haddad Kanembu gave up wandering and settled down (Conte 1986: 133). A century after Nachtigal's visit, all but a few had given up hunting as the main source of nourishment. They subsisted mainly on agriculture, supplemented by hunting and income from the collection of medical plants which might take them on expeditions quite far south into the savanna.

The gradual transformation of the Haddad Kanembu way of life was spurred in part by the same factors which made life difficult for the Haddad Kreda, in particular the drastic decline in game. Population growth may well have played a role as well in forcing the Haddad Kanembu to diversify their economy and increase food production. The transition to agriculture was eased by the fact that the Haddad Kanembu had established rights over land enabling them to settle without facing conflicts over arable soil with other ethnic groups. In the customary law of the ruling Kanemese, usufruct rights over fertile ground are vested in named, locally-anchored or fully localized patrigroups. Traditionally, the leaders of these were office-holders in the administrative set-up of the sultanate, according to Edouard Conte. The Haddad Kanembu enjoyed such rights on a par with the Kanembu as the sultanate used the instrument for taxation (cf. Conte 1983a: 143-153) and they could hence take up farming on suitable land without getting into conflict with the Kanembu.

Contributing to the fairly smooth transition was the considerable strength of Haddad Kanembu clans within the governance system of the Kanemese sultanate in precolonial times. Haddad clans ruled two out of the five chiefdoms which existed in southern Kanem immediately prior to the French colonization: the Darka clan in N'Guri and the Rea, Adia and Bara clans alternating in Bari Kolom. The Darka, in fact, had a solid pre-eminence in respect to the local Kanembu population, a quite unusual situation for the Haddad in Kanem (Conte 1986: 133; 1983a: 38). However, the French failed to acknowledge this state of affairs upon their arrival, probably due to the pervasive European view at the time that invariably perceived of hunters and gatherers as representatives of a lower stage of human evolution. The French established an administrative system similar to the one created by Napoleon in France. Insensitive to the factual political situation and traditional rights of the Haddad, they introduced new territorial divisions and political offices of *chefs de canton* and *chefs de village* which led to an overall erosion of Haddad Kanembu social and political standing. Although the Haddad Kanembu were able to muster some political influence through locally elected *chef de village*, only a few were elected *chef de canton*. Subsequent administrative plans to rectify the situation were never carried out with far reaching consequences for the current position of the Haddad Kanembu (1986: 133-135). This was blatantly clear in the case of those living at N'Guri, a traditional stronghold of the Darka clan of Haddad Kanembu. N'Guri happened to be the first colonial outpost in Kanem. In the initial phase the position of the Darka vis-à-vis the Kanembu proved relatively fortunate, but their luck turned in 1934 when the French decided to transfer this sub-division to the canton of Mao, the center of power of the Kanemese (Catala 1954: 45; cf.

Conte 1986: 135). The transfer implied that the authority and political influence of the Darka chief was seriously diluted as this was intimately tied to the right to collect taxes. Other Haddad Kanembu groups fared somewhat differently, according to Catala,[2] although the net result proved to be similar. In 1899, the allied clans of Adia, Bara and Rea of the chiefdom of Bari Kolom pledged allegiance directly to the Khalif of Mao. For this very reason, they avoided for some time an administrative restructuring of their territories. The clan solidarity broke gradually down, however, as the French army succeeded in curbing the general insurgency. Some of the Adia and Bara decided to move to Dagana and the Bahr el Ghazal leaving their lands to the Rea. The latter were able to maintain their position in Kiwa, until this chiefdom was administratively transferred to the canton of Mao (Catala 1954: 24-25; cf. Conte 1986: 135).

At the time of Conte's fieldwork in the early 1970s, Haddad Kanembu clans were still politically important in some parts of Kanem. The Darka were dominant at N'Guri and Dikara, while the administrative centers at Yalita, Am Dobak and Molimari were ruled by the Bara, Dieri and Rea clans respectively. Taken in the above order respectively, at the time of Conte's study these clans controlled 25, 17, 15 and 12 villages with recognized headmen, total populations of about 1,300 persons and possessed sufficient adjacent fertile lands to remain economically and politically autonomous (Conte 1986: 133; 1983a: 38). Still, by and large, the French had succeeded in eliminating the political standing of the Haddad Kanembu at the cantonal level, in practice relegating them to political domination by the Kanembu. At the time of our study the latter dominated the political, social, economic and cultural life of Kanem. Conte's fine data on clans, marriage alliances and rights to land illuminate the weaker position of the Haddad within the overall Kanemese society. It reveals that Haddad "clans" tend to be territorially more dispersed than their Kanembu counterparts, that local communities are smaller on average, and that the very structure of the:

"clans are different, irrespective of any notion of purported 'genealogical autonomy." A majority of the 'clans' are comprised of only one, two or three small local communities and these are: ..."appendages of larger Kanembu clans to which they are attached by collective and individual patron-client relationships. In many cases, Kanembu and dependent Duu clans share a single name, but this homonymy does not imply common agnatic descent." (Conte 1983: 38)

Conte argues, as previously intimated, that the sedentarization combined with the adherence to strict rules of endogamy by the Haddad and various segments of Kanembu society sustained the pervasive hierarchical order of Kanemese society. This was culturally encoded in categories of opposition such as man versus woman, primogeniture versus second-in-line, Kanembu versus Duu [Haddad]. It was also expressed in gender imagery: oral tradition attributed the origin of the Duu to the illegitimate son of a Bulala woman and a slave who upon birth adopted bow and arrow as his weapon; dancing by hunters was perceived to be feminine by the Kanembu and in contrast to their own aristocratic and masculine demeanor; the long leather dresses traditionally worn by the Haddad are never worn by the Kanembu, etc. The late sedentarization of the nomadic Haddad legitimizes their symbolic feminization in Kanembu worldview, Conte argues (1986: 160).

A far cry from the credo of the French Republic: 'Liberté, Fraternité et Égalité' the administrative practice of French Colonial Rule did not promote social equality but proved supportive of the political ambitions of the Kanembu. From being 'master of their own house' at the time of Nachtigal's travel, the Haddad became increasingly a subordinate group within the wider Kanembu society. The French condoned, if only indirectly, the inequality which permeate Kanembu values and ideology and hence a cultural perception of the Haddad Kanembu as an inferior kind of people.

When Chad gained independence, the new government built its administration on the colonial apparatus and practices and the continued presence of the French. The latter was strongly felt in Kanem and the Bahr el Ghazal due to presence of the Foreign Legion at Mussoro. Finances, development projects and technical assistance at whatever modest level were in the hands of the Quai d'Orsay. Later the World Bank would increasingly assume a say in economic policy, not the least with regard to oil prospecting and development.

The French had taken some steps to curb social discrimination on the basis of race or origin. Still, laws do not change cultural behaviour. In the 1960s the Haddad were held in a caste-like, stigmatized position reinforced by prevailing marriage practices that barred inter-ethnic marriages. The cultural and social discrimination against the Haddad was pervasive throughout society. It prevailed also among people who had gone to school and worked within the public or private sector and hence had some idea of Western way of thinking. We noted this in a range of ways, from the veiled surprise that we would even consider the Haddad worthwhile studying to blatant statements asserting that the Haddad might become citizens with equal rights under the law but they should never be allowed to acquire positions of any importance within the civil service or in any other way move up the social ladder. Such attitudes were conveyed to us at several occasions, for instance when our friendship with a young Haddad was disclosed. He had received some education and spoke French but this was not appropriate, we were told. Some said right out that the Haddad should not even be allowed to attend school, others that it would be wrong to let them get a higher education, and under no circumstances should they be employed to do anything but simple office work. Yet, societies and cultures do change, and so hopefully has the situation of the Haddad.

NOTES

1. The Doko, a hereditary group of hunters living among the Nupe also applied both techniques. In their case, however, the use of these was not monopolized by a specific segment of the Doko, but each family applied nets as well as bows and arrows and traps. The Doko organized large-scale communal hunts in the dry season, a time when game is the more abundant, according to Nadel (1954: 75).

2. I have been unable to access Catala's work via the international library loan service. For this reason I have relied entirely on Conte's references to his work.

17:

17: MATERIAL CULTURE – A CATALOGUE

The ensuing catalogue presents the collection of ethnographic specimens purchased in Kanem and Bahr el Ghazal in 1963 during our – i.e. Ida and Johannes Nicolaisen's – fieldwork. Although Johannes and I worked together on many aspects of our joint fieldwork, we had a division of labour with respect to some topics, one being the analysis and collection of ethnographic specimens, which was undertaken entirely by the author. Johannes and I had but little money at our disposal for the entire trip, as intimated in the introduction, but I had received the modest sum of DKK 2000 from the National Museum in Copenhagen and had also promised to collect specimens for the Moesgaard Museum, if possible. The latter had been established shortly before, its first ethnographic collection being one made by Johannes in 1951 among the Ahaggar and Air Tuareg.

Upon our arrival at Fort-Lamy, we met with the acting director of Institut National Tchadien, Colonel Jean Chapelle, to discuss our research plans. We brought up the issue of ethnographic collections and were assured that there were no specific requirements or strings attached to the purchase of specimens, but that the Institute would be interested in seeing what had been obtained in case there were unique objects in the collection which upon reconsideration ought to revert to the collections at the Institute. We asked Colonel Chapelle whether the Institute would be interested in a duplicate collection free of charge, but were told that this was not the case. However, we did buy some duplicates which we presented to the Institute upon our return, and Colonel Chapelle proved interested in getting 16 items, surprisingly also two of the common spears. At this point in time precisely these common weapons were

being rounded up in the streets of Fort-Lamy by the police and we were told that hundreds of spears had been confiscated in the wake of the prevailing social unrest, so there seemed little need to access these for the Institute. But that happened and the Danish collection does not, therefore, contain four such spears, the number normally carried by adult men at a time.

Upon our return, the collection was divided up between the two museums in such a way that most of the Haddad specimens went to Moesgaard, while those from the Kreda were secured by the National Museum to supplement its rich collections from pastoral peoples. The division was somewhat unfortunate, in that the 'Kreda' specimens to some extent are identical with utensils, dresses and jewellery applied by the Haddad Kreda in daily life. This also applies to tents of which only one specimen was acquired from a pastoralist. A few specimens presented to us as gifts by Haddad and Kreda friends are still in my possession. As they eventually will be donated to the Moesgaard Museum, these items are also included in the catalogue.

Specimens were collected from day one in the field and taken along on whatever means of transportation we were using. Upon reaching Mussoro we were able to store specimens in a house, which was put at our disposal by the government. This proved most convenient, as our travels from then on were carried out on camelback. Camels were not easily available for rent and we did not have sufficient means to buy them. But we were successful in the end, and it proved even possible to get still another one for the latter part of our stay and hence possible for us to acquire a complete tent.

The entire collection was purchased for 39,600 CFA, at that time equivalent of DKK 1,086, or about the same sum as Johannes got per month as a young researcher at Copenhagen University. It cost us 1500 CFA to transport the items by camel to Mussoro and another 25,000 CFA to get them by an old dilapidated lorry to Fort-Lamy, enabling us to give a lift to more than a dozen passengers, who squeezed themselves in on the top of the load. Apart from being stuck for twenty-four hours in the middle of a flooded area due to lack of gum for the repair of a flat tyre, the trip was a joy. From Fort-Lamy the collection was sent by air to Douala at a cost of 18.000 CFA, from where it was shipped free of charge to Denmark by courtesy of the Danish-French Shipping Company.

THE STRUCTURE OF THE CATALOGUE

The catalogue is divided into four parts: 1. specimens from the Haddad Kanembu; 2. specimens from the Haddad Kreda; 3. specimens from Haddad artisans: 4. a tent.

The specimens at the Moesgaard Museum are registered with capital letters (EA) followed by the numerals '69', the identification number of the collection. Ensuing numbers register individual specimens. The collection at the National Museum is registered with a capital letter (G), indicating that it belongs to the African collection at the ethnographic department, a number identifies each speci-

men. Lower-case letters are added if a specimen consists of several items, for example a mortar and pestle. A few specimens, like the Kreda tent, have been given several inventory numbers because of the lack of sufficient letters. Inventory numbers are presented at the end of the description of each specimen.

The descriptions rely on thorough analyses of all specimens and on notes made in connection with the purchase of these. These notes on the acquisition of the collection will be made accessible at the Danish Royal Library. Each description is enriched by data obtained during the fieldwork when deemed relevant. As the entries in the protocols and inventory lists of the two museums are provisory, containing little more information than a listing of the objects, they have not been used except for checking that the inventory numbers on the objects tally with the museum register. Each specimen is described with respect to the materials of which it is made, who made it, its use, where and from whom it was purchased and at what price – except in some cases where several specimens were bought together. A few items could not be retrieved at the time of writing. Descriptions of these are henceforth based on previous notes only and precise measures cannot be given. The ethnic term of each specimen has been mentioned if known to the author; sometimes its name is indicated in Arabic for further reference. Finally, the size and dimensions of the specimen is given in centimetres in respect to height, width and diameter.

HADDAD KANEMBU

17,1. Haddad Kanembu hunter demonstrating how he approaches game, simulating the movements of the ground hornbill. He wears a mask carved to the resemblance of the bird and holds his bow and arrows in the left hand. His quiver can be seen in the foreground.

Hunting and fishing at Lake Chad

1. Iron blade of harpoon, balat (Kanembu), with two solid, very sharp barbs and a socket for fastening on a shaft. The blade was made by a smith at Bol. Harpoons are used for crocodile hunting on the Chari river and at Lake Chad.

Length: 19.6 cm
Prov.: The specimen was bought from a Haddad smith at the market at Bol on July 17, 1963 together with inv. nos. EA 69-2 and EA 69-3 for 150 CFA.
Inv. no. EA 69-1

2. Iron blade of fishing spear, alasa (Kanembu), with socket and two rows of finely made barbs. The socket is pierced crosswise in order that the blade can be lashed to a shaft with a string through the holes. Spears like this one are used for fishing in Lake Chad.

Length: 22 cm
Prov.: Made by a Haddad smith in Bol, from whom it was bought at the market on July 17, 1963 together with inv. nos. EA 69-1 and EA 69-3 for 150 CFA
Inv. no. EA 69-2

3. Iron blade of spear, alasa (Kanembu), used for fishing in Lake Chad. The blade has a socket into which the wooden shaft of the harpoon can be fitted and fastened with a string.

Length: 18.5 cm
Prov.: Bought from a Haddad smith in Bol on July 17, 1963 together with EA 69-1 and EA 69-2 for 150 CFA.
Inv. no. EA 69-3

4. Harpoon known as tjagal in Kanembu. It consists of an iron blade with three barbs known as falat or maraku forged with a socket which can be fitted loosely onto the pointed wooden shaft, jarel. The latter is made of wood of the karikindele tree. The float, bojo, is cut from light wood of the maria tree. It is pierced by a small stick of the same wood. The point and the float of the harpoon are tied together with a cord of finely twined iron thread. Onto this are tied some further metres of cotton line connecting point and float upon harpooning. The line, farey, is kept in a rolled-up state ready for use. Harpoons are used by the Haddad Kanembu primarily for hunting crocodiles at Lake Chad but also used to catch fairly large fish. Crocodile hunting is done at night from boats, kadej, which the Haddad make from the stems of papyrus (Papyrus cyperus or Papyrus antiquorum), known to the Haddad as ma'ara (cf. *Figs. 8,10 & 8,11*).

Length (total): 188 cm
Length (shaft): 138 cm
Length (point): 12 cm
Length (float): 55 cm
Length (iron wire): 160 cm
Prov.: Purchased from a Haddad Kanembu hunter at Baga Sola on July 24, 1963 for 1300 CFA.
Inv. no. EA 69-4

Hunting equipment

5. Mask made to resemble the head of the large Ground Hornbill (Buvorvus abyssinicus), called ngudontule (ngudo meaning bird, ntul being the name) in Kanembu. The mask is used as a means of disguise during hunting. It is carved from wood of the kafi (Kanembu) tree alias Calotropis precera. The beak is open and the bird's forehead is decorated with a piece of blackish sheepskin. A cowry shell (Cyprian moneta), surrounded by tiny red beads glued to the mask with resin, do for the bird's left eye. The corresponding decoration of the right eye is missing. The bird's neck protrudes into a disc-shaped enlargement which is tied to the hunter's forehead with two strings of goat leather. A third string is held in the mouth to steady the mask when closing in on the game (cf. *Figs. 3,2 & 17,2*).

Height: 41 cm
Length (bird's head): 21.5 cm
Prov.: Bought from Haddad Kanembu at N'Guri on July 31, 1963 together with inv. nos. EA 69-9, EA 69-10a-b, EA 69-11, EA 69-12a-l, EA 69-13 and EA 69-14 for 4000 CFA.
Inv. no. EA 69-8

6. Mask, ngudontule, carved in the likeness of the head of the large Ground Hornbill which is known by the same name, ngudontule. The mask is made of wood of the kafi tree alias Calotropis precera except for the beak, the lower part of which is of buffalo horn fastened to the mask with a small piece of sheet metal. The neck of the 'bird' protrudes into a disc-shaped enlargement. When

in use this rests against and is tied to the forehead of the hunter with a coloured piece of cotton cloth. A third cotton string is held between the hunter's teeth to steady the mask when simulating the movements of the large Ground Hornbill in closing in on game (cf. *Figs. 3,2; 5,1 & 17,3*).

Height: 43 cm
Length (head): 24 cm
Prov.: The mask was purchased from a Haddad Kanembu at N'Guri on July 31, 1963 together with inv. nos. EA 69-8, EA 69-10a-b, EA 69-11, EA 69-12a-l, EA 69-13 and EA 69-14 for a total of 4000 CFA.
Inv. no. EA 69-9

7. A pair of pads, n'goromebe, a Kanembu word which implies the function of these devices, namely 'something which protects the knees'. The pads are plaited with strips of old cotton cloth that are sewn together in a spiral. The pads are tied around the knees with cotton strings. One of the pads is made of white cotton cloth - now greyish from dirt, the other of red, blue and formerly white cotton strips. In both cases the pads have a bowl-shape device that fit the form of a knee. The pads are used to protect the hunter's knees against acacia thorns and other prickly material when approaching game.

Diameter: 17 cm
Prov.: Purchased from a Haddad Kanembu at N'Guri on July 31, 1963 together with inv. nos. EA 69-8, EA 69-9, EA 69-11, EA 69-12a-l, EA 69-13 and EA 69-14 for a total of 4000 CFA.
Inv. no. EA 69-10a-b

17,2. Mask of ground hornbill. Cat. no. 12. Photo J.K.   17,3. Mask of ground hornbill. Cat. no. 6. Photo J.K.

8. Bow, kabi or kebi made from a branch of the jujubier tree called sulu or solo (Zizyphus sp.) by the Haddad Kanembu. The bow is fairly simple but the bow leg has been reinforced with bindings of strips of ox hide. The string is of twined sinew of oxen and provided with two small tufts made of cotton thread at one end of the bow. These serve to reduce the vibrations of the string once the arrow is released and hence the noise, which might give away the hunter to the game. The bow is held in a horizontal position when in use (cf. *Fig. 9,9*). At the upper end of the bow leg an Islamic amulet behind a piece of cotton cloth tied around the bow has been concealed. The formula

on this was written by the Haddad owner of the bow, himself a marabout, to enhance the accuracy of the arrow by magical means. The bow was made by the brother of the man from whom it was purchased.

Length: 125 cm
Prov.: Bought at N'Guri on July 31, 1963 with inv. nos. EA 69-8, EA 69-9, EA 69-10a-b, EA 69-12a-l, EA 69-13 and EA 69-14.
Inv. no. EA 69-11

9. Quiver, kara, with arrows. The quiver is made from oxhide and furnished with a leather strap for carrying. The quiver or 'bag' has an almost circu-

lar bottom, some 5.5 cm in diameter, sewn onto the main part with a leather strip. The 'body' of the quiver is narrower near the bottom - with some 19 cm in circumference - than at the opening with 32 cm in circumference. Here the leather has been folded and stitched to the quiver with a coarse, decorative stitching. The rim has been further enforced with a tight stitching of a fine leather string. The arrows are wrapped in indigo-coloured cotton cloth to minimize any rattling sounds which could alert the game. The shafts of the arrows, kayi, are made of reed, enforced at the neck and where the arrow stem is fastened to the shaft with windings of sinew fibres (ox). These are also wound around ledges up and down the shaft. The stem of the arrow head is firmly implanted in the hollow end of the shaft and glued with resin. The quiver contains twelve arrows, kini, one of which is for the hunting of birds like guinea fowl and pigeons. The rest of the lot is for big game like buffalo, an animal which the owner of the quiver had killed several times. Except for the arrow for birds, they are all poisoned with a substance bought at the local market but originally stemming from Mandara in Nigeria (cf. *Figs. 5,2 & 9,12*).

Length (quiver): 42 cm
Circumference (of quiver): 32 cm
Length (arrows): 53 - 58 cm
Length (shafts): 40 - 44 cm
Length (iron points): 13 - 14 cm
Prov.: Purchased from Haddad hunter at N'Guri on July 31, 1963 together with the bow inv. no. EA 69-13 and with inv. nos. EA 69-8, EA 69-9, EA 69-10a-b, EA 69-11 and EA 69-14 for 4000 CFA.
Inv. nos. EA 69-12a-l

17,4. Mask of ground hornbill. Cat. no. 12. Drawing T.O.S.

10. Bow, kabi or kebi made from wood from the jujubier (Zizyphus sp.) known locally as solo or sulu and furnished with a string of twined sinew from oxen. A tiny tuft of cotton thread has been tied to the string at the top end of the bow functioning as a 'cat's-whisker', to reduce the vibrations, the noise of which may give away the hunter when an arrow is released. An Islamic amulet is wrapped around one end.

Length: 129 cm
Circumference (centre): 7.5 cm
Prov.: Purchased from Haddad

hunter at N'Guri on July 31, 1963 together with inv. nos. EA 69-8, EA 69-9, EA 69-10a-b, EA 69-11, EA 69-12a-l and EA 69-14 for 4000 CFA.
Inv. no. EA 69-13

11. Quiver made from the root of the tefi acacia (Acacia raddiana) and then covered by hide except for the very top six centimetres which are painted in a reddish colour. The quiver is furnished with a string of fibre tied to a leather band fastened to the quiver about one third down its body. This enables the hunter to leave the quiver hanging as well

as to bring it along over the shoulder. (cf. *Fig. 9,7*)

Length (quiver): 56 cm
Circumference (quiver): 27 cm
Prov.: Purchased from Haddad hunter at N'Guri on July 31, 1963 together with inv. nos. EA 69-8, EA 69-9, EA 69-10a-b, EA 69-11, EA 69-12a-l and EA 69-13 for 4000 CFA.
Inv. no. EA 69-14

12. Mask, ngudontul, made from wood and the cranium of the Ground Hornbill, (Bucorvus abyssinicus), ngudo, meaning bird and ntul being the name of the Ground Hornbill, as previously mentioned. The cranium is tied to the wooden neck with a tightly fitting leather bandage, which forms both the 'back of the mask's head' and the upper part of its 'neck'. It is further held in place by thin fibre strings wrapped around the bandage at the upper part of the neck and through the bird's beak. A thin leather string is fastened at one end some 8 cm down the neck, while the remaining 40 cm can be used by the hunter to stabilize the mask when creeping up upon the game. The bird has eyes to fool the game, the owner told us. These are made from red beads, unfortunately missing as far as the left eye goes. The beads are fastened to the cranium with resin. The top of the cranium is decorated with ostrich feathers. The slender wooden neck is cut from wood from the douli tree, which grows to the south of Chedra. It ends in an enlargement, the flat end of which rests against the hunter's forehead. The mask is held in place in part with a band of three pieces of goatskin, which have been sewn together with a string of fibre and coarse stitches. The string runs through a hole in the dumb end of the neck, in part by a string of goatskin, which the hunter holds in his mouth to stabilize the mask when moving. A leather string tied just below the head of the mask is for transportation. Before the mask was used the owner treated it with magical plants and smoke (cf. Chapter 10: 273). The mask was carved by a brother of the Haddad man in Chedra from whom it was purchased (cf. *Figs. 3,2; 9,4; 14,2 & 17,4*).

Height: 41 cm
Length (beak and cranium): 31 cm
Prov.: Chedra, September 9, 1963, prize 500 CFA.
Inv. no. EA 69-25

13. Mask, ngudontul, made to resemble the large Ground Hornbill (Bucorvus abyssinicus). The mask is carved from a single piece of wood of Caliotropis precera, known in Haddad as koyo. The bird's beak is open. The left eye is a cowry shell. The one on the right side is missing; instead the eye is marked by two red corals, while there are no such beads decorating the left eye. Both the cowry and the beads have been glued onto the mask with resin. The wooden neck ends in a 12 cm x 5 cm rectangular piece, cut flat at the side where it is to be tied to the hunter's head, while otherwise slightly curved. A leather strap made of two pieces runs through a hole some 5 cm from the lower end of the mask. The hunter applies these to fasten the mask at his forehead, tying each end of the string at the back of his head. Another leather string tied to the 'neck' by

means of two other holes is held in the mouth to stabilize the mask when crawling forwards (cf. *Figs. 3,2 & 9,5*).

Height: 36 cm
Length (neck to beak): 22 cm
Prov.: Purchased from the Haddad hunter, who had carved it himself, at Chedra on September 9, 1963 for 500 CFA.
Inv. no. EA 69-26

14. A pair of pads, nungoromi, for the protection of the hunter's knees. The pads are made from coarsely plaited strips of white cotton cloth, now greyish and dirty from use. The plaited strips have been curled up in a spiral and sewn together to a slightly bowl-shaped form befitting the shape of a knee. They can be tied each with a leather string around the knees of the hunter for his protection, when crawling up upon game (cf. *Fig. 17,5*).

Diameter, a. 10 cm, b. 14 cm
Prov.: Gift from Haddad hunter at Chedra on September 9, 1963.
Inv. nos. EA 69-27a-b

17,5. Protective knee pads used by hunters when creeping up on game. Cat. no. 14.

17,6. Mask of ground hornbill. Cat. no. 15. Photo J.K.

15. Mask resembling the head and neck of a Ground Hornbill (*Bucorvus abyssinicus*). The head of the mask is made from the cranium of one of these birds, its neck from a piece of wood of Calotropis precera, known as kafi or kayo by the Haddad. The two are held together by some of the skin of the dead bird, but mainly by a piece of leather (gazelle) wrapped around the rear end of the cranium and the top end of the neck piece and sewn tightly together. A leather patch covers the forehead of the cranium, while two cowries surrounded by small red beads fixed with resin

do for the bird's eyes. The bird's skull, neck and upper part of the neck are decorated with small ostrich feathers inserted in the leather binding on top of the cranium and tied to the neck further down with a fibre string. A piece of snakeskin is tied around the neck beneath the ostrich feather for further decoration (or perhaps magical function). Two leather strings are fastened to the end of the neck piece. One is applied as a headband, with which the hunter ties the mask around his head, while he holds the end of the other string in his mouth to steady this when moving. The

mask was treated with magic by its owner, who inserted a piece of the plant beitap through the open lower part of the beak and let the mask envelope in smoke from the very same plant, as this is believed to be endowed with magical powers. The mask had also been given a smoke bath over the burning of feathers of a tiny bird known as paké. Either of these two treatments with magic suffices to make game stand still or even approach the hunter, the owner of the mask assured us (cf. *Figs. 3,2 & 17,6*).

Height: 44 cm
Length (neck to beak): 28 cm
Prov.: Bought at Chedra on September 11, 1963 from the owner together with the rest of his hunting equipment inv. nos. EA 69-29, EA 69-30, EA 69-31a-r, EA 69-32a-b. Total cost 1500 CFA.
Inv. no. EA 69-28

16. Bow, kabi or kebi, reflexed and incurved at the middle. The bow leg is of wood from the jujubier tree (Zizuphus sp) known to the Haddad Kanembu as solo or sulu, the string of twined sinew. When not in use the string is wound around the upper end of the bow. The string is fastened at the top of the bow with a loop (cf. *Figs. 9,6 & 9,8*).

Length: 127 cm
Prov.: Purchased at Chedra on September 11, 1963 together with inv. nos. EA 69-28, EA 69-30, EA 69-31a-r and EA 69-32a-b for a total of 1500 CFA.
Inv. no.: EA 69-29

17. Case for bow, ngoldiu, plaited in two pieces from 1.2 cm broad strips of dum palm leaves ngele (cf. Cat. No. 16). Two leather thongs (each the width of about 1 cm) have been 'plaited' into the dum palm 'weaving' close to the centre of the case, each ending with a strap for carrying. Haddad men use such cases to protect the strings of the bow from getting wet during the rainy season. This particular case was made by the Haddad man from whom it was purchased (cf. *Fig. 9,6*).

Length: 136 cm
Length (upper part): 84 cm
Length (lower part): 70 cm
Width: 12 cm
Prov.: Purchased from Haddad hunter at Chedra on September 11, 1963 together with inv. nos. EA 69-28, EA 69-29, EA 69-31a-r, EA 69-32a-b. Total cost 1500 CFA.
Inv. no. EA 69-30

18. Quiver, dju, with seventeen arrows. The quiver itself is made from the root of the kindil or tefi acacia (Acacia raddiana) in the following way: a piece of the root is heated up in a fire until its marrow mellows, after which it can be removed; the remaining hollow piece of root is then suitable for use. The root piece is covered with leather and decorated at both ends with a piece of goatskin, blackish at the bottom, largely white below the lid. The quiver is carried over the shoulder by means of a twined leather string. The latter is tied to a strap cut into the leather cover of the quiver by means of a knot about one third from the top. It has a lid of coiled basketry made of dum palm fibre and rimmed with leather. This is likewise tied to the quiver with a leather string. The quiver was made by a Haddad man together with its content of arrows.

The arrows, kini, are all poisoned. Each arrow consists of a pointed iron head socketed into a shaft made of reed and wound with fine sinew twine. The arrow heads are forged by a Haddad smith in Chedra, from whom they were purchased by the Haddad hunter, as were the shafts and the poison, which he had smeared on the heads of the arrows. The slot has been enforced and embellished with a binding of fine dark sinew twine. One of the arrows has a dumb point for shooting birds (cf. *Fig. 9,7*).

Quiver:
Length: 60 cm
Circumference: 19.5 cm
Diameter (lid): 6.3 cm
Arrows:
Length (total): 58 cm
Length (arrow heads): 14-15 cm
Prov.: Chedra, September 11, 1963 together with inv. nos. EA 69-28, EA 69-29, EA 69-30, EA 69-32a-b for a total of 1500 CFA.
Inv. nos. EA 69-31a-r

17,7. Arrow. Cat. no. 18. Photo J.K.

17,8. Quiver with arrow. Cat. no. 15. Photo J.K.

17,9. Arrows. Cat. no. 18. Photo J.K.

19. A pair of pads for the protection of the knees. Such pads are called nungoromebe, which means 'something which is carried on the knees'. The pads are made from shreds of cotton cloth. They are tied around the knees by means of two pairs of leather strings. One of the pads has been reinforced with a patch of leather on the inside (cf. *Fig. 9,11*).

Diameter, a: 19 cm x 20 cm, b: 17 cm x 20 cm
Prov.: Chedra, September 11, 1963 together with inv. nos. EA 69-28, EA 69-29, EA 60-30 and EA 69-31a-r for a total of 1500 CFA.
Inv. nos. EA 69-32a-b

20. Mortar, pestle, poison and magical wisps.
a. Mortar, kuru kayo, for pounding seeds for the making of poison for arrows, known as kayo. The mortar is carved from wood from the karu or teledi tree (Kreda), a sizeable tree which defoliates during the rainy season. The mortar is crudely cut and only slightly smoothed. A leather strap to be used for transportation and storing is tied around the mor-

tar's foot. The specimen is not decorated except for a simple incision some 1.5 cm below the rim.
b. Pestle, kura, in the form of a simple iron chisel, which the owner used when pounding seeds for the making of poison. Both mortar and pestle were produced by a Haddad smith.
c. Poisonous seeds from a tree called djo, which the Haddad use when producing poison for their arrows. The seeds are imported from Nigeria and can be bought at markets all over Kanem for 75 CFA for an amount corresponding to about one decilitre.
d. A lump of poison, kayo, with which the Haddad owner will smear his arrow heads.
e. Two young dum palm leaves, each with a tying of bast around the petiole. Such wisps are made by hunters to promote hunting luck if they find themselves unable to spot game on an expedition. A hunter will jump over the wisp once to promote his luck. We were not able to obtain any further explanation on this practice or how it fitted into the wider system of Haddad Kanembu knowledge and their understanding of magic (cf. *Fig. 9,14*).

Height (mortar): 17 cm
Diameter (mortar at rim): 9.5 cm
Length (pestle): 20 cm
Prov.: Purchased from a Haddad hunter at Chedra on September 12, 1963 for 300 CFA.
Inv. nos. EA 69-33a-e

21. Horn used for signalling during a hunt, kankagadi, made of a horn of a damalisque antelope, damaliscus korrigum. This has been cut to size and provided with a hole on its concave side with a red-hot knife, a method known throughout

17,10. Horn used for signaling during a hunt. Cat. no. 21. Photo J.K.

North Africa. Not all hunters possess a horn, but the signals are well known to all Haddad. The horn is held in the right hand and placed at the right corner of the mouth when used. The hole is opened and closed with the left hand to interrupt the stream of air, thus producing a consecutive series of sounds. Basically the Haddad make use of two kinds of signals only. The first consists of a tone, a pause, a tone, and a pause. This signals to the other hunters that they can approach. The other signal consists of consecutive sounds made swiftly one after the other. This signals that the hunter has spotted game and calls upon the others to approach swiftly but with care.

Length: 30 cm
Diameter (hole): 0.7 cm
Prov.: Purchased at Chedra, September 12, 1963 for 150 CFA.
Inv. no. EA 69-34

The hunting gear of a specialist

22. Four small nets, sarada (Kanembu), out of an original set of six, for hunting guinea fowl, hare, fox and other small game. Two of the nets were given to the museum at Fort-Lamy. The sticks are made from branches of a tree known as bolokor (Kanembu) or chaw (Arabic), the meshes from cotton thread bought at the local market. These nets were purchased from Chari, a Haddad hunter who, like his father, had specialized in hunting small game, together with a role of cotton thread for repairs (cf. Chapter 9: 237).

Height (sticks): 64-69 cm
Length (nets at top, approx.): 70 cm
Length (nets at bottom, approx.): 82 cm
Width (mesh, approx): 4 cm x 6 cm
Length (reel): 18 cm
Prov.: Bought at N'Guri on July 30, 1963 with inv. nos. EA 69-6 and EA 69-7 for 2000 CFA.
Inv. nos. EA 69-5a-d

23. Bag, sari (Kanembu), for carrying game, made by Chari of twines of dum palm leaves. The bag is cylindrical, narrowing slightly towards the top, and has an almost circular bottom. Two plaited handles are placed opposite one another at the rim, one presumably of a more recent date than the other, judging from the fact that it

is of a different, bluish material, not palm leaf like the other, likely a replacement of the worn out original. The bag is plaited in a loop-like manner, the loops being tied together into a circular, 'loop-stitched' bottom. The bag is reinforced at the rim by means of a thicker string making up the top two centimetres of the bag. A hole in the bottom has been repaired with a simple strip of palm leaf. In general the making of strings and ropes as well as of bags, baskets and bags netted from these is men's work among the Haddad, while other kinds of basketry and the making of mats is done by women. The bag in question was used to carry live game, such as rabbits, fennec and birds to potential buyers. A stick or club was used both

17,11. Bag used for transporting live game. Cat. no. 23. Photo J.K.

to kill the animals caught in nets and - put through the two handles - as a carrying device to put on the shoulder (*Figs. 9,35 & 17,11*).

Height: 40 cm
Diameter (centre): 43 cm
Diameter (at rim): 28 cm
Prov.: Bought at N'Guri on July 30, 1963 together with inv. nos. EA 69-5a-d and EA 69-7 for 2000 CFA.
Inv. no. EA 69-6

24. Simple stick, kar (Kanembu), from a tree known as kawla in Kanembu and Arabic. The stick was used by the hunter to club animals and to carry various gears such as nets, an extra shirt and his game bag over the shoulder. He would put the stick through the handles of the game bag and tie the other items unto this. Occasionally the stick was applied to pester foxes and fennecs in their dens. The stick was stuck in and out of the entrance holes of the underground dens of the animals with a lot of noise to make them leave their hide-outs, although the stick was in fact too short to be of optimal use. In case he opted for a serious try at the game the hunter would take the trouble to cut a branch from a tree of appropriate length of some two to three metres (cf. *Fig. 9,33*).

Length: 79 cm
Prov.: Bought at N'Guri on July 30, 1963 together with inv. nos. EA 69-5a-d and EA 69-6 for 2000 CFA.
Inv. no. EA 69-7

25. Large net, mburu, with fine meshes for catching birds. Such nets are commonly used by the Haddad

Kanembu during the dry season, when birds can be lured more easily into the net with water (cf. Chapter 9: 243-46). This particular net was made by the hunter Chari. The netting is of cotton thread, which he had bought at the market, the meshes being about 1.5 cm in diameter. The net is tied with a cotton string to a 230 cm long rod, some 3 cm in diameter made from a piece of root from a tree known as kindel in Kanembu or irek in Arabic. The root is bent into a semi-circular or bow-like shape by tying the two ends together with a string just after it has been dug out. After a week or so, the branch has dried sufficiently to retain the semi-circular shape. It needs no treatment with fire. The finished net has a skew oval shape measuring some 230 cm x 150 cm. When used the net is placed over a shallow puddle, pegged to the ground with six small wooden pegs, kori, of which the two hold the net at each end of the curved wooden frame, while the remaining pegs hold it to the ground at intervals at the rear end of the frame (EA 69-15a-f). A rope made of twined dum palm leaves, dje in Kanembu, about 9 metres long, is tied to the middle of the wooden frame at one end, the hunter holding the other firmly in his hands in a hideout in a nearby thicket, fada. When one or more birds have come to the puddle to drink, he swiftly pulls it to unleash the net (*Figs. 9,35-9,41*).

Length (frame): 230 cm
Circumference (branch): 3 cm
Length (rope): 900 cm
Prov.: Bought at N'Guri on July 31, 1963 for 2.200 CFA.
Inv. nos. EA 69-15a-f

26. Net, sarada (Kanembu) or segei (Kreda), for the catching of bustards, (Otididae), either Denham's bustard (Neotis cafra denhami), the Sudan bustard (Choriotis arabs stieberi), the northern black-bellied bustard (Lissotis melanogaster melanogaster) or the Nubian bustard (Neotis nuba) - species all hunted by the Haddad. The net itself is made of thread spun from sinews of oxen and tied to and held up by two sticks cut from a tree known as musku (Kanembu and Kreda) or kowlu (Arabic). This is done with a braided string of ox hair. The net can be used by a single person gently driving the bustard towards its fate. A similar but shorter net was purchased among the Haddad Kreda (Cat. No. 48; cf. *Fig. 9,42*).

Length (total): 530 cm
Length (sticks): 188 cm and 151 cm
Width (meshes): 10 cm x 15 cm
Prov.: Bought from a Haddad Kanembu east of Méchimeré on August 14, 1963 for 600 CFA.
Inv. no. EA 69-16

27. Nets for catching jackals. The twine is of fibres from the tefi acacia alias Acacia raddiana, except for a piece of the upper cord, which has been enforced with a piece of twined string of black goat's hair, presumably because the net got torn during a hunt. The net is attached to two sticks made of wood from a tree known as nergi (Kanembu). The sticks taper off to a point at one end, making it easier to stick them into the ground when setting up the net. The Haddad use two or three of these nets when hunting for jackal. They are prone to go hunting if jackals are taking goats from the herds. Normally jackals are caught near water-holes. When the animal approaches the nets, the hunter jumps up and shouts in order to distract the jackal so that it quickens its pace and fails to see the net. Once trapped, the animal is given a blow with a club or stick. Another net was purchased among the Haddad Kreda (cf. Cat. No. 50).

Length: 115 cm
Height (net, approx.): 65 cm
Height (sticks): 108 cm
Width (meshes): 8 cm x 10 cm
Prov.: Bought from a Haddad hunter at Wanagal on August 16, 1963 for 500 CFA.
Inv. no. EA 69-18

Weapons

28. Two out of an original set of four barbed spears, aedi (Kanembu and Kreda) - the number in which they are usually carried by Haddad and Kreda pastoralists alike - together with a leather sheath, karaga (Kanembu and Kreda). The spears were made by smiths in Méchimeré. The shafts are made of roots of the tefi acacia (Acacia raddiana). Each of them has a balancing device at the end consisting of a two milimetre thick iron thread wound neatly around the shaft. The two other spears, now in the collections in Chad have balancing devices of copper, a metal believed to hold magical forces and hence protective powers. The iron blades have two rows of barbs and finely incised geometrical designs. They are fastened to the shafts with sockets into which the shafts have been fitted. For protec-

tion the spears are carried in a sheath made of depilated ox-hide and with a long braided leather strap by means of which it can be carried over the shoulder. The sheath is slightly conical and stitched together with a 3 mm broad leather band. Its bottom end is a roundish piece of leather that has been stitched onto the lower part of the case, also with a leather band. The upper part of the case is enforced and embellished with a 6 cm broad leather band which ends in tiny triangles. Some Haddad and most Kreda men possess such spears and use these as weapons, the former largely for personal protection while the Kreda make use of them in pursuit of cattle thieves or when encountering opposition if they are out to steal cattle themselves - a fairly regular undertaking at the time of our fieldwork. But the spears are also used for hunting if a man gets a chance, for example, of sneaking up on a sleeping gazelle. The spears were made by a Haddad smith in Méchimeré (cf. *Figs. 6,2; 9,1b; 9,1c & 15,12*).

Length (spears, total):
a. 132.5 cm; b. 132 cm
Length (blades): 32 cm
Length (sheath without cord): 39.5 cm
Prov.: Purchased from a Haddad at Wanagal on August 16, 1963 for 500 CFA.
Inv. nos. G.7209a-b

29. Spear, kulai (Kanembu and Kreda), with blade of the antler of a gazelle. The shaft is made of a root of the tefi acacia (Acacia raddiana). Spears like these are used by boys when herding cattle and flocks of small ruminants. The boys carry them

for protection but also to hunt for birds (cf. *Fig. 7,11*).

Length (total): 143 cm
Length (blade with socket): 17 cm
Prov.: Bought from a Haddad hunter at Wanagal on August 16, 1963 for 100 CFA.
Inv. no. EA 69-20

30. Lance, aedi bou (Kanembu and Kreda) with an iron blade. A decoration of simple lines is incised on the lower third part of the blade, which ends in a socket fitted into the shaft. The latter is made of a root of the tefi acacia, Acacia raddiana, and provided with a 3.5 cm long balancing device made of 3.5 mm round iron wire that has been wound around the end of the shaft. The lance was made by Haddad smiths at Méchimeré. Lances like this one are used both as weapons against fellow men and for hunting and protection against wild animals.

Length (total): 215 cm
Length (blade with socket): 48 cm
Circumference (shaft): 6.5 cm
Prov.: Bought from a Haddad at Wanagal on August 16, 1963 for 300 CFA.
Inv. no. EA 69-19

31. Tiny throwing knife, ngili (Kreda and Kanembu) or kurbadj (Arabic) used by Haddad boys. The knife is made of iron and has two blades. The main blade projects from the upper end of the knife's 'stem', the smaller one about one third down from the top. The handle is covered by ox-hide to provide a more comfortable grip. The knife was made by smiths in Méchimeré. Essentially, throw-

17,12. Boomerang. Cat. no. 33. Photo J.K.

ing knives are weapons of defence but they may be used for hunting as well. Boys improve their throwing skills using similar but smaller sized knives for playing and for hunting small birds. With luck they may even get guinea fowl, Nimida meleagris strasseni. The knife was bought from a Haddad, whose son used it quite successfully for hunting (cf. *Fig. 9,3*).

Length (total): 35 cm
Length (small blade): 6 cm
Prov.: Purchased on August 15, 1963 at N'Galu for 100 CFA.
Inv. no. EA 69-17

32. Throwing knife, ngulio (Kanembu), of iron. The blade is curved at the top and the knife has an extra blade that protrudes some 23 cm below the point of the knife. A piece of skin, probably antelope has been wrapped around and stitched together at the 'stem' of the weapon as a handle and for enhancing the grip.

Length: 58.5 cm
Length (handle): 10 cm
Prov.: Purchased from a Haddad man at Chedra on September 12, 1963 for 150 CFA.
Private coll.

33. Boomerang or throwing stick, safarok or sofrok (Kanembu), made from wood of the savonier tree, alou (Kreda) or hadjili (Arabic). It is heavy, slightly curved and adorned with geometrical lines, crosses and some chequered engravings on both sides. The ornaments are merely decorative. A strap for carrying has been inserted near the end of the stick. Boomerangs are occasionally carried by Haddad men. They occur rarely in Kanem whereas they are common in Wadai. This stick was purchased from a Wadai man at Chedra. He claimed that in Wadai boomerangs are used as weapons and only occasionally for hunting. Wadai men often carry several of these weapons at a time (cf. *Fig. 17,12*).

Length: 69 cm
Width: 6 cm
Diameter: 3 cm
Prov.: Bought for 200 CFA at Chedra on September 9, 1963.
Inv. no. EA 69-35

34. Spear, kulai (Kreda), with blade of an antelope horn, damaliscus korrigum. The spear has a wooden shaft made from a root of the tefi acacia, Acacia raddiana, onto which the tip of the horn has been socketed. The horns of the Damalisque are naturally curved with an undulating surface. The Haddad transform the form and surface of these by softening them in embers, after which they are able both to straighten out the horns and to make them smooth. The far end of the shaft is slightly pointed and looks as if originally furnished with a ferrule some 2.5 cm long. Spears like this one are used both by Haddad and Kreda men for protection and as weapons against wild animals, including lions. This particular item was bought from a Kreda pastoralist in a camp at Adjadja; it had been made, however, by a Haddad Kanembu man (cf. *Fig. 9,1a*).

Length (total): 169 cm
Length (blade): 40.5 cm
Circumference (shaft): 5 cm
Prov.: Bought at Adjadja, August 19, 1963.
Inv. no. G.7211

Household items

35. Water skin made from the skin of a gazelle. All hair has been removed from the hide and it has been tanned. The skin is apparently from a male. Holes stemming from the genitals and the anus are sown together with a stitching around an enforcement or leather. The same holds for a long stitching up the animal's neck all the way to where the head has been severed but in this case the hole is left open for the water to pass through. A knot on the hide of each of the fore- and hind-legs ensures that the bag keeps tight. Moreover, the hide of the hind legs have been tied together to facilitate the hanging up of the skin.

Length: 80 cm
Width (at the middle): 42 cm
Prov.: Purchased at Chedra on September 10, 1963 for 350 CFA.
Inv. no. EA 69-36

36. Three wooden bowls, known as bordoa in Kanembu, all with curved lids of coiled basketry rimmed and decorated with red leather strips, known as sende. Each bowl is carved in one piece from a trunk including its four conical feet (about 6 cm tall) and an ear or handle for transportation. The bowls are blackish-brown in colour and decorated from the rim and half-way down their sides with incisions. These run around the bowls in the form of three bands of a herring-bone pattern separated by horizontal lines. The lower part of the bowls has incisions of vertical lines with dots intersected by her-ring-bone bands that run all the way down to the bottom. The lids are of neatly coiled basketry of dum palm strips decorated with a circular red leather patch at the top, red leather rims, and with dots and zigzag patterns sewn onto the basketry with leather strips.

17.14. Decorated bowl with lid of coiled basketry for storage of grain and for display. Cat. no. 37a-b. Photo J.K.

To the Haddad (Kanembu) and the Kanembu alike these bowls are highly prized valuables. They embellish the huts and speak of wealth and status - the more the better. Women stack up the bowls at the back wall of the tent-like construction in their huts, i.e. be-hind the bed, together with brightly coloured enamel basins, bowls and plates. Depending on her wealth a woman may possess one or several rows of these wooden bowls, i.e. up to 12 or 15, many of which will be highly prized heirlooms often given to her by her mother, while others

will be her own purchases (cf. *Figs. 12,24 & 15,14*).

a.
Height (with legs): 35 cm
Diameter (at rim): 33 cm
Height (lid): 12 cm
Diameter (lid at top): 12 cm;
(lid at rim): 34 cm

b.
Height (with legs): 26 cm
Diameter (at rim): 32 cm
Height (lid): 11 cm
Diameter (lid at top): 11 cm;
(lid at rim): 33 cm

c.
Height (with legs): 30 cm
Diameter (at rim): 25.5 cm
Height (lid): 31 cm
Diameter (lid at top): 8 cm; (lid at rim): 32.5 cm
Prov.: Purchased at Chedra, September 12, 1963.
Private coll.

17,13. Waterskin. Cat. no. 35. Photo J.K.

37. Wooden bowl, bordoa, on four conically shaped feet and with a lid, sende, of coiled basketry (cf. *Fig. 17,14*). The bowl is carved from a single piece of wood. It is blackish-brown in colour and decorated with geometrical incisions: Three bands with sets of oblique designs running all around the bowl from the top and slightly past its middle. Further down these are replaced by a band of pyramidal designs, lines and large dots covering the lower part of the bowl. The lid is of coiled basketry with a rim of red leather (goat) and a zigzag decoration here and just above the rim made with a leather strip.

Bowls like these are cherished valuables and traditionally part of the marriage exchanges. Some women buy bowls on their own to embellish their homes. In daily life they solely have a decorative function, being on display against the back wall of the 'tent' placed inside the hut, as well as an indicator of wealth and status. A well-to-do family may possess quite a number of these bowls, so many at times that they are stacked in rows one on top of the other together with polychrome basins of sheet metal. The bowls are not produced locally, but bought at local markets, as are the basins of sheet metal. The bowls may also be obtained from traders from the South where the bowls are produced. They are said to be made by the Kuka, who formerly lived as slaves among the Bulala east of Fort-Lamy around Ati, Kokoro and Lake Fitri.

The bowl was bought from a Haddad Kanembu woman, who had owned it for about 12 years at the time of the purchase. She told us that the bowl had been her mother's and that she in turn had had it for a very long time.

Height (total with lid): 38 cm
Diameter (bowl): 32 cm
Diameter (lid): 35 cm
Prov.: Purchased for 400 CFA at Chedra, September 9, 1963.
Inv. no. G.7215a-b

Implements

38. Hoe, bonu (Kanembu), bon (Kreda), with a triangular iron blade socketed on the tapering end of a shaft made from wood of a tree known as alow in Kreda and Kanembu and as hadjili in Arabic. Hoes are used for a variety of agricultural tasks, first and foremost to prepare the soil before sowing and for weeding millet. The hoe was bought from a Haddad Kanembu family. The man had purchased the item from a smith at the market of Méchimeré (cf. *Fig. 7,20*).

Length (shaft): 45 cm
Width (edge of blade): 17.5 cm
Length (blade from neck to edge): 14 cm
Prov.: Purchased at Wanagal, August 16, 1963 for 100 CFA.
Inv. no. G.7212

39. Small iron awl known as asun (Kreda) or kantan (Kanembu). The awl has a small conically shaped wooden shaft. Awls are indispensable to Haddad women for a variety of tasks. Firstly, they are used when making or repairing coiled basketry, to pierce holes in the already firm coils and to insert new strips of palm leaves, thus adding to and lashing coil upon coil. Secondly, the awls are applied for various tasks including the piercing of holes when working with leather. Thirdly, awls are

indispensable when doing women's coiffure to separate one lock of hair from the other when braiding those scores of tiny braids so characteristic of the look of Kanemese women. The awl was purchased from a Haddad woman together with other of her personal belongings. She, in turn, had bought the awl from a Haddad smith at the market at Méchimeré (cf. *Fig. 13,11*).

Length (total): 11.5 cm
Length (of shaft): 3.5 cm
Prov.: Bought at Wanagal, August 16, 1963 together with inv.nos. G.7195, G.7196, G.7198, G.7199, EA 69-21, EA 69-22, EA 69-23a-b and EA 69-24a-b for a total of 1500 CFA.
Inv. no. G.7200

Adornment and cosmetics

40. Necklace, kiel (Kanembu), made of alternating oblong black and white beads, intersected at five places by three red beads in a row, all double the length of the black and white ones, and at one place by two red beads only. The black and white beads had been bought at the market at Méchimeré by the owner of the necklace, the red ones from a place called Nuku in the préfecture of Mao. The beads are strung on cotton twine and tied around the neck with a short leather string with one yellow bead at the end. Made by the woman from whom it was purchased with other of her personal belongings.

Length (total): 72 cm
Length (black and white beads): 3-4 mm (red beads): 7-9 mm
Prov.: Purchased from a Haddad woman at Wanagal, August 16, 1963

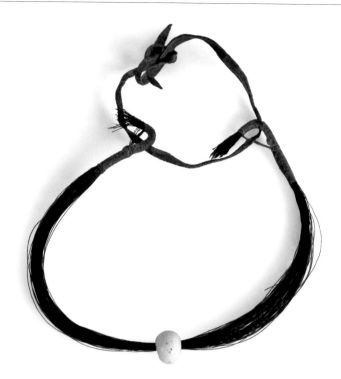

17,15. Necklace of horse-hair with a white bead. Cat. no. 41. Photo J.K.

17,16. Four black glass arm rings.
Cat. no. 42. Photo J.K.

together with inv. nos. G.7195, G. 7196, G.7198, G.7199, G.7200, EA 69-22, EA 69-23a-b and EA 69-24a-b for a total of 1500 CFA. Inv. no. EA 69-21

41. Necklace of horse-hair and a single white glass bead, eri-tjo in Kreda, tjo meaning white. In Kanembu such white beads are known as keri-bul, bul meaning white. The horse-hair is tied together at the ends with a delicate lashing of very fine leather strings ending in loops. The necklace is tied around the neck by making a knot on a leather string inserted through these loops. The necklace is worn pretty tightly around the neck. White beads are highly appreciated. They come in both stone and glass. This necklace had been purchased in Massakory by the Haddad woman from whom it was bought.

Length (minus cord): 30 cm
Prov.: Purchased from a Haddad woman at Wanagal, August 16, 1963 together with inv. nos. G.7195, G. 7196, G.7198, G.7199, G.7200, EA 69-21, EA 69-23a-b and EA 69-24a-b for a total of 1500 CFA. Inv. no. EA 69-22

42. Four arm-rings of black glass, kolia (Kreda), kolio (Kanembu). Arm-rings like these are common in the area. They are bought in pairs at the markets but said to come from Mecca. Haddad Kreda women usually wear this kind of jewellery in pairs on the upper arm, just above the elbow. If a woman wears one only, it will be because the other one has broken. These particular pairs were purchased from a Haddad Kanembu woman together with other personal belongings.

Diameter (inner): 6.6 cm (outer): 7.5 cm
Prov.: Purchased from a Haddad woman at Wanagal on August 16, 1963 together with inv. nos. G. 7195, G. 7196, G.7198, G.7199, G.7200, EA 69-21 and EA 69-22 for a total of 1500 CFA.
Inv. nos. EA 69-23a-b and EA 69-24a-b

43. Calabash, chi (Kanembu) or zi (Kreda), with a lid of coiled basketry used for cosmetics. It is of amphora shape with a neck of coiled basketry. Two 'handles' placed on each side of this are linked with a small braided cord in which the container can be hung. The calabash contains seeds known as argoumi (Kanembu) or teba (Kreda). Women pound these in a tiny mortar. (cf. Cat. No. 46), mix the substance with butter or oil and

17,17. From tool with tweezers, used by women to apply kohl on eye lids. Cat. no. 45.

use the cream for the hair. Teba seeds stem from Nigeria and are sold at local markets in Kanem. The calabash also contains a razor blade. Women clean-shave their forehead to improve their looks. The container was made by the Haddad Kanembu woman and purchased from her with other of her personal belongings (cf. *Fig. 13,11*).

Height: 21 cm
Diameter (lid): 4 cm
Prov.: Purchased from a Haddad woman at Wanagal on August 16, 1963 together with inv. nos. G. 7196, G.7198, G.7199, G.7200, EA 69-21, EA 69-22, EA 69-23a-b and EA 69-24a-b for a total of 1500 CFA. Inv. no. G.7195

44. Small container, known as go-lei (in both Kreda and Kanembu),

made from the tip of an antelope antler (damaliscus korrigum). The horn is used by women to keep kohl or sozerum i.e. the black powder of antimony sulphide which they use as mascara. Kohl is smeared on both the upper and lower eyelid with a tiny iron stick (Cat. No. 45). Although it is not costly, it is not applied daily but only on festive occasions and when women go to the market. The powder is bought at markets, in this case at Méchimeré, and kept in a piece of indigo coloured cotton cloth which is stuck inside the smoothly polished container.

Length: 16 cm
Diameter (at rim): 2 - 1.5 cm.
Prov.: Purchased at Wanagal on August 16, 1963 from a Haddad woman together with other of her personal objects, cf. inv. nos. G.7195, G. 7196, G.7199, G.7200, EA 69-21,

EA 69-22, EA 69-23a-b and EA 69-24a-b for a total of 1500 CFA. Inv. no. G.7198

45. Iron tool, murkat golei (Kreda and Kanembu), used by women to smear kohl at the eyelids (cf. Cat. No. 44). The object has the shape of a blunt awl. It is mostly roundish, but the upper half of the object is square and decorated with geometrical engravings. A few 'ears' are forged at the top end, two of which are furnished with tiny iron rings. From each of these hangs a pair of tweezers, which have seen better days (*Fig. 17,17*).

Length: 15.5 cm
Prov.: Purchased at Wanagal on August 16, 1963 from a young Haddad woman, who herself had bought it from a smith at the market at Méchimeré. The golai was purchased with other of her

17,18. Ornamented mortar and pestle. Cat. no. 46. Photo J.K.

personal items, cf. inv. nos. G.7195, G. 7196, G.7198, G.7200, EA 69-21, EA 69-22, EA 69-23a-b and EA 69-24a-b for a total of 1500 CFA. Inv. no. G.7199

46. Ornamented mortar with pestle, kunusu (Kreda), kunu (Kanembu). The mortar is cut from a single piece of wood. The elliptically formed bowl stands on a conical foot. Three 'pillars' connect the bowl and the foot. The pestle is basically a stick but with somewhat enlarged, conically shaped ends. It is adorned with incisions running parallel all around just below the conical end pieces. Both the mortar and the pestle are decorated with geometrical lines and cross-lines incised in the wood and then blackened with fire.

The mortar is used exclusively to pound seeds of sweet-scented plants which women use for personal hygiene and as cosmetics, be it to make body lotions or conditioner for the hair. Haddad Kanembu and Kreda women alike collect a variety of plants for these purposes (cf. Cat. No. 43).

The mortar had been bought from a Haddad smith by the woman, from whom I bought it.

Height (mortar, total): 27 cm
Height (foot): 7 cm
Diameter (at rim): 21 cm
Length (pestle): 64 cm
Circumference, (pestle at the middle): 11.7 cm
Prov.: Purchased at Chedra, September 7, 1963 for 400 CFA.
Inv. no. G.7194a-b.

HADDAD KREDA

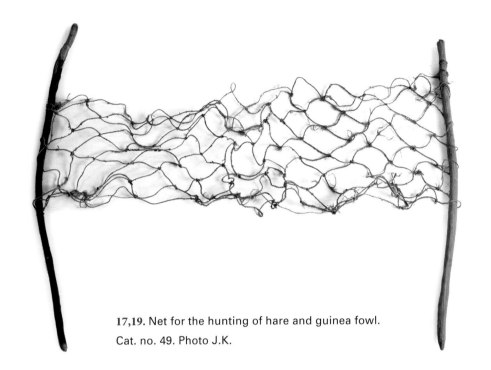

17,19. Net for the hunting of hare and guinea fowl. Cat. no. 49. Photo J.K.

Hunting

47. Net for catching guinea fowl, segia goulaya (Kreda), made from sinews. It is put up between two sticks by means of a cord of oxtail hair, the distance between the two being about 125 cm.

Height (sticks): 85 and 86 cm
Length (net): 125 cm
Width, (meshes): 8 cm x 9 cm
Prov.: Bought from the Haddad Kreda at Sidige Joroso on August 21, 1963 together with inv. nos. EA 69-40a-b, EA 69-42a-g, EA 69-43a-b, EA 69-44, EA 69-45 and EA 69-46 for a total of 2000 CFA.
Inv. no. EA 69-41

48. Net, segei (Kreda), for catching bustards. The net is made of twined strings of sinew. These are

of two different colours, one light brown, and the other beige. It looks as if the net has been put together of two nets, probably for hunting jackals. The strings or thin, twined ropes which hold up the net up have also been mended with two pieces, a fair one of acacia fibres and a black one of goat's hair. The net is suspended between two sticks and rolled up around these during transport and keeping. A similar net was purchased among the Haddad Kanembu (cf. Cat. No. 26).

Length: 260 cm
Width (meshes): 8 cm x 10 cm
Height (sticks): 100 cm
Prov.: Bought at Tatchoma Mada from a young Haddad smith on September 4, 1963 for 200 CFA.
Inv. no. EA 69-58

49. Two nets of an original set of four for the hunting of hares. The nets were fabricated and used by a Haddad boy. Each net consists of two sticks onto which the net is fastened by means of the eyes at each side and a sinew thread tied near the top of each stick. Two of the four nets were made of sinews, the other two of strings twined from bark of the tefi acacia (Acacia raddiana). Nets made of strings of acacia can only be used for catching hares and guinea fowl. Acacia fibres are not strong enough to hold larger game.

a.
Length (total): 91 cm
Height (sticks): 62 cm
Height (nets, approx.): 37 cm
Width (meshes): 6 cm

b.
Length (total): 80 cm
Height (sticks): 58 cm and 62 cm
Height (net, approx.): 35 cm
Width (meshes): 4 - 5 cm
Prov.: Purchased from the owner, a Haddad boy at Gaba, September 3, 1963 for 300 CFA.
Inv. no. EA 69-54a-b

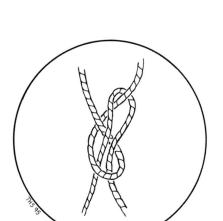

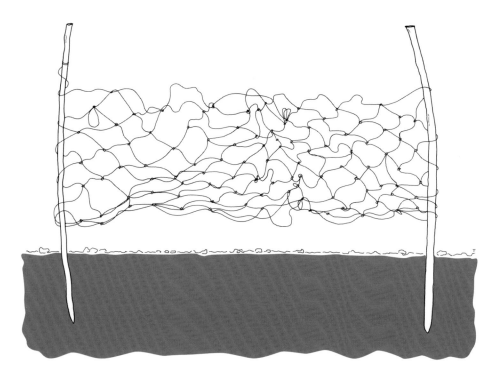

17.20. Net for the catching of hares with detail showing a mesh of the net.
Drawing T.O.S.

50. Net for the hunting of jackals, sarta turka (Kreda) (cf. Cat. No. 27). It is sometimes talked about as mofuin (pl. mofuna), which denotes something 'neither two big nor too small'. The net is made of sinew and stretched between two sticks by means of a string twined from the hair of oxtail. The net was originally bought together with another net now at the museum at Fort-Lamy (cf. *Fig. 17,21*).

Length (net): 160 cm
Length (sticks): 143 cm and 145 cm
Width (meshes): 10 cm
Prov.: Bought from the Haddad Kreda at Sidige Joroso, August 21, 1963 together with inv. nos. EA 69-40a-b, EA 69-41, EA 69-42a-g, EA 69-43a-b, EA 69- 45 and EA 69-46.
Inv. no. EA 69-44

51. Two nets for the hunting of gazelle. These are known by the Haddad Kreda as segia douska. The nets are made from sinews of either oxen or goats or from gazelles. The net is held in place by two sticks with a string of hair spun from oxtails. The sticks are called muska (Kreda) and made of wood from a tree known as koli in both Kreda and Arabic. The nets are placed next to one another so that they close gaps between natural barriers to the gazelle such as tall bushes and trees. The length of the net when put up is approximately 190 cm.

Length (nets): a. 135 cm; b. 145 cm
Height (sticks): 184 - 187 cm
Width (meshes): 10 cm x 15 cm
Prov.: Purchased from the Haddad Kreda at Sidige Joroso, August 1, 1963 together with inv. nos. EA

69-41, EA 69-42a-g, EA 69-43a-b, EA 69-44, EA 69-45 and EA 69-46 for 2000 CFA.
Inv. nos. EA 69-40a-b

52. Four forked sticks, eba, (Kreda) made of wood from the nergi (Kreda) tree. The sticks are used for the hanging of bundles of black goatskin strips to produce a kind of trompe-d'œil that can fool game being chased towards the nets (cf. description below Cat. No. 53; *Figs. 9,50 & 17,27*).

Height: 108 cm - 119 cm
Prov.: Purchased from the Haddad Kreda at Sidige Joroso, August 21, 1963 together with inv. nos. EA 69-40a-b, EA 69-41, EA 69-42e-g, EA 69-43a-g, EA 69-44 and EA 69-45 and EA 69-46 for 2000 CFA.
Inv. no. EA 69-42a-d

53. Three bundles made of strips of black goatskin, tari (Kreda). These bundles are hung on the forked sticks, eba, just mentioned above and form a crucial part of the hunting technology. Before the Haddad Kreda chase game that they have spotted towards the location where they have placed their nets, they put up a considerable number of sticks with bundles of strips of goatskin. The sticks demarcate a kind of passage towards the nets that hopefully induces the game to continue its flight in the right direction towards these. Sticks may also be placed in between nets to 'bar' the game from running between the nets and hence cover greater ground. The bundles are hung on the cleft of the stick, either with a simple leather strap (inv. nos. EA 69.42e and EA 69-42f), or in a plaited leather strap (inv. no A 69-42g). When the 'trompe

17,21. Net for the hunting of jackals. Cat. no. 50. Photo J.K..

17,22. Net set for gazelle.

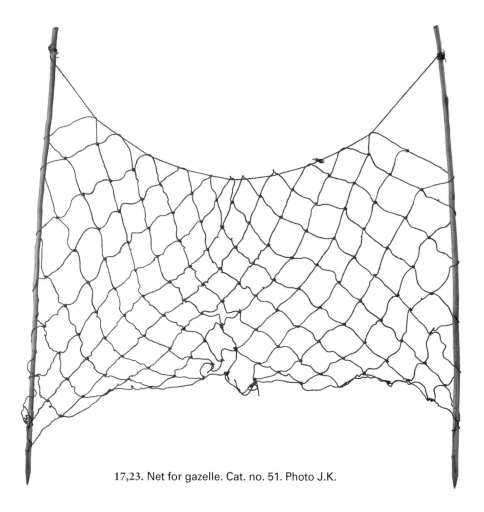

17,23. Net for gazelle. Cat. no. 51. Photo J.K.

17,24. Gazelles that are caught in nets may land some 10-15 metres beyond the place where the nets were placed.

d'œils' are placed in the landscape, the sticks and bundles are called tara-eba. At a distance these are easily taken for human beings (cf. *Figs. 9,50 & 17,27*).

Length: 78 cm - 91 cm
Prov.: Bought from the Haddad Kreda at Sidige Joroso, August 21, 1963 together with inv. nos. EA 69-40a-b, EA 69-41, EA 69-42a-d, EA 69-43a-b, EA 69-44, EA 69-45 and EA 69-46 for 2000 CFA.
Inv. no. EA 69-42e-g

54. Two sticks, one somewhat longer than the other, known respectively as gegere and koltrum (Kreda). Such sticks are used by hunters to make a noise to chase the game into the nets. These sticks are of light, 'porous' wood, which makes the sound both sonorous and loud. The longer of the two sticks, gegere, is also used to club the game caught in the nets, whether this is jackal, gazelle or antelope. They are made from wood of the tjerogo (Kreda) tree, also known as nabak (Arabic) (cf. *Fig. 9,54*).

Length of gegere: 78.5 cm
Length of koltrum: 29.5 cm
Prov.: Purchased from the Haddad Kreda at Sidige Joroso, August 21, 1963 together with inv. nos. EA 69-40a-b, EA 69-41, EA 69-42a-g, EA 69-44, EA 69-45 and EA 69-46 for 2000 CFA.
Inv. no. EA 69-43a-b

55. Bag, tjelli (Kreda) netted of a thin, twined rope of dum palm leaves in a manner which resembles crochet. Such bags are made by Haddad men and used to carry home the spoil of the hunt, a bag of gazelle or antelope.

17,25. A gazelle has been caught, clubbed and had its throat cut.

17,26. Detail of net for gazelle. Cat. no. 51. Photo J.K.

17,27. Forked stick with bundle of goat-skin pieces to be used as scarecrows during the gazelle hunting. Cat. nos. 52 & 53. Photo L.L.

Height: 51 cm
Diameter (top and bottom): 64 cm
Prov.: Purchased from the Haddad Kreda at Sidige Joroso, August 21, 1963 together with inv. nos. EA 69-40a-b, EA 69-41, EA 69-42a-g, EA 69-43a-b, EA 69-44 and EA 69-46 for 2000 CFA.
Inv. no. EA 69-45

56. Small lance, kulai (Kreda), with a conically shaped blade of iron and a shaft made from a root of the tefi acacia (Kreda), alias Acacia raddiana. Used by boys for enhancing their skills at throwing. They practise this by hurling the weapon at bundles of straw which someone throws into the air, simulating the flight of birds or, in a way, the movements of small game (cf. *Fig. 9,1d*).

Length (total): 117 cm
Length (of blade): 22 cm
Prov.: Bought from young man who was training a boy in a Haddad camp on August 11, 1963 for 100 CFA.
Inv. no. G.7210

57. Net for the hunting of antelope, be it the scimitar-horned Oryx (Aegoryx algazel algazel), the Topi (Damaliscus korrigum), or the Addax. The net itself is known as segi urula. Segi (pl. sega) means net and urula big. The net consists of two poles made of the wood from the kolu tree, and the net itself is made from sinew of oxen, gazelle or antelope. The string with which the net is fastened to the top of the poles is spun or twined from the hair of oxtails, as is the case with most

nets. When the Haddad are hunting for these antelopes, they place their nets in rows, one behind the other with a distance of about five metres between each row, in order to be able to catch more than one animal if they succeed in chasing a flock of animals into their nets. This is not difficult, however. In particular the Oryx is not easily fooled by sticks with bundles of goatskin strips (cf. *Figs. 9,52 & 9,57*).

Length (sticks): 228 cm and 215 cm
Height (net approx.): 165 cm
Diameter (meshes): 20 cm
Prov.: The net was purchased at Kulo Jesko on August 30, 1963 for 600 CFA.
Inv. no. EA 69-51

58. Lance, aedi, used i.a. when hunting antelopes. The lance has an iron blade with incised ornaments. This is socketed into a long shaft of bamboo embellished and magically enforced with a 19 cm long winding of a 1.5 cm broad band of scrap metal. A piece of cotton cloth has been coiled around this to offer a better grip when the spear is thrown. The cotton 'grip' covers some 6.5 cm of the middle of the shaft. A balancing device and/or ferrule of 4 mm thick iron wire have been coiled around the rear end of the shaft. It measures 3.5 cm. The blade was forged by Haddad smiths in Mussoro, but provided with a shaft by the owner. Apart from being a powerful weapon, the lance is also used as a measuring device. The length of a lance makes for the distance between nets when these are set up in rows, one behind the other, for the hunting of Oryx antelopes. The Oryx is never

17,28. Bag used by Haddad Kreda hunters for transporting the spoils. Cat. no. 55.
Photo J.K.

17,29. A hunting party.

killed with a club. When the animals have been entangled and caught in the nets, the males are first killed by the Haddad with the lance. Female antelopes are held to the ground by some of the hunters while the owner of the net cuts their throats in accordance with Islamic practice.

Length (total): 298 cm
Length (blade with socket): 53 cm
Prov.: Bought from a Haddad Kreda man at Gaba, September 1, 1963 for 500 CFA.
Inv. no. G.9725

59. Lance, aedi bou (Kreda), with a finely engraved iron blade with socket and a shaft made from a root of the tefi acacia (Acacia raddiana). The shaft is thicker towards the blade than at the end to which a ferrule, ani (Kreda), made of iron wire has been fastened. The shaft has a winding of cowhide just below the place where it goes into the socket of the blade. Below the cowhide the shaft has a winding of sheet metal nailed to it. Right below the socket of the blade the hunter has put a simple brass ring and below this again one of twined copper thread. The Haddad

ascribe magical powers to both copper and brass, believing that these metals empower the lance and ensure that it penetrates whatever object is targeted (cf. *Fig. 9,59*).

Length (total): 226 cm
Length (blade): 48 cm
Prov.: Purchased from a Haddad at Gaba, September 3, 1963 for 500 CFA. Private coll.

60. Boomerang, safarok (Kreda), crudely carved from wood of the olou tree. The boomerang has been

17,30. Basket for collecting seeds and transporting food during foraging expeditions. Cat. no. 63. Photo J.K.

17,31. Collecting the seeds of wild grasses, ogu, with a basket like Cat. no. 63.

17,32. Tray of coiled basketry. Cat. no. 64. Photo J.K.

17,33. Water container. Cat. no. 66. Photo J.K.

bent into a right angle but it is only slightly twisted. Boomerangs are used as toys by boys to go hunting for birds and rabbits, while at the same time furthering their skills at throwing objects with precision, in a similar way as they do with miniature spears (cf. *Fig. 9,2*).

Length (inside angle): 13 cm plus 21 cm
Width: 4 cm
Prov.: Purchased from the Haddad Kreda at Sidige Joroso, August 21, 1963 together with inv. nos. EA 69-40a-b, EA 69-41, EA 69 42a-g, EA 69-43a-b, EA 69-44 and EA 69-45 for a total of 2000 CFA.
Inv. no. EA 69-46

61. Boomerang, safarok, used by boys for playing and enhancing their skills at throwing when hunting birds and small game. The tool is crudely carved. One side of the toy is almost flat, the other curved (cf. *Fig. 9,2*).

Length (inside angle): 14 cm plus 21 cm
Width: 4 cm
Prov.: Purchased in Sidige Joroso on August 21, 1963 for 100 CFA.
Inv. no. EA 69-48

Foraging

62. Basket, sumpu (pl. sumpa), for collecting seeds of the wild grass, ogu. The basket is plaited in a zigzag pattern from split bands of dum palm leaves that are tied to a wooden frame some 2.5 cm in width. The latter is made from a piece of split root of the kolu tree. The basket is further en-

forced by an extra, even thinner piece of split wood tied on the outside some 2.5 cm below the rim. A twined handle of split bands of dum palm leaves solidly tied to the wooden frame, enables a person to swing the basket back and forth through the grasses. Two circular holes, some 7 cm below the rim, both neatly enforced by circular basketry much like sewing, allow a stick to be inserted so that the basket can be carried on the way to the foraging area. Inside the basket runs a thin twined dum palm cord. To this is fastened a circular wicker grid made of similarly twined strings in the manner of a 'cob's net'. The ogu seeds are collected by swinging the basket back and forth through stands of ripe grass. When striking the wicker grid of the basket, the seeds are threshed and drop into it while the straw of the grass is barred by the grid. The collection of this significant nutrient is men's work among the Haddad. Nevertheless, the sumpa baskets are made jointly by women and men. The wicker work of the basket itself is made by women, but the completion of the basket, which involves furnishing it with a circular frame of a thin rod of a tree called kolu, as well as making and attaching the grid and a handle, is all done by men (cf. *Figs. 7,13 & 8,2*).

Height: 27 cm
Diameter (at rim): 28 cm-33 cm
Circumference: 102 cm
Prov.: Purchased at Kulo Jesko, August 30, 1963 together with Cat. No. 63 and still another basket offered to the Museum in Fort Lamy for 700 CFA.
Inv. no. G.7214

63. Basket, sumpu (pl. sumpa), for the collection of ogu seeds cf. description of Cat. No. 62). Unlike the other basket, however, this one is not furnished with holes for the insertion of a carrying stick. Even so, this basket is of what can be considered normal size, the former being on the smallish side (cf. *Figs. 7,13; 8,2 & 17,30*).

Height (from top of handle): 35 cm
Diameter: 40 cm (of grid): 30 cm
Circumference: 130 cm
Prov.: Purchased at Kulo Jesko, August 30, 1963 together with Cat. No. 62 and still another basket presented to the Museum in Fort Lamy for 700 CFA.
Inv. no. EA 69-52

64. Large tray of coiled basketry, afray (pl. afra) (Kreda), made of split bands of dum palm leaves. The rim has been enforced and embellished with an edging of leather (goatskin). A braided leather string tied to the rim makes it possible to hang the tray in the tent or a tree when not in use. Trays like this are used for drying wild seeds in the sun and when cleaning the seeds of debris from other plants. The tray is used in particular for seeds of the grass, ogu. The ogu seeds are nutritionally the most significant of the wild seeds that the Haddad collect (cf. *Fig. 17,32*).

Diameter: 61 cm
Prov.: Purchased from the producer a Haddad woman at Gaba, September 3, 1963 for 200 CFA.
Inv. no. EA 69-56

Weapons

65. Throwing knife, ngili (Kanembu), of a type typically made by Haddad smiths at local markets. This knife was made at the market in Mussoro. It consists of a main knife, which ends in a curved blade while another one springs from its stem 32 cm above the bottom end. There is no handle in the sense of a winding or wrapping to steady the grip of the hand. Throwing knifes are used as weapons by the Haddad (Kanembu) and only occasionally for hunting. Throwing knives are common in southern Chad, where men usually carry several, up to a dozen at times. Until independence in 1963, when the police in Fort-Lamy were granted the right to carry revolvers, they patrolled the streets of the capital armed with three to four throwing knives (*Fig. 9,3*).

Length (total): 57 cm
Length (small blade): 12.5 cm
Prov.: Purchased from a Haddad Kreda at Kurei Iruso, August 27, 1963.
Inv. no. EA 69-49

Household items

66. Calabash, zi (Kreda), used for fetching water. The calabash is placed in a carrying device made of twisted ropes of dum palm leaves. It has a neck of coiled basketry, made from split bands of dum palm leaf. It is closed with a circular lid made from the very piece of the calabash which was cut out to allow for the attachment of the coiled neck. The lid itself has a rim of coiled basketry about 3 cm high (cf. *Fig. 17,32*).

Height: 39 cm
Height (neck): 5 cm
Diameter (neck): 14 cm, (lid): 12.5 cm
Prov.: Purchased from a Haddad woman at Kurei Iruso, August 27, 1963 for 400 CFA.
Inv. no. EA 69-50

67. Bowl-shaped basket with lid, desein (pl. desina) (Kreda) of neatly coiled basketry of dum palm with two ears just 3 cm below the rim. The basket can be hung up in the tent with a braided leather string fastened to the rim to keep it at a safe distance from termites. The lid is decorated with a tiny tuft of black sheepskin and a leather rim of black goat skin. The basket is used for storage of flour made from seeds of the ogu grass, which Haddad men collect and women pound (cf. *Fig. 15,5*).

Height: 29 cm
Diameter (rim): 33 cm, (bottom): 12 cm
Prov.: Purchased from the producer, a Haddad woman at Gaba, September 3, 1963 for 500 CFA.
Inv. no. EA 69-57

68. Bottle-shaped container of coiled basketry with lid of calabash and a carrying device of plaited leather strings. The container is made from dum palm bast and the rim has been reinforced and embellished with a leather plaiting. Just below this four leather ears have been inserted. The lid is made of a circular piece of calabash with a 3 cm tall rim of coiled basketry. This has an edging of leather strips on top of which are placed four tiny leather ears, corresponding to those on the container itself, enabling the owner to tie the lid fairly tightly to the container. The container can be carried in a device made of red braided leather cords. One of these encircles the container just above its middle, i.e. where it gets slightly slimmer, and from this leather straps are tied to another circle of braided leather cords towards the bottom of the container. To the upper circle is tied yet another braided leather cord, in which the container can be hung. The leather appears to be oxhide. The container was made by a Haddad woman, who said that she used it for storage of seeds (cf. *Fig. 8,3*).

Height: 34 cm
Diameter (neck): 12 cm
Prov.: Bought at Gaba on September 3, 1963 for 300 CFA.
Inv. no. G.7185

69. Bowl for milk, desein (Kreda) of coiled basketry made by a Haddad woman. The bowl has been coiled from finely twined strands of palm leaf, and so expertly that it holds milk right away. After some time, when the fat of the milk has lent the inside a fine coating, it may hold water as well. Before usage, the bowl will be turned briefly over the kitchen fire. This lends the fresh milk a smoky taste. Both Haddad and Kreda explained that they hold the bowl into the fire to "take away the smell of uncleanliness" (cf. *Figs. 7,7 & 7,8*).

Height: 17 cm
Diameter (at rim): 25 cm
Prov.: Purchased from a Haddad woman at Kurei Iruso, August 27, 1963 for 400 CFA.
Inv. no. G.7190

70. Double-edged, all-purpose knife, gena. The knife is shaped like a dagger. The handcrafted handle is of wood cut from a species of tree known as alou (Kreda). The blade is decorated with double lines incised from two points where the knife is shafted and some two thirds out along the blade towards its point. Knives of this type are indispensable in any Haddad (as well as in any Kreda and Kanembu) household. They are used by women for all kinds of chores and to scrape

hides before these are tanned. Men and children also make use of these knives for various tasks. The knife was made by a Haddad smith in Mussoro.

Length (total): 32 cm (shaft): 11.5 cm
Width (blade near shaft): 3.3 cm
Prov.: Purchased from at Haddad woman at Gaba, September 3, 1963 for 100 CFA.
Inv. no. G.7191

71. Oval iron scraper, koni (pl. kona), used to soften hides during the final stage of the tanning process, i.e. after tissue has been removed from the hide with a knife and the skin has been treated with tannin. The hide is worked over with the scraper for one day, after which it is ready for use. This work is done by women. A hide can be given a finish by being rubbed with liquid butter, but this is far from always done. Iron scrapers like this one are the preferred tool for the task,

17,34. All-purpose knife. Cat. no. 70. Photo J.K.

17,35. 'Scraper' used for cleaning the ground in and around the tent. Cat. no. 72. Photo J.K.

17,36. Stool used in the tent and when churning butter. Cat. no. 73. Photo J.K.

but a simple piece of wood cut to a similar shape may also do the job.

Length: 11.2 cm
Width: 6.3 cm
Prov.: Bought at the market in Mussoro for 0.50 CFA.
Inv. no. EA 69-59

72. Scraper, kerfe (pl. kerfa) (Kreda), made of wood from the savonier,

alou. The scraper is made in the shape of an ellipse with a convex and a concave side. It is thicker at the middle than along the rim. Scrapers are used by women to clean the floor of the tent and its immediate surroundings. Before a tent is erected anew, a woman will rid the site of debris, removing branches, shrubs and weeds, only then to go over it with the scraper. Scrapers are also used daily to keep

the floor of the tent and its surroundings meticulously clean. They are carved by Haddad smiths and sold at local markets. This tool was made by a smith at Mussoro (cf. *Fig. 17,35*).

Length: 30 cm
Width (middle, concave side): 10 cm
Prov.: Purchased from Haddad woman at Gaba, September 3, 1963 for 50 CFA.
Inv. no. G.7188

73. Stool, ekedela, carved from a single piece of wood. The stool is of a light brown wood and decorated with a geometrical design of fine lines that have been blackened with a hot iron. The seat is of an oval shape with two tiny 'handles' at each end. Stools like this one are used by women when cooking or doing other household chores. Made by a Haddad smith. Gift to IN from a Haddad woman (cf. *Fig. 17,36*).

Height: 11 cm
Length: 37 cm
Private coll.

Personal adornment

74. Tiny brass bell with a cowry shell as a ringer. The bell was tied around the waist of a baby girl with a leather string to cover her pubic region. The bell had been made and was purchased from a Haddad smith in Mussoro (cf. *Fig. 17,37*).

Height (bell): 6.2 cm
Diameter (bell at bottom): 3.5 cm
Prov.: Bought from the girl's mother at Gaba, September 3, 1963 for 250 CFA.
Inv. no. EA 69-55

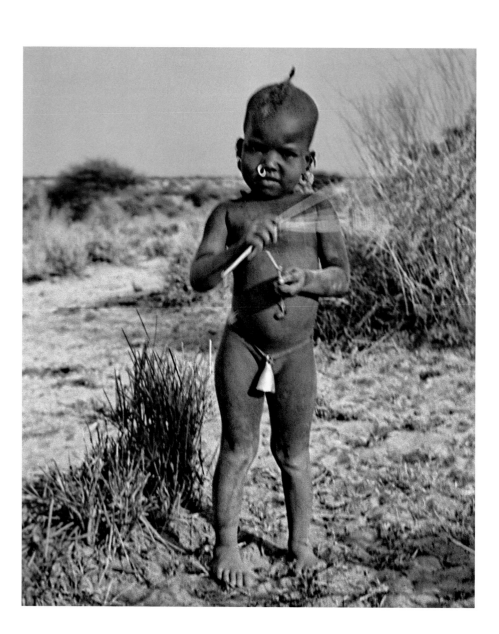

17,37. Little girl wearing only a brass bell. Cat. no. 74.

75. Necklace, karua (Kreda), of big round yellow beads of amber and two oblong red beads strung on a cord of leather. The amber beads stem from Darfur. They are costly and highly esteemed locally. Both the amber and red beads had been bought at the market in Mussoro by a Haddad woman, who strung them herself. Many Haddad women still wear these amber beads, while this no longer so often is the case among the Kreda, we were told - a piece of information which confirmed our observations.

Length (total): 39 cm
Prov.: Purchased from the Haddad owner at Gaba, September 3, 1963 for 2000 CFA.
Inv. no. G.7205

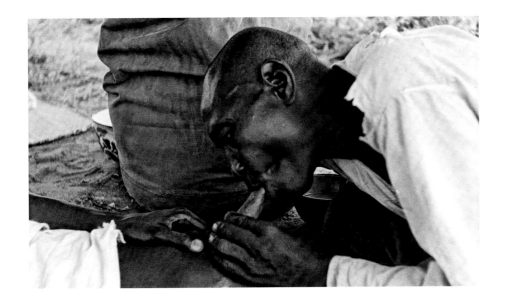

17,38. Haddad Kreda sucking blood from the leg of a relative.

Medical treatment

76. Small greyish-black cow's horn used for blood-letting. The object is called adjam (Kreda). A tiny hole, about 3 mm in diameter, has been drilled at the pointed end of the horn, and two narrow strips of leather, about 8 cm long, have been tied inside this to facilitate the process (cf. *Figs. 17,38 & 17.39*). An incision about 1 cm from the tip of the horn allows for the attachment of a string in case the horn needs to be carried or hung up.

17,39. Cow's horn for blood-letting and medical herbs. Cat. nos. 76 & 77. Photo J.K.

Length: 13 cm
Prov.: Bought from a Haddad woman at Kurei Iruso, August 27, 1963 for 100 CFA.
Inv. no. G.7192

77. Herbal medicine in tiny, cylindrical metal container (cf. *Fig. 17,39*).

Prov.: Bought at the market at Mussoro.
Inv. no. EA 69-60

Music

The musical instrument par excellence of the Haddad Kreda is the three-stringed spike lute, tuluru, played by men, and men only. Spike lutes, similar to the one played by Haddad Kreda foragers and Haddad Kreda smiths are common throughout North Africa. In Morocco, the wandering musicians play spike lutes, practising their skills as they travel from one market to the other or to entertain at religious occasions (Wegner 1984: 136). Spike lutes can be traced back in history to Ancient Egypt, from where they spread to Western Sudan via Meroe. Quoting Farmer, Ulrich Wegner claims that the Arabs only reluctantly incorporated spike lute music into their own, fairly complicated musical culture, leaving it

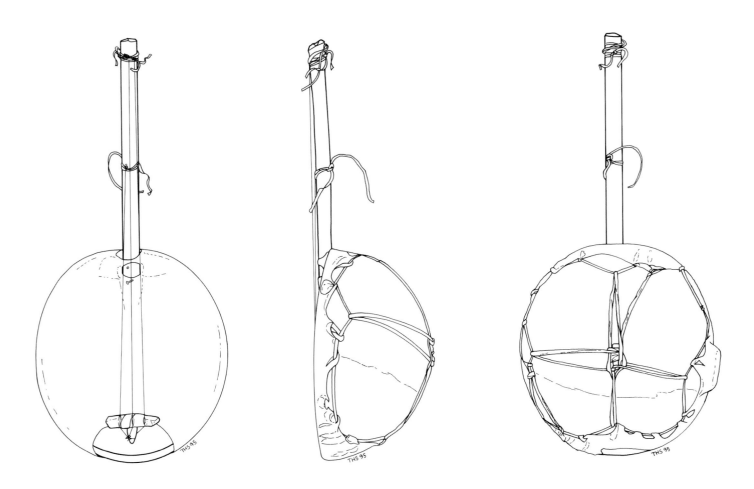

17,40. A three-stringed spike lute. Cat. no. 78. Drawing T.O.S.

17,41. A three-stringed spike lute. Cat. no. 79. Photo J.K.

more or less to its own devices among the general population (ibid. 1984: 136). The three-stringed spike lute is neither played by the Kreda with whom the Haddad Kreda camp for part of the year nor by the Haddad Kanembu. These groups prefer the one-stringed violin. We heard a Haddad Kanembu play this instrument at the village of Wanagal.

78. A three-stringed spike lute, tuluru (Kreda). The resonator of the lute is made of a wooden bowl of the kind used for eating. It is in one piece, carved from a tree known as erei (Kreda) and then charred to acquire the desired black colour. It is decorated on the outside with a series of incisions running from the rim towards the bottom. Each of these consists of from four to six lines, forming a pyramidal design. The resonator is covered by cow hide, achi (Kreda), from which most of the hair has been removed. This covers the opening of the bowl apart from a hole (10 cm x 6.5 cm) where the spike is fastened. The skin is extended beyond the rim for some 2 cm to 9 cm down the outer side of the bowl, where the hide has been cut to make a number of strips that are tied together underneath the bottom and hence keep the skin stretched. The spike is made from a 54 cm long, smooth piece of wood, known as koli (Kreda) alias Acacia raddiana. The strings, siba (Kreda), made from sinews of oxen or gazelle are tied to the spike at the far end of the instrument. From here they run over a small bridge, also tied to the lower end of the spike, to the rear end of the latter, where they are fastened with tiny leather strips. These in turn are tied around the spike with a loop, which enables the player to produce

the desired tune by turning them slightly. The bridge is made from a little wooden stick mostly covered by a strip of hide some 7 cm long and 1 cm in diameter. The shortest of the three strings is 35 cm long, the two longer ones about 47.5 cm. These are in fact made from one single string of sinew, but this is tied so tightly to the spike that each half can be tuned differently. At the other end, each of the strings is tied to the end of the resonator at the place where the hole has been cut.

The bowl was fabricated by a Haddad smith in Mussoro, but turned into a musical instrument by a young Haddad man, from whom we bought it. The fact that young men make their own instruments is normal. It is something which any man in the mood for playing can do. Three-stringed spike lutes are used by the Haddad Kreda all over Kanem and Bahr el Ghazal, be they hunters, farmers, craftsmen or smiths (cf. *Figs. 11,1-11,3 & 17,40*).

Length (total): 54 cm
Diameter (of bowl): 25 cm
Height (of bowl): 12 cm
Prov.: Purchased from a young Haddad Kreda at Sidige Joroso, August 21, 1963 for 300 CFA.
Inv. no. EA 69-47

79. Three-stringed spike lute, tuluru. The resonator is made from a bowl carved of wood from the erei tree and used originally for serving meals. The bowl has a protruding handle (5 cm x 1.2 cm) by which it can be hung on a tent pole safe from termites. It is decorated on the outside with incisions running around the brim in a 3 cm broad band consisting of lines making up a pattern of oblique strokes. A

number of pyramidal designs run from this towards the bottom of the resonator. This is covered by a hide of ox skin, from which the hair has been removed except for the part below the rim. The hide is tied around the resonator with strips of hide that run through holes pierced at intervals in the edge of the hide. It has two holes in it, the spike running through the larger of these - a hole that measures some 8.5 cm x 6 cm - extends beyond the rim ending in a kind of flap that is used for tying the spike. This is a simple wooden stick fastened at the one end some 2.5 cm beyond the rim of the bowl by means of a leather string. It goes under the hide and the over the rim through a narrow hole cut in the hide, projecting some 24 cm from the rim. The flap that is used for fastening the spike also holds in place the instrument's bridge which consists of two small wooden sticks - placed on top of the hide: the larger (8 cm long and approx. 1 cm in diameter) is partly wrapped in the hide - the smaller (6.5 cm x 0.6 cm) is placed on top of the larger. The latter is furnished with three incisions to stabilize the strings of the lute, which are made of finely twined strands of sinew. They are tied at one end to the spike in the bowl, running over the bridge to be tied with leather straps at various places on the spike: one string is placed some 6 cm from the rim, the two others about 4 cm and 6 cm from the end of the spike, respectively.

Length: 51 cm
Diameter (bowl at rim): 25 cm
Prov.: Purchased from a Haddad man at Kurei Iruso, August 27, 1963 for 500 CFA.
Private coll.

HADDAD ARTISANS

80. Large earthenware jar for water, telti, furnished with a lid of coiled basketry and a carrying device of rope. Jars are made by the women of Haddad smiths, who sell them at markets in the towns. The jar has an oval shaped body and a neck which is slightly conical. The ceramic has a dark reddish-bluish finish on the outside, while the inside is black. The lid is plaited from strips of dum palm leaf. The jar is transported in a carrying device of plaited dum palm ropes, a good 1 cm thick. This consists of two circles, a smaller one on which the jar rests and another, bigger one around its middle for stabilization, the two being united at intervals by five pieces of rope. The larger circle ends in a loose piece of rope for tying the jar when it is going to be carried. Jars like this one are commonly used as water containers.

Height: 47 cm (lid): 2 cm
Diameter: 32 cm (lid): 10.2
Prov.: Purchased from a Kreda woman in a camp near Mussoro on September 15, 1963 for 200 CFA.
Inv. no. G.7178

81. Saddle bag for donkeys, used for the transportation of game and of water jars. The bag is in one piece, plaited from twined dum palm rope. The two almost circular bags are joined by a rectangular piece (16 cm x 43 cm) which rests on the back of the donkey when in use (cf. *Fig. 17,43*).

Height: 52 cm – 50 cm
Diameter of bags: a. 52 cm x 62 cm;
b. 54 cm x 66 cm
Prov.: Bought at the market at Mussoro.
Inv. no. G.7216

82. Stool, ekedela, carved from a single piece of wood. It is a fine example, dark brown in colour and with a delicate geometrical design. The seat is oval, with a tiny, protruding triangular 'handle' at each end, onto which a string can be attached so that the stool can be hung during migration. The stool stands on two bars, each connected with the seat by means of three 'pillars', one at each corner of the stool and a thinner one half way along each side. The stool is decorated with incisions that have been blackened to stand out from the brown colour. They are largely pyramidal in shape. At each end of the seat a series of these pyramidal incisions, one on top of the other, are intersected with bands, some of which are decorated with tiny dot-like pyramids. On the top of the pyramidal incisions are four bouquet-like designs. The sides of the seat are decorated in a similar way, but with

17,42. Water jar made by Haddad potters. Cat. no. 80. Photo J.K.

17,43. Saddle bag for donkeys. Cat. no. 81. Photo J.K.

somewhat broader designs. Stools are made by Haddad smiths and bought at markets by the Haddad and Kreda alike (cf. *Fig. 15,13*).

Height: 11 cm
Length: 42 cm
Private coll.

83. Wooden bowl carved in one piece. It has been charred to achieve the desired black colour. The bowl is decorated on the outside with a fine geometrical design. This runs as bands with a herring bone pattern and straight lines below the rim and further on as four pairs of pyramidal incisions towards the bottom of the bowl. Two wooden 'ears' are placed some 4.5 cm below the rim, facilitating the hanging up of the bowl during mi-

gration and in the tent. A fine leather string is tied to one of them, ready for use. Such bowls are made by Haddad smiths and sold at local markets.

Height: 16 cm
Diameter (at rim): 29 cm
Private coll.

84. Blanket of twelve jackal skins lined with red leather. The hides are tanned and very soft. Holes stemming from the hunters' spears are covered by red leather patches stitched to the back side of the skin. Blankets of jackal skin are highly appreciated in Kanem and Bahr el Ghazal. They are used as covers during chilly nights, as are similar covers made from goat- and sheepskin. Jackal skin blankets are also sold by the Haddad Kreda

17,44. Saddle bag for donkeys, detail. The bag is made from twined dum palm rope by Haddad artisans. Only men make baskets of rope. Cat. no. 81. Photo J.K.

17,45. Wooden bowl for the serving/eating of food. Cat. no. 83. Photo J.K.

17,46. Basket. Cat. no. 86. Photo J.K.

17,47. Haddad woman with a sleeping mat made from strips of dum palm leaves cf. Cat. no. 87.

at markets to urbanites, including Europeans, as bedspreads and for decoration (cf. *Fig. 15,4*).

Length: 180 cm
Width: 90 cm
Private coll.

85. Two pairs of boots made of goat-skin made from three pieces of very fine and soft leather: a sole, a shaft which is sewn together at the back and an almost rectangular piece which makes up the uppers. Boots like these are made to measure by Haddad smiths, who measure the feet of the customer with a string (length and width). The boots reach mid-calf and provide some protection against snake bites. This is somewhat assuring as reptiles are plentiful and difficult to spot especially after the rains, when annual grasses cover the grounds. We encountered quite a number of people in Kanem and Bahr el Ghazal who were permanently handicapped from snake bites that had left them with partially lame legs. Boots are not commonly used, as far as I could assess, and are certainly not part of Haddad culture. The Haddad we met all went barefooted (cf. *Fig. 15,15*).

a.
Height: 36 cm
Length: 27 cm

b.
Height: 32 cm
Length: 22 cm

Prov.: Bought at the market at Bol, July 17, 1963.
Private coll.

86. Basket of loosely woven dum palm strips in a herring-bone pattern with an enforced rim, likewise made from dum palm strips. Such containers are made for the markets by some Haddad Kanembu and Kanembu women. They are not used by the Haddad Kanembu themselves.

Height: 30 cm
Diameter (at rim): 35 cm
Prov.: Market at Mussoro.
Private coll.

87. Mat of dum palm strips woven in a herring-bone pattern. The mat is without decoration apart from the borders that are coloured violet (cf. *Fig. 17,47*).

Length: 180 cm.
Width: 100 cm

Prov. Market in Mussoro.
Private coll.

88. Earthenware pot for charcoal and the burning of 'incense'. The bowl-shaped pot has a cylindrical base. It is of a dark, brown-blackish colour decorated with white straight and intersecting lines made with chalk. Pots like these are for sale at all markets. The buyers are Haddad Kanembu and Kanembu women, among others, who use these to 'perfume' their clothes with aromatic smoke to become sexually more attractive. The clothes are hung above the pot in which they have placed charcoal embers and aromatic plants (cf. Chapter 14).

Height: 10 cm
Diameter: 13.5 cm
Prov.: Market in Mussoro.
Private coll.

KREDA PASTORALISTS

89. A 'bowl-shaped' muzzle, kesi (sing.), used to prevent calves from drinking their mother's milk. The muzzle is made of a single, thin rope of twined dum palm leaf. It is tied behind the ears of the calf with another piece of fine rope of twined dum palm leaf. The Kreda make use of such muzzles during migration, to prevent calves from suckling on their way from one camp to the other (cf. *Fig. 7,23*).

Length (muzzle cover): 9 cm
Diameter: 13 cm
Prov.: Purchased from the Kreda man who had made both this item and Cat. No. 90. Kulo Jesko, August 30, 1963 for 150 CFA.
Inv. no. EA 69-53

90. A 'bowl-shaped' muzzle (kesi) for weaning calves similar to Cat. No. 89. The cover is tied behind the ears of the calf with a strap.

Length (muzzle cover): 7.5 cm
Length (total with strap): 27 cm
Diameter: 9 cm
Prov.: Bought at Kulo Jesko together with Cat. No. 89 on August 30, 1963 for a total of 150 CFA.

91. Muzzle (beri) for weaning calves and foals. The muzzle is made of wood of savonier, alou, and twined strings of dum palm fibre in the shape of a semi-circle and provided with a wrapping of coloured cotton cloth. Some twenty-one acacia thorns stuck into the wood will seriously hurt the udder of the mother cow should the calf want to suckle. The device is tied to the head of the calf with two straps of twined fibre from the tefi acacia, (Acacia raddiana) and of dum palm leaves (cf. *Fig. 7,9*).

Length: 32 cm
Length (of thorns): 3.5 cm - 5.5 cm
Prov.: Bought at Gaba, September 1, 1963 for 100 CFA.
Inv. no. G.7193

92. Huge, oval-shaped calabash, zi (Kreda), for churning butter, a task performed by women only and one of those which Haddad women undertake for their Kreda hosts. A circular hole is cut in one end of the calabash, to which is stitched a coiled neck made from dum palm leaves and a rim of

braided leather strips. The neck of the container is closed by means of a circular lid made of the cut-out piece of the calabash. This too has been furnished with a small rim of coiled basketry of dum palm leaves with a leather braid at its rim similar to the one at the neck of the calabash itself. The container is kept in a loosely tied net of carrying strings, made of two sets of twined ropes. One forms a circle around the thickest part of the calabash, the other a smaller circle close to the bottom of the calabash. The latter functions as a stand for the calabash as well, so that it can be placed upright on the ground. The two circles of rope are tied to one another with six pieces of rope some 1.5 cm in diameter. A strap attached to the upper circle makes it possible for the calabash to be hung e.g. in a tree, as women do when they churn butter.

Churning is done much in the same way among the Kreda as among the Tuareg. The butter is kept for twenty-four hours before it is considered ready for churning and can be poured into the calabash, in which the process takes place. Before the work can be carried out, a burning stick or some pieces of glowing charcoal are placed inside the calabash for a few moments for cleansing and to lend it a smell of smoke. This process will eventually make the butter taste slightly smoked, something which people like. The large calabashes are sold at local markets, but they come from an area east of Massakory.

Height (total): 50 cm, (neck): 7 cm
Circumference (with ropes): 137 cm
Diameter (lid): 13 cm
Prov.: Purchased from a woman in a Kreda camp near Mussoro on September 14, 1963 for 500 CFA.
Inv. no. G.7184

Weapons

93. Spear. One of four spears which Kreda men typically carry in a leather sheath for protection and attack. The other spears and the sheath were donated to the museum in Fort Lamy. The shaft is made from the root of the tefi acacia (Acacia raddiana). The spear has a finely engraved iron blade, which is barbed just above the place where it is socketed (cf. *Fig. 15,12*).

Length: 136 cm, (iron blade): 32 cm
Prov.: Purchased in a Kreda camp near Mussoro on September 15, 1963 for 600 CFA.
Private coll.

17,48. Calabash for churning butter. Cat. no. 92. Photo J.K.

94. Throwing knife, ngili (pl.ngila) (Kreda), forged by a smith at Mussoro. The body of the knife is about 3-4 mm thick, slightly curved at the top and whetted above a second blade which protrudes about 23 cm from the top. There is no handle or wrapping to ease the grip, only the rough iron stem of the knife itself.

Length (total): 56.5 cm, (second blade): 12.5 cm
Prov.: Bought from a Kreda man at Gaba on September 3, 1963 for 100 CFA.
Inv. no. G.7207

95. A knife of a type popular among the Tubu and also further west among the Tuareg. It has an oblong, pointed blade decorated with finely incised lines that run in the longitudinal direction. The handle is covered for the most part by an exquisite leather-plaiting of red and black leather strips. The sheath is made from black and red leather, the latter forming a section with an imprinted pattern running longitudinally between the upper and lower black section of the sheath. The sheath ends in a tiny ferrule likewise made of leather. It is furnished with a plaited strap at the top, through which runs another plaited leather strap with which the knife can be tied around the upper arm - the left one if the person is right-handed (cf. *Fig. 3,5*).

Length (total): 31 cm, (of blade): 20 cm
Prov.: Kreda camp near Mussoro, September 15, 1963.
Inv. no. G.7208a-b.

17,49. Digging utensil which women use when making holes for tent poles and to get acacia roots for tent construction. Cat. no. 97. Photo J.K.

96. Small spear, kulai, with a cone-shaped blade of iron. This is socketed onto a shaft made of the root of the tefi acacia (Acacia raddiana). Spears like these are usually carried by boys and not by adult men, although wounds from cone-shaped blades are said to be most dangerous. The spears are used for protection but they also enable boys to hunt for birds and small game. This spear was one of a pair carried by a Kreda boy not yet in his teens.

Length (total): 118 cm (of iron cone): 22.5 cm
Circumference (of shaft): 4.5 cm
Prov.: Purchased at Gaba on September 1, 1963 for 200 CFA.
Inv. no. G.7210

Tools

97. Digging utensil, bon (Kreda), made by Haddad smiths in Mussoro. The implement consists of a wooden shaft with a tapering end onto which a double-edged, slightly curved iron share has been socketed. Digging sticks are used by the Haddad and the Kreda alike. They are applied by women for the digging of holes for

tent poles, for roots of trees for the making of cross-bars for the tents and for a variety of other tasks, including various foraging activities (cf. *Figs. 17,14 & 17,69*).

Length (total): 106 cm, (of share): 17.5 cm
Circumference (shaft): 9.5 cm
Prov.: Purchased in a Kreda camp near Mussoro on September 14, 1963 for 100 CFA.
Inv. no. G.7187

Household utensils

98. Wooden bowl, edei (pl. eda) (Kreda), used primarily for eating porridge but also as container for storing milk. The bowl is cut out of a single piece of wood from the teledi tree. The inside is plain but the outside is decorated with carved geometrical patterns consisting of a band below the rim from where four pairs of pyramidal designs run towards the bottom. The rim itself is decorated with simple lines forming eight cross-split bands. The bowl has small, one times three-centimetre-long ears cut from the same piece of wood, to which a string is attached for hanging up the

17,52. Small basket for carrying and storing cooking pots. Cat. no. 101. Photo J.K.

17,50. Wooden bowl used for serving/eating of porridge. Cat. no. 98. Photo J.K.

17,51. Pot and iron tripod for cooking. Cat. nos. 99 & 100. Photo J.K.

bowl. Bowls like these are made by Haddad smiths in Mussoro.

Height: 14 cm
Diameter (at rim): 25 cm
Width (of rim): 1 cm
Prov.: Bought from a family in a Kreda camp near Mussoro on September 14, 1963 for 300 CFA.
Inv. no. G.7186

99. Earthenware pot, guru (Kreda), of red clay with lid of coiled basketry made of dum palm leaves. The pot has a lip and a leather band is fastened just beneath this to prevent wear and tear. The rim of the lid bends upwards some 2.5 cm, enabling it to fit tightly inside the pot just beneath its lip. The lid can be lifted off the pot by a small handle at its centre. The pot is used daily for cooking porridge. It is transported in a basket (cf. Cat. No. 101).

Height: 20 cm
Diameter (at rim): 21 cm, (of lid): 17 cm
Prov.: Purchased in a Kreda camp near Mussoro on September 14, 1963 for 100 CFA.
Inv. no. G.7181

100. Tripod of iron, muskur (Kreda) used as a stand for cooking pots among both Haddad and Kreda. The cooking pot rests within the tripod's circular iron ring. The legs are made of folded scraps of iron sheet. They are forged onto the flat, circular ring, which initially is made so large that it can be folded around the legs to enforce the structure. The tripod was made by a Haddad smith in Mussoro, who had sold it to the Kreda woman from whom I bought it.

17,53. Wooden stool. Cat. no. 102. Kreda. Kulo Jesko. Photo J.K.

Height: 15.5 cm (of ring): 3.5 cm
Diameter (ring inside): 21 cm
Prov.: Purchased at a Kreda camp near Mussoro on September 14, 1963 for 100 CFA.
Inv. no. G.7180

101. Small basket for carrying and storing pots, plaited from split bands of dum palm leaf, about one cm broad. The rim is enforced by means of a twined string of split bands of dum palm leaf. Two circular holes have been made just below this, opposite one another. Both are neatly enforced with 'button hole' stitching made from strips of palm leaves. A braided leather string with a knot on the outside of each hole, a knot so large that it can-

not go through the holes, functions as 'handle', so that the container can be hung up wherever convenient. Both the Kreda and the Haddad use such baskets for storing cooking pots in the tent, in particular when these contain food to be kept out of reach of ants, dogs and goats which may venture inside. During migrations the Kreda tie the baskets to the saddles of the oxen, the Haddad to the backs of their donkeys with pots and all.

Height: 17 cm
Diameter: 23 cm
Length (leather string): 54 cm
Prov.: Purchased in a Kreda camp near Mussoro on September 14, 1963.
Inv. no. G.7182

17,54. Cage for chickens. These are used primarily during migration. Cat. no. 103. Photo J.K.

17,55. Detail, showing the bottom a the chicken cage. Cat. no. 103. Photo J.K.

102. Stool, ekedela, carved from a single piece of wood. The stool is of a light brown colour and has a decoration of fine black lines charred into the wood. It is provided with a rope for transport. Stools like this one are used primarily by women, for example when cooking or doing other kinds of household chores that require sitting down. Stools are made by Haddad smiths and bought at the markets (cf. *Fig. 17,53*).

Length: 36.3 cm
Height: 11 cm
Prov.: Purchased from a Kreda woman at Kulo Jesko on August 30, 1963 for 200 CFA.
Inv. no. G.7179

103. Cage for chicken, turbulo (Kreda) standing on six legs. The sides and top are plaited from broad strips of dum palm leaves around the main structure in a herring-bone pattern just like the tent mats. The main structure consists of three sticks that are tied together at the middle to form tiny arches, so that the cage rests on each end of these, i.e. on six legs. The structure is furthermore provided with a bottom on which the chicken rests. This consists of a circular wooden frame that is tied to the arches some ten to fifteen cm from the end of these to protect chicken from immediate contact with the ground. A 'spider's web' of finely twined ropes is fastened to the circular frame and constitutes an airy bottom to the cage. A tiny shutter plaited like the rest of the cage allows the chicken to be taken in and out of the cage and closed up at night or when on the move. The cage is hung up in the tent at nightfall, or on the saddle of donkeys or oxen when moving camp or for bringing poultry to the market for sale. This is done by means of a twined rope of split dum palm leaf fastened to the top of the cage. A tuft of hay provides nesting facilities. Chicken cages are plaited by men, poultry, however, is tended by women.

Height: 35 cm
Diameter (bottom): 34 cm x 36cm
Diameter (opening): 12 cm x 14 cm
Prov.: Purchased from a Kreda woman in a camp near Mussoro, September 14, 1963 for 50 CFA.
Inv. no. G.7183

Personal adornment

104. Girl's skirt made of strings of yellow, blue, white and two red glass beads, era, (Kreda). The beads are purchased at markets, in this case at Mussoro. They were strung on cotton threads by the girl's mother in three sections with three strings of beads each: two of entirely yellow beads, one with two strings of largely white beads and one with blue.

Length: 48 cm-50 cm
Prov.: Bought at Sidige Joroso on August 21, 1963 together with inv. nos. EA 69-39, G.7196, G.7197, G.7202, G.7203 and G.7204 for a total of 2000 CFA.
Inv. no. EA 69-38a-c

105. Tiny necklace, bogai (Kreda), consisting of a flattish rhombus-shaped silver bead carried at the centre of a simple leather strip. The necklace was worn by a little girl. The silver ornament had been made by and purchased from a Haddad smith in Mussoro.

17,56. Haddad girl wearing but some coloured beads around her waist and a great many earrings. Girls have their ears pierced at a very young age, often before they are one year old. Cat. no. 104.

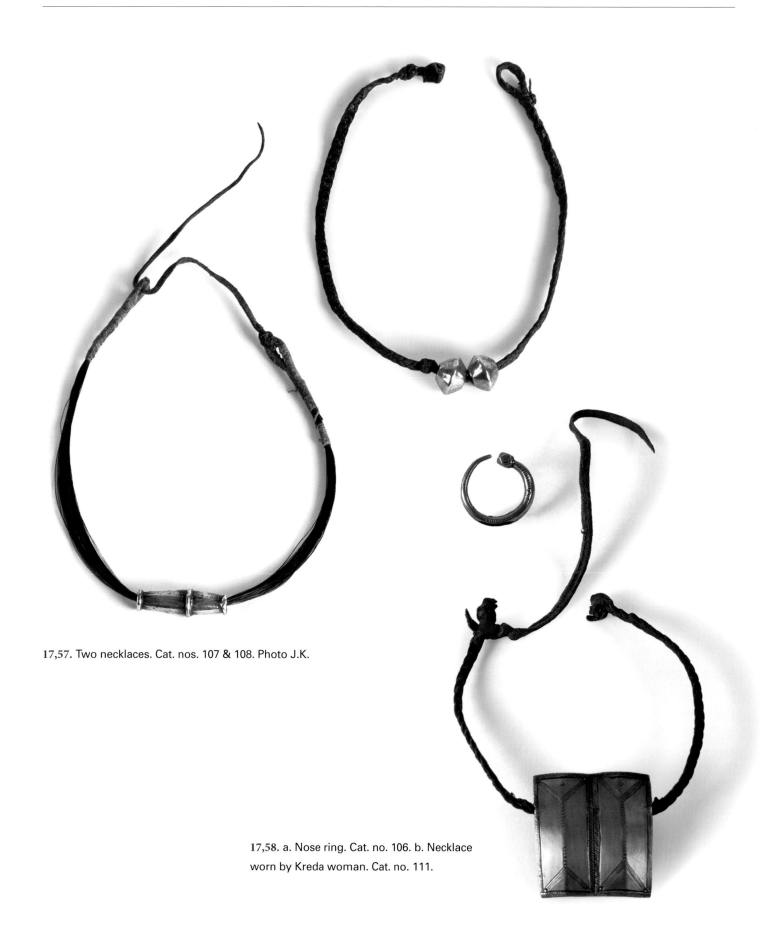

17,57. Two necklaces. Cat. nos. 107 & 108. Photo J.K.

17,58. a. Nose ring. Cat. no. 106. b. Necklace worn by Kreda woman. Cat. no. 111.

Length (of string): 58 cm
Length (silver bead): 3 cm
Prov.: Purchased at Sidige Joroso on
August 21, 1963 together with inv.
nos. EA 69-38a-c, G.7196, G.7197,
G.7202, G.7203 and G.7204 for 2000
CFA.
Inv. no. EA 69-39

106. Nose ring, changai (Kreda), made
of silver. The ring has an opening of
about 2 mm so it can easily be inserted
and removed. The ring is about 4 mm
thick, but thinner at the end that passes
through the right nostril. The other
end has an octagonal knob. The ring
is partly adorned with a finely incised
pattern of simple lines. Nose rings are
worn by most adult women from the
time of marriage. They are made by
smiths, this one by a Haddad smith in
Mussoro (cf. *Fig. 17,58a*).

Diameter: 3 cm
Prov.: Purchased at Sidige Joroso on
August 21, 1963 together with inv.
nos. EA 69-38a-c, EA 69-39, G.7196,
G.7197, G.7203 and G.7204 for 2000
CFA.
Inv. no. G.7202

17,59. Young woman wearing a nose ring and necklaces. The nose is pierced when the girl
is about one year old and almost all women wear this ornament. Cat. nos. 106, 107, 108.

107. Necklace of horsehair with a single oblong silver bead, bogai (Kreda).
The necklace is tied tightly around the
neck with a small leather string attached to the horsehair. This piece of
jewellery was purchased from Haddad
silversmiths in Mussoro by a woman,
from whom I bought it (*Fig. 17,57*).

Length (total): 47 cm, (without
string): 31 cm
Length (silver bead): 3 cm
Prov.: Purchased at Sidige Joroso on
August 21, 1963 together with inv.

nos. EA 69-38a-c, EA 69-39, G.7196,
G.7197, G.7102 and G.7204 for 2000
CFA.
Inv. no. G.7203

108. Woman's necklace, dolta
(Kreda), made of two small, solid
silver beads, rhombic in shape. The
beads are threaded on a finely braided
leather string with a loop and a knot
at the ends respectively for tying.
They were made by Haddad smiths

in Mussoro. The necklace was worn
by a Haddad woman from whom it
was bought (*Fig. 17,58*).

Length (total): 33.5 cm
Size (of beads): 1 cm x 1.5 cm
Prov.: Purchased at Sidige Joroso on
August 21, 1963 together with inv.
nos. EA 69-38a-c, EA 69-39, G.7196,
G.7197, G.7202 and G.7203 for 2000
CFA.
Inv. no. G.7204

109. Oval wicker box, koré, containing a mirror. The box is relatively flat, made fine fibres from dum palm leaves in a coiled basketry technique. The slightly larger lid is adorned on the outside with an oval pattern plaited with pieces of fibre about one centimetre broad. The bottom part is decorated inside with an inserted oval piece of red, tanned leather. A rectangular mirror, woudroum, in a golden frame was kept inside the box, presumably purchased from Nigeria as its back holds an inscription reading: "Nigeria Independence Oct. 1st, 1960" as well as pictures of politicians representing the three parties of the carefully negotiated federation (*Fig. 17,61*).

Length: 19 cm
Width: 14 cm
Height (closed): 3.8 cm
Prov.: Purchased at Sidige Joroso on the 21st of August 1963 together with inv. nos. EA 69-38a-c, EA 69-39, G,7196, G.7202, G.7203 and G.7204 for 2000 CFA.
Inv. no. G.7197

110. Container for scented butter, empi tugortide (Kreda). The container is made from a greyish cow's horn, jaj (Kreda), and furnished with a circular lid. The opening of the horn is decorated with a leather band which has been plaited at the rim and ends as a loose hanging string that functions as a strap for carrying or hanging up the horn. The lid is made of a circular piece of calabash with a circumference of 6 cm and furnished with a rim of plaited split bands of palm leaf with a finish in the shape

17,60. Haddad girls.

of a fine leather braiding and a small leather strap for hanging.

Containers like this one are used by women for butter. They use this to grease their intricate coiffure of tiny braids. The butter, empi, (Kreda), is scented with seeds from nicely smelling plants which the women pound (cf. Cat. No. 46) and mix with the butter and some eau-de-Cologne bought from Arab or Lebanese merchants in the towns. The horn had been furnished with the lid and leather braiding by a woman, from whom I purchased the item together with other of her personal belongings (cf. *Fig. 13,2*).

Length (outer, curved side): 47 cm
Diameter (opening): 7.5 cm, (of lid): 7.5 cm
Width (of lid): 2 cm
Prov.: Purchased at Sidige Joroso on August 21, 1963 together with inv. nos. EA 69-38a-c, EA 69-39, G.7197, G.7202, G.7203 and G.7204 for 2000 CFA.
Inv. no. G.7196

111. Necklace, guluda (Kreda), of silver with a leather cord worn by a Kreda woman. The jewellery is solid, almost rectangular and made from two pieces ornamented with fine geometrical designs. A braided leather cord - prolonged with a simple strip of leather to fit around the neck of the owner - goes through a hole at the upper part of the piece (cf. *Fig. 17,58b*).

Length: 4.4 cm
Width: 4.1 cm
Thickness: 0.7 cm-0.3 cm
Prov.: Purchased at a Kreda camp

17,61. Oval wicker box for cosmetics. Cat. no. 109. Photo J.K.

near Mussoro on September 14, 1963 for 200 CFA.
Inv. no. G.7201

112. Woman's attire consisting of a rectangular piece of black cotton cloth which is draped around the body either around the waist or just above the breasts. One end of the cloth may be drawn up over the head as protection against the sun.

Length: 357 cm
Width: 130 cm
Prov.: Purchased at the market in Mussoro with the assistance of a Kreda woman for 1500 CFA.
Inv. no. G.7213

113. Small calabash for keeping herbs for personal hygiene.

The calabash is provided with a neck of coiled basketry rimmed with a leather band. It has a tiny circular lid also of calabash in the setting of coiled basketry. Like most everyday utensils the container can be hung under the roof or transported by means of a small rope.

Height: 16 cm
Prov.: Gift to the author from Kreda woman at the Kolo camp on August 19, 1963.
Inv. no. EA 69-37

Music

114. Single-stringed fiddle, tchegeni (Kreda), with bow. The resonator is made from a wooden bowl of the kind also used for eating covered with a piece of skin. The neck of the violin is made from a finely polished stick of acacia wood. The string is of horsehair and fastened to the upper end of the violin with a leather strap and to the lower end with cotton and leather straps. The string stretches over a tiny bridge made by a small stone. The key of the string is regulated with another leather cord placed some 15 cm from the upper end of the wooden neck. The bow stick is curved. It is held in place by the horse-hair string which is tied to each of its two ends. Fiddles are played by Kreda men. To our knowledge, Haddad men do not play this instrument, their fa-vourite being the three-stringed spike lute (cf. Cat. Nos. 78 and 79).

Length (total): 71 cm
Diameter (of bowl): 25 cm
Height (of bowl): 14 cm
Length (of bowl): 37 cm
Prov.: Purchased from a Kreda man at Gaba on September 3, 1963 for 500 CFA.
Inv. no. G.7206a-b

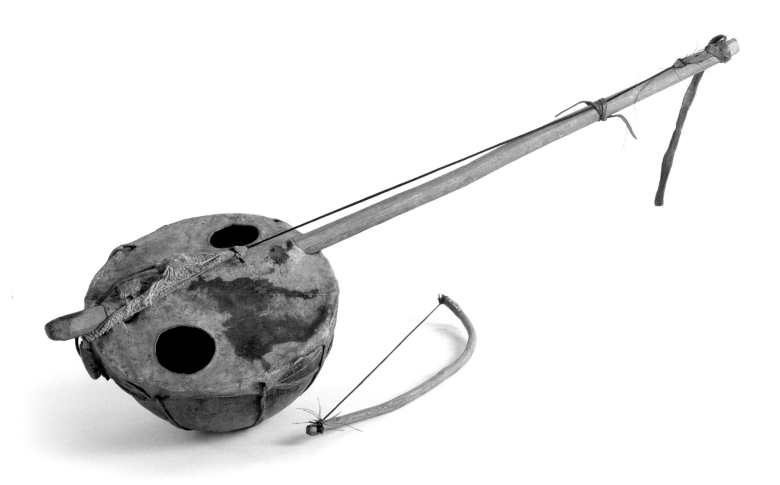

17,62. Single-stringed fiddle used by Kreda pastoralists. Cat. no. 114. Photo J.K.

A TENT

17,63. Haddad tent. The blanket of goatskin that the family uses for cover during the night has been put outside in the sun, perhaps to rid it of lice.

The Haddad Kreda stay in tents all year round except for a short period, if the family is growing millet. Their tents are exactly similar to those used by the Kreda except that they are often a bit smaller and in less good repair. The tents are barrel-vaulted structures made from branches, roots and twined fibres from the tefi acacia, (Acacia raddiana) covered by four mats plaited from split bands of dum palm leaves. They are structurally different from other mat-covered tents of the arch kind found among the Teda, Southern Tuareg and elsewhere in the Sahel area both with respect to the wooden structure itself and the kind of mats applied as cover. It had not even dawned on me that I could purchase a tent for the National Museum in Denmark as the very idea of, so to speak, pulling down the roof over the heads of people was totally alien to me. It so happened, however, that I was offered one by a Kreda family. The purchase was made possible, or so I was told, because the woman was divorcing her husband and was going to leave his camp with her tent for her maternal family. In fact, it was somewhat more complicated, I realized somewhat later. The offer to purchase the tent was made by the husband, who contacted our interpreter Bogar Bechir suggesting the deal. He had noticed that I had acquired some household utensils and found that I might be interested in a tent. He had recently acquired a second, much younger wife with whom he was planning to stay, and while he looked pretty happy, his old wife was not and may well have regretted her threat of divorce and perhaps of departing with her tent, or so I suspected. However, done was done and I bought it from her at Gaba on September 1st 1963 for 25.000 CFA. For a detailed description of how the tent is pitched etc. (Cf. Chapter 13).

The Kreda tent is known as yegé. The total measurements of the tent in the collection of the National Museum are the following: L: 440 cm; W: 265 cm; Distance between rear arch and the one in front of this: 75 cm; Distance between the two central arches: 128 cm; Distance between the arch in front and the first central arch: 112 cm. The overall inventory number is G.7177.

Sleeping platform, kiri

The very first section of the tent that a woman pitches will be the sleeping platform or kiri, as it is known to the Haddad Kreda and the Kreda alike, the very name that also denotes the mat on which one sleeps. The platform consists of the following elements:

115. Four bedposts, which constitute the front row of the structure from left to right. The posts are known as kidichi (sing.) or kidicha (pl.) by the Haddad Kreda and the Kreda alike. They are made from acacia wood and are forked at the upper end to support the bed-board. The posts are raised some 78-86 cm above ground level when in place. They are all decorated with a black, 2-4 cm broad, serpentine coiling that has been burnt into the plain wood.

Length: 130 cm. Inv. no. G.7177a
Length: 135 cm. Inv. no. G.7177b
Length: 121 cm. Inv. no. G.7177c
d. Length: 124 cm. Inv. no. G.7177d

116. Four bedposts, which constitute the supporting structure of the back or eastern side of the bed, numbered from right to left. The posts are called kidichi (sing.) or kidicha by the Haddad Kreda and the Kreda alike. They are made from acacia wood and raised some 79-85 cm above ground level when in place. One part of the fork (Inv. no G.7177e) has been broken off. They are all decorated with a blackish coiling that runs all along the post.

Length: 126 cm. Inv. no. G.7177e
Length: 116 cm. Inv. no. G.7177f
Length: 102 cm. Inv. no. G.7177g
Length: 126 cm. Inv. no. G.7177h

117. Four cross-bars of plain acacia wood that are placed in the forks of the above mentioned bedposts (G.7177a-h). The bars are named kalafu (sing.) or kalafa (pl.) by the Haddad Kreda and the Kreda alike. They run across the short side of the bed and support the long bed-board that runs the full length of this. The bars are about 13 cm in diameter. The bars have no decoration apart from the two that support each end of the bed with slightly conically, 12-13 cm long end-pieces of a circumference of between 19.5 cm and 21 cm.

Length: 165 cm. Inv. no. G.7177aa
Length: 163 cm. Inv. no. G.7177ab
Length: 163 cm. Inv. no. G.7177ac
Length: 164 cm. Inv. no. G.7177ad

118. The board of the platform consists of fifteen long, slender poles, called eriri (sing.) or erara (pl.). They are all of plain, dark wood that has been nicely smoothed. The ends are rounded and provided with an incision some three centimetres from these to facilitate the tying of the poles to the cross-bars at each end of the platform.

Length (approx.): 370 cm
Inv. nos. G.7177ba-bo

119. Two neatly braided strings of thin leather strips that are used to tie the long, slender poles to the cross-bars of the sleeping platform. The strings have a loop at one end, the one with which the tying begins and they are wound consecutively half around each pole. The strings are called agar (sing.) or agara (pl.) by the Haddad Kreda and the Kreda alike, as are all strings and ropes made of leather.

a. Length: 310 cm. Inv. no. G.7177br
b. Length: 370 cm. Inv. no. G.7177bs

120. Cover for the sleeping platform, made from round sticks of acacia root that are held together by 'ropes' made from four loosely twisted strings of dum palm leaf. The sticks each have a

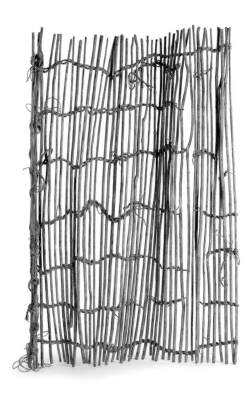

17,64. Cover for the sleeping platform made from round sticks. Cat. no. 120. Photo J.K.

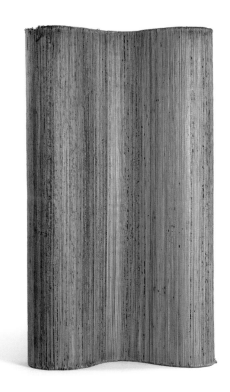

17,65. A beautiful, fine mat used for seating guests. Cat. no. 122. Photo J.K.

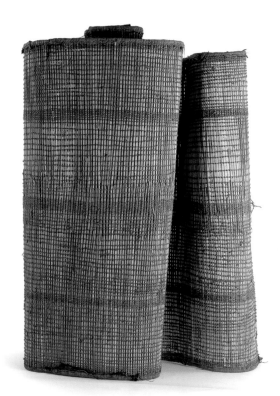

17,66. Mat that covers the sleeping platform. Cat. no. 121. Photo J.K.

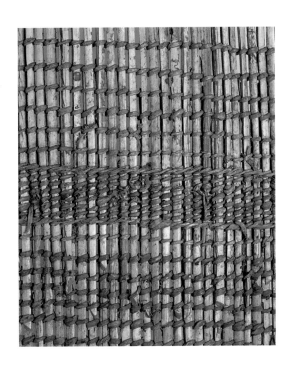

17,67. Detail of the mat that covers the sleeping platform. Cat. no. 121. Photo J.K.

diameter of between 3.4 cm and 4 cm, and they are tied together at an interval of 3 cm by seven bands of ropes. The top and bottom bands run some 12 cm to 14 cm from the edge, respectively (cf. *Fig. 17,64*).

Length: 155 cm
Width: 122 cm
Inv. no. G.7177mb

121. A mat that is placed on top of the cover of round sticks on the platform where the family sleeps (cf. Cat. No. 120). The mat is made from 1 cm thick sticks made of split acacia root held tightly together by leather strings that are wound around each stick the full length of the mat. The strings are wound at intervals that vary between 1.5 cm and 3 cm from one another, except at the edges, where five strings run right next to one another, forming a virtual leather band. The same effect is repeated three more times, one right down the middle of the mat, and two other bands running between the centre and the edges at a distance from these of 28 cm and 34 cm respectively. The mat is furnished with fine edgings of red leather (*Figs. 17,66 & 17,67*).

Length: 362 cm
Width: 143-148 cm
Inv. no. G.7177ma

122. Very fine, long mat made from strips of leaves, which can be used either for seating guests or put inside the tent as protection against the elements. The 140 cm long and 0.2-0.3 cm broad reeds are folded lengthwise and stitched invisibly onto one another with thin strings made from strips of dum palm

leaves at about 5-6 centimetre intervals. The result is a mat with a very smooth surface on both sides. The mat has fine edgings made with a delicate stitching around a string that in turn is stitched to the mat itself (cf. *Fig. 17,65*).

Length: 557 cm
Width: 140 cm
Inv. no. G.7177mc

123. A fine sleeping mat made from reeds that are braided together two and two with 0.8 cm broad leather bands. The stems are a mere 0.2 cm in diameter and the braiding runs over and under two at a time the full length of the mat, with a distance between each leather band of 2.5 - 4 cm. At each end of the mat 12-16 stems of reed are bundled together and covered by a fine braiding with 0.5 cm broad leather bands. The mat can be placed either on the bed or rolled out in the sand for family members or guests.

Length: 175 cm
Width: 140 cm
Inv. no. G.7177md

124. A fine sleeping mat used either on the bed or rolled out in the sand in front of this for family members and guests. The mat is identical with Cat. No. 123. Like this it is made from the stems of a delicate reed by braiding the stems two and two with leather bands. The mat is used either as cover on the sleeping platform or put on the ground for family members or guests (cf. *Fig. 15,8*).

Length: 175 cm
Width: 140 cm
Inv. no. G.7177me

Storage facility

All tents are furnished with a huge 'bag' that functions as a storage facility inside the tent at the northern end of the bed. It is used for trays and other household utensils, for food that has not yet been cooked, such as grain, and for other belongings. The facility is suspended between four or five posts some 40 cm above ground to keep it free of pests. The posts that make up the southern side of the structure can be the posts that also form the northern corners of the bed itself, or the facility relies on separate posts for the southern side and ties the northern to the tent poles at this end of the tent. This was the case with the tent purchased for the National Museum in Denmark in which three posts were placed independently of but parallel to the northern tent poles (G.7177j, G.7177n and G.7177o), while it's other side was attached to this. The posts are forked to provide support for the one cross-bar of the side that stands free, while the other cross-bar is tied with a rope to the tent poles. The support of the hide, that forms the storage 'bag' is made by the thick leather ropes, which the woman winds in such a way that they form long loops corresponding to the depth of the 'bag' between the cross-bars. One loop is made next to the other the full length of the runners. When the ropes have been put in place, an old mat is placed inside the loops. On top of this is placed a large hide in such a way that the centre part rests upon the loops of the rope and hence is kept above the ground, while the sides of the hide

17,68. The basic structure of a Haddad tent. The storage bag is to the right.

hang over and are tied to the two cross-bars.

125. Three pronged posts that support the southern side of the storage facility or 'bag'. The Haddad Kreda and the pastoralists call these kidicha larua (sing.) or kidichi laru (pl.). The posts are all of plain acacia wood and placed some 70-80 cm to the north of the sleeping platform and more or less parallel with this. One of them has a blackish serpentine decoration (Inv. No. G.7177l). The specificities of the posts placed from west to east are as follows:

Length: 176 cm; width (fork): 8 cm; depth (fork): 4.2 cm
Inv. no. G.7177k

b. Length: 166 cm; width (fork): 9.3 cm; depth (fork): 3.5 cm
Inv. no. G.7177l

c. Length: 163 cm; width (fork): 12 cm; depth (fork): 4.5 cm
Inv. no. G.7177m

126. Three poles that constitute the horizontal part of the structure of the storage facility. The Haddad Kreda and the Kreda call these larungudé

(sing.) or larunguda (pl.). Two of them function as cross-bars - one is placed in the prongs of the three posts at the southern side of the facility (G.7177p) and another (G.7177r) tied to the rear, northern tent poles. They are both of plain acacia root. The third pole is of a heavier, darker wood from another species of tropical tree. It is tied some 40 cm above the ground level to the five posts that form the structural support of the storage 'bag'. The bar functions as a kind of board, lending support when the bag is filled with items. The specificities of the three bars are as follows:

a. Length: 171 cm; diameter: 12 cm
Inv. no. G.7177p

b. Length: 165 cm; diameter: 11 cm
Inv. no. G.7177r

c. Length: 174 cm; diameter: 12 cm
Inv. no. G.7177s

127. Three thick pieces of rope, each plaited from three twisted leather strings, lending the ropes a circumference of about 6 cm. The ropes are applied as support for the hide that makes up sides and bottom of the storage 'bag'. Such ropes are known as agar (sing.) or agara (pl.), a word that simply means rope of leather. The ropes are wound around the

two cross-bars that connect the fore- and hind posts of the southern and northern side of the facility respectively. The winding is done in such a way that it forms large loops, their 'depth' corresponding to that of the 'bag'. Inside these loops women place an old mat (cf. Cat. No. 128) and then the hide that forms the sides of the actual storage facility.

Length: 890 cm. Inv. no. G.7177t
Length: 740 cm. Inv. no. G.7177u
Length: 1050 cm. Inv. no. G.7177v

128. Mat or rather an old rag of a mat that is used to protect and support the storage 'bag'. It is placed directly on the loops to stabilize the storage

facility and provides some protection for the hide that makes up the actual storage 'bag'.

Length: 223 cm
Width: 117 cm
Inv. no. G.7177x

129. A large hide used for storage known as dela. The Haddad generally use antelope hides, the pastoralists those of cattle. This hide has been stitched together from two cow hides and a strip of a third one. The latter is added to one side to enlarge the 'bag' even further. The hides are all tanned in such a way that most the brownish hair has been removed. One end of the hide has been folded and stitched and furnished with two 'eyes' for tying. All holes in the hide are neatly repaired with leather patches that have been stitched onto the hide with leather strings.

Length: 235 cm
Width: 165 cm
Inv. no. G.7177v

Tent structure

The structural frame of the tent consists basically of four rows of vertical, pronged posts. In the forks of these are placed the four longitudinal arches, each made from two, sometimes, three plain and smooth acacia roots. To these in turn are tied the cross-arches, the number of which may vary. The tent described here had twenty-four such arches. Most of the vertical poles are plain, with a prong at the upper end. The circumference is more or less the same for all the

17,69. Poles, cross-bars and arches of Haddad tents are made from the roots of accacia raddiana. It is the women who dig up these roots with a digging utensil. Cf. Cat. no. 97.

17,70. Incompletely erected tent. Hides have been put up to provide shade.

vertical poles, i.e. some 12 cm to 13 cm, while the prongs are 7 cm to 9 cm wide and 3.5 cm to 5 cm 'deep'. Some poles are furnished with a winding around the prongs made from quite thin strips of leather to prevent the poles from splitting down the middle. The winding runs around each prong of the fork and around the top of the pole just below this for some 5 - 7 cm. A few poles are decorated with a simple, black serpentine-shaped band that runs up the pole, sometimes full length. Apart from this, decorations on the poles are rare. This tent had only one, more elaborately decorated pole (cf. G.7177fa).

130. The western row of central tent poles is made up by four poles, or six, i.e. if you include the poles at the ends. The Haddad Kreda and the Kreda call the four central poles dual (sing.) or duala (pl.). The poles are registered sequentially from south to north (inv. nos. G.7177db-de). Two of the poles are decorated (G.7177db) or partly so with a blackish meandering decoration that runs from the top of the pole down. Two of the poles have leather windings around the prongs to prevent the pole from splitting lengthwise. That is the case of inv. nos. G.7177dd and G.7177de. The specifics of the poles are as follows:

Length: 217 cm. Inv. no. G.7177db
Length: 235 cm. Inv. no. G.7177dc
Length: 232 cm. Inv. no. G.7177dd
Length: 198 cm. Inv. no. G.7177de

131. The eastern row of central tent poles, known to the Haddad Kreda and Kreda alike as dede (sing.) or deda (pl.) is made up of four poles. These are placed parallel to and only a bit more easterly than the bed posts. Like the poles of the western central row, they are either plain or decorated with a blackish meandering band that runs up the pole full length. One pole has a more delicate pattern of dots and stripes placed right below

17,71. Pronged pole that supports the arches at the south end of the tent. Cat. no. 134. Photo J.K.

the prong (cf. G.7177ef). The poles are registered sequentially from south to north as:

Length: 177 cm. Inv. no. G.7177eb
Length: 188 cm. Inv. no. G.7177ed
Length: 189 cm. Inv. no. G.7177ef
Length: 174 cm. Inv. no. G.7177eh

132. The six poles that make up the very front row of the tent structure, i.e. the entrance part to the west. The Haddad and the Kreda call these poles

for chini kude (sing.) or chini kuda (pl.), kuda meaning in front. The poles are all plain. In three instances the prongs have a winding of thin leather string around and just below the prong to prevent the pole from splitting down the middle. Apparently, the Haddad Kreda and the Kreda do not include the two end poles in the category of poles designated as such, i.e. the three poles at each end of the two central rows of poles plus the two poles located to the south and the north of the bed. This is due to the fact, I suspect, that this row of vertical poles not necessarily are put up each time the tent is erected. The poles may remain unused if the family intends to move camp after a short period of time, or for other reasons. The poles have the following measurements, registered from south to north as:

Length: 109 cm. Inv. no. G.7177ca
Length: 161 cm. Inv. no. G.7177cb
Length: 172 cm. Inv. no. G.7177cc
Length: 167 cm. Inv. no. G.7177cd
Length: 166 cm. Inv. no. G.7177ce
Length: 108 cm. Inv. no. G.7177cf

133. Three vertical poles that support the arches at the eastern rear of the tent. The poles are called chini theréde (singl.) or china theréda (pl.), theréde meaning behind. These poles are not erected vertically but so that they slant slightly towards west to offer maximum support to the tent structure in case of strong winds. The poles are registered from south to north as follows:

Length: 213 cm. Inv. no. G.7177ec
Length: 245 cm. Inv. no. G.7177ee
Length: 226 cm. Inv. no. G.7177eg

134. Three pronged poles erected more or less on line to support the arches at the south end of the tent. The poles are also known in Haddad Kreda and Kreda as chini kulu (sing.) or china kula (pl.). One pole (inv. no. G.7177fa) is placed right opposite its counterpart at the north end (inv. no. G.7177n) the two being on level with the longitudinal central line of the bed. This pole is pronged and has a winding of leather straps around the prong. The two other poles constitute at the same time the end poles of the two central rows of tent poles. Consecutively, from west to east the poles are registered as follows:

Length: 168 cm. Inv. no. G.7177da
Length: 188 cm. Inv. no. G.7177fa
Length: 112 cm. Inv. no. G.7177ea

135. Three pronged tent poles forming the northern end of the tent. Like those constituting the southern end poles these are named chini kulu (sing.) or chini kula (pl.). The terms are applied when the tent is seen as from the outside, so to speak. If observed from within the tent the striking function of the poles is their support of the storage facility, in which case they may be denoted differently, namely as kidicha larua. The central pole (inv. no. G.7177n) is placed just opposite its counterpart at the south end of the tent (inv. no. G.7177fa) and in line with the longitudinal centre line of the bed. All three are made from plain acacia root. Inv. nos. are the following, registered from the location of the post from east to west.

Length: 177 cm. Inv. no. G.7177j
Length: 150 cm. Inv. no. G.7177n
Length: 168 cm. Inv. no. G.7177o

Arches

Only when all of the vertical poles have been erected, including the northern and southern end poles of the two central rows, do women start to put up the arches. The first to be placed are those running in the longitudinal direction of the tent, i.e. from south to north, then the arches that run across these from west to east.

136. The longitudinal arches, erem, (pl. era) do not come in one piece, but are tied together from two, occasionally three slender, slightly bent bars as the construction of the tent structure proceeds. The arches are placed in the prongs of the four rows of vertical poles that make up the tent structure. The longitudinal arches, era, in turn support the twenty-six cross-arches, zewa, that subsequently are placed on top of them.

Length: 290 cm-340 cm
Inv. nos.: G.7177ga, G.7177gb,
G.7177ge, G.7177gf, G.7177gh,
G.7177gj, G.7177gl and G.7177gm

137. Twenty-six plain and slender cross-arches made from acacia roots. They are similar to and can be used interchangeably with the arches used for their support. The cross-arches are called zewé (sing.) or zewa (pl.) by the Haddad Kreda and Kreda alike. The poles are divided into two bundles when travelling, corresponding to whether they form part of the southern or northern section of the tent, respectively.

a. Length: 290 cm-340 cm
Inv. nos. G.7177ha; G.7177hb;

G.7177hc; G.7177hd; G.7177he;
G.7177hf; G.7177hg; G.7177hh;
G.7177hj; G.7177hk; G.7177hl;
G.7177hm; G.7177hn

b. Length: 290 cm-340 cm
Inv. nos. G.7177ja; G.7177jb;
G.7177jc; G.7177jd; G.7177je;
G.7177jf; G.7177jg; G.7177jh;
G.7177jk; G.7177jl; G.7177jm;
G.7177jn; G.7177jo

138. Two long pieces of rope made from twisted leaves of dum palm. These are used for tying the cross-arches to the four arches that run in the longitudinal direction of the tent.

Inv. no. G.7177ho

Mats

The tent is covered by four huge mats, all made from two long sections of dum palm strips. These have been plaited in a herring-bone pattern, as are most plaited items among the Haddad and Kreda. Subsequently, the two mats have been plaited together, leaving a visible band some 6 cm wide and with two thick 'seams' running the full length of the mat. Eyes are placed along some of the edges of the mats to enable the tying of these to poles, or holes with a plaiting almost like a buttonhole are made near the rim to serve the same purpose. The mats are between 420 cm and 600 cm long and about 150 cm to 175 cm wide. The Haddad and Kreda distinguish between different kinds of mats depending on the quality, as far as I understood their explanations, characterizing these as kabatcha, hongo

and raga respectively. The mats are tied with ropes twisted from strips of dum palm leaves. The mat that covers the back or eastern side of the tent is put up first, then the western of the two central mats, followed by the eastern of the central mats. Finally comes the turn to the mat that covers the front of the tent, if this is put up at all. Quite often this is done only during the day.

139. The mat that covers the back side of the tent is called yega tcheredé, yega meaning tent, while the word tcheredé indicates that it is the mat covering the back of the tent. The mat is made from two lengths of plaited strips of dum palm leaves. It has four eyes along one side for the ropes with which it is tied to the rear row of longitudinal arches. As I recall, the mat is also tied near the ground with strings fastened to the corners at each side.

Length: 593 cm-600 cm
Width: 161 cm-175 cm
Inv. no. G.7177kb

140. Mat that covers the western, central part of the tent and the second in turn to be placed when the tent is erected. It is called yega daudé, yega meaning tent, daudé principal or main, indicating the position of the mat as the cover of the central part of the tent. The two lengths that are plaited together to make the mat are somewhat irregular in size, one being about 67 cm wide, the other 85 cm. The mat is partly torn on one side, the one that faces west, while the other, eastern side is furnished with fourteen eyes for the strings or ropes with which it is secured to the longitudinal arches of the eastern row of central poles.

Length: 585 cm
Width: 150-160 cm
Inv. no. G.7177kc

141. Mat that covers the eastern side of the central part of the tent. The mat is known as yega daudé, as is its counterpart for the central, western side of the tent, yega meaning tent, and daudé main or central, indicating its location on the central part of the tent. The mat is made from plaited strips of dum palm leaves, as are the others. It too comes in two lengths that have been plaited together leaving a quite decorative 'seam' running the full length of the mat with a width of some six centimetres. The mat has a minor, rectangular mending. It is furnished with eyes or round holes that are stitched almost like buttonholes along each of the long sides of the mat, sixteen on one side, and seventeen on the other. When put in place the mat will be tied with strings both to the longitudinal arches placed in the prongs of the first, western row of tent poles and to the poles of the rear row of tent poles, i.e. the ones furthest to the east. Here the tying is made near the ground in order to keep the mat tied down as best one can.

Length: 585 cm-595 cm
Width: 162 cm
Inv. no. G.7177kd

142. Mat that covers the front of the tent, known as furgul kudé (sing.) or furgula kuda (pl.). This is usually put up only as a shade against the sun and will otherwise be stored away. Like the other mats, it has been made from two lengths of plaited strips of dum palm leaves, which have subsequently been plaited together, leaving a decorative 'seam' some 4 cm broad running the full length of the mat. The mat is in fine condition, not marked by tear and wear. There are six and seven eyes attached to each of the long sides of the mat respectively, and two eyes at each of the short sides of this for fastening the mat.

Length: 420 cm
Width: 162 cm-168 cm
Inv. no. G.7177ka

Furnishings

143. Stand for storing cooking pots with food, generally left-overs, called oja (sing.) or oja (pl.) by the Haddad Kreda and the Kreda alike. It is made from a simple pole, about 148 cm long and stands in a corner of the tent. The end that is not dug into the ground is split into seven fine 'branches' or prongs, each about 31 cm long. These are held together in an ever wider circle by two rings made from acacia root, the upper and larger some 40 cm x 32 cm in diameter, the lower 21 cm in diameter. The rings are tied to the seven 'branches' by means of a

17,72. Stand for storing pots with food. Cat. no. 143. Photo J.K.

fine binding made from plant fibres. Two of the 'branches' have been repaired with a winding of plant fibres.

Height: 148 cm
Diameter (upper ring): 40 cm, (lower ring): 21 cm
Inv. no. G.7177z

144. Small shelf for storing food and kitchen utensils. It is made from 30 small sticks that are held together by four bands of strings of twisted dum palm strips. The shelf is hung under the tent roof in the kitchen by means of strings.

Length: 64 cm
Width: 53 cm
Inv. no. G.7177y

EPILOGUE

The precarious situation of indigenous people like the Haddad begs the world's attention with ever increasing force, both for humanitarian reasons and as a serious human rights problem. There exist about 375 million indigenous peoples in the world. They count for more than half the 5-6000 languages spoken and for a similar treasure of knowledge systems, ritual forms, artistic expressions and experiments in social organization. It is estimated by UNESCO that more than 50% of the world's languages will disappear within the next few decades and with them the insights, cultural expressions and social forms which it has taken mankind thousands of years to develop. Indigenous peoples carry the brunt of this change the Haddad probably being one of them.

Like the rest of us the indigenous peoples are part and parcel of the ongoing transformation of living conditions on this tiny planet. In general, they have little influence on the course of development, however, and all too often the changes leave them more marginalized and destitute than ever before. All too many indigenous people live in extreme poverty and suffer from ill health and lack of opportunity. Typically, they experience social and economic discrimination - in some nations they do not even hold civil rights on par with other citizens. The reasons for this deplorable situation are many but frequently linked to the fact that indigenous people are few in number and hence without political clout. They live in remote parts of the world and face many difficulties in promoting their rights. Indigenous peoples have limited or no access to the media and are hence barred from drawing attention to their situation and muster political interest in curbing the social injustices, which they experience.

The fragile condition of indigenous peoples is primarily caused by the fast destruction of their natural habitats due to the global quest for natural resources. Hunter-gathering groups are particularly vulnerable and all too many face total destruction of their way of life. Some compete with farming and cattle-raising groups for access to scarce resources, others are threatened by political and economic interventions by the nation states in which they live. A few have retreated into 'voluntary isolation' to avoid cultural extinction as is the case of groups in South America and some of the Andaman Islanders. To most foragers the main threat comes from extractive industries. In th Arctic oil and gas companies seriously disturb the wildlife while timber companies cut down forests in the tropics and roll out large-scale oil palm or other mono-crop plantations for bio-fuel to cater for the world's escalating demand for energy. As a rule these companies have little or no consideration at all for the future existence of indigenous peoples on whose traditional land they operate. One of the last Penan groups still pursuing a nomadic life in the rainforest of Sarawak reached the front page of the *London Times* in May 2006 with a desperate plea to halt the ongoing logging which destroy their livelihood. A month later the *New York Times* reported on its front page that a small indigenous group in South America had given up. They had walked into a township asking for protection because they feared for their lives and saw no other way out than to give up their way of life.

On September 13th, 2007 the UN General Assembly adopted the UN Declaration on the Rights of Indigenous Peoples - 144 states voted for the Declaration, 11 states abstained and 4 states voted against this historic document:

Canada, the USA, Australia and New Zealand. The event marked the culmination of more than eighty years of political struggle by indigenous peoples to commit the international community to their cause. Throughout the history of the League of Nations and the United Nations, indigenous representatives have persistently called upon these institutions to ensure the cultural and social rights of indigenous peoples. Initially, these calls went unheeded. In 1923 Chief Deskaheh of the First Nations of North America returned with empty hands having knocked in vain on the doors of The League of Nations at Palais Wilson in Geneva to draw international attention to the plight of the Iroquois. Other indigenous representatives also tried to obtain permission to speak for this high body but without result. However, in 1957 the International Labour Organization (ILO) adopted the first international legal instrument concerning indigenous peoples and their rights and thereafter, slowly the situation began to improve. In 1970-71 the Commission on the Prevention of Discrimination and Protection of Minorities recommended there be a comprehensive study on the situation of indigenous peoples in response to reports of human rights relations and appointed Special Rapporteur Martinez Cobos to undertake the work. In 1977 nearly 200 indigenous delegates from around the world went to Geneva to attend a conference of non-governmental organizations on discrimination against indigenous people. Four years later the studies of the Special Rapporteur led to the establishment of the Working Group on Indigenous Populations (WGIP) as a subsidiary body of the Sub-Commission of the Human Rights Commission with a mandate to review developments pertaining to the promotion and protection of the human rights and fundamental freedoms of indigenous populations, giving special attention to the evolution of standards concerning those rights. It is the outcome of this work which almost 25 years later was adopted by the UN General Assembly. Still, there is a long way from acknowledging the rights of indigenous peoples to actually ensuring that these are respected and implemented by nation states.

Indigenous peoples' problems are momentous and pressing. This has been proven time and again at sessions of the UN Permanent Forum on Indigenous Issues. This high-level body of sixteen independent experts was established by United Nations Economic and Social Council (ECOSOC) in 2000 to discuss indigenous issues and advice the Council, UN agencies, funds and programs on economic and social development, culture, education, health, environment and human rights pertaining to indigenous peoples and to raise awareness about these issues. No less that 1,400 indigenous observers participated in the Permanent Forum's sixth session in May 2007 together with representatives of 81 states and of 31 UN bodies, making it the largest conference ever held at UN headquarters. The indigenous observers come from all parts of the world representing the rich variety in indigenous cultures and languages, but not matching the number of indigenous peoples. Many groups have no way of getting a representative to New York to speak for them and a fair number have no idea that the UN Permanent Forum exists. Whereas hunting and foraging peoples of the circumpolar region are well represented at the sessions of the Permanent Forum, for example, this is not the case of those living in the tropics. Only one Batwa and one San represented the foraging peoples of Africa. There were no representatives at all from Chad, neither Wodaabe or Tubu pastoralists nor any Haddad.

Human societies have left their imprint on the natural environment and on each other's economic and cultural conditions for thousands of years, of course, but the speed and scale of this transformation in recent years and its impact on and consequences for indigenous peoples are unprecedented. How the Haddad fare at present is uncertain. Their response to the socio-environmental challenges during the last part of the 19th century and the first half of the 20th century has been one of gradually giving up hunting and embarking on a reorientation of their subsistence activities and all that goes herewith, socially and culturally. The strategies have differed, as we have seen. The Haddad Kanembu engaged increasingly in food production, whereas the Haddad Kreda turned to pastoralists for economic assistance and protection perhaps as a step toward a future subsistence based on herding.

How the two groups have coped since Johannes and I lived among them some forty years ago, I have not been able to ascertain. Valid information on social and cultural life in this part of Chad is scarce. It is unlikely that the Haddad have been spared the ravages of drought, environmental pressure and violence. Despite the odds, I can only hope that these kind and wonderful people have been able to live a meaningful life in accordance with their cultural values and that one day Haddad representatives will turn up in New York at the sessions of the UN Permanent Forum on Indigenous Issues to add their voice and wisdom to the cause of indigenous peoples.

APPENDIX: HADDAD CLANS

The Haddad perceive of their social life as largely organ-ized along patrilineal principles, the key structure being the clan. We had no intention of going into any depth with this aspect of Haddad life, knowing quite well that it would be impossible with the relatively short time at our disposal. We made an effort to assess Haddad recollection of the generational depth of clans and knowledge of clan history, an exercise which generally revealed less interest in the subject among our Haddad Kanembu informants than among the Haddad Kreda. Still, an oral tradition of no less than ten generations was common among the Haddad Kanembu.

HADDAD KREDA CLANS

The Haddad Kreda claim that they belong to three distinct and unrelated descent categories: the *Tchatchauma*, the *Ossa,* and the *Bichia Yunussia.* Together these three catego-ries comprise a total of ten clans.

The *Tchatchauma* are split into two major clans, a) the *Tchatchauma Yeska*, i.e. 'the black *Tchatchauma*' and b) the *Tchatchauma Mada*, i.e. 'the red *Tchatchauma*'. Both are said to descend from the same ancestor *Tchatchau*, a name which refers to something which is neither sweet nor sweetened. The clan emblem of the *Tchatchauma Mada* is a gazelle species called *tiguidim,* said to graze to the south of the habitat of the clan. The male has quite small ant-lers, the female is entirely without these, and it is probably the Oribi, or *Ourebia ourebi.* The Oribi prefer open lawns densely populated by large herbivores and decline where

these have been severely reduced. The emblem of the *Tchatchauma Yeska* is the black-bellied bustard. The gen-erational depth of the two clans is around ten to thirteen although there is some uncertainty as to the exact descent and kinship relations of the 'ultimate' ancestors (cf. *Fig. 5,4*). Each of the two *Tchatchauma* clans has a chief, but none of them were invested with but nominal authority at the time of our visit. This had not always been the case, accord-ing to our Haddad informants. In pre-colonial times and the decades that preceded World War II the *Tchatchauma* were not hunting all year round in the Mussoro. They went north during the dry season to hunt antelope, as previously described. These hunts required the collaborative effort of several clans, and the chief was instrumental in the plan-ning and orchestration of these major undertakings. In tune with the abandonment of these major hunting expeditions the *Tchatchauma* ended up staying put in the Mussoro area and directing their hunting activities towards gazelles and other game. In tune with these changes in the subsistence pattern the role and say of the clan chief as an organizer of grand hunts was rendered obsolete.

The *Ossa* comprise four minor clans, all descendants from the same ancestor. The four clans are the *Ossa Éléfima, Ossa Brataya, Ossa Yeska* i.e. the black *Ossa,* and the *Ossa Mada* i.e. the red *Ossa.* We met very few Haddad belong-ing to these clans and were not able to collect substantial information about them.

The *Bichia* are more numerous and comprise more clans than the *Tchatchauma*, yet the generational depth is shal-lower. The *Bichia* all descend from a common ancestor after whom they have their name, *Bichia.* They are divided into four minor clans: the *Bichia Yunussia,* the *Bichia Nguetema,* the *Bichia Becheria,* and the *Bichia Ngamia.* Each of these has an emblem, that of the *Bichia Yunussia* being the black-bellied bustard. The bird should not be killed by clan members, it is believed, or these risk being struck by an illness called *gob,* which causes itching and inflamed skin, probably leprosy. The emblems of the other *Bichia* clans were not known to the *Bichia Yunussia* from whom we obtained our data, just as their knowledge on matters regarding the size, history and organizational character of the other clans was highly fragmentary. We were told however, that they all had about the same generational depth. An elderly man by the name of Mussa traced his descent from the clan ancestor as follows: Bichi - Yunus - Ali - Hassan - Derichi - Deney - Mussa.

The *Bichia* clans do all live together for part of the year and carry out joint hunting expeditions unlike the *Tchatchauma.* We learned bout this among the *Bichia Yunussia,* a clan that is tied to and live together with the pastoral Kreda clan, *Yiria Etama,* for part of the year. The *Bichia Yunussia* number some twenty-two tents, out of which eighteen are dispersed among four different Kreda descent groups or camps. One of these camps had seven Haddad tents, two camp sites had four Haddad tents each, and one camp site had three Haddad tents. When pastures are plentiful and the milk from the cows of the Kreda abundant the *Bichia Yunussia* live with the pastoralists. During the winter time, however, when pastures are scarce and the pastoralists assemble in larger camps, the *Bichia Yunussia* leave their Kreda 'hosts' to set up a joint camp of their own embracing all of the twenty-two tent units. The camp is pitched at a locality called Chakara, but despite the fact that it is an all Haddad campsite this is still, nominally at least, under Kreda authority embodied in the Chef du Canton of the *Yiria* clan. However, the chief of the *Bichia Yunussia* holds authority as well. Winter is also the time for antelope hunting, in particular for flocks of scimitar or white Oryx, *Aegoryx algazel algazel,* which venture south of the 15th northern latitude towards the end of the dry season. The hunting of the Oryx, the Addax and the Dama antelope species require collaboration of a larger number of people than any one of the ordinary camp units can master, and the *Bichia Yunussia* clan chief play a major role in orchestrating these hunts, a role that is acknowledged by his right to an extra part of the game.

Genealogical chart of Haddad Kreda clans

The ensuing genealogical information on the red and black Tchattchauma clans was offered to us by Issaga and Omar respectively. We met the latter at his camp at Gaba on August 31st. Omar proved highly interested in the history of his clan and had made an effort to obtain information on this matter from old people, he told us. The majority of the Haddad were ignorant about their ancestry. They did not care about this but were interested only in eating and sleeping, he argued. The difference in genealogical depth between the two -*Tchatchauma* clan segments is probably due to Omar's insufficient knowledge of his ancestors. It may of course be due to genealogical dislocation. Sar and Tolou are probably brothers.

Tchatchauma Yeska	*Tchatchauma Mada*
Tchatchau	
Sar	NN
Sakine	Tolou
Mussa	Alette
Haroune	Ali
Djeber	Mahamat
Ibrain	Issa
Brahim	Haroune
Issaga	Mahamat
Sale	Hassan
Tchungul	Omar
Hamid	
Issaga	

HADDAD KANEMBU CLANS

We obtained information on Haddad Kanembu clans at two locations. One was at Chedra where we learned of two sets of clan names, the second being at the tiny village of Wanagal where we were told of still another set of clan names. All in all the three lists enumerates fifty-four clans, but this number does by no means exhaust the number of clans. Le Rouvreur lists forty Haddad Kanembu clans, but only ten of these overlap with the names that we noted down, while Conte's survey comprises forty-three Duu clans throughout the eight chieftaincies of South Kanem. The members of these clans were living in 214 villages (Le Rouvreur 1962: 379; Conte 1983: 32: Table 2.).

The key informant at Chedra was an eighty year old man by the name of was Mussa. Our talk with Mussa stirred the interest of almost all the men of the village who sat down with us and eagerly commented on, corrected or supported Mussa's account. According to these informants almost all of the Haddad Kanembu clans stemmed from the N'Guri area. The ensuing tables render the clan names that Johannes and I collected. Specific information on some clans has been added, included that offered by Le Rouvreur's. Clans identified with an asterix are listed by Conte, but twenty-four out of his list of forty-three clans do not occur in our lists (Conte 1983: 32: table 2). Reference is made to the other tables of clans Johannes and I collected, if the names overlap.

Table I

This was collected at Chedra. It embraces the ensuing clans:

*Adia** - cf. table II.

*Asaru**

*Ayuru** - agriculturalists, weavers, and dyers near Djédat southeast of N'Guri. (Le Rouvreur 1962: 379).

*Bara** - agriculturalists and leather artisans near Bari south of N'Guri. (Le Rouvreur 1962: 379); cf. table II.

Bartchilum

*Budasa**

*Brau**

Damkwa

*Darkoa** - located around N'Guri and Darkoa where they support themselves as agriculturalists, weavers, shoemakers, and by petty trading (Le Rouvreur 1962: 379). As is the case of many clans the *Darkoa* are dispersed throughout Kanem and the Bahr el Ghazal. Clan members are numerous around Chedra. The emblem of the *Darkoa* is a cow with black or red back, a white belly, white cornea, and white ears. Cf. table II.

Digeu

*Digeri** - cf. table II.

Jiyumbo

*Kafa** - cf. table II.

*Kanku** - perhaps identical with the *Kaliha* near Soaya who live west of N'Guri and support themselves by fishing, agriculture and weaving, and perhaps the *Kaolia* near

N'Daratioko close to Motoa, who subsist as smiths, agriculturalists and leather artisans. (Le Rouvreur 1962: 379); cf. table II.

Karda - agriculturalists and shoemakers at Kardari near Yalita (Le Rouvreur 1962: 379).

*Keï** - cf. table II.

Kileti

*Kuluru** - a clan from which all smiths are said to originate. Some members support themselves by hunting.

*Kuri** - probably synonymous with the *Kuhuri*, who live near Djiguidada (Liodu), where they support themselves by weaving, fishing and agriculture (Le Rouvreur 1962: 379; cf. table II).

Logia

Magada - perhaps identical with the *Mahada* near Mondo, who are agriculturalists and leather artisans. (Le Rouvreur 1962: 379); cf. table II.

Magi

Malammusaru

*Malaru** - cf. table II.

*Motoa** - who subsist as smiths, agriculturalists and leather craftsmen (Le Rouvreur 1962: 379).

N'Galama

Riga - probably the same as Rëga - cf. table II.

Serau

Tida

Yangu

*Yéya** - who are agriculturalists and weavers near Gallamamé, a place near Mondo. (Le Rouvreur 1962: 379).

Table II

A Haddad Kanembu man near Chedra recalled the following clans and their core area:

*Adia** - at Massakory - cf. table I.

Ayku - at N'Guri

*Bara** - at Massakory. The *Bara* are peasants and leather artisans – cf. table I.

Baraza - at Chedra. The clan emblem is Denham's bustard, *keliru,* which must never be killed by clan members.

*Danka** - at Mussoro. The *Danka* are weavers, shoemakers, and peasants at Marzuk near Mundo. (Le Rouvreur 1962: 379)

*Darkoa** - at N'Guri – cf. table I.

*Digeri** - at N'Guri – cf. table I.

*Kafa** - at N'Guri – cf. table I.

*Kanku** - at N'Guri. The *Kanku* are dyers, weavers, and peasants. According to Rouvreur they live near Munussa near Am Djédat. (Le Rouvreur 1962: 379).

*Kauluru** - at Mao. The *Kauluru* are smiths, who also subsist by hunting with bow and arrow. The totem of the clan is a large lizzard resembling an iguana known as *kuimarfane.* Like other clan emblems this can never killed by members of the clan. Probably the same as *Kuluru.* Cf. table I.

*Keï** - at N'Guri – cf. table I.

*Kuri** - at Massakory – cf. table I.

Magada - at Mondo – cf. table I.

Magui - at Mussoro

*Malaru** - at N'Guri – cf. table I.

*Rëga** - at Massakory, probably the same as Riga – cf. table I.

*Yiyimpu** - at Mussoro, probably the same as Jiyumbo – cf. table I.

Table III

The third listing of Haddad Kanembu clans was noted down in the tiny village of Wanagal east of Méchimeré. The names were forwarded by the men of the village but without any mentioning of an original location of these or the present core location of the clans.

Amzama

Baraza - members of this clan will never eat the black-bellied bustard and to kill the bird entails the death of the hunter.

Baragara

Becher

Bogoma

*Darkoa** - the clan has to emblems: a snake called *kwakwa* and cows with a black back, white horns and ears. Clan emblems must neither be killed nor eaten. Cf. tables I & II.

Gana

Gurdaja

Kalaja

Karda - members of the clan do not eat camels which have not had fodder shortly before they were slaughtered. See list I.

Karea

Kulu - the emblem of the clan is a red goat, which clan members should neither kill or eat.

Kwaka

Mada - the emblem of the clan is that its members never fight with slaves.

Mala

Tolo

Torno

Warda

Wurzama

Zounda

Table IV

An elderly member of the *Darkoa* clan at Chedra by the name of *Brahim* explained how he himself descended from the clan ancestor *Darku* spelling out the genealogical chart as follows:

Darku
Yuno Kura
Yuno Wali
Adama Bossauai
Kindine Mussa
Adam
Kauku
Yussua
Djibrine
Brahim

RÉSUMÉ EN FRANÇAIS

Ce livre traite des Haddad, un peuple autochtone du Tchad, dont tout le mode de vie, la position sociale dans la société qui les entoure et la perception de soi et du monde sont liés à la chasse ou l'ont été. Cette présentation est basée sur des recherches ethnographiques effectuées sur le terrain par l'auteur et son époux Johannes Nicolaisen, aujourd'hui décédé, durant l'été et le début de l'automne de 1963. On ne savait alors que très peu de choses des Haddad, en fait si peu qu'il fut même assez difficile de les localiser. Cette recherche sur le terrain devait être une étude pilote pour préparer une collecte d'informations approfondie à long terme. Pour diverses raisons, celle-ci n'a pas pu être réalisée, mais, vu le peu d'informations disponibles sur les Haddad et sur les sociétés de chasseurs en Afrique de l'Ouest en général, il a été décidé de publier les données que nous avions récoltées.

1: ÉTUDIER LES HADDAD

Le premier chapitre est une introduction sur les Haddad et sur le Tchad, plus particulièrement le Kanem et le Bahr el Ghazal où vivent les Haddad. Cette région était située au carrefour des routes de commerce et de migration. À travers les temps, de nombreuses ethnies y ont trouvé leur subsistance comme pasteurs, agro-pasteurs, agriculteurs, chasseurs et artisans. Ce chapitre décrit l'arrière plan de l'étude sur le terrain et les conditions de sa réalisation, les longs voyages à dos de chameau pour localiser les différents groupes de Haddad et le déclenchement de la guerre civile en 1963 qui mit fin à nos explorations. La section suivante présente les théories anthropologiques dominantes à cette époque ainsi que les discussions clés concernant les sociétés de chasseurs, y compris la tendance à les considérer comme la ligne de référence de l'évolution vers la réalité actuelle hautement diversifiée.

Les études anthropologiques sur les nombreuses ethnies du Kanem sont plutôt rares. Parmi les premières sources européennes, nous trouvons les descriptions d'explorateurs tels que Heinrich Barth et Adolf Overveg qui essayèrent, en 1851, d'atteindre Mao, la ville du sultan du Kanem, et Gustav Nachtigal qui explora la région une vingtaine d'années plus tard, mais ceux-ci ne mentionnent guère les Haddad dans leurs écrits. Après la colonisation française du Tchad à la fin du 19ᵉ siècle, le personnel administratif et militaire rédigea des rapports, mais, à part ceux d'Henri Carbou, ils ne comprennent presque pas d'informations sur les Haddad. Après la deuxième guerre mondiale, on trouve quelques pages les concernant dans les ouvrages du colonel Jean Chapelle et d'Albert Le Rouvreur, tous deux fonctionnaires de l'État. C'est seulement après notre étude qu'un autre anthropologue, Édouard Conte, écrivit quelque chose sur les Haddad. Il effectua, en 1972-73, pour sa thèse de doctorat, une étude sur le terrain parmi les Kanembou et les Duu qu'il définit comme une couche sociale incluant les Haddad kanembou.

La rédaction de notes de terrain 40 ans plus tard pose des problèmes méthodologiques particuliers. En effet, les agendas de recherche ont changé ainsi que les intérêts et les connaissances de l'auteur. Les notes de terrain représentent toujours une appréciation partielle et sélective de configurations sociales et historiques complexes, et la présente analyse y ajoute encore un niveau d'interprétation. Le fait qu'une bonne partie des données ont été collectées par le mari de l'auteur soulève d'autres problèmes méthodologiques ainsi que des considérations éthiques.

Sur le terrain, deux thèmes s'imposaient à l'auteur. D'une part, les différences générales de mode de vie et de culture entre les différents groupes et, d'autre part, la marginalisation des Haddad dans la société du Kanem. La hiérarchie socioéconomique et la complexité culturelle qui caractérisent le Kanem et le Bahr el Ghazal sont la résultante de plusieurs siècles d'histoire, de l'adaptation écologique, de la migration sociale et des processus culturels ainsi que des insurrections, de la chasse aux esclaves, du pillage et de la domination et la subordination politiques. Au Tchad, la violence régit la performance économique, le statut sociopolitique, la formation de l'identité et la politique. C'est dans ce contexte très turbulent que l'on trace les racines de la discrimination dont les Haddad sont victimes.

2: LE KANEM ET LE BAHR EL GHAZAL

Le cadre de vie des Haddad est le bassin du lac Tchad, une vaste échancrure autrefois recouverte d'un lac immense dont le lac Tchad, qui ne cesse de se rétrécir, n'est qu'une pâle réminiscence. Le climat est tropical, mais les précipitations varient et la couverture végétale est différente au nord et au sud du Kanem et dans les massifs centraux du Bahr el Ghazal plus à l'est, ce qui a des implications pour la subsistance des Haddad. Au début du 20e siècle, le gibier était encore abondant, mais la chasse commerciale et les armes automatiques ont prélevé un lourd tribut et ont presque conduit l'autruche, autrefois importante du point de vue économique, au bord de l'extinction. Après la deuxième guerre mondiale, la faune fut encore réduite suite à la sécheresse et à la guerre civile. Dans les années 60, les espèces les plus importantes pour la subsistance des Haddad étaient les antilopes, les gazelles, les crocodiles, les hippopotames, les chacals, les porcs-épics, les outardes, les pintades et d'autres oiseaux.

La composition ethnique est variée en termes de cultures, de langues et de modes de subsistance. La foi musulmane représente un facteur unifiant. Au cours des siècles, d'innombrables groupes sont venus dans la région, certains pour y rester, alors que d'autres sont tombés dans l'oubli

suite aux guerres récurrentes et, jusqu'au début du 20e siècle, à la chasse aux esclaves. C'est dans cet environnement dangereux qu'il a fallu négocier une identité sociale et culturelle distincte, et les Haddad ont dû accepter la perception « d'autres » qui les voient comme socialement et culturellement marginalisés et avilis. Néanmoins, ils revendiquent, en s'appuyant sur leurs traditions orales, une identité distincte qui les définit comme « peuple autochtone ». Cette auto-identification est adoptée comme principe de travail dans l'analyse qui suit.

Les Haddad vivent dispersés sur un vaste territoire dans le Sahel, au Kanem et dans les massifs centraux du Bahr el Ghazal. Ils s'aventurent vers le nord, dans le désert du Sahara, pour chasser l'antilope, et vers le sud, dans la savane, pour faire la cueillette et récolter des plantes médicinales. Des groupes qui leur sont apparentés, généralement connus sous le nom d'Aza ou Azza, vivent au nord-ouest du lac Tchad ou encore plus à l'ouest dans la région de Dillo au Niger oriental. Les Haddad se définissent comme issus de trois « souches », les Haddad kreda, les Haddad kanembou et les Haddad forgerons ou artisans. Aucun d'entre eux n'a de langue propre et chaque groupe parle la langue du groupe ethnique parmi lequel il vit, soit le daza comme les Kreda ou les Kecherda, soit le kanembou comme les agro-pasteurs kanembou. Les artisans utilisent soit l'une soit l'autre de ces langues.

Les Haddad kreda sont nomades et campent pendant la plus grande partie de l'année avec les pasteurs, le plus souvent les Kreda ou les Kecherda. Ils migrent avec les pasteurs en petits groupes de trois à cinq familles, chaque famille montant sa tente juste derrière celle de sa famille « hôte ». La plupart de l'année, ils pratiquent la chasse collective aux filets sur les massifs centraux du Bahr el Ghazal. Pendant la saison sèche, ils s'aventurent cependant vers le nord pour chasser l'antilope. À cette époque de l'année, ils vivent en plus grands groupes et résident parfois dans le campement d'un chef pasteur.

Les Haddad kanembou se sont tous installés dans des villages au bord du lac Tchad ou à l'est de celui-ci, essentiellement dans la région de N'Guri. Ils vivent de la production alimentaire complétée par la cueillette, et ils partagent leur environnement avec les agro-pasteurs kanembou. Ils pratiquent la chasse à l'arc et aux flèches empoisonnées, ce qui est en général une occupation individuelle. L'utilisation d'un déguisement est un trait distinctif de leur méthode de chasse. Le chasseur s'approche furtivement de son gibier déguisé en bucorve avec une ou deux peaux de mouton noir et un masque ressemblant à cet oiseau noir majestueux. Autrefois, ils se déguisaient aussi en autruches.

Il y a un groupe de Haddad vivant dans les villes et gagnant leur vie comme forgerons, artisans et musiciens. Certains d'entre eux pratiquent un peu la chasse pour améliorer leurs revenus. On les trouve non seulement dans tout le Kanem et le Bahr el Ghazal, mais aussi au nord-est du lac Tchad, à Manga et Dillo, où ils augmentent leurs revenus en creusant des puits pour les pasteurs. On trouve aussi des forgerons et des artisans haddad dans les parties nord et nord-est du Tchad.

Le Nord du Tchad a une composition ethnique très variée, mais nous ne mentionnerons ici brièvement que 5 groupes, ceux qui vivent avec les Haddad et interagissent avec eux et, ou bien, ont exercé une influence sur eux au cours de l'histoire. L'un de ces groupes est les Ouled Slimane qui vivent dans le Nord du Kanem et qui exploitaient et contrôlaient le Kanem au 19e siècle. Ils migrent avec leurs troupeaux de chameaux et vendent des dates et du sel, provenant des oasis sahariennes du Borkou et du Kaouar, sur les marchés du Kanem. Ils font partie d'un groupe de pasteurs et semi-pasteurs arabes comprenant aussi les Juhayna, Hassaouna et Tunjur qui possèdent du bétail. Les Arabes représentent au total entre 14 et 20 pour cent de la population du Tchad. Au sud et au nord-est des pasteurs arabes, on trouve les Toubou, nombreux et propriétaires de bétail, qui sont connus sous le nom de « nomades noirs ». Ils sont divisés en de nombreux clans qui ne forment pas d'unités spatiales et n'ont pas de politique commun, mais qui sont unis par leurs traditions orales liées à une ascendance commune qui s'exprime symboliquement par l'utilisation des mêmes marques pour les chameaux. Ils n'ont pas de terme propre pour désigner leur identité commune. Les linguistes distinguent deux groupes. D'une part, les groupes parlant le teda qui vivent au-dessus du 18e parallèle, c'est-à-dire le massif Tibesti ou ses environs, Koufra, Djado, Kaouar, Borkou, Erdi-Ma, Mourdi et Basso Erdébé. D'autre part, les groupes parlant le daza qui font paître leur bétail au sud du 18e parallèle, c'est-à-dire Manga, Chitati, le Kanem et le Bahr el Ghazal où l'on trouve, entre autres, les Kreda et les Kecherda. Les Kreda sont organisés en 9 clans principaux et comptaient entre 50.000 et 66.000 personnes dans les années 60. Les campements kreda rassemblent de cinq à plus de vingt tentes, habituellement habitées par des parents pa-

trilatéraux. Des unités ou campements pour s'occuper des troupeaux sont établis et dissous selon des considérations de parenté ou de mariage ou des considérations personnelles. Ainsi, les Kreda sont beaucoup plus flexibles que tous les autres pasteurs du Tchad. Les Kanembou sont le groupe ethnique le plus important au Kanem même. Au moment de notre étude, ils étaient environ 42.000 dans cette région et environ 65.000 au total. Ils parlent le kanembou, un dialecte du kanouri, et affirment que leur terre ancestrale est au Yémen. Ils sont apparentés aux Kanouri vivant à l'ouest du lac Tchad et certains maintiennent des liens avec ceux-ci à travers la frontière actuelle entre le Tchad et le Nigeria. L'histoire des Kanembou a été turbulente et a donné lieu à beaucoup de migrations, de déplacements et de mariages avec d'autres groupes. La plupart des Kanembou vivent dans de petites agglomérations de huttes en forme de ruches et tirent leur subsistance d'un mélange d'agriculture et d'élevage. Le dernier groupe que nous mentionnerons sont les Yedina, ou Boudouma, qui résident sur les rives et les îles du lac Tchad et vivent de la pêche, de la culture saisonnière de plantes comme le millet et le maïs et d'un peu d'élevage, principalement de bétail. Ils se déplacent entre les îles et les rives du lac avec leurs chevaux et autres animaux dans de simples canoës de papyrus ou à la nage en utilisant des bottes de papyrus comme flotteurs. Au début des années 60, on pensait qu'ils étaient environ 25.000, mais il existe peu d'écrits sur ces populations.

3: DANS LE MIROIR DU TEMPS

Ce chapitre étudie de plus près l'histoire politique et socioculturelle du Kanem et du Bahr el Ghazal. Aussi bien l'histoire lointaine, y compris les données révélées par l'archéologie moderne, que l'histoire plus récente des 19e et 20e siècles, afin de présenter le cadre permettant de comprendre la société et la culture des Haddad ou plus spécifiquement les facteurs qui influent sur leur vie actuelle. Un de ses traits caractéristiques est la persistance, tout au long des trois mille dernières années, de la coexistence entre les activités agro-pastorales et la chasse-cueillette. Un autre trait caractéristique est l'importance de la production du fer pour la subsistance des populations en général et pour l'ordre politique du Kanem en particulier, et, par conséquent, pour l'existence des forgerons haddad. Un troisième élément est l'ensemble complexe de forces qui sont à l'origine du développement de la hiérarchie du Kanem et leur impact sur les relations socioéconomiques. Le commerce à longue distance était l'une de ces forces et l'expansion de l'Islam en était une autre. On allègue que l'existence et le destin des Haddad sont étroitement liés aux processus historiques susmentionnés, aux structures politiques hégémoniques qui se sont développées dans la région et aux troubles civils constants qui s'ensuivirent.

4: LES HADDAD – QUI SONT-ILS ?

Le caractère insaisissable des Haddad

Notre première impression, qui était que les Haddad étaient considérés comme périphériques par la société environnante, fut amplement confirmée tout au long de notre étude sur le terrain. Il était difficile d'obtenir des informations valides sur les Haddad en général et, en ce qui concerne les Haddad kreda, il fut même difficile de les localiser. Les autres groupes ethniques ne savaient que peu ou rien d'eux et ne leur montraient que peu ou pas d'intérêt. C'est peut-être compréhensible car les Haddad n'étaient pas particulièrement remarquables. Ils n'étaient pas réputés pour leur bétail ou leurs raids de bétail comme les pasteurs kreda et kecherda ou pour avoir régné sur un empire comme les Kanembou et les Kanouri. À cette époque, ils étaient dispersés géographiquement et marginalisés économiquement, et leur importance politique était donc négligeable. Nous ne savons pas s'ils ont connu des jours meilleurs autrefois. Les annales du Kanem et du Bahr el Ghazal ne leur accordent pas une grande importance, mais, comme l'ont montré les historiens modernes et les auteurs féministes, les archives historiques sont des rapports sélectifs qui, le plus souvent, reflètent les intérêts, les connaissances et les points de vue de ceux qui sont au pouvoir. Les sources historiques fournies par les savants arabes et les explorateurs et administrateurs européens s'intéressent surtout aux affaires dynastiques et aux activités des personnalités éminentes. Nous ne pouvons pas exclure la possibilité que les Haddad aient joué un rôle plus important à un moment donné, mais il nous semble raisonnable de supposer qu'en général leur destin a été marqué par l'asservissement. Les Haddad kreda et les Haddad kanembou que nous avons rencontrés différaient les uns des autres du point de vue

de la distribution spatiale, de la socialité, de l'habitat, des moyens de subsistance, des méthodes de chasse, de la nature des relations d'échange avec les autres groupes, ainsi que de la perception et de l'expression culturelle.

Noms et lieux

Dans les sources existantes sur le Kanem, les Haddad sont identifiés par un nombre étonnant de noms. Haddad, qui est le nom habituellement utilisé par ces populations elles-mêmes, est dérivé du mot arabe *ḥaddid* signifiant fer et désigne un forgeron, mais dans tout le Nord du Tchad, il est utilisé dans un sens plus large pour désigner les chasseurs ou cueilleurs. Parmi les autres noms, on trouve Aza, utilisé par les pasteurs daza et, selon Nachtigal, Dânoâ ou Dânawa, utilisé par les Kanouri. L'administrateur français Carbou n'a pas rencontré ce dernier terme, mais il mentionne Duu, le nom que les Kanembou donnent aux Haddad. Les sources françaises datant d'après la deuxième guerre mondiale utilisent toutes le terme Haddad, sauf Annie M.-D. Lebeuf qui réserve le nom de Dânoâ aux Haddad kanembou, et Edouard Conte qui utilise le terme kanembou Duu, mais dans un sens plus large désignant une couche sociale de la société kanembou. Les différents groupes que nous avons rencontrés sur le terrain s'identifiaient eux-mêmes comme Haddad, que ce soit des chasseurs-cueilleurs, présents ou passés, ou des artisans urbains. Ils faisaient cependant une distinction entre les « archers » et les « chasseurs au filet » qui correspond à la différence entre les Haddad kanembou et les Haddad kreda. À l'époque de notre étude sur le terrain, l'anthropologie était encore dominée par les structuralistes et la théorie et les paradigmes structure fonctionnaliste. Cependant, des doutes commençaient à germer concernant l'applicabilité de ces théories bien nettes pour expliquer des processus sociaux dynamiques et l'ambiguïté des étiquettes sociales. Ce chapitre discute certains problèmes se rapportant aux paradigmes et propose d'utiliser le terme Haddad en accord avec la perception de ces populations elles-mêmes et d'y ajouter kreda ou kanembou pour préciser le groupe de Haddad duquel il s'agit.

Langue et démographie

Les Haddad n'ont pas de langue propre et parlent la langue du groupe dominant parmi lequel ils vivent. Ainsi, les Haddad kreda parlent le teda des pasteurs kreda ou kecherda, les Haddad kanembou parlent la langue des Kanembou et les artisans urbains parlent soit l'une soit l'autre de ces langues tonales. Les estimations diffèrent en ce qui concerne la taille de la population haddad. Nachtigal estimait la population dânoâ à environ 6.000 personnes. Cent ans plus tard, l'administrateur français Chapelle estimait la population haddad à 7.600 personnes, alors que son collègue Le Rouvreur avançait qu'ils étaient près de 100.000 en tout. Nous avons estimé le nombre de Haddad kreda à 2-3.000 personnes et le nombre de Haddad kanembou à environ 25.000, ce qui correspond à peu près aux estimations de Conte. Les chercheurs ne s'entendent pas non plus sur la question de savoir si les Haddad peuvent être distingués des autres groupes par leur apparence physique. La plupart affirment que non, mais nous nous sommes aperçus que nous pouvions distinguer les Haddad des groupes dominants parmi lesquels ils vivaient, comme pouvaient le faire les membres de ces groupes eux-mêmes.

5: ORIGINE ET IDENTITÉ

Aux yeux de l' « européen d'autre »

Cette section discute les théories relatives à l'origine et à la spécificité des Haddad proposées au cours des temps par les explorateurs, les chercheurs et les administrateurs familiers avec la région du Kanem et du Bahr el Ghazal, tout en mettant en garde contre une extrapolation trop peu critique à partir des traditions orales. Un des premiers auteurs, Gustav Nachtigal, retrace une ascendance commune Haddad-Manga au Niger oriental. Cette théorie sur l'origine des Haddad est réfutée par l'administrateur français Henri Carbou qui, en accord avec la tradition orale des Kanembou, avance que les Haddad kanembou et les Boulala du lac Fitri ont le même « sang », les ancêtres des premiers étant issus d'une mésalliance entre une femme de la famille royale boulala et un esclave. Ce mythe justifie la domination des Kanembou sur les Haddad et le bas statut de ces derniers. Carbou pense que les Haddad kanembou descendent en fait d'un mélange de captifs boulala et de forgerons païens. Aux yeux de Carbou, ceci explique la discrimination généralisée à l'égard des Haddad. Le Rouvreur observe simplement que « nous sommes confrontés au mystère de leur origine », alors que Chapelle associe l'origine des chasseurs-cueilleurs haddad au métier de forgeron. Il avance que les Haddad, comme le métier de for-

geron, sont originaires d'Ennedi et qu'ils constituent une « caste » dans la société tchadienne par ailleurs égalitaire. L'anthropologue allemand Peter Fuchs pense le contraire, à savoir que toutes les populations connues sous le nom de Haddad peuvent tracer leur ascendance à une culture et un mode de subsistance de chasseurs-cueilleurs. Il avance que le rendement de la chasse étant devenu insuffisant suite à la raréfaction du gibier, les clans haddad du Kanem ont été forcés de se mettre à l'artisanat pour vivre, d'abord en tant que forgerons et plus tard d'autres métiers artisanaux. L'anthropologue français Edouard Conte considère les Haddad kanembou comme un sous-groupe de roturiers du Kanem, endogame et distinct professionnellement et rituellement, qu'il appelle Duu, mais il admet qu'une partie de cette couche est issue de communautés de chasseurs-cueilleurs.

L'héritage des Haddad

Les traditions orales propres aux Haddad se rapportent d'une part à l'histoire immédiate des différents clans et groupes et d'autre part à un passé mythique indéfini. Les récits des Haddad kanembou s'accordent avec ceux des Kanembou dominants. Ils affirment que les Haddad vivent au Kanem depuis les temps immémoriaux. Il y a un mythe qui trace leur ascendance aux Boulala qui, à une certaine époque, se sont dirigés vers le sud jusqu'au lac Fitri. D'après ce mythe, un homme, Anna, est resté quand les autres sont partis et c'est l'ancêtre des Haddad kanembou et des Kanembou eux-mêmes. Anna eut trois fils, deux d'entre eux choisirent la lance, ce sont les ancêtres des Kanembou. Le troisième eut un fils, Méle, et il choisit l'arc et les flèches comme armes et depuis, les Haddad kanembou pratiquent la chasse à l'arc. Nous n'avons trouvé aucun mythe d'origine chez les Haddad kreda, mais ceux-ci soulignaient que leur origine et leur histoire diffèrent de celles des Haddad kanembou. Ils étaient arrivés au Bahr el Ghazal il y a longtemps, peut-être, autant que nous puissions en juger, au cours du 17e siècle, et certains disaient qu'ils étaient venus avec des pasteurs kreda.

Marques d'identité

Comme nous l'avons décrit, le tableau dressé par les sources existantes de l'histoire et de l'origine des Haddad n'est pas simple, mais il prouve l'existence des Haddad, en tant que groupe identifiable et distinct, dans le contexte socioculturel complexe et très instable du Nord du Tchad. À la fin du 19e siècle, les Haddad étaient essentiellement nomades et vivaient de la chasse et de la cueillette ou comme forgerons itinérants. Nos discussions avec des individus haddad qui pratiquaient encore la chasse et la cueillette, ou disaient les avoir pratiquées, nous ont convaincus que les Haddad kreda et les Haddad kanembou, respectivement, se percevaient comme des unités ethniques distinctes. Ces identités se voyaient renforcées par les règles d'endogamie et le stigmate culturel qui régissaient l'interaction des Haddad avec les groupes ethniques avoisinants.

6: DESTIN ET INÉGALITÉ

Les stéréotypes ethniques font partie de la vie, au Kanem comme ailleurs. Les Haddad kanembou et les Haddad kreda connaissent différentes formes de discrimination culturelle, mais pas au même degré. La différence est liée à leurs modes de subsistance respectifs, leurs valeurs et leurs modes d'interaction avec la société environnante. La société du Kanem est caractérisée par l'asymétrie, et les perceptions culturelles des phénomènes sociaux, professionnels, physiques et religieux s'inscrivent invariablement dans un plus vaste discours sur l'inégalité. Les relations sociales sont perçues comme des dichotomies hiérarchiques entre hommes libres et esclaves, patrons et clients, partenaires de mariage éligibles ou non, chasseurs et pasteurs, peau noire et peau blanche, musulmans et païens, porteurs de lances et porteurs d'arcs, et ainsi de suite. Un examen plus approfondi montre comment les marqueurs culturels servent à justifier la relégation des Haddad au plus bas de l'échelle sociale. Les Kanembou et les Kreda justifient le peu d'estime qu'ils ont pour les Haddad en se référant à la tradition orale. Ils racontent, par exemple, comment le prophète lui-même, lors d'une rencontre avec les Haddad, les a condamnés à vivre pour toujours comme de pauvres chasseurs. Ce chapitre discute les signifiants culturels de l'inégalité et les formes symboliques du stigmate. Il montre comment l'utilisation des armes est dotée d'une signification symbolique et utilisée comme marqueur d'identité ethnique et de rang. Il mentionne l'attitude ambivalente des Kanembou qui, bien qu'ils admirent la dextérité des Haddad comme chasseurs à l'arc, les placent au bas de la structure hiérarchique de la socialité kanembou. De leur côté, les Kreda n'ont que peu d'estime pour les Haddad qui vivent parmi eux parce que ces derniers sont supposés manquer de courage. On note que les Aza du Niger semblent être victimes d'une stigmatisation similaire.

Ordre politique et hiérarchie

La section qui suit analyse le contexte historique de la socialité haddad et l'institutionnalisation de l'inégalité sociale. Les modes de vie des Haddad sont façonnés par les ressources de gibier disponibles et l'accès à d'autres ressources, ainsi que par les conditions sociales et politiques régnant au Nord du Tchad. Au 19e siècle, le sultan de Mao régnait sur le Kanem et le Bahr el Ghazal. Le Califat détenait l'autorité religieuse et exerçait des droits fiscaux sur la population du Kanem par l'intermédiaire de ministres de noble descendance, de chefs des clans principaux et d'une armée privée. En principe, le sultan avait un droit prééminent sur tout le territoire, y compris les pâturages sur lesquels les pasteurs faisaient paître leur bétail. Le pouvoir colonial français reprit ces droits d'investiture qui passèrent ensuite à l'État tchadien.

Quand les Français sont arrivés dans la région, celle-ci connaissait une période très agitée à cause des groupes de maraudeurs ouled slimane et toubou, des marchands d'esclaves arabes et de l'impact de la Sanūsiyya. Les Français étouffèrent la révolte et restructurèrent le système administratif sur le modèle napoléonien en institutionnalisant une série d'unités administratives d'après leur taille et leur importance sociopolitique : *préfecture, sous-préfecture, canton* et *village*. Au premier abord, les Français ne réalisèrent pas que la politique au Kanem et au Bahr el Ghazal était dominée par la parenté, l'affiliation, la solidarité et l'opposition. Les Kanembou, les Kreda et les Haddad furent organisés, et ensuite réorganisés, en cantons, définis spatialement, qui coïncidaient parfois avec la structure politique traditionnelle et parfois non (cf. Chapelle 1957 : 368-9). Le système établi par les Français avait des implications différentes pour les Haddad kreda et les Haddad kanembou. Chez les Kreda et autres pasteurs, les clans et lignages étaient reconnus en tant qu'épine dorsale des nouvelles unités administratives, et cette politique soutenait les liens de dépendance traditionnels entre les familles haddad kreda et leurs « hôtes » pasteurs. Les Haddad kreda, peu nombreux et dispersés sur toute la région du Bahr el Ghazal, n'étaient pas à même de se constituer en unités sociopolitiques indépendantes avec leur propre *chef de village* et *chef de canton*. Ils devinrent donc une couche subordonnée au bas de l'échelle sociale chez les pasteurs. La situation des Haddad kanembou était différente. Ils étaient plus nombreux, en grande partie sédentarisés, et furent donc capables de former des unités géopolitiques qui, dans certains cas, furent reconnues par les Français. La très bonne étude de Conte montre que, bien que certains Haddad kanembou furent élus chefs de village, très peu atteignirent la position plus élevée de *chef de canton*. Les Français établirent leur première unité administrative au Kanem à N'Guri, c'est-à-dire au cœur du pays des Haddad kanembou, mais la chefferie fut très vite divisée et réorganisée d'une façon qui ne servait que les intérêts de la noblesse kanembou, ce qui mit fin à la primauté des Haddad. Au cours du temps, les pratiques administratives changeantes entraînèrent une plus grande centralisation et les Haddad ne réussirent jamais à se regrouper et à influencer la politique française en leur faveur. Selon Conte, les Haddad sont probablement le groupe qui a été le plus profondément influencé par le colonialisme français dans le Kanem du Sud.

Esclaves et dépendants

L'esclavage était une partie intégrale et importante de la société du Kanem jusqu'à ce que les Français mettent un terme à la chasse aux esclaves et au commerce des esclaves et limitent graduellement son existence formelle. Néanmoins, l'esclavage et la servitude ne furent abolis formellement par la loi qu'en 1956, c'est-à-dire à peine quelques années avant l'indépendance du Tchad. La stigmatisation et la privation économique dont souffrent les Haddad sont en surface similaires à la situation des esclaves affranchis, mais culturellement la rationalité est différente. Les esclaves étaient intégrés dans l'économie et les ménages kanembou d'une manière radicalement différente de la relation existant entre les Kanembou et les Haddad kanembou. Les différences sont décrites en se référant à l'étude de Conte et la conclusion est que l'abolition formelle de l'esclavage chez les Kanembou entraîna un élargissement de la classe des roturiers (cf. Conte 1983a : 74). Il n'y a cependant pas eu de changement parallèle dans les normes définissant la position sociale et juridique des Haddad kanembou. La situation était différente pour les Haddad kreda. Contrairement aux pasteurs touareg et toubou, le système social et économique des Kreda et des Kecherda n'était pas basé sur l'esclavage et les relations des Haddad kreda avec leurs « hôtes » pasteurs, bien que tout à fait asymétriques, ne portaient pas le stigmate culturel de l'esclavage.

Relations sexuelles et restrictions au mariage

Les règles d'endogamie et de mariage prescriptif sont des facteurs clés pour le maintien des frontières ethniques et de la hiérarchie des groupes sociaux au Kanem. Elles empêchent la mobilité sociale et assurent que les Haddad restent une unité sociale autonome. Les relations sexuelles entre personnes de différentes couches sociales, bien que problématiques, peuvent être traitées avec discrétion, mais pas le mariage. Le mariage est un contrat social qui a des implications non seulement pour l'homme et la femme concernés, mais aussi pour leurs familles et pour leurs futurs enfants. Les Haddad sont strictement endogames et ne se marient qu'avec des Haddad. Le mariage entre un Haddad et une personne de descendance kanembou ou kreda est absolument interdit. Il en va de même pour les hommes et les femmes des autres groupes ethniques. Un homme arabe fut forcé d'abandonner ses projets de mariage avec une femme haddad, car son frère menaçait de le tuer s'il les réalisait. Quelle que soit la nature des relations entre les Haddad et les deux groupes dominants, les contacts quotidiens semblent être faciles et les enfants jouent ensemble. La communication entre les familles chasseurs-cueilleurs et les pasteurs est libre et facile, mais les différences de statut social sont marquées symboliquement de plusieurs façons. Par exemple, ce sont les Haddad qui rendent visite aux Kreda et pas l'inverse. Certains Haddad affirmaient que la facilité avec laquelle les gens communiquent à travers les frontières ethniques est née dans le sillage du changement politique intervenu en 1965.

La vie avec les Kreda

Les Haddad kreda campent une bonne partie de l'année avec les pasteurs nomades, la plupart avec les Kreda, mais certains avec les Kecherda. Chaque famille a développé d'étroites relations d'échanges avec une famille de pasteurs particulière et monte sa tente juste derrière celle de cette famille « hôte ». Les échanges sont à l'avantage des deux parties, mais la relation est asymétrique dans le sens que les Kreda pourraient se passer des Haddad, alors que l'inverse n'est pas toujours vrai. Les Haddad recherchent la compagnie des pasteurs pour leur protection physique, mais un avantage subsidiaire du campement commun est qu'il leur est possible d'échanger du travail contre des produits. La famille Haddad reçoit une ration de lait du troupeau de son « hôte » kreda, ce qui apporte un complément essentiel à leur diète pendant la saison des pluies où la chasse est difficile parce que les filets ne supportent pas l'humidité. Les Haddad peuvent aussi recevoir des petites portions de viande. En échange, ils fournissent différents services aux pasteurs, en premier lieu la tannerie des peaux, un processus que les Haddad maîtrisent parfaitement. Les femmes peignent les cheveux des femmes et des filles kreda en échange de petits cadeaux, peut-être un peu de thé, un luxe auquel elles n'ont pas souvent accès. La relation existant entre les familles kreda et les familles haddad est reconnue symboliquement au moment des mariages, chez les Kreda ou chez les Haddad, par des échanges entre les deux parties (cf. chapitre 14). Les Haddad ne se déplacent pas toute l'année avec leurs hôtes pasteurs, mais vont camper avec un chef kreda à la saison sèche quand les troupeaux ne donnent que peu de lait. Durant cette période, ils reçoivent du millet du chef kreda et organisent des expéditions de chasse vers le nord pour chasser l'oryx et d'autres antilopes.

La vie avec les Kanembou

Dans les années 60, le mode de vie des Haddad kanembou et celui des Kanembou eux-mêmes présentaient beaucoup de similarités, car les premiers dépendaient de plus en plus de l'agriculture, certains ayant des chèvres et quelques têtes de bétail. Les deux groupes menaient cependant des vies séparées et leur interaction se limitait aux endroits neutres tels que les marchés ou autres lieux publics. La plupart des interactions étaient sporadiques et court terme comme par exemple au moment de la vente ou du troc des produits des Haddad, que ce soit les produits des artisans ou des chasseurs-cueilleurs ou le sel extrait par les hommes haddad des puits appartenant aux Kanembou. Les relations entre les Kanembou et les Haddad ont été marquées historiquement, et le sont encore de nos jours, par les efforts déployés par les Kanembou pour exercer leur pouvoir sur les Haddad et leur soutirer des services, de la main-d'œuvre et des impôts. Les Kanembou ont fait cela avec succès et ils étaient toujours politiquement dominants à l'époque de notre étude sur le terrain, comme ils l'étaient pendant le Califat. Dans certaines parties du Kanem, les villages kanembou dominent entièrement alors que dans d'autres, les villages des deux groupes se trouvent les uns entre les autres. Les Haddad ont conservé leur avantage numérique autour de N'Guri et dans quelques autres poches du Kanem. Les villages des Kanembou sont situés au sommet de dunes et comprennent en moyenne

trente huttes disposées en cercle autour d'une place publique. Les villages des Haddad kanembou sont plus petits et moins structurés. Les huttes sont éparpillées, en général à une certaine distance les unes des autres. Dans les années 60, les Haddad kanembou pratiquaient beaucoup des activités de subsistance pratiquées par les Kanembou, alors qu'au début du siècle, la chasse-cueillette jouait encore un rôle dominant. Ce qui distinguait l'économie des Kanembou de celle Haddad dans les années 60 était en partie l'inégalité de l'accès aux terres convenant à l'agriculture sous pluie, un fait intimement lié au caractère hiérarchique de la socialité du Kanem. Les droits fonciers sont collectifs, mais ils sont distribués de manière inégale entre les différents groupes. Conte affirme qu'environ trois quarts de la population kanembou et une proportion encore plus élevée des Duu sont des agriculteurs pauvres et dépendants qui ne tirent que très peu ou pas de surplus de leur travail suite à l'expropriation systématique du travail et des produits dans le cadre de relations hiérarchiques institutionnalisées (cf. Conte 1983a : 38-9). Conte écrit que, jusqu'au décret de 1956, la plupart des Duu/Haddad étaient tenus de donner la moitié de leurs produits agricoles aux chefs ou aux aristocrates kanembou (cf. 1983a : 43).

7 : STRATÉGIES DE SUBSISTANCE

Aussi longtemps que nous puissions remonter dans l'histoire, les modes de subsistance du Kanem et du Bahr el Ghazal ont été caractérisés par des techniques adaptables et changeantes. Les populations ont développé de nombreuses stratégies de subsistance allant de la production pastorale et une gamme d'activités agro-pastorales à une production essentiellement agricole ou, comme les Haddad, la chasse-cueillette et l'artisanat spécialisé. Ces stratégies de subsistance adaptables n'ont pas seulement été utilisées à différentes périodes, mais, vu les conditions microclimatiques et les différences dans la qualité du sol, elles sont également toutes vitales à chaque période donnée. Bien que l'élevage de chameaux et de bétail domine dans le Nord, et la culture du millet, du doura et du maïs dans le Sud, la plupart des groupes ethniques pratiquent aussi bien l'élevage que l'agriculture, mais à des degrés différents. Le Kanem et le Bahr el Ghazal connaissent régulièrement des périodes de sécheresse plus ou moins longues qui affectent l'écosystème, tuant le gibier et le bétail, asséchant les champs de millet et de doura, et montant les groupes pasteurs et les groupes sédentaires les uns contre les autres. En 1851, quand Heinrich Barth a tenté d'atteindre Mao, le Kanem du Nord-Ouest prospérait grâce à la transhumance à longue distance et l'élevage intensif du bétail. C'était à l'aube de quatre décennies de pluies abondantes et Barth vit des troupeaux d'environ mille têtes de bétail. Néanmoins, à l'arrivée des Français, au début du siècle, il n'y avait pratiquement pas de bétail dans la région après dix ans de diminution rapide des précipitations, des périodes de troubles sociaux et les effets dévastateurs de la peste du bétail. Les années 60 furent caractérisées par des précipitations moyennes, mais la région fut à nouveau sévèrement touchée par la sécheresse dans les années 70.

8 : LA CUEILLETTE

La cueillette est une activité importante au Kanem et au Bahr el Ghazal, et pas seulement pour les Haddad. La récolte de plantes comestibles, graines, fruits et noix permet néanmoins rarement aux familles de stocker des provisions pouvant les nourrir pendant de longues périodes. Récolter des plantes comestibles est en général le travail des femmes dans toutes les sociétés de chasseurs, un fait que la théorie anthropologique n'a pleinement pris en compte que dans la deuxième moitié du 20e siècle. C'est aussi le cas chez les Haddad, mais il y a une exception intéressante, c'est la récolte saisonnière des graines d'*ogu*, une herbe ayant une valeur nutritive élevée, effectuée par les hommes à l'aide d'un panier spécial (*cf. figs. 8,1 & 8,2*). Les graines sont préparées et mangées en bouillie. Ce chapitre fait l'inventaire des plantes récoltées par les Haddad à diverses périodes de l'année et décrit leur mode de préparation ainsi que la signification qui leur est associée. Pendant la saison des pluies, les œufs d'oiseaux représentent une autre source de nourriture, en particulier ceux d'espèces faisant leur nid à même le sol comme la pintade. Par contre, les rongeurs, les reptiles et les sauterelles sont moins intéressants pour les Haddad, mis à part les tortues.

Exploitation du lac Tchad

Les Haddad kanembou qui vivent sur les rives du lac Tchad bénéficient d'une variété de plantes vivant sur l'eau du lac et de la végétation abondante poussant sur ses rives. Ainsi, ils peuvent récolter du riz sauvage, des racines de nénuphar, des caroubes, des noix de karité, et des fruits de baobab et de tamarin sauvages. Ils exploitent également l'unique environnement aquatique et pratiquent en outre l'agriculture, la cueillette, diverses activités artisanales et, dans une certaine mesure, la chasse, une source de nourriture dont l'importance est allée en s'amenuisant au cours du 20e siècle. Certaines familles subsistent uniquement en exploitant le lac Tchad, en pêchant et en chassant le crocodile. Les Haddad chassent les trois espèces de crocodiles ainsi que les varans et les hippopotames. La pêche se pratique avec des filets faits des fibres du *calotropis*, des trappes et des harpons ainsi qu'avec des filets modernes en nylon. La chasse au crocodile se pratique la nuit dans des bateaux faits de bottes de tiges de papyrus. Les chasseurs partent en général deux par deux, chacun étant armé d'un harpon (*cf. figs. 8,9-8,11*) et d'une torche, et ils cherchent les animaux qui sont sur les rives ou tapis dans les bas-fonds. Il faut que l'eau soit calme pour pouvoir capter la réflexion de la lumière dans les yeux des animaux. L'un des chasseurs conduit le bateau à la perche dans les eaux peu profondes et l'autre se tient prêt, à la proue, avec le harpon. Les chasseurs savent comment leurrer les crocodiles en imitant l'appel plaintif du bébé crocodile ou sa manière de nager en remuant leurs mains dans l'eau d'une façon particulière.

9 : LA CHASSE

Le gibier était abondant au Kanem et au Bahr el Ghazal jusqu'au début du 20e siècle. Ensuite, les exigences commerciales, les armes automatiques, l'accroissement de la population et la sécheresse réduisirent considérablement les populations d'autruches et de gros mammifères desquelles vivaient les Haddad et qu'ils connaissaient très bien. La dépendance des Haddad du monde animal et leur fascination pour celui-ci trouvent leur expression culturelle dans la poésie, la musique et de très belles fables. Il existe des différences significatives entre la manière de chasser des Haddad kreda et celle des Haddad kanembou, d'une part au niveau technologique et organisationnel et, d'autre part au niveau de la conceptualisation et contextualisation spirituelles et magico-religieuses du monde animal.

Technologie et savoir-faire

Les Haddad possèdent de vastes connaissances sur l'environnement en général et sur les animaux et leur comportement en particulier. Ils ont la patience et les techniques nécessaires pour s'approcher furtivement du gibier, l'expérience leur permettant de placer leurs filets de la meilleure façon possible et la dextérité requise pour atteindre leurs proies avec une flèche empoisonnée ou une lance. La chasse est généralement une activité pratiquée par les hommes comme c'est le cas chez la plupart des chasseurs-cueilleurs. Chez les Haddad kreda, les femmes participent parfois à la chasse collective, mais chez les Haddad kanembou, les femmes ne chassent jamais. La chasse représente l'une des principales sources de nutrition ainsi que de revenus grâce à la vente des peaux, des ramures, de la viande et des tendons. On chasse aussi des animaux à des fins médicinales ou, dans quelques cas, pour les vendre comme animaux de compagnie, par exemple des singes ou des guépards. Pour les garçons et les jeunes hommes, la chasse est également un sport. Auparavant, les Haddad kreda avaient beaucoup de chiens qu'ils utilisaient pour la chasse, en particulier pour la chasse à l'antilope. Avec le déclin des ces magnifiques animaux, les revenus de la chasse baissèrent et il devint difficile et peu rentable d'élever des chiens. Au moment de notre étude, il n'y avait que quelques familles qui possédaient encore des chiens. Les hommes et les garçons les plus âgés sont toujours armés, ils portent des armes pour leur propre protection et pour la chasse. Les Haddad kreda portent des lances barbelées ou des lances faites en corne de gazelle ou d'antilope, parfois des lances longues, l'arme des Haddad kanembou par excellence. Ces derniers utilisent également un couteau à lancer en fer ou, plus rarement, un boomerang en bois. Les deux groupes ont des couteaux. Les techniques de chasse comme les pièges ou les trappes ne semblent être utilisées que pour les oiseaux. Les Haddad utilisent deux techniques principales : les Haddad kanembou utilisent l'arc et les flèches et les Haddad kreda utilisent différents types de filets selon les espèces qu'ils veulent chasser.

Le déguisement
– chasser à la manière des Haddad kanembou

Durant les premières décennies du 20ᵉ siècle, les Haddad kanembou tiraient une grande partie de leur subsistance de la chasse. À cette époque, les autruches et les gros mammifères tels que les buffles et différentes espèces d'antilopes étaient abondants. Il en était de même pour les éléphants et les lions qui, parfois, quand ils menaçaient des communautés, étaient chassés de façon collective. Parallèlement au déclin du gibier, la chasse devint une activité de plus en plus individualisée et d'autres stratégies de subsistance acquirent une plus grande importance.

La caractéristique la plus remarquable de la chasse pratiquée par les Haddad kanembou est l'utilisation d'un déguisement et la simulation du comportement animal pour s'approcher furtivement de leurs proies. Au début du 20ᵉ siècle, ils utilisaient des parures de plumes d'autruches, mais après le déclin radical de ces animaux, ils se déguisèrent uniquement en bucorve, un oiseau noir majestueux d'environ 107 cm de hauteur. Ils s'attachent un masque ressemblant à l'oiseau sur le front et une peau de mouton noire sur le dos pour s'approcher furtivement de leurs proies. Les Haddad utilisent l'arc réflexe recourbé au milieu. La corde n'est en place que lors de l'utilisation. Le tir se fait à genoux. L'arc est tenu à l'horizontale et la plupart des chasseurs tirent deux flèches à la fois quand ils chassent la gazelle ou d'autres animaux de grande taille.

Les Haddad sont des archers renommés. Ils savent comment s'approcher du gibier et suivre la trace des animaux blessés. Les chasseurs haddad pensent qu'au bout du compte, outre les compétences techniques et le déguisement, les poisons puissants et la magie sont essentiels à la réussite. Chaque chasseur prépare son propre poison dont il garde la recette secrète. Le poison le plus puissant est fait à base d'os de serpent, mais on utilise aussi des ingrédients végétaux. Comme décrit dans cette section, le processus de production consiste à dissoudre des petits morceaux d'une masse sèche dans l'eau quand il faut réenduire la pointe d'une flèche. Ceci est nécessaire quand la flèche a pénétré profondément dans la chair d'un animal. Le temps nécessaire pour qu'un animal succombe à ses blessures dépend de la nature et de l'emplacement de la blessure ainsi que de la quantité de sang perdue. La viande se trouvant près de la blessure devra être jetée.

Comme nous venons de le mentionner, la magie est aussi importante à la réussite que le poison. La magie est personnalisée et gardée très secrètement. Les chasseurs haddad n'appliquent pas seulement leur magie à leurs arcs, mais ils l'utilisent aussi quand ils préparent leur poison, et surtout, ils l'appliquent à leurs masques. Un masque d'oiseau au fort pouvoir magique permet au chasseur de s'approcher très près de n'importe quel animal, si près, disent les Haddad, qu'ils partageront la fraîcheur de l'ombre du même arbre. Les chasseurs prennent également différentes précautions d'ordre magique pour mettre la chance de leur côté pendant la chasse. Les chasseurs haddad ne mettent leur déguisement que lorsque le gibier a été repéré : une peau de mouton fixée avec une corde couvre la poitrine, une autre couvre le dos et un masque est attaché au front. Quand il s'approche de sa proie, le chasseur avance en rampant sur les genoux, baissant la tête avec le masque d'oiseau tantôt d'un côté tantôt de l'autre pour imiter les mouvements du bucorve qui picore des graines et autres choses comestibles sur le sol. De temps à autres, le chasseur s'arrête net, comme le font tous les oiseaux et animaux toujours en alerte, puis, après quelques instants, il reprend tranquillement son chemin vers sa proie tout en « picorant ».

Chasser le porc-épic dans sa tanière

On chasse le porc-épic régulièrement pour sa viande et ses épines. Des groupes d'hommes, et peut-être aussi des grands garçons, partent à sa poursuite, sans autres armes qu'une pelle et une torche, car ils vont le chercher dans sa tanière. Le porc-épic vit dans une tanière se trouvant environ quatre mètres sous terre et il peut y avoir jusqu'à dix mètres de galeries d'accès. Si la galerie est trop étroite pour que le chasseur puisse passer, il faudra creuser un ou plusieurs puits permettant le passage. Le chasseur tape sur le plafond de la galerie pour signaler sa position aux autres chasseurs qui pourront commencer à creuser le puits, ce qui est une tache ardue. On répète cette procédure quand la tanière est localisée. Alors, on bloque les accès et on creuse la tanière pour attraper le porc-épic vivant. Ce travail laborieux est une indication de la dureté du mode de vie des Haddad.

Chasser avec Chari

Au cours de nos voyages, nous n'avons rencontré que peu de Haddad kanembou qui chassaient au filet. Quelques familles, à l'est de Méchimeré, avaient récemment emprunté cette méthode aux Haddad kreda et pratiquaient la chasse de manière similaire. Nous avons également passé quelques jours avec Chari, un homme qui, comme son père, s'était spécialisé dans la chasse au filet d'animaux relativement petits, en particulier le renard pâle et le lièvre, ainsi que d'oiseaux qu'il vendait au marché soit pour leur viande

soit comme animaux de compagnie. Le renard était chassé dans sa tanière. Ce chapitre décrit les techniques utilisées par Chari pour faire sortir les renards de leurs tanières ainsi que la manière dont il posait ses filets pour attraper les lièvres dans leur environnement préféré, c'est-à-dire une dense végétation de jeunes palmiers doum.

Attraper des oiseaux

Certaines espèces d'oiseaux sont attrapées avec des pièges, en particulier les colombes et des volailles telles que la perdrix, le ganga et le francolin. On étend un grand filet sur une flaque artificielle pour attraper différents oiseaux et parfois des pintades et des perdrix ou même, une fois de temps en temps, un lièvre assoiffé. La perdrix, le ganga, le francolin, la pintade et l'outarde, le gibier préféré des Haddad kreda, sont attrapés dans des filets spéciaux. Chari ne chassait pas l'outarde. L'outarde est un grand oiseau terrestre de 74 à 90 cm de hauteur. Elle était encore relativement répandue dans les années 60 mais très farouche. Le chasseur rabat l'oiseau très lentement vers un long filet d'environ 550 cm suspendu entre deux poteaux à une distance appropriée de l'endroit où il a été repéré. Quand l'outarde est près du filet, le chasseur lui fait peur de sorte qu'elle coure droit dans le filet. Une technique similaire est utilisée pour attraper les pintades.

Attraper des mammifères au filet – la spécialité des Haddad kreda

La caractéristique de la chasse aux mammifères pratiquée par les Haddad kreda est l'utilisation de différentes sortes de filets. Cependant, tout homme haddad se contentera d'un bâton de jet, d'une pierre ramassée sur place ou d'une lance s'il tombe sur du gibier par hasard. La chasse au filet est pratiquée dans tout le Bahr el Ghazal ainsi que par les Haddad vivant avec les pasteurs kecherda dans la partie orientale du Niger. Chez les Haddad kanembou, la chasse est fondamentalement une rencontre entre l'homme et l'animal. Par contre, chez les Haddad kreda, la chasse est une activité commune et collective, sauf la chasse aux outardes, pintades et autres oiseaux comme indiqué ci-dessus. Les Haddad kreda utilisent une technique qui demande plus de main-d'œuvre et d'équipement que ce dont dispose un seul ménage, du moins quand il s'agit de la chasse aux grands mammifères comme la gazelle et l'antilope. La chasse à l'antilope, en particulier, demande un grand nombre de chasseurs et beaucoup de matériel. Chaque chasseur prépare son propre matériel, c'est-à-dire des filets de différentes tailles adaptés aux différentes espèces et les poteaux entre lesquels ils seront suspendus. Les filets sont noués de cordes faites de tendons provenant des pattes de gazelles ou d'antilopes. Seuls les filets destinés à la chasse au lièvre ou au chacal sont parfois faits de fibres provenant de l'*acacia raddiana*.

Lièvre et chacal

La chasse au lièvre se pratique comme chez les Grecs anciens. Les chasseurs cherchent l'animal dans son terrier et quand ils l'ont trouvé, soit ils le rabattent vers des filets placés au préalable sur ses pistes, soit ils le forcent à terrain découvert. En général, le lièvre est chassé collectivement par des petits groupes de garçons, qui sont d'ailleurs ceux qui en mangeront la viande, mais un chasseur peut également attraper un lièvre, surtout si les filets peuvent être placés en demi-cercle (cf. cat. n° 49). Les Haddad font la chasse au chacal assez fréquemment, les Haddad kreda avec des filets en tendons et quelques Haddad kanembou avec des filets en fibres d'acacia (cf. cat. n° 50). La viande de chacal est appréciée par tous les Haddad et sa fourrure rapporte bien. La chasse au chacal se fait seulement pendant la saison sèche quand les animaux ont besoin de boire de l'eau et qu'il est possible de les trouver aux points d'eau. Elle peut se faire de jour ou de nuit, mais la chasse de nuit est préférable. Un ou plusieurs filets sont placés à proximité du point d'eau en travers des pistes suivies par le bétail et les animaux sauvages. Le ou les chasseurs se mettent à couvert du côté le plus éloigné des filets dans un endroit d'où ils peuvent observer tous les mouvements sur la piste. Quand un chacal s'approche d'un filet, le chasseur bondit et se met à crier, envoyant ainsi le chacal surpris et effrayé droit dans le filet où il sera achevé à la massue. Par une bonne nuit, un chasseur ou un groupe de chasseurs peut prendre jusqu'à cinq animaux.

Gazelle

La source de viande la plus sûre pour les Haddad tout au cours de l'année est la chasse à la gazelle à front roux (*Gazella rufifrons*) qui pèse de 25 à 30 kg, la gazelle dorcade (*Gazella dorcas*) qui est plus petite et la grande gazelle dama (*Gazella dama*). Les filets pour la chasse à la gazelle font environ 135-145 cm de large, et les poteaux auxquels ils sont suspendus font environ 184-187 cm de haut (cf. cat. n° 51-53). La chasse se pratique en groupes de, préférablement, six ou sept personnes, et c'est plus que ce qui

peut être fourni par une seule famille. Il faut en outre un bon nombre de filets. Chaque famille possède entre dix et vingt filets, ce qui est suffisant vu le grand nombre de rabatteurs participant à la chasse, mais plus il y a de filets, mieux le terrain de chasse est couvert, et, le plus souvent, on utilise les filets de deux ou plusieurs familles. Le facteur décisif est cependant toujours la main-d'œuvre disponible. Pour compenser la pénurie de main-d'œuvre inhérente, les Haddad utilisent beaucoup de poteaux fourchus, *eba*, sur lesquels ils suspendent des bandes de peau. Ces poteaux sont alignés de différentes façons, soit en forme d'entonnoir menant aux filets, soit entre les filets, comme trompe-l'œil simulant des rabatteurs, car, à une certaine distance, ils font de très bons substituts de personnes vivantes (*cf. Fig. 9,50*). Les expéditions de chasse se mettent en route dans une ambiance d'anticipation joyeuse et les montures, qui sont de petits ânes gris, semblent disparaître sous leurs lourdes charges composées de filets, de poteaux et de plusieurs personnes. Un homme adulte mène l'expédition, à pied ou sur sa monture, 100 ou 200 mètres en avant des autres. Quand l'expédition s'approche du terrain de chasse, les échanges verbaux deviennent des murmures, puis s'arrêtent complètement. Dès qu'elle entend le signal imitant le cri de la pintade, qui indique qu'une ou plusieurs gazelles ont été repérées, l'expédition s'arrête pour mettre au point une stratégie. La stratégie de chasse tient compte non seulement des caractéristiques de l'environnement, de l'emplacement de la gazelle et de la direction du vent, mais aussi du nombre de filets et de personnes disponibles. Chaque groupe possédant des filets pose ses filets et plante ses poteaux fourchus sur un emplacement différent afin d'éviter, par la suite, les discussions de savoir à qui appartient la prise. La chasse sur terrain découvert pose un défi particulier. Si la gazelle broute dans une plaine, les Haddad essayeront de la rabattre calmement vers un endroit avec quelques arbres et arbustes où ils peuvent poser leurs filets. Le texte décrit un certain nombre d'expéditions de chasse et les stratégies utilisées à chaque occasion (*cf. fig. 9,55*). La chasse au filet est basée sur une division du travail bien définie qui sera mise en œuvre quand on s'est mis d'accord sur la stratégie de chasse. Chaque propriétaire de filets doit poser ses filets seul, sans aide du reste de l'expédition, pendant que les autres participants plantent les poteaux fourchus en deux rangées et y accrochent les bandes de peau destinées à tromper le gibier. Tout ceci doit être fait aussi rapidement et aussi discrètement que possible afin de ne pas alerter le gibier. Quand tout le matériel est en place, les propriétaires de filets se cachent derrière leurs filets, alors que les autres participants vont se positionner derrière le gibier. À un signal donné, le rabattage commence, les enfants crient le plus fort possible et les hommes frappent deux bâtons l'un contre l'autre tout en imitant l'aboiement des chiens. Quand une gazelle agitée se fait prendre dans un filet, le propriétaire saute sur l'animal, lui casse le cou, puis lui coupe la gorge pour respecter la coutume musulmane. Lorsque la chasse est terminée, toute l'expédition se réjouit, les chasseurs se rassemblent et bavardent joyeusement, parlant de leur succès et soulignant, à maintes reprises, certains détails de la chasse. Le gibier est ramené au campement où il sera écorché et coupé en morceaux et la viande partagée. Cependant, si la chasse n'a pas été un succès, il est probable qu'une grande dispute s'ensuivra. Les campements Haddad que nous avons visités partaient à la chasse trois ou quatre fois par semaine et ramenaient à chaque fois de une à trois gazelles.

Antilope

La chasse à l'antilope était l'un des fondements de la subsistance des Haddad kreda jusqu'à la première partie du 20e siècle où ces animaux ont connu un déclin catastrophique. Au moment de notre visite, certains clans pratiquaient encore cette chasse, bien qu'elle soit loin de donner le même rendement qu'autrefois. Les Haddad kreda chassent trois espèces d'antilopes : le damalisque ou topi qui paît en troupeau de quinze à trente têtes et dont on sait qu'il a formé des troupeaux comptant plusieurs centaines de têtes ; l'oryx blanc qui paît aussi en troupeaux d'une douzaine de têtes et qui formait également de beaucoup plus grands troupeaux autrefois ; et enfin l'addax que les Aza de Termit et Dillia chassaient de façon saisonnière avec beaucoup de succès.

La chasse à l'antilope se pratique généralement pendant l'hiver dans le désert où paissent les troupeaux. C'est une opération de grande envergure qui pose un défi de taille aux compétences des Haddad et à leur organisation. Elle requiert de la main-d'œuvre, beaucoup de filets grands et solides et, de préférence, un grand nombre de chiens (cf. cat. n° 57 ; *figs. 9,57-9,61*). La chasse à l'antilope est organisée par des chefs de clans ou des aînés qui, en coopération avec les autres participants, décident de la stratégie à suivre dans chaque cas selon le terrain, la direction du vent et le nombre de filets et de chasseurs disponibles. Les filets des membres du clan sont placés sur plusieurs rangées, chaque rangée appartenant à un homme donné. La distance entre les rangées correspond à une longueur de lance. Selon nos informations, l'oryx n'a aucun respect pour les trompe-l'œil faits de poteaux et de bandes de peau simulant des rabatteurs, mais seulement pour les hommes et les chiens. En outre, il galope à une telle vitesse et avec une telle force qu'il faut plusieurs rangées de filets pour arrêter un seul animal, sans parler de tout un troupeau. Au premier tour de la chasse, les filets de l'aîné de l'expédition sont placés au devant, ensuite ceux du plus jeune chasseur et ensuite ceux des autres participants par ordre d'âge. Au tour suivant, les filets du plus jeune participant sont placés devant ceux de l'aîné, puis suivent ceux des autres chasseurs. Au troisième tour, les filets du deuxième plus jeune sont placés au devant, puis ceux du plus jeune, puis ceux de l'aîné et ainsi de suite. De cette manière, tous les chasseurs auront, à un moment ou à un autre, leurs filets en avant, c'est-à-dire là où on a le plus de chance d'attraper un animal. Souvent, les filets sont marqués pour éviter les disputes. Les filets sont placés en tenant compte des caractéristiques du terrain, de la végétation et de la direction du vent vu que le rabattage devra se faire dans cette direction. La méthode est plus ou moins la même pour les trois espèces et la chasse se fait de façon à donner à tous les ménages la même chance de prendre un animal. Habituellement, on chasse pendant les chaleurs de la mi-journée, quand les antilopes ralentissent leur activité et se reposent.

10: PARTAGE, MAGIE ET MÉFIANCE

Les différences qui existent entre les Haddad kreda et les Haddad kanembou en ce qui concerne la technologie et l'organisation de la chasse sont reflétées dans la façon de partager le gibier et le rôle de la magie chez les deux groupes. La plupart du temps, le collectivisme domine quand les Haddad kreda répartissent le gibier, mais différentes règles s'appliquent aux différentes espèces d'animaux et ces règles sont étroitement liées à la façon dont les filets sont placés, l'organisation générale de la chasse et, surtout, les valeurs des Haddad kreda. La chasse au lièvre est généralement perçue comme une activité récréative et le butin est donné aux garçons qui le feront griller sur le feu. Quand on chasse la pintade de façon collective, les filets sont placés en une seule rangée, mais les oiseaux seront donnés au propriétaire du filet dans lequel ils ont été attrapés et ils ne seront normalement pas répartis entre les chasseurs. Par contre, les autres types de gibier sont partagés. Les chacals sont répartis également entre les hommes participant à l'expédition, à l'exception des fourrures qui vont au propriétaire du filet dans lequel l'animal a été pris. Il existe des règles très strictes pour la répartition des parties de la gazelle, celles-ci tiennent compte du filet dans lequel l'animal a été pris. Ainsi, le propriétaire du filet reçoit la tête, le cou, la peau et les pattes jusqu'aux genoux, c'est-à-dire jusqu'aux tendons dont sont faits les filets, même s'il n'a pas participé à la chasse lui-même. La viande est répartie de façon égale entre tous les participants à l'expédition, quel que soit leur âge ou leur sexe. Les personnes âgées, hommes et femmes, qui ne sont plus capables de chasser, reçoivent aussi une part égale. Si l'on a pris plus de trois gazelles, la viande de l'un des animaux doit aller au chef du clan, que celui-ci ait participé à la chasse ou non, mais la tête, le cou, la peau et les tendons reviennent toujours au propriétaire du filet dans lequel la gazelle a été prise. Le découpage d'une antilope est effectué par le propriétaire du filet dans lequel l'animal a été pris. Il se réserve la tête, le cou, la peau et les pattes et divise la viande en portions égales, qui seront attribuées aux participants par tirage au sort.

La courtoisie et la discipline caractérisent le partage du gibier. Par contre, si la chasse n'a pas été un succès, les esprits se déchaînent, les accusations et contre-accusations fusent et les injures volent. Nous avons entendu un homme dire à son frère : « Si Dieu n'a rien de mieux à faire aujourd'hui, il lui semblera peut-être bon de te tuer !». Les bagarres et les coups et blessures sont cependant inconnus parmi les Haddad kreda, ce qui n'est pas le cas chez leurs hôtes pasteurs. Le chasseur Haddad kanembou, lui, est habituellement seul et peut disposer de sa prise à sa guise. Il n'y a pas de règles compliquées régissant le partage et l'échange de gibier comme chez les Haddad kreda.

Les Haddad sont musulmans, mais ils n'ont adopté l'Islam qu'au début du 20e siècle et des concepts préislamiques relatifs à la nature et à la faune ont encore une signification pour leur façon de voir le monde. Les deux groupes croient aux mauvais esprits et affirment, par exemple, que les métaux possèdent des pouvoirs magiques. Par contre, ils n'ont pas d'idées très développées sur le monde animal et ne perçoivent pas de liens entre des clans et des espèces d'animaux spécifiques, comme les totems. La chasse au filet des Haddad kreda est perçue comme une activité purement séculaire et une mauvaise chasse sera toujours attribuée à des erreurs humaines. Par contre, chez les Haddad kanembou, la chasse est étroitement associée aux croyances magiques. La connaissance des propriétés magiques et de leur application pour accroître ses chances à la chasse représente une « propriété » individuelle tenue très secrète et passée de père en fils. Les chasseurs traitent leurs arcs et leurs flèches avec des substances magiques, par exemple en les plaçant dans les braises de plantes magiques pour qu'ils en prennent le pouvoir magique. Les pouvoirs magiques sont considérés particulièrement importants pour les masques utilisés dans le déguisement. D'après la croyance, les masques dotés de pouvoir magique assurent que les animaux ne s'enfuient pas et même, dans certains cas, s'approchent d'eux-mêmes du chasseur. Ce chapitre décrit ce savoir ésotérique et son application au matériel de chasse et aux masques.

11: POÉSIE ET PERFORMANCE

Ce chapitre est consacré à la poésie des Haddad qui nous donne une idée de leurs valeurs et de leur façon de voir le monde. Elle reflète leur connaissance intime de la vie animale et l'importance du gibier pour leur mode vie. Il y a des poèmes sur les éléphants, les autruches et les lions, qui sont maintenant tous des choses du passé. D'autres poèmes parlent de chacals et de phacochères, ridiculisent la hyène, ou nous chantent l'histoire du chasseur qui offre une belle pintade bien grasse à sa bien-aimée qui, elle, le trompera. Les animaux les plus chers au cœur des Haddad sont l'oryx blanc et la gazelle. En général, les poèmes sont récités accompagnés d'un luth et parfois de danses. Chez les Haddad, les hommes dansent seuls alors que les femmes dansent en groupes. Il y a une danse populaire, connue sous le nom de *ajewibarie*, qui est exécutée par les hommes et les femmes ensemble.

12: ESPACE ET LIEU

La vie familiale tourne autour de l'habitation, la tente recouverte de nattes dans le cas des Haddad kreda et la hutte en forme de ruche dans le cas des Haddad kanembou. La disposition spatiale favorise différentes formes d'interaction sociale et de perception esthétique, et elle est étroitement liée aux stratégies de subsistance et à l'organisation sociopolitique générale. Les campements des Haddad kreda sont situés au sommet de dunes, et les tentes sont placées en ligne, les unes à côté des autres, et grandes ouvertes aux yeux des autres habitants du campement. Les huttes des Haddad kanembou, en forme de ruches au toit de chaume, sont dispersées entre les champs de millet et protégées des regards curieux par des grandes nattes ou des palissades de paille.

Les Haddad kreda campent pendant la plus grande partie de l'année avec les pasteurs kreda. Chaque famille monte sa tente juste derrière celle de la famille kreda avec laquelle elle a une relation d'échange, main-d'œuvre contre lait et protection. Les tentes sont montées dans la direction nord-sud et l'entrée face l'ouest ou l'ouest nord-ouest, quels que soient les vents dominants. Ce sont les femmes qui fabriquent les tentes, qui en sont propriétaires et qui les montent. La famille fournit les tentes au moment du mariage et elles seront transportées d'un campement à un autre à dos d'âne. La tente a une structure voûtée comme un tonneau faite des racines de l'*acacia raddiana* et couverte de quatre nattes tissées avec les feuilles du palmier doum (cf. catalogue à la fin du résumé). Elles diffèrent des tentes des Tibou et des Touareg du Sud, aussi bien en ce qui concerne la construction de la voûte que l'emplacement des nattes. Ce chapitre décrit en détail comment les tentes sont montées : la préparation du site, la construction de la plate-forme de couchage et du dispositif de stockage, ainsi que la structure de la tente elle-même. On plante deux rangées centrales de poteaux auxquels sont arrimés des arceaux longitudinaux, puis des arceaux transversaux. Ensuite trois poteaux fourchus verticaux sont plantés à l'arrière de la tente et les arceaux transversaux y sont arrimés. Enfin, quatre longues nattes recouvrent la structure de telle façon que l'arrière et les côtés de la tente soient complètement couverts alors que le côté ouest reste ouvert et constitue l'entrée de la tente.

13: L'EXPRESSION PERSONNELLE ET L'IDENTITÉ

Les Haddad portent moins d'intérêt à leur apparence personnelle que les pasteurs kreda et kanembou, peut-être parce qu'ils ont moins de moyens économiques, mais il est pos-

sible que la culture joue aussi un rôle. L'apparence modeste des Haddad pourrait être l'un de ces marqueurs, à peine perceptibles mais tacitement acceptés, de leur position comme une sorte de caste. Cette différence s'exprime très clairement dans la coiffure des femmes qui est un signe de statut social. Il faut avoir le temps et les moyens pour se faire sa coiffure fréquemment. Les femmes haddad sont des coiffeuses expertes. Elles se peignent les unes les autres gratuitement, mais elles sont payées quand elles coiffent les femmes d'autres groupes ethniques, avec du beurre par les Kreda ou de l'huile par les Kanembou. Cette tâche laborieuse qu'elles effectuent pour les femmes kreda est un élément important dans la relation d'échange entre les Haddad kreda et leurs « hôtes » pasteurs. La coiffure des femmes est composée de nombreuses petites tresses. Deux grosses tresses descendant du front au cou indiquent qu'il s'agit d'une femme mariée. Les Haddad portent des vêtements de coton. Traditionnellement, les femmes portaient du indigo bleu foncé, mais maintenant on les voit aussi avec des tissus à fleurs enroulés autour du corps. Les hommes ne portent qu'un pantalon large et, seulement rarement, un poncho de coton blanc. Les bijoux sont simples, de même que les marques corporelles chez les deux sexes. Ces dernières sont faites pour la décoration et pour des raisons de santé. On perce les oreilles et les côtés du nez des filles à un jeune âge avec des épines d'acacia. Par contre, les odeurs corporelles revêtent une grande importance culturelle et les jeunes femmes, en particulier, utilisent des parfums doux pour se rendre désirables aux yeux de leurs maris. Elles « baignent » leurs corps et leurs vêtements dans la fumée d'un feu d'écorce de jujubier ou d'autres arbres et utilisent également des pommades, du beurre et du parfum. Les femmes Haddad se mettent aussi du henné sur les mains et sur les pieds et du khôl, poudre noire de sulfure d'antimoine, sur les paupières.

14: VIE SOCIALE ET PERCEPTIONS CULTURELLES

Rites de passage

La vie sociale et l'expression culturelle des Haddad soulignent les prérogatives des mâles et l'importance des parents en ligne paternelle, ce qui est également le cas chez d'autres groupes ethniques du Kanem. Les rites de passage suivent les pratiques musulmanes et les règles du Hadith. Ils sont célébrés à différents stages de la vie d'un individu, à savoir l'attribution d'un nom, la circoncision, le mariage et les funérailles, de préférence par un marabout ou un aîné pouvant offrir un sacrifice en règle. Étant donné que les Haddad ne possèdent que rarement des animaux domestiques, on n'offrira probablement des sacrifices que dans des cas très rares. L'enfant reçoit son nom dans la semaine qui suit sa naissance, l'événement social important suivant est sa première coupe de cheveux, et idéalement, cet événement sera marqué par la bénédiction d'un marabout. Les garçons sont circoncis entre l'âge de sept et douze ans, probablement sans grande cérémonie.

Partenaires de mariage et échange

Les Haddad sont endogames et choisissent leurs époux dans leur propre groupe. L'endogamie est respectée à tel point qu'un mariage entre un Haddad et un Kanembou sera considéré comme nul juridiquement et, dans certains cas, même criminel. La polygamie est acceptée en principe, mais ne semble pas être pratiquée. Par contre, la monogamie sérielle est commune. Un homme ne doit pas se marier avant un frère plus âgé et une femme ne doit pas se marier avant une sœur plus âgée. Pour que cette coutume fonctionne sans problèmes, les jeunes frères travaillent dur pour assurer le mariage de leurs frères plus âgés et rassembler les moyens nécessaires. Cette coutume est liée à l'autorité des frères et sœurs plus âgés. Les Haddad pratiquent aussi le lévirat qui signifie qu'un homme a le droit de reprendre la veuve et les enfants d'un frère plus âgé décédé, mais ils ne pratiquent pas le sororat permettant à un homme d'épouser une plus jeune sœur de sa femme défunte. Normalement, les mariages haddad sont moins ostentatoires et les échanges et les célébrations beaucoup moins importants que chez les groupes ethniques dominants qui profitent de telles occasions pour afficher leur richesse. La question du prix de la fiancée se pose rarement, peut-être parce que les Haddad sont généralement tellement pauvres qu'ils n'ont pas grand chose à échanger à l'occasion des mariages. Les échanges dont nous avons connaissance étaient tous en argent, sous forme de « Maria Theresa Thalers », car les Haddad ne possèdent pas de bétail et peu ou pas de petits ruminants. Les Haddad kreda et les Haddad kanembou expliquent que le prix de la fiancée sert à compenser le père de la fiancée pour le coût de la dot. Celle-ci reste la propriété de la femme et la suit toute sa vie. En cas de divorce, elle ramènera ses filets avec elle en retournant au campement de ses parents.

Les Haddad kanembou préfèrent se marier avec des parents, en particulier la fille du frère du père. Au début des années 1970, environ 75 pour cent des mariages haddad kanembou étaient entre cousins patrilatéraux et 24 pour cent entre cousins matrilatéraux (Conte 1983a : 388). Chez les Kanembou, les fêtes de mariage peuvent durer jusqu'à une semaine et des échanges très élaborés ont lieu avant et pendant les célébrations. La quantité et le type d'échange varient selon le statut social, mais ces échanges ne représentent pas, comme c'est le cas dans un certain nombre de sociétés, un mécanisme de base pour transférer du capital d'une génération à une autre ou d'un lignage à un autre. Le premier échange formalise les fiançailles. Puis, la famille du fiancé fait une série de cadeaux à la fiancée et à sa famille, le plus important étant le prix de la fiancée lui-même, qui est une somme d'argent, remise par la mère du fiancé à la mère de la fiancée. Enfin, le fiancé présente le *sadau* à la fiancée, un cadeau fait le jour du mariage en présence des parents de celle-ci (Conte 1983a : 229). Par contre, il semble que, dans certains cas, les Haddad kanembou ont conclu des mariages pratiquement sans aucun échange, à part l'offrande faite pour marquer le changement de lieu de la fiancée.

Les Haddad kreda, comme les pasteurs kreda, préfèrent se marier avec des non-parents. La femme restera deux ans dans le campement de ses parents, où elle recevra de temps en temps la visite de son mari, avant d'aller habiter avec lui. Le mari n'est pas tenu d'effectuer des services pendant la période d'attente. Cependant, si la femme tombe enceinte, elle ira habiter dans le campement de son mari pour que l'enfant naisse là et puisse prendre sa place en tant que membre du lignage agnatique du mari, en accord avec la règle répandue disant que « l'enfant n'est pas là où est le prix de la fiancée ». Cette période de deux ans pendant laquelle la femme reste dans le campement de ses parents correspond au temps nécessaire pour rassembler la dot qui comprend une tente et son ameublement. Idéalement, le prix de la fiancée doit être remis le jour du mariage. Son montant est fixé à 8 filets pour la chasse à la gazelle et quatre filets pour la chasse à l'antilope oryx, que la femme remettra immédiatement à son mari.

Les mariages sont des occasions où les liens unissant les Haddad et les Kreda sont symboliquement renforcés. Les Haddad kreda n'arrangent pas de mariage sans informer les « hôtes » kreda de la famille de la fiancée. L'accord formel est donné symboliquement par un échange où la famille du fiancé offre 4 lances aux « maîtres » kreda de la famille de la fiancée. L'échange de lances souligne symboliquement l'obligation des Kreda à défendre et à protéger les Haddad. La situation est inversée pour les mariages kreda où le futur mari kreda et sa famille doivent offrir un âne à la famille haddad qui reçoit du lait de la famille de sa future femme. Nous n'avons noté aucune indication que les liens entre les Haddad et les Kreda étaient doublés de relations de parenté fictive comme celles qui existaient entre les Kreda et leurs esclaves autrefois.

Parenté et clans

La structure sociale des Haddad met l'accent sur la patrilinéarité et la prééminence des groupes de parenté et des clans paternels. Cela se manifeste dans la terminologie relative aux relations de parenté et dans les règles de succession et d'héritage qui sont en accord avec l'idéologie arabo-musulmane. Les termes haddad désignant le père et le frère sont étendus à une série de parents paternels, de sorte qu'un homme désigne aussi bien ses cousins germains que ses cousins plus éloignés par le terme de « frère aîné » ou de « jeune frère » selon leurs âges relatifs. Conformément à cette terminologie, le code de comportement met l'accent sur le respect dû aux parents paternels plus âgés. Les beaux-parents et les gendres et les brus doivent s'éviter.

Après le mariage, les Haddad kreda s'installent le plus souvent patrilocalement, mais certains hommes choisissent de vivre dans le campement de leur femme, ce qui veut dire que les familles qui vivent dans un même campement ne forment pas forcément un groupe de parenté paternel. Les Haddad kanembou font preuve de la même flexibilité en ce qui concerne le choix de résidence. Selon les Haddad, le fait que le principe de patrilocalité ne soit pas strictement appliqué implique que la solidarité parentale est faible. C'est une situation où les griefs éclatent facilement au grand jour, et les querelles sont dites plus fréquentes chez les Haddad que chez les Kreda ou les Kanembou. Chez ces derniers, le clan constitue la trame même de la structure sociale hiérarchique. Ils forment la base sur laquelle on distingue entre les segments dirigeants et les segments non-dirigeants de la société chez les Kreda, et entre les aristocrates, les roturiers et les esclaves chez les Kanembou. Chez les Haddad, les clans ont une fonction un peu différente. La société haddad est fondamentalement égalitaire et habituellement, chaque clan est dispersé sur un vaste territoire de sorte que ses membres vivent entre les membres d'autres clans. Chez les Haddad ka-

nembou, même un petit hameau peut abriter des hommes de différents clans. Néanmoins, les clans ont eu une importance politique chez les Haddad kanembou dans certaines régions du Kanem, notamment N'Guri et Bari Kolom, aussi bien à des époques précoloniales que coloniales. Chez les Haddad kreda, les clans jouent un rôle politique moins important, mais ils maintiennent un lien avec un noyau central identifiable par la présence d'un chef de clan. (Le chapitre 16 traite ce sujet de façon plus approfondie.)

Animaux et identification

De même que d'autres groupes de chasseurs-cueilleurs, les Haddad s'identifient eux-mêmes en référence au monde animal qu'ils exploitent et dont ils sont dépendants. Tous les clans haddad ont des emblèmes animaux. La relation particulière existant entre un clan et son emblème est normalement tracée à un ancêtre du clan, même si son origine est parfois entourée de mystère. Le rôle joué par l'animal du clan ou son emblème dans la façon de voir le monde des Haddad s'est avéré être relativement vague. Ce manque d'intérêt et de connaissance apparent est peut-être lié au peu d'importance que revêtaient les clans et leur organisation au moment de notre étude sur le terrain, ce qui réduit le besoin de donner une représentation symbolique à ces unités de parenté. Stimulés par les débats anthropologiques importants soulevés par ce sujet au cours des temps, de Tylor, Durkheim, Radcliffe-Brown et Lévi-Strauss aux travaux académiques modernes, nous avons essayé de trouver des informations s'y rapportant. L'identification des clans haddad avec des plantes ou des animaux prend différentes formes. Il est généralement accepté que ces relations ne peuvent être expliquées exclusivement comme des expressions religieuses et/ou associée à l'identification symbolique de groupes ou de systèmes de mariage, mais qu'elles sont aussi l'expression d'une réflexion intellectuelle visant à classifier les objets de l'expérience. Les Haddad expliquaient que les relations entre les clans et des espèces animales spécifiques remontaient à des événements passés, mais sans approfondir le sujet. À leurs yeux, la plupart de ces relations avaient été forgées quand un ancêtre avait sauvé animal ou quand un animal était intervenu au bénéfice de sa famille. Les emblèmes des clans haddad ne faisaient pas l'objet de rites et les membres du clan ne leur offraient pas non plus de sacrifices. Néanmoins, il était interdit de tuer l'emblème du clan, et on pensait qu'un tel acte pourrait causer la mort ou une maladie grave.

15: L'ARTISANAT ET LE COMMERCE

Les chasseurs-cueilleurs haddad sont de très bons artisans. Ils s'entourent d'objets simples et fonctionnels, mais, en même temps, délicats et esthétiquement agréables, qui témoignent de leur ingénuité et de leurs compétences techniques. Les Haddad kreda, en particulier, sont de très bons vanniers, surtout en ce qui concerne la vannerie spiralée. Les femmes produisent des plateaux exquis, des récipients en forme de bouteille pour la farine, ainsi que des bols à lait d'une telle qualité qu'ils peuvent contenir aussi bien de l'eau que du lait. Ces objets n'ont en général pour seule décoration que des bordures de cuir. Les Haddad kreda, comme les Haddad kanembou, produisent la plupart des objets dont ils ont besoin dans la vie quotidienne. Outre les habitations, tente ou huttes, les hommes et les femmes produisent des ustensiles, des nattes, des cordes, des outils et le matériel de chasse dont ils ont besoin à partir de matériaux naturels comme les peaux, le bois, les feuilles de palmier doum, les racines d'acacia et autres matières végétales. Les Haddad kreda, hommes et femmes, sont également des experts en tannerie. Ils ne tannent pas seulement les peaux des animaux qu'ils tuent eux-mêmes mais également celles des pasteurs. Ni les Haddad kreda ni les Haddad kanembou ne forgent, tissent ou teignent les tissus, travaillent le bois pour faire des mortiers, des tabourets ou des bols, et ils ne font pas non plus de poterie. Ils laissent ces tâches aux artisans professionnels qui vendent leurs produits sur les marchés des villes. Certains de ces Haddad urbains améliorent leurs revenus comme musiciens.

Tannerie et travail du cuir

Les Haddad utilisent la peau de la plupart des animaux qu'ils chassent. Les peaux tannées et apprêtées sont cousues ensemble et placées sous les nattes des tentes pendant la saison des pluies, offrant ainsi une protection supplémentaire contre la pluie. Le cuir est utilisé pour faire des outres, des fourreaux de couteaux ou de lances, des sacs, des courroies, des lanières et des cordes et, autrefois, des vêtements. Les Haddad utilisent deux techniques de tannage différentes selon qu'ils souhaitent enlever les poils ou les conserver. Les femmes s'occupent du tannage des peaux d'animaux comme les gazelles, les chèvres et les moutons, alors que les femmes et les hommes s'occupent ensemble du tannage des peaux d'antilope et de bétail. Le tannage de grandes peaux prend plusieurs jours. Le processus utilisé quand les poils doivent être enlevés complètement consiste à laisser tremper la peau dans le tannin, dans une fosse creusée dans le sol, en la battant régulièrement, pendant 24 heures, puis à racler les poils de la peau, la faire sécher et finalement enlever les pellicules restantes avec un racleur, une tâche ardue qui est exécutée par les hommes.

Vannerie

Les Haddad fabriquent différentes sortes de paniers, de récipients et de boîtes servant pour le transport, le stockage, la traite du lait et autres. Ils utilisent des techniques anciennes comme la vannerie spiralée, le tressage, le torsadage et le nouage. Ils torsadent et tressent les feuilles de palmier et les fibres d'acacia pour faire des lanières et des cordes. Ils font des nattes pour s'asseoir ou dormir dessus et, dans le cas des Haddad kreda, pour couvrir les tentes. La vannerie est en général une occupation féminine, mais les hommes participent à certaines tâches comme par exemple la fabrication des paniers destinés à ramasser les graines de l'herbe sauvage appelée *ogu*.

Les artisans urbains

Dans tout le Kanem et le Bahr el Ghazal, on trouve, sur les marchés des villes, des artisans haddad fabriquant leurs produits ou les vendant dans de très petits stands ouverts. Le nombre de familles pouvant vivre ainsi dépend bien sûr de la taille de la ville et de sa zone d'attraction. Il y a des forgerons qui travaillent avec des soufflets doubles, des enclumes, des lanières et des marteaux de différentes tailles et qui transforment les déchets de métaux en houes, couteaux, lances, pointes de flèches, harpons, caveçons et étriers, ainsi que divers ustensiles ménagers tels que des tripodes pour faire la cuisine, des braseros, des casseroles et des louches. La forge, tout comme le travail du bois, est un métier exclusivement masculin. Les artisans haddad font des quenouilles de lit, des tabourets, des mortiers et des pilons, des armatures pour les selles et des manches pour les armes et les outils. La plupart de leurs produits en bois sont sans décoration, mais certains portent des motifs géométriques gravés avec un outil en fer chauffé au rouge. Il y a aussi des joailliers qui vendent leurs collections de bracelets, d'anneaux pour le nez, de colliers et de bagues en argent, ainsi que des bourreliers et des cordonniers travaillant sous un arbre ou dans un stand. Ils teignent les peaux en blanc, noir, rouge, vert et jaune et les transforment en produits divers à l'aide de marteaux, de tenailles, de limes et de brosses, des outils qui sont fait en Europe maintenant, ainsi que des ciseaux, divers couteaux, des aiguilles et un instrument pointu en forme d'amande pour lisser et redresser les bords. Il y a aussi des tisserands, ainsi que des teinturiers avec leurs grandes jarres remplies d'un mélange de colorant indigo, de natron et d'eau. Il est intéressant de noter que les Haddad ne tirent aucun prestige de la teinturerie. Carbou note que : « … alors que la teinturerie est un métier très respecté dans la région voisine de Bornou, il est méprisé par les Kanembou qui, par conséquent, le laissent aux Haddad. » (1912, I : 39). Autrefois, les Haddad faisaient le commerce des tissus de couleur indigo à grande échelle, mais de nos jours ces tissus ont été complètement remplacés par des tissus importés produits industriellement. Ce développement a également eu un impact négatif sur le métier de tisserand. En fait, nous n'avons pas rencontré de tisserands haddad, bien que l'on dise que certains pratiquent encore ce métier, mais nous avons rencontré un petit nombre de tisserands issus d'autres groupes ethniques. Ils utilisaient des métiers à cartons pour tisser des couvertures de coton et de poils de chèvre.

La poterie était par contre toujours florissante et un métier exclusivement féminin. Toutes les potières que nous avons rencontrées étaient sœurs ou parentes ou femmes de forgerons ou de travailleurs du cuir haddad. Les potières haddad travaillent dans tout le Kanem et le Bahr el Ghazal sauf à Baga Sola où les pots sont faits par les Kotoko. On trouve de l'argile localement à plusieurs endroits, mais certaines potières importent de l'argile. La technique du modelage est utilisée pour les petites pièces, mais on utilise la technique du colombin pour les plus grandes pièces comme les jarres à eau. D'autres techniques sont aussi utilisées, mais le tour est inconnu dans toute la région.

Les marchés et les marchandises
Les Haddad kreda et les Haddad kanembou sont en grande partie autosuffisants et couvrent tous leurs besoins de base grâce à la chasse, la cueillette et les activités agro-pastorales. Néanmoins, ils dépendent du marché pour se procurer du sel, du tissu, des outils en fer, des ustensiles, des pointes de flèches et des armes. Les Haddad kreda vont au marché pour acheter du millet et pour échanger, petit à petit, des petits ruminants, et ils y vont aussi pour vendre de la viande et des peaux. Certaines femmes haddad produisent aussi de la vannerie à vendre au marché. Les marchés ne sont ouverts tous les jours que dans les grandes villes, ailleurs, ils sont

ouverts un jour par semaine sur la base d'une rotation entre les petites villes d'une même région. Ce chapitre décrit la disposition d'un marché, la répartition des producteurs et des commerçants selon l'appartenance ethnique et comment elle coïncide avec les variétés de produits.

16: PERSPECTIVES

Dans ce chapitre final, l'auteur présente une plus vaste perspective théorique sur la culture et la société des Haddad en se focalisant sur deux éléments clés. D'une part, les différences existant entre les deux groupes en ce qui concerne les méthodes de chasse et les modes de subsistance. D'autre part, l'impact des insurrections et des interventions politiques au cours des siècles passés sur la société des Haddad ainsi que le manque d'égalité des droits et d'acceptation culturelle dont ils sont victimes.

Les méthodes de chasse des Haddad sont des méthodes anciennes en Afrique. La spécialisation dans la chasse au filet ou dans la chasse à l'arc combinée avec le déguisement, existe dans plusieurs sociétés de chasseurs, les mieux connues étant les divers groupes batwa en Afrique centrale. Différentes théories ont été avancées pour expliquer cette spécialisation technologique en se basant sur des facteurs comme l'environnement naturel et sociopolitique ainsi que d'autres facteurs clés tels que la visibilité du gibier dans l'habitat, la situation relative à la sécurité alimentaire, le rendement par rapport à l'effort fourni et la question de la diffusion culturelle. Ce chapitre discute la pertinence d'un certain nombre de théories pour comprendre les différences entre les deux groupes haddad en ce qui concerne la technologie de la chasse. Il conclut que, bien que la spécificité de l'environnement, y compris la visibilité et la composition du gibier, influent sur le choix de la technologie et des méthodes de chasse, d'autres facteurs entrent également en jeu. La sécurité alimentaire, le rendement par rapport à l'effort fourni et la pression démographique sont tous des facteurs importants. En outre, dans les conditions données, la chasse au filet semble être une stratégie plus viable que la chasse à l'arc et aux flèches. La question de la diffusion culturelle est écartée.

L'état d'insurrection et de violence général au Kanem et au Bahr el Ghazal sont également des facteurs importants qui influent sur la société haddad. Les Haddad kanembou, plus nombreux, étaient en état de se défendre à l'époque précoloniale, mais ils furent de plus en plus obligés d'abandonner la chasse, suite à la pression démographique et à la rareté du gibier, et à se mettre à la production alimentaire. Les Haddad kreda, très peu nombreux, cherchaient la protection contre les attaques auprès des groupes pasteurs. Avec la raréfaction du gibier, ils devinrent de plus en plus dépendants du lait que les pasteurs leur donnaient en échange de leur travail. La transition au pastoralisme pose un certain nombre de problèmes. L'ultime menace au mode de vie des Haddad est néanmoins l'interdiction de la chasse au filet imposée par le gouvernement. La taille respective des deux groupes haddad et les différences de mode de vie sont reflétées dans leur influence politique, celle des Haddad kreda étant négligeable.

ÉPILOGUE

L'épilogue discute l'avenir de la société et de la culture haddad dans le cadre plus général de la situation des populations autochtones, comptant 375 millions de personnes, dans le monde actuel et leur lutte pour les droits autochtones. Il exprime l'espoir que les Haddad seront acceptés comme des citoyens égaux au Tchad dans un avenir pas trop lointain, et qu'il leur sera possible d'assister aux sessions du Forum Permanent des Nations Unies sur les questions autochtones à New York.

CULTURE MATÉRIELLE – UN CATALOGUE

Les choses matérielles, habitations, armes, ustensiles, vêtements, bijoux et objets rituels, constituent des éléments clés de toute culture, aussi bien en tant qu'éléments essentiels au maintien d'un certain mode de vie qu'en tant que manifestations culturelles et expressions de l'identité ethnique et personnelle. Durant notre étude sur le terrain, nous nous sommes efforcés d'explorer la culture matérielle des Haddad et de noter les différences entre les différents groupes haddad dans ce domaine. Nous avons rassemblé des spécimens ethnographiques en accord avec l'Institut national tchadien à N'Djemena pour ses collections et pour des musées danois. L'Institut national tchadien sélectionna les spécimens intéressants pour son travail et le reste de la collection fut réparti entre le Musée National et le Musée Moesgaard au Danemark.

Ce chapitre décrit en détail les spécimens rassemblés chez les Haddad kanembou, les Haddad kreda, les artisans haddad et les pasteurs kreda, y compris une tente kreda identique à celles utilisées par les Haddad kreda. Ces descriptions sont basées sur l'analyse approfondie de tous les objets ainsi que sur les notes prises au moment de leur achat. Chaque spécimen est catalogué avec un numéro et un texte comprenant des informations sur les matériaux utilisés, la personne qui l'a produit, son utilisation, le lieu où il a été acheté, à qui et à quel prix. Le terme ethnique est indiqué lorsqu'il est connu de l'auteur. Les dimensions sont indiquées en cm, H indique la hauteur, W la largeur et D le diamètre. Les spécimens se trouvant au Musée National du Danemark sont marqués d'un (G) majuscule indiquant qu'ils font partie de la collection africaine du département d'ethnographie. Des lettres minuscules sont utilisées quand plusieurs spécimens sont catalogués sous le même numéro. Les spécimens faisant partie de la collection se trouvant au Musée Moesgaard sont marqués des lettres majuscules (EA).

Les Haddad kanembou

Les spécimens rassemblés chez les Haddad kanembou sont analysés sous les rubriques suivantes :

Chasse et pêche au lac Tchad (cat. nos. 1-4), comprenant la description de harpons utilisés pour la chasse au crocodile au lac Tchad et les lances utilisées pour la pêche.

Équipement de chasse (cat. nos. 5-21) comprenant la description de masques utilisés, en même temps que des peaux de mouton, par les chasseurs haddad quand ils se déguisent en bucorve. Les masques (cat. nos. 5, 6, 12, 13 & 15) sont sculptés en bois et ornés de différentes façons pour parfaire la ressemblance avec la tête de l'animal. Deux de ces masques (cat. nos. 12 & 15) sont faits avec le crâne de l'oiseau. Le catalogue décrit aussi des arcs (cat. nos. 8, 10 & 16); un étui à arc tressé de bandes de feuilles de palmier doum (cat. no. 17); des flèches, faites de tiges de roseaux, avec des pointes de fer enduites de poison, placées dans des carquois faits de cuir de bœuf (cat. no. 9) ou de racines d'acacia raddiana recouvertes de cuir (cat. nos. 11 & 18). Cette section décrit aussi les protège-genoux utilisés par les chasseurs (cat. nos. 7, 14 & 19); un mortier avec pilon utilisé pour préparer le poison destiné aux flèches (cat. no. 20); et une corne de damalisque utilisée pour faire des signaux pendant la chasse aux lions et autres gros animaux. Elle décrit en outre les filets utilisés par un chasseur spécialisé dans la chasse aux petits mammifères et aux oiseaux (cat. nos. 22-27). Ensuite, les armes utilisées par les hommes haddad kanembou pour leur propre protection ou, parfois, pour tuer du gibier; des lances barbelées avec des lames de fer (cat. no. 28); des lances en bois de gazelle (cat. no. 29); une lance longue avec une lame de fer (cat. no. 30); un couteau à lancer en fer utilisé par les garçons (cat. no. 31); des couteaux plus grands pour les hommes (cat. no. 32) et une lance avec une lame en corne d'antilope (cat. no. 34). Parfois, les hommes haddad sont armés de bâtons de jet ou de boomerangs en bois, des armes courantes au Ouaddaï (cat. no. 33). La section suivante décrit des objets ménagers : une outre (cat. no. 35); des bols en bois décoratifs avec des couvercles bombés en vannerie spiralée, bordés et décorés de bandes de cuir rouge (cat. nos. 36a-c et 37). Puis des outils ménage: une houe (cat. no. 38) et un petit poinçon en fer, un outil indispensable aux femmes haddad pour faire la vannerie spiralée, pour faire des trous dans le cuir et pour coiffer les femmes. Ensuite, elle décrit des bijoux Haddad: des colliers simples faits d'une seule ou de plusieurs perles noires et blanches (cat. nos. 40-41); quatre bracelets de verre noir (cat. no. 42); une petite calebasse avec un couvercle en vannerie spiralée pour les produits de beauté (cat. no. 43); une autre, connue sous le nom de *golei* et faite de l'extrémité d'une corne d'antilope, pour mettre le sulfure d'antimoine noir que les femmes utilisent comme mascara ; un outil en fer pour l'appliquer (cat. nos. 44 & 45) ; et un mortier et un pilon ornés pour piler les graines que les femmes utilisent pour faire du lait de corps (cat. no. 46).

Les Haddad kreda

Cette partie du catalogue commence par la description de différents types de filets faits de tendons torsadés et suspendus entre deux poteaux ou piquets que les Haddad utilisent pour chasser les pintades (cat. no. 47), les outardes (cat. no. 48), les lièvres (cat. no. 49), les chacals (cat. no. 50), les gazelles (cat. no. 51) et les antilopes (cat. no. 57); des poteaux fourchus et des ballots de bandes de peau de chèvre que les Haddad utilisent pour simuler des êtres humains quand ils rabattent le gibier (cat. nos. 52 & 53); deux bâtons que les chasseurs battent l'un contre l'autre pour rabattre le gibier dans les filets (cat. no. 54); un sac de cordes tressées de feuilles de palmier doum fendues pour transporter les animaux tués (cat. no. 55); une petite lance avec une lame de fer conique que les garçons utilisent pour pratiquer leur technique de lancement; une lance de 226 cm de long pour tuer les antilo-

pes et, autrefois, les lions et autres gros animaux (cat. no. 59); et enfin, deux boomerangs en bois, un pour les garçons et un pour les hommes adultes (cat. nos. 60 & 61). La section suivante décrit des outils pour la cueillette : des paniers tressés de bandes de feuilles de palmier doum fendues, faits par les hommes qui les secoueront à travers des touffes d'herbe *ogu* pour en récolter les graines qui représentent une source nutritive importante chez les Haddad kreda (cat. nos. 62 & 63); et un grand plateau en vannerie spiralée utilisé pour faire sécher les graines d'*ogu* au soleil (cat. no. 64). Ensuite, elle décrit quelques objets ménagers: une calebasse pour aller chercher l'eau placée dans un dispositif de transport fait de cordes tressées (cat. no. 66); un panier en forme de bol avec un couvercle en vannerie spiralée très bien travaillé fait par les femmes avec des feuilles de palmier doum pour stocker les graines sauvages; un récipient similaire, mais en forme de bouteille, qui sert aussi à stocker les graines (cat. no. 68); un bol à lait spiralé très bien fait (cat. no. 69); un couteau tous-usages à double tranchant (cat. no. 70); un racleur ovale en fer pour lisser les peaux au stade final du processus de tannage (cat. no. 71); un racleur léger en bois utilisé par les femmes pour nettoyer le sol de la tente (cat no. 72); et un petit tabouret en bois décoré utilisé par les femmes quand elles font la cuisine ou pour d'autres tâches ménagères (cat. no. 73). Ensuite, elle décrit des ornements personnels : une toute petite cloche en laiton avec des coquillages comme battant qui est attachée au poignet des bébés filles (cat. no. 74); un collier de grosses perles jaunes que les femmes haddad ne possèdent que rarement (cat. no. 75); et une corne de vache utilisée pour la saignée (cat. no. 76). Finalement, elle décrit l'instrument de musique des Haddad kreda par excellence, à savoir le luth à pique à trois cordes qui n'est joué que par les hommes (cat. nos. 77, 78 & 79).

Les artisans haddad

Un certain nombre de spécimens furent achetés à des artisans haddad et parmi ceux-ci une grande jarre à eau faite par des potières haddad (cat. no. 80); une sacoche d'âne tressée par des artisans mâles avec des cordes torsadées de feuilles de palmier doum et principalement utilisée pour transporter les jarres à eau (cat. no. 81); un tabouret en bois finement décoré (cat. no. 82); et des bols à bouillie de même finement décorés (cat. no. 83); tous ces articles sont faits par des forgerons haddad. Cette section décrit également une couverture faite de douze peaux de chacal doublées de cuir rouge (cat. no. 84); deux paires de bottes en cuir faites par des tanneurs haddad (cat. nos. 85a-b); et des paniers et des nattes tissés sans serrer avec des bandes de feuilles de palmier doum par des vannières (cat. nos. 86 & 87). Les potières haddad fabriquent des récipients pour le charbon de bois et pour faire brûler l'encens (cat. no. 88).

Les pasteurs kreda

Le catalogue contient également la description de certains outils utilisés par les pasteurs kreda : des muselières en forme de bol pour empêcher les veaux de téter le lait de leur mère (cat. nos. 89, 90 & 91); et une énorme calebasse ovale utilisée pour baratter le beurre, une des tâches que les femmes haddad exécutent pour leurs « hôtes » kreda (cat. no. 92). Les autres spécimens sont des lances dont les lames ont des barbelures finement exécutées et que les hommes portent, en général par quatre, dans des fourreaux en cuir, pour leur protection personnelle et pour attaquer (cat. no. 93); un couteau à lancer (cat. no. 94); un couteau dans un fourreau de cuir fin qui est attaché au haut du bras (cat. no. 95); et une petite lance utilisée par les garçons pour leur protection quand ils rassemblent le bétail (cat. no. 96). Enfin, il y a un ustensile pour creuser fait d'un manche en bois et d'un soc en fer du genre qui est utilisé par les Haddad, hommes et femmes, pour creuser les trous pour les poteaux des tentes, déterrer des racines d'acacia pour faire les barres transversales des tentes et un certain nombre d'autres tâches, y compris des tâches liées à la cueillette (cat. no. 97). Tous ces ustensiles (cat. nos. 93-97) sont fabriqués par des forgerons haddad.

La collection kreda comprend aussi un bol en bois pour manger la bouillie et stocker le lait (cat. no. 98); un pot en terre rouge avec un couvercle de vannerie spiralée et un panier pour le transporter (cat. nos. 100 & 101) ; un tabouret en bois (cat. no. 102); et une cage à poulets tissée de larges bandes de feuilles de palmier doum (cat. no. 103). Elle comprend également des ornements personnels : une jupe de fille faite avec des chaînes de perles de couleur (cat. no. 104); un anneau de nez en argent porté par la plupart des femmes adultes après leur mariage et trois colliers simples composés de quelques perles en argent faits par des forgerons haddad (cat. nos. 105, 107, 108 & 111); une boite en osier ovale avec une glace (cat. no. 109); un récipient fait d'une corne de vache pour mettre le beurre parfumé (cat. no. 110); une petite calebasse pour mettre les herbes utilisées pour l'hygiène personnelle (cat. no. 113); et un vêtement de femme consistant en un rectangle de coton noir (cat. no. 112). Il y a également un violon à une corde avec son archet. La caisse de résonance est faite à partir d'un bol en bois, comme ceux qui sont utilisés pour manger, recouvert d'un morceau de peau, et la corde et l'archet sont faits de racine d'acacia et de poil de cheval (cat. no. 114).

Une tente, yegé

Les Haddad kreda habitent dans des tentes toute l'année, sauf pendant une courte période si la famille cultive le millet. Leurs tentes sont identiques à celles utilisées par les Kreda, mais elles sont un peu plus petites et souvent en moins bon état. Elles ont une structure voûtée comme un tonneau construite avec les branches, les racines et les fibres torsadés de l'*acacia raddiana* et recouverte de quatre nattes tissées avec des bandes de feuilles de palmier doum fendues. Elles sont structurellement différentes des autres tentes voûtées et recouvertes de nattes que l'on trouve chez les Tibou et les Touareg du Sud et ailleurs dans le Sahel.

Ce chapitre décrit en détail le spécimen acheté à une famille kreda pour le musée Moesgaard. Comme les autres tentes, elle comporte une plate-forme de couchage surélevée (cat. nos. 115-120) couverte de nattes (cat. nos. 121-124) et un dispositif de stockage pour le grain, les graines, les plateaux et autres ustensiles ménagers, suspendu entre cinq poteaux (cat. nos. 125-126). Il est fait d'une natte et de peaux suspendues par un système de cordes de cuir torsadées (cat. nos. 127- 129). La structure de la tente consiste en quatre rangées de poteaux fourchus verticaux (cat. nos. 130-135) dans la fourche desquels on place quatre arceaux longitudinaux, chacun étant fait de deux, parfois trois racines d'acacia lisses sans décorations (cat. no. 136). Vingt-quatre arceaux transversaux (cat. no. 137) y sont arrimés avec des cordes torsadées (cat. no. 138). L'ossature est recouverte de quatre nattes immenses, chacune consistant en deux sections tissées avec des feuilles de palmier doum (cat. nos. 139-142). La tente est meublée d'un stand pour la batterie de cuisine (cat. no. 143) et d'une petite « étagère » de cuisine faite de trente petits bâtons (cat. no. 144). Notre spécimen fait au total 440 cm de long et 265 cm de large.

BIBLIOGRAPHY

Anon.
1997 EIU Country Report CHAD. *The Economist Intelligence Unit Ltd.*

Abruzzi, William S.
1980 Flux among the Mbuti Pygmies of the Ituri Forest: An Ecological Interpretaion. In: Ross, Eric B. (ed.): *Beyond the Myths of Culture: Essays in Cultural Materialism:* 3-31. New York: Academic Press.

Ajayi, J.F.A. and M. Crowder (eds.)
1971 *History of West Africa, I-II.* London: Longman.

Allan, J.A. (ed.)
1981 *The Sahara, Ecological Change and Early Economic History.* London: Menas Press.

Alexander, Boyd
1907 *From the Niger to the Nile,* I-II. London: Edward Arnold.

Ankermann, B.
1905 Kulturkreise und Kulturschichten in Afrika. *Zeitschrift für Ethnologie,* 37: 54-90.

Arkell, A.J.
1961 (1955) *A History of the Sudan. From the Earliest Times to 1821.* London, University of London. The Athlone Press.

Azevedo, Mario J.
1998 *Roots of Violence. A History of War in Chad.* The Netherlands: Gordon and Breach Publishers.

Bahuchet, Serge and Henri Guillaume
1982 Aka-farmer relations in the north-west Congo Basin. In: Leacock, E. and R. Lee (eds.): *Politics and History in Band Societies:* 189-211. Cambridge: Cambridge University Press.

Bailey, R.C. and R. Aunger
1989 Net hunters vs. archers: variation in women's subsistence strategies in the Ituri forest. *Human Ecology,* 17: 273-297.

Baker, Samuel. W.
1875 *Ismalia. Berättelse om den af Ismail, khediv af Egypten, för undertryckande af slafhandeln i Centralafrika utsände expedition.* Stockholm: Bonnier.

Banton, Michael (ed.)
1965 The Relevance of Models for Social Anthropology. *A.S.A Monographs,*I. London: Tavistock Publications.

Barich, B.E.
1987 *Archaeology and Environment in the Libyan Sahara: The Excavations in the Tadrart Acacus 1978-1983.* Oxford: British Archaeological Reports, International Series, 368.

Barker, G.
1981 Early Agriculture and Economic Change in North Africa. In: Allan, J.A. (ed.): *The Sahara. Ecological Change and Early Economic History:* 131-145.

Barnard, A.
1992 *Hunters and Herders of Southern Africa: A comparative Ethnography of the Khoisan Peoples.* Cambridge: Cambridge University Press.

Barnard, A. and James Woodburn
1988 Property, Power and Ideology in hunter-gathering societies: An introduction. In: Ingold, Tim, David Riches and James Woodburn (eds.): *Hunters and Gatherers Vol. 2: Property, Power and Ideology:* 4-31. Oxford: Berg Publishers Limited.

Barnhart, Jim (ed.)
1994 *Manual for the National Bowhunter Education Program.* United States: National Bowhunter Education Foundation.

Baroin, Catherine
1972 Les marques de bétail chez les Daza et les Azza du Niger. *C.N.R.S.H. - Etudes Nigeriennes* 29. Niamey.

1985 *Anarchie et cohésion sociale chez les Toubou. Les Daza Kĕšerda (Niger).* Cambridge: Cambridge University Press.

1987 The Position of Tubu Women in Pastoral Production. *Ethnos,* 52, 1-2: 137-155.

1990 Pourquoi les Daza assimilent-ils leurs voisins? *Actes du IIIème Colloque Mega-Chad,* 95-102. Paris: ORSTOM

1991 Dominant-Dominé: Complementarité des rôles et des attitudes entre les pasteurs Teda-Daza du Niger et leurs forgerons. *Actes du IVéme Colloque Méga-Tchad*, I: 329-381. Yves Moñino (ed.): Forge et Forgerons. Paris: ORSTOM.

1997 Droit foncier et aménagement agricole. Le cas des sources du Borkou Occidental. In: Jungraithmayr, Herrmann, Daniel Barreteau and Uwe Seibert (eds.): *L'Homme et l'eau dans le bassin du lac Tchad*. Paris: ORSTOM.

1997 *Tubu: the Teda and the Daza*. New York: Rosen Publication Groups.

Baroin, Catherine and Pierre-François Pret
1997 Le palmier du Borkou, végétal social total. In: Barreteau, Daniel, René Dognin and Charlotte von Graffenried (eds.): *L'Homme et le milieu végétal dans le bassin du lac Tchad*, 349-363. Paris: ORSTOM.

Barreteau, Daniel and Henry Tourneux (eds.):
1990 Relations interethniques et culture matérielle dans le bassin du lac Tchad. *Actes du IIIème Colloque Mega-Tchad*. Paris: ORSTOM.

Barreteau, Daniel
and Charlotte von Graffenried (eds.):
1993 *Datation et chronologie dans le bassin du lac Tchad*. Paris: ORSTOM.

Barreteau, Daniel, René Dognin and Charlotte von Graffenried (eds.):
1997 *L'Homme et le milieu végétal dans le bassin du lac Tchad*. Paris: ORSTOM.

Barth, Fredrik
1954 Father's brother's daughter marriage in Kurdistan. *Southwestern Journal of Anthropology*, 10: 164-171.

1956 Ecological Relationships of Ethnic Groups in Swat, North Pakistan. *American Anthropologist*, 58: 1079-1089.

1969 Introduction. In: Barth, F. (ed.): *Ethnic Groups and Boundaries: The social organization of cultural differences*: 9-38. Boston: Little Brown.

Barth, Heinrich
1857-58 *Reisen und Entdeckungen in Nord- und Zentral-Afrika in den Jahren 1849 bis 1855*, I-V. Gotha.

Baumann, Hermann
1940 *Völkerkunde von Afrika*. Essen.

Baumann, Hermann and D. Westermann
1948 *Les peuples et les civilisations de l'Afrique*. Paris: Payot.

Bender, Barbara and Brian Morris
1991 Twenty years of history, evolution and social change in gatherer-hunter studies. In: Ingold, Tim, David Riches and James Woodburn (eds.): *Hunters and Gatherers*, I: 4-14. New York/Oxford: Berg.

Bicchieri, M.G. (ed.):
1972 *Hunters and Gatherers Today*. New York: Holt, Tinehart and Winston.

1974 Hunters and Gatherers Today: A socio-economic study of eleven such cultures in the twentieth century. *American Anthropologist Review*, 1974, 76: 3.

Blackburn, Roderick H.
1982 In the land of milk and honey: Okiek adaptations to their forests and neighbours. In: Leacock, E. and R. Lee (eds.): *Politics and History in Band Societies*: 283-305. Cambridge: Cambridge University Press.

Boas, F.
1888 The Central Eskimos. *Report of the Bureau of Ethnology 1884-1885*, 399-669. Smithsonian Institution.

1897 The Decorative Art of the Indians of the North Pacific Coast of America. *Bulletin of the American Museum of Natural History*, IX. New York.

1916 The Origin of Totemism. *American Anthropologist*, 18: 319-26.

Bond, George C.
1990 Fieldnotes: Research in Past Occurences. In: Sanjek, Roger (ed.): *Fieldnotes. The Makings of Anthropology*: 273-289. Ithaca/London: Cornell University Press.

Bonte, Pierre
1975 Esclavage et relations de dépendance chez les Touareg Kel Geres. In: Meillassoux, C. (ed.): *L'esclavage en Afrique précoloniale*: 49-76. Paris: Maspero.

1979 Segmentarité et pouvoir chez les éleveurs nomades sahariens: élément d'une problématique. In: *Pastoral Production and Society*: 171-199. Cambridge University Press.

Bouchardeau, A.L.R. Lefevre
1957 *Monographie du lac Tchad*. Paris: ORSTOM.

Bouillié, R.
1937 Les Coutumes Familiales au Kanem. Thèse pour le Doctorat. *Université de Paris - Faculté de Droit*. Paris: Domat-Montcrestien.

Bourdieu, Pierre
1977 *An Outline of a Theory of Practice*. Cambridge University Press.

Bovill, E.W.
1958 *The Golden Trade of the Moors*. 2nd. edn. London.

Brandily, Monique
1974 Instrument de musique et musiciens instrumentistes chez les Teda du Tibesti. *Koninklijk Museum voor Midden-Afrika - Tervuren, België Annalen - Reeks IN-8 - Menselijke Wetenschappen*, 82. Belgium.

1988 Traditional Music of Rwanda. *Yearbook for Traditional Music*, 20: 246-247. New York: Int. Council of Traditional Music. Columbia University.

Briggs, Lloyd Cabot
1960 *Tribes of the Sahara*. Cambridge: Harvard University Press.

Brooks, George E.
1993 *Landlords and Strangers: Ecology, Society, and Trade in Western Africa, 1000-1630*. Boulder: Westview Press.

Brouin, G.
1950 Notes sur les ongulés du Cercle d'Agadez et leur chasse. *Mém. de l'IFAN. Contribution à l'étude de l'Aïr*, 10: 425-455. Paris.

Bruel, Georges
1935   *La France Équatoriale Africaine.* Paris.

Buchwald, Vagn Fabritius
1996   *Grundrids af jernets historie indtil år 1900.* Xerox. DTU, Afd. for Metallære. Copenhagen.

Buffon, Georges Louis Leclerc de
1770-1786 *Histoire naturelle des oiseaux.* Paris.

Buijtenhuijs, Robert
1987   Le Frolinat et les guerres civiles du Tchad (1977-1984). Paris: Karthala.

Bulliet, Richard W.
1990 (1975) *The Camel and the Wheel.* Cambridge, Mass.

Burch, Ernest S. Jr. and Linda J. Ellanna (eds.):
1996   *Key Issues in Hunter-Gatherer Research.* Oxford: Berg.

Buschan, Georg
1914-1916 *Die Sitten der Völker,* I-III. Stuttgart: Union Deutsche Verlagsgesellschaft.

Cabot, Jean and Christian Bouquet
1973   *Le Tchad.* Paris: Presses Universitaires de France.

Carbou, Henri
1912   *La Région du Tchad et du Ouadaï,* I-II. Publications de la Faculté des Lettres d'Alger. Bulletin de Correspondance Africaine, 47-48. Paris: Ernest Leroux.

Catala, R.
1954   I'évolution des chefferies africaines du district de Mao de 1899 a 1953. *Mémoire de C.H.E.A.M. no. 2328.* Paris.

Caulk, R.A.
1984   Islam and Christianity in North-East and East Africa. In: Oliver, Roland and Michael Crowder (eds.): *The Cambridge Encyclopeida of Africa:* 117-123. Cambridge: Cambridge University Press.

Chang, Cynthia
1982   Nomads without cattle: East African foragers in historical perspective. In: Leacock, E. and R. Lee (eds.): *Politics and History in Band Societies:* 269-282. Cambridge: Cambridge University Press.

Chapelle, Jean
1957   *Nomades Noirs du Sahara.* Paris: Librairie Plon.

1980   *Le Peuple Tchadien - ses racines, sa vie quotidienne et ses combats.* Paris: Édition l'Harmattan.

1987   *Souvenir du Sahel.* Paris: Éditions l'Harmattan.

Chevalier, A.
1907   *Mission Chari-Lac Tchad, 1902-1904. L'Afrique Centrale Française. Récit de Voyage de la Mission.* Paris: Challamel.

Childe, Gordon V.
1935   *New Light on the Most Ancient East.* London: Kegan Paul, Trench, Trubner & Co.

Childs, S. Terry and David Killick
1993   Indigenous African Metallurgy: Nature and Culture. *Annual Review of Anthropology,* 22: 317-334.

Clanet, Jean
1975   *Les éleveurs de l'ouest tchadien. La mobilité des éleveurs du Kanem et leurs réponses à la crise climatique de 1969-1973.* Université de Rouen.

1977   Les conséquences des années sèches 1969-1973 sur la mobilité des éleveurs de Kanem. In: Gallais, J. (ed.): *Stratégies pastorales et agricoles des Saheliens durant la Secheresse 1969-1974:* 237-259 (no publisher).

Clark, J.D.
1976   The domestication process in Sub-Saharan Africa with special reference to Ethiopia. In: Higgs, E. (ed.): *Origine de l'Élevage et de la Domestication:* 56-115. IXth Congress IUSPP. Nice.

Cline, Walter
1950   *The Traders of Tibesti, Borku, and Kawar in the Eastern Sahara.* Wisconsin: Banta Publishing Co.

Close, Angela E.
1980   Current Research and Recent Radiocarbon Dates from Northern Africa. *Journal of African History,* 21: 145-167.

1987   Overview. In: Close, Angela E. (ed.): *Prehistory of Arid North Africa. Essays in Honor of Fred Wendorf:* 317-324. Dallas, Texas: Southern Methodist University Press.

Close, Angela E. and Fred Wendorf
199   North Africa at 18000 BP. In: Gamble, C.S. and O. Soffer: *The World at 18000 BP.:* 41-57. London: Unwin Hyman.

Coe, Michael T. and Jonathan Foley
2001   Human and natural impacts on the water resources of the Lake Chad basin. *Journal of Geophysical Research - D: Atmospheres.* February: 106 (4): 3349-3356.

Coeur, Charles Le
1950   Dictionnaire Ethnographique Téda. *Mémoires de l'IFAN,* 9. Paris: Larose.

Coeur, Charles Le and M. Le Coeur
1955   Grammaire et textes téda - daza. *Mémoires de l'IFAN,* 46. Paris: Larose.

Coeur, M. Le
1970   Mission au Niger - juillet-decembre 1969. *Journal de la Société des Africanistes,* 40, 2: 160-168.

Cohen, A.P.
1985   *The symbolic construction of community.* London: Tavistock Publications.

Cohen, Ronald
1978a   Introduction. In: Cohen, Ronald and Elman Service (eds.): *Origins of the State: The Anthropology of Political Evolution.* Philadelphia: Institute for the Study of Human Issues.

1984   Warfare and State Formation: Wars Make States and States Make Wars. In: Cohen, Ronald and Elman Service (eds.): *Origins of the State: The Anthropology of Political Evolution:* 329-358. Philadelphia: Institute for the Study of Human Issues.

Collingwood, R.G.
1961   *The Idea of History.* London: Oxford University Press.

de Colombel, V.
1997 Noms et usages des plantes. In: Barreteau, D., René Dognin and Charlotte von Graffenried (eds.): *L'Homme et le milieu végétal dans le bassin du lac Tchad:* 289-310. Paris: ORSTOM.

Conkey, Margaret W.
1984 To Find Ourselves: Art and Social Geography of Prehistoric Hunter-Gatherers. In: Schrire, C. (ed.): *Past and Present in Hunter Gatherer Studies:* 253-76. New York: Academic Press.

Connah, Graham
1981 *Three thousand years in Africa: man and his environment in the Lake Chad region of Nigeria.* Cambridge: Cambridge University Press.

Conrad, David C. and Barbara E. Frank (eds.)
1995 *Status and Identity in West Africa.* Bloomington: Indiana University Press.

Conte, Edouard
1979 Politics and Marriage in South Kanem (Chad): A Statistical Presentation of Endogamy from 1895 to 1975. *Cahiers de l'Office de la recherche scientifique et technique outre-mer. Série sciences humaines,* 4: 262-275. Paris.

1983a *Marriage Patterns, Political Change and the Perpetuation of Social Inequality (In South Kanem [Chad]).* Paris: ORSTOM.

1983b Castes, classes et alliances au sud-Kanem. *Journal de la Sociétés des Africanistes,* 53, 1-2: 147-169.

1984 Taxation et tribut au Kanem. Considérations sur l'accumulation inégale dans une société agropastorale. *Paideuma,* 30: 103-121.

1986 La dynamique de l'alliance parmi les chasseurs sédentarisés Duu Rea du Sud-Kanem (Tchad). *Paideuma,* 32: 129-161.

1988 *Macht und Tradition in Westafrika. Französische Anthropologie und afrikanische Geschichte.* Frankfurt/New York: Campus Verlag.

1991 Herders, Hunters, and Smiths: Mobile Populations in the History of Kanem. In: Galaty, John G. and P. Bonte: *Herders, Warriors, and Traders. Pastoralism in Africa,* 221-247. Boulder: Westview Press.

Coppens, Y.
1969 Les cultures protohistoriques et historiques de Djourab. *Actes du premier colloque international d'archéologie africaine,* 129-146. Fort-Lamy: I.N.T.S.H.

Cordell, Dennis
1985 *Dar al-Kuti and the Last Years of the Trans-Saharan Slave Trade.* Madison: University of Wisconsin Press.

Cornet, Jean
1963 *L'histoire politique du Tchad de 1900 à 1962.* Paris: Pichon & Duran.

Cuoq, J.M.
1975 *L'histoire des sources arabes concernant l'Afrique occidentale du VIII à XVI siècles.* Paris: CNRS.

David, N.
1983 The archaeological context of Nilotic expansion: A survey of the holocene archaeology of East Africa and the southern Sudan. In: Vossen, R. and M. Bechhaus-Gerst (eds.): *Nilotic studies. Proceedings of the International Symposium on Languages and History of the Nilotic Peoples, Cologne, January 4-6, 1982. Kölner Beiträge zur Afrikanistik,* 10: 1. Berlin.

Deacon, H.J.
1989 Late Pleistocene Palaeoecology in the Southern Cape, South Africa. In: Mellars, Paul and Cris Stringer (eds.): *The Human Revolution - Behavioural and Biological Perspectives on the Origins of Modern Humans.* Edinburgh: Edinburgh University Press.

Decalo, S.
1977 *Historical Dictionary of Chad.* New York/London: Scarecrow Press.

Decorse, J.
1905 La chasse et l'agriculture chez les populations du Soudan. *L'Anthropologie,* XVI: 457-473.

Delhoyo, J.D.
1992-2005 *Handbook of Birds of the World, vol. 6.* Barcelona: Lynx.

Denham, D., H. Clapperton and W. Oudney
1826 *Travels and Discoveries in Northern and Central Africa in 1822, 1823, and 1824, I-IV.* London: Murray.

Dentan, Robert
1988 Band-Level Eden: A Mystifying Chimera. *Cultural Anthropology,* 3, 3: 276-284.

Dentan, Robert, Kirk Endicott, Alberto G. Gomes and M.B. Hooker
1957: *Malaysia and the Original People.* U.S.A.: Allyn and and Bacon.

Denyer, Susan
1978 *African Traditional Architecture.* London: Heinemann.

Derricourt, Robin M.
1984 The African Past. In: Olwir, Roland and Michael Crowder (eds.): *The Cambridge Encyclopedia of Africa,* 87-99. Cambridge: Cambridge University Press.

Donnan, Hastings and Thomas M. Wilson (eds.)
199 *Border approaches: anthropological perspectives on frontiers.* Oxford: Berg.

Dorst, Jean and Pierre Dandelot
1972 *A Field Guide to the Larger Mammals of Africa.* London: Collins.

Doutressoulle, G.
1947 *L'élevage en Afrique Occidentale Française.* Paris.

Dowling, John H.
1968 Individual ownership and the sharing of game in hunting societies. *American Anthropologist,* 70, 3: 502-507.

Dumas-Champion, Françoise
1980 Le rôle social et rituel du bétail chex les Massa du Tchad. *Africa,* 50, 2: 161-181.

Durkheim, Emile
1915 (1912) *The Elementary Forms of Religious Life: A Study in Religious Sociology.* J.F. Swain transl. London: Allen & Urwin.

Echard, Nicole (ed.):
1991 Les Relations Hommes-Femmes dans le Bassin du Lac Tchad. *Actes du IVe colloque Méga-Tchad, CNRS/ORSTOM. Paris, du 14 au 16 septembre 1988,* II. Paris: ORSTOM.

The Economist
2001, January 6-12.

EIU Country Report
1997

Ember, Carol R.
1978 Myths About Hunter-Gatherers. *Ethnology,* XVII, 4: 439-449.

Encyclopædia Britannica
1993

Evans-Pritchard, E.E.
1937 *Witchcraft, Oracles, and Magic among the Azande.* Oxford: Oxford University Press.

1949 *The Sanusi of Cyrenaica.* Oxford: Oxford University Press.

Fanon, Frantz
1969 *The Wretched of the Earth.* New York: Grove Press.

Fartua, Ahmed Ibn
(1970 transl.) *History of the first twelve years of the reign of Mai Idris Alooma of Bornu (1571-1583).* London: Frank Cass.

Feit, A. Harvey
1996 The Enduring Pursuit: Land, Time and Social Relationships in Anthropological Models of Hunter-Gatherers and in Subarctic Hunters' Images. In: Burch, Ernest S. and Linda J. Ellanna (eds.): *Key Issues in Hunter-Gatherer Research:* 421-439. Oxford: Berg.

Financial Times,
2001, June 21.

Fisher, H.J. and Virginia Rowland
1971 Firearms in the Central Sudan. *Journal of African History,* XI: 215-239.

Flannery, K.V.
1969 Origins and Ecological Effects of Early Domestication in Iran and the Near East. In: Ucko, J. and Gj.W. Dimpleby (eds.): *The Domestication and Exploitation of Plants and Animals:* 73-100. Chicago: Aldine Publishing Company.

Forbes, R. J.
1950 *Metallurgy in Antiquity. A Notebook for Archaeologists and Technologists.* Leiden: E. J. Brill.

Foucauld, Charles de and de Motylinski
1922 *Textes tuareg en prose. Dialecte de l'Ahaggar.* Algiers.

Foureau, F.
1905 *Documents scientifiques de la Mission saharienne (Mission Foureau-Lamy) 1898-1900.* Paris: Masson & Cie.

Fowler, Brenda
2004 Scientists Explore Ancient Lakefront Life in the Sahara. *The New York Times,* January 27.

Franz, Charles
1975 Contraction and expansion in Nigerian bovine pastoralism. In: Monod, Theodore (ed.): *Pastoral Societies in Tropical Africa:* 338-353. London: Oxford University Press.

Fratkin, E., K.A. Galvin and E.A. Roth
1994 *African Pastoralist Systems: An Integrated Approach.* Boulder: Lynne Rienner.

Frazer, J.G.
1887 *Totemism.* Edinburgh: Adams and Charles.

1890 *The Golden Bough,* I-XII. London: MacMillan & Co.

Freydenberg, H.
1908 *Étude sur le Tchad et le bassin du Chari.* Paris.

Frobenius, Leo
1933 *Kulturgeschichte Afrikas.* Zürich: Phaidon Verlag.

Fuchs, Peter
1961 *Die Völker der Südost-Sahara. Tibesti, Borku, Ennedi.* Wien: Braumüller.

1962 Zwei dringende Aufgaben in Afrika (Kara [Birao] und Haddad). *Bulletin of the International Committee on Urgent Anthropological and Ethnological Research,* 5: 52-53.

1966 *Tschad.* Bonn: Kurt Schroeder.

1970 Eisengewinnung und Schmiedetum im nördlichen Tschad. *Baessler Archiv, Neue Folge,* XVIII: 295-335.

1972 Tubu (Ostsahara, Tibesti). Errichten und Abbrechen eines Zeltes. *Encyclopedia cinematoghraphica.* Göttingen.

Gabus, Jean
1977 *Oulata et "Gueimare" des Nemadi.* Neuchâtel: Musée d'Ethnographie.

Gaillard, R. and L. Poutrin
1906-1909 Études anthropologiques des populations des régions du Tchad et du Kanem. *Documents Scientifiques de la Mission Tilho (1906-1909),* 3: I-III.

Galaty, John G.
1986 East African hunters and pastoralists in a regional perspective - an "ethnoanthropological" approach. *Sprache Geschichte Afrikas,* 7 (1): 105-131.

Galaty, John G. and Pierre Bonte (eds.):
1991 *Herders, Warriors, and Traders. Pastoralism in Africa.* Boulder: Westview.

Gallais, J.
1975 Pasteurs et paysans du Gourma (Mali). La condition sahélienne. *Mémoires du CEGET:* Bordeaux

Gautier, Achilles
1984a Quaternary Mammals and Archaeozoology of Egypt and the Sudan: A Survey. In: Krzyzaniak, L. and M. Kobusiewicz (eds.): *The Origin and Early Development of Food Producing Cultures in North-Eastern Africa,* 43-56. Poznan: Polish Academy of Sciences.

1987 Prehistoric Men and Cattle in North Africa. In: Close, Angela E. (ed.): *Prehistory of Arid North Africa. Essays in Honor of Fred Wendorf:* 163-187. Dallas: Southern Methodist University Press.

Gautier, Achilles and W. Van Neer
1982 Prehistoric fauna from Ti-n-Torha (Tadrart Acacus, Libya). *Origini,* II: 87-127.

Gentil, P.
1946 *Confins libyens, lac Tchad, fleuve Niger.* Paris: Charles Lavanzelle.

Gibbon, Edward
1909 (1776) *The Decline and Fall of the Roman Empire.* London: Methuen & Co.

Gillis, John (ed.):
1994 *Commemorations: The Politics of National Identity.* Princeton.

Godelier, Maurice
1972 *Rationality and Irrationality in Economics.* New York: Monthly Review Press.

Grall, Lieutenant
1945 Le secteur nord du Cercle de Gouré. *Bulletin de l'IFAN,* VII: 1-46. Paris.

Graebner, F.
1911 *Methode der Ethnologie.* Heidelberg.

Grébénart, Danilo
1987 Characteristics of the Final Neolithic and Metal Ages in the Region of Agadez (Niger). In: Close, Angela E. (ed.): *Prehistory of Arid North Africa. Essays in Honor of Fred Wendorf:* 287-316. Dallas.

Greenberg, J.H.
1955 *Studies in African Linguistic Classification.* Branford, Conn.: Compass Pub. Co.

1966 (rev. edn.) The Languages of Africa. Bloomington: Indiana University Press.

Gregg, Susan Alling
1988 *Foragers and Farmers.* Chicago: University of Chicago Press.

Griaule, Marcel and Jean-Paul Lebeuf
1948, 1950 Fouilles dans la région du Tchad, I-II. *Journal de la Société des Africanistes,* XVIII: 1; XX: 1.

Grimes, Barbara (ed.):
1992 *Ethnography.* Austin, Texas: Summer Institute of Linguistics.

Grinker, Roy Richard
1994 *Houses in the Rainforest. Ethnicity and Inequality among Farmers and Foragers in Central Africa.* University of California Press.

Gusinde, Martin
1946 *Die Feuerland Indianer,* I-III. St. Gabriel-Mödling bei Wien. Verlag der internationalen Zeitschrift Anthropos.

1961 *The Yamans: the life and thought of the water nomads of Cape Horn.* New Haven: Human Relations Area Files.

Haaland, Randi
1992 Fish, Pots and Grain: Early and Mid-Holocene Adaptations in Central Sudan. *The African Archaeological Review,* 10: 43-64.

Harako, R
1976 The Mbuti as hunters: A study of ecological anthropology of the Mbuti Pygmies. *Kyoto University African Studies,* 10: 37-99.

Harlan, Fred, J. M. de Wet and K. A. Stemler
1976 *The Origins of African Plant Domestication.* The Hague: Mouton

1982 The Origins of Indigenous African Agriculture. In: Clark, Desmond (ed.): *The Cambridge History of Africa,* I: 624-657. Cambridge: Cambridge University Press.

1989 The Tropical African Cereals. In: Harris, David and Gordon Hillman (eds.): *Foraging and Farming:* 335-43. London: Unwin, Hyman.

1992 Indigenous African Agriculture. In: Cowan, C.W. and P.J. Watson (eds.): *The Origins of Agriculture: An International Perspective:* 59-70. Washington: Smithsonian Institution Press.

Hart, J.A.
1978 From subsistence to market: a case of the Mbuti net hunters. *Human Ecology,* 6: 325-353.

Headland, Thomas N. and Lawrence A. Reid
1989 Hunter-Gatherers and Their Neighbors from Prehistory to the Present with CA* Comment. *Current Anthropology,* 30, 1: 43-66.

The Herald Tribune
2000, January 26.

Heuglin, Theodor von
1869 *Reise in das Gebiet des Weissen Nil und seiner westlichen Zuflüsse in den Jahren 1862-1864: 201.* Leipzig und Heidelberg: C.F. Winter.

Hilbert, John
1962 *Les Gbaya.* Studia Ethnographica Upsaliensis, XIX. Lund.

Hindess, Barry and Paul Q. Hirst
1975 *Pre-capitalist modes of production.* London: Routledge and Kegan Paul.

Hodgkinson, Edith
1997 Economy. In: *Regional Survey of the World - Africa South of the Sahara. CHAD.* (27th edn.)

Hoffman, Carl L.
1984 Punan Foragers in the Trading Networks of Southeast Asia. In: Schrire, C. (ed.): *Past and Present in Hunter-Gatherer Studies:* 123-149. Orlando: Academic Press.

Holub, E.
1881 *Sieben Jahre in Süd-Afrika.* Wien.

Hultkrantz, Åke and Ørnulf Vorren (eds.):
1982 *The Hunters. Their Culture and Way of Life.* Tromsø Museum Skrifter, XVIII. Tromsø-Oslo-Bergen.

Iliffe, John
1995 *Africans. The History of a Continent.* Cambridge: Cambridge University Press.

Ingold, Tim
1987 *The appropriation of nature: Essays on human ecology and social relations.* Iowa City: University of Iowa Press.

1990 Comment on Solway and Lee. *Current Anthropology,* 31: 130-131.

Ingold, Tim, David Riches and James Woodburn (eds.)
1991 *Hunters and Gatherers,* I-II. Berg: New York/Oxford.

Jungraithmayer, Herrmann Daniel
1997 *L'Homme et l'eau dans le bassin du Lac Tchad.* Paris: ORSTOM.

Kazadi, Ntole
1981 Méprisés et admirés: L'ambivalence des relations entre Bacwa (Pygmées) et les Bahemba (Bantu). *Africa,* 51, 4: 836-47.

Kenny, M.
1981 Mirror in the Forest. The Dorobo hunter-gatherers as an image of the other. *Africa,* 51, 1: 477-495.

Killick, D.J., N.J. van der Merwe, R.B. Gordon and D. Grébénart
1988 Reassessment of the evidence for early metallurgy in Niger, West Africa. In: *Journal of Archaeological Science,* 15: 367-394.

Kingdon, James
2004 *The Kingdon Pocket Guide to African Mammals.* London: A. & C. Black.

Kleinman, A., V. Das and M. Lock (eds.)
1996 *Social Suffering.* Berkeley: University of California Press.

Konrad, Walter
1957 Die Wasserjahrzeuge der Tschadsee-Region. *Baessler Archiv,* 5, 1: 121-43.

Krarup Mogensen, A.
1963 Kulturgeografiske studier i det sydlige Kanem. Unpbl. MS. Copenhagen: The Royal Library.

Kriger, Colleen E.
1999 *Pride of Men. Ironworking in the 19th Century West Central Africa.* Heineman, Currey & Philip.

Kronenberg, Andreas
1958 *Die Teda von Tibesti.* Wiener Beiträge zur Kulturgeschichte und Linguistik, XII. Wien.

Krzyzaniak, Lech
1978 Early Farming in the Middle Nile Basin: recent discoveries at Kadero (Central Sudan). *Antiquity,* 65: 515-532.

Krzyzaniak, Lech and M. Kobusiewicz (eds.):
1984 *The Origin and Early Development of Food Producing Cultures in North-Eastern Africa.* Poznan: Polish Academy of Sciences.

Köhler, Harry
1964 Mode de capture chez différentes tribus de chasse et de pêche au bord de la Rivière Sangha. *Studia Etnographica Upsaliensis,* XX, Varia I.: Lund.

Lagercrantz, Sture
1938 *Beiträge zur Kulturgeschichte der afrika-nischen Jagdfallen.* Stockholm.

1974 Om fällor och fångst. Review of James Bateman: Animal traps and trapping. *Rig,* 58: 18-23.

Lamphear, John
1986 The persistence of hunting and gathering in a "pastoral" world. *Sprache Geschichte Afrikas,* 7 (2): 227-265.

Landeroin, M.
1910-1914 Du Tchad au Niger. Notice historique. In: *Documents scientifiques de la mission Tilho (1906-1909),* II: 309-552. Paris: Impr. Nationale.

Lange, Dierk
1977 *Le Dīwān des Sultans du [Kanem-] Bornu. Chronologie et histoire d'un royaume afri-can (de la fin du Xè siècle jusqu'à 1808).* Wiesbaden: Franz Steiner Verlag.

Last, Murray
1978 Reform in West Africa: The Jihad movements of the nineteenth century. In Ajavi, J.F.A. and M. Crowder (eds.): *History of West Africa:* 1-30. Great Britain: Longman.

Law, Robin
1967 The Garamantes and Trans-Saharan Enterprise in Classical Times. *Journal of African History,* VIII: 181-200.

1980 *The Horse in West African History.* London: Oxford University Press.

Leacock, E. and R. Lee (eds.)
1982 Introduction. In: *Politics and History in Band Societies:* 1-20. Cambridge: Cambridge University Press.

Lebeuf, Annie M.-D.
1959 Les populations du Tchad (Nord du 10e parallele). *Monographies Ethnologigues Africaines. Institut International Africain.* Presses Universitaires de France: Paris.

Lebeuf, Jean-Paul
1962 *Archéologie Tchadienne.* Paris.

Lee, Richard B.
1968 What Hunters Do for a Living, or How to Make Out on Scarce Resources. In: Lee, Richard B. and I. DeVore (eds.): *Man the Hunter:* 30-48. Chicago: Aldine.

1969 !Kung Bushman Subsistence: An Input-Output Analysis. In: Vayda, Andrew (ed.): *Environment and Cultural Behaviour:* 47-79. New York: Natural History Press.

1982 Politics, sexual and non-sexual, in an egal-itarian society. In: Leacock, E. and R. Lee (eds.): *Politics and History in Band Societies:* 37-59. Cambridge: Cambridge University Press.

Lee, Richard B. and Richard Daly (eds.)
1999 *The Cambridge Encyclopedia of Hunters and Gatherers.* Cambridge: Cambridge University Press.

Lee, Richard B. and Irven DeVore (eds.)
1968 *Man the Hunter.* Chicago: Aldine.

Leisinger, Klaus M. and Karin Schmitt (eds.)
1995 *Survival in the Sahel. An ecological and developmental challenge.* ISNAR.

Levaillant, François
1806 *Histoire Naturelle des Oiseaux d'Afrique.* Paris: Delachaussée,

Lévi-Strauss, Claude
1949 *Les structures élémentaires de la parenté.* Paris: Presses Universitaires de France.

1955 *Tristes tropiques.* Paris: Librairie Plon.

1962 *Le totémisme aujourd'hui.* Paris: Presses Universitaires de France.

1963 *Totemism .* Boston: Beacon Press.

1967 Structural Analysis in Linguistics and in Anthropology. In: *Structural Anthropology*. New York: Doubleday & Co.

Lévy-Bruhl, Lucien
1951 (1910). *Les fonctions mentales dans les sociétés inférieures*. Paris: Presses Universitaires de France.

Lhote, Henri
1951 *La Chasse chez les Touaregs*. Paris: Amiot - Dumont.

1958 *À la découverte des fresques du Tassili*. Vichy.

1970 Le Peuplement du Sahara Néolitique d'après l'Interprétation des Gravures et des Peintures Rupestres. *Journal de la Société des Africanistes*, XL, 2: 91-102.

Lindblom, Gerhard
1925 & 1926 *Jakt- och fångstmetoder bland afrikanska folk*, I-II. Stockholm: Etnografiska Riksmuseet.

Lukas, J.
1936 The linguistic situation in the Lake Tchad area in Central Africa. *Africa*, 11, 3: 332-349. London.

1967 (1937) *A study of the Kanuri language*. London: Dawsons of Pall Mall.

1939 Linguistic Research between the Nile and Lake Tchad. *Africa*, 12: 335-349. London.

Lyon, Captain G. F.
1821 *Narrative of Travels in Northern Africa in the Years 1818, 1819, and 1820*. London: John Murray.

Mabogunje, A.L.
1968 *Urbanization in Nigeria*. London.

Maclatchy, Alain
1945 L'Organisation Sociale des Populations de la Region de Mimongo (Gabon). *Bulletin de L'Institut D'Études Centrafricaines*: 53-86. Brazzaville.

Magnant, Jean-Pierre
1997 Gens de la terre et gens de l'eau au Tchad. In: Jungraithmayer, H. D., D. Barreteau and K. Seibert (eds.): *L'Homme et l'eau dans le bassin du Lac Tchad*: 403-418. Paris: ORSTOM.

Maillard, P.
1951 Les redevances coutumières au Tchad. *Mémoires des C.H.E.A.M.*, no. 1906. Paris. MS.

Malbrant, René
1952 *Faune du Centre Africain Français*, 2. edn. Paris.

Malinowski, Bronislaw
1925 Magic, Science, and Religion. In: Joseph Needham (ed.): *Science, Religion, and Reality*: 19-84. London: Sheldon Press.

Maret, Pierre de
1980 Ceux qui jouent avec le feu: La place du forgeron en Afrique Centrale. *Africa*, 50, 3: 263-279.

Marks, Stuart A.
1976 *Large mammals and a brave people. Subsistence hunters in Zambia*. Seattle/London: University of Washington Press.

Marshall, Fiona
1994 Archaeological Perspectives on East African Pastoralism. In: Fratkin, E., F.A. Galwin and E.A. Roth (eds.): *African Pastoralist Systems. An Integrated Approach*, 17-43. London: Lynne Rienner Publishers.

Martin, M. Kay and Barbara Voorhies
1975 *Female of the Species*. New York: Colombia University Press.

Mason, O.T.
1913 Trap. *Encyclopædia Britannica*, 13th edn., 27: 212.

Matthey, Piero
1966 Brief Notes on the Nò-èy, a Former Tribe of Hunters and Fishers in Southern Chad. *Bulletin of the International Committee on Urgent Anthropological and Ethnological Research*, 8: 37-38.

Mauny, Raymond
1961 Tableau géographique de l'Ouest Africain au Moyen Age. *Mémoires de l'IFAN*, 61. Paris.

Mauss, Marcel and H. Hubert
1950 Esquisse d'une théorie générale de la magie. In: *Sociologie et Anthropologie*, 3-141. Paris: Presses Universitaires de France.

McDonald, M.
1991 Technological Organization and Sedentism in the Epipalaeolithic of Dakhleh Oasis. *African Archaeological Review*, 9: 81-109.

McIntosh, Susan K. and Roderick J. McIntosh
1988 From Stone to Metal: New Perspectives on the Later Prehistory of West Africa. *Journal of World Prehistory*, 2: 89-133.

McNaughton, Patrick R.
1988 *The Mande Blacksmiths*. Bloomington: Indiana University Press.

Meakin, Budgett
1902 *The Moors*. London.

Meek, C.K.
1931 *A Sudanese Kingdom*. London: Kegan Paul, Trench, Trubner & Co.

Meillassoux, Claude
1964 Essai d'interprétation du phénomène économique dans les sociétés traditionnelles d'autosubsistance. *Cahiers d'Études Africaines*.

1972 From reproduction to production. *Economy and Society*, 1, 1: 93-105.

1973 The Mode of Production of the Hunting Band. In: Alexandre, Pierre (ed.): *French Perspectives in African Studies*: 187-203. London.

Mellars, Paul and Cris Stringer (eds.)
1989 *The Human Revolution - Behavioural and Biological Perspectives on the Origins of Modern Humans*. Edinburgh: Edinburgh University Press.

Meyers, Fred R.

1988 Critical trends in the study of hunter-gatherers. *Annual Review of Anthropology,* 17: 261-288.

Migeod, F.W.H.

1924 *Through Nigeria to Lake Chad.* London: Heath Cranton Ltd.

Miller, Duncan E. and Nikolaas J. Van der Merwe

1994 Early Metal Working in Sub-Saharan Africa: A Review of Recent Research. *The Journal of African History,* 35, 1: 1-36. Cambridge: Cambridge University Press.

Milton, Katharine

1985 Ecological Foundations for Subsistence Strategies among the Mbuti Pygmies. *Human Ecology,* 13: 71-78.

Morgan, Herbert Lewis

1877 *Ancient Society.* London

Moulinard, Commandant

1947 Essai sur l'habitat indigène dans la colonie du Tchad. *Journal de la Société des Africanistes,* XVII: 7-18. Paris.

Murdock, George P.

1968 The Current Status of the World's Hunting and Gathering Peoples. In: Lee, Richard B. and Irven DeVore (eds.): *Man the Hunter:* 13-20. Chicago: Aldine.

Myers, Fred R.

1988 Critical Trends in the Study of Hunter-Gatherers. *Annual Review of Anthropology,* 17: 261-282.

Nachtigal, Gustav

1879 1881, 1889 *Sahara und Sudan. Ergebnisse sechsjährigen Reisen in Afrika.* I-III. Berlin: Paul Parey.

Nadel, S.F.

1954 *Nupe Religion.* London: Routledge & Kegan Paul.

Needham, Rodney

1962 *Structure and Sentiment. A Test Case in Social Anthropology.* Chicago: University of Chicago Press.

New York Times

2006 May 5. Parry, Richard Lloyd and Devika Bhat: Dying tribe takes on timber giants over

Nicholson, Sharon E. and Hermann Flohn

1980 African Environmental and Climatic Changes and the General Atmospheric Circulation in Late Pleistocene and Holocene. *Climatic Change,* 2: 313-348.

Nicolaisen, Johannes

1962 Afrikanske Smede. *KUML,* 33-79.

1963 *Ecology and Culture of the Pastoral Tuareg.* Copenhagen: Nationalmuseets Forlag.

1964 Kreda - et sudanesisk hyrdefolk. *Naturens Verden,* April: 97-128.

1964 *Haddad. Et jægerfolk i Tchad.* Unpbl. MS.

1968 The Haddad - a Hunting People in Tchad. Preliminary report of an ethnographical reconnaissance. *FOLK,* 10: 91-109.

1975 The Negritos of Casiguran Bay. Problems of affluency, territoriality and human aggressiveness in hunting societies in Southeast Asia. *FOLK,* 16-17: 401-434.

1976 The Penan of Sarawak. Further Notes on the Neo-evolutionary Concept of Hunters. *FOLK,* 18: 205-236.

1978 The Pastoral Kreda and the African Cattle Complex. Notes on some Culture-historical and Ecological Aspects of Cattle Breeding. *FOLK,* 19-20: 251-307.

Nicolaisen, Johannes and Ida Nicolaisen

1997 *The Pastoral Tuareg. Ecology, Culture, and Society,* I-II. Copenhagen/Londong and New York: Rhodos International Publishers and Thames & Hudson.

Oliver, Roland A. and Brian M. Fagan

1975 *Africa in the Iron Age, c. 500 B.C. to A.D. 1400.* New York: Cambridge University Press.

Palmer, H.R.

1926 (1967) *Sudanese memoirs: being mainly translations of a number of Arabic manuscripts relating to the Central and Western Sudan,* III. London: Cast.

1936 *The Bornu, Sahara and Sudan.* London: Murray.

Petit-Maire, N., J.-G. Celles, D. Commelin, G. Delibrias and M. Raimbault

1983 The Sahara in Northern Mali: Man and His Environment Between 10.000 and 3.500 Years BP. *African Archaeological Review,* 1: 105-125.

Phillipson, David W. and Laurel Phillipson

1984 The development of mankind. In: Oliver, Roland and Michael Crowder (eds.): *The Cambridge Encyclopedia of Africa:* 57-74. Cambridge: Cambridge University Press.

Phillipson, David W.

1985 *African Archaeology.* Cambridge: Cambridge University Press.

Plutarch

1982 *Lives.* The Loeb Classical Library. Harvard University Press.

Prussin, Labelle

1995 *African Nomadic Architecture. Space, Place, and Gender.* Washington/London: Smithsonian Institution Press.

Quellec, Jean-Lois le

1993 *Symbolisme et art rupèstre au Sahara.* Paris.

Raa, Eric ten

1986 The Acquisition of Cattle by Hunter-Gatherers: A Traumatic Experience in Cultural Change. *Sprache und Geschichte in Afrika,* 7, 2: 361-374.

Radcliffe-Brown, A.R.

1922 *The Andaman Islanders.* Cambridge: Cambridge University Press.

1952 *Structure and Function in Primitive Society.* London: Oxford University Press.

Reader, John

1999 *Africa. A Biography of the Continent.* New York: Alfred A. Knopf.

Reiter, Rayna R. (ed.)

1975 *Toward an Anthropology of Women.* New York: Monthly Review Press.

Revkin, Andrew C.
2001 Lake's Rapid Retreat Heightens Troubles in North Africa. *New York Times,* March 27.

Reyna, S.P.
1990 *Warsw without End. The Policical Economy of a Precolonial African State.* Hanover, NH: University Press of New England.

Richter, Dolores
1980 Of Caste in West Africa. The Senufo. *Africa,* 50, 1: 37-54.

Richter Nielsen, Lars, Erik Larsen og Jes Kramer
1999 *Lærebog i buejagt.* Copenhagen.

Robertshaw, Peter
1999 Archaeology. In: Lee, Richard B. and Richard Daly (eds.): *The Cambridge Encyclopedia of Hunters and Gatherers:* 87-99. Cambridge: Cambridge University Press.

Robinson, Charles Henry
1897 *Hausaland or fifteen hundred miles through the central Sudan.* London: Sampson Low, Marston & Co.

Rohrlich-Leavitt, Ruby, Barbara Sykes and Elizabeth Weatherford
1975 Aboriginal Woman: Male and Female Anthropological Perspectives. In: Reiter, Rayna R. (ed.): *Toward an Anthropology of Women:* 110-126. New York & London: Monthly Review Press.

Roscoe, Paul B.
1990 The Bow and Spreadnet: Ecological Origins of Hunting Technology. *American Anthropologist,* 92, 3: 691-701.

Roset, Jean-Pierre
1974 Contribution à la connaissance des populations néolithiques et protohistoriques du Tibesti (Nord Tchad). *Cahiers ORSTOM. Série sciences humaines,* XI, 1: 47-84.

1987 Paleoclimatic and Cultural Conditions of Neolithic Development in the Early Holocene of Northern Niger (Aïr and Ténéré). In: Close, A.E. (ed.): *Prehistory of Arid North Africa:* 211-234. Dallas: Southern Methodist University Press.

Rouvreur, Albert Le
1962 *Sahéliens et Sahariens du Tchad.* Paris: Éditions Berger-Levrault..

Rubin, Gayle
1975 Traffic in Women: Notes on the "Political Economy" of Sex. In: Reiter, Rayna R. (ed.): *Toward an Anthropology of Women:* 157-210. New York & London: Monthly Review Press.

Rüppell, Eduard
1835-1840 *Neue Wirbelthiere zu der Fauna von Abyssinien geh¨rig.* Frankfurt am Main.

Sadie, Stanley (ed.)
1997 (1984) *The New Grove Dictionary of Musical Instruments.* London: Macmillan.

Sadr, Karim
1991 *The Development of Nomadism in Ancient Northeast Africa.* Philadelphia: University of Pennsylvania Press.

Sahlins, Marshall D.
1972 (1968) The Original Affluent Socitey. In: *Stone Age Economics:* 1-39. London: Tavistock Publications.

Sanjek, Roger (ed.)
1999 *Fieldnotes. The Makings of Anthropology.* Ithaca/London: Cornell University Press.

Santandrea, Stefano
1964 *A Tribal History of the Western Bahr el Ghazal.* Verona: Editrice Nigrizia.

Sato, Hiroaki
1992 Notes on the distribution and settlement pattern of hunter-gatherers in Northwestern Congo. *African Study Monographs - the Center for African Arid Studies, Kyoto University,* 13, 4: 203-216.

Schildkrout, E. and C. Keim
1990 *African Reflections: Art from Northeastern Zaire.* Seattle/London: University of Washington Press.

Schmidt, Wilhelm
1926-55 *Der Ursprung der Gottesidee,* I-XII. Münster.

Schneider, David M.
1965 Some Muddles in the Models: or, How the System really Works. In: *The Relevance of Models for Social Anthroplogy.* A.S.A. Monographs, 1: 25-85. London: Tavistock Publi-cations.

Schrire, Camel
1984 Wild Surmises on Savage Thought. In: Schrire, C. (ed.): *Past and present in hunter gatherer studies:* 1-25. Orlando, Fl.: Academic Press.

Sclater, Philip Lutley and Oldfield Thomas
1894-1900 *The Book of Antelopes,* I-IV. London.

Scott, James
1990 *Domination and the Arts of Resistance. Hidden Transcripts.* New Haven & London: Yale University Press.

Sentance, Bryan
2001 *Basketry. A world guide to traditional techniques.* London: Thames & Hudson.

Serle, W., G.J. Morel and W. Hartwig
1983 *A Field Guide to the Birds of West Africa.* London: Collins.

Service, Elman R.
1962 *Primitive social organization: an evolutionary perspective.* New York: Random House.

1966 *The Hunters.* London: Prentice-Hall Inc.

Shaw, Thomas
1981 The late Stone Age in West Africa. In: Allan, J.A. (ed.): *The Sahara. Ecological change and early economic history.* London: The School of Oriental and African Studies.

Sikes, S.K.
1972 *Lake Chad.* London: Eyre Methuen.

Silberbauer, G.B. and A.J. Kuper
1966 Kgalagari masters and Bushman Serfs: Some Observations. *African Studies,* 25, 4: 171-179.

Slocum, Sally
1975 Woman the Gatherer: Male Bias in Anthropology. In: Reiter, Rayna R. (ed.): *Toward an Anthropology of Women:* 36-50. New York & London: Monthly Review Press.

Smith, Andrew B.

1980a The Neolithic Tradition in the Sahara. In: Williams, Martin A.J. and Hugues Faure (eds.): *The Sahara and the Nile:* 451-465. Rotterdam: Balkema.

1980b Domesticated cattle in the Sahara and their introduction into West Africa. In: Williams, Martin A.J. and Hugues Faure (eds.): *The Sahara and the Nile:* 489-501. Rotterdam: Balkema.

1984 Origins of the Neolithic in the Sahara. In: Clark, J.D. and J.A. Brandt (eds.): *From Hunters to Farmers: The Causes and Consequences of Food Production in Africa:* 84-92. Berkeley, Calif.: University of California Press.

1986 Cattle Domestication in North Africa. *African Archaeological Review,* 4: 197-203. Berkeley: University of California Press.

1992 Origins and Spread of Pastoralism in Africa. *Annual Review of Anthropology,* 21: 125-141.

Smith, C.S.

1981 *A Search for Structure.* Cambridge: MIT Press.

Smith, H.F.C. Abdullahi

1971 The early states of the Central Sudan. In: Ajayi, J.F.A. and M. Crowder (eds.): *History of West Africa,* 1: 158-201. London.

Smith, M.G.

1965 *The Plural Society in the British West Indies.* Berkeley: University of California Press

Solway, Jacqueline S. and Richard B. Lee

1990 Foragers, Genuine or Spureous? Situating the Kalahari San in History with CA* Comment. *Cultural Anthropology,* 31, 2. 109-146.

Soper, R.C.

1965 The Stone Age in Northern Nigeria. *Journal of the Historical Society of Nigeria,* III, 2: 176-194.

Stiles, Daniel

1981 Hunters of the Northern East African Coast: Origins and Historical Processes. *Africa,* 51, 4: 848-862.

Stow, G.W.

1905 *The Native Races of South Africa.* London.

Street, F.A. and F. Gasse

1981 Recent Developments in Research into the Quaternary Climatic History of the Sahara. In: Allen, J.A. (ed.): *The Sahara, Ecological Change and Early Economic History,* 8-28. London: Menas Press.

Sutton, John

1977 The African Aqualithic. *Antiquity,* 51: 13-29.

Swift, Jeremy

1977 Sahelian Pastoralists: Underdevelopment, Desertification, and Famine. *Annual Review of Anthropology,* 6: 457-478.

Tamari, Tal

1991 The development of caste systems in West Africa. *Journal of African History,* 32: 221-250.

1995 Linguistic Evidence for the History of West African "Castes". In: Conrad, David C. and Barbara E. Frank (eds.): *Status and Identity in West Africa:* 61-85. Indiana University Press.

Tauxier, L.

1931 Les Dorhosié et Dorhosié-Finng du cercle de Bobo-Dioulasso (Sudan-Français). *Journal de la Société des Africanistes,* 1, 1: 61-115.

Testart, A.

1982 The Significance of Food Storage among Hunter-Gatherers: Residence Patterns, Population Densities, and Social Inequalities. *Current Anthropology,* 23: 523-537.

Thomas, Roger G.

1973 Forced Labor in British West Africa: The Case of the Northern Territories of the Gold Coast, 1906-1927. In: *Journal of African History,* 14, 1: 79-103.

Tiéga, Anada

1991 Contribution à l'ébauche du plan d'aménagement de la réserve naturelle nationale de l'Aïr et du Ténéré: La faune dans l'Aïr et le Ténéré: Potentialités et contratives. *Projet de conservation et de gestion des ressources naturelles dans l'Aïr et le Ténéré.* Niamey: UICN.

Tilho, Capt.

1906 *La Géographie.* Paris.

Tilly, C.

1975 *The Formation of National States in Western Europe.* Princeton: Princeton University Press.

Treinen-Claustre, F.

1982 *Sahara et Sahel à l'Âge du Fer: Borku, Tchad.* Paris: Journal de la Société des Africanistes.

Tremearne, Major A.J.N.

1912 *The Tailed Head-Hunters of Nigeria.* London: Seely, Service & Co. Ltd.

Trimingham, J. Spencer

1959 *Islam in West Africa.* London: Oxford University Press.

1962 *A History of Islam in West Africa.* London: Oxford University Press.

Tubiana, Marie-José

1964 Survivances préislamiques en pays Zaghawa. *Travaux et Mémoires de l'Institut d'Ethnologie,* IXVII. Paris.

Turnbull, Collin M.

1962 *The Forest People.* New York: Doubleday.

1965 *Wayward Servants: the Two Worlds of the African Pygmies.* New York: Natural History Press.

1968 The Importance of Flux in Two Hunting Societies. In: Lee, Richard B. and Irven DeVore (eds.): *Man the Hunter:* 132-137. Chicago: Aldine.

1973 *The Mbuti Pygmies: change and adaptation.* New York: Holt, Rinehart & Winston.

Turney-High and Harry H. (eds.)
1971   *Primitive War: Its Practice and Concepts.* Columbia: University of South Carolina Press.

Ucko, P.J. and G.W. Dimbleby (eds.)
1969   *The domestication and exploitation of plants and animals.* London.

UNDP
1994   *Human Development Report.* Washington, D.C.

Urvoy, Y.
1942   Petit Atlas Ethno-Démographique du Soudan entre Sénégal et Tchad. *Mémoires de l'Institut Français d'Afrique Noire,* 5. Paris: Librarie Larose.

1949   Histoire de l'empire du Bornou. *Mémoires de l'Institut Français d'Afrique Noire,* 7. Paris: Librairie Larose.

Vansina, Jan
1982   Towards a History of Lost Corners in the World. *The Economic History Review, Second Series,* 2: 165-178.

1985   *Oral Tradition as History.* Madison: University of Wisconsin Press.

Vayda, Andrew P.
1965   Anthropologists and Ecological Problems. In: Leeds, A. and Andrew P. Vayda (eds.): *Man, Culture and Animals. The Role of Animals in Human Ecological Adjustment.* The American Association for the Advance-ment of Science, 78: 1-25. Washington, D.C.

Vierich, Helga I.D.
1982   Adaptive flexibility in a multi-ethnic setting: the Basarwa of the southern Kalahari. In: Leacock, E. and R. Lee (eds.): *Politics and History in Band Societies:* 213-223. Cambridge: Cambridge University Press.

Weekendavisen
2002, April 2. Skull of earliest man found in Tchad.

Wegner, Ulrich
1984   *Afrikanische Saiteninstrumente.* Berline: Staatliche Museen Preussischer Kulturbesitz, Museum für Völkerkunde.

Wendorf, Fred and Romuald Schild
1984   The Emergence of Food Production in the Egyptian Sahara. In: Clark, J.D. and S.A. Brandt (eds.): *From Hunters to Farmers. The Causes and Consequences of Food Production in Africa,* 93: 102. Berkeley: University of California Press.

Wendorf, Fred, Romuald Schild and Angela Close
1987   Early Domestic Cattle in the Eastern Sahara. In: *The Palaeoe-cology of Africa and the Surrounding Islands,* 18: 441-448.

Wente-Lukas, Renate
1977   *Die materielle Kultur der nicht-islamischen Ethnien in Nordkamerun und Nordost-nigeria.* Wiesbaden: Franz Steiner Verlag.

White, Lesley A.
1959   *The Evolution of Culture.* New York: McGraw-Hill.

Williams, Martin A.J. and Hugues Faure (eds.):
1980   *The Sahara and the Nile.* Rotterdam: A.A. Balkema.

Wilmsen, Edwin N.
1990   *Land filled with flies.* Cambridge: Cambridge University Press.

Wilmsen, Edwin N. and James R. Denbow
1990   Paradigmatic History of San-Speaking Peoples and Current Attempts at Revision with CA* Comment. *Current Anthropology,* 31, 5: 489-524.

Woodburn, James
1968   An Introduction to Hadza Ecology. In: Lee, Richard B. and Irven DeVore: *Man the Hunter:* 49-56. Chicago: Aldine.

1980   Hunters and gatherers today and reconstruction of the past. In: Gellner, Ernest (ed.): *Soviet and Western Anthropology:* 95-117. New York: Colombia University Press.

World Bank
1974   *Chad: Development Potential and Constraints.* Washington, D.C.

Wordsworth, William
1800   *Lyrical Ballads.* London.

Wulff, Hans E.
1966   *The Traditional Crafts of Persia.* Cambridge, Mass.: M.I.T. Press.

Zeltner, J.C.
1980   *Pages d'histoire du Kanem.* Paris: L'Harmattan.

GENERAL INDEX

GEOGRAPHIC INDEX

NAMES INDEX

SOCIAL INDEX